THE POSTWAR MOMENT

ISSER WOLOCH

The Postwar Moment

PROGRESSIVE FORCES
IN BRITAIN, FRANCE,
AND THE UNITED STATES
AFTER WORLD WAR II

Yale

UNIVERSITY PRESS

NEW HAVEN & LONDON

Published with assistance from the foundation established in memory of Henry
Weldon Barnes of the Class of 1882, Yale College.

Yale University Press books may be purchased in quantity for educational,
business, or promotional use. For information, please e-mail sales.press@yale.edu
(U.S. office) or sales@yaleup.co.uk (U.K. office).

Set in Times Roman by IDS Infotech Ltd., Chandigarh, India.
Printed in the United States of America.

Library of Congress Control Number: 2018943983
ISBN 978-0-300-12435-4 (hardcover : alk. paper)

A catalogue record for this book is available from the British Library.

This paper meets the requirements of ANSI/NISO Z39.48-1992
(Permanence of Paper).

10 9 8 7 6 5 4 3 2 1

But can those have been possible seeing that they never were?
Or was that only possible which came to pass?

James Joyce, Ulysses

What we are looking for are characteristics held in common,
which will make whatever is original stand out by contrast.

Marc Bloch, French Rural History

CONTENTS

Illustrations follow page   252

PROLOGUE

HERE ARE A YOUNG FRENCHMAN, AMERICAN, and Englishman, unknown to each other and destined for starkly different fates, who could stand in for millions as they fought Nazi barbarism. But the three are also set apart because, well before Germany surrendered, they belonged to small cohorts committed to progressive change in their respective nations after victory.

A Catholic youth activist before the war, Gilbert Dru brought his moral intensity into the anti-Nazi Resistance in Lyon as founder of a small group known as the Young Christian Combatants. Apart from his other Resistance activities, which earned him a place on the Gestapo's wanted list, Dru articulated a social-Catholic vision for post-Liberation France. When he proclaimed it the right and duty of the Resistance to become "the artisans of a total Renaissance for our fatherland" after the war, Dru spoke for *résistants* across the political spectrum. For his own part, he joined a circle of Catholic resistors reaching up to Georges Bidault, the second president of the clandestine National Council of the Resistance, an umbrella group formed in 1943 that linked various internal resistance movements to General de Gaulle's Free French in London and Algiers.

Dru's laboriously typed and hand-circulated manuscript of 1944, "Project for a Revolutionary Action by the Youth of France," would have barred the door against any return to prewar normalcy. Dru refused to cede the future to the communists, whose current high standing in the Resistance he recognized as well-earned but whose exclusive sway would negate "the integrity of the French soul." In his "Project," Dru sketched the broad doctrinal bases for the "grand assemblage" he hoped would replace France's prewar political parties, which he deemed morally bankrupt.

Young Dru's language melded Christian humanism with social democracy. He championed a republic at once individualist and communitarian, based on individual dignity and social rights. For capitalism to act as a positive force in the future, the notorious trusts ("that occult force that lay over political life") must be smashed and the corroding spirit of "money as king" banished. Liberty also entailed freedom from "disgraceful slums" and "proletarian slavery" and required a guaranteed social safety net. In this quest for equity, however, a due regard for personal dignity precluded overreliance on the state, with its potentially oppressive bureaucracies. In sum, Dru's social-Catholic values demanded respect for the individual and the family, but equally for the community and the common interest. French liberty must be restored in tandem with greater equality.[1]

Gilbert Dru did not live to see the flowering of the new political movement he anticipated. The Germans arrested him in July 1944, and later that month, in retaliation for the bombing of a restaurant frequented by German officers (which in fact killed no one), the Gestapo dragged Dru and four other Resistance prisoners into Lyon's central square, the Place Bellecour. In a savage act of reprisal, they machine-gunned the five and ordered that the bodies be left lying for the entire day in the pools of their blood.[2]

Dru never saw the handbills that his comrades of the Republican Movement for Liberation would shower on the capital on August 25, proclaiming that "Paris Is Free" and encapsulating his vision for the future, with the primacy of the family, respect for individual dignity, and "an end to the all-consuming power of money as king."[3] Four months later the social-Catholic wing of the Resistance convened the founding congress of a new political party in the progressive spirit of Dru's project. Avoiding the Christian label while incorporating social-Catholic values, it called itself the Popular Republican Movement (MRP). Over the next three years the MRP would be France's most influential non-Marxist political party and a faithful vessel for the Resistance ideals of postwar transformation and social justice.

While the war enmeshed, inspired, and devoured Gilbert Dru, American Charles Bolté went forth to find the war. A student leader in the class of 1941 at Dartmouth, an editor of the college newspaper, and an outspoken interventionist on campus, Bolté upon graduation acted on his convictions. While some like-minded Americans headed north to join the Canadian air force, Bolté and four fellow collegians crossed the Atlantic to enlist in the King's Royal Rifles. Their motivations were not especially grandiose. Instinctive antiwar sentiment had finally given way to revulsion against the fascist threat. "We fought for America in the English Army because we felt that if England fell America would be next. . . . We fought a holding action to save for America the last best hope. . . . We didn't expect to be disappointed because we didn't hope for much."

The British army trained and commissioned the five friends and in April 1942 sent them off to the Egyptian front. Of the five, "two got death and three got limps." During the campaign around El Alemain shrapnel tore up one of Bolté's legs. In the course of a painful year military doctors amputated his leg and fitted a prosthesis. By the summer of 1943 he was back in the United States, free of crutches but using a cane. Fighting off the depression that might engulf any amputee, Bolté settled into the comforts of home and a good job with the Office of War Information. But the question of what this global upheaval was supposed to mean for his country vexed him.

America's first objective was simply victory over its enemies, which alone justified the deaths and maiming of its soldiers. But "winning the war and reaping the fruits of victory were two different things. By winning the war, the victors would win the chance to determine the shape of the future. We could then decide how much or how little we wanted the deaths of the young men to mean. The fight for freedom would not be won when the shooting stopped; that was a battle each generation of Americans had to be prepared to fight again." As it now stood, the war was being fought solely to defeat the aggression of Germany and Japan, without much of a positive vision for the future. For Bolté, optimism won out over cynicism. Regardless of all signs to the contrary, he concluded that "we had a wonderful chance to win something more [than] victory alone."

Through a chance connection, Bolté learned of a correspondence circle of serving soldiers, orchestrated by Corporal Gilbert Harrison (later to become editor of the *New Republic* magazine). Numbering around 100 men, they were groping to determine "how they might achieve the world they wanted to live in after the war." The correspondents had just decided to formalize their quest with a new organization, and they needed a sympathetic veteran, recently discharged, to take on the task. It was a perfect match. Charles Bolté became the point man for the American Veterans Committee (AVC), a veterans organization in a new key. Within months he gave up his job and took on the work of the AVC full time.[4]

The contours of the organization gradually took shape. What began as a small affinity group of servicemen grew into a full-fledged veterans organization when peace finally came. To World War II veterans with progressive instincts it offered an alternative to the American Legion, an organization "that would look ahead, not back," with the motto "Citizens first, Veterans second." The AVC's positions remained vague at this point, but its members knew what they opposed: a return to the prewar world "just as it was." They would resist the inevitable "power grabs" by special interests; support policies that fostered full employment; demand fair treatment for all World War II veterans without excessive special pleading; and resist "reactionary" political forces. In 1945 the AVC won its modest place in the public sphere as a dogged David to the American Legion's Goliath. As intended, it would give veterans the collective heft to advocate progressive causes in their communities and in Washington. In the broadest terms it could breathe some energy into the fading New Deal during America's postwar moment.

Oxford University was a more intense place than Dartmouth College in the late 1930s, the shadow of Hitler far more immediate. After a first-rate Grammar school education, Denis Healey went up to Balliol College, Oxford, in October 1936, where he proved an outstanding scholar in the demanding "Mods and Greats" double major in ancient literature and philosophy. Political activism nonetheless trumped his studies and led to his presidency of the Oxford Labour Society, by far the largest political group on campus. Healey's leftish views also propelled him, along with about 200 members of the society, to join the Communist Party (CP) in 1937 when the party line had moved well into its Popular Front phase.

Healey's Oxford generation was shaken without respite by the Spanish Civil War in 1936, Munich in 1938, the Nazi-Soviet pact in 1939, and the outbreak of war. "For the young in those days," he recalled, "politics was a world of simple choices. The enemy was Hitler with his concentration camps. The objective was to prevent a war by standing up to Hitler. Only the CP seemed unambiguously against Hitler." Healey was slow to drop his communist affiliation when circumstances changed; he rationalized the Nazi-Soviet pact of August 1939 "as a reaction to the failure of Britain and France to build a common front against Hitler." But his commitment to the CP did not run deep, and after the fall of France in June 1940 it ended. Meanwhile, despite all the distractions, Healey wound up his studies with a First in his final examinations. Graduation, more waiting, and finally his military call-up arrived.

Commissioned a lieutenant, he was assigned to Movement Control for training in combined operations. In due course he became a military landing officer, or beach-master, during the British invasion of Southern Italy and in the Anzio landing. He then moved to a staff position with the British Eighth Army in its ambulatory headquarters, where he planned other operations and saw a great deal of Italy in the process. The gulf between the generally collaborationist middle classes and the peasants and workers struck him forcefully. Altogether, Healey's service lasted five years: in the thick of the Italian campaign from beginning to end, exposed on occasion to real danger, good at what he did (with eventual promotion to major), yet emerging without injury.

For Denis Healey prospects for postwar renewal depended on the fortunes of the Labour Party. In 1944 he received an inquiry from a Labour MP asking if he would like to be put on a list of potential candidates for the election that would come right after the war. He replied enthusiastically and in February 1945 had his name submitted to the selection meeting in the normally Tory constituency of Pudsey and Otley. As he wrote to the committee from Italy:

> I am only one of the hundreds of young men, now in the forces, who long for the opportunity to realise their political ideals by actively fighting an election for the Labour Party. These men in their turn represent millions of soldiers, sailors and airmen who want socialism and who have been fighting magnificently to save a world in which socialism is possible. . . . We have now almost won the war, at the highest price ever paid for victory. . . . [But] the defeat of Hitler and Mussolini is not enough by itself to justify the destruction. Only a more glorious future can make up for this annihilation of the past.

The constituency adopted Healy as its candidate, and he later received leave to return to England for the election.

Healey arrived from Italy just in time for the Labour Party National Conference on May 21. "The Blackpool Conference was remarkable for the number of young candidates in uniform . . . determined to make a better Britain and a better world," he recalled. But it was Healey whom the party tapped for a keynote address, immortalized in an iconic photo of the young major in uniform, looming above the delegates as he exhaled socialist fire and brimstone. "The upper classes in every country are selfish, depraved, dissolute and decadent," he cried. "The struggle for socialism in Europe . . . has been hard, cruel, merciless and bloody. The penalty for participation in the liberation movement has been death for oneself, if caught." Leaders from all factions of the party were impressed.

Healey went on to campaign with zest. "It was a wonderful campaign. I spoke with total confidence, based largely on total ignorance. . . . But my central theme was sound enough: we must solve the problems of the peace by applying the same planning techniques as we had used to win the war. . . . Churchill was handicapped by his obvious inability to understand the men and women he had led in war." To everyone's surprise, Healey came close to winning, as the Tory margin in the district dropped from the previous 10,000 to 1,650 votes. Despite his predictable loss, Healey felt part of the great Labour victory. While he had to wait until 1952 to win a seat in Parliament, Healey now rode the Labour tide at party headquarters. Backed by several party stalwarts, he successfully applied for the post of international secretary of the Labour Party. With some knowledge of the Continent's political movements, Healey would be building bridges to the socialist parties of Europe, energetically promoting democratic socialism at home and abroad.[5] Like Dru and Bolté, Healey personified progressive aspirations for the postwar moment.

THE WARTIME EXPERIENCES OF FRANCE, BRITAIN, and the US differed profoundly from one another. Nazi occupation and the Vichy regime triggered a heads-down accommodation by most French citizens, collaboration with the Nazis by some, and resistance from a small but growing minority of others. British or American civilians did not face such fateful choices in daily life. As a battleground in 1940 and again in 1944, France suffered extensive physical damage and casualties, and the deportations of Jews and resistors to Nazi concentration and death camps increased the toll. Across the Channel, Britain endured six years of exhausting, all-out economic mobilization and austerity; continuous military and naval battles in Europe, the Atlantic, and across the British Empire; and on the home front, waves of devastation and death from German bombing and rockets. The United States committed itself in 1940 to prodigious industrial output for the Allied cause and, after Pearl Harbor, to massive military deployments in Europe and the Pacific. Americans paid a steep price in military deaths and maimings but had few civilian casualties and little physical damage at home.

Victory over Nazi barbarism, justification enough for the titanic conflicts of World War II, would not in itself determine what followed in the allied democracies. After the war's upheavals—plainly different as they were for Britain, France, and the US—most citizens wished to return to a familiar life after all the casualties, miseries, and dislocations they had endured. In contrast (like Gilbert Dru, Charles Bolté, and Denis Healey), others insisted that victory should on no account bring a return to the prewar civic order. Their hopes, channeled in different ways according to circumstances in the three countries, ran roughly parallel courses. This book is about progressive forces in the three allied democracies in the postwar moment, forces that nurtured an impetus for transformation and resisted a return to normalcy.

I use the umbrella term "progressive" in this book as a flag of convenience, one more suitable than the alternatives although not without its own problems. In the US the label had a specific trajectory over time. Between roughly 1890 and 1920, the urban politicians, academics, lawyers, and journalists who pushed for nonpartisan reforms from the top down usually called themselves Progressives, and in Wisconsin the LaFollette family launched an insurgent state party under that banner. Later, the leftists who rallied around Henry Wallace's national third party in 1948 appropriated that designation for themselves. But in the 1930s and 1940s the general run of New Deal activists referred to themselves interchangeably as progressives or liberals. "Liberals," however, would not work in this book. In Britain the term evokes the Victorian-era reformers of the Liberal Party, whose signature issue was free trade. In shrunken form the Liberals barely survived into the World War II era, although their milieu bequeathed the influential ideas of William Beveridge and J. M. Keynes. But the Labour Party, which displaced the Liberals in 1929 as the chief rivals of the Conservatives, is our major protagonist here. The Labourites generally referred to themselves simply as "Labour," but the party's 1945 electoral manifesto appealed for support to "all men and women of progressive outlook," and I take them at their word. In France "liberal" pointedly designates the advocates of laissez-faire, free-market capitalism. "The Left" is a protean term that usually refers in modern times to Marxists of various kinds, but it can also encompass the non-Marxist center-left, as it did during the Popular Front of 1935–38; "progressives" is rarely used in France as a label for anything. Still, the term works well for the postwar moment in France because it aptly accommodates a new generation of social-Catholics who joined coalition governments with socialists and communists after the Liberation. In all, although the term "progressive" can be ambiguous, it best describes the transformational impetus coming out of World War II in the three historic democracies.

The three parts of the book examine the character of progressive forces in the interwar decades and during the war; the struggles over postwar change that began in each country in 1944–45; and the mixed outcomes. In Britain, France, and the US, the interwar years, the wartime experience, and the postwar period have been the subjects of extensive and excellent study. But no book with a comparative view has encompassed the postwar moment in the three democracies. For narrative interest and interpretive perspective, this threefold approach will, I hope, enrich the usual recounting of those national histories in isolation.

The stakes in the three societies were comparable, but progressive forces in each nation of course had particular centers of gravity. In Britain before, during, and after the war, the Labour Party (conjoining a large trade union wing and a smaller political wing) manifestly dominates any account of the progressive impetus. In France the mutating strands of the Left, all inscribed to some degree under the heritage of the French Revolution, were varied and contentious, especially after the Bolshevik Revolution split the Marxist Left between rival socialists and communists. But the progressive impetus reemerged in transfigured and temporarily unified form in the Resistance and after the Liberation. In the US the impetus for progressive renewal in the postwar had two obvious foundations: Roosevelt's long sway over Washington, and the CIO's remarkable unionization of the mass production industries in the 1930s. In selective detail Part 1 of the book introduces these protagonists and sets the stage for considering the struggles of progressives after victory over the Axis. The three chapters of Part 1 (one on each country) are, in other words, essential background to the main event.

The focal point and architecture of the book crystalized when I aligned three nearly contemporaneous manifestos, anchored in progressive values and aspirations for the postwar. Independent and uninfluenced by one another, yet strikingly similar, the manifestos effectively carry us over the threshold to the postwar moment: the *Common Program* adopted in Paris by the clandestine National Council of Resistance (CNR) in March 1944; *The People's Program for 1944* of the CIO Political Action Committee for the US election of November 1944; and the British Labour Party's long-gestating electoral manifesto for 1945, *Let Us Face the Future.* Each program rested on expansive visions of human dignity, equal opportunity, and social rights. Each offered an agenda to promote full employment, enhanced social security, decent wages for workers, trade union rights, and educational reform. Each insisted that a healthy democracy must oversee and regulate its economic system to promote greater productivity and a sounder distribution of wealth that would undergird mass purchasing power—to increase economic growth in comparison to past performance and to better distribute its bounties.

The forms and details of these programs varied in each country, but they hinged on a common assumption: victory over Nazism would be drained of its meaning if society, economy, and government at home simply reverted to their customary prewar ways and inequities. While any illusion about a new dawn immediately gave way to grinding political and social struggles, the end of the war still brought a period of fluidity and opportunity. Peace offered the prospect of social, economic, and political renovation in these societies reeling from privation and sacrifice but relieved by victory. The challenges and struggles in the aftermath of victory had no guaranteed timetables or outcomes. The postwar moment began early in France with the Liberation and ended there convulsively by late 1947; in Britain and the US it came to an end less dramatically by 1951. Although the momentum for transformation during the postwar moment proved to be meteoric in character—intense, dramatic, but short-lived—it still had lasting impacts in these societies.

In due course the three Western allies resumed a normal democratic politics with deep roots despite their varied historical trajectories. A vigorous free press, political parties, legislative battles, independent trade unions, labor-management conflicts, veterans organizations—all became arenas in which the struggles of the postwar moment played out. Sharp conflict or stalemate are the common coin of any electoral democracy. Normal democratic politics in the three nations neither extinguished the impetus for postwar transformation nor assured it. Hanging in the balance were such matters as the priorities for postwar reconstruction or reconversion; the possibilities for national planning to stimulate economic growth and "full employment"; what sectors (if any) of the infrastructure and economy to nationalize and on what terms; trade union powers as against the prerogatives of management; the relationships among business, labor, and the state; the potential reach of social security benefits; the allocation of veterans benefits; the expansion of educational opportunity at various levels; and how to meet desperate needs for new housing. In the broadest terms, at stake in each country was the degree to which the elusive notions of greater equity and social solidarity would become core democratic values.

ABBREVIATIONS

Britain

AEU	Amalgamated Engineering Union
ARP	Air Raid Precautions (Civil Defense)
BMA	British Medical Association
CPGB	Communist Party of Great Britain
CSCA	Civil Service Clerical Association
ILP	Independent Labour Party
LCC	London County Council
LEAs	Local Education Authorities
MFGB	Miners Federation of Great Britain (after 1945: NUM)
M-O	Mass Observation
NALT	National Association of Labour Teachers
NCL	National Council of Labour
NEC	National Executive Committee of the Labour Party
NHI	National Health Insurance (1913)
NHS	National Health Service (1947)
PLP	Parliamentary Labour Party (Labour MPs)
SMA	Socialist Medical Association
TGWU	Transport and General Workers Union
TUC	Trades Union Congress

France

AMGOT	Allied Military Government of Occupied Territories
CAS	Comité d'Action Socialiste
CFLN	Comité Française de la Libération Nationale (Free France)
CFTC	Confédération Française des Travailleurs Chrétiens
CGT	Confédération Générale du Travail
CGT-U	CGT-Unitaire (pro-communist)
CNR	Conseil National de la Résistance
COMAC	Commission d'Action Militaire (CNR)
FFI	Forces Françaises de l'Intérieur
FN	Front National (communist dominated)
FO	Force Ouvrière (anti-communist)
GPRF	Gouvernement Provisoire de la République Française
IC	Internationale Communiste (Comintern)
MEN	Ministre de l'Économie Nationale
MLN	Mouvement de Libération Nationale
MRP	Mouvement Républican Populaire (social-Catholic)
MUR	Mouvements Unis de la Résistance
MURF	Mouvement Unifié de la Renaissance Française (pro-PCF)
OCM	Organisation Civile et Militaire
PCF	Parti Communiste Français
PRL	Parti Républicain de la Liberté (right wing)
SFIO	Section Française de l'International Ouvrière (formal name for the PS, the Socialist Party)
STO	Service du Travail Obligatoire
UDSR	Union Démocratique et Sociale de la Résistance

United States

AAA	Agricultural Adjustment Act
ADA	Americans for Democratic Action
AFL	American Federation of Labor

AMA	American Medical Association
AVC	American Veterans Committee
CIO	Congress of Industrial Organizations
CIO-PAC	CIO-Political Action Committee
CNH	Committee on the Nation's Health
CPUSA	Communist Party USA
CWA	Civil Works Administration
DNC	Democratic Party National Committee
FEPC	Fair Employment Practices Commission
FERA	Federal Emergency Relief Agency
FHA	Federal Housing Administration
HUAC	House Un-American Activities Committee
ILGWU	International Ladies Garment Workers Union (AFL)
NAACP	National Association for the Advancement of Colored People
NAM	National Association of Manufacturers
NC-PAC	National Citizens PAC
NIRA	National Industrial Recovery Act
NLRB	National Labor Relations Board
NNC	National Negro Congress
NRPB	National Resources Planning Board
NWLB	National War Labor Board
OES	Office of Economic Stabilization
OPA	Office of Price Administration
OWMR	Office of War Mobilization and Reconversion
PCA	Progressive Citizens of America
PWA	Public Works Administration
SOC	Southern Organizing Committee (CIO)
SWOC	Steel Workers Organizing Committee (CIO)
TVA	Tennessee Valley Authority
TWUA	Textile Workers Union of America (CIO)
UAW	United Auto Workers (CIO)
UDA	Union for Democratic Action
UE	United Electrical Workers (CIO)
UMW	United Mine Workers Union

USHA	United States Housing Authority
USWA	United Steel Workers of America (CIO)
VA	Veterans Administration
WPA	Works Progress Administration
WPB	War Production Board

PART I

FACING DEPRESSION, FASCISM, AND WAR

Britain: Labour's Long Apprenticeship

IN MAY 1940, TO STAVE OFF CASCADING parliamentary opposition to his war leadership, Prime Minister Neville Chamberlain pressed the Labour Party to join in a national unity coalition. Party leader Clement Attlee, a sharp critic of Chamberlain's for the past two years, replied that he would take it to the party. After an official consultation, Attlee tersely told Chamberlain that Labour would serve under any Conservative leader but himself. The PM then resigned, and when Winston Churchill was designated to replace him, Labour joined Churchill's cabinet as a major partner. An opposition party of trade unionists, political progressives, and socialists had suddenly become pivotal in Britain's national life. What developments marked Labour's lurching ascent since its founding at the turn of the century? As a vessel for progressive aspirations, what did the party contribute to the British people at war, and what promise did it offer for a postwar future?

An Uncertain Ascent: From 1900 to the Depression Decade

The roots of the Labour Party go back to 1900, when Britain's labor federation, the Trades Union Congress (TUC), sought to increase the political influence of the working class in Parliament. A conference convened by the TUC launched the Labour Representation Committee, which changed its name to the Labour Party in 1906 after it had established a toehold in the House of Commons. The new party conjoined a growing trade union movement with kindred cooperative associations and small socialist organizations. Two of the leading figures in the new party, Keir Hardie and Ramsay MacDonald, had risen from humble origins in their native Scotland and used the small socialist group known as the Independent Labour Party (ILP) as a way station for their political ambitions. Hardie won a parliamentary seat in 1900, becoming the Labour Party's first member of Parliament and inspirational elder statesman. MacDonald took longer to win his seat but went on to become party leader in 1911.

Given the fusion of elements in Labour—the trade unionists (known as the industrial wing) and the progressives outside the trade unions—conflicts over power and policy were bound to arise. MacDonald, for example, believed that to achieve any influence at all in Westminster, Labour had to seek some kind of accord with the Liberal Party, long the rivals of the dominant Conservatives. To gain an electoral foothold MacDonald negotiated a commitment from the Liberals in 1903 to offer a clear field for Labour candidates in two score working-class constituencies in the next general election. Similarly, only sponsorship by the Liberals could achieve such short-term Labour goals as salaries for parliamentary deputies (enacted in 1911) or legislation nullifying the Osborne judgment of 1909—a court ruling that inhibited trade unions from engaging in political action. But should Labour collaborate indefinitely in this "Lib-Lab" mode or, as it sank its electoral roots, should the party assert full independence in the belief that it could eventually achieve power on its own? This dilemma persisted even after 1922, when Labour displaced the imploding Liberal Party as the second largest party in Britain, because Labour's accession to power in a new three-party system might still depend on the Liberals' cooperation.[1]

In the long term Labour faced a more fundamental question: could the movement transcend its status as a special interest pressure group? Putting it another way, was Labour destined to remain in essence a class party—in British usage, a "sectional party"—or could it become a truly national party? On the party's industrial side, the trade unions were perforce "sectional" or class based. The bulk of the party's voters came from the working class, and in its early years most Labour MPs were trade unionists or others sponsored by individual trade unions, such as the railwaymen and coal miners, which paid salaries to their MPs until 1911. In trade union eyes, the Labour Party existed to advance working-class interests which, workers had every reason to believe, did not diverge from the veritable national interest. But this outlook could still lead in two directions: toward greater socialist militancy for structural change in the face of a hostile capitalist establishment, or to a quest for modest but cumulative advantages for working people. In its political wing, the party included the pragmatist intellectuals and socialist reformers of the Fabian Society, but also socialists of a more anti-capitalist, ideological and confrontational bent. The ILP, for example, pivotal in launching the Labour Party, had a rocky relationship with it over the years and finally disaffiliated from the party in 1932 in a fit of leftish impatience.[2]

As the party struggled to establish its political presence and define its socialist identity, the Great War posed a crisis but also an opportunity of sorts. While most Labourites rallied to the patriotic cause, a pacifist current in Labour set some of its stalwarts against the prevailing tide. Keir Hardie agitated passionately against the war until his death in 1915. Opposing the war if less stridently, MacDonald had to resign from the party leadership and entered a kind of political wilderness; in the reckoning that came with the 1918 election he was viciously denounced and lost his parliamentary seat. On the other hand the wartime governments had to accommodate trade union interests in their plans for all-out mobilization and regulatory controls over the economy. As a gesture, the Liberals brought Labour's leading trade unionist and general-secretary Arthur Henderson into the cabinet—a first taste for the party of influence on the inside, although one that soured by 1917.

After the armistice, the popular wartime leader David Lloyd George called an election in November 1918 to renew the mandate for the National Government he had forged from elements of the Liberal and Conservative parties. The PM offered Labour some places (or "coupons") for his cross-party national ticket, but the party refused and went before the voters as a straight-out opposition party. Considering Lloyd George's juggernaut tactics, Labour did not do badly. It won 23 percent of the votes from the new mass electorate, and 57 seats (a gain of 15), almost to a man "sponsored" trade union candidates. Lloyd George, however, rapidly dismantled the regulatory apparatus of wartime that might have cushioned the dislocations of demobilization. After a brief boom, massive and prolonged unemployment in certain regions of the country greeted demobilized soldiers and workers, rather than the disingenuous promise of "homes fit for heroes."[3]

In its response to the Bolshevik Revolution at that time, Labour did not experience the trauma of the French Socialist Party, which split French socialists and gave birth to a large and militant French Communist Party, as we shall see. Labourites were leery of the Bolsheviks, and the new Communist Party of Great Britain (CPGB) remained small and negligible politically, although influential in certain social movements, intellectual life, and the affairs of some trade unions. Yet there was no lack of intense class feeling in 1920s Britain. The economic slump, concentrated in northern England, Scotland, and Wales, intensified industrial conflict, especially in the coalfields. Recalcitrant mine owners would not yield an inch to the bitter grievances of the miners or, for that matter, to national needs for greater efficiency in that key economic sector. In this atmosphere Labour began to gain ground; in the general election of 1922 it surpassed the fractured Liberals by winning 142 seats, of whom only 85 were candidates sponsored by trade unions. In December 1923 the Conservatives called a snap election over the issue of protective tariffs, with surprising results: the Tories lost over 100 seats and were down to 258; the reunited Liberals won 159 seats; but Labour won 191 seats. The king invited Ramsay MacDonald (who had returned to Parliament in 1922) to form a government. As a minority government with no mandate, the party accomplished little during an interlude lasting less than a year, but under its appealing new leader it gained experience, public standing, and self-confidence.

Meanwhile, the TUC and its constituent unions were growing apace, despite conflicts over how to build trade union power. Certain unions encouraged a confrontational posture of direct action, with the ultimate weapon being a general strike that could paralyze the country. Other unions put their faith in collective bargaining, with strikes as a last resort. On the terrain of organizing, the general union model (amalgamation of varied unions across different sectors) produced two of Britain's largest unions: Ernest Bevin's Transport and General Workers Union (TGWU), and the General and Municipal Workers Union. But other activists organized smaller unions based on craft specializations, especially in the new mass production industries. A parallel struggle, which would continue for decades, pitted shop-floor activism against the power of union officials at central headquarters—"labor bureaucrats" to their opponents. Opinions also varied on the role of the TUC's governing body, the General Council. Some saw the council as a general staff leading the entire trade union movement, while others advocated more modest functions as a clearing house to assist individual unions if asked, coordinate research and policy debates, and generate propaganda to influence public opinion.[4]

These cross-currents converged in the general strike of 1926. For several years, the Miner's Federation of Great Britain (MFGB) had been vainly resisting wage cuts, layoffs, and demands by the owners for longer hours in the pits, while the owners did little to modernize the organization, management or technology of their vital but inefficient industry. Blue-ribbon government commissions of inquiry came and went, their recommendations for overhaul in the coal industry gathering dust as successive governments failed in pressuring the owners to modernize. Driven to desperation by their appalling working conditions, the miners finally launched a national strike and appealed to the TUC for support. In 1925 dockers and railwaymen attempted to embargo the movement of coal to no avail. The next year the TUC's General Council decided to play their ultimate card: mobilization of a unified labor movement in solidarity with striking miners.[5]

"General strike" is technically a misnomer for the TUC's action in May 1926; the General Council did not call out all its unions and did not use the term, although the government insisted on that label. But with railway workers and dockers in the vanguard, this broad-based support strike for the miners brought out 2.5 million workers and, like the mythic general strike, was intended to immobilize the economy and force the government to intervene in the coal dispute. Despite the risks, and without much advance planning by the TUC, rank-and-file trade unionists rallied with remarkable discipline and high spirits. On the other side, the Conservative government's response proved equally determined in the battle for public opinion and in logistics. Arguing that this was a strike against the state itself, the government would not negotiate let alone capitulate. Instead, it mobilized public authorities and large numbers of volunteers to keep essential food, milk, and fuel flowing, and thus limited the potentially paralyzing impact of the strike.

The government would not negotiate but neither would the miners. The MFGB would accept no reduction of wages under any circumstances: "Not a minute of the day, not a penny off the pay," expressed the miners' immovable position. No government commissions or vague promises of future redress would persuade the union to back down. Ernest Bevin had taken a leading role in bringing the TUC and his own TGWU into this support strike, but he quickly recognized that unanticipated rigidity on both sides made the TUC's position untenable. Following Bevin's lead, the TUC's General Council called the workers back after nine days. They could take pride in their solidarity and discipline, but they had lost the battle. The miners, however, would not go back, and continued their increasingly bitter strike for six months, until their endurance finally collapsed and they were forced to accept a punishing settlement in which pay fell back to the levels of 1921.[6]

The general strike of 1926 thus ended in a severe if honorable defeat for the TUC. With some unions nearly bankrupted by the burden of strike pay, workers also faced reprisals that threatened hard-won gains of the past on the railways and other sectors, and which local union leaders scrambled to mitigate. Nationally the unions absorbed a backlash of punitive, though not crippling, legislation. Parliament resisted the call of some Tories to repeal whatever protections trade unions had won over the years, but the Trade Disputes and Trade Unions Act of 1927 prohibited secondary strikes and boycotts, placed limits on organizing in the public sector, and banned the automatic transfer to the Labour Party of a portion of dues payments in affiliated unions. Instead, the new law obliged individual workers to "contract in" if they wished part of their dues to be used for that purpose. The impact was dramatic: in 1927 the party had counted 3,239,000 trade unionists as dues-paying members; the following year the number dropped to 2,025,000, and it hovered around that level for the next decade.[7]

Ernest Bevin had played a central role in launching, conducting, and calling off the general strike of 1926. In those tense days he displayed fierce dedication to labor solidarity, deft leadership of his own union, and a talent for reading complex situations and making hard decisions. Though not without critics and rivals, Bevin emerged from this drama as an iron man of the trade union movement and, in consequence, a major power in the Labour Party. A son of the working class from the very humblest origins—a family of farm laborers— Bevin was orphaned as a youth and his formal schooling ended at age eleven. Settling in Bristol, he worked as a drayman or deliveryman in the area of the docks, while he took adult education courses and attended public lectures where he absorbed the precepts of reformist socialism. Eventually he found his vocation as branch secretary in Bristol of the Dockers Union. Pugnacious and fearless, Bevin achieved legendary success in organizing the nation's dockers and from that foundation went on to expand his union by a series of amalgamations into a powerhouse of the labor movement. As general-secretary of the TGWU, Bevin proved a stubborn but shrewd negotiator, a master at the collective bargaining that he viewed as the workers' surest route to progress.[8]

For someone without much education, Bevin had a remarkable intellectual capacity, and was a powerful if sometimes ungrammatical speaker with a kind of "rough eloquence." In due course he operated as effectively in the corridors of power as he had on the docks, in the union halls, at TUC General Council meetings, or on the floor of the annual Labour Party conference. Bevin distrusted ideologues and Labourites who spouted ideological pieties, but the dignity and well-being of working people remained his supreme value and the moral core of his socialism. A man of intense prejudices and blunt to a fault, one crossed him at one's peril. (When a colleague declared after a fractious meeting that Bevin's frequent critic Nye Bevan "is his own worst enemy," Ernest Bevin was heard to mutter, "not while I'm alive.") But most opponents respected him as a pivotal figure in the trade union movement and the party. The opening of Transport House in 1928 symbolized Bevin's ascendancy: this capacious and impressive new home for his TGWU also provided central headquarters facilities for both the TUC and the Labour Party national executive.[9]

Facing the Depression

With the prolonged slump as its chief campaign issue, Labour emerged from the general election of 1929 with 37 percent of the vote and 287 seats, and as the largest party was invited by the king to form a government. Without an actual parliamentary majority, however, its duration again depended on the unpredictable will of the other parties. Soon after Ramsay MacDonald settled into 10 Downing Street, his cabinet faced the repercussions of the Great Depression. As unemployment surpassed 2.5 million in 1930, MacDonald and his Chancellor of the Exchequer Philip Snowden proved to be in thrall to orthodox monetary and fiscal doctrines. They accepted as dogma the need to maintain a strong currency based on the gold standard (as opposed to devaluing so as to stimulate the economy), and the necessity of balancing the budget at whatever cost. Novel state interventions lay beyond their ken, while their improvised austerity measures proved fruitless. Finally the international banking crisis in the summer of 1931 seemed to cause a dangerous run on the pound sterling, and MacDonald concluded that only more drastic budget cuts could restore confidence in the financial community and save the pound. Alongside new taxes and cost-cutting measures, Snowden insisted on slashing the level of unemployment insurance benefits by 10 percent. Most Labourites balked at this misguided move to balance the budget on the backs of the most vulnerable citizens, and in the cabinet this proposal created a paralyzing crisis of political conscience.

Meanwhile, Bevin had been a member of a blue ribbon Committee on Finance and Industry, appointed by the Treasury in 1929. Listening to the testimony, he grasped and embraced certain unorthodox notions of financial management and deficit spending, including those expounded by fellow committee member, economist J. M. Keynes. Though not an MP let alone in the cabinet, Bevin in the summer of 1931 led the opposition to MacDonald's rigid austerities. But his representations in behalf of the TUC were to no avail since MacDonald and Snowden would not budge. With his cabinet split and seemingly immobilized over the slash in unemployment benefits, the PM decided to form a multi-party cabinet instead of relying exclusively on his balky Labour comrades. In response, all but three members of the cabinet resigned, and the party in turn expelled MacDonald and Snowden. Labour then stood with its face to the wind in the snap election that MacDonald called to legitimize his new "National Government," one dominated by Conservatives. The Labour Party suffered a devastating defeat, losing a fifth of its voters and over four-fifths of the seats it had won in 1929, including almost the entire front bench of the party. The election returned a mere fifty-two Labour deputies to Parliament as against 556 for MacDonald's National Government bloc. MacDonald remained PM, but past and future Conservative leaders such as Stanley Baldwin and Neville Chamberlain dominated his cabinet. The political vehicle for progressive aspirations in Britain had been shattered in 1931 by this unimaginable series of betrayals and reversals.[10]

This debacle did have positive repercussions. Like the TUC after the general strike of 1926, the party had to take stock and clarify its strategies. Labour recognized that the lack of clear doctrines and priorities underlay the missteps of MacDonald's tenure. Over the next few years, with input from progressive young economists working with the Fabian Research Bureau and with Hugh Dalton (chair of the party's subcommittee on Finance and Trade), the party defined its brand of democratic socialism more clearly. Since 1918 (in Clause 4 of its charter) Labour had vaguely committed to "the common ownership of the means of production and distribution" as a long term goal; now the party considered specific actions that would guide it if and when it returned to power. The new program that emerged in 1936–37 espoused a nonauthoritarian or democratic form of economic planning by way of a National Investment Board to oversee an efficient allocation of resources. The program espoused a tempered redistribution of wealth; Keynesian-style pump-priming and management of "aggregate demand" to combat unemployment; and the nationalization of certain key economic sectors. Specifics on these matters remained vague, it is true, and the program said almost nothing about pricing mechanisms, how to combat inflation should it develop, or how public ownership should actually be organized.[11]

Between 1918 and 1935 the party had evolved from a federation of affiliated trade unions and socialist societies into a party where individuals could also find their place in local constituency branches. After the punitive Tory labor law of 1927 and the debacle of MacDonald's government in 1929–31, the party's membership sank to an interwar low of 1.9 million and rebounded to only 2.6 million in 1938, since a majority of workers in affiliated trade unions had still not "contracted in" to dues-paying party membership as the 1927 law required. But the constituency membership was growing, and surpassed 400,000 in 1935, when the party increased branch representation on the National Executive Committee (NEC).[12] Some branches thrived as fraternal organizations with social activities such as dinners, dances, and fetes, alongside discussion groups and local publications; at the extreme, members in some branches verged on fencing themselves off into an hermetic subculture or "alternative society." At the other extreme, however, some branches remained creaky from factionalism or apathy.[13]

As the Depression deepened and social cleavage hardened, the general election of 1935 brought a partial recovery in the party's fortunes. Its share of the total vote rebounded to 38 percent, more or less back to its 1929 level, which netted Labour 154 seats against the National Government's 431. Among the losers in 1935 was Ramsay MacDonald. Having won in 1931 by 6,000 votes against his local Labour opponent in the Seaham mining district, this time MacDonald faced the tough Labour veteran Emmanuel Shinwell, who had cut his teeth on the Glasgow docks. Shinwell acidly reminded embittered voters that their misguided confidence in the PM in 1931 had been rewarded by four years of stagnation, unemployment, and continuation of the detested means test for poor relief. Shinwell carried the poll in Seaham by 38,380 to 17,882 for MacDonald.[14] Among the other victors in 1935 was Herbert Morrison, a junior minister in MacDonald's original cabinet who had lost his seat in the 1931 tidal wave, but who remained one beacon for Labour with his effective ground level socialism as head of the London County Council.[15]

Under Morrison's influence, the NEC worked to combat Labour's image as a "sectional (i.e., class) party" and to present itself as a national party appealing

beyond its base to middle-class voters, they too being "workers." Labour headquarters in Transport House astutely nurtured a more favorable treatment of the
party in the press. Among the five largest-circulation London dailies, for
example, Labour long held a beachhead through its direct sponsorship of the
Daily Herald, which reached a circulation of 2 million in 1933 and continued
to grow. Now the party cultivated friendly coverage from the populistic *Daily
Mirror* and developed a comfortable relationship with two other newspapers;
only the tabloid *Daily Mail* remained implacably hostile. The party also pursued
a marketing strategy of sorts, initiated in a conference on "selling socialism" in
1937. This led to production of a picture magazine called *Your Britain,* which
used modern graphic art and photojournalism to amplify Morrison's spirit of
cheerful optimism and outreach.[16]

Facing Aggressive Fascism: From Pacifism to Rearmament

In 1935 international relations began to overshadow other issues in the
Labour Party as in Europe at large. Abhorrence of capitalist militarism and
outright pacifism had deep roots in Labour. Labourites like Keir Hardie, the
party's revered founding father, and MacDonald denounced the war of 1914
and paid a political price in the short term. Draft-age pacifists paid a steeper
one. The future lawyer and left-wing Labour MP Sydney Silverman, for
example, was a member of the No-Conscription Fellowship. When his preliminary draft notice came in 1916, Silverman applied for conscientious objector
status but was denied. When called up next year he refused to go, was court-
martialed, and served over two years of hard prison time. Antiwar sentiment
had strong personal roots in some quarters of the Labour party.[17]

In the 1920s and early 1930s, during its brief periods in government or in
opposition, most Labourites comfortably advocated disarmament and international accords to keep the peace. But as fascist aggression blighted the dream of
a world at peace, the party became mired in wishful thinking and evasions.
Certain figures in Labour gauged the fascist threat clearly and early. Bevin
understood that the rise of Nazism imperiled everything Labour stood for; trade
unions and socialists would inevitably be among its first victims. (A bloody
assault on working-class, socialist neighborhoods in Vienna under its right-wing
government struck Bevin as an early warning sign and aroused his fury.) Hugh
Dalton, an economist from the party's political wing who lost his parliamentary

seat in 1931 but returned in 1935, and who played a leading role on the party executive throughout the decade, argued relentlessly for strong measures against fascist aggressors. But the party as a whole remained immobilized by antiwar sentiment and by its distrust of the Conservatives. Between 1931 and 1935 Labour's shrunken contingent of MPs—known as the Parliamentary Labour Party, or PLP—chose as party leader George Lansbury. One of only three front-benchers to survive the electoral debacle of 1931, Lansbury was a venerable but dogmatic Christian pacifist. Arthur Ponsonby, Labour leader in the House of Lords, was an even more doctrinaire pacifist.

At the party's annual conference in September 1935, Bevin bluntly attacked Lansbury's "parading" of his pacifist conscience as unbefitting his role as party leader. The aging Lansbury, recognizing that his position was growing untenable, resigned—free now to travel the world with his blinkered and increasingly quixotic pleas for reconciliation and unilateral disarmament. To replace Lansbury, the PLP chose Clement Attlee, another front-bench survivor of the 1931 landslide and Lansbury's deputy leader. Educated at a second-tier public school and at Oxford, a one-time social worker in London's East End, and, like Dalton, a serving officer in the Great War, Attlee was a moderate but deeply committed socialist. After the 1935 election tripled the Labour contingent, many expected Attlee to step down in favor of a more forceful personality like Herbert Morrison, who had recovered his seat. But the PLP voted 88 to 48 to stay with the low-keyed Attlee, a man easily underestimated. Dalton, who had lobbied for Morrison, deplored this "wretched and disheartening result." "And a little mouse shall lead them!" Dalton vented to his diary.[18]

During the protracted Abyssinian crisis in 1935–36, when Mussolini invaded that independent African nation in quest of a colony for Italy, Labour endorsed the vague notion of "collective security" through the League of Nations but skirted around the issue of military sanctions against the fascist aggressor. In this the party seemed to be in accord with the British public at large, which gave qualified support to collective security in the remarkable "Peace Ballot" organized by the League of Nations Union in 1934. (Half a million volunteers distributed this questionnaire, and over 11.6 million British citizens, 38 percent of the adult population, responded. The organization released preliminary tallies of the Peace Ballot in November 1934 and announced the final results at a grand rally in June 1935.) Unsurprisingly, the ideal of disarmament through the League of Nations won resounding support in this comprehensive survey of British public opinion.

Respondents overwhelmingly favored international agreements to promote disarmament: all around arms reduction; abolition of military air fleets; prohibitions on the manufacture and sale of armaments for private profit. The Peace Ballot then asked citizens about sanctions: "Do you consider that if a nation insists on attacking another, the other nations should combine to compel it to stop by (a) economic and non-military measures? [yes: 87 percent]; (b) if necessary, by military measures? [yes: 59 percent, no: 20 percent, no answer: 20 percent]."[19]

Pacifists opposed military sanctions against aggressors even through the League of Nations, because they regarded war as an utterly hateful and unacceptable option regardless of its provenance. On the left of Labour a basic distrust of the League of Nations on political grounds also entered the mix. The party's outspoken left-wing gadfly, the upper-crust barrister and MP Sir Stafford Cripps, repeatedly denounced the League as a tool of imperialist power, "an International Burglar's Union." To most of Labour's national executive, however, Cripps seemed a loose cannon whose incendiary comments went beyond the pale; as Dalton put it, "Tory H.Q. regard him as their greatest electoral asset." But like Lansbury's pacifism, Cripps' anti-imperialist attack on the League blunted the party's response to fascist aggression.[20]

In any case, the golden moment in Britain for "collective security" through the League of Nations came and went with the Peace Ballot. By 1936 collective security seemed a hopeless cause after the League's failure to stop Mussolini in Abyssinia with an oil embargo on Italy. By July 1936, after Hitler's unilateral remilitarization of the Rhineland elicited no response, Dalton darkly confided to his diary: "The Hitler rearmament races on. Few people in the Labour Party seem to know or care anything about it. . . . The Nazis look like getting away with it everywhere. Perhaps, since collective security is off the map since the Abyssinian affair, collective surrender will seem better than collective suicide."[21]

Labour's evasion extended to another front when the rightist General Franco attacked the republican government of Spain and set off a civil war. Labour's sympathies lay entirely with the republican or loyalist side. Yet Labour supported the Conservative's policy of nonintervention in the Spanish Civil War, ostensibly in deference to French socialists who had to go that route for domestic political reasons, as we shall see. But Labour also managed to convince itself that nonintervention would preclude Spain from becoming the pretext for a general European war instigated by the fascist powers.

For those who would resist the fascist tide, then, rearmament and bilateral diplomacy stood as the last resort by 1937. This came as an extremely painful realization: after the Great War, rearmament reasonably seemed tantamount to a revival of the great power rivalries and arms races that had helped precipitate that nightmare in the first place. But even as Labour got past its principled opposition to rearmament in the face of bellicose fascism, it could not bring itself to support actual rearmament under the auspices of a Conservative government. Led by Cripps, the party's vocal left wing had long maintained that only a people's government could be trusted to rearm, lest the armed forces be used for nefarious imperialist adventures or even against the working class itself. But without resort to such extreme rhetoric, even the party's mainstream would not trust the Conservatives to enlarge or deploy the armed forces wisely and in good faith.[22]

Impetus for digging out of this conundrum came in 1937 from the trade union wing of Labour. At the TUC's annual conference, General Secretary Walter Citrine (who marched in tandem with Bevin) urged a change of course. Citrine paid lip service to the League of Nations but effectively dismissed its current relevance. Instead, his official report put forward the unpopular case for rearmament: "It may be that the primary responsibility for the maintenance of peace will fall upon one or two countries who are adequately prepared and ready to shoulder their responsibility. How in these circumstances can we escape the conclusion that some measure of rearmament is indispensable if this country is to face its obligations?" After impassioned debate, the conference overwhelmingly endorsed Citrine's report. The following month delegates to the annual Labour Party conference (dominated as usual by trade union block votes) adopted a similar position by a margin of eight to one.[23] Conference policy did not automatically dictate how the party's MPs would actually vote, although the party could and did expel deputies who deviated excessively from its positions. But the party's parliamentary deputies (the PLP) also took this turn in 1937 and abstained instead of voting against the government's annual military estimates as they had done in 1936.[24]

Hitler's annexation of Austria in March 1938 and the final throes of the Spanish Republic set Labour on the anti-appeasement road, and the Czech crisis of that year made the shift explicit. As Hitler's bullying of the Czechs to cede the German-speaking Sudetenland region came to a climax, the National Council of Labour (NCL: an umbrella group representing the TUC, Labour's

NEC, and the executive committee of the PLP) issued its joint "Blackpool Declaration" on September 8: "The British Government must leave no doubt in the mind of the German Government that they will unite with the French and Soviet Governments to resist any attack upon Czechoslovakia. . . . Whatever the risks involved, Britain must make its stand against aggression. . . . Labour cannot acquiesce in the destruction of the rule of law by savage aggression." Prime Minister Chamberlain felt free to ignore this advice. He likely believed that the Soviet Union posed a greater potential threat than Germany; felt he could drive a wedge between Mussolini and Hitler; and clung to the hope that with enough concessions the Führer would stand down. After a trip to see Hitler in Berchtesgaden, Chamberlain spurned a second plea against further appeasement by a delegation from the NCL (Citrine, Morrison, and Dalton), and a few days later he flew to meet Hitler in Munich.

The Munich pact, which agreed to Hitler's annexation of Sudetenland, was the last straw for Labour. While the irrepressible Lansbury blessed the Czechs as Christ-like martyrs in the cause of world peace, most Labourites denounced Munich as a craven act of appeasement that brutally sacrificed the sovereignty of a democratic nation to Hitler's will. Attlee led the party into all-out opposition. When Chamberlain asked for a vote of confidence in Parliament on the Munich agreement, even Churchill abstained but Labour voted overwhelmingly no. While admitting to a momentary spasm of relief that the conflict in central Europe had not precipitated a general European war, Attlee denounced Munich as "one of the greatest diplomatic defeats that this country and France have ever sustained. . . . It is a tremendous victory for Herr Hitler. Without firing a shot, by the mere display of military force . . . he has destroyed the last fortress of democracy in Eastern Europe, which stood in the way of his ambitions." Even the staunch war resistor Sydney Silverman acknowledged that harsh reality: "Munich is not the triumph of negotiation or reason," he wrote in his weekly newspaper column; "it is the triumph of naked force. This is not pacifism, it is anarchy."[25]

Labourites now demanded a rapid and meaningful alliance with the Soviet Union as the only way to make good on the guarantees that the British and French governments had offered to Poland. Chamberlain's obvious reluctance to negotiate that pact further shredded his credibility with Labour. After the PM recognized Franco's fascist government in Spain, Cripps and Nye Bevan launched a campaign for a Soviet-oriented popular front against fascism. The

NEC frantically tried to squelch this démarche as dangerously naïve and harmful to Labour's future electoral prospects; early in 1939 the party expelled Cripps and Bevan, but it could not silence them or their organ *Tribune*.[26] Yet even Ernest Bevin and Dalton would not support the military conscription proposed by Chamberlain in April 1939 as a logical part of his belated rearmament program. Labour balked because, in their view, recruitment of volunteers (which they did support) was proving adequate and because they feared that military conscription could quickly lead to domestic labor conscription. Once the war began Labourites would cross that line as well and support conscription, but in April their visceral distrust of the Conservatives held them back.

When the thunderbolt of the Nazi-Soviet pact came down in August 1939, most Labourites excoriated the Soviet Union but insisted that Chamberlain had contributed mightily to creating this ghastly situation. Secure for the moment on his eastern frontier, Hitler ordered the invasion of Poland to proceed. Disabused by now of his illusions about the Führer, Chamberlain led Britain into a state of war against Germany in alliance with France. Profoundly disgusted with Chamberlain, Labour nonetheless endorsed this course. Remnants of pacifism still survived in the party; a score of deputies formed an informal peace caucus to oppose the war and conscription and to press for a negotiated peace in the months ahead. But Sydney Silverman held back. While regarding the coming war as hateful, he glumly accepted it and implicitly rebuked his pacifist colleagues: "We must win because if we do not, all hope for our ideals is dead. . . . How dare we contemplate a world under Hitler's heel?"[27] Silverman's enduring pacifist convictions caused him to agonize over every step along this route, but his qualified support for the war can be taken as symbolic of Labour's odyssey. Putting antiwar idealism and equivocations behind by the time of the Munich pact, Labour had positioned itself against the appeasement of Hitler even at the price of war.

War and Coalition

After the declaration of war Churchill dropped his feud with Chamberlain over appeasement, joined the PM's cabinet as first lord of the Admiralty, and served under him loyally. Though invited to do the same, Labourites would not enter a unity coalition under Chamberlain, whom they continued to revile. *Guilty Men,* a short book by three left-wing British journalists published in 1940, summarized Labour's indictment against the appeasers. Had the general election due that year been held, this attack might have been a potent campaign weapon.[28] But while staying at arm's length from Chamberlain, Labour immediately entered into an "electoral truce" with two components. First came an agreement, to be renewed year by year, that no general election would be held under wartime conditions, even though this would perpetuate the Conservatives' overwhelming parliamentary majority of 1935. Second, the three parties to the truce (Tories, Labour, and Liberals) would not contest by-elections. Instead, whenever a vacancy occurred by death or resignation, the party that held the seat could field a new candidate unopposed by the other two. Of course this did not preclude independents or candidates from minor parties like the Communists from contesting a by-election. Such candidates, including several from a group of socialistic reformers in 1943 called the Commonwealth Party, scored a few notable victories. But the electoral truce kept the three established parties on a common course without the heat of by-election campaigns. This did not entail a suspension of political activity. Party activity at the grass roots diminished considerably but did not cease, and discussion on the meaning of the war continued robustly. Still, many constituency activists chafed at the electoral truce and feared that the party would atrophy.[29]

The months of the "phony war" (September 1939–April 1940)—when the armies of France and Britain faced those of Germany without fighting—brought a frustrating foretaste of war on the home front. Mass evacuations of schoolchildren and of infants and their mothers from London and other cities began almost immediately in anticipation of bombing raids by the Luftwaffe. A stressful situation for all concerned, the evacuation in the end proved to be a gigantic false alarm, since no bombing raids materialized, and in due course most urban refugees trooped back home. This dramatic exodus from the cities, however, forced into intimate contact two subcultures that inhabited the same nation with little knowledge and less understanding of each other. The cultural clashes between working-class evacuees and their provincial middle- or upper-class hosts—on everything from personal hygiene to table manners and child rearing—strained the inspiriting premise that all Britons were now pulling together. The evacuation also demonstrated deficiencies in logistical planning by the government. Like the bumbling propaganda efforts of the new Ministry of Information, the evacuation did little for Whitehall's credibility.[30]

Nor did the Allies' tepid military and naval efforts raise the country's spirits. There was no movement at all on the western front, as the French burrowed into defensive positions along the Maginot Line and elsewhere, while the British regiments and fighter squadrons deployed to France adopted the same defensive posture. The seeming stalemate finally broke when both the Allies and the Germans realized that control of Norway might be of genuine strategic value. Both sides rushed forces into that hapless country to preempt the other, but the Germans prevailed and the Allies evacuated on May 2—the first military fiasco of the war for Britain. Churchill had as much to do with the failure in Norway as anyone, but it was Chamberlain's overall leadership that now came under fire.

As the House of Commons held a two-day debate on the Norway campaign, Labour's speakers bitterly attacked the prime minister's record of incompetence, his "almost uninterrupted career of failure," as Attlee put it. While Churchill duly defended Chamberlain, backbench Tory dissidents, including a number of serving officers, rounded on the prime minister over strategic and related issues. Chamberlain retained the support of rank-and-file Conservatives but the PLP still decided to risk a division (vote) of the House, in effect posing a no-confidence motion. In the vote on May 8, 41 usual government supporters defected, to taunts from their Tory colleagues of "quislings!" and over 80 abstained, at least 40 in a studied gesture of protest. The government's normally huge majority shrank embarrassingly as Chamberlain won the vote by only 281 to 200.[31]

Though not forced out by this vote, Chamberlain felt he could salvage his tenuous position only by bringing Labour into a coalition. He queried Attlee, who tersely replied that he must put the question to the party. It came as no surprise that Labour's executive spurned the offer and urged Attlee to respond that the party would enter a coalition but not under Chamberlain. The PM then resigned, and on the question of who would replace him Labour stood to the sidelines. Chamberlain met with the two leading figures of his cabinet, Churchill and the foreign minister Lord Halifax, along with the chief Tory whip. By most accounts Halifax resolved a potential impasse by stating that it would not do in these times to have a peer as prime minister. Back channels indicated that Labour, notwithstanding its low regard for Churchill as a bombastic imperialist and occasional scourge of working people, would willingly serve under him. And so the king asked Winston Churchill to become prime minister. Churchill continued his respectful treatment of Chamberlain (who remained party leader) and insisted that he accept a top post in the new cabinet. On assuming office, Churchill famously promised Parliament victory at any cost—a stance that appealed to the broad public but which made some Tory insiders squirm, since they regarded "Winston" as a bellicose loose cannon with boundless personal ambition.[32]

Having helped bring down Chamberlain, Labour now shifted from "constructive opposition" to coalition partner. Attlee won the overwhelming endorsement of Labour's annual conference, which happened to be meeting at Bournemouth at that very moment, for the new course: "Labour," he explained, "should take its share of responsibility as a full partner in a new Government which under a new Prime Minister commands the confidence of the nation."[33] But did the new government in fact command that confidence? For the change in leadership coincided with the sudden German *Blitzkrieg* on the western front, and within days the "phony war" gave way to an extreme military crisis. Churchill's war cabinet and chiefs of staff became the exclusive locus of debate and decision for the moment. Sitting with Churchill in the five-member war cabinet were Chamberlain, Halifax, Attlee, and his deputy leader Arthur Greenwood. As the military situation in France deteriorated alarmingly, and Holland and Belgium capitulated, nothing could be taken for granted, including Churchill's wisdom or primacy. Chamberlain and Halifax retained considerable leverage since a protest resignation by either might precipitate a vote of no confidence in Parliament on Churchill.

As the Wehrmacht decimated Allied forces, it seemed likely that France would capitulate and take itself out of the war, leaving Britain completely isolated. There was no argument in the war cabinet against disengaging from the collapsing French front and evacuating the British expeditionary force before the Germans trapped it. During the last week of May, however, the prime embarkation point of Calais fell into German hands, leaving a shrinking beachhead at Dunkirk as the sole exit. The odds seemed depressingly long for a successful evacuation from Dunkirk under German air and artillery bombardment. But with good fortune (a one-day halt by the Germans) the evacuation succeeded.

What *did* cause debate in the war cabinet was whether to use the imminent capitulation of France as a pretext for entering negotiations with Hitler. At first, the PM did not close the door completely on this notion, nor did its proponent Halifax insist on that defeatist move. But according to two historians who have sifted the evidence, Halifax definitely leaned toward that course, and Chamberlain seriously pondered the possibility of negotiation as well, but in the end followed Churchill who had no intention seeking a parlay. Attlee and

Greenwood said relatively little, but their presence acted as a kind of ballast for Churchill as he fenced with the wavering Chamberlain and the more determined Halifax. When Churchill insisted to the war cabinet that "nations which went down fighting rose again, but those which surrendered tamely were finished," Attlee endorsed that view. Britain's will to continue the fight would be destroyed, Attlee maintained, if the government now pursued back-door truce negotiations. Attlee thus helped the PM isolate Halifax and rein him in without causing an open rift.[34]

With the Dunkirk evacuation complete, talk in the war cabinet of negotiating with Hitler at an end, and France out of the war by mid-June, Britain now faced the prospect of sustained bombing and invasion. There was no disguising the debacle—the collapse of continental resistance to Hitler; the abandonment of all heavy weapons and transport on the beaches of Dunkirk; the casualties and trauma of a rout ending in frightful disorder; and the brute fact that France would now become a German base for assaults on Britain. Still, even if the rescued soldiers were "more thankful than proud," the story of Dunkirk could be read in a positive light. The evacuation of the expeditionary force in the face of such dire odds in itself constituted a notable feat—not a victory, as Churchill acknowledged, but a deliverance. Although destroyers and other naval ships carried the bulk of the troops back to Britain, the participation of Channel ferries, pleasure steamers, fishing trawlers, and other civilian vessels imparted to the evacuation a dramatic air of British fighting spirit, studiously cultivated in press coverage and government propaganda. That version of the story, "the myth of Dunkirk," was thus a benign myth of exaggeration and positive spin, not of fabrication, and signified the refusal to accept defeat.[35]

A BBC broadcast by J. B. Priestley on June 5 made a singular contribution to this benign myth of Dunkirk. The metamorphosis of blunders and near disaster at Dunkirk into an epic of gallantry was symbolized for Priestley by the paddle steamer *Gracie Fields,* which he had frequently ridden before the war as it plied between Portsmouth and the Isle of Wight. The vessel (which had been requisitioned as a minesweeper shortly before) found its way into the Dunkirk flotilla and ended up bombed to the bottom of the sea, although most of the 750 evacuees on board survived. After fondly reminiscing about the steamer, Priestley concluded: "Our great grand-children, when they learn how we began this War by snatching glory out of defeat, and then swept on to victory, may also learn how the little holiday steamers made an excursion to hell and came back glorious."[36] After this performance, the BBC slotted Priestley into a prime listening hour— the ten-minute "Postscripts" following the nine o'clock news on Sunday evenings.

An established playwright, novelist, and essayist of leftish sentiment, this well-connected man of letters and veteran of the Great War proved superbly equipped for the task. Priestley wrote his own scripts and then broadcast them in a rich and agreeable Yorkshire voice, with a sense of timing and modulation from his experience with stagecraft. He understood that cultivating morale depended on plain speaking and the authenticity of personal observation. His skills as a broadcaster, his calm yet passionate radio persona, won him a huge audience comprising about 30 percent of Britain's adult population, second only to Churchill. An anti-fascist and anti-appeaser in the 1930s ("the disguised war of the Thirties became the open war of 1940," he maintained), Priestley vividly assailed Nazi barbarism, with its hallmarks of lies and torture and its underlying nihilism. Britain had to become "a fortress" to defeat this reign of darkness.[37] Priestley's "Postscripts," however, were no mere exercise in upbeat propaganda. Though it was scarcely the BBC's intention, Priestley (who was not a member of the Labour Party) infused his broadcasts with the leftist view that this was not simply a war for survival and the defeat of the Nazis, but a war to build a better world, which alone would justify the hardship and sacrifice. The war was not "a terrible interruption" from which we would one day "go back to where we started from," he declared; "My own personal view [of the future]: we must stop thinking in terms of property and power and begin thinking in terms of community and creation."[38]

At times Priestley referred to men in combat, at times to civilians toiling in arms factories or living through the Blitz. "I was shocked to learn," he told his listeners, "that some middle-class women, with any amount of room to spare in their houses, made every excuse to avoid receiving mothers and babies who'd been bombed out of the East End." This led Priestly to conclude, "We're fighting not merely to keep the German jackboot off our necks but also to put an end once and for all to that world [of greed, privilege, and love of power], and to bring into existence an order of society in which nobody will have far too many rooms in a house and nobody will have far too few." Priestley evoked a future in which "free men could combine, without losing what's essential to their free development, to see that each gives according to his ability, and receives according to his need." This sentiment, he admitted, may have shocked our fathers and grandfathers, but we, "who've seen all hell let loose," take this notion as "no mere propaganda but the blazing truth of the mind and heart." Priestley courted his listeners with an inspirational sense of a "people's war" and a people's peace.[39]

Labour ministers could insert "fair shares" socialism into coalition discourse only in the most gingerly and oblique fashion at this juncture, but Priestley candidly expounded that sentiment to a mass audience and conveyed the sustaining myths of wartime with a socialist inflection—the Dunkirk spirit (which emphasized the positive in this debacle); the stoic popular response to the Blitz (which elided Londoners' inadequate resources, bad behavior, and demoralization); and the hopeful notion of the war's larger purpose. In due course Priestley therefore provoked a Conservative backlash. In his broadcast on October 20, he told his audience that he was stepping down voluntarily "because I am in danger of becoming one of the war bores myself." But Priestley left the distinct impression that his alleged partisanship had offended Conservatives, although "I am not a member of any particular party" and it was not himself but his critics "who put party before country." In his mind he had simply promoted a deeper understanding of the causes and consequences of the war, of "real democracy," and of "obvious elements of social justice."[40]

Although Priestley left the air voluntarily that October, the axe did fall on him in 1941 after the BBC called him back for a new series but then cancelled it after his eighth broadcast under pressure from Conservatives.[41] The Priestley affair illustrates in miniature the fragility of the coalition government. Up to a point, egalitarian input from Labourites bolstered the war effort by promoting cooperation and encouraging optimism about the future. But whenever it became too explicit, forward looking, or threatening to traditional verities, such sentiments provoked a Tory backlash.

Labour's Wartime Presence: Civil Defense

In Churchill's coalition the PM himself ran the war and personally made important military and diplomatic decisions. Conservatives headed the traditional prestige ministries, the Treasury (Kingsley Wood) and the Foreign Office (Eden, after Halifax became ambassador to Washington). Churchill appointed his ruthless crony, the press baron Lord Beaverbrook, to run the critical Ministry of Aircraft Production, later amalgamated with the Ministry of Supply, and the respected Lord Woolton became minister of food. The veteran civil servant Sir John Anderson was Home Secretary, responsible since 1939 for civil defense as well.[42] Labour's front bench totaled about nineteen cabinet members, junior ministers and parliamentary secretaries. Attlee was Lord Privy Seal and later deputy prime minister; Bevin minister of labor; Morrison, after a stint as minister of supply, replaced Anderson at the Home Office in October 1940; and Dalton, minister of economic warfare, then head of the Board of Trade.

Churchill successively entrusted two of his Tory intimates with the new Ministry of Information, which monitored morale and tried to shape it. But the early efforts of that operation became legendary for ineptitude, with ham-handed campaigns, slogans, and posters based on dubious psychological premises and a patronizing "we know best" attitude.[43] In the end, of course, morale really depended on how the war was going and on the handling of vital matters on the home front, such as food supplies, civil defense, and the treatment of labor. Daily contact between government and people in their respective offices, therefore, made Morrison and Bevin the public face of Labour during the war. With their zeal and common touch, the two Labour veterans came to personify home-front grit, patriotic dedication, and generally effective leadership.

Controversial matters continuously passed through Morrison's hands as home secretary, including whether or not to release the ailing British Fascist leader Oswald Mosley from prison and what to do about the anti-government posturing of the *Daily Worker;* in the event Morrison released Mosley and banned the communist newspaper, to outcries on both scores from many Labourites. But civil defense—or ARP (Air Raid Precautions), in the official designation—occupied most of Morrison's energy. When Churchill shifted him to the Home Office in October 1940, as the bombing of London became relentless, Morrison inherited a daunting assignment. Despite the best efforts on civil defense of his starchy predecessor Anderson, obvious shortcomings in the organization, facilities, and personnel of civil defense persisted. The government had laid down general policy, imposed mandates on local authorities, then left them to execute and (in many cases) pay for them.

When the Luftwaffe failed to obliterate the airfields and fighter squadrons of the RAF during "the Battle of Britain" in the summer after Dunkirk, it impulsively changed tack and began the sustained bombing of London. After one massive daylight raid, for fifty-seven consecutive nights, starting on September 7, German bombers assaulted the metropolis. By May 1941, when the Germans put this campaign on hold in anticipation of invading the Soviet Union, over 20,000 Londoners had been killed and 70,000 injured.[44] In those months civil defense seemed to be the central front of the war. As Stephen Spender later observed, "In this war, by War Pictures we mean, pre-eminently, paintings of the Blitz. . . . The background to this war, corresponding to the Western Front in the last war, is the bombed city."[45] The lack of a commanding figure in charge of this front became a glaring deficiency. In Morrison the PM identified an experienced leader popular with Londoners and dedicated to their welfare.[46]

Civil defense (ARP) consisted of defensive measures—the blackout, enforced by air raid wardens; the peal of warning sirens; provision of shelter; plans for evacuation—and damage repair: firefighting services, rescue squads, first-aid posts, mortuary facilities, rest centers, and relocation for those bombed out. In a broadcast on assuming office Morrison admitted that he could not guarantee the public's safety, but he vowed "to ward off danger and to lessen hardship" as much as possible. Sheltering and firefighting demanded the most urgent attention.

Government policy in 1939 had emphasized surface shelters or basements in public buildings where people could take cover for short periods when the sirens went off. For nighttime air raids, the government advised sheltering at home and promoted a simple backyard shelter consisting of a shallow excavation topped by corrugated metal. Known as "Anderson shelters," their downside included susceptibility to water seepage. Initially the government opposed "deep sheltering" in underground facilities, which would (in this view) engender passivity and defeatism in the population. Accordingly, Anderson placed underground tube tunnels and stations off limits for civil defense and ordered the stations locked after hours. But when certain London neighborhoods came under bombardment, citizens ignored this prohibition. In numbers soon approaching 200,000 they either descended to the stations during the day and refused to leave or forced their way in en masse as evening came. Once underground they were left on their own in overcrowded spaces lacking provision for sleeping and sanitary facilities. Being shut out of the subways may have seemed insupportable, but sheltering in such disorderly and unhealthy conditions was itself demoralizing.[47]

Morrison reversed government policy on deep sheltering. He convinced the cabinet to begin construction of reinforced underground shelters in London and elsewhere, permitted sheltering in the subway system, and brought the government into its management.[48] By Christmas 200,000 bunks had been provided along with sanitary facilities, canteen services, and official supervision of access by ticketing. Since an estimated 85 percent of Londoners still remained in or near their homes during air raids, however, Morrison also sought an alternative to the outdoor "Anderson shelters." His staff soon devised a table-like construction with a steel top and wire mesh sides that could accommodate a family of four and double as a dining table. These indoor "Morrison shelters," inexpensive and easy to fabricate, were useless against a direct hit and provided no respite from the frightful noise of the bombing raids, but they deflected falling debris and offered a new option to families sheltering at home.[49]

To head his shelter policy committee, Morrison appointed one of his parliamentary secretaries, Ellen Wilkinson, a Labour MP famous for leading the Jarrow hunger march of 1936 by her unemployed rust-belt constituents. After visits to tube shelters and bomb-damaged neighborhoods the two helped restore basic services to bombed-out areas and offered the reassurance that sympathetic people were actually in charge.[50] Their experience in London then helped Morrison and Wilkinson deal with the devastation from German bombing campaigns in the provinces that began in earnest that November. Concentrated raids on ports and cities like Coventry, Plymouth, and Portsmouth produced proportionately vaster devastation—human, material, and psychological—with far scantier resources than London had for responding. As the magnitude of the destruction dazed and dispirited communities and their leaders, Morrison and his aide visited the scenes and provided practical assistance in getting those places back on their feet.[51]

Firefighters were the front-line troops of civil defense, their working environment one of danger and exhaustion, as depicted in Humphrey Jennings's memorable docudrama *Fires Were Started*, which followed one small unit in 1940 London.[52] But when the Blitz began, the nation's firefighting services comprised a hodge-podge of small professional forces, new full-time auxiliaries, and a large number of part-time volunteers, all with varied standards and capabilities and fragmented into more than 1,600 local fire-service authorities. Morrison led a grinding campaign to transform these disparate resources into a high-quality National Fire Service, which he officially launched in May 1941 and which would endure long after the worst circumstances of its creation.

On a parallel track, and under cabinet prodding, he and Wilkinson instituted compulsory civilian fire-watching in 1941. This practice began in certain large factories and other sites, the purpose being to spot and extinguish incendiary bombs before they set off a major conflagration. The value of fire-watching was manifest during a huge raid of September 29 on central London, when a volunteer team saved St. Paul's Cathedral from destruction by a rain of incendiary bombs. Morrison compared this duty to enrollment in the Home Guard during the invasion scare following Dunkirk. To begin with he promoted voluntary participation in this line of defense against incendiary bombing. After his ministry had laid the groundwork, he then instituted a compulsory system that incorporated some six million men and women. Each was responsible for forty-eight hours a month of this tedious but potentially vital duty in their neighborhood or workplace. In characteristic language, Morrison emphasized that "compulsion will apply to everyone, of every grade—managers and office workers as well as manual workers—as the needs of the situation may require."[53]

Just after the war, a lavishly illustrated volume by Stephen Spender (himself an auxiliary fireman), with a foreword by Morrison, celebrated the saga of civil defense, even while acknowledging early missteps along the way. The book combined a poet's human interest perspective with a concise history and organizational account of civil defense. The volume stood as a testament to the "fourth arm" of wartime service, this "rank-and-file army" that comprised (apart from the fire-watchers) 1.5 million men and women, four-fifths unpaid volunteers. Emphasizing "the breakdown of social barriers among neighbors" in this work, Spender regarded civil defense as "a vast social movement in which civilians have become aware that they are citizens." "Civil Defence workers," he maintained, "feel vividly that it would be a misfortune if the local patriotism, the neighborliness, the social tasks undertaken during these years, should be forgotten and dissolved with the peace."[54] Morrison, of course, felt the same way; in a radio address on "Civil Defense Day" in November 1942 he had already linked civil defense with pious Labour sentiments: "It is for you to strive against selfishness, idleness, greed in yourselves and in others, as you strove against the Nazi bombers."[55] In charge of this vast assemblage of men and women operating in small units among their neighbors and co-workers, Morrison could claim to have led his countrymen in a people's war (a phrase he often used) with implications for the future.

Labour's Wartime Presence: The Mobilization of Workers

Most Labourites lifted to prominence in Churchill's coalition came from the party's political wing, but the PM wished the industrial wing to be represented as well, and he enthusiastically co-opted Ernest Bevin, the trade unions' towering figure. Offered the Ministry of Labor and National Service, Bevin at first hesitated. Historically a low-ranking ministry, it administered unemployment insurance and occasionally served as "a glorified conciliation board"; starting in 1939 it oversaw military conscription. Broad domestic manpower policies were not in the ministry's brief. But Bevin accepted the post on the understanding that this would change, and the cabinet soon approved his proposal for sweeping Labor Ministry authority to shape the civilian labor mobilizations that lay ahead. Bevin also expected his ministry to help determine "the conditions in which we shall start again" after the war. (To normalize his status as a cabinet minister, the government ran Bevin for a vacant seat in the House of Commons, a first in his career.) Bevin bade his comrades in the TGWU a fond farewell; now serving the entire nation in its war effort, he brought to the task his profound identification with working people, with "my people" as he often put it.

Under his new mandate, Bevin had three main tasks: to allocate scarce labor among war production facilities and the armed forces; to contain the pressure for wage inflation that scarcities of labor ordinarily produced; yet to assure the fair and dignified treatment of workers for the sake of equity as well as industrial efficiency.[56] Although armed with statutory authority to impose directives under the Emergency Powers Act of May 1940, Bevin intended to honor trade union traditions of collective bargaining and opposition to the compulsory direction of labor. Conversely, he shared the labor movement's belief that strong government controls over food supplies, prices, and profits would alone make it possible to win the cooperation of workers in the battles for production— policies quickly enacted by the government, including higher income taxes, excess profits levies, food subsidies, and an expanding regimen of rationing. In the sphere of labor relations and manpower policy, consultation with trade unions preceded most decisions and legal compulsion would be a last resort. Trade union membership grew from around 6.3 million in 1939 to 7.8 million in 1945.[57]

During Chamberlain's tenure, employers had scrambled for labor by luring workers away from rivals and bidding up its price. In Bevin's hands government policy fell short of the outright industrial conscription favored by some business interests and Conservative politicians, but it still entailed far-reaching authority over labor. The difference lay in the spirit with which Bevin applied various mandates. As the war situation darkened in 1941 the population accepted greater direction in work assignments so long as they were made fairly. In effect his leadership produced consensus for compulsion or, in the fanciful term he coined, "voluntaryism."[58]

Collective bargaining over wages and working conditions remained the norm, rather than the military-style fiat that would have prevailed under all-out labor conscription. Bevin's Order No. 1305 of July 1940 banned strikes and lockouts and required that if collective bargaining in any sector or factory ended in an impasse, the dispute must go to binding arbitration. Yet the government did not limit let alone freeze wages, while under Bevin's prodding it did impose higher minimum wage floors for the coal mines, agricultural labor, and the railways. Something more than voluntary wage restraint yet less than wage controls, Bevin's approach worked reasonably well in tamping down wage inflation while satisfying most workers. By the end of the war, wage levels had increased overall by about 50 percent compared to September 1939, while the cost-of-living index under price controls had risen about 31 percent. Actual earnings in war production industries grew even higher thanks to overtime pay and production incentives, despite higher income taxes and excise taxes on staples of working-class life, beer and tobacco.[59]

After months of piecemeal interventions, the groundwork was ready in March 1941 for two comprehensive initiatives for recruiting and placing workers in war-related jobs. Under the Essential Work Order system, in enterprises designated by the ministry as essential to the war effort, no worker could quit or be dismissed without ministerial consent. By the end of the year over 30,000 enterprises, employing about six million workers, had won that designation, but only after the companies pledged adequate compensation, training, and on-site welfare for their workers. With this leverage Bevin, for example, insisted on a guaranteed weekly wage for construction workers and dockers traditionally treated as casual labor.

The Registration for Employment Order of March 1941 required the registration of all men over the military age of forty-one and all women twenty and twenty-one years of age (later expanded in both directions). Registrants would be called for interviews at their local labor exchange and would be asked to consider filling vital job vacancies. Relatively few compulsory directions were necessary under this system, except for war-related construction projects in isolated locations. With new streams of workers being mustered, the ministry could revise the list of "reserved occupations" that had kept many younger men out of military service. For the armed forces were due to expand in 1941 to about 7 million men and women, even as the war-production industries required an estimated 1.5 million new workers to arm and supply those forces.

The solution was obvious: at least half these new workers had to be women. At first the Labor Ministry looked to single young women, and to volunteering and persuasion as the method of recruitment. Then wives without children and older single women were included, and the ministry ultimately made about 88,000 involuntary assignments. Women constituted between 30 and 50 percent of the labor force in war industries such as engineering, chemicals, and metallurgy, while almost 500,000 women joined the armed forces and 80,000 went to work for short-handed farmers.[60]

The influx of new workers (male and female) into the labor force, and the exhaustingly long hours and weekend work to meet production targets, strained industrial relations and caused spurts of absenteeism. But Bevin tried to offset demoralization by mandating joint labor-management committees to deal with issues on production lines or work sites, and joint welfare committees to enhance workplace environments. On its own authority, the ministry intervened to improve canteen facilities and on-the-job health care and to upgrade skills with serious job-training programs. Yet Bevin stopped short of adopting a veritable corporatist model. The state did not involve itself directly in collective bargaining or ground-level industrial relations. In keeping with Bevin's core beliefs, ample space remained for trade union autonomy and authority.[61]

There were of course hard bumps on this road. The ministry did little to assure pay equity for new female workers. Nonofficial or wildcat strikes erupted frequently, especially among overworked coal miners. But the ministry simply rode out most of these short, localized strikes, and Bevin rarely resorted to government coercion. Only 109 workers were prosecuted under Order No.1305 with scarcely any jailings at all or even the levying of fines. Faced with an increasing incidence of rank-and-file walkouts, however, Bevin issued a draconian order in April 1944 criminalizing incitements to wildcat strikes. But again, he thought better of actually using this power, his instincts perhaps reinforced by a scathing attack on the order in the House of Commons. Nye Bevan undoubtedly enraged the minister with his claim that Bevin's order abetted "trade union officials . . . [in] invoking the laws against their own members." But in practice the minister of labor implicitly accepted Bevan's view that "small strikes, small disputes are the vent valves of society; they do not hold up the war."[62]

The Limits of Coalition

Even with the Blitz abating, and the Soviet Union and the US now in the war, 1942 was the low point of Britain's fortunes. U-boats were decimating supply convoys in the Atlantic. Yugoslavia and Greece had fallen to the Axis. In the Pacific, the Japanese army laid siege to Singapore, the great redoubt of British naval power in the Far East, whose surrender in February 1942 was a world-historic event that stunned the British Empire. And in North Africa, after prolonged British resistance to a siege at Tobruk in Libya, the fortress fell to the Germans in June. That event touched off a debate in Parliament in July that exposed Churchill to severe criticism from Tory backbenchers, but the opposition faltered and the government prevailed in the confidence vote, 476 to 25 with 40 abstentions.[63]

The inner circle of that government—the war cabinet—looked different at the end of that trying year from the group Churchill had assembled in May 1940. On the Labour side, Greenwood had been eased out, a casualty of his alcoholism and ineffectiveness. Stafford Cripps had enjoyed a brief starring moment as a fresh face when he returned early in 1942 from being ambassador to Moscow, but by the end of the year Cripps was gone from the war cabinet. That left Labour's "big three" as the party's representatives at the summit: Attlee, Bevin, and Morrison.[64]

This is not to say that Labour's triumvirate was inherently harmonious. Morrison still considered Attlee an "accidental" party leader and retained his ambition to take Attlee's place. Bevin, on the other hand, was one of Attlee's staunchest supporters and maintained an unyielding antipathy for Morrison. Among other things, when Morrison took the greater London transportation system into the public domain in the 1930s, his plan antagonized Bevin because it precluded the representation of workers in the new public corporation. Paradoxically, Morrison's reputation as a political tactician and conciliator in the party also fed Bevin's animus. In Bevin's judgment, which he barely bothered to conceal, the man simply could not be trusted.[65]

Whatever the tensions among them, however, these three party stalwarts and veteran socialists stood together in sustaining the coalition. Each was personally loyal to Churchill and considered coalition unity at almost any price an overriding wartime imperative. In effect, the three played by Churchill's rule. As the PM recapitulated it in 1943: "Everything for the war, whether controversial or not, and nothing controversial that is not *bona fide* needed for the war."[66] In the Tory lexicon, "controversial" meant anything that smacked of the dreaded socialism. Yet Attlee insisted to his comrades in the PLP "that if the test was effective prosecution of the War the Government were willing to take all necessary steps, but ideological considerations were ruled out." Morrison too understood the prime minister's position. Churchill "was not going to tolerate any possible division within the Conservative Party because of alleged pressures by Labour to prepare schemes of reform." As head of the Conservative Party since Chamberlain's death, Churchill had no wish to arouse or mediate between two outspoken factions in his own party: the doctrinaire reactionaries of The 1922 Committee, and the young Turks who coalesced in 1943 as the Tory Reform Committee.[67]

Many rank-and-file Labourites and dozens of their MPs felt little compulsion to accept Attlee's restraint. Hence Labour Party leaders engaged in a running battle with dissident backbenchers, such as Nye Bevan, Shinwell, and Silverman, who regarded the terms of coalition as entirely one-sided. The invaluable diary of Chuter Ede (a Labourite junior minister who worked harmoniously with his Tory boss R. A. Butler, president of the Board of Education) documents this conflict, as does historian Stephen Brooke more comprehensively. Labour pulsated with resentment over the need to rein in its demands for equity and to defer socialist objectives for the duration of the war. And within the party at large, the electoral truce caused a restless discontent since local constituencies were obliged support Tory "government" candidates in by-elections rather than more kindred left-wing independents.[68]

Demands for principled action kept welling up among party activists and in the PLP, even at the risk of unsettling the coalition. When Labour entered Churchill's coalition, for example, it anticipated remedial action on the punitive restraints of the Trade Unions Act of 1927 and on the humiliating Household Means Test that required applicants for relief to prove that virtually the entirety of their household's assets had been consumed. Tories insisted, however, that the Trades Union Act had no relevance to the war effort and would therefore stand. The same held for the means test, although Conservative leaders agreed on minor alterations. Similarly, the cabinet agreed to modest raises in the abysmally low level of old-age and widows' pensions for the neediest citizens, but not to double them as Labour reasonably demanded. In a caucus preliminary to a vote in the House of Commons on the government's pension bill, only

51 Labourites backed the leadership compromise while 49 voted against it. As historian Brooke puts it (evoking memories of Ramsay MacDonald in 1931), "compromise and betrayal became interchangeable terms for Attlee's back-benchers." To Attlee and his supporters, unwillingness to back the Labour ministers once the cabinet reached a decision meant that "the Party was heading for ruin." In a commonly used phrase, "if Labour broke up the Government it would commit suicide."[69]

Labourites had also expected that in joining the coalition they could promote structural changes in the economy to enhance the war effort, which could carry over into peacetime. With the inefficient railways and coal mines central to the war effort, and with the trade unions in those sectors demanding action, Labour ministers made the case in cabinet for major steps toward nationalization. Adamant business and Tory resistance stopped them short. But backbench Labourites defied their leadership and tabled an amendment to Bevin's manpower bill that called for the nationalization of coal and transport. Much to Attlee's discomfort they mustered forty-two dissident votes for their amendment.[70]

Coal became a great bone of contention that strained the coalition to its limits. Fearing impending coal shortages, Dalton at the Board of Trade hoped to reduce consumption through a system of coupon rationing. While coal rationing won public support for fairness (70 percent in an opinion poll), it ran into fierce opposition from the mine owners' lobby and certain Tories. Dalton reasonably interpreted this response as a blend of traditional Tory hostilities, but he also discerned "a fear that I am trying to put through nationalisation of the mines by a side wind [of rationing]." Yet Dalton also had to watch his left flank: "those Labour Members who feared that the rationing proposals were a dodge to shelve reorganization [of the mines]."[71]

Dalton eventually circulated a proposal combining a modified version of the rationing scheme and a plan for state intervention in the industry short of outright nationalization: the mines could be "requisitioned" for the war effort— in Bevin's vague term—a temporary conscription of property to parallel the conscription of men. This might appease the miners who demanded state control because, as a spokesman put it, "the men must feel that they are not working for the profit of the owners" as they met backbreaking quotas and overtime and saw their wages lag behind those of munitions workers. For a while Cripps argued "that [coal rationing] is an issue on which we should be prepared to break [from the coalition]." But Churchill saw pockets of implacable Tory opposition to coal rationing, which he personally opposed as well. The PM finally insisted that rationing be postponed, in effect blocking it. As Dalton recorded, when the moment of decision finally came, "The P.M. only asks on what page it is stated that rationing will not be introduced at once. When satisfied that this is [the case], he takes no more interest." The Tories prevailed, but Dalton saved the coalition by not turning coal rationing into a make-or-break issue as Cripps had urged.[72]

On the production side, the government finally accepted a kind of dual power for the state and the mine owners. A new National Coal Board had authority to allocate supplies and regulate working conditions without modifying the archaic structures of mine ownership. For Dalton and Bevin this arrangement sufficed to improve conditions in the mines, stimulate production, and lay the ground for an eventual transition to state ownership: "Both of us were sure that if the owners lost control of the pits now they would never get it back."[73] But Nye Bevan spoke for angry Labour backbenchers who took the opposite view: "If it is not possible in the exceptional conditions of war, to nationalize the coal pits, it will never be possible in peacetime." Ridiculing the new joint coal board, he concluded: "The state steps in not in substitution of private interests but as their guardian."[74]

Having bested Dalton on coal, the Tory 1922 Committee now tried to face down Bevin, another bête noire, over his catering wages bill. The catering industry (comprising hotels, cafes, bars, and restaurants) was largely low-wage and nonunion. Bevin's bill of January 1943 set up a Catering Wages Commission to encourage collective bargaining in the industry, barring which the ministry could appoint arbitration panels to set standards of pay and hours. The cabinet finally agreed, but Tory diehards tried to block this unwelcome advance in state intervention by forcing a parliamentary debate and division. Only 283 deputies voted for the government's bill while 116 Tory dissidents voted no against their own leadership.[75] Bevin relished this victory, but it offered small comfort to Labour's leaders, who faced continuous sniping in the constituencies and the PLP against their own frequent accommodations.

The Beveridge Report and Its Aftermath

The greatest trouble for the Labour leadership arose over the Beveridge Report. This landmark initiative was the unanticipated product of an interdepartmental committee quietly established by the cabinet to reassess the current jumble of unemployment insurance, workman's compensation, old-age pensions, and workers health insurance. In this accretion of provisions since the reform era of the 1890s, some were private and others public; some national and some local; some contributory, some taxpayer funded. Coverage in various schemes extended to certain workers but not to others, and even the best type of medical insurance covered the worker but not his family. Amid this welter of limited benefits, no income maintenance provision existed for working-class children living in poverty.

To head this committee, Greenwood and Ernest Bevin proposed Sir William Beveridge, who had moved between academe and government service for over three decades. An economist, Oxford don, and one-time director of the London School of Economics, Beveridge had served in various government posts and commissions of inquiry since the Great War. Not simply a technocrat (though he could be so regarded), Beveridge was a political man in the reformist Liberal Party tradition of the late Victorian era. His principal expertise lay in manpower questions, and at the Ministry of Labor he had produced a report on the use (and waste) of skilled manpower in the armed forces. Dalton then enlisted him to draft the plan for coal rationing. But Bevin did not warm to the flinty and self-important Beveridge, and he was happy to shunt him out of the Labor Ministry to chair this new ad hoc committee.

Once into his assignment, Beveridge unilaterally altered its scope in the hope of producing a grand gesture toward social reform that would lift morale in the armed forces and at home. The vague mandate for his committee encouraged him to go beyond a "sort of tidying up operation." Instead, Beveridge shaped his committee's report into a proposal for an entirely new comprehensive and universal system of social security. In fact, when his approach became known, the government insisted that the ministerial delegates to the committee refrain from signing the final report lest they commit their ministers to its recommendations. Initially chagrined at the government's directive, Sir William quickly turned it to his advantage. Published in December 1942 under the title *Social Insurance and Allied Services,* Beveridge's name alone appeared on the cover, and the report became known simply as the Beveridge Report. Beveridge astutely bracketed its copious technical detail between an accessible twenty-page introduction and an adventurous conclusion that went far beyond the subject of social insurance. Long accustomed to writing for newspapers and lecturing publicly, Beveridge energetically promoted his vision, with initial boosts (soon regretted) from the War Office and the Ministry of Information. Thus did the basic ideas in this long, technical government report gain extensive press coverage and enthusiastic public response.[76]

Beveridge framed his work in the context of the war: "Now, when the war is abolishing landmarks of every kind, is the opportunity for using experience in a clear field. A revolutionary moment in the world's history is a time for revolutions, not for patching." Sir William described his report as a first step toward "a comprehensive policy of social progress. Social insurance fully developed may provide income security; it is an attack upon Want. But Want is one only of five giants on the road of reconstruction and in some ways the easiest to attack. The others are Disease, Ignorance, Squalor and Idleness." (Or, to put it positively, health care, education, housing, and unemployment had to be dealt with.) Beveridge promoted his plan as an assault on Want, the first of these "five giants"; social security "could be achieved now without waiting for the whole of that policy." The incomplete patchwork of existing social provisions for some groups covering unemployment, disability, sickness, or old age should be replaced by an entirely new contributory system of social security entitlements. "It is, first and foremost, a plan of insurance—of giving in return for contributions benefits up to subsistence level, as of right and without means test, so that individuals may build freely upon it." As a logical first step, he proposed that the government establish a new Ministry of Social Security to implement the plan.[77] In his conclusion Beveridge reiterated that the abolition of Want was a practicable and imperative war aim, and he set out three complimentary "assumptions" to go along with a new system of social insurance: family allowances (to be paid from the Treasury); a comprehensive national health service; and maintenance of full employment (with government planning to counter prospective unemployment). For as he put it in a later paper, "Unemployment insurance as a means of palliating mass unemployment is a confession of failure."[78]

Churchill would have preferred to shelve the Beveridge Report, but he could not ignore it after all the publicity.[79] The cabinet circled around the report, commended its basic vision, and endorsed sixteen of its recommendations in principle but resolved that their implementation must await the peace and be preceded by a general election. Kingsley Wood, the Chancellor of the Exchequer, insisted that any major postwar commitments must wait until the state of Britain's postwar finances and the likely costs of such initiatives could be forecast.[80] For while the Beveridge Report sketched a social insurance system funded mainly by contributions from employees and employers, the Treasury would have to shoulder large expenditures to get these entitlements up and running.

Bevin had reservations about the report's particulars, maintained that the trade unions would as well, and saw no need to rush into any of this. But other Labour ministers greeted the report enthusiastically and voiced dismay at the Tories' procrastinating response and possible bad faith. When a three-day House of Commons debate on the Beveridge Report began on February 16, 1943, deputy Labour leader Greenwood laid down a vaguely evasive motion that welcomed the report "as a valuable aid in determining the lines on which developments and legislation should be pursued as part of the Government's policy on post-war reconstruction."[81] Then the debate began and things fell apart.

Anderson opened for the government and, despite his sympathy for the report, by all accounts did a poor job that only raised Labour's hackles. As he droned on reading from an interminable typescript "he emphasized nothing," Dalton opined: "a most miserable and inept presentation." A Tory friend of Dalton's similarly deemed the speech "ludicrously inept. [It] gave the impression that the Govt were both shifty and hostile to the Beveridge Report." Chuter Ede too believed that Anderson "made everyone think that the Govt would shelve the whole matter." Conservative MP Harold Nicholson complained that "to accept the Report in principle, and then qualify that acceptance by all manner of dodges, merely creates suspicion." Anderson's performance galvanized the PLP, which voted in caucus to put down an aggressive amendment by Labourite Jim Griffiths "expressing its dissatisfaction with the now declared policy of the Government" and urging "the reconsideration of that policy with a view to the early implementation of the plan."[82]

Kingsley Wood's speech on the second day further infuriated the Labourites and reformist Tories as well. On day three Morrison closed for the government, giving by all accounts a fine speech that emphasized the positive in the cabinet's response, underlined how many of Beveridge's proposal had been accepted in principle, and realistically addressed the question of costs to the Treasury without implying that the costs would scuttle the plan in the future. But it was too late to alter the mood and pacify backbench Labourites. In the division on Griffith's amendment calling for "early implementation," the PLP overwhelmingly repudiated the Labour ministers. In a vote of 119 for the amendment versus 335 for the Government, 98 Labour deputies voted against their own leaders, while another 24 backbenchers abstained. Ede was shaken by the dramatic spectacle of the entire Labour front bench gathering in the No lobby to oppose the Griffiths amendment, while almost 100 rebellious members filed into the Yes lobby. "Such an example of all tail and no dog was quite futile," he confided to his diary. "The value of Labour ministers to the Govt was that they represented the rank & file of the Party." With more votes like that one, he worried, the party would be "thoroughly discredited."[83]

Could the party survive such a stark schism? In caucus before the vote Bevin had been furious over the impending revolt, took it personally as a vote of censure, and rumbled about boycotting the party. Dalton feared that "Churchill might appeal to the country, on the ground that he must know where he stands, with the result that Labour would be scrubbed out as completely as in 1931." When the Labour ministers met a few days later, they displayed a bad case of nerves. Morrison "said the Labour Party was a Suicide Club. . . . If we broke up the Govt, the P.M. might call a general election on whether winning the war or planning for after the war was the more immediate practical issue." If this kind of discord persisted or was carried to a higher level the party might indeed be immolating itself.[84] From that point forward, however, emotions cooled and a new understanding of this episode began to take hold. By defying its hamstrung coalition ministers and voting overwhelmingly for the Griffiths amendment, the PLP had positioned Labour for the next general election, whenever it might come, as the party standing solidly behind the Beveridge Report.

At the time, such tempests within the PLP seemed to threaten the cohesion of the party, its viability as a coalition partner, and (in the minds of some) its electoral future. Yet the leadership survived continuous harassment by dissidents and occasional embarrassments in the division lobbies, and the coalition endured. Despite outbursts of frustration and worry over future political advantage on both sides of the House, each party was heavily invested in the wartime coalition and loath to risk its breakdown. Admittedly, as Morrison recalled in his memoirs, "constructive planning [for the postwar] of a kind which was bound to be politically controversial was almost impossible—an inherent weakness of a coalition."[85] The disputes in cabinet over coal and the Beveridge Report in 1942–43 illustrate the point. But as the military situation improved in 1944–45, Churchill became less adamant about exclusive concentration on the war and allowed two initiatives in social policy to make their way into law. At the Board of Education Tory Rab Butler and his Labourite deputy Chuter Ede hammered out a substantial if far from comprehensive education reform bill in the face of the vested interests and inertia deployed against them (to be discussed in chapter 7).[86] Then, after a protracted struggle, Parliament enacted family allowances into law in June 1945.

The leading advocate for family allowances—social reformer, feminist, and independent MP since 1929 Eleanor Rathbone—had pressed her case for nearly three decades. The war provided new openings for her cause. In April 1941 Rathbone helped form an all-party caucus in the House of Commons to push for family allowances "as a means of safeguarding the health and well-being of the rising generation." Besides the usual opposition from the Treasury over affordability, the TUC had been a major obstacle. During the thirties certain unions feared that such a child-centered entitlement would make it harder to demand higher wages, that is, a better "family wage" for (male) breadwinners. Family allowances would therefore undercut the clout of trade unions and their value to workers. Instead, the TUC argued, the government should increase social services for families in trouble. Labour had deferred to this trade union position in the thirties, but activists from the women's section and elsewhere campaigned to win support for family allowances after the war began. Under pressure from Labour's national executive and from Walter Citrine, general secretary of the TUC, the General Council of the TUC by a split vote finally endorsed the idea in March 1942. Labour could now declare its unambiguous support at the party conference that year, and further impetus came when Beveridge listed family allowances among his report's three "complimentary proposals."[87]

In the bill proposed to Parliament, a non-contributory, income support program funded by the Treasury would entitle every family to a cash allowance for its children, without any means test and with the expectation that payments would start as soon as possible. In this outcome, advocates like Rathbone compromised on one question and prevailed on a second. First, how generous and therefore how significant would this entitlement be? To limit its cost and its scope, officials drafting the bill excluded the first child from the benefit and set the rate for the others at a "niggardly" 5s per week. Thus the bill would not provide the guaranteed subsistence for *all* children that Rathbone and Beveridge had envisaged. Second, insofar as family allowances had long been a feminist cause, it was crucial that the payments go directly to the mothers of these children. But the government's draft bill bolstered traditional paternal control in the

family by making fathers the statutory recipients. In the final round of parliamentary debate, however, Rathbone declared that she could not vote for the bill
in its present form. Proponents of vesting the allowance with mothers (in the
name of child welfare and of women's rights) successfully amended the bill in
that sense.[88]

Beyond these two landmark parliamentary acts on education and on family
allowances, various ministerial and cabinet study committees prepared for
reconstruction with a flurry of white papers in 1944–45 on such subjects as full
employment, housing, health care, and town planning. But rather than veritable
products of coalition, these position papers generally reflected the prescriptions
that a moderate Conservative government might offer in the postwar moment.[89]
Meanwhile, the same subjects and others were being studied within the Labour
Party, and the view from there would look quite different, as we shall see.[90]
Reform-minded Tories may have become more open to change in the crucible
of the war, but as Britain neared the threshold of peace in 1945, Labour would
advocate a distinctively progressive path for the nation. In the long run, the
recurrent challenges from backbenchers and party activists during the coalition
years constituted an annealing process that clarified and toughened Labour's
position on fundamental issues. As the war drew to an end, and with it the
inhibiting imperatives of coalition, the Labour Party would emerge surprisingly
unified and determined. Apprehensive about Churchill's popularity but otherwise self-confident from its experience in office, and chaffing at self-imposed
restraints during the coalition, Labour was a coiled spring awaiting the first
general election since 1935.

2

The Travails of the French Left

THE CONTRAST COULD NOT HAVE BEEN STARKER. In May 1940 Clement Attlee led a united Labour Party into a coalition government under Churchill pledged to resist the Nazis. Two months later, after the fall of France, the French parliament convoked in the town of Vichy granted "full powers" to Marshal Pétain, thereby interring the Third Republic and accepting French collaboration with Hitler. Astoundingly, over two-thirds of the Socialist parliamentarians ignored the pleas of their leader Léon Blum and voted yes. The French Left was again in disarray, more profoundly than ever. What were the fault lines running through the Left since the turn of the century, and what drove its lurches between unity and division in politics and the labor movement? In the wake of the Bolshevik Revolution the Socialist Party split apart, and the CGT labor confederation experienced a comparable schism. Fifteen years later a reunited Left forged a Popular Front alliance that won a remarkable electoral victory in 1936. Yet within two years the Popular Front collapsed; Munich bitterly divided the Socialist camp; and the French Communist Party went its own way. Under the extreme circumstances of the German occupation and Vichy, however, the French Resistance created new openings for the Left, in tandem with General de Gaulle's Free France in London. With the coming of the Liberation, what then would be the prospects for progressive forces in France, new and old?

Pillars of the Modern French Left: The CGT and the Socialist Party

It took almost a century for the French revolutionary heritage to subside into a stable democratic and republican regime. After a succession of upheavals (1789, 1792, 1830, 1848, 1870), two Napoleonic coups, and violent civil conflicts, it is not surprising that French republicans, socialists, and labor activists at the turn of the twentieth century were riven by factionalism and conflicting values. Over time, moves toward unity and fissure alternated on the French Left with seeming regularity.[1]

For workers, a durable trade union federation, the Confédération Générale du Travail (CGT), came together only at the turn of the century. With little more than 100,000 members in 1902, the CGT claimed about 600,000 members on the eve of the Great War. The war and its immediate aftermath brought a dramatic surge in membership, which peaked in 1920 at 1,600,000, only to plummet after a wave of failed strikes that year. In contrast to labor federations in Britain and the US (the TUC and the AFL), the CGT at its 1906 congress in Amiens codified a radical doctrine known as revolutionary syndicalism. Trade unions must remain independent from all political parties since progress for workers depended entirely on their own efforts (a stance, to be sure, largely shared by the moderate AFL in America). But the CGT sought not simply to improve the conditions of employment (as in its long-running campaign for an eight-hour day) but to promote the transformation of society. CGT militants regarded strikes not only as tools of negotiation but as the radicalizing weapon of choice. When the time was ripe, they believed, a paralyzing general strike could arouse the working masses and force dramatic change on an inertial society and a hostile state. When actual strikes failed (as they often did), however, less committed members deserted their unions.[2]

In 1909 the CGT chose as its general secretary Léon Jouhaux (1879–1954), who had gone to work in a cigarette factory at the age of sixteen and then climbed his way up his union's hierarchy. Yet even as he espoused the CGT's revolutionary syndicalism, Jouhaux's pragmatic temperament gradually diluted it. Over time, while maintaining the federation's political autonomy, he edged closer to reformist socialism. The portly Jouhaux would remain at the CGT's helm for decades and provided the French Left with one durable if far from fixed coordinate.[3]

* * *

At the turn of the century, meanwhile, French socialists reached an extreme
level of sectarian division, at one point fielding three distinct political parties
alongside socialists who stood independently in their own constituencies
as advocates of the working class. Some socialists forged their political careers
in the broad republican front during battles with right-wing anti-republicans,
whose victory over the latter included the separation of church and state in
1905 and the exoneration of Alfred Dreyfus.[4] By then many socialists had
wearied of their fragmentation and heeded a call from the Second Workingmen's
International in Geneva to provide France with a unified socialist party. Their
new party in fact called itself the French Section of the Workingmen's
International (Section Française de l'Internationale Ouvrière)—the SFIO. The
party's titular head was Jules Guesde, who had made Marxism a common
vernacular of socialist discourse in France and who, as a would-be revolutionary, scorned mere parliamentary reformism. But if Guesde was the SFIO's
elder statesman, its effective leader and guiding voice was Jean Jaurès. A former
philosophy teacher, Jaurès too had incorporated Marxist theory about class
struggle into his own thinking and duly referred to the new party as proletarian
and revolutionary. But he also insisted that egalitarian socialist values could
best be nurtured within the democratic and republican legacy of the French
Revolution. Conversely, the democratic promises of the French Revolution
could only be consummated, he argued, through the gradual achievement of
socialism. Besides being parliamentary leader of SFIO deputies and editor of
the party's daily *L'Humanité*, Jaurès wrote an influential *Socialist History of the
French Revolution* to make that case.[5]

While the SFIO presented itself as proletarian, most of its leaders and many
of its militants were middle class. Although it proclaimed itself a revolutionary
party, its own internal organization was eminently democratic, and the party
operated comfortably in the electoral and parliamentary system of the Third
Republic. But it drew one important line in the sand: under Guesdist doctrine,
the party would not participate in governing cabinets formed by any bourgeois
party, although it might support them in parliament as the occasion warranted.
Should the republic seem in imminent peril, however, that distinctive marker of
socialist political identity might have to be reconsidered.

Though emotionally patriotic, like the revolutionary Jacobins he admired,
Jaurès shared with most socialists an aversion to militarism and war, and socialist
deputies routinely voted against military budgets. As the hardening alliances

within the European state system seemed to foreshadow a general war, the Second International strove mightily to interpose proletarian internationalism as a barrier against that cataclysm. Like Keir Hardie in Britain, an anguished Jaurès worked tirelessly to hold back the tide of war, for which he was vilified as a traitor in the right-wing press. On July 31, 1914, as Europe hurtled toward an explosion, a nationalist fanatic shot Jaurès dead. This shocking event had the paradoxical effect of deflating the French antiwar movement, as the government rushed to enfold the martyred Jaurès into the national cause. In any case, the socialist antiwar movement collapsed in both Germany and France. With war declared in August, the SFIO joined a patriotic *union sacrée* of French parties, and three socialists entered a coalition cabinet with the party's consent.[6] Léon Blum, the future socialist leader, gained his first governmental experience when the socialist minister of public works invited this skilled constitutional lawyer to become his chief of staff. Simultaneously, Jouhaux pivoted from his previous antiwar stance and led the CGT into support of the *union sacrée.* As in Germany and Britain, socialist and labor cooperation helped rally the home front and promoted efforts by workers for robust industrial war production.

Despite France's victory in the war, the *union sacrée* ended badly for socialists and trade unionists. The prolongation and unimaginable carnage of the war caused a sharp revival of anti-militarism in their ranks. When a center-right *bloc national* swept the November 1919 French election, its leaders showed no interest in rewarding labor's wartime cooperation. Earlier that year parliament had enacted labor's long-standing demand for the eight-hour day, but the new government declined to enforce this new standard, which employers stubbornly resisted. When embittered railwaymen launched a series of aggressive strikes, militant syndicalists pushed the CGT into supporting them with a general strike. The government faced down the waves of strikers in various sectors with unflinching hostility, and the general strike collapsed after two weeks, bringing in its wake severe employer reprisals.[7]

The good faith and participation in the wartime *union sacrée* now appeared to many socialists and workers as a disastrous mistake, especially in light of what was occurring in Russia. The Bolsheviks—uncompromising in their commitment to class struggle and antiwar agitation—had seized power in the name of the proletariat, taken Russia out of the war, and beaten back domestic and foreign efforts at counterrevolution. Most French socialists instinctively rallied around their Russian comrades.

A Fractured Left, 1919–1934

Under Guesde and Jaurès the SFIO had incorporated Marxist language of class struggle and proletarian revolution into its vision of socialism alongside a commitment to democratic politics, support for specific reforms, and (in some quarters) Jacobin patriotism. Postwar reaction at home coupled with the example of the Bolshevik Revolution abroad exposed the tensions in this amalgam. The Bolsheviks then forced European socialists to confront such ambivalence directly when they launched the Third or Communist International (IC), soon to be known as the Comintern. But if the SFIO chose to join the IC, what would the IC demand of French socialists as the price of admission?

In the spring of 1920 the party's National Council dispatched its general secretary L.-O. Frossard and *L'Humanité*'s editor Marcel Cachin to Moscow, to report back on the situation in Russia and to sound out the IC on its attitude toward the SFIO. Impressed by what they were shown of Soviet society, the Frenchmen also absorbed a good deal of hectoring by IC leader Zinoviev about the laxness of their party, the heresy of reformism, and the need for unconditional support of the Russian Revolution.

The IC insisted that the SFIO must become a truly revolutionary party. It must forego democratic procedures in favor of centralized leadership acceptable to Moscow and adopt a firm party line as laid down by the Comintern. Zinoviev made crystal clear that the French party could no longer include reformists. Leading antiwar militants such as Jean Longuet and Paul Faure were caught in the middle. Longuet (Marx's grandson) became a litmus test for the impending conflict: he extolled the proletarian revolution in Russia and wished to bring his party under the IC's umbrella, but he defended the traditional internal democracy and toleration for dissent in the SFIO. The Comintern's executive, however, insisted that affiliated parties could not indulge in such luxuries.[8]

With an influx of new and restive members after the war (perhaps half the 180,000 SFIO members joined at that time),[9] sentiment in the party ran heavily toward unconditional affiliation with the IC. Upon their return the two emissaries recommended this course. "We remained with the working class, at the side of the world's first Socialist revolution," Frossard recalled. Moscow deserved deference as the world center of proletarian revolution, they argued, and the SFIO must accept the Comintern's conditions. When the Comintern finally made its twenty-one conditions for affiliation explicit and public, its demands amounted to a draconian transformation: the exclusion of "reformists and centrists" from any position in affiliated parties regardless of their previous status (specifying Longuet by name as an example); infiltration by the party of trade unions; the renunciation of "social-patriotism"; subordination of the party's parliamentary deputies to its central committee; a centralized party organization wielding "iron discipline"; an obligation to implement the decisions of the Comintern; adoption of the name "Communist Party"; and the exclusion of those who opposed these conditions.[10] Some of these specifics made Frossard uncomfortable but he framed the issue in general terms: "that you fight with the greatest possible energy against opportunism and social reformism." The more fervent Cachin declared that there was only one condition Moscow really cared about: "to break decisively with class collaboration, to act like Socialists to prepare for the coming revolution."[11]

The annual SFIO Congress, meeting in Tours in December 1920, would decide the issue. After the local socialist federations had expressed their preferences, it was obvious that unconditional affiliation with the IC would carry the day at Tours. The speeches in support of various motions took up four days. Longuet and Faure still hoped to prevent a schism by moving for *conditional* affiliation to the IC—an unrealistic attempt at compromise, as a brutally blunt telegram from Zinoviev to the congress made clear.[12] Frossard and Cachin backed the motion for unconditional affiliation, without which French socialism would be severing itself from the Soviet triumph. Léon Blum, elected as a socialist deputy from Paris for the first time in 1919, emerged as the strongest voice opposed to any affiliation with the IC, and he delivered a remarkable speech comparing traditional French socialism with Moscow's new model.[13]

Blum categorically rejected the notion that socialists everywhere must now subordinate themselves to Moscow. The Bolshevik Revolution did not comport with Marxist theory, he argued, and could certainly not be generalized as a model for Western Europe. Blum denied that this was an argument "between the reformist and the revolutionary idea." The goal of socialism remained the transformation of capitalism, and a seizure of power might well be appropriate down the road to consolidate an imminent socialist revolution, but only under two circumstances. First, that the long maturation of industrial capitalism must be nearing completion, during which time the party will have been publicly educating and preparing the masses. At that point, but only then, might there be a revolutionary act, as the socialists consolidated this imminent transformation "by any means, excluding neither legal nor illegal means." This scenario Blum contrasted to the error of the Bolsheviks, who deemed the seizure of power an end in itself, to be accomplished through armed attack prepared clandestinely.

Secondly, Blum insisted, when and if the time came for a final revolutionary action, it was crucial that the instrument of this action, the socialist party, be itself impeccably democratic. Blum extolled the decentralized and democratic traditions of French socialism. "The collective will of our party rose from level to level, from the [local] section to the [departmental] federation, from the federation to the National Council, from the National Council to the [annual] Congress. . . . Leaders were only interpreters, representatives of the collective will and the thinking developed by the rank and file of the party." In contrast, "The Bolshevik system of centralization entails the subordination of each organism to the organism hierarchically above it . . . a kind of military command formulated on high. . . . The central power will finally belong to a secret committee designated under the control of the . . . International itself. . . . [Our] party was an appeal to all workers, while the one you want to establish is the creation of small, disciplined, homogeneous avant-gardes subject to rigorous control."

In sum, Blum argued, when the time for the proletarian revolution arrived, "we accept [a transitional] dictatorship if the conquest of power is not pursued as an end in itself. But . . . you imagine, against the entire Marxist conception of history, that it is the only way to bring about that transformation on which neither capitalist evolution nor our own propaganda work has had an effect." In the Bolshevik model, the seizure of power became tantamount to the social revolution itself. Worse yet, their dictatorship would not be temporary or provisional but "is a stable system of government behind whose shelter you wish to do all the work." Moscow's system elevated violence and terror to a routine, indefinite method of rule.

As he prepared to leave the rostrum Blum expressed feelings of "tragic anxiety, sadness and fear," yet he ended on an optimistic grace note of fraternity, at polar opposites from the wrathful belligerence of Zinoviev and company: "Let all of us, even separated, remain socialists; in spite of everything, let us remain brothers, brothers separated by a cruel quarrel, but a family quarrel, and whom a common home may once again bring together." Maudlin in the extreme at the time, these words would yet prove uncannily prophetic some years later, not once but twice over.

For the moment, the delegates heard out Blum, Longuet, Cachin and others, then by a margin of more than three to one they voted for unconditional affiliation to the IC. The party of Jaurès, it seemed, would become the party of Lenin. At any rate the unified Socialist Party of 1905 now split apart. The majority willingly surrendered the name SFIO to become the Parti Communiste Français (PCF), and legitimately retained the party's treasury and the newspaper once edited by Jaurès, *L'Humanité.* The ousted minority (for such it effectively was) immediately found another venue in Tours and convened to shore up what was left of "the old house," as Blum nostalgically called it.

Initially the trend and the numbers would favor the communists. But as the formulae for "Bolshevization" laid out in the twenty-one conditions took hold in the PCF, the new style engendered counterproductive tactics, as in the party's focus on workplace cells rather than local sections. Among the early casualties was Frossard, who quietly left the PCF in 1924. After a harsh new Comintern line of 1928 demanded an unbending "struggle of class against class," the PCF began hemorrhaging. As the Socialist Party picked itself off the ground after Tours, it still held the advantage over the communists in the electoral arena. Only thirteen of the SFIO's sixty-eight parliamentary deputies had deserted to the new PCF after the schism, and most of its mayors stayed with "the old house" as well. Going forward, the communists' subservience to Moscow and scorn toward "bourgeois democracy" gave them little traction in the next three national elections (1924, 1928, 1932) outside a few bastions in industrial suburbs.

Meanwhile the SFIO found its new equilibrium under a co-leadership team of Léon Blum and Paul Faure. Blum provided doctrinal direction as head of the socialist parliamentary delegation and political director of its new organ, *Le Populaire,* while Faure served as the party's general secretary and master organizer. They could scarcely resolve the party's longstanding identity crisis— ostensibly Marxist, proletarian, and in some sense revolutionary yet committed to democracy, the republic, and the need for interim reforms. For the moment they clung to non-participation in bourgeois cabinets as their political totem, and they assured places on their National Council and voices at party congresses for dissident factions (*tendances*) of the militant but non-communist left. Blum and Faure proved adept at maintaining party unity at the congresses by mollifying dissenters with face-saving compromises known as "synthesis motions."

Back in 1920–21 a fissure comparable to the one at Tours also split the CGT. A minority of militants in the confederation remained furious at the betrayal of syndicalist values when Jouhaux led the CGT into the *union sacrée* in 1914. The postwar national government's hostility to workers stoked this anger, which exploded in the convulsive strikes of 1920, the government's repression, and employer retribution. Tension mounted between so-called reformers (personified by Jouhaux) and radical factions newly inspired by the Bolshevik example. Whether or not to affiliate with Moscow's new Red trade union federation posed a symbolic fork in the road for the CGT. But with membership in most trade unions in steep decline, the radical tendencies gained ground. When anti-reformists formed a pressure group within the CGT called the Revolutionary Syndicalist Committee in 1920, the federation's leadership was tempted to expel these dissidents, even at the risk of a schism in the labor movement.

Since 1914 Jouhaux's majoritarian side held sway at CGT annual congresses by margins of three to one, but delegates to the Lille congress in July 1921 supported the leadership by the minuscule margin of only 1,556 to 1,348 *mandats*.[14] Traditional attempts to split differences and paper over conflicts for the sake of labor unity no longer suited anyone. Schism did not come in one dramatic moment as it had in the Socialist Party at Tours, but during the following year certain trade unions and departmental labor federations dominated by militant tendencies pulled out of the CGT and soon formed a rival, pro-communist federation calling itself the CGT-Unitaire (CGT-U), with particular strength in the regions around Paris and Lyon. When the schism had run its course, the CGT could count an estimated 488,000 members and the CGT-U about 349,000. In 1920 Moscow had hoped to dominate a united CGT. In due course the PCF and Moscow established control over the CGT-U, which drove out the radical syndicalists still faithful to unadulterated worker independence. The most damaging result of the schism was of course all the energy spent on competition instead of cooperation to build up the labor movement, as the rival confederations proved "incapable of conducting the smallest common action."[15] Thus did the schisms of 1920–21 in the Socialist Party and the CGT brutally fracture progressive forces in France.

From Schism to Unity

Potentially in the progressive camp as well, the Radical Party (formally the Radical-Socialist Party) was the traditional centrist or center-left party of rural and small town republicans and secularists. The Radicals congenitally vacillated over policies, lacked party discipline, and tended to opt for the most painless or politically advantageous short-term choices. In their temporizing, however, the Radicals knowingly reflected the nature of French society, with its exceptionally large numbers of farmers, shopkeepers, small businessmen, and public employees, alongside conservative big business and financial elites and an alienated industrial labor force. This underlying structure produced France's "stalemate society," as it has been called, and the Radical Party responded to these discordant social interests with inertial caution.[16] In the electoral arena the Radicals profited from the Third Republic's single-constituency, two-round runoff, voting system (apart from an experiment in proportional representation in 1924), which overrepresented rural and small town districts.

The electoral results in 1928, 1932, and 1936 indicate the returns for the three protagonists on the left of the political spectrum: the Socialists, the Communists and the Radicals (table 2.1).[17] In 1932, with almost 2 million votes, the SFIO became the leading vote-getting party in France, although it ended up with fewer seats than the Radicals. With support from the Socialists, the Radicals won a fragile mandate in the Chamber of Deputies to form a government, which proved unstable and short lived in part because the Socialists would not join the cabinet and could not be relied on to support objectionable government policies going forward.

Despite the Great Depression and the Nazi's ascendancy in Germany, business as usual continued in France on most fronts in the early 1930s. The Third Republic emitted an aura of torpor and dysfunction with its unstable parliamentary coalitions, revolving door governments (over thirty cabinets between 1919 and 36), opportunistic political horse-trading, and episodes of public corruption—a state of affairs encapsulated by one critic as "the Republic of Cronies."[18] As cabinets came and went, political ineffectiveness fueled extra-parliamentary agitation that

Table 2.1. Votes and Seats for the Three Major Parties of the Left in France

	Election of 1928	Election of 1932	Election of 1936
SFIO	1.7m / **101 seats** (17%)	1.95m / **129 seats** (22%)	1.9m / **147 seats** (25%)
PCF	1m / **14 seats** (2.4%)	.79m / **12 seats** (2%)	1.5m / **72 seats** (12%)
Radicals	1.7m / **113 seats** (19%)	1.8m / **155 seats** (26%)	1.4m / **109 seats** (18%)

sometimes smacked of fascism, notwithstanding the absence of any figure on the Right in France comparable to Mussolini or Hitler. In the popular right-wing press, incendiary rhetoric about extruding decadence and corruption from France targeted its purported carriers: foreigners, Jews, freemasons, financiers, communists, or all of the above. Right-wing leagues and veterans organizations like the Croix de Feu sought to create a transformative political crisis with raucous demonstrations and violent street actions.

This charged atmosphere engulfed the SFIO itself. Disgruntled right-wing dissidents or neo-socialists (as they came to be called) at a minimum hoped to enhance the party's appeal to rural and middle-class voters, and they considered "non-participation" in governing cabinets to be pointless. Rejecting Marxism altogether as an ideological foundation for their party, some neo-socialists advocated instead new ideas about central planning and a mixed economy. More ominously, however, two of the prominent socialist deputies in this camp, Marcel Déat and Adrien Marquet (who doubled as the mayor of Bordeaux), displayed severe ideological confusion. At a confrontation during the party congress of 1933, they insisted that the appeal of fascism arose from society's hunger for order and authority and went beyond the need for a strong state to manage capitalism. As Marquet put it, "Order and authority are the foundations of the action we must undertake to win over the masses." Blum found such sentiments "frightening," insisted that "one does not combat fascism by adopting its principles," and wondered aloud if he hadn't strayed into a Nazi meeting.[19] Later that year the SFIO expelled the neo-socialist deputies who repeatedly broke party discipline. Some eventually returned to the fold, but Déat's disaffection from traditional socialism escalated. "Order, Authority, and Nation" eventually ended up as the slogan of a fascistic, anti-Semitic movement led by Déat, irredeemably hostile to the Third Republic.

The PCF also contributed its share to the overheated political atmosphere in France. Under the strategy of "class against class" adopted by the Comintern in 1928, the PCF and the CGT-U treated leaders of the SFIO and the CGT not simply as rivals and reformist sellouts but as the most dangerous of enemies. Under this rigid party line, communists viciously attacked socialist leaders as "social fascists."

A violent and bloody night of rioting on February 6, 1934, brought the menace of anti-parliamentary politics in France to a head. A few days earlier, a Radical-led cabinet had fallen amidst a financial scandal centered on a swindler named Stavisky, who had bribed a number of politicians. For the extreme Right this offered a lush target for attack, with a final spark added when the new premier-designate, Radical Edouard Daladier, removed the Paris prefect of police, who had been indulgent to right-wing demonstrators in the past. Whipped up by the right-wing media, angry crowds from various leagues poured into the streets on February 6. Some converged on the Place de la Concorde and attempted to storm the Chamber of Deputies across the river, despite police units barring the bridge that led there. Pitched battles ensued throughout the night, violence spread to other neighborhoods, and the Ministry of Marine was set ablaze. In the end the police killed 14 rioters, and between 1,500 and 2,300 civilians and police were injured. The next day, in the wake of brutal hectoring from the Right, Daladier resigned.[20]

The riot of February 6, 1934, was not a fascist uprising or an actual plot to overthrow the republican government, but to the Left it seemed close enough at the time. At the least, the riot displayed the radicalization of the extreme Right in France, and it was a milestone "in a prolonged and unfolding crisis of the Third Republic comparable to parallel developments elsewhere [on the continent]." While the leader of the Croix de Feu tried to restrain his legions during and after the event, they still projected an intimidating presence that had to be reckoned with.[21]

The communists responded to the sixth of February with a demonstration of their own three days later, which the government banned and which turned into another riot with fatalities. For their part, the SFIO and the CGT concerted to organize mass demonstrations and a one-day general strike on February 12. This initiative carried a huge risk: if it fizzled, the extremists would surely be emboldened. But these demonstrations "to block the route to fascism" succeeded beyond expectations in the capital and across the country. Impressive crowds turned out in over 340 cities and towns, including 19 cities that saw over 5,000 demonstrators.[22]

Great obstacles remained to any sustained cooperation on the Left, however, since the Communist Party line had not changed one whit. Maurice Thorez—elected a deputy from Paris in 1932 and being groomed by Moscow for leadership—reiterated this line before the PCF's central committee on the eve of the February 6 riot: "All the parties of the bourgeoisie, including the various factions of social-democracy, are cooperating in the work of fascisization. . . .

In no case will we seek an accord with the leadership of the Socialist Party." As for Daladier, Thorez derided him as a major facilitator of fascism. On the very day of the riot *L'Humanité* declared, "One cannot fight against fascism without also fighting against social-democracy." Such fulminations continued well after the riot. "Defend the Republic, says Blum?" opined *L'Humanité* on February 19: "As if fascism is still not one and the same as the Republic, as if the Republic wasn't already fascism."[23] Yet some rank-and-file communists were eager to undertake joint anti-fascist actions. Socialist leaders, having absorbed years of venomous attack, responded with caution, but some local socialist and trade union militants also pressed for common action and established ad hoc anti-fascist committees with local communists.

Then, in July 1934, Moscow changed its party line to a popular front strategy in which socialism and bourgeois democracy no longer figured as leading enemies. The shift flowed from Stalin's dawning conviction that a strong republican France might be an effective ally in containing a Nazi Germany dangerous to them both. Once the popular front strategy became fixed, the PCF could exit from the political wilderness, serve the working class more effectively, yet still defend the strategic interests of the Soviet Union to the maximum. The PCF could now call off its war with the socialists; promote labor solidarity; and respond to the concerns of the lower middle classes potentially susceptible to fascism's appeal.

Momentum for "barring the route to fascism" galvanized the divided labor movement as well. Impetus for reunification percolated up from rank-and-file trade unionists in the rival confederations, and the new Communist Party line then impelled leaders of the CGT-U to push for reunification from the top down. Jouhaux remained leery during protracted negotiations that began in October 1934 and demanded concessions from the CGT-U, such as a ban on leaders of a reunited CGT doubling as officials of a political party. By September 1935 the CGT and the CGT-U each endorsed a merger plan at parallel congresses and authorized individual trade unions and departmental federations to execute formal mergers locally. At the final national unity congress in Toulouse in March 1936, the relative size of each confederation initially favored the non-communists (the *ex-confedérés* of the CGT) in allocating leadership posts and in resolving the "incompatibility" issue: a vote of 5,508 to 2,411 barred future leaders from holding positions in a political party. Jouhaux was named secretary general of the reunified CGT, while Benoît Frachon became his co-secretary but had to resign from the PCF central committee. Having been the last to embrace reunification, Jouhaux now committed himself to maintaining labor unity and paid little mind to complaints by some former comrades about communist tactics. The reunified CGT quadrupled total union membership within one year, with communist-dominated unions gaining a preponderant share of new adherents, especially in future growth areas such as the metallurgical and chemical sectors.[24]

The Triumph of the Popular Front

The new popular front line from Moscow also permitted French communists to embrace republican patriotism and to cooperate with the Radical Party. An astonishing if fragile union on the French Left ensued, publicly sealed in two very different venues. In Paris on July 14, 1935, a huge demonstration of republican solidarity unfolded on the streets, as Blum, Thorez, and Daladier stood together on a platform in the Place de la République to address the vast throngs. In Moscow later that month, at the Seventh Congress of the Communist International, Thorez extolled "the success of the anti-fascist united front" in the pugnacious language uniquely suited to a communist audience.[25]

The three parties of the Left still remained wary of each other. But the Nazi ascendancy in Germany, the February 6 riots, and the failure of successive governments to combat the economic slump impelled them to mute their differences. By January 1936, the anti-fascist reflex of 1934–35 had evolved into a formal, tri-party political alliance known as the *rassemblement populaire* or Popular Front, which also encompassed the two labor federations (shortly to merge), a venerable civil rights organization (the League of the Rights of Man), and two associations of anti-fascist intellectuals. In prospect of the coming national election, the parties thrashed out a vague common program focused on the defense of republican liberties in France, the maintenance of peace via the League of Nations, and economic reform to foster "the restoration of purchasing power destroyed or reduced by the crisis." The program pleased none of the parties completely but avoided any fatal impasse.[26] Even so, alliance with the communists posed considerable risks to the two other partners. For despite the PCF's public moderation, a drumbeat from the right-wing press denounced the Popular Front as paving the way for the Bolshevization of the country, economic anarchy, perhaps civil war.[27]

The electoral campaign of 1936 crested with a national radio address by Blum on April 21. In his didactic yet passionate style, Blum elaborated the Popular Front's overriding themes: maintaining peace by containing fascism through collective security; defending republican liberty against the threat of fascism at home; responding to the ravages of the depression by repudiating failed deflationary policies and stimulating mass purchasing power.[28] The alliance did not preclude competition among its parties in the first round of voting—especially from traditionalist Radicals who accepted the Popular Front with great reluctance. But the spirit of cooperation generally held through the runoffs of the second round and produced a clear majority of seats for Popular Front candidates.[29] Within this majority, the SFIO garnered the most votes and seats (see table 2.1) The communists reaffirmed that they would not accept positions in the cabinet but would support it in parliament. Socialists and Radicals then formed a government with Blum as prime minister.

Léon Blum was more than ready to lead. Back in 1926 he had proposed to modify socialist "non-participation" doctrine in a novel fashion. While participating in a government formed by the Radicals should remain taboo, he argued, the party should be willing to form a cabinet on its own or in coalition with the center-left so long as socialists headed this government and had the dominant voice. Dangers lurked in this stance, he admitted, for it would enmesh the socialists in managing a capitalist system that they opposed in principle. Still, should it find itself in such a situation, Blum argued, the party must accept the responsibilities of office, where it could "accelerate the rhythm of reform." As a corollary, if it came to power the party must adhere scrupulously to legality. With misgivings, both the militant and reformist wings of the party accepted this doctrine at the party congress of 1926. A decade later the socialists thus stood ready to "exercise power" following the Popular Front's victory at the polls.[30]

Even before Blum's cabinet formally took office, rank-and-file workers, energized by the new political climate, launched a strike movement as extensive, creative, and effective as any in European history. It began with factory occupations or sit-down strikes in the Renault works, other auto plants, and metallurgical factories in the industrial suburbs of Paris, then spread across the country and into numerous sectors public and private, including nonunionized workplaces such as department stores. In June 1936 official statistics counted over 12,000 strikes involving 1.8 million strikers. The novel forms and buoyant energy of the strikes gave this social explosion an air of theater and festivity. A distinct lack of violence against persons or property went hand in hand with fierce resolve by the workers to prevail. Ultimately they returned largely undamaged factories and workplaces to their owners, but the social fabric appeared permanently altered by the upsurge of worker confidence and by the terms of a national settlement brokered by Blum's government.[31]

For any government, this strike wave would have posed the worrying prospect of a national economic breakdown. But for the Popular Front it also served as a multiplier of sorts. Since the tidal wave of strikes stunned and frightened business interests and opposition politicians, it imparted unforeseen leverage to Blum's government in achieving an immediate impact. Settling these conflicts decisively in labor's favor became a distinct possibility even though the government had no direct control over the workers. In marathon negotiations held at the Matignon (the prime minister's official residence), shaken representatives of big business effectively capitulated to labor's broad demands. The Matignon Agreements won a forty-hour week for workers, wage increases, two weeks of paid vacation, and unprecedented negotiating rights for trade unions in the future. Both houses of parliament quickly approved the agreements, for the unique circumstances deterred even the Senate, the bastion of conservatives, from its habitual obstructionism. Implemented immediately, paid vacations amounted to a sociocultural revolution of sorts and in due course engendered new vacation colonies, package tours, and summer camps for working people who had never enjoyed such opportunities. Paid vacations became a palpable symbol and durable legacy of the Popular Front. But in retrospect it could be argued that the forty-hour week became a poisoned chalice for the Popular Front legacy.

The Collapse of the Popular Front

Notwithstanding its spectacular electoral success, the Popular Front rested on shaky foundations. The great strike wave of 1936 and the Matignon Agreements had stunned conservatives into momentary impotence, but they left a residue of bitter enmity. Resentment from big business, small proprietors, and political conservatives of all stripes hardened into a thirst for retribution. The communists backed Blum's government loyally but kept their options open by declining to join his cabinet. At the core of the Popular Front, the socialists suffered their perpetual identity crisis over how aggressive or reformist the party should be;

leftish *tendances* repeatedly roiled party conclaves with demands for greater militancy and class struggle. The Blum-Faure leadership deflected this pressure, but their own consensus was itself destined to implode in a conflict over how to deal with international fascism, as we shall shortly see. The Radicals held great leverage in the Popular Front with their 115 deputies who stood between the Marxist Left (with 263) and the parties of the Right (with 236). Daladier had led the Radicals into the Popular Front, but elements of the party never embraced this tilt and awaited the opportunity for a reversal. Moreover, the Radicals too would shortly split over how France should respond to fascist aggression abroad.[32]

From the start, economic stagnation and financial problems bedeviled the Popular Front government. In the election campaign of 1936, Blum used the slogan "neither deflation nor devaluation." He attacked previous deflationary budget cutting and advocated new public works to stimulate purchasing power, but he ruled out the unpopular if sensible option of realigning the overvalued franc with other currencies. By September, however, Blum reluctantly concluded that the franc had to be devalued, and Finance Minister Vincent Auriol negotiated a monetary accord with the US and Britain as a framework for devaluing the franc by over 25 percent.[33] As hoped, devaluation provided short-term economic stimulus, but it soon petered out. In February 1937, with rearmament now high on his agenda, Blum sought to consolidate his gains and avoid further political contention by announcing a "pause," a moratorium on further social and economic reforms. But he still faced severe budgetary shortfalls, speculation on the franc, and capital flight, which limited the state's borrowing power. Having broken the political taboo on devaluation, Blum prepared to breach a second: public hostility to currency-exchange controls. Shunning more draconian measures, he proposed that certain corporations and banks be required to maintain a portion of their reserves in state securities.[34] Blum requested from parliament "full powers" (as the French called it) to enact decree-laws on credit and borrowing that would not require legislative approval—a standard but always contentious tool of govern-ance in the Third Republic. In the Chamber of Deputies the Popular Front coali-tion held and approved these powers by a vote of 346 to 247. But the Senate, dominated by the Right and the most hidebound Radicals, balked by a vote of 168 to 98. The state's financial duress thereby precipitated a political crisis.

What could Blum do to prevail? Left-wing militants looked to the masses to break the impasse; pressure in the streets might help Blum push back at the

Senate. But mass demonstrations against the Senate could easily turn violent, and with his scruples about legalism Blum would "at no price" condone such tactics. A possible solution would be the dissolution of the Chamber and new elections, but the Senate would have to agree and had no reason to give Blum a way out. In exasperation, Blum decided to submit his cabinet's resignation on the understanding that a reshuffled government of Socialist and Radical ministers headed by his vice premier, the opportunistic Radical Chautemps, would give the Popular Front a second chance. A National Council of the SFIO approved that option by a three to one margin, and in attenuated form the Popular Front limped on.[35] By January 1938, however, when the communists in the Chamber of Deputies balked at one of his policies, Chautemps effectively told them he didn't care about their support. At this, the Socialist ministers resigned from his cabinet. Chautemps, in any case, was losing his will to lead and in March, at the first sign of difficulty in getting his way, he resigned, just as Hitler executed his *Anschluss* of Austria.

At this moment of grave domestic and international perils President Lebrun again turned to Blum, who proposed to form a national unity government extending from the Communists to the Right. Blum made a patriotic appeal to an unprecedented meeting of about 200 rightist deputies—a Daniel in the lion's den. Almost alone, the fiscal conservatives Paul Reynaud and Joseph Laniel spoke in favor of the idea. The other rightist deputies in the room showered Blum with contempt and viciously rebuffed his proposal. At Lebrun's request, Blum then formed a new Popular Front cabinet, but his government quickly fell when the Senate again blocked Blum's financial measures.[36]

Eduoard Dalladier then became the man of the hour. On July 14, 1935 Daladier, as the new head of the Radical Party, had stood on the platform with Blum and Thorez to herald the Popular Front alliance. Now he led his party and his country into a dramatic reversal as the impresario of a center-right "national union" government—entirely different from the broader patriotic union envisioned earlier by Blum. Over the coming months Daladier and his Finance Minister Reynaud, governing through decree-laws, repudiated the spirit of the Popular Front. The forty-hour week became the focal point of this change. The trade unions that had pushed for it in the first place had insisted on a rigorous application: "Forty hours for everyone and at once," as Jouhaux put it. Workers generally resisted flexible overtime arrangements as well as an arguably more efficient six-day working week in factories; employers denounced the forty-hour week as an obstacle not simply to profitability but to the enhanced productivity on which economic recovery and rearmament depended.[37] Daladier took it as his mandate to scrap the forty-hour week; when his moves provoked a one-day general strike his resolve hardened and he crushed the strike.

Facing International Fascism and Flinching

Daladier is most remembered as Chamberlain's counterpart in the appeasement of Hitler at Munich. But as historians agree, he did not actually reverse the Popular Front's foreign policy since it never had a coherent one to begin with.[38] The Popular Front arose in response to a perceived threat of fascism at home, and on coming to power it dissolved the paramilitary leagues, which resurfaced as extremist political parties. But how to deal with aggressive fascism abroad proved to be a fault line running through the alliance.

The disarray began early and brutally, with General Franco's rebellion against the Spanish Republic in June 1936. After Franco's surprise attack, the Spanish government requested immediate assistance from France in the form of aircraft and arms. On moral and political grounds Blum quickly authorized such shipments to a legitimate democratic government fending off an internal rebellion with fascist overtones. Blum could do this without parliamentary approval, but he had to consult his cabinet and quickly realized that providing such aid was by no means a self-evident response.

The communists supported active assistance, but they had not joined the cabinet, hence were absent where it most counted. Prominent Radicals split over the issue. Strong advocacy for aid to the Spanish Republic came from Radical Air Minister Pierre Cot and Education Minister Jean Zay, but Vice Premier Camille Chautemps and Foreign Minister Yvon Delbos pressed Blum to maintain neutrality and stay out of it. Some Socialists too insisted that avoiding war trumped all other considerations in dealing with this international crisis. If France took one side in Spain's civil war, they argued, Franco's fascist supporters in Germany and Italy would actively intervene, potentially turning Spain into a cockpit for a European war. Blum recognized this risk, but he believed that unequivocal support for the Spanish Republic might best avert that possibility. To such pacifist Socialist ministers as Paul Faure and Charles Spinasse, however, aid to the Spanish Republic would heighten the threat of a general war.[39]

On both sides of the divides over Spain within the Radical and Socialist camps sympathy for Franco played no part. But in the conservative opposition and in French opinion at large, support for Franco as an anti-communist crusader abounded, stoked by leftist anti-Catholic atrocities in Spain amplified by the right-wing press. Even the Catholic writer François Mauriac, usually known for moderation, joined this chorus: "If it were established that our rulers are actively collaborating in the massacres of the Peninsula, then we would know that France is governed not by statesmen but by gang leaders. . . . Take care: we will never forgive you for this crime."[40] French assistance in opposing Franco, it seemed, might incite civil strife in France itself. Finally there was Britain's position. For Blum a tacit alliance with Britain was the bedrock of collective security to contain Nazism short of war. But the Conservative government signaled its strong disapproval of any effort to aid the Spanish loyalists. Britain would not risk being dragged into a conflict with Germany over Spain, and if France chose to run that risk it would do so on its own.

What seemed like an obvious choice for a socialist prime minister, then, quickly became intensely contentious. When a dispirited Blum convened his cabinet on July 25, he did not defend his instinctive response but instead found himself playing mediator. Like a synthesis motion at an SFIO party congress, the cabinet's unanimous decision finessed the issue. It foreswore any large-scale, public program of arms aid to loyalist Spain; tacitly accepted that shipments already in the pipeline would quietly go forward by way of Mexico; and offered a pledge "not to intervene in the internal conflict in Spain."

Over the next fortnight, however, it became manifest that fascist Italy and Germany were providing men, materiel and aircraft for Franco. So on August 8 the cabinet met to reassess the situation. This time Defense Minister Daladier joined fellow Radicals averse to any risk of being drawn into a war over Spain, who therefore demanded strict French neutrality. Blum would not contemplate a break with the Radicals that might rupture the Popular Front. He thought of resigning in conscience, but the Spanish prime minister assured Blum that he preferred having a friendly government in Paris even if it could not openly aid his republic. As a Blum biographer concludes, besides the pressure from pacifists in his own party and the outcry of pro-Franco sentiment in France, "the domestic veto which Blum confronted from the majority of the Radical party and the foreign veto formulated in London certainly tied his hands."[41] Out of his divided cabinet came the notorious plan for international negotiations to embargo arms shipments to both sides, with France setting an example in advance. Blum (always "with anguish") swallowed the embargo in the hope of precluding an arms race focused on Spain, which Germany was bound to win.[42] The arms embargo constrained the democracies, but the fascist powers did not in the least honor their nominal and mendacious commitment to the embargo.

As long as the Popular Front lasted the Socialist Party maintained a façade of unity over foreign policy, but with Daladier's ascendancy in 1938 and Hitler's mounting aggressiveness, polarization over appeasement deepened. Pacifists in the SFIO, led by General Secretary Faure, dreaded the prospect of war above all other considerations: "The heaviest concessions would be better than the most victorious of wars," wrote one of his allies. Nazi Germany's aggressiveness, they argued, derived from legitimate grievances over the Versailles Treaty on such issues as borders, colonies, and raw materials. International negotiations and concessions to Germany could redress the situation and thereby blunt Nazi aggressiveness. Pacifist socialists still claimed to be anti-fascist but argued that war would provide the most favorable domestic environment for the fascist virus in both Germany and France. Besides, many pacifist socialists detested the communists and shared with appeasers from the center and Right a fear that France could be drawn into a war that only served the interests of the Soviet Union. The Fauristes regarded French communists, with their belligerent anti-fascist stance, as blatant warmongers [bellicistes], with the Blumiste anti-appeasers not far behind.[43]

Anti-appeasement socialists, however strong their own revulsion against war, believed that in this unprecedented era of aggressive fascism, to preserve peace one must be willing to risk war. They agreed that the Versailles Treaty was unfair but insisted that Hitler's attempts to revise it by force threatened injustices for other nations. Conversely Blum advocated strengthened ties with Russia. True, when Blum was in power he had dragged his feet on this matter. A French pact with the Soviet Union in 1935 had no operative military accord, and as prime minister Blum had failed to negotiate one in the face of opposition from France's military and diplomatic establishments.[44] But by 1938 military alliances with the Soviet Union and Czechoslovakia seemed incumbent for the "collective security" that alone might deter Hitler. At the socialist congress of Royan in June 1938 Blumistes and Fauristes could still paper over their differences. A synthesis motion combined pledges to stand by Czechoslovakia, to negotiate with the fascist powers, to do everything possible to maintain peace yet "without bowing before all the undertakings of the dictators."[45]

The Czech crisis in September (when Hitler demanded the incorporation of Czechoslovakia's German-speaking Sudetenland into the *Reich* under threat of force) strained unity in the socialist camp to the breaking point. After Chamberlain's first meetings with Hitler to defuse the crisis by concessions to the Führer, Blum expressed his personal anguish in *Le Populaire* on September 20 with these famous lines: "War has probably been averted. But in conditions such that I, who has never stopped fighting for peace . . . am unable to experience any joy, and feel myself torn between a cowardly relief and shame."[46] After the Munich accord fashioned by Chamberlain, Daladier, Hitler, and Mussolini for the cession of the Sudetenland, and the acquiescence of the Czechs who were barred from the negotiations, Blum admitted that by forestalling a war, Munich "stirred an immense movement of joy and hope" among the people of Britain and France. But when Daladier presented the Munich pact to the Chamber of Deputies for a vote of confidence, the socialist caucus divided bitterly. Blum and Auriol argued against endorsing Munich, but the growing ranks of the Fauristes easily prevailed.[47] Under party rules, socialist deputies had to unite behind the majority view of their caucus, and for Blum the "religion of [socialist] unity" remained sacred. About a dozen socialist deputies nonetheless entered the Chamber ready to break party discipline and oppose the Munich pact, compelling Auriol to twist the arms of his anti-appeasement comrades.[48] In the end Daladier won an overwhelming vote of confidence on Munich with 537 votes against 75 nays (including all 73 communists).

After Munich the divide in the party could not be disguised. The Fauristes argued that democracies must coexist with the dictatorships, insisted that ideological crusades led to war, and warned against the hardening of international blocs as in 1914. The Blumistes countered that "peace at any price is inevitably war at any price." "We will find peace [only] by justice and by force," wrote one of Blum's allies; "Germany's dream of hegemony is a reality. It is futile to bury our heads in the sand."[49] At an extraordinary party congress in the Paris suburb of Montrouge that December, Blum and Faure personally sponsored rival motions—a discordant step by these co-leaders without precedent. After acrimonious debate, neither side would support a synthesis motion for the sake of party unity. As historian Nathanael Greene summarizes it, Blum's motion would commit socialists to pursuing alliances to resist fascist aggression, while

Faure's would commit socialists to negotiations with and concessions to the fascist powers. Blum's motion finally won 53 percent of the *mandats* as against 35 percent for Faure's—a final bow to Blum's personal stature and seeming indispensability to the SFIO.[50]

Hitler's brazen occupation of the remaining Czech state in March 1939 did not give the pacifists pause. On the contrary it impelled them to denounce "the insanity of war" with ever-growing zeal—especially a war likely to be fought on French soil. Among rank-and-file socialist federations this position was gaining ground, with a push from the teachers union, whose anti-nationalist pacifism harped on the linkage between capitalism, militarism, and fascism.[51] By the time of its next annual congress, at Nantes in May 1939, the SFIO seemed immobilized over the most urgent issue of the times. The exhausted delegates finally settled for a contradictory synthesis motion that cobbled together the Blumiste's "unbreakable will of resistance" to fascist aggression and the Fauriste faith in "peaceful negotiation" with the dictators. This contorted stalemate announced that socialism, isolated politically from the communists and from Daladier's center-Right government alike, was a spent force in French public life.[52]

The Fall of France and of the French Republic

Germany's occupation of Czechoslovakia in March 1939 did little to shake French pacifists of the Left or appeasers of the Right, but the Nazi's entry into Prague did cause Daladier to abandon appeasement, and France now joined Britain in pledging to defend Poland. Ruling largely by executive decree with parliament's consent, the French government seemed to function reasonably well in 1939.[53] Rearmament, begun under Blum, accelerated. Without a Franco-Soviet military alliance, however, effective support for Poland in a future war was a geo-military fantasy. Still, when Hitler invaded Poland, after the Nazi-Soviet pact of August cleared the way, the British and French governments felt honor-bound to declare war on Germany.

The Nazi-Soviet pact (which took the PCF by surprise), and a new party line from the Comintern, obliged the party to pivot abruptly from its anti-fascist militancy. The PCF now claimed that war against Germany would be an imperialist conflict of no interest to the working class. Hoping to shore up his support on the Right, Daladier enacted an escalating series of sanctions against these defeatists: he immediately banned the PCF's organ *L'Humainté;* soon banned the party itself; dissolved Communist municipal councils; expelled Communist deputies from parliament; arrested over 3,000 activists; and for good measure interned many left-wing anti-fascist refugees. Finally in March 1940 the government put on trial forty-four ex-deputies who had not renounced their PCF ties. (On orders from Moscow, General Secretary Thorez escaped this fate by deserting from his military unit and making his way to the Soviet Union.) Stalin's new policy had totally changed the PCF's situation: it was now illegal, clandestine, isolated, and verging on treasonous behavior.[54]

Having strengthened the fixed border defenses of the Maginot Line in the 1930s, France went to war in a defensive posture intended to preclude the ghastly carnage of the Great War. French strategic thinking held that a war with Germany would be protracted, and that superior economic resources and production would ultimately prevail, despite the military power demonstrated by Germany in its lightening conquest of Poland. The extended lull or "phony war" on the western front provided time for Allied war production, but Allied leaders still hungered for action and considered aid to Finland against Russia or the defense of Norway against German invasion as promising arenas. When such initiatives miscarried, the leadership of Chamberlain and of Daladier foundered. In late March 1940 Daladier demanded a vote of confidence in the Chamber of Deputies, but abstainers outnumbered his supporters, Daladier resigned, and his feisty finance minister Paul Reynaud became prime minister.

When Germany suddenly attacked on the western front through the Low Countries in May, the Allies rushed their best armies, reserves and all, for a prepared blocking action in Belgium—only to find the Germans invading as well through the Ardennes forest and Sedan, where the Maginot defenses ended and where the Germans faced second-tier French units. Startled British and French forces in Belgium were outflanked, cut off from their rear, and faced entrapment with no prospect of reinforcement. The Dunkirk evacuation saved many of these men to fight another day, but this rout tilted the battle decisively in Germany's favor. When the Wehrmacht broke apart France's last line of defense along the Somme/Aisne Rivers on June 12, the entire country starting with Paris lay open to conquest.

In postmortems on the collapse of France, eyewitness testimony evoked incompetence and demoralization within a French army ill-prepared for Germany's tactics. Panic figured heavily in this drama: panic at command and field levels in the face of unexpected and dire setbacks, and panic flight from

German forces by huge, road-choking masses of civilians. This exodus expanded as the Germans advanced, greatly complicated military logistics, and undermined morale. In a different register, some projected the French collapse back onto the political and social polarizations of the 1930s, epitomized by the February 1934 riots and the sit-in strikes of 1936. Class hatreds, defeatism on the Left or Right in the 1930s, and the alleged "decadence" and opportunism of Third Republic political culture were all adduced as underlying causes of the debacle in 1940. Soon enough the new Vichy regime would insist that the policies of the Popular Front had hobbled France's capacity to confront Germany but that Daladier's government recklessly plunged France into war anyway.

The historical consensus today supports a different framing of the issue. The utterly unexpected fall of France, in this view, was first and foremost a military phenomenon. It was as much a "strange victory" for Germany as a "strange defeat" for France, a victory that German generals themselves considered something of a miracle.[55] France's military collapse resulted from such liabilities as the strains of coalition warfare, for example, how to deploy British RAF fighter wings in France; poor handling of military intelligence about German preparations in the Ardennes; the inability of the high command to respond quickly to the new situation; defective communications at all levels; and (as Charles de Gaulle long insisted) obsolete tactical doctrines about how to use tank forces that matched Germany's in quality and numbers. As recapitulated by historian Julian Jackson, however, there is also a crucial corollary to this perspective. If social and political malaise in the 1930s was not a proximate cause of this epic military catastrophe in 1940, such malaise did influence the *response* to the defeat. With the astonishing collapse of France's formidable military force, the question became: how would the government and people of France deal with German victory?[56] We have already seen the unflinching response from Churchill's coalition war cabinet to the Allied collapse in France; under far greater direct pressure, the French response would be different.

Right after Dunkirk Reynaud sounded much like Churchill in vowing to continue the fight. But as the Germans swept through the Somme/Aisne defenses, the French government had to flee Paris and ended up in Bordeaux. By then hope of regrouping the army to hold a portion of the national territory in Brittany was fading. Continuing the fight alongside Britain could only mean evacuating the government, the French navy, and whatever military forces could be transported to French North Africa. An assortment of politicians advocated this course—nationalist conservatives like Reynaud and his interior minister Georges Mandel (Clemenceau's chief of staff in 1917); a smattering of Blumiste socialists and anti-appeasement Radicals; and Reynaud's new undersecretary of war Charles de Gaulle, just promoted from colonel to brigadier general. In early June the head of the navy, Admiral Darlan, also seemed to be in that camp—ready to send the French fleet to England if necessary—but he quickly did a complete volte-face. To shore up his government Reynaud replaced Daladier's failed commander-in-chief Gamelin with General Weygand and brought the venerable Marshal Philippe Pétain out of retirement as minister of state. It quickly became clear that those appointments embedded defeatism and anti-republican sentiment at the very heart of the government. For several days the cabinet temporized over whether remove the government to North Africa and fight on. First it brushed aside Churchill's proposal (endorsed by de Gaulle) of a political union of the two allies: why, asked Pétain, should France "merge with a corpse"? Then it tarried until the predictably evasive response came from Roosevelt to Reynaud's appeal for his intervention. The cabinet proved to be deeply divided: eight ministers probably favored carrying on the struggle from North Africa (including Reynaud and Mandel), nine were ready to capitulate (including Pétain and Chautemps), and four remained uncertain.[57]

Hovering over the cabinet, General Weygand opposed an evacuation of the government across the Mediterranean and demanded instead a formal armistice with Germany to preempt further battlefield surrenders by defeated French forces. From his perspective, only civilian responsibility for an armistice would save the army's honor and its ability to preserve social order. As the clock wound down, the cabinet still discussed plans to fly top personnel to Casablanca, with members of parliament to follow by ship and join the score of deputies who had already debarked from Bordeaux on the *Massilia*. (By the time they landed they would be interned and stigmatized as traitors.) On June 16, however, a distraught Reynaud, unable to forge a clear consensus around evacuation, resigned. Thwarted by the weighty opposition of Pétain and Weygand, Reynaud "was genuinely opposed to the armistice but lacked the inner conviction that there was a viable alternative." Lebrun, the weak figurehead president of the republic, bowed to circumstances and named Pétain as prime minister. With the support of Chautemps and Weygand, the Marshal approached the Germans for an armistice with only minimal preconditions, and on June 22 he accepted what Hitler offered.[58]

The armistice provided that slightly under half of French territory, as well as the entire French Empire, would constitute an "unoccupied zone" under the sovereignty of the French state; the French fleet would be neutralized but not handed over to Germany. Punitive features of the armistice included the internment in Germany of over 1.5 million French prisoners of war; the annexation of Alsace-Lorraine; a "forbidden zone" in the Northeast under strict German military control; and the occupation of the remainder of France outside of the unoccupied zone, including Paris, Bordeaux, and the entire Atlantic littoral. Pétain then moved the seat of government to the spa town of Vichy just south of the demarcation line. In certain respects the sway of his Vichy regime (as embodied by the departmental prefects) extended into the occupied zone as well—much to the advantage of Germany, since routine administrative continuity facilitated the occupation in the North. Apart from the absence of German troops in the South, the two zones differed in other ways. When it came to propaganda and news management, for example, the Nazis kept exclusive control over all authorized media output in the occupied zone, while Vichy controlled the media in the Southern zone. When necessary the Germans could overrule, preempt, or exclude altogether any Vichy or French authority in either zone. Clearly the unoccupied zone and the Vichy state existed at Hitler's sufferance. Thus after the Allied invasion of French North Africa in November 1942, Hitler kept the collaborationist Vichy regime in place but extended military occupation to the whole country, while agreeing to a small Italian occupation zone in the Southeast.

In the months after the armistice Pétain insisted that his personal ordeal of submission served the greater good of the French people in its extreme moment of adversity. The Marshal presented himself as a father figure interposing himself as a shield against the harshest potential repercussions of the German victory, and most French citizens willingly accepted this balm. But the armistice also offered his regime an opportunity to settle domestic political accounts by its own lights. Pétain immediately named the mercurial (rogue) politician Pierre Laval as his deputy prime minister and enforcer for a project to inter the Third Republic, with its allegedly corrosive values, empty traditions, corruption, and gross incompetence that had led to the debacle. Vichy was not simply a regime that capitulated to Hitler and then collaborated with him, but was on its own terms a reactionary one. Its "National Revolution" would empower a conservative "old guard," with at least passive support from a broad swath of citizens dismayed over the military collapse but more relieved at the cessation of war than anguished by the loss of French honor. Pétain would replace the Third Republic by a new kind of regime called simply "L'État français," which could take its place in Hitler's European order as the old republic could not.[59] Nor would this mutation be effected simply by force or fiat. Rather, Laval orchestrated a collective suicide for the republic.

Laval convoked the deputies and senators of the French parliament for an extraordinary session in Vichy that July. His plan eerily resembled the scenario that Sieyès and General Bonaparte had fashioned for the self-immolation of the first French Republic in 1799. On July 9 the Senate and Chamber of Deputies would meet separately to vote on a motion declaring the need for revision of the republic's constitution (technically, the organic laws of 1875 that founded the Third Republic). If both houses agreed—a foregone conclusion in the wake of the armistice—the two houses would meet jointly on the following day as a "National Assembly." But there it would end, since Laval intended to demand that the National Assembly vote full powers to Marshal Pétain to carry on, without any further scrutiny let alone approval by either the parliament or the people. Everyone who considered Pétain the indispensable or irresistible savior was ready to collude in this coup with a veneer of legality.

Committed republicans of all stripes faced a disheartening dilemma, but for the socialists it was an especially brutal moment. Four years of recrimination between Blumiste "warmongers" and Fauriste "appeasers" reached its climax. The vulnerability of Blum and his coterie, papered over in the past by his national prominence and by party discipline, now came into full view, heightened by undercurrents of anti-Semitism. True, at a socialist caucus on July 8 anti-Pétain sentiment seemed widespread, but only half the socialist deputation attended and the impression proved highly misleading. (Faure did not come to Vichy at all, and Spinasse pointedly skipped the caucus.) The caucus realistically agreed that the coming votes must be a matter of individual conscience, not party unity.[60]

For Blum this entire event was one long Calvary. As party leader, Blum was accustomed to being surrounded and cheered on by his fellow socialist deputies. Now, at the Chamber of Deputies' pro forma session of July 9, in an atmosphere pervaded by anxiety, only a handful of intimates such as Auriol and Jules Moch sat with their leader. In Moch's graphic recollection, "an empty space formed around us. Far from gathering around Blum, most of the socialists scattered as far as possible from him."[61]

At the joint session the next day Laval's masterly use of intimidation and high-handedness permitted no debate before a vote on the blank check, enabling motion for Pétain, authorizing the demise of the Third Republic. Present at the improvised meeting hall in Vichy's casino were 666 deputies and senators, with about 260 absent counting the banned communists. The enabling motion received 569 yes votes, including over 100 socialists. Eighty parliamentarians voted no, including only 37 socialists out of the 149 present. (Twenty-seven socialists were absent for the vote, including seven who had sailed on the *Massilia.*)[62] As for the Radicals, the quintessential party of the Third Republic for decades, several high-profile ministers of the Popular Front—Daladier, Delbos, and Zay—had sailed on the *Massilia,* leaving 178 Radicals and allies from the two chambers present at Vichy for the vote on July 10: 152 voted yes and only nineteen voted no. Edouard Herriot—longtime Radical Party leader, mayor of Lyon, and president of the Chamber of Deputies—abstained as did his venerable counterpart in the Senate, independent Jules Jeanneney.[63]

What qualities set apart the eighty no voters from their compliantly fatalistic, opportunistic, or craven brethren, not to speak of the vengeful rightists? Perhaps it was an extraordinary optimism. A deputy or senator who went against the tide on July 10 might have believed against all odds that France would one day soon regain its liberty from the Nazis. He would then be inscribing himself on an honor roll instead of a likely proscription list. Or perhaps most of "the eighty" acted simply as stoics, voting their conscience in a futile but honorable gesture, ignoring arguments of circumstances, and girding themselves for unpleasant consequences, starting with possible assault by rightist thugs when they left the hall.[64]

Stirrings of Resistance

Charles de Gaulle made his legendary radio broadcast on June 18 from London calling on the French people to continue the fight against Hitler for their own honor and the Allied cause. Hardly anyone heard that broadcast, but other radio appeals followed from "Free France," and in the minds of Vichyites and their opponents alike, "Gaullism" became synonymous with resistance. The social-Catholic Pierre-Henri Teitgen, for example, had been mobilized as a reserve lieutenant. After the surrender of his unit, his superior ordered him to stay put, but Teitgen escaped from captivity and made his way to Montpellier in the unoccupied zone. "Understanding what 'the National Revolution' and

Pétainism would be," he recalled, "I knew that de Gaulle alone was going to resist and continue the war, and thus that I was a gaullist." No-voting socialist André Philip considered the earliest form of resistance in France as "gathering around the radio set and listening to the BBC."[65]

Improbable beginnings and early setbacks bedeviled de Gaulle's Free France in London, and plausible questions about his legitimacy, haughty personality, and ultimate intentions persisted for a long time, not least in the White House.[66] But from the start Churchill viewed Free France as a potential military asset, if only within the French Empire, and he supported de Gaulle's operation. With Churchill's backing (despite occasional blowups between these two strong-willed men), the general in due course took the fight to various corners of the French Empire. Free French units lost a mortifying early round when Vichy loyalists repelled their attempt to invade Dakar, but they succeeded in Brazzaville, and won admiring headlines for a two-week stand in the Libyan desert at Bir-Hakeim against Rommel's superior forces.[67]

Most men in de Gaulle's inner circle were conservative patriots or military officers who could not abide Pétain's dishonorable capitulation. But an early trickle of more diverse individuals also won de Gaulle's confidence, including the republican businessman René Pleven; the liberal jurist René Cassin; and the social-Catholic, anti-Munich journalist Maurice Schumann, who became the voice of Free French broadcasts beamed to the homeland by the BBC French service.[68] In the summer of 1940 de Gaulle intended to lead a purely military effort and certainly could not claim that Free France was a government-in-exile. With the *Massilia* politicians interned upon their arrival in Vichy-controlled North Africa, none of the early Gaullists in London were ex-deputies let alone ex-ministers. De Gaulle's initial apolitical stance minimized partisan wrangling and kept the focus on patriotic struggles against Germany and Vichy. Besides, de Gaulle and others in Free France held ambivalent or negative views about the Third Republic and did not wish to cast their defiant stand as a defense of that regime. Free French letterheads bore the patriotic slogan *Honneur et Patrie,* and for well over a year avoided the old republican watchwords *Liberté, Égalité, Fraternité.* While de Gaulle emphatically denounced Hitler and fascism, he did not do so as a defender of traditional French republicanism.[69]

Churchill hoped to broaden the leadership of Free France to constrain the prickly de Gaulle, and at the PM's urging the general announced in September 1941 the formation of a French National Committee in London. With himself as president it had seven other members: his potential rival Admiral Muselier, two generals, Cassin, Pleven, and two former government aides. But instead of allowing the committee to evolve into a kind of collective leadership, de Gaulle simply used it to enhance his own stature while countering the impression that Free France was a one-man affair.[70] Free France remained patriotic rather than political, but that was about to change. Various political figures, including socialists and even communists, began making their way to London in 1942 to consult with de Gaulle, as did emissaries from several internal Resistance organizations. Cumulatively they reinforced de Gaulle's inclination to expand his destined role from the purely military to the political.

Back in France the earliest acts of resistance came from scattered individuals, not established groups, and they scarcely dented the groundswell of relief at the armistice or the confidence in Pétain as a "shield" against further misfortune. As most French men and women put their heads down and went about their daily lives, the earliest resistors comprised tiny islets in a sea of *attentisme* (waiting it out) and accommodation.[71] Organized defiance grew very slowly at first, but as the German occupation became more oppressive, and as the prospects for Allied victory began to come into view, Resistance cadres slowly expanded. Methodical economic exploitation by Germany sent the French standard of living plummeting (except among farmers and well-placed collaborators) with food, fuel, and clothing in drastically short supply. The obliteration of personal liberty; the plague of anonymous denunciations for venting personal resentments; the execution of hostages in reprisal for attacks on Germans; the harsh roundups of Jews, including children, that started in 1942 (the earlier extrusion of Jews from public life by Vichy having provoked scarcely any response); the strident activity of fascistic collaborators at the margins of the regime, including thuggish members of a new paramilitary *milice*—all this created a backlash that turned some people from their instinct for accommodation to one of sympathy for the Resistance. Above all the STO (Service du Travail Obligatoire), or forced draft of French labor for work in Germany, which Vichy began to implement for the Nazis in 1943, eroded support for Pétain. Hundreds of thousands of young men ended up in Germany, leaving resentful families behind, while the STO drove thousands of others into hiding or flight to mountains and forests where some coalesced into armed Resistance bands known as *maquis*. Increasing opposition in turn stepped up repression by the Gestapo, the German military, the Vichy police, and the *milice*. While Resistance cadres grew in 1942–44, some were decimated by mounting arrests, torture, prison, deportation to concentration camps, and executions. For good reason, courage, sacrifice, and martyrdom became hallowed themes in Resistance circles.

Hindsight permits us to spotlight two early gestures of protest, which prefigure the roles in the Resistance and the Liberation of social-Catholics (notwithstanding their relative marginality in the political battles of the thirties) and of socialists (notwithstanding the party's implosion between Munich and the Vichy coup). Edmond Michelet—a social-Catholic civic activist, father of seven, and commercial traveler by profession—had been anti-fascist in the late thirties without being much involved in politics. He responded to the prospect of Pétain's capitulation by mimeographing an exhortation to moral and patriotic backbone, which he distributed clandestinely with the help of a few trusted friends in mailboxes around his hometown of Brive.[72] In the occupied zone, a few weeks later, the socialist journalist Jean Texcier composed a pamphlet he described as "a manual of dignity and proper conduct for use by the French people." *Conseils à l'occupé* urged Frenchmen to adopt a nonconfrontational but purposeful style of passive hostility to the Germans.[73] Both men went on to participate in sustained Resistance efforts. In the Vichy zone Michelet linked up with a handful of social-Catholic intellectuals such as Teitgen in a group they called "Liberté," which published one of the earliest clandestine newssheets. In the occupied zone Texcier worked with socialist trade unionist Christian Pineau to organize a movement called Libération (Nord). From such tiny acorns, two progressive forces would blossom after the Liberation.

This is not to imply that social-Catholic or socialist activists provided the leadership that put the internal Resistance on the map. On the contrary, the early Resistance chiefs in France were often singular individuals of conservative background. In the Southern zone, for example, career officer Henry Frenay initially had no problem with Pétain's "National Revolution," and for a time he worked under the Vichy regime. But he considered the armistice a blot on French national honor and took it as his patriotic duty to prepare for eventual military action to free French soil of the Germans. His organization, eventually known as Combat, became the first all-purpose Resistance movement involving extensive underground propaganda, intelligence gathering, sabotage, and clandestine military preparation. Influenced by his leftish companion, however, Frenay welcomed social-Catholics and socialists into his movement and soon disavowed the Vichy regime completely. In due course "Liberté" folded itself into Combat, and

Michelet and Teitgen took on perilous jobs as regional coordinators for Combat; when Frenay had to leave France for London in 1943, the left-wing journalist Claude Bourdet replaced him on the ground. Eventually the Gestapo arrested Michelet and Bourdet and deported them to concentration camps; Teitgen eluded capture but learned that his like-minded father had been caught and deported.[74]

The clandestine PCF, meanwhile, had been forced into a contorted position during the first year of the occupation because of the Nazi-Soviet pact. Communists could denounce the reactionary Vichy usurpation, but the party line welcomed the armistice (which restored peace after a pointless war among imperialists), and it dictated prudence toward the German occupiers, now ostensible allies of the PCF's Soviet patrons. After Hitler invaded the Soviet Union, of course, French communists threw themselves into all-out struggle against the Nazis and their Vichy collaborators. They injected into the fray a fierce rhetoric of uncompromising resistance and a program of direct action. The Front National, a non-military umbrella group, attracted members across the political spectrum despite its communist leadership by astute organizing, effective propaganda, and a gospel of patriotic unity. Small paramilitary action groups operated on a separate track, but an initial spate of assassinations cost them dearly as savage Nazi reprisals shook the public.[75]

Intense communist activity in the Resistance galvanized some socialists to establish their own imprint. But where the communists were disciplined, experienced in operating clandestinely, and coordinated by an established if thinned leadership, the socialists were habituated to acting lawfully and bereft of their traditional organizations and leaders. Léon Blum, it is true, provided a moral compass for loyal remnants of his party even if he could do little else. Blum had considered debarking on the *Massilia* but could not make it in time, and once Pétain signed the armistice Blum would not leave the country despite the obvious personal danger. For Blum now saw his duty as defending the record of the Popular Front against a cascade of slanders from Vichy. Arrested in September 1940, he was allowed to maintain contact with friends and family, but in 1942 Vichy put him on trial before a special High Court at Riom along with Daladier and General Gamelin. While the Germans wanted to punish these men for unleashing the war, Vichy's priority was to blame them for France's defeat, by implication leaving Pétain to pick up the pieces. Thus the prosecution accused Blum's Popular Front of causing France's "material and moral unpreparedness" for the war. An able lawyer, Blum defended himself so effectively that the government abruptly terminated the trial in midstream as a public relations disaster. But in March 1943 Vichy handed him over to the Germans for deportation to the Buchenwald concentration camp. Blum would survive Buchenwald, where he was permitted to read and write; repatriated to France in mid-1945, physically weak but morally commanding, Blum could resume symbolic leadership of his party.[76]

But what party? When last seen on July 10, 1940, in the Vichy casino, the Socialist Party was in ruins. Even before the ban on its legal existence—when Vichy dissolved all republican political parties and national trade union federations—party activists were hopelessly at odds, seething with recriminations. Vichy then permitted antiwar socialists such as Faure and Spinasse to publish their accommodationist views and enlisted their support for Vichy's corporatist labor policies.[77] Many other socialists, of course, loathed Vichy and the German occupation. Early on Blum had counseled one young disciple, the journalist Daniel Mayer, to do his resisting in France instead of slipping off to England, and Mayer set out to build a socialist presence in the Resistance. First enlisting a few trusted comrades in the South, he then made contacts in the occupied zone where militants such as Texcier had the same idea. The two minuscule groups eventually coalesced to form the Committee for Socialist Action (CAS), with a council that straddled the two zones. In December 1941 the first number of a CAS underground newssheet, *Socialisme et Liberté,* appeared, to be followed later by occasional issues under the more familiar title of *Le Populaire.*

Initially, the CAS did not imagine itself as a clandestine resurrection of the Socialist Party. Given its ad hoc, self-constituted nature, it understood that "nothing authorizes us to consider ourselves as qualified representatives of the Socialist Party." Nor did its founders intend CAS as an all-purpose resistance movement. On the contrary, socialists were expected to join any effective movement operating in their localities[78]—the same approach that led social-Catholic *résistants* to merge their *Liberté* group with Combat. But unlike *Liberté,* the CAS retained its distinct identity and organizational presence, and it hoped to build a foundation for relaunching a purified socialist party after the Liberation.[79] To leaders of Resistance movements like Combat, however, the CAS had its priorities backward. Its political positioning clashed with the stated credo of the Resistance movements: "to place immediate concerns of action against the enemy before political concerns for the future." In the same vein, the Southern movements dismissed the clandestine *Populaire* as "more of a political leaflet than an organ of combat."[80]

Socialists resistors in France had been grappling with an interlinked set of dilemmas for some time: should they fully embrace the enigmatic figure of de Gaulle as the de facto head of the Resistance, despite the right-wing nationalist aura surrounding Free France? If so, how might they push de Gaulle in a direction compatible with democracy and socialism? They also shared a conundrum with all *résistants* on the ground, who daily risked their lives: did it make sense to accept direction from a distant Free France, along with the money, radios, and weapons that they desperately needed and that de Gaulle could provide? Two veteran socialists close to Léon Blum, the no-voting deputies André Philip and Félix Gouin, who reached London in 1942 and would not be returning to occupied France, helped resolve those questions. Philip was eager to bring socialists under de Gaulle's umbrella, Gouin initially more hesitant,[81] but soon enough, in keeping with Blum's advice, both threw in their lot with de Gaulle, rose to prominence in his operation, and helped shape its political posture. When Daniel Mayer made his way to London in April 1943 on a liaison mission for the CAS before returning to France, he too helped align socialist *résistants* with de Gaulle's organization.[82]

Forging a Unified Resistance

The impetus to fuse Free France with the internal Resistance came most forcefully from Jean Moulin. An intrepid republican prefect soon ousted by Vichy, and before that an aide to Radical Popular Front air minister Pierre Cot, Moulin took it upon himself in 1941 to contact and learn as much as possible about the diverse Resistance groups in the unoccupied zone. He then made it over to London by way of Lisbon and prepared a detailed report about those movements. The British clandestine warfare section was establishing small networks of its own in France and sought to enlist Moulin, but he submitted his report directly to de Gaulle instead. By conveying so much firsthand information, he dispelled the haze of ignorance in Free France about Resistance activities back home. Moulin impressed de Gaulle by his status as a patriotic, high-level ex-official, and by the force of his personality, commitment, and intelligence. Moulin convinced de Gaulle that the internal Resistance could be a major force in the eventual liberation of France if it achieved a measure of unity. Armed with cash, radios, and authorization from de Gaulle to speak in his behalf, Moulin parachuted back into France in January 1942 and remained there for over a year, a uniquely placed intermediary between Free France and the Southern Resistance movements.[83] By sheer persistence in consultations with the chiefs of Combat, Libération, and Franc-Tireur, he gradually overcame their instinct to preserve their freedom of action. Under Moulin's suasion the three agreed in late 1942 to coordinate their organizations, and early in 1943 they formally federated into the United Movements of the Resistance (MUR). While each movement still published its own clandestine newspaper (*Combat, Libération,* and *Franc-Tireur*), they merged their intelligence, infiltration, sabotage, and propaganda activity, as well as their efforts to build the "Secret Army" for an eventual uprising.[84]

Moulin returned to London in February 1943 to push his agenda to the next level: unifying the internal Resistance, North and South, under the umbrella of a National Council that would be the counterpart in France of de Gaulle's French National Committee in London. Moulin prevailed over obstructionism and turf battles within de Gaulle's organization, then dropped back into France to fight similar battles on the ground. Objections, foot dragging, and counterproposals put up by the Resistance movements eventually gave way before the resolve and negotiating skill of de Gaulle's delegate.

Moulin's second mission took on particular urgency in the wake of the Allied landing in North Africa in November 1942, when Roosevelt's convoluted relationship with Vichy posed a serious threat to de Gaulle's future position. America's priority was to win the cooperation of the Vichy French officer corps in North Africa, to secure the landing and Allied lines going forward. The Americans first enlisted as their cat's paw a top Pétainist official, Admiral Darlan, who happened to be in Algiers at the time—a move that scandalized anti-fascists. When Darlan was assassinated in late December, Washington turned to the ambiguously anti-Vichy General Henri Giraud, who outranked de Gaulle and whom most fellow officers in North Africa held in higher regard than the London rebel. Roosevelt could not abide the headstrong figure of de Gaulle, let alone his arrogant claim to incarnate the true France in his own person. During his meeting with Churchill at Casablanca, FDR found de Gaulle "rigid and unresponsive to my urgent desire to get on with the war." The Casablanca conference therefore left Giraud in a superior position for the moment, although the two Allied leaders saved the appearance of unity by pressuring the rival generals into a public handshake.[85] Earlier in 1942 de Gaulle had in fact affirmed to the Resistance his commitment to democratic and republican values in a way that Giraud never did.[86] Ultimately Giraud proved to be no match for de Gaulle politically, and de Gaulle eventually eased Giraud out of the picture. But the issue was in doubt for several months, which coincided with Moulin's second mission to France, whose success would certainly bolster de Gaulle's position.

That success did not come easily. Serious differences over strategy between London and the movements in France never abated. The Resistance believed that its impact, its morale, and its very honor required continuous direct action—demonstrations, propaganda campaigns against outrages like the forced labor draft, sabotage of rail lines and the like. But the dominant view in Free France held that most such actions dissipated the energy of the Resistance and imperiled its cadres. For London, the primary task in France was to quietly organize and prepare the "Secret Army" for D-Day.[87]

On Moulin's second mission to France in early 1943, the specific composition of his proposed Resistance council also proved extremely contentious. With de Gaulle's support Moulin intended to offer places on the new council, and thus an acknowledged standing, to representatives of the old republican political parties. Prominent *résistants* in London and in France balked at the prospect. After all, men and women had joined forces in the Resistance movements as individuals; differences in political orientation faded before the unitary, patriotic goal of liberating France from the Nazis and Vichy. To be an effective *résistant,* what counted was not past political commitments but dedication and temperament—courage, calmness under pressure, and resourcefulness. Not only was nonpartisan unity axiomatic for effectiveness, but action-oriented Resistance leaders, such as Frenay, Bourdet, and d'Astier in the South, and Blocq-Mascart and Lecomte-Boinet in the North, viewed the political parties of the Third Republic as enablers of the debacle in 1940 that had nothing to contribute to the current struggle. In their eyes the political squabbling, corruption, and evasions of the interwar decades condemned those parties to oblivion. Conversely, the patriotism, bravery and sacrifice of the Resistance created new claims to democratic political power that should trump any resurrection of the old parties.[88]

On the other side in this debate, socialists like Blum, Philip, and Mayer drew an opposite conclusion about how to build the broadest front against Nazism and Vichy: the Resistance should reach out and incorporate patriotic elements of the old political parties who "had not dishonored themselves." More fundamentally, how could there be a viable democratic future after the Liberation without experienced republican parties as part of the mix?[89] Moulin, at first skeptical about this idea, finally accepted it as a strategy for broadening the Resistance politically and thereby reassuring the Allies about its representative character. When he returned to France on his second mission he insisted that the national Resistance council must include delegates representing the patriotic elements of six Third Republic "political families" (as he prudently called them), as well as the two trade union federations banned by Vichy. The Resistance movements uniformly resented Moulin's attempt to shoehorn the old parties into the new council; at one point Frenay actually called Moulin "the gravedigger of the Resistance."

In London and then again in Paris Moulin faced a formidable adversary on this question in the person of Pierre Brossolette. A former socialist and early *résistant* in the occupied zone, Brossolette like Moulin had made his way to London in April 1942 to inform de Gaulle about the Resistance movements in the North, with the hope of aligning them with Free France. Brossolette too won de Gaulle's confidence. But unlike the ex-prefect, Brossolette had an abiding animus against the old parties. Brossolette returned to France several times to liaise with Resistance movements in the North and to create a coordinating committee for them as a counterpart to the MUR in the South. When Moulin and Brossolette crossed paths in Paris in March 1943, the latter believed himself a coequal of Moulin, when in fact Moulin had just been empowered as de Gaulle's *national* delegate with supreme authority in all of France. The two engaged in a furious shouting match, part rearguard turf battle by Brossolette, part differing visions of democracy's future in France. Moulin prevailed, since his authority could no longer be thwarted short of breaking with de Gaulle himself.[90]

De Gaulle had long been a symbol of Resistance, and the internal movements were ready to accept his leadership along with his material support; for months the masthead of *Libération* had read: "*Un seul chef: DE GAULLE.*" As part of the bargain, albeit with great reluctance, the movements swallowed Moulin's plan for the composition of the Resistance council. (The Communists liked Moulin's approach, which gave them two places at the table: one for their party and one for its Front National.)[91] Moulin's endless cajoling, tactical compromises, but unshakable resolve finally yielded success. Sixteen delegates would represent eight Resistance movements (the three in the South, four action-oriented Northern movements, and the Front National); the two banned trade union federations (CGT and CFTC); and six "political families" of the Third Republic: the PCF, the Socialists, Radicals, social-Catholics, and from the center-right the Fédération Républicaine ("nuance Marin") and the Alliance Démocratique ("nuance Reynaud").[92]

In a perilous operation organized by Moulin's aides on May 27, 1943, these sixteen men made their way in small groups and by serpentine routes to an apartment in Paris. There they proclaimed the birth of the National Council of the Resistance (CNR), with Moulin combining the roles of president and of de Gaulle's official delegate to France. At this inaugural meeting the CNR, after a brief discussion of Giraud's claims, formally acknowledged de Gaulle not simply as a symbol of the Resistance but as its leader.[93] Each side needed the other. De Gaulle's legitimacy increased with the creation of the CNR and its acceptance of his leadership. Not only did it help as his jousting with Giraud came to a head, but it could strengthen his hand in future dealings with Roosevelt and Churchill. Conversely, in forging this entente, the general bound himself to the democratic values of the Resistance and opened the door for their input in shaping the Liberation. When the Nazis were expelled from France, a provisional government led by de Gaulle would act in behalf of a united Resistance, refusing any accommodation whatsoever with the Vichy regime and preempting any Allied plans for imposing a military government in France. Then together internal and external *résistants* would begin a process of national renewal.

Moulin did not live to see this outcome, and neither did Brossolette. Having returned to Lyon, Moulin called a meeting of local Resistance leaders for June 11, but on a tip the Gestapo raided the meeting and swept Moulin up in its net. At first the Germans did not know who he was, but within a few days they identified him as the elusive Max (his nom de guerre), the most wanted man in the Resistance. To Berlin's chagrin, Moulin died from prolonged torture without revealing his secrets. (His achievements and martyrdom cast him as the most authentic of heroes, and in 1964 the government transferred Moulin's remains to the Panthéon alongside Voltaire and Rousseau.) For his part Brossolette continued his liaison activities in France but was arrested in February 1944. Taken to Gestapo headquarters, he managed to throw himself out of a third floor window to his death rather than risk breaking under torture.

The calamity of Moulin's arrest coincided with intense maneuvering by de Gaulle who was about to move his headquarters to Algiers. As a result the general neglected for weeks to appoint a replacement as his national delegate in France. Two lesser emissaries on the ground received scant instructions and in any case had limited influence with the internal Resistance. In the face of this void the CNR decided in August to designate a new president on its own, and chose Georges Bidault. A social-Catholic militant, Bidault was a former lycée history teacher, outspoken opponent of Munich, early activist in Combat, and head of the clandestine press information bureau established by the Southern movements. A bachelor, Bidault had long since gone underground and had worked closely with Moulin during his two missions to France. In May 1943 he was the delegate to the CNR for the social-Catholics, and he had joined the communists' Front National in the spirit of Resistance unity.[94]

The Common Program of the CNR

The CNR was perforce completely clandestine, any meetings of the council fraught with danger; after its founding session the full council met only twice more before the Liberation. Instead it designated a five-man bureau to act in its behalf, but only after the bureau canvassed all council members on important matters, laborious as that procedure would be. The socialists hoped for a place on the bureau but were thwarted by the lingering animus of the Resistance movements against the old parties. The bureau consisted of President Bidault, the centrist Blocq-Mascart of OCM (for the Northern movements), the MUR's leftish Pascal Copeau (for the Southern movements), communist Pierre Villon of the Front National, and the CGT's Louis Saillant.

Despite an increasingly brutal Nazi/Vichy repression, 1943–44 was a good time for discussion of postwar prospects in France, as Allied victory began to come into view but before the chaos D-Day would unleash. De Gaulle had recruited a small group of legal scholars and ex-functionaries in France, including social-Catholics such as Teitgen, to deliberate on such matters. On its own initiative, the OCM was doing the same; first out of the gate, it published some ponderous position papers in 1942–43, collectively entitled *Études pour une Nouvelle Révolution française.*[95] Finally, in the Consultative Assembly that de Gaulle convened in Algiers in September 1943, members kept busy in committees addressing postwar policy issues. But none of the plans emerging from these efforts gained much standing or traction, and they entirely lacked the post-Liberation resonance of the CNR's initiative.

In January 1943 the CAS had published a sketch of a political, economic, and social program for the postwar in its clandestine newspaper. Between the lines of this proposal, one can discern the socialists already jousting with their communist rivals for the political high ground. In July the Free French commissioner for the interior, socialist André Philip, sent an emissary to Paris bearing a "Project for an Economic and Social Charter" for consideration by the new CNR. This proposal initiated months of intermittent discussion among the council's members, which produced impasses, alternatives, revisions, and finally in March 1944 an historic agreement.[96]

The effort by the CNR to forge a "common program" for the Resistance in fact had two major components. The more urgent matter, "The Immediate Plan of Action," dealt with mobilizations for the coming military insurrection and management of the rolling liberation that would follow upon D-Day, including the formation and roles of departmental liberation committees. The second part, "Measures to be Applied after the Liberation of the Territory," laid out the CNR's postwar vision. Although not inherently secret like the first part, the manifesto received scant publicity before the Liberation,[97] yet it would prove totemic and remarkably influential in post-Liberation politics.

In the CNR's program, once de Gaulle's provisional government installed itself, the first order of business had to be the punishment of traitors and the purge of active collaborators. Then, when the war was over, and POWs and surviving deportees had returned home, a constituent assembly would be elected by universal suffrage. Parallel to this reestablishment of democracy, far-reaching reforms would begin, aimed at eliminating "the great economic and financial feudalities" and creating "a veritable economic and social democracy." Like progressives in Britain and the US, the CNR envisioned "a rational organization of the economy in order to assure the subordination of particular interests to the general interest . . . [and] the intensification of national production under the lines of a plan decreed by the State." Alongside this notion of state planning, regulation, and intervention—what the French would call *dirigisme*—the CNR Common Program also called for nationalizations, albeit in slippery language: "the return to the nation of the large monopolistic means of production" in energy, mining, insurance companies, and large banks.[98]

The insistent socialist call for nationalization had almost been a deal-breaker. For the SFIO, nationalization or "socialization" of key financial and industrial sectors was a longstanding goal, although the party had muted it for the sake of unity during the Popular Front. When nationalization resurfaced in Philip's proposal to the CNR, spokesmen for the two conservative "political families" on the council objected on the grounds of liberal economic principle. At that point Villon ruled out nationalization in the absence of unanimity in the CNR.[99] But communist disapproval had deeper roots as well, since the PCF had historically shown little enthusiasm for nationalization. On the eve of the Popular Front, French communists scorned the prospect of "islands of socialism" in a sea of capitalism, and in debates over the Popular Front's program they joined the Radicals in opposing nationalizations. In the communist view public ownership of a few sectors was a reformist palliative, insufficiently revolutionary, which would nonetheless pointlessly alarm the bourgeoisie.[100]

Over time, however, other members of the CNR weighed in with their belief that bold social and economic reforms, including nationalizations, would be crucial to the renovation they anticipated. In November 1943 Villon reopened the debate with a proposal that used vaguer wording on nationalization better calculated to win broad acceptance than the socialists' more pointed language.[101] The CNR bureau hammered out a comprehensive draft for the Common Program in January and, after taking further criticisms, a final version. When the bureau again canvassed all the delegates to the CNR council, Laniel (the last holdout) now agreed in the name of Resistance unity.[102] On March 14, 1944 the bureau could announce the council's unanimous approval of a two-part "Charter of the Resistance." Given the diverse composition of the CNR, the negotiated unanimity on this document represented a consensus unique in French political history. The imperative for unity in facing down the Nazis and Vichy undoubtedly impelled the quest for consensus, but unanimous approval of the program stemmed as well from a common desire to assure "democratic and popular institutions" after the Liberation.

Beyond the calls for state economic planning and nationalization, the CNR Common Program made security and dignity its watchwords for the postwar future. It called for the right to a job and to leisure, job security, and wages sufficient to yield a decent standard of living; monetary stability to protect purchasing power; independent trade unions with substantial roles; "a complete plan of social security," guaranteeing to everyone the means of existence throughout the life cycle regardless of circumstances; policies to promote the well-being of farmers and farm workers; compensation for the victims of "fascist terror"; and access to appropriate levels of education regardless of parental means, which alone would produce "a veritable elite" based on merit.

Before renewal, however, must come liberation, as the closing line of the charter made plain: "Forward to combat! Forward to Victory!" In February 1944 the

CNR established a Military Action Commission (COMAC) to coordinate preparations for the armed action of the "Secret Army" parallel to the Allied invasion. With its strong communist presence, COMAC became a front line in skirmishing between de Gaulle's emissaries and Resistance organizers over operational control of this paramilitary activity.[103] On parallel tracks, de Gaulle's headquarters and the CNR planned for filling the vacuum of civil authority as French territory was liberated from the Germans and Vichy. The Resistance worked from the bottom up, designating local and departmental liberation committees that to some extent would draw on the variety of local anti-collaborationist forces. With crucial roles to play during the invasion, the uprising, and the German retreat, the liberation committees were then supposed to cede power to officials designated by the CFLN in Algiers. In the name of de Gaulle's provisional government (the GPRF, which replaced the CFLN after D-Day) seventeen "commissioners of the republic" would wield supreme authority in their regions as territory was liberated, assisted by new departmental prefects also named in Algiers to replace Vichy's prefects.[104] The departmental liberation committees would then serve as advisory bodies to the prefects and, unofficially, as local pressure groups. The degree of tension between liberation committees and de Gaulle's appointees would depend on local circumstances. But the committees did not question the legitimacy of the GPRF—manned at the center by a spectrum of ministers, including communists, socialists, social-Catholics, Radicals, and non-party men. The committees also shared de Gaulle's determination to prevent interference by Allied military government (AMGOT) personnel, who might use clashes among GPRF officials, liberation committees, or units of the armed Resistance, the Forces Françaises de l'Intérieur (FFI) as an excuse to intervene in the name of security for allied forces.

The staggering American and British Empire casualties on the Normandy beachhead and in the ensuing campaign raise the question: what did the French contribute to their own liberation? The unwillingness of Roosevelt and Churchill to recognize de Gaulle's GPRF in advance as the de facto authority in liberated France gave an added edge to this question. For the Allied leaders continued to insist that nothing could be settled before the French people had regained their liberty and could freely decide their future, leaving the impression that some sort of AMGOT operation might yet follow in the wake of the Allied landing. On the eve of the invasion de Gaulle and Churchill bitterly clashed over issues of French authority, with the PM exploding against de Gaulle's "monstrous failure to understand the sacrifice of the young Englishmen and Americans who were about to die for France." De Gaulle still threatened to stand down by refusing to address his countrymen over the BBC on D-Day and by holding back the Free French liaison teams assigned to work with Allied troops. In the end he did make a terse broadcast calling the French people to arms but not to a potentially anarchic general uprising (which pleased the Allies); mentioned without specifics the need to obey "the orders given by the French government and by the French leaders it has named for that purpose"; and never once referred to the Americans.[105] Regardless of that unseemly tempest, however, the French people were in the thick of the fight on several levels.

After its perilous years of preparation, the French Resistance was raring for action. The coded personal messages broadcast on the eve of D-Day over the BBC to the small British-led networks and to the internal Resistance movements (the likes of "it is warm at Suez" or "her skirt is red") finally unleashed waves of planned sabotage against German transport and communications and specific armed actions.[106] (Well before the invasion *maquis* units had begun challenging German units in certain localities; some tragically miscalculated their relative strength, took heavy casualties, and in the case of the large Vercors *maquis* in the Southeast suffered near annihilation.) After the invasion, FFI units harassed enemy troops in retreat, exacting a toll in German casualties and morale but in some places provoking reprisals against hapless civilians.

On D-Day itself 177 Free French rangers attached to the Fourth British Commando were the first men ashore on Normandy's Sword Beach, where they incurred heavy casualties and took their assigned objective.[107] Apart from that symbolic gesture, Free France landed army divisions in Normandy for the buildup of forces after the first invasion waves and provided several divisions to spearhead Operation Anvil, the invasion of Southern France in August. Still other French units continued fighting their way up the Italian peninsula with the Allies.[108]

These two types of action against the Germans—by regular units of the Free French army and by Resistance paramilitary units—came together in unanticipated fashion that August in Paris. Within COMAC, the CNR, and the Paris Liberation Committee, fierce arguments raged over just when and how to launch their own armed uprising in a city still under German occupation. Pushed by communists such as Charles Tillon and the local commander of the FFI, the insurrection began but stalled, with a distinct possibility of defeat in the balance. While its leaders argued over whether to negotiate a temporary truce, they appealed for help to Allied headquarters. Allied forces, including the Second French Armored Division under General Leclerc, had planned to skirt Paris in pursuit of the main German armies. De Gaulle and his emissaries had strongly opposed what they deemed a premature uprising in Paris, but he now convinced the high command to divert Leclerc's unit to Paris where it could assist the beleaguered rebels. De Gaulle then embraced the uprising for its supreme propaganda value as a heroic example of self-liberation. Before and after this event tense confrontations were occurring in other places, especially over summary executions, jailings, and head-shavings of collaborators carried out by elements of the Resistance. Yet for all their local drama, such incidents almost never escalated into prolonged civil strife.[109]

Once Paris and a good part of the national territory were liberated, and the threat of AMGOT had faded, de Gaulle had three immediate priorities: *la guerre, le rang, l'État*.[110] With his Free French divisions reinforced by newly incorporated elements of the FFI, the general's top priority was continuing the war to final victory in concert with the Allies. This would in turn help de Gaulle reclaim for France its rightful place at the postwar table alongside the three other Allied powers. At the same time, his provisional government would work to restore the authority of a purified French state, the fundamental requirement in his view for reviving the battered nation. In this domain above all the Resistance would be looking over de Gaulle's shoulder, its Common Program in hand as a roadmap for its hopes and expectations.

3

The Roosevelt Era: From the New Deal to D-Day

AS NECESSARY BACKGROUND TO THE POSTWAR MOMENT, we have considered the evolution of the British Labour Party and the French Socialist Party, conduits in those countries for a progressive impetus. We have seen those forces wax and wane, unify and split, and the crises domestic and international that they faced—including the impact of communism on the French Left, responses in both countries to the Great Depression and to the rise of aggressive fascism in Europe, and the profoundly different experience of Hitler's war in France and Britain.

In the US Franklin Roosevelt's presidency became the prime force for progressive gains. In the New Deal's ascendant phase from 1932 to 1936, the agricultural and industrial recovery strategies of the "Hundred Days" came first and foundered. Later, Roosevelt's administration enacted social security, inventive new programs for work relief, and the Wagner labor relations act that changed the rules of the game for trade unions. As conservative opposition in both major parties mounted after 1938, the White House retreated, and during the war the New Deal went into suspended animation.

As in Britain and France the specter of aggressive fascism collided in America with antiwar sentiment; as a counterpart to British and French appeasement, anti-interventionist sentiment intensified in the US and Roosevelt strove to keep the US out of any European war. But after Munich, as in Britain and France, the US started to rearm. Once the European war began in 1939 the US gradually became "the arsenal of democracy." But only on a fraught and twisting path did Roosevelt finally lead America into the crucible of World War II.

Meanwhile, a new social movement reinforced the progressive thrust of Roosevelt's presidency—the rise of new trade unions in the mass production industries impelled by the CIO (Congress of Industrial Organizations), a new labor federation. The close but bumpy relationship between the New Deal and the CIO lies at the core of this chapter. No fusion comparable to that of political progressives and trade unionists in the British Labour Party occurred in the US. New Deal laws enabled the rise of the CIO, yet FDR at times clashed with the CIO in action before and during the war. Overall, however, the New Deal and the CIO in tandem brought a distinct progressive tilt in American society, which would be sorely tested in the postwar moment.

Any comparative account of the US in this period is complicated by the distinctive features of its political system: a president elected by the people stood at the center of American government and political life; the Constitution's federal system vested a substantial degree of sovereignty in the several states; and the Supreme Court had power to strike down acts of Congress or the president that were challenged on constitutional grounds, and to hear claims against state legislation when individuals contested such acts for abridging their individual rights.

Notwithstanding these unique features of the American republic, the center of gravity for political power in all three historic democracies lay in directly elected legislative houses. In the 1930s each used single constituency systems for their elections, although their procedures differed substantially: first past the post in Britain; second-round runoffs in France; state party primaries in the US, tantamount in the one-party South to election for the Democratic nominees. In France women did not have the vote until 1945, and in US black citizens were disenfranchised in the South before and after 1945. Representatives from large northern cities might be elected by ten times the number of voters as colleagues from rural districts of the South. Upper legislative houses existed in all three countries, but even more than the French Senate the US Senate was coequal.

The US had an unvarying cycle of congressional elections every two years overlapping with a presidential contest every four years. Quadrennial party conventions chose their candidates for president in the back rooms and on the floor of these conclaves; the nominees then ran in tandem with local candidates of their parties. The parties often chose presidential candidates who would not threaten the dominance of political barons in the big cities, state capitals, or Congress. Periodically, however, strong personalities advocating change pushed to the top in both major parties.

"Progressivism" and "Normalcy"

In the late nineteenth century, waves of agrarian populism in the South and West attacked big banks and railroads for exploiting America's farmers. Among other things, populist dissidents demanded inflationary monetary policies to free indebted farmers from the oppression of the gold standard. They found an advocate in William Jennings Bryan and helped propel him to three presidential nominations in the Democratic Party (1896, 1900, 1908), and three losing campaigns against Republican monetary and social orthodoxy.

Lacking the focused intensity of agrarian populism, the elite reformers known as Progressives also shook the status quo. "Muckraking" journalists around the turn of the century formed an advanced guard, as they exposed nefarious practices by cartels and big businesses in such industries as oil and meatpacking, which exploited consumers, crushed small producers, and despoiled the environment. Urban reformers campaigned for "good government" against big city political machines that seemed to thrive on graft. They worked to ameliorate the squalid conditions of urban slums, a product, to some Progressives, of untrammeled immigration. They deplored the exploitation of workers in sweatshops or other substandard employment, especially of women and children. To cure such ills, Progressives put their faith in disinterested expertise at the state and local levels to frame reforms free of ideological posturing.

Nationally, Republican Theodore Roosevelt (TR) and Democrat Woodrow Wilson harnessed such impulses into rival programs for new kinds of government activism. TR, president between 1901 and 1908, accepted the inevitability and advantages of business concentration but pushed for more regulation to curb its excesses ("the ferocious scramble in which greed and cunning reap the largest rewards"). Wilson instead backed strong laws against trusts and monopolies to promote competition. Progressive reformism reached its high-water mark in the election of 1912. In the wake of his tenure as president, TR had come to view the conservatism of his Republican successor, William H. Taft, as hopelessly retrograde. TR shouldered his way back onto the national scene by forming an insurgent third party in 1912, while Wilson narrowly won the nomination of the Democrats. In the ensuing three-sided election, Taft finished third, TR came in second, and Wilson won with 42 percent of the popular vote.

Wilson's era saw constitutional amendments for the direct election of senators, a federal income tax, and women's suffrage, and such domestic reforms as a new antitrust law and the creation of a central bank. But Wilson is best remembered for his roles in the international crisis that eventually enveloped his presidency. Re-elected in 1916 as a leader who had kept America out of the Great War, he then reversed course, brought the US into the conflict, and mobilized the economy for war with an unprecedented collaboration between big business and government orchestrated by Bernard Baruch's War Production Board. After the allied victory, Wilson set an idealistic tone for the future of international relations, but he could not stop his allied partners from pursuing traditional geopolitical and colonial interests or from imposing harsh peace terms on their vanquished foes. As American opinion turned sourly isolationist, the US Senate rejected participation in the League of Nations, the capstone of Wilson's hopes for keeping the future peace.

The Great War brought an era of domestic reform to an abrupt halt, as TR and Wilson faded from the scene. The US savored its global financial and economic dominance at the expense of a shattered Europe, but the war's carnage provoked a backlash against future entanglements in Europe's rivalries. Workers, meanwhile, saw temporary economic gains from wartime mobilization evaporate. As in France, they responded with a wave of strikes in 1919 involving over four million workers, but the collapse of the strikes assured the authority of large corporations over their labor.[1] Wartime censorship and the alarm caused by the Bolshevik Revolution provoked repression against pacifists and radicals, especially "reds" of European origins, while a surge of racist and anti-Catholic fundamentalism reenergized the Ku Klux Klan.

Out of this mix came the legislative monument of the decade: a pair of draconian immigration laws in 1921 and 1924, driven by nativist and racialist doctrines espoused on both sides of the congressional aisle. Through arbitrary geographic quotas, the new laws drastically restricted future entry into the US not only of Asians (as in the past), but of southern and eastern Europeans, especially Italians and Jews, implicitly denying the capacity of such foreigners to adapt to American mores and values.[2] Meanwhile, native-born, middle-class Americans basked in their vaunted individualism. Newspapers and magazines—in tune with the US Chamber of Commerce, the American Bankers Association, and the National

Association of Manufacturers (NAM)—preached devotion to untrammeled free enterprise as the engine of American prosperity.

In the 1920s both major political parties largely embraced this orthodoxy. Since Democrats offered scant alternative, voters generally chose the Republicans' more reliable version of "normalcy." (The spirit of earlier populist insurgencies briefly flared in 1924 in a third party led by two maverick senators, Robert La Follette, a progressive independent from Wisconsin, and Burton K. Wheeler, a Democrat from Montana. Their campaign attracted almost five million votes but still ran a distant third.) Against a backdrop of high employment, prosperity in all but the agricultural sector, and boundless opportunities for speculative investment, Republican political supremacy continued in 1928 under the well-credentialed Herbert Hoover. Democrat Al Smith, the reform but pro-business governor of New York, lost to Hoover in 1928 in part because of who he was: an urban politician of Irish-Catholic background and a "wet" opposed to the prohibition of alcohol. With the Ku Klux Klan nipping at his heels in the South, the Midwest, and states like Montana, Smith even lost five states to Hoover in the "solid" Democratic South.[3] Much like Ramsay MacDonald, however, Hoover would be blindsided by the Great Depression, and his response would prove futile.

For three long years before voters returned to the presidential polls in 1932, the Great Depression devastated the economic and social fabric of the United States. The bursting of speculative bubbles heralded by the New York Stock Exchange crash of October 1929 only marked the beginning, as contractions in every economic sector and geographic region multiplied and fed on one another. Sinking world commodity prices deepened an already grave US agricultural slump. Consumption and business profit plummeted in tandem. As industrial production shrank by almost 50 percent between 1929 and 1932, shuttered factories, stores, offices, and construction sites created unprecedented levels of unemployment, reaching somewhere around 25 percent of the labor force. And just when the states had to step up expenditure on relief for the unemployed, their revenues fell precipitously. Worse yet, a loss of confidence in an under-regulated banking sector eventually led to panic runs on deposits and an epidemic of failures by undercapitalized banks that wiped out lifetimes of savings.[4] The Great Depression shook habits of mind as well. In business and finance, the aura of complacency seemed to evaporate. In the population at large, the comforting American ethos of individual self-reliance and opportunity now rang hollow, although what could possibly replace it remained a mystery. Yet the grip of those bedrock attitudes lingered to compound the Depression's psychological damage: in countless families of the unemployed a misguided sense of personal failure intensified the stress and humiliation of privation.

The bare statistics for the US presidential elections of 1928 and 1932 convey the dramatic reversal of political sentiment triggered by the Great Depression (table 3.1). Where the election of 1928 had reaffirmed the sway of "normalcy" with a resounding 58 percent of the popular vote for Republican Hoover, the contest in 1932 registered a desperate vote against such illusions, as Democrat Franklin D. Roosevelt won by an almost identical margin. Whatever voters did or did not expect from Roosevelt, they could at least turn out the ineffective Hoover. But what did FDR's victory portend for progressive forces in the United States going forward?

Table 3.1. US Presidential Elections, 1920–1940

1920	James Cox (Democrat)	9,140,000 (34.1%)
	Warren Harding (Republican)	16,144,000 (60.3%)
	Eugene Debs (Socialist)	914,000 (3.4%)
1924	John W. Davis (Dem)	8,386,000 (28.8%)
	Calvin Coolidge (Rep)	15,724,000 (54%)
	Robert LaFollette (Progressive)	4,800,000 (16.6%)
1928	Al Smith (Dem)	15,015,000 (40.8%)
	Herbert Hoover (Rep)	21,427,000 (58.2%)
	Norman Thomas (Soc)	267,000 (0.7%)
1932	Franklin D. Roosevelt (Dem)	22,821,000 (57.4%)
	Herbert Hoover (Rep)	15,761,000 (39.6%)
	Norman Thomas (Soc)	885,000 (2.2%)
1936	Franklin D. Roosevelt (Dem)	27,753,000 (60.8%)
	Alf Landon (Rep)	16,682,000 (36.5%)
	William Lemke (Union Party)	892,000 (1.9%)
	Norman Thomas (Soc)	188,000 (0.4%)
1940	Franklin D. Roosevelt (Dem)	27,314,000 (54.7%)
	Wendell Willkie (Rep)	22,348,000 (44.8%)
	Others	240,000 (0.5%)

The Rise of Franklin Roosevelt

Son of a patrician family and a distant relative of TR, Roosevelt had cast his lot with the Democratic Party and began an ambitious political climb by winning a seat in the New York State Senate in 1910. An appealing young figure in the party, he passed to the national stage with appointment as an assistant secretary of the navy in Woodrow Wilson's administration, and in 1920 he was the vice presidential nominee in the party's losing campaign. Then a singular event threatened to derail his career. Felled by polio in 1921, he lost the use of his legs. Roosevelt drew on a reservoir of personal grit to carry him through a long ordeal. With exhaustive physical therapy and willed optimism, he eventually managed a few steps using heavy metal braces and sticks, but he remained confined to a wheelchair for the rest of his life.

A toughened Roosevelt reemerged publicly in 1928 as a floor manager in Governor Al Smith's bid for the Democratic presidential nomination, after which the New York Democratic Party drafted FDR to run as Smith's successor for governor. His Republican opponent in the contest harped on Roosevelt's "health," but with Roosevelt's narrow victory his disability faded as a political liability. When FDR ran for re-election in 1930, he campaigned on the challenges of "insecurity" spawned by the Depression and won the largest plurality of any gubernatorial candidate in the state's history.[5] During his second term he kept his promise to establish bold state relief programs, "not as a matter of charity but as a matter of social duty." An activist, progressively oriented, and popular governor of the Empire State, Roosevelt vaulted onto the short list of potential Democratic presidential candidates for 1932.

That roster scarcely foretold a dramatic political shift led by the Democratic Party. Besides FDR the two leading aspirants were the increasingly conservative Al Smith and the veteran Speaker of the House, conservative Texan, and unabashed "dry" John Nance Garner. Democratic presidential conventions in the recent past had deadlocked under a party rule requiring the nominee to win at least two-thirds of the delegate votes; as delegates wilted in the summer heat they held repeated ballots until deals were finally cut behind the scenes. Deadlock again loomed in 1932, but the amiable and eager-to-please New York governor had the advantage of a fresh face that might bridge geographic and political chasms in the party. During recuperative sojourns at a spa in Warm Springs, Georgia, Roosevelt cultivated southern politicians and had become a trusted, honorary citizen in his second home.[6] In 1932 Roosevelt won several primaries in the seventeen states that chose convention delegates in that fashion, although Garner carried the delegate-rich primaries in Texas and California. Meanwhile, FDR's operatives outmaneuvered Smith to gain control over the party in their common bailiwick of New York. Roosevelt also won the backing of two forceful Democratic populists, Senators Huey Long of Louisiana and Wheeler of Montana (who would both give FDR grief once in the White House).

Still, a first, second, and third ballot yielded no winner at the 1932 Chicago convention and no obvious path for resolving the impasse. When the convention opened, diehard "drys" and "wets" still believed Prohibition to be an issue that could derail FDR's candidacy, with its evasive, state-option position. But the fierce party debate of 1924 and 1928 over Prohibition—a surrogate for cultural clashes between urban and rural cultures—was actually dissipating, and Prohibition no longer loomed as a make-or-break issue for either side. FDR's operatives finally brokered a deal by getting Garner to accept the vice presidential nomination. After winning on the fourth ballot, Governor Roosevelt ended the "foolish tradition" whereby presidential nominees waited at home to be officially notified days later and flew to Chicago to accept the nomination in person. His speech, broadcast over a national radio hookup, concluded with the resonant pledge of "a New Deal for the American people."[7]

For the moment Roosevelt remained mentally and politically tethered to a traditional Democratic Party platform, which promised new initiatives for relief and recovery yet reaffirmed the verities of balanced budgets and government cost cutting; indeed FDR attacked Hoover for running up federal budget deficits. In hindsight, FDR's hazy campaign, designed to offend no major region or voting bloc, occasionally foretold the kind of energetic if unpredictable president he would be. Intimations of new thinking surfaced in some of his speeches: on the need for "imaginative and purposeful planning" or, alternatively, for "bold, persistent experimentation" to combat the Depression. While vague on policy, the tone of his speeches conveyed an appealing blend of anger (at the utter futility of the Hoover administration) and of hopefulness for a new start, made credible by FDR's jaunty yet sober personality.

The First New Deal

In 1932 the fabled New Deal electoral coalition of the near future—that improbable amalgam of votes from southern whites, urban ethnic groups, organized labor, northern blacks, and aggrieved farmers—had yet to cohere or become manifest. Trade unions remained a negligible political force, most northern black votes went to Hoover, and FDR's top priority was to retain the "solid South" for Democrats. Yet Roosevelt's victory in 1932 extended across much of the country, urban and rural, and Democrats won their largest majorities ever in both houses of Congress—311 Democrats (including 131 freshmen) to 116 Republicans in the House, and 60 to 35 in the Senate (with several progressive Republicans also apt to support New Deal policies). Thanks to a rigid seniority system, it is true, the elections of 1932 gave conservative Southern Democrats disproportionate influence in Congress as committee chairmen, along with a sprinkling of liberals. But FDR had amicable rapport with the key southern players and good political instincts about when to press forward and when to compromise. He could generally bring along conservative Democrats as long as he avoided any challenge to race relations in the South (which he had no inclination to do) and did not blatantly threaten congressional prerogatives. But from day one an anxious Congress understood that combating the Depression's devastation required not only new policies but new powers for the executive branch.

Roosevelt eased into his role by enlisting a bipartisan range of personalities for cabinet-level positions. He named a Republican industrialist who backed him in 1932 as secretary of the Treasury (soon replaced by FDR's devoted Hyde Park neighbor Henry Morgenthau); veteran Wilsonian Senator Cordell Hull (Tenn.) as secretary of state; the fiscal conservative Lewis Douglas as his budget director; two Republican Progressives, conservationist Harold Ickes (secretary of the interior) and agronomist Henry Wallace (secretary of agriculture); veteran New York reformer Frances Perkins (secretary of labor); and Democratic Party stalwarts Homer Cummings (attorney general) and James A. Farley (postmaster general and chief patronage dispenser).[8] In the White House, a small "palace guard" of staffers acted as a buffer for the president but had little influence on policy.

For policy FDR relied on his cabinet and an eclectic group of advisors from his gubernatorial days dubbed his "brains trust" by the press. These advisors nurtured FDR's pragmatic, experimental bent. Along with Harvard law professor Felix Frankfurter they also created—parallel to Farley's traditional patronage system— a recruitment network which brought in lawyers, academics, and state officials new to Washington as counsels, staff, sub-heads, and heads of agencies new and old.[9] These newly minted federal officials, often young, full of idealism, and administratively creative, became Washington's "New Dealers," alongside a few senior figures. Chief among the latter: FDR's relief administrator Harry Hopkins, and Columbia professor Rexford Tugwell, an ex-"brains truster" devoted to the gospel of planning. Those two men personified the New Deal's initiatives to aid the most vulnerable citizens and to save American capitalism from itself by transforming it into a force for the public good.

Roosevelt's inaugural address in March memorably encouraged hope over fear and promised vigorous action; behind the scenes as he spoke, his collaborators met to fashion emergency legislation. The opening act of the New Deal would unfold in two scenes. The first took a mere ten days, as Roosevelt addressed the vicious cycle of the banking crisis: the cascading collapse of undercapitalized banks accelerated by the panic runs of depositors. The president declared an extended bank holiday and convened a special session of Congress to enact emergency federal support for banks, new banking regulation, and federal depository insurance that would calm the public. The breathtaking speed and huge majorities that Congress provided in adopting those measures prompted Roosevelt to extend the special session to address other issues. Scene one thus merged into scene two, together known as the Hundred Days. Fifteen pieces of legislation on financial, economic, and social issues emerged from Congress with FDR's signature by the end of the special session—some like rural electrification long under congressional debate, and others originating in the White House after brief but intense internal debate—including policies to stabilize the severely depressed agricultural sector; to stimulate industrial recovery; and to inject a new federal presence into the realm of public relief.[10]

As Senator Wheeler recalled, "When FDR first came into office and the depression was on, the only question when a bill came before a congressional committee was: What does the President say? If he wanted it, the committee would approve the bill even without finding out what was in it."[11]

The New Deal's muscular response to the prolonged agricultural depression came first and hinged on an unprecedented kind of government intervention. The Agricultural Adjustment Act (AAA) created a new agency in the Department of Agriculture to establish crop quotas (called acreage allotments) and to subsidize farmers for respecting these limits—paying them, paradoxically, for not growing as much as they could. If farmers collectively refrained from overproducing such commodity crops as wheat, corn, cotton, hogs, and milk, they could reduce the present gluts and put floors under sagging prices; in combination, subsidies and better prices should raise farm income.

The big farm lobby (the Farm Bureau Federation) pushed for passage of the AAA, reflecting what its architects—Tugwell and Secretary Wallace—understood all too well. The AAA's benefits would go primarily to large-scale farming and do little to rescue desperate small holders, tenant farmers, share-croppers, or agricultural laborers. Other New Deal programs would later address the epidemic of farm mortgage foreclosures, the drought of credit, and the inability of tenant farmers to relocate to more promising environments. But even if those other programs ultimately helped some small farming families to survive, they would not produce the transformative benefit of the AAA for large-scale agriculture or ameliorate the dire straits of most white tenant farmers and sharecroppers, let alone rural blacks in the heavily agrarian South.[12]

Roosevelt entered the White House without plans for addressing industrial recovery. Hugh Johnson (an acolyte of Bernard Baruch's and a party official in the 1932 campaign) got to work on this question, as did Tugwell; they soon fused their efforts and presented Roosevelt with a scheme to stabilize industrial production, restore its profitability, sustain employment, and improve the lot of workers. The key was to curb excess competition among manufacturers and their race to the bottom in cost cutting at the expense of workers. As Roosevelt put it in a fireside chat of May 7, "Well-considered and conservative measures will be proposed, within a few days, that will attempt to give to the industrial workers of the country a more fair wage return, to prevent cutthroat competition, to prevent unduly long hours for labor, and at the same time to encourage each industry to prevent overproduction." The proposed National Industrial Recovery Act (NIRA) authorized collaboration between government officials and businesses in a kind of voluntary corporatism that sanctioned cartel-like arrangements and perforce would scale back antitrust enforcement.

The administrative arm of this program—the National Recovery Administration or NRA—was to broker agreements in a host of industries to reduce overproduction and predatory price-cutting and to assure standards of pay and hours for workers. Signatories of an industry-wide NRA code would accept production limits and pricing guidelines (including pledges not to sell goods below cost) and would agree to avoid child labor and substandard wages. The administration did not support Senator Hugo Black's bill to cap the national work week at thirty hours as a way to spread work around, but the NRA would encourage companies to limit the workday by voluntary agreement. At the behest of Labor Secretary Frances Perkins and others, section 7a of the NIRA affirmed labor's rights to organize unions and to bargain collectively, though without establishing mechanisms to compel employer cooperation.[13]

Designed largely by Tugwell, the AAA had been an entering wedge for government economic planning, but Hugh Johnson later claimed that the NRA was different: "AAA thinks that government should run [agri-]business. NRA thinks that business should run itself under government supervision"; the NRA would broker and review industrial codes, not impose them.[14] Like the AAA, the NIRA tilted the balance against small producers, since the government would negotiate industry codes with trade associations dominated by the large corporations. Consumers too might have trouble seeing the advantage of higher stabilized prices as against competitive price-cutting. In a lively Senate debate veteran progressives attacked the NIRA's tendency toward cartelization and the resultant "ultra concentration of wealth." Senator Robert Wagner of New York, the administration's point man on many New Deal measures, gamely responded that the NIRA was an experiment meant to "purify and strengthen competition," not abolish it. It sought to make competitive practices "constructive rather than ruinous," especially as regards the hours and wages of workers. "The task is not to check efficiency but to reap its full benefits," he argued.[15] But Wagner, like most other proponents, recognized the flaws in the NRA's heterodox strategy for recovery: it favored big business at the expense of small producers; was impossible to enforce where voluntary agreement failed; and promised benefits for workers that could not be guaranteed against recalcitrant employers. Proponents also feared that down the road a refractory Supreme Court might rule the whole project unconstitutional despite its voluntary patina. In fact, the court did strike down the NRA in 1935.

When Congress enacted the NIRA, after a close vote of 46 to 39 in the Senate, FDR named as head of the NRA the intense Johnson, a man with inordinate faith in his own capacity to produce results. Well before the industrial codes were in place, Johnson launched a publicity blitz for the NRA. Marketing the program to citizens as a collective, patriotic effort to combat the Depression, Johnson organized rallies, parades, and relentless propaganda, which were reinforced with a deft fireside chat by the president in July. The NRA enlisted stores and businesses large and small to display the NRA's Blue Eagle logo with its motto "We Do Our Part" and urged consumers to patronize vendors who signified their adherence and to shun those who did not. This whirlwind of public hype set the bar of expectations for the NRA very high, and it ended up squandering political capital on a policy courting failure for its intrinsic shortcomings even before the Supreme Court struck it down. But Johnson's handling of the NRA immediately projected the New Deal into the fabric of daily life across the country and perhaps contributed to public confidence that recovery was possible.[16]

The voiding of the NRA in 1935 did not include the public works section of the NIRA approved by Congress. Roosevelt had considered a large public works program from the outset but ran into opposition from Budget Director Douglas in the name of balanced budgets and deficit reduction. For his part, Johnson viewed public works as a relatively minor tool in his recovery strategy. Advocates, however, persuaded the president to give public works a high priority, and he finally overrode Douglas and Johnson. FDR decided that public works should constitute a separate title of the NIRA, command huge appropriations from Congress, and not be under the NRA. From his base in the Department of the Interior, Secretary Ickes would head the new PWA (Public Works Administration). The PWA was not intended to produce a quick economic stimulus; Ickes would take his time in overseeing the selection, design, and letting of contracts for major projects like bridges, tunnels, dams, airports, hospitals, water projects, and urban slum clearance. But in due course the expenditures on large public works would stimulate construction industry employment and leave a legacy of infrastructure improvements. Between 1933 and 1937, 80 percent of all public construction came out of the PWA, with funds going to all but 3 of the nation's 3,071 counties.[17]

In the congressional election of 1934 Democrats could campaign on an extraordinary range of accomplishments evoked by the New Deal's alphabet of new agencies like the AAA, NRA, PWA aimed at economic recovery, along with FDIC, FERA, NYA, and CCC.[18] Atypically, Democrats increased their majorities in Congress from 313 to 322 seats in the House and from 59 to 69 in the Senate, clearly a vote of confidence in the Roosevelt administration. Ardent New Dealers felt emboldened to strike out in new directions: "a works program, wages & hours law, social security—now or never," as Hopkins put it, in accord with Tugwell and Ickes, though not necessarily with the president himself. But when FDR finally agreed to launch a "second New Deal," it encompassed a social justice agenda: social security (in early gestation before the election), a reconfiguring of federal relief and employment programs, and a new labor relations law encouraging trade union organization.

Social Security

Reformers had long advocated mandatory unemployment insurance and old-age pensions, but bills in Congress languished. New pressure for such benefits now came from grass-roots movements responding to the Depression's miseries. Novelist Upton Sinclair's "End Poverty in California" campaign, with its advocacy of "production-for-use," lifted his maverick gubernatorial run to striking distance of victory. Senator Huey Long's populist crusade to "share the wealth" excoriated New Deal moderation and directly threatened FDR's leadership. "Social security" thus promised to be a weapon for the administration to fend off radical challenges from its flanks.[19]

The saga of the Social Security Act captures the ambivalent qualities of the New Deal, starting with the mind of the president himself. If one takes FDR's most generous sentiments as a baseline, he imagined a comprehensive umbrella of social security "from cradle to grave," including unemployment insurance, old age pensions, and national health insurance. As he told Frances Perkins, "There is no reason why everybody in the US should not be covered . . . from the day he is born." "Everybody ought to be in on it," he mused, including farmers and their families.[20] Yet Roosevelt's instinctive deference to state governments, his aversion to anything resembling a permanent "dole," and his political calculations led him to downshift from this sweeping vision, notwithstanding the thunder on his left.

Unlike the precipitous initiatives in the Hundred Days, Roosevelt slowed the momentum by appointing a cabinet Committee on Economic Security (CES) chaired by Perkins, with a staff of experts and an outside advisory panel, to study "social security" over the summer of 1934 and to fashion a consensus for congressional action. Even discounting business opposition, social security faced resistance from conservatives in both parties leery about federal preemptions of state power, while southern lawmakers would balk at any side effects the legislation might have on race relations. Alongside sentiment for bold federal programs, the CES also had to accommodate a preference among some veteran reformers for experimentation on social policies at the state level that took into account "the prejudices of our people and our legislative habits." Finally, the elephant in the room for the CES was not the Republican Party but the threat of Supreme Court nullification: the US government had the necessary taxing powers, Perkins believed, "but could it distribute its funds on a basis of social benefit?"[21]

The Social Security Act that finally emerged in 1935 from the CES report and congressional deliberation included three distinct elements: new state unemployment insurance programs; federal old-age pensions to begin in 1942; and federal matching funds to states for aid to various kinds of dependent persons, such as needy single mothers and the disabled, blind, or elderly indigents—matching funds to encourage the states "to develop more liberal eligibility requirements and more adequate assistance standards."[22] National health insurance, part of Roosevelt's list, all but disappeared in the CES report in the face of adamant opposition from the American Medical Association.[23] Even as Social Security became one of FDR's vaunted legacies, his signing statement for the act on August 14, 1935, made no extravagant claims. The Social Security Act, he believed, would provide "some measure of protection to the average citizen and his family against the loss of a job and against poverty-ridden old age."[24]

The limitations of the Social Security Act unfolded in its details. The unemployment insurance title was simply an enabling law and an incentive for the states. The act levied a federal payroll tax on employers of eight or more persons, but only 10 percent of the income would be retained in Washington for administrative purposes, the rest sent to individual states that established unemployment compensation programs. At present only Wisconsin had such a program, but the act correctly anticipated that even the most recalcitrant states would set up counterparts, since the money awaited them, and the cost of the payroll tax would not put employers in their state at a competitive disadvantage. The IRS collected the payroll tax as a kind of trustee and passed the revenue to the states for that purpose alone.

The act left the modalities of unemployment compensation almost entirely up to the individual states. No federal standards determined the scale or duration of benefits, waiting periods before payments began, eligibility requirements, minimum or maximum levels of wages subject to the tax. (In due course the duration of payouts ranged from 13 to 26 weeks, averaging 16 weeks, with a benefit roughly equivalent to half the wage level up to $15 a week.)[25] The act stipulated, however, that benefits could not be denied to an unemployed worker who refused to fill a vacancy arising from a strike or to take a job that paid substandard wages or barred membership in a labor union.[26]

In contrast to unemployment insurance, the old-age pensions for future retirees created by the Social Security Act constituted a national program, uniform and portable across the states. Following the president's preference, the CES and Congress used private insurance plans as a template: after a reserve had been built up, and in keeping with actuarial calculations, the inflow and outgo of funds over time should roughly match; to use an imprecise shorthand, old-age pensions should operate on a pay-as-you-go basis. But from where would the funding come? In Britain the Beveridge Plan later proposed a three-legged stool of contributions from employers, employees, and the exchequer—for Beveridge the only way to assure an adequate payout.[27] But Roosevelt's aversion to what he called "the dole," along with his discomfort over deficit spending, led him to oppose Treasury expenditure to support old-age pensions. Rather they should be funded solely by contributions from employers and employees, an arguably regressive kind of tax on workers. Roosevelt stuck to this approach even though it meant hiking payroll taxes beyond the comfort levels initially discussed, thereby increasing the act's potential deflationary effect.[28] Equal contributions from employees and employers would begin immediately, each rising over time from 1 to 3 percent of wages. The initial payouts, extremely modest when slated to begin in 1942, would not be at a flat rate for every eligible worker (as proposed in the Beveridge Plan) but would reflect the individual's earnings history and would range from a minimum of $10 monthly up to $85.[29]

In speeches and radio addresses, the three Social Security commissioners appointed to oversee implementation of the act stressed that old-age pensions would be paid as a matter of right to qualified individuals who had been contributing. As one explained, younger workers would now be able to count on "a definite income upon retirement." As another put it: "These benefits should not in any way be confused with any kind of relief. They are dividends which belong to the recipient."[30] Here was the positive side of Roosevelt's resistance to injecting Treasury funds to build up the trust fund. The payroll taxes might bite, but individual workers would have their own social security accounts going forward. Thirty-eight million people were in the system by 1938, their dossiers filling an acre of floor space,[31] and the program could not easily be dismantled in the future no matter how the political winds might shift.

Different as they were, the unemployment insurance program and the federal old-age pensions had one huge deficiency in common. In the CES blueprint no large categories of workers would be excluded from coverage for either benefit, apart from the special case of government employees. By the time both houses of Congress did their work, however, agricultural and domestic workers were excluded from both programs. Treasury Secretary Morgenthau began the retreat in testimony to Congress by raising no objection to leaving out agricultural and domestic workers on the grounds that collecting payroll taxes from their small employers would be impossibly cumbersome. But even if administrative difficulties were a bona fide consideration,[32] they disguised the veritable reason that Congress enacted the exclusions. Southern legislators feared that such liberalities would undermine race relations, which rested on the profound dependency of southern blacks employed as low-wage farm laborers or domestic servants. An estimated 65 percent of black workers ended up outside the scope of unemployment insurance and old-age pensions (with an even higher proportion in the South), as did 40 percent of whites. Southern lawmakers may have veiled the role of race relations here, but the indignant protests of black journalists at the time make this interpretation incontrovertible.[33]

Federal Work Relief

As governor of New York Roosevelt stretched shrinking state resources to relieve the poverty and hunger spawned by the Depression. Once in the White House he asked Congress for large federal subventions to besieged state and local relief agencies and named Harry Hopkins, his New York relief administrator, to head a new Federal Emergency Relief Administration (FERA). From his experience directing social service organizations and his stint in Albany, Hopkins brought to Washington a dynamic amalgam of administrative skill and bold progressive thinking, along with an instinct for political maneuvering. Hopkins could work the system to maximum effect even as he tried to transform it. He detested the inadequacies and demeaning practices of local relief agencies: the stringent means testing to prove destitution; the proffer of assistance in kind or in vouchers rather than cash; the intrusive supervision by his fellow social workers. For the moment Hopkins swiftly disbursed $500 million in FERA funds to local relief agencies for cushioning the worst misery of their clients. But exclusionary and humiliating requirements kept millions of newly unemployed workers beyond the reach of those agencies.

Hopkins believed that with a different kind of program and an infusion of new funding, the government could put four million unemployed people to work that winter. In his own mind Hopkins faced a devilish conundrum. "The indignity of public charity" might still relieve desperate need, but the state of "worklessness" came a close second in demanding remedy. Subsistence relief to the unemployed might alleviate destitution and hunger, but getting people back to work would be the best form of aid. Ordinarily government could do little to provide jobs, but Hopkins proposed an interim "works program" to tide over the unemployed during the coming winter. In effect, government would become a temporary employer of last resort. Under this Civil Works Administration (CWA) the unemployed person "is paid wages and the social worker drops out of the picture."[34]

Hopkins convinced Roosevelt to launch the CWA by executive order in November 1933, using funds siphoned from FERA and the PWA, to be supplemented in February with a new congressional appropriation. Lasting only the intended four winter months, CWA was a successful test run for a new federal response to Depression unemployment. Immediately after the green light from FDR, Hopkins convened a conference of state and local officials in the Mayflower Hotel, where his keynote speech described a novel works program for the unemployed that bypassed the usual hurdles for public assistance. "For heaven's sake," he replied to one question, "we don't want to go through investigations [by relief offices]." Two million unemployed persons currently on local relief would be rebooked into CWA programs, along with two million unemployed not on relief, to be enrolled via the US Employment Service. The CWA work would pay standard hourly wages varying across three zones (Southern, Central, and Northern), with differentials between skilled and low skilled workers, and with a maximum workweek of thirty hours.[35]

The CWA would still use local relief agencies to execute this program, but federal officials could initiate CWA projects. Hopkins's illustrative list included clerical, professional, and research jobs; the sewing of clothing; pest control; maintenance or refurbishment of public buildings, parks, playgrounds, roads, and water supplies —although CWA would not preempt public services such as street cleaning or garbage collection. Just how CWA projects would differ from those being planned by Ickes's PWA may not have been self-evident. But Ickes personally addressed the Mayflower conference, called CWA "a great scheme," and explained that while his PWA had to proceed methodically with its project designs, bids, and contracts, he would shift $400 million from his $ 3.3 billion appropriation to CWA for immediate expenditure.[36] Marked by speed and improvisation, CWA put to work over four million unemployed men and women that winter, including 33,000 laid off teachers channeled into adult education and nursery classes. Forty thousand school buildings were upgraded, along with countless roads and recreational facilities.[37] The CWA's local projects in thousands of communities created a new model for government support of the unemployed.

As FDR's relief administrator, Hopkins understood the special circumstances of unemployed women and blacks. With FERA's director of women's issues, veteran Progressive Ellen Woodward, he convened a second conference in November on the emergency needs of women, and he would continue this attention going forward.[38] How to incorporate blacks into federal work relief schemes posed a greater challenge. With a vastly disproportionate place among the destitute, blacks received subsistence relief via FERA in twice their proportion to the population.[39] But how would they fare in CWA projects? At the Mayflower conference an official from Florida asked if there would be "difference in the minimum wage rate between colored and white labor?" To which Hopkins answered: No. But the limited number of CWA jobs caused tensions in the South. Reports from South Carolina forced Hopkins to admit "the possibility of rioting and the fact that the white people will run the Negroes off their jobs, as they will not stand for the Negroes earning $36 a month while the whites are unemployed."[40] No anti-discrimination sentiments or policy guidelines from Washington could conjure away such raw racial tensions.

Roosevelt had agreed to launch CWA as a temporary expedient during the winter of 1933–34. Hopkins hoped to renew the program, but Budget Director Douglas opposed renewal in extremely blunt language: "I recommend that in lieu of the continuation of CWA," he wrote to FDR in January 1934, "you revert to direct relief, applying the 'means test.' It is interesting to note that England, having had ten years of experience in this field, has adopted it." Inarguably correct about Britain's reliance on the means test—whose humiliations infuriated the British Labour Party and Harry Hopkins alike—Douglas also addressed the push and pull among the federal government, the states, and private enterprise. The states have a vested interest in shifting relief expenses onto the federal government through programs like CWA, he cautioned, while CWA pay rates made it harder for private employers to hire workers at customary wages when needed, especially in rural areas. Douglas won the argument and FDR decided that "with the coming of seed time on the farms, we can confidently look forward to a reduced necessity for civil works and its consequent demobilization." He also expected "a considerable increase in the employment of private industry."[41]

Hopkins lost the battle for extending CWA, but the election of 1934 changed his prospects. As noted, Hopkins, Ickes, and Tugwell pushed for a second New Deal: "a works program, social security, wages & hours [laws]—now or never." In a message to Congress in January 1935 the president called for a shift from traditional relief for unemployed workers to a new works program.[42] Administrative complications and turf wars between Hopkins and Ickes briefly stalled the new initiative. (Famous for using subordinates in overlapping ways that assured his own final say, FDR purportedly took perverse pleasure in choosing the awkward title of WPA [Works Progress Administration] for Hopkins' new program—leaving it easily confused ever since with Ickes's PWA.) After some jousting Hopkins emerged as director of a well-funded, vaster, and more durable version of the CWA.[43] Unlike CWA, the WPA could undertake small-scale construction projects such as new post offices and schools, farm-to-market roads, and water and sewer systems. Over 400,000 women found work in the WPA, the majority in sewing rooms but also dispensing hot school lunches and running adult literacy classes. Under WPA, wage rates again varied by region, as did sporadic efforts to mitigate racial discrimination.[44] At its zenith in 1937–38, 3.3 million unemployed people of various sorts earned over $2 billion working for the WPA.

Besides devastating the blue-collar and low-skilled workforce, Depression-era unemployment hit hard at the professions and the arts; an estimated 90 percent of architects in New York, for example, lost their positions.[45] Through its four Federal Arts Projects covering writing, theater, music, and the visual arts, the WPA helped sustain American cultural life during the Depression. Unemployed writers collected oral slave narratives or prepared superb local guidebooks; artists painted murals on public buildings; theater troupes commissioned and mounted new works. The arts projects of the WPA had a multiplier effect, as when painters taught free art classes. But as the arts projects of WPA enriched their communities, some stirred controversy, most conspicuously under the Federal Theater Project. To its advocates the Theater Project was a lifeline for unemployed actors and theater professionals and a great experiment in offering theater to a new popular audience. But the leftist or communist ties of some theater people; the populist tenor of certain productions ("made in Russia," their opponents mocked); and the interracial activity in a few troupes became lightning rods for anti-New Deal conservatives. Opponents deplored the whole program as one big "frill," subversive at its core. Their attacks brought a few resignations by WPA arts officials and brutal hectoring during congressional hearings in 1938–39. Congress zeroed out the Theater Project when it finally renewed funding for WPA.[46]

As Social Security and the WPA neared adoption in 1935, Roosevelt mused that if another long depression occurred, the unemployed would not simply be left to their fate. "First a cash benefit [from unemployment insurance], then use up his savings, then a work benefit," he told Perkins.[47] When Congress finally terminated the WPA during World War II, only Social Security remained. But another leg of Hopkins's vision for a second New Deal had come to fruition: new labor laws that facilitated organizing drives and collective bargaining by trade unions and that established federal labor standards.

Labor on the Move

In a radio pitch for the NIRA, FDR endorsed a simple, if not simplistic, way to combat unemployment and substandard wages. "If all employers will act together to shorten hours and raise wages, we can put people back to work. . . . The essence of the plan is a universal limitation of hours of work per week for any individual by mutual consent, and a universal payment of wages above the minimum, also by common consent."[48] These standards would be established in industry codes. Something of an afterthought, section 7a of the NIRA encouraged the organization of trade unions and collective bargaining.

William Green, president of the American Federation of Labor (AFL), had lobbied for 7a and impulsively hailed it as "the Magna Carta of labor." A spurt of organizing followed under the impetus of 7a, but the NRA could not compel employers to recognize unions or bargain collectively. Some large corporations responded by bolstering employee representation plans or company unions that they could control. As Green subsequently complained to a Senate committee in 1935, the feeble mechanisms of 7a, including a federal conciliation board, had no powers to curb abusive practices by employers such as planting spies in local unions, discriminating against union supporters, or threatening to close a plant and not rehire pro-union workers if the plant reopened.[49] And as later documented by Senator La Follette's committee on the abuse of civil liberties by big business, some firms used armed violence if unionization threatened. Replete with such details as the weapons in Republic Steel's private arsenal (245 shotguns, 552 revolvers, and 2,707 tear-gas grenades), the La Follette hearings offered up a gripping narrative of anti-union coercion.[50]

The White House showed little concern over obstacles to the labor movement, but this became Senator Robert Wagner's priority issue. At FDR's request, Wagner had chaired the NRA's conciliation or National Labor Relations Board (NLRB) and saw firsthand its utter inability to support organizing drives under 7a or to deter violence around picket lines. Wagner therefore introduced a "Bill to Promote Equality of Bargaining Power between Employers and Employees, to Diminish the Causes of Labor Disputes, to Create an [effective] NLRB." The bill languished in the 1934 session, but Wagner expected the gates to open after the 1934 mid-term election. FDR remained uncommitted but let Wagner proceed in the Senate on his own. Against intense lobbying by the NAM and the US Chamber of Commerce, Wagner steered his bill to adoption in the Senate after turning back crippling amendments.[51] He could not, however, fend off the insertion by southern lawmakers of a clause (similar to their altera-tion of the Social Security Act) excluding agricultural and domestic workers from coverage by his proposed law, a modification meant once again to insulate prevailing race relations in the South.[52]

In a nice twist of timing, the Senate acted just days before the Supreme Court struck down the NRA and its toothless section 7a. At that point FDR finally came out for Wagner's bill, and in July 1935 it became law. The National Labor Relations Board now became an independent federal agency that could super-vise union representation elections and certify winners. The NLRB could also hear charges against employers for "unfair labor practices," with power to order their cession, impose fines for violations, and order reinstatement and back pay to workers fired for union activity. The National Labor Relations, or Wagner, Act was no Magna Carta for labor. Employers could still combat unionization (Henry Ford and Bethlehem Steel held out until 1941); they could appeal certain NLRB decisions to federal courts; they could absorb sanctions for unfair practices; and even if a union won recognition, a company could stalemate contract negotiations. In short the NLRB created greater opportunities for trade unions but did not guarantee outcomes. The Wagner Act tilted the balance in favor of unionization drives only if workers on the ground shed their distrust of unions, risked employer wrath by signing up for union representation, and stayed the course.[53]

What, then, was the profile of US trade unionism in 1935 and its potential for expansion? How did the contested terrains for organization look from the top down and the bottom up? The structure of organized labor seemed simple enough at this point in time: trade unions had about three million members, most (apart from the railroad brotherhoods) in national unions affiliated with the AFL. Unions were strongest in skilled and semi-skilled trades, their members usually native-born or at any rate not from the most recent immigrant communities. The AFL craft unions included carpenters, plumbers, machinists, printers, brewers, teamsters, specialists in certain metal trades, and the all-black Brotherhood of Sleeping Car Porters, along with more diverse unions such as the United Mine Workers (UMW), ladies' garment workers (ILGWU), and men's clothing workers. Union officials worried over skill dilution and raiding by other unions; turf battles and border disputes were part of their stock-in-trade. While the AFL nominally backed the goal of organizing the mass production industries, many of its barons doubted the prospects. The leaders of craft unions tended to view mass production workers as unpromising constituencies for trade union membership, too volatile and unreliable.

William Green came to personify the AFL's failure to act effectively in the mass production industries. Ostensibly an American counterpart of Ernest Bevin in Britain's TUC or Léon Jouhaux in France's CGT, Green had attained his position not by force of personality or record of achievement, but was in effect the AFL's accidental if long-term president. Starting out as secretary of a coal miner's local in 1891, Green became president of the UMW's Ohio district in 1906 and detoured into politics in 1910–14 as a Democratic state senator in Ohio. After he returned to the UMW, its current president John White named him secretary-treasurer of the union, and then chose Green to fill an unexpected vacancy as an AFL vice president in Washington (White himself being uninterested in the post). After the death of the AFL's founding president Samuel Gompers in 1924, Green, without any power base or elective mandate of his own, was chosen as president by the AFL's executive council. For good reason, then, Green believed that his role was simply to represent the will of the federation's council; the majority view of those union leaders on any issue constituted his marching orders. Green's adherence to a Protestant version of the social gospel reinforced the federation's aversion to militancy; the common interests and potential harmony of business and labor, he believed, must be promoted through moral suasion and industrial peace.[54]

In the early 1930s under 7a, organizing in nonunion industries such as autos, rubber, and electrical manufacturing sprang from local islands of militancy in a sea of indifferent or fearful workers. The AFL recognized some ad hoc unions formed by activists, known as "federal" locals because they answered directly to federation headquarters. But the AFL would not accept an "industrial union" or plant-wide strategy for organizing the mass production industries. In a tire plant, for example, unskilled production line workers and skilled mechanics who serviced the machines might join forces, unity being their source of leverage. But AFL headquarters would soon insist that the mechanics be moved from the "federal" local into the AFL machinists union. Mass production workers on the ground considered this a ridiculous policy that undercut their unity and doomed them to arcane turf battles among themselves. Members of new AFL "federal" locals often drifted away.[55]

Unlike most AFL leaders, John L. Lewis (president of the United Mine Workers) and Sidney Hillman (president of the Amalgamated Clothing Workers of America) prioritized "organizing the unorganized." Lewis was America's best-known labor leader in the 1930s—theatrical, sharp-tongued, intimidating, an effective public advocate, and an astute negotiator. Like Green, Lewis was a native-born Protestant, committed to capitalism, and impatient with radical ideologies; in a contest for the presidency of the UMW in 1926 he had routed John Brophy, an advocate for the nationalization of the troubled coal industry, and for good measure purged him from the union. But Lewis was cunningly opportunistic; he understood that rank-and-file militancy could incline management to see him, in contrast, as a reasonable broker. Hillman became Lewis's improbable partner in dissidence within the AFL. A Russian-born immigrant, battle-scarred veteran of struggles with the communists in his own union, a social democrat by conviction but comfortable in alliances with urban progressives.[56]

Lewis and Hillman insisted that mass production industries must be organized without concern for jurisdictional claims of existing AFL unions. After arguing in vain for a more expansive strategy at AFL conventions in 1934 and 1935, Lewis and Hillman finally balked. With a handful of other leaders they went off on their own to form a Committee on Industrial Organization. These founders did not intend to commit the capital heresy of splitting the labor movement but simply to bypass the AFL and get started.[57] Within two years, however, their unions, new and old, were gone from the AFL and had formed a full-fledged, rival federation—no longer a "committee" but now the Congress of Industrial Organizations (CIO).

With funding from UMW and other union coffers, the CIO hired 200 organizers, and Lewis named as director of organizing John Brophy, whom he had recently brought back to the UMW from exile. The CIO launched top-down organizing drives in steel and textiles—two largely unorganized industries linked to the respective interests of Lewis (coal) and Hillman (the garment trades). But the CIO also provided funds, personnel, and advice for rank-and-file organizing in such industries as autos, rubber, and electronics. In its formative phase the CIO thus combined two top-down organizing drives with support for activists in other mass production industries. From each type of intervention large new national unions eventually emerged, permanently transforming the landscape of organized labor.[58]

Lewis and Hillman also saw the CIO's role in political terms. Millions of newly organized workers would not only be helping themselves directly, but as voters could bolster political allies in state and national government. Under Gompers AFL doctrine kept political parties and government at arm's length in the belief that what politicians gained for workers they could take away. Nonetheless certain established union leaders had ties to the political parties. Teamsters president Dan Tobin, for example, was the official labor delegate to the Democratic National Committee, while the head of the carpenters' union supported the Republicans, as had Lewis in the1932 election. Philip Murray, UMW vice president, on the other hand, had backed Roosevelt in the 1932 campaign. Hillman still voted the Socialist ticket in 1932, but he soon became an ardent New Deal supporter. By the CIO's inception in 1936, its founders stood squarely in Roosevelt's corner, worked for FDR's re-election, and helped put states like Pennsylvania into the Democratic column.

Steelworkers and Autoworkers

In June 1936 the CIO formed a Steel Workers Organizing Committee, or SWOC, headed by Lewis's UMW lieutenant Philip Murray. SWOC launched an invasion of the "open-shop" or nonunion terrain of modern industry's key sector.[59] In steel mills and fabrication plants across states like Ohio, Illinois, and Pennsylvania, which often grew in tandem with company towns, steelworkers generally distrusted unions after the crushing defeat of a unionization drive in 1919. They tended to rely instead on the solidarity of their ethnic and religious communities, and to assume that only the companies could assure their economic security.[60] But SWOC provided new ingredients to the mix: dedicated, full-time organizers (UMW veterans along with communists and other radicals), seed money, and tactical experience.

In the face of initial worker indifference or hostility, its "mass meetings" attended only by handfuls of men, SWOC persisted. Eventually SWOC organizers found the local activists they needed in an unexpected quarter—the leaders of company unions within the empire of the United States Steel Corporation (or as it was known, Big Steel), whom SWOC organizers pushed to embrace independent trade unionism. Even as SWOC gained momentum, however, only 7 percent of US Steel's workers had signed union cards and fewer were committed enough to pay dues; SWOC was not ready to petition for an NLRB election at US Steel let alone launch a major strike.[61] Yet Myron Taylor, president of US Steel, feared a strike and was averse to confronting picketers with the customary violent methods. In the spirit of the moribund NRA, Taylor sought a stabilized wage-price structure for the industry. Closeting himself with Lewis in February 1937, Taylor agreed to recognize SWOC and negotiate a contract for US Steel's largest plant, an astonishing accord announced to the public on March 2, 1937, with a wage increase quickly following. Initially SWOC represented only its own members, but the NLRB soon certified SWOC as the exclusive bargaining agent at US Steel.[62]

Yet this dramatic breakthrough did not open a path for SWOC in the rest of the industry. The other major firms (known collectively as Little Steel) granted the same wage raise as US Steel but with one exception would not recognize the union. Driven by pressure from impatient local activists, SWOC authorized the risky strike weapon. At Republic Steel—"the filthiest cesspool of labor relations in America," according to Murray—armed company thugs and city police, claiming to protect a Republic plant in Chicago from being stormed, viciously attacked SWOC pickets and their families on Memorial Day 1937, killing several and with them the strike. Managers of Bethlehem Steel plants in Johnstown, Pennsylvania, and of Youngstown Sheet and Tube in Ohio used varied but comparably brutal methods to break their strikes.[63] One piece of collateral damage from the Little Steel strikes would later cause serious trouble for the CIO. During the confrontations at idled steel mills, and with no prospect of compromise in sight, FDR in frustration had publicly declared "a plague on both your houses"—for which Lewis would never forgive him.

After the failed Little Steel strikes, SWOC union-building continued in the far-flung US Steel empire, with organizing of other plants, dues picketing to collect dues from balky union members, and wildcat strikes over grievance procedures.[64] More broadly, however, the situation for all steelworkers deteriorated as the "Roosevelt Recession" deepened in 1938 (see below). No additional wage increases could be extracted from the steel companies after 1937, and fears of unemployment again gripped steelworkers. Only with the rearmament program that FDR enacted in 1940 did the picture brighten. One by one the Little Steel companies then recognized SWOC to secure their positions in seeking defense contracts, and Republic and Youngstown reinstated with back pay union members fired in 1937. Recognition of SWOC did not in itself guarantee expeditious or good-faith contract negotiations. But by the eve of Pearl Harbor, 90 percent of the steel industry was unionized, and this collective strength would bring gains for steelworkers during the war and after.[65]

In 1935 the American auto industry formed another vast "open-shop" terrain. Its big three corporations—General Motors, Ford, and Chrysler—loomed over small competitors and a host of parts suppliers and subcontractors. Bodies, engines, power trains, and other components were manufactured in separate plants; workforces included low-skilled European immigrants and southern migrants, white and black. Union-building in this variegated industry therefore posed severe challenges.[66] Organizers could focus on parts factories or auto assembly plants; the brass ring would be a strategy to pressure a major auto company into recognizing a union across its domain.

The CIO offered its help, but it did not launch a top-down organizing drive on the SWOC model. The first major breakthroughs came from local sit-down strikes or factory occupations—a novel form of leverage by which small groups of union activists could challenge local management, uncommitted fellow workers, and public authorities. Sit-downs had spread in France right after the election of Blum's Popular Front government in June 1936 as we saw, and US workers trying to organize a few auto parts companies and Goodyear's Akron tire plants also pioneered this tactic. In the winter of 1936–37 autoworkers in West Detroit and in Flint, Michigan, independently launched large-scale sit-downs, culminating with an occupation of GM's Fischer Body assembly plants in Flint that, if sustained, could have choked off much of GM's production.

The high drama of the Detroit and Flint sit-downs included intrepid physical resistance by the occupiers against attempts to retake plants; community support to provide food, drink, and reinforcements for the strikers; and deft legal foot-work to stymie court actions against building occupations of questionable legality. The CIO general counsel Lee Pressman, sent to Michigan by Lewis, found that a state judge who had issued an injunction against the occupiers held over $200,000 worth of GM stock; Pressman thereby got the injunction voided.[67] Lewis, meanwhile, lobbied Michigan's new Democratic governor to refrain from using his national guard to clear the factories. As the usual methods of resistance to union organizing failed, a demoralized GM management decided to negotiate with Lewis, acting in behalf of the autoworkers. On February 11 GM recognized the CIO's fledgling United Auto Workers (UAW) and signed a six-month contract. Within the space of one month two giants of American industry, GM and US Steel, seemed to abandon their historic resist-ance to unionization, as did General Electric a few weeks later.[68]

Energized by the GM contract, the UAW emerged from the sit-down strikes as a major presence in the CIO. But unlike SWOC, where leadership flowed from Murray and Pittsburgh headquarters down, power in the UAW rose upward from its locals and districts. The UAW paid a price for its democratic proce-dures, with relentless shop-floor activism, kaleidoscopic factional conflicts, and leadership rivalries. Conflicts between rival caucuses allowed Communist Party cadres in the UAW to leverage their effective organizing into influence far beyond their numbers—at first in cooperation with Walter Reuther, one of the UAW's rising stars. A skilled tool-and-die maker of social-democratic convic-tions, Reuther began organizing for the UAW in 1935, led his West Detroit local during the sit-down strikes, and in 1939 won a solid power base as head of the UAW's GM division.[69]

The New Deal Peaks and Falters

The election of 1936 produced a landslide for FDR and congressional Democrats. The thunder on the left dogging Roosevelt eventually fizzled into a huge anticlimax, starting in September 1935 when an embittered Louisianan assassinated the demagogic Senator Huey Long, the president's strongest poten-tial challenger. Several populist organizations still mounted a third-party campaign, but it floundered amid clashing priorities and ugly crosscurrents of anti-Semitism. With a colorless North Dakota congressman at the head of its ticket, the Union Party ended up with fewer than 900,000 votes in November.

Roosevelt, meanwhile, mocked the reactionary bankers and big businessmen who had railed against him for three years as a radical traitor to his class and potential dictator. FDR taunted his wealthy foes as "economic royalists," whose American Liberty League would "make Long Island safe for polo players." Roosevelt's Republican opponent, Governor Alf Landon of Kansas, was no creature of such interests but a fiscal conservative more comfortable with small-town traditionalism than Wall Street. But with almost 61 percent of the popular vote, Roosevelt inundated Landon, who carried only two states (see table 3.1). Roosevelt attracted millions of first-time voters as well as converts from old political habits. His electoral coalition swept cities like New York, Chicago, and Pittsburgh where political machines mobilized Catholics, Jews, and blacks. The growing ranks of organized labor now voted Democratic, and the South remained rock solid. The Democratic majority in the House grew to 334 against a mere 89 Republicans, and in the Senate Republicans held only 19 seats out of 96.[70]

Democrats of all stripes had embraced FDR's coattails during the 1936 campaign, but after the election, while liberals hoped to extend the New Deal, conservative Democrats (secure in their congressional sway) backed away from the president, having long resented his overbearing executive activism. FDR then stoked congressional opposition with several misconceived initiatives. The aftermath of the 1936 electoral landslide therefore unfolded paradoxically: instead of producing a victory lap for the president, the election started a downward slope in his sway.

Roosevelt's greatest problem in 1936, besides his re-election, was the Supreme Court. Its conservative majority, unchanged since he took office in 1933, had by 1935 struck down the New Deal's centerpiece recovery programs: the poorly crafted NIRA (by a unanimous vote) and the AAA (by a more typical 5–4 vote). Looking ahead, the White House expected the court to overturn the Wagner Act and the Social Security Act, along with any federal law to regulate wages or working hours. Roosevelt expressed his dismay at a press conference; the court, he said, still lived in "the horse and buggy era," while the challenges of modern society demanded heightened governmental regulation of the economy. Then, on a parallel track in May 1936, by a 5–4 vote the court overturned a carefully drafted New York State minimum wage law for women workers. *Morehead v. Tipaldo* extended a thirty-year cycle in the court of nullifying most state laws to protect workers on the grounds that such laws violated the freedom of contract or "substantive due process" of employers.[71] When

Tipaldo came down, FDR complained that the court had created a "no-man's land" where neither federal nor state governments could protect the economic and social welfare of citizens. Still, he kept the issue of the Supreme Court out of the 1936 election campaign.

With the election behind him, however, FDR placed "reform" of the Supreme Court at the top of his agenda. Some advisors counseled that the court's vetoes of New Deal legislation under its vague powers of judicial review required a constitutional amendment to rein in that power. Others argued that the adverse decisions were products of the court's current composition, especially the four rigidly conservative justices known as "the four horsemen," whose "personal economic predilections" dictated these outcomes; the president should simply wait out the aging justices. But FDR finally decided neither to seek a constitutional amendment nor to wait for one of the justices to retire. Spurning those prudent if time-consuming strategies, Roosevelt instead sent a bill to Congress drafted by Attorney General Cummings to enlarge the Supreme Court with amenable new judges. Based on the specious premise that with six justices over the age of seventy the court could not cope with its crowded docket, this proposal would authorize the president to appoint one new justice for each judge over seventy who chose not to resign.[72]

Tampering with the historic independence of the Supreme Court had long been taboo in American politics, and FDR's high-handed proposal aroused a storm of congressional and editorial anger that offset the liberals' frustration at the court's decisions. Even as Ickes and a few liberal senators defended the plan, it severely discomfited other New Dealers. Democratic maverick Wheeler agreed to lead the senatorial opposition, allowing Republicans to keep a low profile. Even among allies from FDR's New York home base, Senator Wagner refused to state his position on "court packing," and Governor Lehman denounced it.[73]

The chief justice prepared a memo for Senator Wheeler demonstrating the speciousness of allegations about inefficiency in the court, which undercut the main rationale for the bill. Then Justice Roberts, the court's frequent swing vote, appeared to change sides. In *West Coast Hotel v. Parish,* a 5–4 vote sustained a Washington State protective labor law similar to the one struck down by the court only months before in *Tipaldo.* In due course decisions by narrow majorities upheld key elements of the Wagner Act and the Social Security Act. Roberts's reason for switching were best known to himself.

Perhaps it was the sobering effect of FDR's 1936 landslide; or the cumulative impact of sharp dissenting opinions in previous decisions; or the more skillful way the second wave of New Deal laws had been drafted or defended before the court.[74] In any case, after Roberts's switch one of the "four horsemen" announced his retirement and further defused the constitutional deadlock. Yet even with the rationale for court packing in tatters, the political urgency removed, and head counts in Congress showing poor prospects for the bill, FDR simply would not back down. Forced to vote, the Senate recommitted the bill to committee, handing the president a humiliating defeat.[75]

True, the president acquired a more tractable Supreme Court as he filled several vacancies between 1937 and 1941. The court now interpreted the due process, interstate commerce, and "general welfare" clauses of the constitution expansively and thereby upheld New Deal legislation and regulatory activity. The collateral political damage of the court-packing struggle, however, proved substantial. After Roosevelt's humiliation, transient conservative coalitions resisting the president became more commonplace.[76]

The New Deal's triumph of 1936 soured in the 1938 mid-term election in part thanks to a steep new recession. With his qualms about government deficits, Roosevelt in 1937 spurned the counsel of liberal advisors and submitted a balanced budget that scaled back New Deal programs like the WPA and PWA. Washington thus reduced the government "pump priming" that had propped up purchasing power and consumption at the depth of the Depression. Arguably this retrenchment helped plunge a still shaky economy back into recession. J. M. Keynes certainly believed that to be the case when he chided FDR in February 1938 for "the error of optimism" in prematurely cutting back on public works and other government programs, thereby helping to stall the recovery.[77] Conservative critics countered that the New Deal had overregulated and overtaxed business and that business confidence had never truly recovered; only balanced budgets that reflected fiscal responsibility would encourage businesses to invest and to hire. In any case, at the first sign of a serious economic downturn, businesses retrenched and unemployment soared.

By June 1938 the president swung back to pump priming. In a radio address Roosevelt recalled how "government spending acted as a trigger to set off private activity" in 1933–36 and had to do so again. He now proposed large appropriations for New Deal agencies, work relief, and construction projects "to turn the tide of national income upward" so as to rekindle consumer demand and business activity.[78] The budget change was either belated (in the liberal view) or utterly misguided (in the conservative view), but either way the "Roosevelt recession" of late 1937–38 shadowed Democrats in the mid-term election of 1938 and contributed to a rebound by Republicans.

A move by the president to bolster liberal allies also backfired when he campaigned against a few conservative Democratic incumbents in their primaries. His hopes of strengthening the party's progressive wing failed conspicuously, as all but one of his targets won their primaries and re-election. In tandem with the Republican rebound in the November election, resentment at the abortive purge sapped the president's clout in his own party. Veritable political realignment and further progress for the New Deal both became problematic.[79]

America Faces European Fascism

As the "Roosevelt recession" weighed on voters in the mid-term elections of 1938, foreign relations remained a comfort zone for FDR, although that would change drastically within a year. With a congressional exposé of profiteering by American financiers and arms manufacturers during the Great War as a backdrop, Congress in the mid-thirties had codified the nation's antiwar sentiment. The Neutrality Act of 1935 prohibited exporting or transshipping "arms, ammunition, or implements of war" to any belligerent in a time of war. Roosevelt wanted discretion for the president to distinguish between aggressors and their victims, but Congress balked at such latitude and he did not insist. FDR sidestepped the early international crises created by aggressive fascism (Abyssinia, the Spanish Civil War, Munich) and in his own way supported "appeasement" by Britain and France.

During the Abyssinian crisis the League of Nations (to which the US did not belong) sponsored a prospective oil embargo on Italy, a sanction designed to halt Italian aggression in Africa. As the Neutrality Act did not cover oil, FDR responded that American companies could not be compelled to join the embargo; in due course the League's effort collapsed, Britain and France backed away from confrontation, and Mussolini had a free hand.[80] Privately the president grew increasingly alarmed at fascist aggression and considered the Neutrality Act a regrettable straightjacket, but it provided protective covering when he next faced the potential snares of the Spanish Civil War.

Like Léon Blum, Roosevelt sympathized with the Spanish Republic as it reeled from Franco's uprising backed by Hitler and Mussolini. As in France, however, Catholic sentiment pulled in Franco's direction, and FDR was loath to antagonize that key element of his electoral coalition. Although the Neutrality Act had not included civil wars in its purview (an omission remedied by a revision in 1937), the administration willingly followed its spirit: the US embraced the embargo on arms to both sides of the Spanish conflict, adopted (as we saw) by the Conservative government in Britain and a divided Popular Front cabinet in France. Washington could not prohibit private citizens from supplying arms to either side, but Roosevelt lashed out at one selling airplanes to the Spanish Republic "for his perfectly legal but thoroughly unpatriotic act."[81]

From time to time Roosevelt publicly denounced the fascist menace, but he struck no insistent chord. In a celebrated speech of October 1937 he described fascist "lawlessness" as an affront to the civilized world meriting "quarantine," but he concluded with the pledge "to pursue a policy of peace and adopt every practicable measure to avoid involvement in war."[82] The Czech crisis of September 1938 and Europe's dance of evasion around the fascist dictators soon put FDR to the test. From a safe distance across the Atlantic, and with no commitments to Czechoslovakia, Roosevelt became a leading advocate of peace through negotiation.

With the world at large, FDR feared a drift toward war. He understood that Hitler would risk military confrontation over the Sudetenland, while the democracies would be extremely reluctant parties to any war. Even so, Roosevelt addressed nearly identical messages to Chamberlain and the Führer: no matter what, do not break off negotiations. The Munich accord badly split French Socialists and drove the British Labour Party into outright opposition to appeasement. But since Munich averted a general European war, the pact seemed to vindicate FDR's brief for negotiation, although the president privately deplored the annihilation of Czech sovereignty. At any rate, Chamberlain and his enthusiasts in the British press lavished high praise on Roosevelt's "magnificent, wise, timely and perhaps decisive intervention at an instant when peace seemed impossible."[83]

American "isolationism" and Anglo-French "appeasement" both arose from antiwar sentiment. Roosevelt loathed the Nazi dictatorship and sympathized with the quandary of Britain and France. But he shared his countrymen's abhorrence of war, and as a political pragmatist he recognized the determination of

Congress to keep Europe's quarrels at arm's length, despite the menacing novelty of aggressive fascism. After joining the arms embargo on Republican Spain, FDR bolstered appeasement at Munich without saying so. Washington then shared with France and Britain the great sigh of relief when the Czech impasse was settled without war. But after Munich the three democracies recognized the need for serious rearmament.

In the US, foreign relations began to dominate politics in 1939 and FDR's comfort zone shrank. In a confidential meeting on January 31 with the Senate Military Affairs Committee, Roosevelt stressed the threat of an "offensive and defensive alliance" among Germany, Italy, and Japan, which materialized two years later as the Berlin-Rome-Tokyo Axis. He presented a geopolitical domino theory of sorts to the committee, with Europe's nations the first domino, their African possessions the second, and Central or South America the next. America must rearm itself and aid its potential allies against this prospect of world domination. But when his candid assessment was leaked (and exaggerated) to the press, the president backed away from a contentious push to revise the Neutrality Act let alone repeal it.[84]

The outbreak of an actual war in Europe in September 1939 between the dictatorships and the democracies hardened the resolve of veritable isolationists: only genuine neutrality and statutory barriers against involvement in European belligerency on any level could assure that the US did not get sucked into this European conflict, an involvement that might jeopardize American democracy itself.[85] But for Roosevelt the outbreak of war challenged the evasions and pieties of neutrality. While the isolationists insisted on American neutrality when it really mattered, Roosevelt wanted greater freedom for Washington to bolster the Allies because their struggle to contain Hitler, in his view, served the vital long-term interests of the US.

To Roosevelt isolationism or strict neutrality in the age of the airplane was a "fallacy." He worried that Hitler might gain a toehold in the Western Hemisphere, perhaps by seizing Newfoundland or dominating a Central or South American republic. The US had to defend the whole of the Western Hemisphere from Nazi inroads.[86] Under the umbrella of neutrality, according to the isolationists, America could remain impregnable regardless of what happened in Europe. Roosevelt reversed this logic and used hemispheric defense as a rationale for abandoning the pretense of neutrality and tilting publicly against Germany.

As the European war began FDR believed that Britain and its fleet were America's first line of defense against Hitler's ambitions. In September 1939 Roosevelt called a special session of Congress and by November finally won a revision of the Neutrality Act that repealed the blanket arms embargo in time of war. Britain and France could now purchase armaments from US companies, albeit only on a "cash-and-carry" basis, with no credits and no utilization of American ships to transport them, although the re-flagging of American vessels might be condoned. Meanwhile, America's own rearmament began in earnest with huge appropriations for the navy and air force, the defensive bulwarks of the country on its two vulnerable coasts, and not inconsistent with FDR's pledge "to keep America out of this war."

The fall of France in June 1940 reshuffled the deck. As the British Empire stood alone against Hitler, Britain faced aerial bombardment and a likely invasion from across the Channel. Still, ambivalence bedeviled the president's thinking. His deference to antiwar sentiment limited his support of Britain. Restraining the all-out interventionists in his circle, FDR equivocated before a skeptical Congress and a mercurial public opinion on the most urgent issue facing the country: how could a progressive administration stand up to Hitler and defend democracy without actually going to war?

Over the summer and fall of 1940 British tenacity, amplified by the media, stirred American opinion. After the fall of France few Americans expected the UK to prevail, but the British still won admiration from the saga of the Dunkirk evacuation; from the RAF's stellar performance in the "Battle of Britain"; and from the fortitude of ordinary Londoners during the relentless bombing ordered by Hitler in September. Yet even as sympathy swung toward Britain, the clear desire of most Americans to stay out of the war remained unshaken. Now, moreover, the dilemma would be enmeshed with the presidential election of 1940.[87]

The Election of 1940 and the Clouds of War

General elections, also due in Britain and France in 1939–40, had been suspended by the British Parliament for the duration and abolished altogether by Pétain after France's capitulation. The US electoral cycle proceeded apace but with two startling turns. On the Republican side, an outsider—never elected to any office and nominally a Democrat until 1938—came out of the Philadelphia convention in June with the GOP's nomination. Prevailing over well-known senators from the party's isolationist wing, Wendell Willkie was drafted after an intensive organizing drive by activists in the party's internationalist wing. Their maneuvers climaxed during the sixth convention ballot with a demonstration in the galleries that stampeded deadlocked delegates toward this new face in American politics. Willkie's stance on the European war seemed fairly close to FDR's, and Willkie accepted some New Deal programs, such as Social Security, but he had come to distrust Roosevelt profoundly. Like most Republicans he detested the preemptory style of the Roosevelt administration; as a Wall Street lawyer and utilities executive he had fought FDR's public electric power initiatives and draconian tax policies.

On the Democratic side Roosevelt's candidacy remained a question mark going into the summer. The president repeatedly signaled a lack of desire to seek an unprecedented third term, and a yearning to return to Hyde Park and write his memoirs. But he also insisted that the legacy of the New Deal had to be consolidated in this election—that only the social solidarity nurtured by the New Deal now allowed the US to stand tall in a world menaced by totalitarianism. Yet Roosevelt would not identify a potential successor to carry the torch. He flirted with having Harry Hopkins assume his mantle, and he shifted Hopkins out of the controversial WPA to become secretary of commerce. But Hopkins had grave medical problems that erupted in the spring of 1940 and foreclosed his potential candidacy.[88] Party activists remained in limbo, waiting for FDR to claim the nomination or unambiguously renounce it, neither of which he would do. The present consensus holds that Roosevelt genuinely wished to retire; believed that the supreme peril of the times ruled out that preference; and expected the Democratic convention to resolve his conundrum by drafting him by acclamation.

Awkward at best, this scenario played out in ragged fashion. When the Democratic convention opened, FDR sent a personal message for the delegates about his desire to retire, but with the implication that a spontaneous draft could alter this. In blunt words Ickes telegraphed FDR his dismay on the first day: "This Convention is bleeding to death. . . . Nine-hundred leaderless delegates are milling around like worried sheep waiting for the inspiration of leadership that only you can give them." In this vacuum, Ickes continued, the convention is "dominated by men who are bent on betraying you" either by nominating someone else or creating a situation where you will not accept the nomination.

In effect he advised the president: stop playing games, declare your intention to run, insist on a hard-hitting platform "of your own dictation," and name your preferred vice presidential candidate.[89]

Following two days of confusion, the popular senator Alben Barkley (Ky.) read FDR's statement to the delegates. After a moment's stunned silence, most grasped that the time had come to shout their acclaim for Roosevelt. The president's renomination now became certain, but exasperation at Roosevelt was displaced onto the matter of his running mate. The White House had announced no preference, and several aspirants believed that FDR had previously encouraged them. At the last hour the president quietly settled on Agriculture Secretary Henry Wallace as his man—a choice unpopular with party regulars (as Wallace had been a progressive Republican before 1932) and with conservatives (although he had shown himself to be a team player rather than a self-immolating liberal).[90] Disarray in the convention reached a crescendo when conservative Speaker of the House William Bankhead (Ala.) refused to withdraw his candidacy for the vice presidential spot and in the ensuing balloting seemed to be winning nearly half the votes. Only a calming speech by Eleanor Roosevelt, and rumors that if his belated choice was rebuffed FDR would decline his own nomination, finally put Wallace over the top.[91]

Despite Willkie's relative moderation, the election became a highly charged referendum on Roosevelt's character and leadership. His quest for a third term fed into Republican charges that Roosevelt was devious and dictatorial. Willkie argued that New Deal programs (even the beneficial ones) were tyrannically administered by inept idealists or dangerous cynics. Huge federal debts, fiscal mismanagement, and overregulation of American business, he claimed, had stymied a real recovery.

Democrats viewed Willkie's astonishing rise as a mixed blessing. True, he did not wish to roll back the New Deal in its entirety and shared the administration's desire to aid Britain. But Willkie's fresh face and plain-spoken style appealed to moderates and therefore posed a threat to the president's re-election. Until late October Roosevelt himself did not actively campaign; he staked his re-election on confidence that voters would opt for familiar, steady leadership in an exceedingly perilous world. His appointment of two Republican internationalists to his cabinet in June—Henry Stimson (Hoover's secretary of state) as secretary of war and Frank Knox (Landon's running mate in 1936) as secretary of the navy—gave FDR's novel above-the-fray aura a degree of credibility. Having Willkie as an opponent instead of an isolationist also helped FDR through a high-risk period in defense policy.

Along with aerial bombardment and the threat of invasion after the fall of France, Britain faced strangulation of its seaborne lifeline of food, armaments, and supplies from heavy losses of transports and naval escorts to enemy submarines. (A chance to mitigate that problem was lost when the French government refused to sail its fleet to Britain before concluding an armistice with Hitler, and Roosevelt had done little to help at that time.)[92] Pleas from Churchill for surplus American destroyers started in June and became more desperate by August. Then the idea arose that in exchange Britain might provide bases for the US in British colonies in Newfoundland and the Caribbean. Roosevelt liked this "destroyers-for-bases" concept but it was fraught with difficulties. Must the president go to Congress, where the isolationists would reasonably put up a fight? Should the deal be packaged as a quid pro quo, with various strings that might appear to abridge British sovereignty or make America seem mercenary? With creative thinking and some deviousness, Roosevelt quietly negotiated details with Churchill to minimize embarrassment to either side, and then announced the agreement in September without going to Congress. Willkie blasted FDR's executive order as "arbitrary and dictatorial," but he did not attack the substance of the destroyers-for-bases deal, which isolationists denounced as tantamount to an act of war against Germany. Nor did Willkie oppose the Selective Service Act passed by Congress in divided but bipartisan votes, although it established the first peacetime draft in American history.[93]

Still, partisan rancor mounted. The Democratic Party machinery piled on to Willkie as a man bought and bossed by Wall Street and big business and as a magnet for unsavory reactionaries. Democrats trumpeted FDR's leadership in opposing Hitler, aiding Britain, yet keeping the US out of war. On both international relations and domestic policy they portrayed Willkie as an opportunistic master of "weasel words."[94] As Willkie stumped the country his folksy but improvised speeches produced gaffes and inconsistencies; in October, pressured by party regulars, his campaign became more strident. He accused Roosevelt of manipulating foreign crises and of "warmongering," and finally blustered that "on the basis of his past performance with pledges to the people, if you re-elect him you may expect war by April 1941." Furious at these attacks, Roosevelt finally left his White House cocoon for giant campaign rallies in Philadelphia, New York, and Boston. He gleefully attacked certain congressional Republicans as obstructionists in matters of national security and reiterated his pledge to America's mothers that "your boys are not going to be sent into any foreign wars." But he did not bother to add the qualifier he had insisted on back in July for the Democratic Party platform: "except in case of attack." By now those words seemed to Roosevelt either self-evident or meaningless. "If somebody attacks us, then it isn't a foreign war, is it?" he told a skittish speechwriter.

His peace pledge apparently reassured FDR's voters, and his electoral coalition held. Roosevelt's familiar radio voice and image of leadership; the manifest benefits of the New Deal; and his canny mix of anti-fascism and antiwar sentiment prevailed over the promise of his appealing but inexperienced and equivocal opponent. With the largest voter turnout ever yet, Willkie drew 5 million more votes than Landon had in 1936, but FDR still outpolled him 27 million to 22 million, and carried thirty-eight states to Willkie's ten (table 3.1), while the party composition of the House barely changed (267 Democrats to 162 Republicans).[95]

In an unstable tandem after the election, US policy and public opinion crystallized around Roosevelt's support for all-out aid to Britain short of war. His previous initiatives had come up short: "cash-and-carry" was too late and restrictive to help stave off France's defeat; "destroyers-for-bases" gave a psychological lift to Britain without staunching its punishing losses in the Atlantic. Now the British were running out of hard currency to pay cash for vital supplies from the US as required by the Neutrality Act. But the president deftly turned that corner. In a fireside chat and his annual address to Congress he described three basic American goals. Without entering the war, the US would become "the arsenal of democracy" for itself and its allies. More broadly, the US would seek a world based on "four essential human freedoms": freedom of speech and of religion, freedom from want and from fear. And the US would supply the cash-strapped British by means of "lend-lease"; in FDR's homey metaphor, it would be like lending a garden hose to a neighbor whose house was on fire, not asking to be paid on the spot but expecting the hose to be returned after the emergency.

This time FDR risked isolationist ire and turned to a Congress whose political complexion had subtly changed despite the continuities of the 1940 election. Veteran progressive Republicans had generally backed the New Deal, but as hard-core isolationists most were now lost to Roosevelt on defense issues, along with comparable Democrats like Wheeler. For the isolationists the Great War still cast a frightful shadow: not only the slaughter on all sides, but the manipulative allied propaganda; the profiteering by American financiers and munitions makers; the censorship and assault on civil liberties once the US entered the war. But southerners who had given FDR grief over domestic policies after 1936 generally supported the president's defense policies. Lend-lease therefore passed by comfortable margins with congressional amendments that constrained but did not cripple the president's latitude.

Isolationists understood that lend-lease put the US firmly in the British camp. Inexorably, strategic measures to cement America's commitment followed: occupation of Greenland and then Iceland by American forces to anchor naval patrols in Atlantic sea lanes and the arming of US merchant vessels. Finally, after trying for months to avoid it, Roosevelt ordered American warships to escort supply convoys to Britain. Meanwhile, the US stepped up industrial mobilization to rearm the nation while keeping arms flowing to Britain and, after some hesitation, to a Soviet Union under German attack in June 1941. The US expanded its two-ocean navy, began building a huge new air force of bombers and fighters, and accelerated the transformation of its small and drowsy professional army into a large, expandable force of draftees. When Congress renewed the Selective Service Act of September 1940 a year later, it dropped the one-year term of service.[96]

Well before it faced an actual two-front war, the administration had effectively embraced a Europe-first strategy. Simmering conflicts with Imperial Japan over its invasion of China and aggressiveness in Southeast Asia took a back seat to the challenge of Nazism. Roosevelt avoided the most bellicose responses to Japanese threats, and even authorized shifting elements of the Pacific Fleet to the Atlantic. In August 1941 he met personally for the first time with Churchill, on a warship off Newfoundland, to coordinate relations and issue a vague declaration of principles known as the Atlantic Charter. On the seas, at least, US convoy escorts skirmished with Germans in an undeclared war months before Pearl Harbor. Which perhaps helps explain the gift that Hitler gave Roosevelt by declaring war on the US three days after Pearl Harbor put America into a war with Japan but not necessarily with its Axis ally.[97]

Labor and Economic Mobilization for War

Long after the fact, in early 1943, Roosevelt told his countrymen that he was no longer Doctor New Deal but Doctor Win-the-War. Doctor New Deal had faced difficulties with Congress since 1937, and he shelved any major progressive initiatives after his re-election in 1940. The low turnout, mid-term election in November 1942 strengthened conservative forces. Republicans gained forty-four seats in the House and seven in the Senate, almost all adamant conservatives, who bolstered their party's informal cooperation with conservative Democrats.[98]

While Roosevelt did not enjoy the benefits of a British-style electoral truce or formal coalition government, as a wartime president he implicitly followed the axiom laid down by Churchill and accepted by Attlee to guide their coalition: everything for the war, whether controversial or not, and nothing controversial that is not truly needed for the war. As commander in chief the president usually secured the military appropriations and defense measures that he sought from Congress, but problems at home created by economic mobilization for defense generated chronic discord among the American people and their representatives. Roosevelt tried to set a lofty, patriotic tone on such issues, and after 1941 he could invoke the sacrifices of men and women in the armed forces to justify austerities on the home front. But before and after Pearl Harbor conflicts kept erupting, and battles between liberals and conservatives within his own administration were displaced onto this novel terrain.

As "the arsenal of democracy" during the defense period of 1940–41 and the war effort of 1942–45, America's vast productive potential was mobilized for allied military needs. But among the four notional partners in this effort—the military, government, business, and labor—how would the balances be struck? The old-line army and navy procurement agencies, somnolent in the 1930s but suddenly operating at full tilt, held the whip hand. Their civilian superiors in the War and Navy Departments backed them even when a case could be made for better cushioning the domestic impacts of conversion, or for placing more orders with small businesses seeking defense contracts instead of the largest corporations that the agencies almost invariably favored.[99]

Organized labor seemed at first glance well positioned to defend its interests in this environment. To be sure, its alliance with Roosevelt had briefly frayed in 1940 when, like the country at large, labor split over FDR's tilt in foreign policy. CIO president Lewis had been furious at the president's "a plague on both your houses" stance during the Little Steel strikes, and in 1940 Lewis vented his long-held isolationist views to denounce Roosevelt's entanglement in Britain's war. Lewis finally endorsed Wilkie, and to rally his members he vowed to resign the CIO presidency if FDR won re-election.

After the election Lewis kept his rash pledge and turned the CIO presidency over to his disciple Phil Murray—a veteran UMW vice president, Lewis's handpicked head of SWOC, and a CIO vice president. Despite their deep personal ties, however, Murray did not share his mentor's views on the European war or on Roosevelt. Both Murray and the CIO gradually emerged from Lewis's domineering shadow in a drama of intensifying mutual estrangement. By 1942 the federation had freed itself from dependence on UMW personnel and funding, and Lewis took his UMW out of the CIO. In a spiteful coda, Lewis subjected Murray to a ritual expulsion from the UMW, Murray's home-away-from-home since his youthful days in the Pennsylvania coalfields.[100]

Utterly devoted to the cause of organized labor; Catholic, patriotic, and anti-totalitarian; tough but pragmatic, and (unlike Lewis) low-keyed, Phil Murray in the 1940s became a pivotal figure not only in the labor movement but in American history. By 1940 Murray held a comprehensive vision for "industrial democracy," situated somewhere between parochial trade union traditions and militant left-wing attitudes about class conflict. In an address to the Wharton School of Business, at the crest of CIO organizing in the spring of 1937, Murray had explained CIO goals: organize the unorganized; follow up with serious collective bargaining; "establish a stable, progressive, modern relationship between capital and labor." The SWOC did not like strikes and did not want them, he said, but the bad faith and stubborn resistance being mounted by the Little Steel companies were bound to ignite strikes "with all their turmoil and sacrifice." "Powerful, militant, and aggressive industrial trade unions," he concluded, would expand democracy.[101] In effect he advocated a new moral economy for modern American capitalism.

In a 1940 book written jointly with Morris Cooke—an engineer and veteran government official of progressive views—Murray articulated "labor's struggle for status and the good life." The psychology of class warfare, the authors agreed, must give way to "constructive industrial statesmanship" in labor relations. Murray believed that the "scrappiness" of trade unions, the strikes and tough-guy tactics, were apt in the early, contested stages of unionization, "where employers generally get the kind of labor relations they ask for," but would likely abate in unionized companies. Murray flavored his outlook with the new Keynesian vocabulary: increased productivity via innovation need not threaten workers but could benefit them by lowering prices on consumer goods, thereby enhancing labor's purchasing power. To promote that outcome, however, the authors agreed that government oversight must be applied to capital as well as labor, since big business would otherwise raise prices whenever it wished.[102]

As economic conversion slowly began in 1940, Murray and Walter Reuther (head of the UAW's General Motors division), called for the creation of "industrial councils" with equal representation for business, labor, and government to oversee expansion in such sectors as steel and aircraft production. Tripartite councils, they argued, would assure rational planning and restrain corporations from putting profits first as they took on defense work. Reuther then folded the idea of "industrial councils" into a proposal for producing fighter planes in converted auto plants.

Reuther's plan, outlined in summer 1940 and publicly launched in December, arose from Britain's desperate need for American fighter planes to assure its survival. Roosevelt had already called for a huge expansion of military aircraft production, but the construction of new plants was expected to take eighteen months to complete. Reuther noted that about 50 percent of the auto industry's plant capacity was currently unused, either seasonally or permanently. Idle auto factories, machinery, and workers, he argued, could be converted for aircraft production within six months by adopting one standard model for fighter planes across the whole industry. This effort would be possible, however, if and only if individual auto manufacturers were "treated as one great production unit" for national defense. Moreover, in Reuther's view, this conversion could be speeded by incorporating into production decisions the skilled tool and die makers of the auto industry, not incidentally his own craft background. Reuther presented the plan in a national radio address, and when he and Murray published it as a pamphlet early in 1941, its catchy title of *500 Planes a Day* garnered wide publicity.[103]

Despite a good press, the plan was stillborn. When Murray presented it to the White House, Roosevelt passed it along to Walter Knudsen, his current point man on economic conversion in the Office of Production Management (OPM). A former GM executive, Knudsen rejected the plan categorically, while current auto company executives did not bother to react publicly. By February—responding to national shortages of rubber, steel, and gasoline—Reuther vainly called on auto manufacturers to forego retooling for the 1942 model year in order to pour machinery, materials, plants, and manpower into defense production. But only after Pearl Harbor, with no choice left in the matter, did the manufacturers abandon planning for the 1943 model year. Then, as the auto companies organized themselves and their subcontractors for full-scale defense conversion, the Reuther plan resurfaced. This time GM's president Charles Wilson agreed to a national debate and press conference with Reuther, broadcast on the *Town Meeting of the Air.*

During this remarkable day-long event Wilson charged that the Reuther plan was a stunt "proposed for publicity and political purposes" and was never a practical conversion plan. Wilson disputed the ready adaptability of auto machinery and assembly lines for production of aircraft engines or bodies. And he balked especially at the notion of a tripartite "aircraft production board" that would override corporate autonomy in planning defense work. He dismissed the board as likely to end up as "a debating society . . . or an alibi committee"; introducing a labor voice "in matters of policy and administration" would divide responsibility and create confusion. As for "putting selected groups of workmen in charge of production"—even our Russian allies, Wilson quipped, have tried and abandoned that: "It is certainly not the American way."[104] The idea of "industrial councils" thus received a public airing at the moment of its final interment. The administration appointed trade unionists to staff or advisory positions on various agencies and boards overseeing the wartime economy, but it never came near to adopting tripartite industrial councils for defense production let alone for postwar reconversion.

Britain had not adopted that model either, but Ernest Bevin represented labor at the highest level, as he strove doggedly to maintain the welfare of home front workers. During the defense period Roosevelt brought CIO co-founder Sidney Hillman to Washington in a comparable gesture, and when the president established the OPM in January 1941 he named Hillman its co-director for labor issues. But without Bevin's standing in the British cabinet or the mandate he had negotiated for his office, Hillman's role in Washington remained hazy. At the OPM he was supposed to promote stable labor relations in defense industries by sensitizing managers and bureaucrats to the needs of workers, while using his influence within the unions to tamp down labor strife. In marked contrast to Bevin, Hillman's vague responsibilities far exceeded his limited powers.[105]

Meanwhile the CIO rebounded. As the economy heated up with defense contracts, CIO unions resumed the organizing drives in mass production industries that had foundered with the Roosevelt recession. A wave of victories came in 1941, as Bethlehem and other Little Steel giants recognized the USWA, and the implacable Ford Motor Company negotiated a contract with the UAW. Even when union organizers won recognition from the NLRB, however, employers could stonewall on negotiations. The unions might then bring lawsuits before the NLRB for unfair labor practices or call strikes over wages or working conditions even if this disrupted military production. With increasing frequency in 1941 unions used both tactics.[106]

After Roosevelt formally declared a national emergency in May 1941, however, the service departments would not abide aggrieved workers impeding the production of aircraft, ships, military vehicles, or weapons with strikes or slowdowns. The president established a National Defense Mediation Board to defuse such situations, but many trade unionists were loath to surrender their strike weapon when the US was not actually at war. Hence 1941 approached all records for numbers of strikes and man-hours lost to strikes. Communists and their supporters in certain CIO unions constituted a particular problem after the Nazi-Soviet pact. Long excelling as organizers and advocates for the rank-and-file, they now made no concession to the imperatives of defense production for a so-called imperialist war. A dramatic confrontation at an aircraft company in Inglewood, California, in the spring of 1941 brought matters to a head for all to see.

As aircraft manufacturing expanded exponentially on the West Coast, North American Aviation hired thousands of new workers, mostly at minimal wage levels. Rival organizing drives by the AFL machinists and a communist-influenced staff sent west by the UAW elbowed each other in courting these workers. After NLRB elections narrowly confirmed the UAW as the bargaining agent, negotiations deadlocked when the company categorically refused the union's key wage demand. National leaders of the CIO and of the UAW in Detroit were ready to refer the dispute to Washington's defense mediation board. Fearing a sellout, however, local activists opposed that move and prepared for a massive strike to shut the plant, while the War Department was equally determined to keep the plant open. Caught in the middle, Hillman tried but failed to head off a final confrontation. Pickets shut down the plant; Washington deployed troops with fixed bayonets to force it open; and the War Department sent in officials to run the plant. Hillman, Murray, and UAW president R. J. Thomas detested such blatant strikebreaking and were profoundly embarrassed, yet they implicitly accepted that new rules of the game now existed in defense industries. As Thomas's envoy ousted the leaders of the striking UAW local, Hillman lobbied the War Department to pressure the company into compromising on the workers' wage demands. Under duress, workers began returning, management finally agreed to some wage increases as the price for regaining control of their plant, and the White House breathed a sigh of relief.[107] After the North American Aviation strike was broken, leaders of organized labor, apart from Lewis, all but renounced the weapon of strikes by national unions, although local wildcat strikes kept erupting. The Nazi invasion of the Soviet Union reinforced this change, as a new party line directed communist cadres to maximal support for defense production, much as their French comrades could finally pivot into all out resistance against the occupation.

Government pressure on industry and labor intensified after Pearl Harbor. Roosevelt replaced the OPM with a more powerful War Production Board (WPB), headed by Donald Nelson, a former Sears Roebuck executive, and Hillman found himself sidelined. A more powerful National War Labor Board (NWLB) replaced the defense mediation board. Headed by William H. Davis—a patent attorney and sometime progressive public servant—the NWLB drew its members from business, labor, and government. Unlike its predecessors, the board could issue regulations and settle disputes in defense industries rather than merely mediate them. Then in April 1942 the White House established a War Manpower Commission to allocate scarce labor and to oversee retraining for defense work. (It could also pursue or, as it largely chose to do, ignore issues of racial discrimination in hiring.) Manpower allocation was a key part of Bevin's portfolio as Churchill's labor minister, but instead of naming Hillman, who wanted that job, Roosevelt chose as his "labor czar" Paul McNutt, a moderate Democrat and ex-governor of Indiana, linked neither to business nor labor. Hillman lost all institutional leverage and was left with the honorific post of special advisor to the president. Accentuating this shift of influence away from organized labor and New Dealers, Roosevelt in October 1942 appointed former South Carolina senator James F. Byrnes as director of Economic Stabilization and (in May 1943) as head of a new Office of War Mobilization (OWM) standing somewhere above other wartime economic agencies. Working out of the White House, Byrnes became FDR's gatekeeper and point man on economic issues and his primary political advisor in trying to balance competing interests on the home front.[108]

Strains in Labor's Grand Bargain

After Pearl Harbor Roosevelt asked the AFL and CIO to call a truce in their organizing rivalries, and to tender formal pledges from their federations renouncing strikes for the duration.[109] In exchange for the no-strike pledge by Green and Murray, the National War Labor Board issued "maintenance of membership" regulations that effectively kept workers new and old on the rolls of certified unions, unless a worker almost immediately opted out. Union membership swelled during the coming years of labor scarcity and full employment—especially in the CIO steelworkers, autoworkers, and electrical workers unions and in the AFL machinists union. This grand bargain of sorts between Washington, big business, and organized labor made union membership the default position in the war production industries. Prices, however, were creeping up despite the rigors of a new price control and rationing system shared by the entire population. At newly organized Little Steel plants, the USWA demanded wage increases based on rising price indices and estimates of corporate profits, but the NWLB rejected those wage demands and permitted only a much smaller raise. Seeking to prevent a dangerous wage-price inflationary spiral, the NWLB then generalized its calculations into the "Little Steel Formula" for restraining wage increases across the country. FDR's "hold-the-line" executive order of April 1943 later elevated the capping of wage increases to a kind of national priority.

Meanwhile the War Production Board convinced most unions to drop double time or "premium pay" for Saturday and Sunday shifts, so that plants could more readily operate all week. But some unions such as the AFL machinists refused to comply and FDR had to issue an executive order to that effect in September.[110] Like their British counterparts, American workers would gain ground during the war by well-paid overtime work, but severe housing shortages for relocated defense workers and the punishing pace of production took a serious toll in fatigue, spasms of absenteeism, and stoppages over localized grievances against management.

The WPB also promoted "incentive pay" plans or productivity bonuses that could bring larger pay packets for some workers at the cost of speed-ups in the factories. While younger workers in West Coast aircraft plants tended to welcome the prospect, experienced Midwest auto- and steelworkers generally opposed incentive pay as a throwback to exploitative piece-rate systems and as a ploy of management to divide-and-rule workers. The AFL flatly opposed incentive pay, but the CIO was willing to let its unions consider it as a way around the Little Steel Formula wage ceilings.[111] To old hands in certain CIO locals, however, the Roosevelt administration seemed to be defaulting on its bond with labor. The Michigan UAW—a cauldron of rank-and-file militancy— denounced incentive pay and rounded on communist activists who awkwardly supported it in the name of maximizing defense production. A shifting coalition of dissidents also attacked the no-strike pledge as a kind of unilateral disarmament for workers, who faced unyielding managements over local plant practices, and national economic policies crafted in Washington by dollar-a-year men from industry.

For his part, John L. Lewis categorically rejected both the no-strike pledge and the writ of the Little Steel Formula. In 1943 he called a potentially crippling strike in the nation's soft coal fields to win a two-dollar-a-day wage increase and portal-to-portal pay (wages for time in a mine getting to and from the coal face). His defiance of patriotic sentiment made Lewis the most unpopular man in America in opinion polls, but his miners did not flinch. "Local CIO folk are pro-union, pro-mine worker but anti-Lewis," two CIO regional directors told Harold Ickes. Green and Murray feared "being overshadowed by a man [Lewis] who fought the Administration and won. . . . We are sure that the President will give [on loosening wage stabilization], because if he doesn't, he will only help Lewis," they warned.[112]

On the opposite side, conservative congressmen from both parties pounced on wildcat strikes in defense industries and Lewis's defiant coal strike. In June 1943 both houses of Congress quickly adopted the Smith-Connally War Labor Disputes Act. A poorly crafted catchall of punitive measures, Smith-Connally placed new curbs on future strikes (workers had to observe a thirty-day "cooling off period" and approve a strike in a secret ballot by majority vote); created obstacles to political action by trade unions; and like Bevin's executive order of 1944 threatened draconian punishments to deter wildcat strikes at defense plants. The War and Navy departments and the WPB urged the president to sign the law, which reinforced his power to seize struck defense plants and might discourage local strikes by its harsh sanctions. Perkins, Ickes, and Davis, however, urged FDR to veto the law, which would do little to prevent strikes but "injected complication and dangerous provisions in the handling of future strike situations" and might paradoxically "stimulate industrial unrest and thus interfere with the production of essential war materials."[113]

Murray and Green immediately demanded a veto of Smith-Connally for its coercive provisions. "The War Labor Disputes Act is a wicked, vicious bill," they jointly wrote to the White House. "It is the worst anti-labor bill passed by Congress in the last hundred years. It is the very essence of fascism. It destroys the philosophy of voluntarism on which free trade unionism is founded. . . . Compulsion, civil damages, and criminal [conspiracy] penalties are the unholy trinity." They objected as well that Smith-Connally's curbs on political contributions by labor unions had nothing to do with war production.[114] In the end FDR vetoed Smith-Connally, burnishing his credibility with organized labor, but Congress promptly mustered the two-thirds votes for an override. As predicted by its opponents, the new law did not stop localized walkouts, nor did it bring Lewis to heel, as he deftly avoided prosecution with on-again, off-again strike tactics that finally won a good settlement for his miners.[115]

The no-strike pledge continued to roil the CIO and its largest constituent, the UAW (half of whose members lived in Michigan). In the 1943 convention of the Michigan CIO, dissidents swept the union council elections and ratcheted up criticism against Murray and R. J. Thomas over their capitulations to Washington. Dissidence peaked at the UAW's national convention in September 1944. After intense maneuvering, CIO and UAW leaders agreed to hold a mail referendum among UAW members on the no-strike pledge, but only after the November 1944 election. Ballots duly went out in January 1945, the results announced in March. Only 23 percent of the members bothered to return their ballots, but those who did voted by 64 percent to sustain the pledge.[116]

The combined abstentions and support for the no-strike pledge presumably registered the patriotism of American workers. Trade unionists scorned the cant in government appeals for sacrifice, but in 1944–45 US armed forces were massively exposed to death and maiming in Europe and the Pacific. Washington had rushed a high-level delegation of trade union leaders to the battlefields of Normandy in July 1944. Touring the invasion beaches, contested hedgerow country, and field hospitals, they saw the carnage and the enemy's ferocity. They returned to spread the word and to rouse their members to maintain all-out production.[117] Despite significant dissent, workers generally sustained wartime demands on their labor, and they backed union leaders who cooperated with the administration—a temporary equilibrium for labor to be tested after the peace, when the no-strike pledge and the powers of the NWLB would lapse.

Induced to cooperate in defense production by Washington's carrots and sticks, big business and organized labor nursed reservoirs of pent up hostility as the war ran its course. Local grievances over personnel decisions or work rules led to thousands of local stoppages between 1940 and 1945 even under wartime regulations. Coping with relentless production schedules, industrial workers enjoyed full employment and substantial overtime pay, but both seemed likely to end abruptly as war production wound down. Workers did not feel secure in their postwar job prospects and feared being left behind in a future wage-price inflation cycle. Big business had temporarily ceded its powers over corporate planning, product choices, and pricing yet managed to secure wartime profits through cost-plus contracts and subsidies for new plants. But corporate America chaffed to recover the full range of its "right to manage." For most companies in the mass production industries, union recognition would continue, but employers were likely to be aggressive in future negotiations and plant management.

Based on its experience between 1935 and 1945, how might organized labor act in the postwar moment? By 1945 the idea of tripartite industrial councils in selected industries was dead. Wage increases would clearly head the list of insistent union demands, even if they might seem inflationary to Washington and public opinion. Work rules and grievance procedures would figure heavily in organizing drives and collective bargaining. But management and labor might yet finesse conflict over wages and work rules by opening novel fronts for negotiation over such new matters as health care benefits, pensions, or cushions for seasonal unemployment. Finally, would the CIO remain an effective anchor for the Democratic Party's progressive wing in future electoral battles and in legislative struggles over such issues as full employment, housing, expansion of social security, education, racial discrimination, and postwar international relations?

DESCENT FROM VICTORY: CHARTING NEW PATHS

4

Labour's Moment: The Election of 1945 and After

DURING THE DARK YEARS OF 1940–42, Britain's government worried a great deal about home-front morale. As the Ministry of Information puzzled over the very definition of good morale, its opposite was obvious enough in France, where defeatism and panic flight compounded the Allied military collapse. Back home, an often uncomprehending officialdom feared comparable contagions among their own citizens. As we have seen, that did not happen despite a dire sequence of events: the jarring urban evacuations in 1939; acute invasion fears after Dunkirk; the material and psychological traumas of the Blitz; and the unrelieved string of military setbacks in Western Europe, North Africa, the Atlantic, the Balkans, and Asia. Notwithstanding bouts of demoralization and pockets of bad behavior, defeatism did not seize the British people. While official versions of Dunkirk and the Blitz exaggerated popular fortitude, the British people coped impressively well in this period of great trials and dangers.[1] But what of the long haul—of popular hopes and fears for the postwar at the end of the tunnel?

The British could take pride in their stubborn endurance over six long years of war, but the toll and the scars ran deep by 1945: over 950,000 wartime casualties, including 357,000 killed (about 3 percent of civilians and between 7 to 10 percent of the armed forces);[2] massive bombing destruction of already scarce housing; pervasive shortages and bleak austerities; an empty treasury. Lingering memories of the economic slump after the Great War and of endemic class differences thickened these clouds on the postwar horizon.

The shared austerity and purposefulness of wartime had briefly blurred or diluted social divisions in Britain, but well before the guns fell silent George

Orwell, for one, detected stirrings of the old ways. In his weekly *Tribune* news-paper column in the summer of 1944 Orwell observed that certain railroad carriages again carried designations as "first-class," while formal evening dress had reappeared out on certain London streets. Most alarming, the gated private parks dotting London's fashionable neighborhoods, which had been opened to the public when the government requisitioned their iron railings for scrap metal in 1940, were again being closed off, if only as yet by makeshift wooden fencing.[3] Orwell may have been singularly pessimistic about holding back such tides, but he was far from alone in his gray mood. Most immediately, people wondered how military and civilian demobilization would be organized. More fundamentally, how would future recovery be managed and to what ends?

Hopes and Fears

In early 1944, Mass-Observation (M-O)—a prewar organization that assessed public attitudes and opinions for private clients or for the government—reported on what soldiers and civilians seemed to want, expect, and fear about postwar prospects. (Founded by two social scientists and a documentary filmmaker in 1937, M-O drew on two types of informants—some who kept diaries and others who interviewed people on designated subjects or listened in on conversations in public places. More cultural anthropology than opinion polling, M-O did not rely on the statistical sampling methodology of the Gallup Poll, established in Britain that same year.)[4] In a slim volume called *The Journey Home,* M-O gave due attention to competing claims over timetables and priorities for bringing soldiers back to "civvy street" after the peace. Consensus prevailed on avoiding either a heedlessly rapid or ponderously slow process for military discharges, but issues of fairness over how individuals would be treated (such as first-in, first-out criteria, or how a veteran might regain a prewar job) naturally proved contentious.[5] But demobilization was only the minor theme in M-O's inquiry.

The Journey Home instead dwelled on the "underlying mood," the uneasy ambivalence of people caught between hope and fear, between optimistic desires and pessimistic expectations, between concern for their own future situations and for the larger society. At the least, M-O argued (or hoped), "the conflict of ideas over demobilization and over the future of Britain is a conflict between the necessity of finding private security and purposefulness for self in a world threateningly insecure, and the desire to help make the world secure and purposeful for everyone." Drawing on its archive of earlier wartime inquiries, M-O posited a "growth of cynicism" following an initial mood of enthusiasm in 1940 when the war began in earnest. By 1944, it claimed, growing pessimism or apathy was providing a protective shell against future disappointment.[6]

Concretely, people wanted good housing, good pay, and security but also something beyond that—a sense that they were "going someplace," which postwar prospects simply did not seem to offer. More than once M-O used the fate of the Beveridge Report to illustrate the point. People *want* a full-scale Beveridge social security system to be implemented, but they generally *expect* only a bit of Beveridge, "a compromised, emasculated Beveridge." In political terms, M-O maintained, "the assumed power of vested interests to prevent change darkens people's horizons." From conscription to rationing, most wartime controls and infringements of liberty had been widely accepted as fair, useful, and consonant with democracy if they applied equally to all. But soldiers and civilians alike feared that after the war the motto would become "each for himself;" that the wartime embrace of communal effort would evaporate or even prove to have been "phoney." Forebodings over "the potential contrast between wartime cooperation and postwar selfishness, conflict, and disunity" seemed to feed "a protective crust of cynicism about the post-war world . . . [a] dead weight of distrust" over the future.[7]

In a pamphlet of his own, M-O co-founder Tom Harrisson pondered "the political set-up which will eventually have to face this reconditioned public . . . [with its] mixed doubt and hope, apathy and alertness . . . [now that] the siren's wail is dim and unity less vital."[8] Harrisson anticipated what Orwell would write a few months later: that the "revolutionary" shift in sentiment of 1940–41 (as conveyed, for example, in Priestley's BBC broadcasts)—a new spirit which Orwell hailed at the time as the linchpin of Britain's war effort—was in fact circumstantial rather than durable, and that any general turn in opinion toward socialism was pure illusion.[9]

The inquiries by M-O suggested that Churchill might remain in power if he headed an ongoing coalition, or that a Labour victory was possible if the party "played for success" and overcame its old "fear of power." "Labour nervousness, Churchill overshadowing," Harrisson argued, were but symptoms of a demo-cratic system verging on exhaustion, because "the whole basis of our democracy has been shelved dangerously." A Parliament lasting an unprecedented nine years, drawing its mandate from a general election in 1935, left a "strained and stale electorate" suspended in the amber of the electoral truce. Yet Harrisson sensed that even as Britons esteemed Churchill as war leader, "his position as post-war figure is far from certain in the public mind. . . . Most people do not expect he will be the primary post-war leader."[10] More broadly Harrisson saw "confused doubt about *all* political parties over the past 16 months" and lots of negative sentiment. In a vague and befuddled manner political sentiment among soldiers and civilians seemed to be tilting leftward, but not necessarily to the Labour Party per se. Warming to his pessimistic theme, Harrisson foresaw growing "indifference and negativism" among the citizenry, with a deficit of "political vitality . . . which is the lifeblood of healthy mass life." At the last moment, however, Harrisson pivoted to a more hopeful note: "Yet I doubt if this cynicism is so deep-seated in relation at least to the small act of voting, as it seems." He concluded with his first-ever political prediction: the Conservatives even if led by Winston Churchill will not continue in power "unless the alternatives commit suicide."

The postwar moment in Britain would unfold against a background of hopefulness for change and inertial pessimism. But even if the Labour Party navigated through this unsettled atmosphere to win the next general election, it remained to be seen whether it had the effective policies, political skills, and sheer good fortune to lead Britain forward.

Toward the 1945 Election

When V-E Day finally arrived on May 8 1945, the political question of the day was: how long should the coalition and its electoral truce continue? On both sides of the House some chafed to end the coalition. Nye Bevan, for one, had long denounced the compromises and sellouts that Labour's front bench accepted for the sake of coalition, and in 1944 he was elected to the party's executive committee (the NEC), where he continued to press his critique.[11] Attlee and Bevin tentatively supported prolongation of the coalition until V-J Day or at least until October, by which time updated electoral registers could be readied. (Bevin favored prolongation perhaps in fear of a Conservative victory that would roll back the gains for organized labor he had overseen during the war.)[12] In any case, maintenance of the coalition until October emerged after V-E Day as Labour's consensus. Churchill himself hoped to extend the coalition, at least until victory in the Pacific—likely a grim, long slog at that pre-A bomb juncture. Tories pressed Churchill to insist on an extension until V-J Day or else to call an election immediately, presumably to capitalize on the PM's popularity. On May 23 Churchill decided to resign and set in motion the first general election since 1935.

Churchill would head an interim "caretaker" government composed entirely of Conservatives; Parliament would be dissolved on June 15; and the election would be held on July 5, although ballots would not be counted until July 26 in order to include votes cast overseas by the armed forces. Whatever misgivings either side may have had about its prospects, the time had now come. To mark the coalition's end, Churchill convened a moving, even tearful farewell meeting of his cabinet, where he extolled "the most glorious five years in our history" and offered the kindest of words for Attlee and his comrades. But as the Labour junior minister Chuter Ede observed in his diary, "The coalition had served its end. It could not produce [future] measures to deal with policies on which the two major parties had fundamental differences."[13]

Labour's rebound from its mere 52 parliamentary seats in the post-MacDonald wipeout of 1931 to 154 seats in 1935 had buoyed the party but still left Conservatives in complete control, which opinion polls and by-elections reinforced in the late 1930s. During the war, however, the Conservative grip on the electorate eroded, although just when, why, and how extensively remains unclear. Historian Ross McKibbin argues persuasively that the change came early and fast, as a direct result of the crisis in May-June 1940, between the Norway debacle and Dunkirk. Those events finally brought the war home and retrospectively revealed the disastrous diplomatic and military consequences of earlier Conservative leadership. (Chamberlain's Gallup approval rating plunged from a reassuring 65 percent at the beginning of May 1940 to 33 percent at month's end.)[14] The crisis in Westminster that led to Chamberlain's resignation converged with a collapse of public confidence in the Conservative Party; as McKibbin puts it, "Labour would have won any election held after July 1940"— well before the full impact of wartime experience on the British people, which is often credited with the shift of political sentiment leftward.[15]

As the demands for sacrifice on the ground multiplied, the coalition's electoral truce papered over any such shift. To be sure, several wartime by-elections signaled a flight from Conservatism, but not necessarily to the Labour Party's benefit, since the electoral truce ensured that insurgent winners were independents. Most dramatically, a new left-wing party called CommonWealth, unbound by the electoral truce and with the appeal of a fresh political face, resoundingly won three key by-elections between late 1943 and early 1945.[16] Meanwhile and more fundamentally, however, Churchill's coalition government provided Labour's front bench with experience, patriotic respectability, and considerable credit for the planning of economic mobilization, the improvement of civil defense, and the equitable management of wartime austerity. One way or another, then, the entitlement of Conservatives to govern—comparable to the Republican version of "normalcy" in 1920s America—was falling into doubt.

On the day Churchill called the election, the annual Labour Party conference was meeting at Blackpool in an atmosphere electric with optimism, despite the wartime displacements that had seen Labour's constituency membership briefly drop to 266,000 in 1944.[17] Labour now launched its electoral manifesto, which set the tone for its upcoming campaign. Aptly titled *Let Us Face the Future,* it entirely left behind the wartime spirit of bipartisanship. A bitter historical prologue reminded voters that after the Great War "the people lost the peace," as postwar reconversion left "too much power in the hands of too few men" with no sense of responsibility for the people's well-being. Eliding MacDonald's ill-fated minority government of 1929–31, the manifesto turned a famous wartime phrase of Churchill's to Labour's account in stigmatizing the interwar decades: "Never was so much injury done to so many by so few." During World War II, in contrast, Labour's presence in the coalition insured at least an approximation of "fair shares" as the moral basis for the struggle and specific policies "that took the profit out of war." On the cusp of the postwar moment, Labour accused the Tories of preparing to scrap wartime controls, thereby guaranteeing a "profiteer's paradise."[18]

Instead, Labour demanded ongoing public controls and planning: "The sphere of public action must be extended . . . [with] a firm constructive hand on our whole productive machinery . . . [and planning] which will win the Peace for the People." While emphatically committed to individual liberty, the party "will not tolerate freedom to exploit, to pay poor wages." Labour linked the vague coalition goal of "full employment" to the notion that under-consumption caused depressions. Full employment could be assured only by maintaining purchasing power and by rationally channeling the investment of capital. But as a self-described socialist party, Labour also insisted that "each industry must have applied to it the test of national service." Having reaffirmed its commitment to nationalization in heated debates at its 1944 conference, Labour now called for public ownership of the Bank of England, coal mines, electric and gas utilities, inland transportation, and iron and steel production. But the manifesto offered scant detail on how central planning would actually work or how public ownership would be organized.

Similarly, *Let Us Face the Future* offered only the haziest markers on two other high-priority issues: housing and health care. Always topping the public's list of concerns in 1944–46, housing would be "a great test," and Nye Bevan had already set a tone on the issue in a fierce pamphlet of late 1944: "The interests represented by the Tories are not primarily concerned with building you a house," he declaimed. "Their primary concern is to make a profit out of building it, and then afterwards to exploit you as a tenant."[19] The party's election manifesto called for the allocation of scarce building materials by the state (a crucial and contentious policy, as far as it went) but had little more to say. Likewise, it insisted that "the best health services should be available free for all" and alluded to clinics and hospitals, but its vision for a National Health Service remained otherwise vague. No doubt prudently, the party would not bind itself in advance to specific plans for fulfilling its promises on these two vital issues, even as it spurred its candidates to stress them.

Notwithstanding such studied vagueness, Labour's postwar vision came across clearly as it advocated "great national programs" to promote health, education, and social services, in place of the "mean and shabby treatment" under the Tories. While such programs would assuredly be costly, it argued, "there is no good reason why Britain should not afford them; but she will need full employment and the highest possible industrial efficiency in order to do so." Thus Labour's program firmly linked social justice to the advance of economic efficiency. Only greater productivity through planning and controls could sustain greater fairness and security in the social order.[20]

If much of this sounds familiar, it should. True, there is no evidence that the Labourites at Blackpool knew anything of the Common Program of the CNR in France—approved clandestinely in March 1944 and publicly released that autumn after the liberation of Paris. Yet by almost any measure *Let Us Face the Future* ran parallel to that Resistance vision for the postwar future of France. If there was a socialist core in both programs, it was non-Marxist and unrigorous, designed in both cases to appeal to broad cross sections of citizens. The two manifestos can be labeled progressive, but their watchwords and goals did not require such labels. On the social side, fairness, equity, and dignity; on the economic side, planning and a measure of control from the center to promote efficiency. Both versions advocated nationalization of certain key economic sectors, albeit in a vague, unspecified process. And in both cases (to anticipate the outcomes) nationalization would unfold as a means for enhancing economic efficiency and redistributing economic power but not as a strategy for transforming the structures of work or consumption.

The General Election of 1945

Labour's manifesto concluded with an appeal "to all men and women of progressive outlook": whatever attraction the Liberals or other small parties might have, cast your votes for Labour—do not waste them and court the risk of a hung parliament or a Tory victory. As the campaign unfolded Labour politicians anticipated solid gains, but only a few expected to come out on top, for it was still hard to believe that the voters would repudiate Churchill. When the PM toured the country in June, large, enthusiastic crowds turned out to cheer him; only in retrospect was it clear that the tour had been a personal victory lap for Churchill and not an effective campaign circuit for his party. True, the Gallup Poll accurately caught the electorate's inclinations. While it found an 83 percent approval rating for Churchill's leadership, it discerned a tilt toward Labour in the coming vote. But few Labourites credited these polls predicting their victory.[21]

The electorate generally displayed a sober mood, and potentially boisterous crowds at political rallies seemed averse to the hooliganism of old on the hustings, although voters still complained to the Gallup Poll that there was "too much heckling, vote-catching stunts, and mud-slinging." A series of radio broadcasts allotted to the rival parties drew impressively large audiences. Here Churchill famously stumbled by linking socialism with totalitarianism and making an ill-conceived crack about "Gestapo" tactics that might follow a Labour victory. Attlee responded in his next broadcast with dignified mockery, in effect clucking his tongue at such a "lurid travesty" and underscoring the difference between Churchill as a great war leader and as a partisan Conservative leader for the postwar. As they awaited the delayed tally on July 26 Labour candidates expressed guarded optimism, restrained expectations, and nervous-ness. Then the stunning results began to come in. First a gratifying trickle—Leo Amery and Brendan Bracken, two of Churchill's most prominent cronies, had gone down. By evening the returns exploded into a torrent of victories in marginal constituencies and suburbs as well as traditional blue-collar bastions.[22]

In certain contrasts with 1935, the election of 1945 may not appear as quite the seismic landslide one supposes, but historically it was close enough. The percentage turnout of eligible voters, for example, was only a shade above the percentage in 1935—in part because the service vote (either direct postal votes from overseas or prearranged proxy votes by family members) fell surprisingly short of anticipated levels. In the end only about 60 percent of personnel in the armed forces, some of whom had not received ballots at all, cast their votes. Labour's aggregate popular vote surged by 10 percent between 1935 and 1945, but the party still fell short of a majority with a total vote of 47.8 percent (table 4.1).

Table 4.1. British General Elections of 1935 and 1945

Election of 1935

Total eligible electorate	31,379,000		
Total votes cast	21,997,000 (70.1 percent)		
	Number of votes	Percentage of votes	MPs
Conservatives	11,810,000	53.7	432
Labour	8,325,000	37.9	154
Liberals	1,422,000	6.4	20

Election of 1945

Total eligible electorate	33,240,000		
Total votes cast	25,086,000 (75.5 percent)		
	Number of votes	Percentage of votes	MPs
Conservatives	9,988,000	39.8	213
Labour	11,995,000	47.8	393
Liberals	2,248,000	9.0	12

Sources: D. and G. Butler, *British Political Facts, 1900–1985* (NY, 1986), 226; R. B. McCallum and A. Readman, *The British General Election of 1945* (Oxford, 1947/1964), ch. 15.

In an electoral system using first-past-the-post, single constituencies in all but a handful of special cases, however, the tides in aggregate national voting often produced disproportionate allocations of parliamentary seats. When Labour had rebounded in 1935 with 38 percent of the aggregate vote, that success brought the party only 25 percent of the seats in the House of Commons. In 1945 the same electoral system produced an opposite, arguably disproportionate result. As the electoral preference swung to Labour, its 48 percent of the total vote gave it 393 seats, yielding a formidable majority of 146 over a combined opposition of 247. Finally, in what ostensibly remained a three-party competition, the Liberals' share of the aggregate vote increased by over 50 percent between 1935 and 1945 (from around 1.4 to 2.2 million), but they won only 12 seats compared to 20 in 1935, with the losers including their party leader and Sir William Beveridge. For close students of elections these are interesting nuances, but in the end the swings in voting and in parliamentary seats were landslides by any standard.[23]

Below the tested if narrow layer of party veterans with government experience in the coalition, the new Parliamentary Labour Party (PLP) included the usual phalanx of "sponsored" trade union deputies, mainly former officers funded by their unions. But where union-sponsored deputies made up over half the PLP in 1931 and 1935, in 1945 they numbered only 120 out of the 393.[24] In the new parliament 46 Labour MPs had Oxbridge educations, and 21 of the 42 female MPs were Labourites. At the age of thirty-four the dynamic, photogenic, and leftish Barbara Castle was the youngest of the female MPs; those ahead of her in line included the veteran Ellen Wilkinson and Jennie Lee, the MP wife of Nye Bevan.[25]

The largest cohort in the 1945 PLP was of course the 250 or so deputies new to Parliament—some noticeably more independent or ambitious than their trade-union colleagues; most relatively young; and some still wearing military uniforms before they took the oath of office. (In the 1945 Parliament, however, only 63 Labourites had served in World War II's armed forces, compared to 110 Tories.)[26] Many Labour freshmen had informal connections to trade unions, however, even if they themselves were of middle- or upper-class background, as were Attlee, Dalton, and Cripps before them. Numerous examples could evoke the diverse backgrounds and trajectories of Labour's new deputies and the routes by which they arrived in Parliament in 1945. Sketches of two promising newcomers will highlight some of the way stations on the party's road to power in 1945.

Two New Faces in Parliament

From his modest background as the son of Russian immigrants, Ian Mikardo (1908–93) received a good secondary education but could not go on to university. A self-taught management consultant, his first success came in turning around a failing local laundry with production efficiencies. Mikardo subsequently worked for the aircraft industry and settled in Reading, where factory output soared during rearmament and war. Meanwhile, as he later recalled, "I served my busy but unremarkable political apprenticeship in three separate little classrooms—in a constituency Labour Party, in a Fabian Society group, and in a small and struggling trade union."[27] Mikardo threw himself into branch party activism, where the wartime electoral truce channeled his energy into discussion and reading groups and local publications. As he made his mark in local Labour circles, the Reading party chair favored him for selection as Labour's parliamentary candidate (in a currently Tory constituency), to be on tap whenever the next election was finally called. His supporters fended off maneuvers by an NEC operative to have an outsider designated for Reading (naval officer Jim Callaghan, as it happened), and the Reading selection committee finally chose "local man" Mikardo.

The Fabian Society's Industrial Group for Postwar Research, founded by socialist professor G. D. H. Cole of Oxford, also recruited Mikardo. As chair of the civil aviation subcommittee, Mikardo drew on his experience in manufacturing management and a commitment to planning and industrial democracy. Participating as well in the summer and weekend schools of the Fabian Society, Mikardo soon became the society's treasurer. On a third front he was active in his white-collar trade union, ASSET (Association of Supervisory Staff and Engineering Technicians), a small union founded years back by railway foremen, which through mergers and affiliations would later grow to almost 400,000 members, and which Mikardo would head in 1968–73. Just as groups of socialist physicians and school teachers lobbied the party, so did "socialist managers" like Mikardo, who advocated greater consultation with workers, smoother adjudication of factory disputes, and enhanced roles for works councils—in short, "the democratic side of management."[28]

From this three-sided political apprenticeship Mikardo briefly emerged into the national party spotlight during Labour's annual conference in December 1944. The NEC had been vacillating over the party's program for nationalization;

in its most recent iteration—a brief policy paper for the 1944 conference—
the NEC backpedaled somewhat on Labour's commitment to public ownership
by employing vaguely equivocal language. Angry delegates placed a total of
twenty-two motions on the table to oppose this dilution, one having originated
with Reading railway workers and constituency activists. Mikardo was named
to a conference "compositing group" to sort out the motions, and the Reading
version emerged as the likeliest to win conference support. The party leadership
scrambled to avoid a floor vote over this matter but failed. A public debate then
pitted Emmanuel Shinwell for the NEC against Mikardo for the amending motion,
which carried decisively. After the session adjourned, Herbert Morrison came up
to Mikardo and in the heat of the moment told him: "Young man, you did very
well this morning. That was a good speech you made—but you realize, don't you,
that you've lost us the general election." Mikardo, on the contrary, believed then
and always that only a bold program without waffling could provide a winning
strategy—that "nothing so undermines our credibility as spending years decrying
our opponents and then adopting policies which make us look a bit like them."[29]

Mikardo also pioneered a tactic for waging electoral campaigns in individual
constituencies. "The Reading system" (as it came to be called) refined selective
campaigning: canvass to identify voters who were pro-Labour or at least
"doubtful," revisit to bring them out on election day, but avoid all further
contact with other households, which might catalyze potential Tory or Liberal
votes.[30] Canvassing, printed electoral propaganda, stump speeches, and public
meetings were still the coin of electoral campaigns. Mikardo proved a forceful
speaker with a sense of humor, and he was invited to campaign in other districts,
including an address to overflow crowds attending a speech indoors by Attlee
in Swansea. Mikardo's eve-of-poll rally astutely included appearances by a
soldier, a sailor, and an airman. With over 62,000 votes cast, Mikardo prevailed
in his marginal Reading constituency with a plurality of 6,390 votes, although
the combined Liberal and Tory votes exceed his own by 1,400—the national
story writ small.

Sharing the euphoria of that summer, Mikardo understood that he was likely
to remain a backbencher—too independent, too unwilling to follow the leadership if it went astray. After an initial year of remarkable unity, Mikardo would
in fact join such left-wing MPs as Michael Foot and Barbara Castle in protests
on policies foreign and domestic. Such dissidence barely dented party unity,
but it convinced Attlee to keep such "pesky rebels" off the front benches.[31]

Later those dissenters would rally around Nye Bevan in a conflict over party policy that did threaten Labour's unity at its core, as Bevan dueled for primacy in 1950–51 with Hugh Gaitskell, another new face of 1945 but one on the fast track to power.

Hugh Gaitskell (1906–63) came from a comfortable and well-connected family, with a father in the Indian Civil Service. Hugh received the best education Britain had to offer in a top prep school, a first-tier public school (Winchester), and New College Oxford. At Oxford he studied "the modern greats" with emphasis on economics; imbibed the influence of socialist professor G. D. H. Cole; and graduated with first-class honors. Gaitskell had a conversion to socialism along the way, crystallized by the general strike of 1926 during which (unlike most Oxonians) he sided with the workers. In this spirit, before beginning a promising academic career, he spent his first year after Oxford as an adult education lecturer near the Nottingham coalfields, which brought his first sustained exposure to working-class life. Here he established lasting affective bonds with stalwarts of the general strike, the bitter and often blacklisted miners.[32] Only in 1928 did he take up a lectureship in economics at University College, London, where he rose to head of department and became an early proponent of Keynes.

Gaitskell had ties with the Fabian Research Bureau and the Fabian summer school, and with Labour figures such as Bevin and Dalton who were redirecting the party toward clearer socialist policies after the MacDonald debacle. With his young economist friends Douglas Jay and Evan Durbin, Gaitskell was among the apostles of economic planning gathered by Dalton at party headquarters in the 1930s. Together they honed a doctrine of democratic socialism free of Marxist dogma, which promoted social justice without class warfare: redistribution of wealth, full employment, demand management through fiscal policy, and a parallel insistence that Labour totally embrace political democracy.[33] While avoiding any truck with the CPGB, Dalton and his circle were resolute anti-fascists even if this meant advocating rearmament. An early omen of the looming conflict came for Gaitskell (as for Bevin) with the brutal assault by the Austrian right on the vibrant community of Viennese social-democratic workers in 1934. Gaitskell happened to be in Vienna at the time and did what he could to aid his Austrian comrades. With Bevin and Dalton, he raised an early voice in Labour against appeasement, while the opportunistic behavior of the Austrian Communist Party set Gaitskell unshakably against communism.

Gaitskell's first foray into electoral politics came in 1935, when the party in Chatham adopted him (as a candidate of the left), but where the Tories won the seat handily by 19 to 13,000 votes. Then in 1937 the South Leeds constituency had a prospective Labour retirement for whenever the next general election would come. The incumbent's agent recruited Gaitskell to vie for the designation with a candidate sponsored by the National Union of Railwaymen—the latter's advantage being that the union would defray his campaign and constituency service expenses. But Gaitskell won the nomination, spent some of his independent means for the same purposes, and began to cultivate his future constituency.[34]

When the coalition government took shape in 1940, Dalton recruited Gaitskell into his Ministry of Economic Warfare, where he helped plan clandestine operations for the Special Operations Executive. (Like fellow economists Jay, Durbin, and Harold Wilson, Gaitskell's priority job kept him out of military service.) When Churchill shifted Dalton to head the Board of Trade, Gaitskell moved with him. He initially worked in the Mines Department, and then was moved to a price-control desk. Admired by colleagues for his intensity and administrative skills, an overworked, exhausted Gaitskell suffered a mild heart attack in April 1945. But the South Leeds constituency continued to back Gaitskell's candidacy for the coming election even if he had to limit his campaigning drastically. With the help of surrogates, and some fatiguing personal appearances in the last ten days, he swamped his two opponents.[35]

Gaitskell took his seat in the House, but his temporary ill health sidelined him during the jockeying among his comrades for junior ministerial positions, even as he remained a well-connected confidante and future prospect. Attlee kept his eye on Gaitskell and when he decided on a minor shuffling of cabinet posts in May 1946, he concluded that Gaitskell had fully recovered his health and named him as parliamentary private secretary (effectively deputy) to the notoriously prickly minister of fuel and power, Shinwell. With the great crisis over coal and electricity that would come in the winter of 1946–47, Gaitskell thus found himself in the thick of events and began his steady if bumpy rise to the top. Along with Harold Wilson, another freshman economist of 1945, Gaitskell was being groomed by Attlee for rapid elevation to ministerial rank.[36]

The Labour Government: Hopes and Challenges

In the Parliamentary Labour Party (PLP) of 1945, the "big five"—Attlee, Bevin, Morrison, Dalton, and Cripps—formed the incontestable top echelon, an aging but seasoned leadership, and in current parlance "a team of rivals." All featured in the upheavals of the 1920s and 1930s and were ministers in the wartime coalition. Their family backgrounds ranged across the British social structure, from Bevin's working-class depths, Morrison's policeman father, and Attlee's solid middle-class upbringing through the upper-class advantages of Cripps and Dalton. They differed too in personality, Bevin and Dalton being notoriously abrasive in different ways; Cripps brilliant, mercurial, and strikingly ascetic; and Attlee deceptively low-keyed. But all were profoundly embedded in Labour's history, and for a day or two after the election the exact role each would play hung in question. As chairman of the NEC's policy committee and of its campaign committee in 1945, Morrison had been the prime architect of Labour's electoral victory. To dramatize his belief in making the broadest political appeal, he had abandoned his own safe seat to run in East Lewisham, a traditionally Conservative and demographically mixed inner suburb of London, where he won an impressive majority.[37] Morrison considered Attlee to be the "accidental" leader of the PLP (after the 1931 election had decimated Labour's front bench, including Morrison himself), and he still aspired to become party leader. Rumors now swirled about a possible challenge. Apart from personal ambitions, the issue of democratic procedure arose: instead of Attlee automatically passing from party leader in the old Parliament to prime minister in the new one, shouldn't the newly-elected PLP freely choose its own leader and thus the next prime minister? But Attlee and his stalwarts easily quashed that notion; the first caucus of the new PLP immediately hailed Attlee with a standing ovation and no challenge materialized.[38]

Notwithstanding his moment of ill-judged ambition, Morrison became Attlee's unofficial deputy prime minister, head of the "Lord President's Committee" (chief coordinator of domestic policy), and leader of the House of Commons, where he proved supremely effective in translating the cabinet's voluminous agenda into legislation. For the two highest-profile cabinet posts, it seemed likely that Bevin would become Chancellor of the Exchequer and Dalton foreign secretary, given their strong predilections in those respective domains. But Attlee believed that the smooth functioning of his government would suffer if Morrison faced daily negotiation on domestic issues with his nemesis Bevin, and perhaps too that Bevin could stand up to the Russians more effectively than Dalton.[39] Attlee therefore arranged a switch in those expected roles, naming Bevin foreign secretary (where he proved a quick study) and Dalton Chancellor of the Exchequer. Cripps, who had formally rejoined the party only in 1945, headed the Board of Trade and quickly emerged as a cabinet strongman on economic and financial issues.

To fill out his front bench Attlee turned to other veterans of the coalition whom we've encountered, including Chuter Ede (shifted to home secretary from education) and Ellen Wilkinson (as minister of education). Party veteran Emmanuel Shinwell, who had blustered himself out of a ministerial post in 1940, now became the minister of fuel and power, charged with supervising the nationalization of coal mines and the electric and gas utilities. Nye Bevan, who had kept Shinwell company on the wartime backbenches, had been a relentless and sharp-tongued critic of the Tories and Attlee alike. But the prime minister understood Bevan's potential value to his government and forgave him. In the other surprise served up by Attlee after the election, he named Bevan to a second tier but critical cabinet post as minister of health (charged with designing a new National Health Service), which also carried a portfolio for housing.

After successive moments of euphoria at the obliteration of the Third Reich and at their resounding electoral victory, Labourites took the reins with a clear mandate to govern and an unprecedented level of party unity. The first caucus of the PLP and the first day of the new Parliament had decidedly festive airs, but such bliss could only be short-lived given the parlous state of their country. In the political diary that Hugh Gaitskell began just after his election, for example, he recounts a private dinner hosted by Dalton on July 30, 1945, for twelve freshman Labour MPs—including seven still in uniform and all but one university graduates. As they discussed challenges facing the new government, even this compatible group had opinions ranging all over the map.

The economist Evan Durbin, for one, was especially gloomy over the outlook for food, housing, and fuel and argued that the Labour government should release only candid information and avoid soothing propaganda. Eonomist Harold Wilson agreed but maintained that coal and housing should be presented

as the inherited problems they truly were. He also made the surprising suggestion that the government should order refrigerators and vacuum cleaners to help
the transition to peacetime production. John Wilmot (the only sitting MP in the
group) urged that moving from "war work . . . to housing work" be the top
priority, but the others did not seem to rally around that slogan. A worried Major
Younger, meanwhile, hoped that people had not voted Labour in expectation of
more pay and less work in current conditions. With a different inflection,
Gaitskell himself cautioned about establishing high-production targets at a
moment when control of labor had to be loosened. He advocated subsidizing
coal (in part to support the wages of miners), spurring new housing with an
early demobilization of building workers in the armed forces, focusing on
social security or Beveridge Plan issues, and preparing to reform the House of
Lords in case it tried to thwart the new government. Dalton's anodyne wrap-up
stressed that nothing would come easily in such straitened times—not even the
obvious need to increase old-age pensions.[40]

Public opinion initially offered breathing room for Attlee's government. In a
post-election Gallup Poll in July asking what the election results meant, 30
percent responded that the British people wanted Labour "to govern along
existing lines only more efficiently," but an encouraging 56 percent anticipated
the introduction of "sweeping changes such as nationalization." In a November
poll, 57 percent thought the government was doing well and only 16 percent
that it was doing badly; 59 percent approved the early round of proposed nationalizations, while only 25 percent disapproved.[41]

When a large plurality of voters turned to Labour in June, what actually
did they want from a new government? On the level of sentiment they must
have endorsed Labour's emphasis on equity and fair shares. In practice they
anticipated "full employment" (a goal ostensibly shared by Conservatives),
new stocks of affordable housing (a consistently high priority), and the comprehensive social insurance of the Beveridge Plan, including a new National
Health Service. The public expected to be asked for continued sacrifice during
reconstruction but with a gradual easing of austerity. For their part Labour
ministers, MPs, economists, and functionaries no doubt shared these objectives, but managing the postwar economy had to be their dominant concern.
Economic policy would be driven not simply by the party's long-standing if
vague social-democratic agenda but by the terms of international trade: Britain's
desperate need for imports of food, raw materials, and machinery; the shortage

of gold and dollar reserves to pay for these crucial imports; and the consequent need to direct as much manufacturing production as possible for export rather than home consumption in order to build up those reserves.

The impediments to economic recovery would have bedeviled any postwar British government. But it could be argued that Labour's commitment to planning for maximal economic efficiency in a "mixed economy" put it in a better position to deal with these problems than the Conservative opposition, with its tropism for unfettered free-market forces. (As the government negotiated bulk purchases of various imports, for example, the Tories called for "a resumption of healthy competition through normal trade channels.") While Attlee's government carried out the pledged nationalizations, it also sought to channel capital into the modernization of obsolescent industrial plants in both the nationalized and the private sectors. Forced into prolonged and dispiriting postwar austerity, the government would allocate or ration foodstuffs, clothing, and other scarce items of mass consumption in the fairest possible way. Meanwhile, national budgets would calibrate revenue and expenditure to support both economic growth and modest redistribution of income.

On a parallel track the Labour government carried out most of its other programmatic commitments, which we will examine in a subsequent chapter: initiating a program to replenish the housing stock (with policies starkly at variance from Conservative prescriptions); creating and launching a comprehensive National Health Service to round out social security; and (far less impressively) grappling with the reform of education. It goes without saying that on another level any postwar government would be beset from beginning to end by the pressures of international relations, defense policy, and rebellious colonies, which together posed the question of how Britain would play its role as a greatly weakened world power situated between the US and the USSR.

Labour had made the case for "democratic planning" since the mid-thirties, and it had redoubled this theoretical effort after F. Hayek's *Road to Serfdom* in 1944 had tarred all forms of central planning as an infringement of liberty. Yet for all its commitment to the mantra of planning, the Attlee government took office without actual blueprints or administrative mechanisms to carry out the task.[42] Compounding this lack of forward preparation, disputes arose among officials already on the ground, such as civil servants in the Treasury and economists in the Cabinet Office. Over time the Labour government created the instruments for economic planning, but they retained an improvised, ad hoc feel and did not produce a consistent or durable design.[43]

Some of the mechanisms Labour initially relied on were little more than peacetime adaptations of emergency wartime bodies, including the Labor Ministry's National Joint Advisory Council, with representatives of the employer's federation and the TUC, and the Board of Trade's National Production Advisory Council on Industry. A less familiar (and understudied) innovation was a series of boards called "Working Parties" in such non-nationalized sectors as cotton, wool, heavy clothing, textile machinery, cutlery, glassware, and linoleum.[44] Numbering about twenty by 1948, the Working Parties resembled on a smaller scale the "voluntary" industrial code-making bodies assembled under Roosevelt's abortive NIRA of 1933. To counsel the Working Parties and other industrial enterprises, the government established a Production Efficiency Service in March 1946, headed by a former official in the Amalgamated Engineering Union who had worked in the wartime aircraft industry. With a staff of twenty-eight, and no charges to the companies that enlisted its aid, it was in effect a free consulting service for industry; in its first year the staff fielded over 600 inquiries and made 200 site visits to offer technical advice. But it was not until mid-1947 that the threads for Labour's project of democratic planning were finally gathered into an "economic general staff"—a joint planning staff that would work with the Cabinet Office and the new Central Statistical Office to coordinate sector-wide planning initiatives and to balance policy requirements and actual resources.[45]

Short of Dollars and Short of Coal

The lack of forward preparation for directing the "mixed economy" was bad enough, but the cabinet soon faced successive crises of one sort or another, piled atop the aftermath of wartime devastation, dislocation, and deficits. Most of these crises were predictable, but were no less brutal when they actually struck. The first blow, the termination of American lend-lease, came as a rude shock only because of its timing. America's vital pipeline of food, supplies, and credit under its lend-lease program was due to end with the peace, but at the time of the British election no one expected the surrender of Japan to come just three months after V-E Day. J. M. Keynes, Britain's unofficial point man on wartime finance, had indeed privately hoped that "the Japanese would not let us down by surrendering too soon," so that American aid would continue. And when peace finally came, he hoped, a large American grant or interest-free loan would carry an otherwise strapped Britain through the postwar transition. Such a generous gesture, Keynes felt, would help repay Britain's disproportionate costs in that titanic struggle—"a retrospective redistribution of the costs of the war." Such continued assistance, he added, would in turn allow British movement toward the other side of the bargain—the liberal, multilateral postwar trade and currency exchange systems that Washington demanded.[46]

In that sense the atomic bomb hit Britain's finances as well as the Japanese people. The unexpected arrival of V-J Day in August brought the immediate cessation of lend-lease aid as dictated by the original congressional legislation. It thereby presented the Attlee government with its first crisis, because the US then took a much tougher negotiating position than Whitehall or Keynes had hoped for. With a wary eye on a restive, potentially isolationist Congress, Truman's officials sought to extract the maximum concessions on any future loan short of causing a complete financial collapse in Britain. Negotiations with Washington dragged on painfully for almost a year. Keynes, for whom an accord with the US could alone avoid a "financial Dunkirk," led the mission to Washington but lacked the power to accept terms without referring them back to a divided and skittish cabinet, some of whose members seemed ready to forego US assistance altogether if pushed too hard. In the end Britain received a $3.75 billion loan at a 2 percent interest rate, rather than the larger grant or no-interest "credits" that it sought, interest and principal payments to be deferred, however, for five years.[47] The US loan negotiations made clear that British economic policy would be driven in good part by the inexorable terms of international trade: dependence on imported foodstuffs and raw materials and the need to build gold and dollar reserves to pay for the imports.

Dollars were in short supply, and so was coal. Britain's bountiful advantage in fuel for the industrial revolution had by the 1920s morphed into an economic liability, with a coal industry fragmented into more than 900 firms, obsolete technology, and poisonous labor relations. The bitter miners' lockout/strike of 1926 and the general strike it had spawned did nothing to foster modernization in the industry. During the wartime coalition, as we saw, Labour ministers used the desperate need for coal to advocate immediate nationalization of the mines, along with "fair shares" coal rationing for domestic consumption. Churchill blocked both demands and would approve only the creation of a National Coal Board to allocate production from the mines, a step (as Bevan observed) that actually shored up the position of the owners. With Labour's victory in 1945, however, the coal industry stood near the front of the line for nationalization, although no actual blueprint had been prepared for this long-heralded step.

Attlee had given the ministry of fuel and power to veteran Labourite Shinwell, who made resounding speeches that endeared him to party activists but was otherwise ill-suited to the job. Inattentive to detail, prone to blame others when things went wrong, and "ravaged by suspicion" of colleagues in almost paranoid fashion (as his deputy Gaitskell plausibly recorded in 1946), Shinwell lacked the requisite administrative and interpersonal skills.[48] Nationalization nonetheless moved forward on the Morrison model of a quasi-autonomous public corporation. With the owners compensated and their profit motive now removed from the mix, and with a National Coal Board to set overall policy, implementation devolved on eight new regional coal boards that would presumably have the local knowledge to oversee this variegated industry. The ministry, the cabinet, and Parliament were to have no direct role in setting policy once nationalization was complete, but they retained vague oversight powers to defend broader public interests.

Miners, meanwhile, would not be directly represented on the national or regional coal boards that set policy, although individuals from the labor movement were occasionally appointed to comparable boards in their own right. (Walter Citrine, long the general secretary of the TUC, for example, was named head of the National Electricity Board.) In keeping with the orthodox view of collective bargaining, labor and management would remain potential adversaries across the table, although both sides presumably had more incentive now for cooperation. As a prelude to nationalization, a new "Miner's Charter" promised a five-day week and other long-sought ameliorations of working conditions.

By January 1947 Shinwell could preside over vesting day, as signs went up around the country's coal mines: "This colliery is now managed by the NATIONAL COAL BOARD on behalf of the people." Which, of course, was only the beginning. Production lagged far behind a rising curve of industrial and domestic demand for coal, thanks in part to decades of inadequate investment in new technology. Mining still suffered from labor shortages (despite the temporary importation of Polish miners) and from a paucity of experienced, capable managers. The effects of fragmentation in mine ownership were ameliorated only to a degree by the board's initial amalgamations and economies of scale. And the miners' deeply ingrained distrust of management lingered. So it was hard to organize the "battle for production" in that vital sector. While fulfilling the promise of the Miner's Charter for better compensation and working conditions, the coal boards had to push for increasing levels of output per man and for increased volumes of production through well-paid but exhausting overtime work.[49]

For two months, however, an immediate crisis in the supply and distribution of coal eclipsed this structural challenge. Government economist Douglas Jay had been warning about a dire shortfall of coal for the coming winter of 1946–47, warnings which Shinwell dismissed and the cabinet largely ignored. When an acute shortage actually materialized it was too late to respond because of extraordinarily harsh winter weather that no one had foreseen. Prolonged frigid temperatures, gales, and record-breaking snows brought land and water transport of coal to a halt, leaving electric power plants without adequate supplies, thereby forcing them to curtail the generation of electricity for homes and industry. This in turn caused factory closures and a temporary spike in unemployment of perhaps 15 percent, along with two months of blackouts, dark and unheated homes, and utter misery for consumers until conditions finally thawed out.[50]

As the pain of this winter agony receded, leaving scars on the collective memory of the public, the battle for coal production resumed. (The only reference to the crisis in the monthly *Labour Party Bulletin* was an apology for a delay in publication because of "the suspension of printing during the fuel crisis"!) During the war coal output had fallen from 231 million tons in 1939 to 174 million tons in 1945, as the workforce had contracted and output per man had decreased. Nationalization and better labor relations would help, but they were offset by increasing industrial and consumer demand for electricity. In that other nationalized sector, new regional electricity boards were supposed to pay their way, and their priority was to sell more power and not to husband scarce coal supplies.[51]

Increased coal production ultimately depended on the goodwill of the miners and their unions. The national president of the NUM (National Union of Miners), Will Lawther, was amenable but his new interlocutors did not consider him an effective leader. On the other hand, the NUM's general secretary, Arthur

Horner, and the heads of several regional miners federations were communists who cooperated for the moment but might pivot at any time to become obstructive. Gaitskell, who became Shinwell's deputy at fuel and power in 1946 and replaced him as minister in October 1947, acted as a kind of diplomat at large in the industry, shuttling between visits to coal mines, regional union federations, and meetings of the regional and national coal boards. He admired and got along well with most local union leaders of whatever political coloration, even as they ranged from ineffective, mercurial, or inebriated to reliable and skillful. But given the deep-seated distrust and grievances of the miners, he understood that their cooperation on issues such as absenteeism (in response to the punishing conditions of work in the mines) or Saturday work at overtime pay was always precarious. Nationalization could ameliorate labor relations only up to a point.[52]

The Three Economic Battles

"Purchasing power was shortage number one in the pre-war economy and employment was shortage number two. These shortages were so vast that they swamped all others," Morrison declared in October 1946, but now they had been overcome.[53] In their place, three interrelated economic challenges faced Attlee's government: "the battle of the gap" against the unfavorable balance of trade caused by the need to import almost half of necessary food and raw materials; "the battle for production" of coal and of manufactured goods for export to help pay for the imports; and the threat of wage-price inflation from the combination of full employment and scarcities of consumer goods.

When the protracted negotiations for the American loan had finally ended with US congressional approval in July 1946, Dalton commented that the funds would be used to buy foodstuffs for a more varied diet and raw materials for industry, giving "a breathing space and a new reserve of strength to enable us to reach our export targets." Soon even this modest optimism abated as a world food shortage took hold and the aforementioned fuel crisis struck. Despite early success in the export drive, monthly trade deficits rapidly devoured the US and Canadian loans of 1946. Foreign demand initially absorbed Britain's manufactured goods such as autos, but soon British firms would face severe competition on the quality and pricing of their exports. At the Board of Trade Cripps waged public campaigns, akin to the dubious home-front morale propaganda of the war years, featuring such slogans as "We're up Against It" and "We Work or Want." As one poster of 1947 put it, "We need more imports from abroad (cotton, rubber, tea and the like) than our exports now pay for. This can't go on. We must export one third more this year or get less and fare worse."[54]

Labour might boast that as black markets ran rife in countries like Italy and France, Britain was holding down prices and ensuring fair shares by subsidies and rationing. (This was true but only comparatively so, as the "spiv" or black-market street hawker was a notorious presence in postwar Britain.)[55] In any case, the balance of payments or trade gap kept growing, forcing further cutbacks in imports and therefore in food supplies for consumers. Where the prewar daily diet averaged approximately 3,000 calories, it had fallen to 2,870 calories in 1946, and in late 1947 the government reduced its targeted average to 2,700 calories. Reluctantly the cabinet instituted bread rationing, which even wartime conditions had not required, and rationed potatoes after a wet spring followed by an abnormally dry summer reduced the potato harvest by about 20 percent. The government also lowered existing rations of meat, bacon, and sugar; tried to compensate for severe shortages of fish by promoting the unfamiliar and repellent fish from South Africa known as snoek; and ended altogether the minimum individual allotment of petrol, causing a furor in the middle class.[56]

In August 1947 the House of Commons held a "State of the Nation" debate centering on the deteriorating balance of payments and the consequent threats to the import program. As Cripps bluntly put it: "The time for the realisation of our aims and hopes has been set back by the inescapable facts of world development. . . . The battle of the balance of payments is as tough a proposition as this country has ever faced [!]." The global impact of the war's effects had become painfully evident—in Europe and elsewhere, scarcities and the need to import basic necessities; in the Western Hemisphere, plentiful basic resources (food, raw materials, dollars). A steep rise in the price of American export commodities starting in 1947 drained Britain's Canadian and American credits even faster than anticipated in the midst of a worldwide "dollar famine."[57]

Worse yet, as a condition of the US loan agreement of 1946 Britain had pledged to permit the free convertibility of pounds sterling into dollars starting in July 1947. Before that date, the government could at least control private currency movements, as in the Exchange Control Bill of 1946 for the conservation and allocation of exchange resources and overseas income.[58]

As convertibility loomed and then kicked in, however, it set off the equivalent of a run on a bank, as investors and speculators liquidated their British stocks and bonds and sent their pounds sterling abroad to places like Belgium for conversion into dollars. Albeit predictable, this "convertibility crisis" stunned the cabinet. After a few days of panic and flailing, the cabinet finally suspended convertibility in the sterling area. The US Treasury denounced this unilateral scrapping of the 1946 agreement, then conceded Britain's need to suspend convertibility "on an emergency and temporary" basis, which in fact lasted many years. In this unsettling sequence of events—the acceptance of convertibility under coercion by the US during the loan negotiations of 1946 and the subsequent need to renege or default on its word—Britain effectively acknowledged its pitiful position in the global economy.[59] After the suspension of convertibility, the government was drawing down the last tiers of currency reserves and the credits remaining from US, Canadian, and IMF loans. A glimmer of hope at this dire moment—that "further American help" might come from the seed planted in Secretary of State Marshall's recent speech about aiding European recovery—was only that, for as Attlee warned, "We cannot and will not base our plan on that assumption."

The strains of managing the economy now erupted among the big five ministers in an abortive move to replace Attlee with Bevin in September 1947. The PM deftly survived, in the main by detaching Cripps from the cabal. Attlee offered to create a new Ministry of Economic Affairs for Cripps, thereby making him the czar for economic policy in place of Morrison, who had not been up to the task. Dalton, continuing as Chancellor of the Exchequer, would concentrate on budget matters. Cripps got along well with Dalton, but unexpectedly replaced him in November when Dalton had to resign as chancellor because of a minor but unpardonable indiscretion—a thoughtless leak to a journalist hours before he unveiled his budget in Parliament.[60]

In November Cripps's first "Crisis Report" explained that the drops in dollar reserves and in daily caloric consumption were nearing "the irreducible minimum beyond which we could not go without facing the possibility of widespread hunger and unemployment." Reluctantly he announced reductions in new capital projects, including desperately needed housing and factory construction. In other words, the problem of disappearing gold and dollar reserves was forcing the Labour government to cannibalize its resources, hopes, and priorities—reconstruction and industrial modernization on one side, and a rise in living standards on the other.[61] Cripps still insisted, as Morrison had a year earlier, that Britain's rationing and fair shares system "has remained the envy of Europe . . . where massive black markets are rife." Food subsidies at least kept the prices of scarce necessities steady and low, even as the Tories kept demanding that controls be eased and subsidies cut. Worse yet, coal production kept lagging behind industrial and consumer demand for the fuel, putting Britain in "the deplorable position" of requiring imports of coal from the US and Poland. Now, as the trade deficit still kept rising despite the growth of exports, the cabinet finally balked at further cutbacks in imports of foods and raw materials, but it agreed to scale back imports of such products as tobacco, newsprint, and (much to Hollywood's dismay) motion pictures.[62]

The export drive centered on vehicles, rubber, footwear, and textiles but extended to 23 manufacturing groups with 153 distinct products. "The Labour government of so-called pipe-dreamers," Cripps boasted, "is busily overtaking a generation of capitalist decay." (Labour's ultimate target for exports was an ambitious 175 percent of the prewar level, using 1938 as the benchmark.) Export records were set in car and truck sales and shipbuilding; the 41,000 cars exported in October 1947 surpassed by three times the highest prewar monthly figure, with similar levels in bicycles and textiles.[63] But Cripps had to report that after the gratifying industrial bounce of 1946–47 "there is an apparent flattening out of the curve of production." So at the end of 1947, despite the heightened austerities, Attlee's government called for yet more patience by consumers and redoubled efforts by labor and management to increase productivity.[64]

The Sisyphean struggle continued across 1948. Unlike the US, Italy, or France, inflation had so far been held in check by tax policy, price controls, rationing, and subsidies. But closing the gap in the balance of payments by increased exports and reduced imports meant fewer goods for the home market even as income rose. "When it comes to a race between rising prices and personal incomes," warned Cripps, "prices will always win in the long run," especially for wage earners. "Higher production and lower costs are the prime safeguards." For the short term, however, Cripps concluded that "we must avoid a further rise in personal incomes in the face of continuing shortages in the home market." He would have preferred a capital levy to that end (which Mendès France had advocated for France in 1945), but it would take too long to assess and implement. In his first budget as chancellor Cripps instead proposed, along-side existing profits taxes and surtaxes on high incomes, a one-time levy on "unearned income." The tax would cover investment income from rent, dividends, and interest collected in 1947-48 for those earning over £2,000 a year and with over £250 of such income. Conversely, workers with moderate income would receive "substantial reliefs" in taxation—reflecting Labour's commitment to "progressive democratic policies . . . [which] our people demand and deserve."[65] In his budget for 1950 (his last) Cripps made Keynesian-style demand management via fiscal policy even more explicit: "The Budget itself can be described as the most important control and as the most powerful instrument for influencing economic policy [under democratic planning]." "Excessive demand produces inflation and inadequate demand results in deflation. . . . The fiscal policy of the Government is the most important single instrument for maintaining the balance [and avoiding these twin evils]."[66]

Attlee's government intended to raise productivity and keep industrial prices as low as possible "not by the traditional Tory method of slashing wages, but by . . . greater efficiency." It was easy enough for the government to call for more and better machines, greater standardization of components and end products, and better management—all of which had recently been emphasized by the Anglo-American Council on Productivity.[67] As minister of fuel and power after replacing Shinwell, for example, Gaitskell bemoaned the "appalling" lack of capable colliery managers and board members drawn from business or engineering backgrounds, most "without any conception of leadership or administration."[68] But that same trans-Atlantic Council on Productivity also criticized the fragmentation and parochialism of British trade unions. Clearly Attlee's government had to tread cautiously around labor issues, but Cripps was just the man to confront them. If production stagnated at present levels, Cripps warned, the standard of living cannot rise. But new efficiencies would require "the abandonment of anti-social restrictive practices of all kinds"—a barely coded phrase certainly not be found in trade union playbooks.

The Labour Government and the Unions

In pursuit of higher productivity and an improved standard of living, Attlee's government could in good conscience dismiss Conservative cant about unfettering the free market or about the need for workers "to apply more elbow grease." But the belief in individual responsibility ran deeply in the Labour Party. As Morrison put it: "It is not enough to socialise the physical assets of an industry. The outlook of the men and women must be social too, while preserving individual enterprise and initiative."[69] With a moral earnestness that combined unimpeachable idealism, wishful thinking, and mystification, Attlee, Morrison, Cripps, and most of their colleagues believed that democratic socialism rested not simply on social justice and economic reform but on a "responsible society" nurturing a virtuous citizenry.[70] In that frame of mind Cripps in early 1948 addressed the inflationary potential of rising wages—the havoc from a wage-price inflationary spiral that might arise from the combination of full employment and shortages of consumer goods. His potential partner or chief obstacle in this matter would be the Trades Union Congress (TUC).

Like its counterparts in the US, the TUC had grown and strengthened during the war. Total trade union membership rose from 4,460,000 in 1938 to 6,642,000 at the end of 1944. Bevin had assured that collective bargaining was preserved without the imposition of wage controls, and had brought union officials into unprecedented levels of consultation on industrial mobilization. In exchange the TUC accepted government direction of labor; tendered no-strike pledges (which did little to stop local wildcat strikes); and accepted compulsory arbitration when negotiations deadlocked. Bevin's loyalty to Churchill's coalition ran so deep, however, that he almost resigned from the party after the backbench rebellion over implementing the Beveridge Report, and he virtually boycotted the party apparatus for the next year. Meanwhile, other rifts erupted. At the annual party conference of 1944 (where Ian Mikardo gained the attention discussed earlier) delegates battled over the urgency of nationalizations. Then Bevin's bill to deter wildcat strikes by the threat of draconian measures not only split the PLP (with Nye Bevan's slashing attack on Bevin's proposal) but roiled the TUC as well. A vote at the annual TUC convention to accept its General Council's endorsement of Bevin's policy passed by only 3,686,000 to 2,802,000 mandates.[71]

Soon after, however, such conflicts abated, and the trade unions and party reknit their alliance as Labour prepared for the general election. The six biggest unions of the TUC, whose combined membership topped 3.5 million, dominated the union votes at the annual Labour Party conference and emphatically supported the party leadership before the election and after. At the same time, the TUC and its unions always pursued specific professional objectives beyond the ken of their political comrades, and the question of wages in 1948 was bound to test their kinship.

The Labour government, as promised, had repealed the punitive Trade Disputes and Trade Unions Act of 1927 (which had outlawed sympathy strikes and secondary picketing, banned union shops in the public sector, and required workers to "contract in" for the political levy). On the issue of wage levels, Attlee's cabinet appealed to the unions for restraint against the self-defeating prospect of an inflationary wage-price spiral. As Morrison put it, "Higher wages and lower hours before the goods are there to be bought—that is worse than useless. They give no more real income and by inflation . . . may wreck the whole structure we are trying to build." Attlee exhorted the unions to link their wage demands to gains in productivity, but he tried to avoid any clash with the TUC's primal commitment to free collective bargaining by not proposing any preconditions on wage negotiations. For as Arthur Deakin, Bevin's handpicked successor as general secretary of the mighty TGWU, put it an address to America's AFL in 1947: the government should "not even offer an opinion as to whether a particular wage claim should be conceded or turned down."[72]

But the dire economic situation changed the equation for the government and for Deakin and the TUC. In February 1948 the cabinet endorsed a white paper that ruled out an outright wage freeze, but it proposed a national "wages policy" with guidelines for limiting negotiated wage increases. This was a hard decision to take. Some ministers believed that only Bevin's absence from cabinet meetings while on foreign policy missions made it possible to move forward at all; when the subject had been broached earlier Bevin had indeed balked at any government "wages policy" that infringed on the TUC's historic commitment to unfettered collective bargaining in peace and war.[73] Now the cabinet adopted Cripps's call for a kind of prior restraint on collective bargaining, reminiscent of the Little Steel Formula of 1942 for labor negotiations in the US.

To the government's relief, the General Council of the TUC agreed to confer with Cripps over implementing this policy, so long as there were complementary restraints on food prices, dividends, and profits;[74] that the lowest paid workers were excepted from any preset ceiling; and that "differentials based on craftsmanship, training, and experience" were maintained. Then by a ratio of more than 5 to 2, a TUC conference of affiliated union executives approved this remarkable turnabout by its leadership, and it renewed the endorsement the following year by an even larger margin of 6.5 to 1. While this entente between

the TUC and the government precluded a general wage freeze or direct government control over wages, the guidelines decisively moderated wage raises over
the next eighteen months to an average of only 2.8 percent. But worker sacrifice
and "responsibility" in solidarity with the Labour government had its limits.

In September 1949 the cabinet once again entered crisis mode over "the
battle of the gap," this time debating the distasteful expedient of devaluing the
pound sterling to reduce the cost of British exports. The cabinet's irresolution
over violating the devaluation taboo echoed the distressed responses during
debates on the American loan of 1946 and the convertibility crisis of 1947. And
again the cabinet finally swallowed the bitter pill and devalued the pound by
almost a third.[75] As export prices temporarily gained the anticipated competitive advantage, prices of goods at home predictably began to climb. In response,
one trade union after another sought to annul the TUC's official support of
wage restraint. By June 1950, spurning a plea by Deakin, the TUC renounced
the leadership's commitment to Labour's "wages policy" by a vote of 3,898000
to 3,521,000 mandates, although most unions still maintained a measure of
restraint in their own collective bargaining during the next year.[76]

Another fissure between workers and the Attlee government unfolded on the
docks of London and other ports, where labor relations were historically as
volatile as in the coal mines. Bevin had pushed through significant changes on
the waterfront during the war, notably a "decasualization" of labor that guaranteed stevedores a minimum wage whether or not they worked on a particular
day. A National Dock Labour Scheme that went into effect in 1947 created a
condominium of TGWU officials and employers to regulate procedures for
hiring and discipline. But rank-and-file dockers, like miners, viscerally
distrusted the bosses in this dangerous and contentious occupation, and they
tenaciously clung to hard-won work rules, which might have struck outsiders as
restrictive barriers against new efficiencies. Flashpoints included the customary
size of work gangs for particular cargos, arbitrary assignment to distasteful
tasks, disputes about overtime, and disciplinary procedures. Over such issues
dockers broke free from their TGWU locals, which now seemed remote and
collusive with the employers, and formed ad hoc associations quick to call
walkouts. The TGWU opposed such unofficial strikes as a form of sabotage
against national economic interests, and so too did the government. The cabinet
(with the support of both Bevin and Bevan) responded to a potentially crippling

dockers' strike in June 1948 by invoking emergency power statutes and mustering troops to act as replacement workers if necessary. In the summer of 1949 another, more militant unofficial strike erupted over work issues, but it was also stoked by communist organizers suspected of serving other agendas. This time the government actually deployed 15,000 troops to unload cargo and thereby broke the strike.[77]

In some manufacturing sectors tensions escalated between aggressive shop stewards and officials of the national unions who could not control them. While the TUC argued for "responsibility" and sought to tamp down potential embarrassment to the Labour government, shop stewards pushed plant managers to the maximum with (as Deakin put it) "smash and grab tactics." The indispensable but sometimes contentious alliance between the trade unions and the Labour Party hinged on a measure of restraint by the unions in channeling the class consciousness and the material interests of their members.[78] That relationship was now strained, but it did not snap. The labor barons responded to shop-floor militancy and rank-and-file disdain with tactics fair and foul, including charges that their opponents were dupes of communist agitators. The established leaders rarely lost control of national unions let alone the TUC.[79] From this shaky but secure base, union officials in turn aided Labour Party leaders in resisting pressures from the left under Attlee and his successor after he stepped down in 1955.

From day one, inexorable postwar economic and financial constraints enveloped the Labour government, apart from its self-inflicted wounds such as the winter coal crisis in 1946–47 and the convertibility fiasco. But across its five-year term of office Labour stood by its proclaimed egalitarian values. Labour honored its unprecedented commitment "to raise the living standards of the people as a whole," and it linked that goal to the imperative of raising the economy's productive capacities. As Attlee put it: "For years we had been fighting to see who should get the largest slice of the loaf. Now that we are in a position to give everyone a fair share, the vitally important thing is to increase the size of the loaf."[80]

5

Starting Over, with de Gaulle or without Him

IN ONE RESPECT THE POSTWAR MOMENT BEGAN earlier in France than else-where with the gradual liberation of French soil in the summer of 1944. Alongside the Allied armies, de Gaulle's Free French units and the paramilitary forces (FFI) of the Resistance helped drive out the Nazis and oust Vichy's collaborators. Still a decided minority when the Liberation began, the Resistance in due course brought over most of the *attentistes* who had kept their heads down for four years. But liberation of the national territory was the first of two steps necessary to make France whole again. Only the conquest of the Reich would allow the repatriation from Germany of more than two million French POWs, forced laborers, and surviving concentration camp deportees. Once that was achieved the progressive project of renewal, the "peaceful revolution" envisaged by the CNR Common Program, could begin in earnest.

Liberation and Provisional Government

The commissioners of the republic named by de Gaulle's provisional govern-ment (the GPRF) to take charge of various regions as they were liberated had three immediate tasks: to support Allied military operations, to establish order and "republican legality," and to help meet the desperate needs of the popula-tion for food, fuel, and the like. Certain local liberation committees and para-military units sometimes took actions that clashed with the directives of the GPRF. But localized conflicts and spasms of popular retribution against collaborators never escalated into anything like the potential civil war that some had feared. Meanwhile, French officials answering to the GPRF in liberated territory facilitated the progress of Allied armies across France, and Allied sector commanders generally reciprocated with de facto recognition of those officials.

For de Gaulle, national recovery and France's standing in the world depended on quickly establishing effective state power to fill the vacuum left by the collapse of Vichy. The stubborn refusal of FDR to recognize the GPRF impeded de Gaulle's quest. The general visited the US in July 1944 and was enthusiastically feted by American progressives in events rich with symbolism. In New York City, for example, de Gaulle accompanied the popular mayor Fiorello LaGuardia to a packed outdoor concert where Marian Anderson sang the Marseillaise, an anthem "of new found freedom and friendship among free peoples."[1] But when the general met with Roosevelt, the White House did not treat de Gaulle like a head of state. The president regarded the French National Committee merely as a de facto authority in France that did not yet merit legal and diplomatic recognition. Only in October did Roosevelt finally relent.

Setbacks still followed, down to France's exclusion from the Potsdam Conference after V-E Day. De Gaulle claimed that Potsdam would merely be filling in the agreements of "the big three" at Yalta, where France regrettably had been excluded and where de Gaulle therefore could not help forestall the unfortunate results. But in the US skepticism about France lingered into the Truman administration. In a briefing paper for Potsdam, the new president was warned that France "may precipitate trouble and threaten peace because of its relations to Europe, its imperial ambitions, and the mercurial and sometimes paranoiac attitude of its leadership."[2] Nevertheless, the general's relentless drive to reclaim great power status for France prevailed. France had its own occupation zone in Germany and membership on the four-power allied control commission as well as a prominent place in the United Nations. Despite some snubs during the planning process for the UN, de Gaulle recalled, "We achieved in San Francisco all that we were most eager to obtain." France received one of five permanent seats with veto power on the UN Security Council, and French would be one of the UN's three official languages.[3]

Such international status still left the French economy in shambles, devastated by the successive blows of the occupation and the destruction of battle— its food, fuel, and resources systematically looted by Germany, its commercial networks and industrial capacity upended, its finances in disarray, and its transportation infrastructure bombed and sabotaged into ruins. France's reclaimed "rank" also left untouched a large question mark: how would France's political forces regroup and effect a return to democracy after the traumas and self-lacerations of the occupation?

With its links to the departmental liberation committees and FFI paramilitary forces, the CNR sought to stay relevant after Vichy's collapse, the Parisian uprising of August, and the return of de Gaulle to the capital. The CNR never made any claim to dual power alongside the GPRF, but it hoped to maintain the voice, influence, and prestige of the internal Resistance after the Liberation. But as de Gaulle's provisional government settled in, the CNR's role now seemed to him problematic, a lame duck whose writ had expired. As its institutional relevance and functionality waned, however, the CNR's Common Program of March 1944 took on a life of its own as the embodiment of Resistance ideals for "peaceful revolution" and civic renewal.

De Gaulle's initial encounters with the CNR upon his return to Paris seemed marked by wariness. True, he invited CNR president Bidault and conservative CNR member Laniel to walk alongside him on his triumphal march down the Champs-Elysées, and he would shortly appoint Bidault as foreign minister in his provisional cabinet. But de Gaulle soon decided to discourage any major role for the CNR going forward.[4] At the height of Liberation fervor, at a grand public meeting at the Palais de Chaillot on September 12, the general acknowledged the CNR's indispensable contribution to preparing for the Liberation, but he implicitly relegated it to the margins: until a National Assembly could be elected down the road, he said, "the [Provisional] Government will continue its work with the help of the [appointed] Consultative Assembly, in which the CNR is represented."[5]

As for the CNR Common Program, the general rarely alluded to it specifically although he did embrace some of its broad principles, as in that very address at the Palais de Chaillot. Then, during a visit to Lille in October, where he faced a sea of emaciated and desperate workers laid low by the occupation's privations, he explicitly endorsed the CNR's commitment to economic and social democracy, national planning and economic intervention. The Resistance press hailed the speech as an important milestone. (America's reactionary Hearst press ignorantly headlined the Lille speech as "De Gaulle in His True Color: Red!"—claiming that while he did "not advocate out-and-out Communism," he was "Trojan-horsing" his communist-like objectives.) Unlike many of its votaries who considered the CNR program totemic, de Gaulle regarded it prag-matically, but he certainly did not try to instigate a backlash against it.[6]

In naming cabinet ministers for his provisional unity government de Gaulle drew mainly on participants in Free France or the internal Resistance, including socialists (4), social-Catholics (3), communists (2), Radicals (2), and non-party men (4). For months these ministers tried to avoid partisan bickering among themselves or with the general, but eventually the aggressive post-Liberation press began to snipe at the minister of information (over allocation of scarce newsprint and confiscated presses), the minister of justice (over the slowness and missteps of the promised purges), and the minister of supply (over severe shortages including bread). This eventually pushed de Gaulle, who did not like being pushed, into a minor cabinet shuffle for those posts, but without any acknowledged changes of policy.[7]

The Purges

As French territory was liberated, the CNR program called for punishing traitors, purging collaborators from administrative and professional realms, and confiscating ill-gotten economic gains during the occupation. These strands quickly became aggregated as *l'épuration* (the purge), which unfolded as a series of scripted and unscripted dramas. The purge envisioned by the GPRF aimed for "justice" as against retribution. It relied for fairness on the procedures of special and regular courts, and on formal definitions of treason and other offenses that had arisen during the exceptional circumstances of the occupa-tion. Local actions on the ground, in contrast, gave vent to unmediated views of culpability and to quests for revenge or retribution. Justice and retribution might often overlap but were not always identical.

The GPRF intended to prosecute the central figures of the Vichy regime and the most notorious collaborationists as soon as possible. Proceedings against high-level Vichyites actually began well before the Liberation with Pierre Pucheu, a collaborationist minister of interior notoriously implicated in the selection of French hostages executed in a reprisal by the Germans at Châteaubriant in 1941. Pucheu had traveled to French North Africa just as Free France was consolidating its grip there. With de Gaulle's approval he was arrested, tried by a military court, and executed as "a swift example" to high-level collaborators.[8] After V-E Day in 1945 Pétain and Laval were apprehended

and put on trial. Initially public opinion favored indulgence toward the octoge-
narian hero of the Great War, but as the trial neared and unfolded, opinion
turned against Pétain, no doubt to the GPRF's relief.[9] In separate trials, a special
High Court of Justice sentenced Pétain and Laval to death; Laval was duly
executed but de Gaulle reprieved the Marshal from his capital sentence.

Well before those of Pétain and Laval, the first trials by the High Court
started in October 1944. Georges Suarez, a notorious collaborationist journalist
who "constantly supported the German viewpoint ... and worse still, advocated punishment of Patriots" was the first to stand in the dock; sentenced to
death after a one-day trial, he was executed in November.[10] Soon after, Robert
Brasillach, a writer for the viciously anti-Semitic and aggressively collaborationist newspaper *Je Suis Partout,* stood trial. Brasillach had been a serious
literary and cultural critic before the war, however, and his capital sentence
elicited a clemency petition from certain intellectuals led by François Mauriac.
Eliding the issue of incitement, the petitioners argued that even the most hateful
words, as opposed to actual criminal deeds, did not merit the death penalty, but
de Gaulle refused a reprieve. For the general, a few such high-profile trials and
punishments seemed necessary (and perhaps sufficient) to exorcise high-level
collaboration. Thereafter the pursuit of most collaborating journalists, writers,
artists, and entertainers would be far milder in outcome.[11]

In July 1944 de Gaulle had promised the Consultative Assembly in Algiers
that the GPRF would proceed "with necessary dismissals" in the state apparatus
and would draw replacements "from among the very able organizations of the
Resistance." But, he cautioned, his government "has no intention whatsoever
of suddenly dismissing the great majority of State officials most of whom
during the terrible years of occupation and usurpation did try as best they
could to serve the public cause."[12] A plausible point of view, perhaps, which
still provoked a great deal of clamor to go further. The same discord arose over
the treatment of economic collaboration. The GPRF quickly took over a few
collaborationist companies, including auto maker Renault and truck maker
Berliet in Lyon, whose patriarchs were arrested but died before their fates could
be settled.[13] But what about managers and directors of such companies, or the
gamut of profiteers and black-marketers at all levels, rural and urban. With
some justification, a sentiment grew among the public that most big economic
fish were escaping the purge while small fry opportunists bore the brunt of
punishment.

To deal with broad swaths of less egregious collaborationist behavior, the GPRF added the notion of "national unworthiness" (*indignité nationale*) to the categories for purge trials. Under an ordinance of August 26, 1944, the stigma of "national unworthiness" could be affirmed as a court's verdict after a trial or by professional review panels (*juris d'honneur*). Conviction would entail disqualification: loss of civic rights (voting or eligibility to run for office) and ouster from governmental, professional, cultural, military, or trade union positions for varying lengths of time—but with the proviso that individuals could remove that stigma if they had "rehabilitated themselves [later] by their active participation in the Resistance or having proved extenuating circumstances for their equivocal behavior."[14] Most dramatically, the Third Republic deputies and senators who had voted yes on plenary powers for Pétain in July 1940 were subject to that stigma. But as historian Olivier Wieviorka has shown, a surprisingly large number of those men were spared from the dishonor of "national unworthiness" under various circumstances, including 113 (mostly from prewar conservative parties) who were exonerated by special *juris d'honneur.*[15]

In the early months of the Liberation, in advance of the slow-moving mechanisms for official proceedings by courts and *juris d'honneur,* the ad hoc acts of retribution meted out locally came to be known as the *épuration sauvage,* the savage purge. In a high-profile foretaste of such summary justice, Philippe Henriot, the hectoring Parisian radio voice of all-out collaboration with the Germans, was assassinated in the capital by the Resistance on June 28, 1944. As the Liberation moved across France, the paramilitaries of the collaborationist French *milice* became particular targets for summary execution in reprisal for their sprees of torturing and murdering *résistants* and Jews over the previous months. People believed to have informed on their neighbors to the Vichy or German authorities, or of blatant profiteering, were also marked for reprisals. In the most publicized acts of the *épuration sauvage,* women who had consorted with Germans had their heads shaved in public rituals with misogynistic overtones.

The GPRF's commissioners tried to halt the *épuration sauvage* as they took control of their regions. Some arrested potential targets for their own protection as well as for future prosecution. The commissioners launched inquiries to determine in systematic fashion who actually deserved to stand trial and worked to get special or regular courts up and running—no easy task given the tainted bench and bar of the Vichy years that they inherited. But since legal procedures and amassing evidence delayed many trials, and since capital sentences were often commuted once trials were held, demands from aggrieved citizens and local liberation committees for expedited proceedings and firmness mounted. At the extreme, enraged citizens more than once stormed a prison and lynched a collaborator as in Lyon, where the capable (and left-wing) commissioner Yves Farge had commuted a death sentence against a *milicien*. Generally well regarded in the region, Farge defended his action at a raucous public meeting yet could not stop a crowd from forcing the jail and executing the culprit.[16] But just as delays or leniency in the official purge provoked sharp criticism, certain episodes of retributive violence also caused a backlash.[17]

A retrospective balance sheet of verdicts and sentences by the courts in the official purge as of December 1948 shows that over 73,000 cases (45 percent of the total) resulted in dropped charges or acquittals; 26,000 cases (16 percent) in prison or detention; 13,000 cases (8percent) in the harsher punishment of forced labor; and 7,000 cases (4 percent) in death sentences (mostly decreed in absentia), of which only 767 were actually carried out. In comparison to the proportions of prosecutions and convictions for collaboration in Belgium, the Netherlands, Norway, or Denmark, France's *épuration* was mild. But subjective perceptions of leniency or harshness at the time counted most. For many the purge went on too long and reached too far. Most French citizens were neither outright collaborators nor veritable *résistants;* they had experienced the occupation in "silent and massive acquiescence" or accommodation. The grinding of the purge likely discomfited many such people because it implicitly cast a shadow over their own behavior under the occupation, notwithstanding the comforting post-Liberation myth propagated by de Gaulle of France as nation of resistors.[18]

Mendès France: "Redress and Reconstruction"

With the collapse of Vichy, the GPRF had responsibility for the basic needs of the French people. On the plus side, the drain of French food, fuel, manufactures, and labor from forced transport to Germany came to an end. But the devastating disruptions of production, market networks, and finances during the occupation, compounded by the wreckage of transportation infra-structure and housing during the German and Allied invasions, prolonged the population's severe deprivations. Pierre Mendès France would be the GPRF's point man confronting these problems after the Liberation.

A doctor of law and economics, Mendès France (1907–82) won election to the Chamber of Deputies in 1932 as a Radical in Louviers (Eure) and was re-elected under the Popular Front banner in 1936; in the second and short-lived cabinet of Léon Blum in 1938 he served as deputy secretary of the Treasury. A captain in the French air force, Mendès France was on leave from his unit when he joined a score of fellow deputies sailing on the *Massilia* in June 1940 to continue the fight from North Africa. Interned with the others upon landing, he was singled out for allegedly abandoning his military unit, was sent back to France for trial as a deserter, and against the evidence was convicted. He subsequently escaped from jail and reached England in February 1942, where he joined the Lorraine Group of light bombers in the Free French air force. Invited in September 1943 to sit in de Gaulle's Consultative Assembly in Algiers, the captain declined, explaining that he had fled to England to fight Germany not engage in politics. But in December de Gaulle summoned him to Algiers to tap his economic expertise as Free France's commissioner for finances, and that assignment he could not refuse.[19]

From day one in the new post Mendès France worried that shortages of provisions and the excess of occupation-era currency chasing scarce goods threatened to create severe, even crippling inflation. (The Finance Ministry later estimated that a currency supply totaling 142 billion francs just before the war in 1939 had expanded to 632 billion by September 1944.)[20] Hence Mendès France argued that after the Liberation the money supply must be reduced with draconian methods, including a forced currency exchange and the blocking of suspect bank accounts. This would not only shrink the artificial surfeit of currency engendered by the occupation but could flush out the illicit profits of collaborators and profiteers. Finally, he insisted, the government must not sugar coat the dismal situation facing the French people, tempting as that might be.

Mendès France's calls for extreme rigor and complete candor raised various objections within Free French circles. Some colleagues feared the dire effects on morale of an excessively gloomy tone and of draconian, deflationist currency measures piled atop four years of privation and stress. A few liberals (in the French sense) favored greater reliance on free-market incentives even if basic controls were necessary. Some on the Left objected to Mendès France's readiness to restrain long overdue and desperately needed wage increases for workers because of their self-defeating inflationary potential. Finally, the communists may have opposed his banknote scheme because their own wartime caches of currency might be compromised in the process.

Faced with such sniping, Mendès France proffered a letter of resignation in which he underlined his stance as "a revolutionary attempt at social equality . . . for redress and reconstruction."[21] Thus Mendès France, who played no role at all in drafting the CNR Common Program, came to embody its transformational spirit as much as anyone in de Gaulle's inner circle. For his part the general remained well disposed to his finance commissioner, offered him vague reassurances, and insisted that he remain at his post. In July 1944 Mendès France accompanied de Gaulle to North America and then attended the Bretton Woods conference, where found himself jousting with his hero Keynes.

The real struggle began with the Liberation, when the GPRF moved to Paris. Mendès France wanted economic policy to be the domain of a single minister, preferably himself. De Gaulle gave him a new, high-sounding title—minister of the national economy (MEN)—but not the concentration of actual powers that the MEN sought; as a practical matter the finance minister held the stronger hand. De Gaulle's appointee to that post, Aimé Lepercq, admired Mendès France and gave him wide latitude, while Lepercq himself concentrated on the GPRF's "Liberation Loan," whose bond sales were meant to absorb some of the excess currency tucked away in bank accounts and strong boxes. While on the road to promote the loan, however, Lepercq died in an automobile crash on November 9. De Gaulle replaced him with the Breton businessman René Pleven, one of the general's closest associates in Free France.[22]

The more "liberal" Pleven resisted Mendès France's draconian calls for the forced replacement of banknotes and the freezing of bank accounts, and he criticized the timetable and modalities for the first nationalizations proposed by the MEN.[23] For a while the wrangling between the two occurred behind the scenes, but it eventually leeched into public view as the press reported on a private meeting with de Gaulle lasting over four hours where the two ministers argued it out. But those accounts did not explain that Pleven made a succinct presentation of about half an hour, while the MEN expatiated didactically for three hours to the increasingly numbed general.[24] Pleven's cautious position meshed better with de Gaulle's political instincts and his indifference to technical details. For the moment, however, de Gaulle brokered a face-saving compromise, and Mendès France withdrew the second letter of resignation he had offered.

Mendès France remained the government's public spokesman on economic issues by way of his weekly radio broadcasts between November 11, 1944 and March 31, 1945—part basic economics, part moral exhortation. After the extreme privations endured under the occupation, it was asking a lot for citizens to accept further austerities, yet Mendès France insisted that "it is imperative to accept sacrifices on consumption" and that producers must accept price controls over their goods even if they see their own costs rising. Ever-rising prices would at the least devastate the mass of people with limited or fixed incomes.[25]

After the economic damage from the occupation, France confronted earlier than Britain and the US what Mendès France called (as would Morrison and Cripps in Britain and Chester Bowles in the US) "the infernal cycle where prices and wages chase each other without ever linking up. . . . Controlling prices is the dam, the blow that will halt the infernal cycle." Farmers certainly needed better prices for their products but could attain them, the MEN claimed, without raising retail prices for consumers. How could this alchemy be accomplished? "Thanks to a compression of intermediary costs . . . which weigh on prices between production and consumption." Increased prices for farmers who raise beef, pork, or lamb, for example, did not have to be passed through to consumer if wholesale butchering and other meat distribution costs could be streamlined. Everyone could contribute to this battle by increased productivity, for which he specifically praised coal miners, railroad workers, stevedores, and metal workers. And with the pathetically low bread ration of 350 grams daily, farmers must on no account withhold their grain crops in prospect of higher prices. Above all, the black market of "profiteers and parasites" must not be allowed to dominate the economy. Since consumption demands far exceed supplies, the gap must be bridged by rationing and obligatory savings. Public sector employees, for example, had just won much deserved raises, but the higher tiers had to participate in a mandatory savings scheme (carnet de pecule). To be sure, he admitted, regulation does not create goods; "it [only] promotes equity, it equalizes." The denunciations of regulation that flowed into his ministry were misguided, he insisted; they resembled a man who broke his leg blaming his crutches for his troubles.

Mendès France consistently presented problems of economic recovery as moral-civic challenges, matters of social justice and solidarity, as well as economic imperatives. In his final broadcast on March 31 he dwelled again on the supreme danger of a wage-price inflationary spiral in view of promised wage increases and relentless pressure from the black market, which drove goods out of the regulated, open market. He seized a final chance to sermonize on the social and moral dimensions of France's predicament: "The fewer the goods that are available in the normal marketplace . . . the more the privilege of the rich is confirmed and the condition of the poor, of workers deteriorates." Inflation does not create wealth but only shifts the distribution in favor of "the egoists, the parvenus, the selfish. . . . Inflation is the triumph of immorality and social iniquity." The temptation to extract higher wages from higher prices and vice versa will lead France into a crisis "from which we can only exit materially weakened and morally degraded."[26]

Mendès France lost most of the policy arguments over economic and monetary issues with the more flexible Pleven and other critics, including some on the Left wary of alienating future voters among workers, farmers, or retailers with overly rigorous wage or price controls. While ever the trained economist, Mendès France remained an austere, progressive, and politically lonely moralist, who cast his technical arguments against inflation and laissez-faire in terms of equity. His draconian deflationist approach to monetary policy, his fury at the black market, and his defenses of rationing were driven in the first instance by his assessment of sheer economic necessity. But they spoke as well to a vision of social solidarity linked to the spirit of moral responsibility and sacrifice that had animated the Resistance. This moral high ground availed little against the political backdrafts to his prescriptions from various economic liberals, socialists, and communists or against the technical objections of even sympathetic economists at the time.[27] Yet the consensus among later economists and biographers seems to be that the nation's chance of effectively checking the "infernal" wage-price spiral evaporated when Mendès France left the GPRF in April 1945, and it would haunt his successors for the next three years.[28]

The Regrouping of Political Forces: The Consultative Assembly

To help build a political foundation under Free France, de Gaulle's French National Committee had created a provisional Consultative Assembly, which convened in Algiers in September 1943 "to furnish as broad as possible an expression of national public opinion." Of the 102 members recruited, almost half were men linked in some fashion to the Resistance, and 20 were ex-parliamentary no-voters against plenary powers for Pétain. Their presence in Algiers, like the

CNR in Paris, contributed to the aura of legitimacy that de Gaulle was creating around himself despite the skeptics. Conjoining men of varied political backgrounds and experience (who elected socialist Felix Gouin as their president) the Consultative Assembly had no actual powers. Although purely advisory, it usefully debated policy issues that loomed over the coming liberation. The body did much of its work in committees and generally avoided sharp partisan controversy; it occasionally nettled de Gaulle but he almost always had the last word.

In October 1944 the GPRF moved the Consultative Assembly from Algiers to Paris, where it would meet in the Luxembourg Palace that formerly housed the Third Republic's Senate. In the heady atmosphere of the Liberation the Assembly's presence in Paris initially seemed of little to no importance. As a British Embassy observer recalled, the members had taken no active part in the Parisian uprising or the lethal fighting in the provinces and could claim none of the Liberation's glory; "they returned to their country almost as exiles."[29] But the GPRF expanded the Consultative Assembly's membership from 102 to 248 to give it an infusion of relevance. The enlargement could be counted as a small gesture toward the restoration of democracy short of an election precluded by the chaos of the moment. Internal Resistance organizations would hold 148 seats in the body, and the cohort of no-voting ex-parliamentarians would expand from 20 to 60. Although the Consultative Assembly was unelected and lacked any legislative powers, de Gaulle now tasked it with examining the budgets of his GPRF's ministries.

De Gaulle named the 16 current members of the CNR as members of the Assembly, intending this to undercut the CNR's independent existence. The six "political families" that Jean Moulin incorporated into the CNR had additional representatives in the Assembly, as did the trade union federations that reemerged from clandestinity. Among the Resistance movements, the Front National got 12 seats, the seven other movements in the CNR 6 members each, and 1 to 3 seats went to several smaller Resistance groups. The executive committees of all those organizations were to appoint their delegates.[30]

To oversee the enlargement of the ex-parliamentary group, de Gaulle tapped Jules Jeanneney, already serving the GPRF as minister of state without portfolio. A venerable figure in the Third Republic and president of its Senate, Jeanneney had abstained from the 1940 vote on Pétain and had then maintained an aloof but legalistic stance toward Vichy. He finally rallied to Free France in August 1942 when Laval scrapped the last fig leaf of accommodation for the defunct parliament by abolishing its administrative office.[31] The designation of Jeanneney served de Gaulle's desire to link his authority with pre-Vichy republicanism despite the general's scorn for the Third Republic's record. Jeanneney also exemplified de Gaulle's mythic yet shrewd pretense that the majority of French citizens had opposed the Nazi occupation and the Vichy usurpation.

The Regrouping of Political Forces: Communists and Socialists

In late 1944, the regrouping of political forces began in earnest despite the overwhelming material hardships of the French people, the ongoing prosecution of the war, and uncertainty over when elections could finally be held. The state of play initially centered around the two old parties of the Left and the two largest Resistance organizations—the Mouvement de Libération Nationale (MLN) and the Front National (FN). By year's end a fifth contender burst on the scene and altered it dramatically, when social-Catholic *résistants* organized a new political party called the Mouvement Républicain Populaire (Popular Republican Movement, or MRP).

Communist militants stood in the front ranks of the armed struggles in France, especially in the Paris uprising of August, but their intentions for the post-Liberation future seemed uncertain. By October many organized units of the FFI were being incorporated into the Free French army, but no control existed over local paramilitary units known as patriotic militias, which had formed in the spring of 1944 as back up forces and generally operated as adjuncts of local liberation committees. In tandem, liberation committees and patriotic militias constituted a potential base independent of GPRF officials. On October 27 communist leader Jacques Duclos hailed the patriotic militias at a public meeting, but the next day de Gaulle signed an ordinance (countersigned by his socialist minister of the interior Tixier) ordering those forces to disarm and effectively dissolving them. This move outraged the communists (among others), but in the end the PCF political bureau accepted the policy and thereby laid to rest any notion that communists might mount an armed challenge to the GPRF. In a quid pro quo of sorts de Gaulle authorized the return from Moscow of PCF general secretary Maurice Thorez, previously considered by Vichites and Gaullists alike as a military deserter in 1939.[32]

In effect the communists renewed their Popular Front posture of 1936, except that they now seemed to hold the leading position based on their resistance record after June 1941; the role of the Soviet Union in vanquishing the Nazis; and communist influence in a trade union movement growing explosively after the Liberation.[33] The communists at first waltzed gently with rivals in the CGT and with the SFIO. On the momentum of Resistance solidarity, both parties even talked publicly about seizing the moment to undo the schism of 1920 at Tours. With an armed seizure of power by the communists off the table, and an unspecified degree of cooperation with other political forces possible, the battle for public opinion and future electoral influence began.

But how far could trust and cooperation between socialists and communists actually go, beyond rhetorical or tactical gestures by both sides? This question hung over the entire postwar moment, but an answer implicitly lay near the surface. For the communists held to an abiding assumption that their party was the only authentic voice of the working class and constituted its political surrogate. Certain fellow-traveling intellectuals and labor leaders (such as CNR president Louis Saillant) seemed to accept this assumption and therefore refused to do ideological battle with the communists. Others, receptive to working with communists up to a point, rejected that assumption and its implications.

Their dilemma is hauntingly conveyed in the memoirs of Claude Bourdet, a non-communist, leftist leader of Combat and its representative on the CNR in 1943. Bourdet recalled an extremely candid conversation in the autumn of 1943 (before he was apprehended and deported to an SS concentration camp) with his respected communist comrade Pierre Villon, a member of CNR bureau and a director of the Front National. Villon's words were so striking that Bourdet could convincingly recall them years later.

> For us, [Villon told him] the Communist Party is not just some party of the left, it is the party of the working class, it is the political expression of the working class, it is that class in political form. There cannot be any question of another party of the working class. That would be illogical, and it would only serve to divide the popular forces confronted by the bourgeoisie. Alongside the communist party, there can only be large formations that do not have a veritable driving role, or to put it another way, formations representing other social groups with which, in effect, the working class may ally itself to win the battle: the middle classes, certain intellectuals, etc. Your future party can represent that [alliance], but it must choose that position knowingly [*franchement*], or else we will not be able to accept it and will combat you.

That thesis, Bourdet commented, "determined the attitude of the communists without being formulated overtly, lest it arouse indignation among their allies, especially the socialists." To Bourdet, this theory of the *parti unique* rested on a misguided military analogy that required unity of command, reinforced by Marxist dogma about class struggle. Worst of all it implied that "all political pluralism, when it is a question of representing the interests of a class, can only be an aberration or a mere maneuver." Bourdet himself was leery of all the old parties and their dogmas, but he remained *socialisante* (of socialistic bent) and favored a reliance on *experimentation,* as he italicized it.[34]

In the short term the PCF's chief tactical priority was forging joint Resistance lists of candidates for the coming local elections, an idea with wide appeal outside the party's ranks as well. As the fellow-traveling editor of *Front National* (Jacques Debû-Bridel) put it: "To oblige voters to decide on one or another [Resistance] group . . . will mean that rival candidates will again be forced to use all the old apparatus of political quarrels. Free rein will then be given to bluff, demagogic biddings-up, and solicitations by political barkers."[35]

The SFIO began its comeback with a National Congress in November 1944 that carried out a rigorous purge of its own parliamentary veterans. The congress banned and expelled 84 of the 90 socialist deputies and senators (the solid majority of their delegations in July 1940) who had voted plenary powers for Pétain.[36] Other questions facing the SFIO proved more challenging. Initially the Resistance spirit of brotherhood washed over the congress. With seeming goodwill the party's new secretary general Daniel Mayer, along with other Blum allies like Vincent Auriol and Jules Moch, extended their hands to Christians and communists. With the proviso that Catholic comrades of the Resistance accept the secular character of the state's schools, socialists looked forward to a future alliance where "the nobility of the revolutionary tradition joins with the nobility of the Christian tradition." Mayer also made "a solemn offer in good faith of sincere friendship, alliance, and union . . . to the PCF, which no longer questions the duty of national defense or the principles of democracy, the reasons for the split at Tours in 1920."[37]

The congress proposed a *comité d'entente* (cooperation committee) with the PCF, and the PCF political bureau agreed. The committee did most of its work in a subcommittee on "unity of action," but another on "organic unity" never got off the ground. Activists in each party generated position papers and public statements that revealed the ambivalence on both sides of the divide, but discussions on unity of action continued for many months.[38] Some socialist militants truly hoped to effect a merger with the PCF that would undo the schism at Tours. The majority of socialists, however, saw their party as historic rivals of the communists for the support of workers and republicans of all stripes. Thus the socialist congress of 1944 rejected the idea of single lists in the first rounds of local elections but accepted the prospect of coalitions in second-round runoffs "to defeat reaction and ensure the success of the Resistance." By the next socialist congress in August 1945, distrust of the communists had hardened. The SFIO definitively buried the possibility of a fusion with the PCF by a vote of 10,000 mandates against the idea versus 270 in favor, without excluding the possibility of cooperation.[39]

The Future of the Resistance

Now that France had been liberated, the Resistance movements struggled to define their future. Socialist Adrien Tixier, de Gaulle's minister of the interior, for example, urged the movements not to vie directly for office in the coming elections but rather to serve as "a leaven and a watchdog." Even Combat and Franc-Tireur seemed to reduce their expectations. As the latter acknowledged: "Although it is impossible to rule in opposition to the Resistance, it may be possible to rule without it." One obvious impediment to future political influence for the Resistance movements lay in their inability to unite effectively. Relations between the two largest organizations, the MLN and the Front National, were especially problematic.

The MLN had its roots in 1943 when, under Jean Moulin's prodding, the three southern movements—Combat, Libération, and Franc-Tireur—agreed to coordinate their clandestine activities, while maintaining their own newspapers and cadres and, in due course, their own representatives on the CNR. In 1944 the troika invited four smaller groups not represented on the CNR to join their ranks and renamed their federation the MLN. At the MLN's first National Congress in January 1945 the keynote speech by André Malraux, a non-party man of the Left and an FFI brigade commander, set the tone in exhorting the delegates to "a fresh mobilization of French energy . . . [to build] a real democracy and an effective socialism." Competing programs originating in Paris and Lyon vied to put flesh on those bones, but the activists had not resolved two basic questions. Should the MLN remain a federation of autonomous Resistance organizations or should it promote a genuine fusion that effaced those separate identities? And how should the MLN deal with the broad-based but communist-dominated Front National, which the MLN had so far kept at arm's length? Some delegates opposed that separation as self-defeating for the postwar aspirations of the Resistance. But Malraux, Frenay, and certain other MLN notables argued against any merger with the FN and warned against an "inferiority complex" in the face of the FN's disciplined communist cadres.[40]

The Front National had been founded by communists immediately after the Nazi invasion of the Soviet Union in 1941. Effectively led by Pierre Villon, the FN promoted a single-minded dedication to Resistance unity, and it drew adherents from across the historic divides in France between secularists and Christians, Marxists and anti-Marxists. The FN's effective organizing and uncompromising propaganda created an appealing umbrella movement under the conditions of the occupation. The successive heads of the CNR after Moulin, social-Catholic Bidault and the CGT's clandestine operative Saillant, both joined the FN in 1943 as did conservatives like Joseph Laniel. The FN's marquee names (revealed after the Liberation) included several well-known priests, Catholic laymen like François Mauriac, and the veteran Radical Justin Godart, alongside communists and fellow travelers like the scientist Joliot-Curie and the poet Louis Aragon. When Saillant replaced Bidault as head of the CNR in September 1944 he projected the FN's mantra of unity into the post-Liberation. In a standard speech (this version on October 14) Saillant evoked the unprecedented unity of spirit at the core of the Resistance, which brought together "adherents of the Christian concept and devotees of materialist socialism." Such people, Saillant declared, "never had met except to clash and then part back to back. [But] in the shadows of underground France they found each other."[41] For all its sentimental hyperbole, this image of unprecedented cooperation was reasonably accurate for the years of the occupation.

At the FN's first National Congress (January 30–February 2, 1945), where 1,800 delegates represented a claimed membership of two million, the rhetoric of Resistance unity suffused the proceedings. Villon himself personified the PCF's shift of late October away from any challenge to the GPRF that might have dashed such unity. As a member of the CNR's military committee he had initially resisted the blanket incorporation of FFI units into the Free French army and had been faced down by de Gaulle himself on that issue.[42] Like the PCF in general by late 1944, Villon ceased his defiant gestures and pivoted into staunch support for the GPRF. A huge banner across the stage at the congress affirmed the priority shared by de Gaulle and the FN: "Everything for the war / to hasten victory." The congress avoided divisive issues; speakers emphasized local efforts to deal with food shortages and relief for the neediest citizens and downplayed criticisms of the purge common in the Resistance press. Neither de Gaulle, nor even the so-called Palewski cabal of right-wingers around him, came in for criticism.[43]

The FN aggressively recruited new members after the Liberation, including blocs of trade unionists; at the close of its congress the FN set a target of doubling its membership to four million. The MLN found this post-Liberation recruiting to be indiscriminate, opportunistic, and highly suspect, which made the prospect of uniting with the FN all the more problematic. The FN responded that the MLN was being sectarian and exclusivist, and defended its membership drive as consistent with the ideals of national unity and postwar renewal. But the decisive barrier to any merger remained the domination of the FN by the communists. So when the FN broached the idea of a fusion with the MLN into a "grand movement of the Resistance . . . a vast unified organization," the majority of delegates to the MLN congress had responded with a "visceral anti-communism" (in Villon's words) and spurned the approach by a vote of 250 to 119.[44] Instead the MLN would explore such options as a union with the socialists (a *rassemblement travailliste* in the spirit of the British Labour Party) or alliances with other Resistance movements groping to chart their own futures.

Two of those movements had originated in the occupied Northern zone and were now considering a merger despite their differing provenance and coloration. Libération-Nord had been organized by socialist and trade union activists, while the OCM was led by conservative patriots, some of whom had injected a tinge of Vichy-style anti-Semitic sentiment into their earliest proclamations. But by early 1944 both groups strongly supported the social democracy of the CNR Common Program, and some activists now hoped to federate as a *Union Travailliste*—yet another wistful tribute in post-Liberation France to the inspiration of the British Labour Party. A third Northern movement called Ceux de la Résistance held a National Congress in Paris on December 21–22, 1944, where it claimed to have over 100,000 members, including 20,000 men of the FFI now incorporated into the Free French army. Its dilemma: should it seek closer ties with the MLN or push for a broader Resistance front that included the FN? In the end the congress could reach no consensus.[45]

The MLN had rejected a merger with the FN at its January 1945 congress, and in June the MLN's executive committee voted 26 to 15 to explore federation with any Resistance movement *other* than the FN. At this point the minority faction in the MLN walked out, protesting that this decision only encouraged reaction. Ready to join forces with the FN, however, the bolters found that the FN was on the verge of dissolving itself, having lost its non-communist members, who by now saw the FN as simply a front for the soft power of communism. Rebranding itself as a new *Rassemblement de la Résistance,* the remnant of the FN focused on mobilizing for the future national election.[46]

The schism in the MLN soon resulted in the formation of two new but narrowly based political parties, each appropriating the mantle of the Resistance even while abandoning the core notion of a grand, unified movement of renewal. Some adherents of the anti-communist MLN majority created the UDSR (Democratic and Social Union of the Resistance), an opportunistic coalition of Resistance notables such as Frenay, Capitant, Pleven, and Mitterand. These individuals would eventually go off in various directions, but initially the UDSR allied itself with the Socialist Party.[47] Meanwhile the fellow-traveling activists of the minority MLN faction formed the MURF (Unified Movement of the French Renaissance), which immediately became a satellite of the PCF.

Notwithstanding its solid support for the GPRF while the war still raged, the FN advocated a continuing role for the liberation committees on the grounds that they were representative of local opinion and attuned to local needs. It also supported an initiative by the CNR to convene a National Congress of departmental liberation committees, which met in Paris in December 1944. The 250 delegates may well have wondered what their roles might be after the local elections expected that spring, but in concert with the CNR, the FN, and the PCF, they endorsed the convocation of an "Estates General of the French Renaissance" in Paris on July 14, 1945, entirely independent of the GPRF. Delegates would be selected in meetings of local liberation committees, Resistance movements, and trade unions, which would presumably channel ground-level enthusiasm into a great national conclave in the capital. As the FN newspaper in the Nord department put it, "Like those of '89, the Estates General will build the new France."[48]

The Estates General of the French Renaissance convened on July 14 in the Palais de Chaillot with 2,100 delegates, chaired by the ubiquitous Louis Saillant.

After the opening speeches the Estates divided into policy commissions and subcommittees, which produced a spate of position papers for future reference or, as happened, neglect.[49] When the conclave reconvened in plenary session it adopted resounding motions about the rights of man and citizen, economic and social democracy, and an apt pledge "to remain true to the ideal for which men, fighting for freedom, gave their lives." In a prospective conflict with de Gaulle, the plenary demanded that the future National Assembly "select and control the responsible government" to foreclose the possibility of a strong independent executive. The Estates General had no official standing when it began or when it ended. Despite a great deal of earnest effort, it was essentially stillborn. Coincidentally, the Consultative Assembly was about to dissolve as well after some bitter exchanges with de Gaulle about the national election being planned by the GPRF.[50]

The Birth of the MRP

The great success story of the Resistance impetus after the Liberation came from an unexpected direction when prominent social-Catholic *résistants* launched a new political party called the MRP in November 1944. In the interwar years, social-Catholic activism in France had spread through a variety of political and cultural organizations. These included an energetic youth movement; a thinly rooted political party (the PDF), which never elected more than twenty deputies; the civic movement called Jeune République; *L'Aube,* a newspaper founded by Francisque Gay that peaked at about 15,000 subscribers but created a stir when it attacked the Munich pact; and a Christian trade union federation (the CFTC) that inscribed fewer than 10 percent of unionized workers. Altogether, the social-Catholic presence in interwar France was far from negligible, but it did not achieve a substantial national impact. The traditionalist clergy and laity on the Right, secular republicans of the center, and the Marxist Left all kept their distance from the social-Catholics and the distrust was doubtless mutual for the most part.[51]

The occupation revealed the mettle and intensity of certain social-Catholic stalwarts and aroused new cohorts of activists. The ones who emerged with a degree of prominence from the Resistance got there by various routes, some flagged earlier in chapter 2. The anti-Munich journalist Maurice Schumann rallied immediately to de Gaulle in London and became an official radio voice

of Free France. Law professor Pierre-Henri Teitgen became a regional organizer for Combat, and with his fellow professor François de Menthon he
was coopted into Free France's select underground study group for postwar
planning. De Menthon eventually joined de Gaulle's inner circle in Algiers,
while Teitgen remained in France and barely escaped deportation. The social-
Catholics had their outright martyrs (like the youth activist Gilbert Dru,
executed by the Gestapo in Lyon in July 1944), their deportees to Nazi concentration camps (like Edmond Michelet, another regional organizer for Combat,
and Louis Terrenoire), and clandestine operatives (like Bidault, who survived
the Vichy/Nazi repression and who, with communist endorsement, succeeded
the martyred Moulin as president of the CNR).

Social-Catholics did not form any large-scale civil or military resistance movements of their own, and like socialists they joined organized movements in their
areas. But small local networks of activists were coalescing by 1943 in such
places as Lyon and the Nord/Pas-de-Calais region, drawing on cadres from the
Catholic youth movement or former CFTC activists. During the Paris uprising in
August 1944 a small social-Catholic group leafleted the capital to exhort Parisians
to action and to set out their distinctive credo: respect for the family, for individual dignity, and for liberty, alongside the common Resistance demands for
social and economic justice. "We must break free of the capitalist system," their
handbill demanded, "and bring to an end the all-powerful reign of King Money."[52]
Writing to Bidault in April 1944 from his vantage point in Algiers, de Menthon
shrewdly had assessed the prospects of social-Catholics. He had helped convince
de Gaulle to incorporate communists into the future provisional government
despite the risks, de Menthon explained, since that was "the sine qua non of a real
revival." Meanwhile, "the weakness of the Socialists and the Radicals as political
forces is evident. . . . Our side carries a considerable weight in opinion. . . . You
know, in reality, how few in number we are and how little [political] experience
we possess. . . . [But] circumstances have never been so favorable for us."[53]

At the critical juncture of late 1944, such men broke free from the dream of a
grand post-Liberation political movement emanating from the Resistance, but
they also spurned the idea of simply resurrecting their prewar organizations. Led
by Bidault, de Menthon, and Teitgen (all newly minted ministers in de Gaulle's
provisional unity cabinet) along with Schumann, trade unionist Paul Bacon,
and youth leader André Colin, among others, they steered a promising course
between political fantasy and business as usual. Far more effectively than the

Front National, the Estates General of 1945, or the MLN and its schismatic offshoots, the MRP carried the Resistance ideal of a new start into the political arena of the postwar moment. As one electoral poster would put it: "Created in secrecy in order to reestablish the Republic and reconstruct France according to the basic principles of the Resistance, the MRP presents itself to you."[54] In 1946 the party's executive committee would remind its adherents: "We should not allow the genesis of the MRP to be explained solely by reference to '50 years of social Catholicism.' Without the Resistance there would be no MRP."[55]

In the new party's manifestos, long-held social-Catholic beliefs about liberty, individual dignity, and the primacy of the family now meshed with pervasive Resistance demands for moral renewal, real democracy, social justice, and economic reform. As Teitgen recalled, it was not religious faith but Christian values that animated the nascent party. In its coming glory days, he believed, a third of its adherents were not practicing Catholics at all.[56] Above all, the Common Program of the CNR constituted a political lodestar for the MRP, a new party with old principles but little doctrinal or strategic heritage to build on. Though it was not central to de Gaulle's conception or practice of leadership, the CNR Common Program already functioned as a cement for his unity government, which ranged across the political spectrum from the center to the far Left, and would remain an anchor for the successor governments of 1946–47. Both before and after de Gaulle's departure in January 1946 the MRP's role in maintaining a progressive center of gravity was critical.

In contrast to the floundering MLN and FN, the MRP fashioned itself four-square as a political party and embarked on a precociously successful enterprise of party-building from the top down and from the bottom up. Between its founding in November 1944 and the election for a Constituent Assembly in October 1945, the MRP organized 87 departmental federations comprising 1,280 local sections with 235,000 members, of whom it reckoned that about 10,000 could be described as militants.[57] Like the British Labour Party and the SFIO, the MRP had three centers of power atop its local federations: its parliamentary deputation (once elections had occurred); the annual party congress (where floor debate and voting could not always be scripted), which elected an executive committee to steer the party between those congresses; and the permanent headquarters staff in Paris. In its early years, central headquarters energetically organized study groups; departments for youth, for rural members, and for women; a press relations bureau; and a propaganda bureau. The latter issued one mimeographed bulletin for local party officials and another for activists, to explain issues under debate and decisions taken by the leadership. The party naturally got off to a shaky start in the early local elections of 1945 but did supremely well in the ensuing national elections. Initially it emphasized its loyalty to de Gaulle. After his departure the MRP soldiered on without him and then, as we shall see, despite him.[58]

Elections and More Elections

Citizens (including women for the first time) went to the polls repeatedly in 1945–46 for a variety of elections and referenda, all in the cause of reestablishing republican democracy. Even before V-E Day, municipal elections began on April 29, 1945, to replace unelected local officials from the Vichy or Liberation periods in town halls. From the largest cities to the smallest rural communes, voters elected municipal councils. About 80 percent of France's 36,000 communes had populations under 1,500, and in most of those rural places citizens opted for the comfort of familiarity and tended to vote for veteran local figures even if their behavior during the occupation had been equivocal.[59]

Le Monde tried to evaluate these unwieldy results, despite the fluidity of political labels in 1945 and the huge variations in municipal populations. Its tally indicated that the PCF more than quadrupled its control of municipal councils compared to 1935, while the SFIO more than tripled its majorities. Yet together they now controlled only about 5,500 communes. Conversely the Radical Party, which had dominated over 9,000 councils in 1935, lost more than 2,500 of them, while the conservatives (mainly the Fédération Républicaine and the Alliance Démocratique), who controlled roughly 22,700 municipal councils before the war, won majorities in 1945 in about 15,000. The newspaper concluded that even these relatively parochial elections "confirmed the defeat of Vichyism and the trend toward the left, though the latter trend was far less marked in rural communes than in cities."[60]

Paris and its suburbs, at any rate, exemplified that trend. In the capital, balloting involved proportional representation for the 90 seats on the municipal council, 9 of which now went to women. The communists won 27 (up from 8 in 1935); the MRP 13; the Republican Federation 13; the Socialists 12; "Resistance" candidates 8; the Radicals 6; the Democratic Alliance (which led with 20 seats in 1935) only 4; "others" 7. And in the suburbs of Paris communist-led slates under the banner of the "Union Patriotique Résistante et Antifasciste" carried 60 of the 80 municipalities, while conservatives (who controlled 34 of those councils in 1935) won only 3.[61]

The next round of voting came at the end of September 1945: the two-round cantonal elections to choose members of the general administrative councils for each of the nation's 90 metropolitan departments. The departmental councils loomed large in the political culture of the Third Republic, and Vichy had dissolved them. During the occupation the idea was floated in the corridors of Free France to reconvene the prewar general councils immediately after the Liberation as a first step toward reestablishing republican legality, but de Gaulle opted for new elections. The voice of local interests par excellence, the councils gave disproportionate weight to the rural cantons, and reflected the sway of local personalities, including members of the Third Republic's indirectly elected Senate.

With a total of 3,006 general council seats up for decision in the cantons nationwide, the victors came from across the spectrum of parties and ad hoc alliances. Socialists could claim the most seats, but there was no decisive political trend. In combination the socialist and communist Left more than doubled their seats on the general councils compared to their prewar numbers, while the prewar Right lost roughly half of its former seats, but a good number of "moderate" (i.e., conservative) candidates still won election.[62]

These first two rounds of elections in effect picked up from where Vichy had scrapped republican institutions in 1940 and through their familiar templates restored republican legality locally. But neither de Gaulle nor other elements of the Resistance desired a simple revival of Third Republic institutions on the national level. A return to democracy and republicanism?—without question; a reversion to the Third Republic's procedures for national elections and parliamentary governance?—to be avoided. But what would take their place? How could a new system be legitimately established? And after that, how would the habits of Third Republic political behavior and Resistance-inspired impulses for change play out on a national scale?

From Provisional Rule to Democracy

In July 1945 de Gaulle brought before his cabinet the issue of a new constitutional order. After the fall of France he had heaped scorn on the sterile partisanship of the Third Republic's parliamentary regime, and he continued to portray it as impotent and unstable, as "divided and enfeebled by intrigue, invective and the exploitation of discontent." He had no wish at all to revive its parliamentary system, which would have been easy enough to do: simply hold elections for a new Chamber of Deputies and Senate. De Gaulle and most Resistance veterans instead wished to call an election for a Constituent Assembly that would draft a new constitution and serve in the interim as the nation's legislature. In de Gaulle's enigmatic formula, he and the French people "desired something new and something reasonable."[63] "Reasonable" signified that in starting over the general did not wish to empower an entirely uncon-strained or "sovereign" Constituent Assembly; he did not want that Assembly to be all-powerful either in its interim governmental functions or in its constitution-making. Once the Assembly named a provisional head of state, he and his cabinet should be as independent as possible. Nor did de Gaulle wish the Constituent Assembly to be entirely sovereign in fashioning the new consti-tution: he wanted a time limit on its deliberative life, and he wanted its consti-tutional draft submitted to a national referendum for approval or rejection. In one of its last and liveliest debates the Consultative Assembly greeted the GPRF's proposals uneasily. The communists found allies among other members suspicious of de Gaulle's agenda and argued that "the executive power must necessarily be subordinate to the elected legislature." As a British observer wrote: "Though the debate was confused and the outcome inconclusive . . . the delegates seemed sincerely to feel that they were performing a national duty by combatting an attempt at the seizure of personal power [by de Gaulle]."[64]

De Gaulle decided to resolve these foundational issues in a preliminary refer-endum, despite the objections of the Radicals who historically opposed the resort to referenda because the two Napoleons had buried republicanism twice with abusive plebiscites. The GPRF authorized a preliminary referendum along with the simultaneous election of an Assembly. On October 21, 1945, French citizens would face two referendum questions and a ballot for the election of representa-tives. The first question asked: "Do you wish the Assembly that we elect today to be a Constituent Assembly?" A yes vote would definitively inter the old repub-lican "constitution" (i.e., the organic laws) of 1875. The second question asked: "If the electorate has answered yes to the first question, do you agree that the public powers—until the implementation of the new Constitution—shall be organized according to the *projet de loi* appended to the back of this ballot?" The latter stipulated a duration of seven months for the Constituent Assembly; the submission of its constitutional draft to the voters in a referendum; and an interim government whose acting president the Assembly would name but who would then be more independent than a Third Republic prime minister, since a vote of no confidence would be very difficult to bring about. A yes vote on the second question would signify an acceptance of de Gaulle's blueprint, while a no vote would mean that the Constituent Assembly (as approved on the first ballot question) would be unconstrained or fully "sovereign" in both its roles.[65]

With these choices looming, the political parties adopted a spectrum of positions on the two ballot questions:

YES/YES: Supported by the SFIO; its allies in the new UDSR; centrists in the CGT; and the MRP. Non-communist progressives wanted a new start and accepted de Gaulle's blueprint for the Constituent Assembly.

YES/NO: Advocated by the PCF and the dominant element of the CGT. Communists and fellow travelers wanted a new start, of course, but vigorously campaigned for a fully "sovereign" Constituent Assembly.

NO/YES: Most Rightist groups on the scene, notably the ad hoc alliance of the moment known as the *Entente Républicaine*.[66] Conservatives were comfortable with the old Third Republic. But if the voters opted for a new start, they wanted the restraints on the Constituent Assembly established by the second proposal.

NO/NO: Some prominent Radicals, as doctrinaire in their way as the communists, stuck by their investment in the Third Republic and a "sovereign" Assembly.[67]

When the ballots were tallied (after an impressive turnout of over 75 percent of eligible voters), the proposal for a Constituent Assembly carried with an overwhelming vote of 96.4 percent, while de Gaulle's proposals to limit its sovereignty carried by a vote of 66.3 percent. The opposition of communists and their allies on the second question had a noticeable impact but was easily offset by the tacit alliance of de Gaulle's partisans, the socialists, and the MRP. In the process the Radicals suffered a crushing repudiation, and conservative voices were marginalized as well. The simultaneous election of a Constituent Assembly produced a parallel outcome with a somewhat different valence.

Before that balloting, however, a serious conflict had erupted over the procedure for electing representatives. The three major parties (PCF, SFIO, MRP) approved de Gaulle's notion that proportional representation should replace the two-round, single-constituency system used for electing the Chamber of Deputies during the Third Republic (with two brief exceptions)—a single-constituency system congenial to conservatives of various stripes and to the Radicals. The three parties also agreed that departmental party slates rather than national slates should be the vehicle for proportional representation. The conflict arose over several details, especially the proposed apportionment of seats, which favored less populous, rural departments at the expense of large urban areas, to which the Left vehemently objected.[68]

After a flurry of threats to scuttle the whole process, the Left backed down and de Gaulle had his way, apart from the minor concession of adding 16 extra seats for the urbanized departments without reducing the overrepresentation of rural ones. Other details of the electoral ordinance provided that the most populous departments would be subdivided into *arrondissements* for the balloting; that party slates had to include a list of candidates equal to the number of allotted seats (a difficult task for the disorganized party remnants on the Right); and, as in Britain, that parties had to pay a security bond, nonrefundable if their slate won less than 5 percent of the departmental vote.[69]

The outcome of the national election had no precedent. The three major parties, all to the left side of the normal political spectrum in France, swept the field with about 75 percent of the total vote. Each drew between 4.5 and 5 million votes across the nation and won roughly similar numbers of the 522 seats for Metropolitan France in the Assembly:

Communists and MURF allies	148 (142 + 6)
Socialists and UDSR allies	143 (133 + 10)
MRP	143
Radical Party	19
Parties of the Right and others	69

Results for the 64 seats from the overseas territories (including 26 for Algeria) trickled in later and did not substantially alter the outcome; about half the overseas representatives were either socialists or UDSR.[70]

The wipeout of the Radicals, traditionally an anchor party for centrist republican coalitions, was stunning considering that they managed to field slates in almost all departments. The conservatives of the Right (often called "moderates" in French nomenclature) were so fragmented, and their improvised alliances so shaky, that they had trouble fielding full slates and were overwhelmed in the final results as well.[71] Thanks in good part to the *épuration,* which had rendered so many of the parliamentarians of 1940 ineligible, only 117 representatives elected in 1945 had served in a prewar parliament, while 85 had been members of de Gaulle's Consultative Assembly. All the ministers but one in de Gaulle's provisional government who stood for election to the Assembly won, while only a handful of well-known personalities were defeated, including Daladier and Mendès France, among the Radicals, and two independent left-wing Resistance figures, Claude Bourdet and Yves Farge.[72]

The MRP had the most remarkable success, with results exceeding the party's rosiest expectations of winning about 100 seats. Its spectacularly large deputation was collectively new to national politics and young. Only 11 had sat in a previous parliament, and 90 of the MRP deputies were forty-five years of age or younger. Unusually diverse in their social profile as well, they included 21 farmers, 21 blue- and white-collar workers, 18 teachers, 16 businessmen, and 15 doctors, but only 17 lawyers. Though the MRP's female candidates were generally listed well down in the "sacrificial portion" of departmental slates, a surprising total of 9 women won election.[73]

No doubt the MRP's meteoric victory reflected the unique alignment of the political stars at that juncture: the breakdown of the leading prewar conservative parties under the taint of Vichy and the exclusions of the *épuration;* the prestige of the MRP's best-known Resistance figures; its slogan as the *parti de fidelité* to de Gaulle (and of being the general's implicit party of choice without his ever saying so). No question that the MRP helped fill a temporary vacuum in French politics, as it drew "moderates" among first-time voters (women and young men) as well as many prewar voters ordinarily at home somewhere toward the Right.

During the campaign the Communists sought to isolate the MRP with such wedge issues as their desire for state aid to Catholic schools, and denigrated them with a cascade of mud. Posters and hecklers across the country traduced the MRP with its own initials as a "Machine à Ramasser les Pétainistes" and as a party of "Mensonge, Réaction, Perfidie."[74] But as the British Embassy astutely reported, the PCF assaults on the MRP (to which the latter barely responded) probably led many conservatively inclined citizens to ignore the shards of the old conservative parties and vote instead for the MRP as "a solid-looking barricade against what they feared most. In their eagerness to support anti-communism, [however,] these electors were willing to overlook the fact that they were at the same time supporting a party pledged to a program of nation-alizations and social reform equivalent to that of the Socialists and Communists." In other words, such conservative citizens voted for the MRP notwithstanding its self-presentation as a progressive party of the Resistance with a vaguely *travailliste* outlook, leavened certainly with the family-oriented, educational, and libertarian values of traditional social-Catholicism, but avoiding any religious emphasis.[75]

Back in August Charles Closon, de Gaulle's able commissioner of the republic in the Nord and Pas-de-Calais, had noted this tension between an avowedly progressive party and a potential electorate with many voters of a more conservative bent: the MRP "against its inclinations and with a heavy heart, is the beneficiary of this situation." Closon recognized the party's poten-tial kinship with the socialists, "if the MRP is not held back by the exigencies of their political clientele." He considered the MRP "an unstable party, senti-mentally oriented toward the center-left but pulled by an important element of its electoral interests toward the center-right." Either way, he recognized its precocious success in party-building in his region with "a solid and effective organization, something new among the [social-]Catholics."[76]

In the long view, most historians interpret the MRP's character in the light of where it indisputably ended up after the election of 1951: as a smaller centrist party with shrinking claims on the electorate, pried from its progressive moorings by the collapse of tripartism (as we shall see), and eroded by compe-tition from revived conservative parties and especially from a hostile Gaullist movement launched in 1947. But should one judge the initial promise, perform-ance, and significance of the MRP by its eventual fate as a small centrist, pro-Europe, Christian Democratic party? If so, one would underestimate the progressive coloration of the new party during the postwar moment, and its capital role in sustaining a bumpy but notable progressive turn in France's history.[77]

The British Embassy assessed the election results incisively—if only by virtue of an inspired guess: "The elections have shown that there is an urgent desire among all classes in France for a fundamental reform, and *the people have mostly voted as far Left as they dared.*"[78] If true, as seems likely, this helped all three victorious parties. The PCF emerged at the top of the poll with a total vote more than triple its previous maximum in 1936, while the SFIO, despite its perpetual identity crisis, maintained an impressive parity even if it failed to emerge at the very top as it expected. But if citizens had indeed voted "as far Left as they dared," the MRP benefited the most. Its electorate no doubt sprawled across a gray area between the center-right and the center-left, but the vote empowered an array of new political figures who identified unequivocally with a progressive agenda and emerged from October with a redoubtable political presence.

Reports from the British Embassy also speculated accurately on what lay immediately ahead. "At the moment it would appear that all depends on whether the Communists participate in the Government and shoulder their responsibility ... or whether they prefer to remain outside and to form a strong Opposition." Strong because "the Communists now control the CGT and would be able, if in opposition, to make the life of the Government extremely difficult by provoking labor unrest. It may be expected therefore that every effort will be made to induce the Communists to enter a coalition Government based on the CNR program, and the only major stumbling block may be the bitter enmity between Communists and MRP."[79]

In this situation the socialists ended up for the moment as the political fulcrum. By a hair's breadth, the PCF and the SFIO could have combined to muster a majority of about 300 out of 586 votes in the Constituent Assembly for a government exclusively of the Left, which could have then dispensed with de Gaulle altogether. The communists briefly imagined such an outcome, but the socialists indicated that they would not participate in any coalition that excluded either the PCF or the MRP.[80] This effectively prompted both of those parties to step back from their animus during the election campaign. Since the attacks by the PCF had been tactical for the most part, they did not preclude a post-election détente, especially since the MRP had largely held its own fire and was ready to continue the de facto tripartite coalition initiated by de Gaulle. Whatever the amorphous nature of its electorate, the power centers of the MRP (its newly anointed parliamentary delegation and its executive committee) were leading a progressive party in a new key. They insistently shared a public commitment to the CNR Common Program with socialists and communists and plausibly stood for a new kind of constructive politics.[81]

The Constituent Assembly

The electoral victory of three large, relatively coherent parties seemed a big change from the multiplicity of loose parties and fluid factions in most Third Republic parliaments. Although by no means monolithic, the three parties each insisted on discipline among their deputies. The socialists required a united front by their deputies once a majority opinion cohered in their caucus. The MRP too required discipline from its parliamentarians, in contrast especially to the free-wheeling individualism of Third Republic Radicals once elected, "where each will pursue his personal agenda," ever-ready to cut self-interested deals.[82] For its part, Communist deputies could be counted on to vote as their leadership decided in keeping with the party line.

It took almost two weeks of maneuvering to sort out the basis for a new government. The Left challenged de Gaulle to present a program before the Assembly named him as provisional president of the republic. The general, insistent on having no connection to any party, refused to tie his hands in that fashion and made the first of his proffers to walk away. But counter-pressures to maintain national unity soon led all the principals back from the brink.[83] The communists dropped their maximalist goal of an exclusive socialist/communist government; the MRP took part in new tripartite negotiations despite communist sniping; and de Gaulle kept his freedom of action. On November 13 the Constituent Assembly unanimously named the general as provisional president of the republic, with a commitment on his part to form a cabinet reflecting the election's outcome.

A historic photo captures the urgency of this next step: it shows a session of the Constituent Assembly before de Gaulle's investiture, with the traditional two rows of government benches at the front starkly vacant. But another tempest now threatened to derail the process. Since it had won the most seats, the PCF demanded one of the three key ministries that in de Gaulle's view guarded France's place in the world: foreign affairs, war, and interior (which controlled the national police forces). Implying that the PCF's ties to the Soviet Union created a potential conflict, he would not entrust it with any of those posts. A brief stalemate with another implicit threat of resignation ensued.

Fearing political isolation, however, the PCF accepted a face-saving compromise brokered by the socialists. De Gaulle would recognize communist parity by naming PCF general secretary Maurice Thorez as one of four ministers of state without portfolio—in effect vice premiers—along with three others repre-senting the SFIO, the MRP, and a surrogate for the rest of the electorate. Each of the three major parties would have four additional ministers, and the cabinet would be rounded out by five others with roots in the Resistance along with one technocrat. De Gaulle himself would be minister of defense; serving under him, along with the uniformed heads of the three services, would be a new minister of armed forces charged with personnel issues (the MRP's Edmond Michelet) and a new minister of armaments charged with weaponry and supply (commu-nist Charles Tillon), both notable *résistants.*[84]

All well and good. But as the British ambassador commented, de Gaulle had questioned the patriotism of the communists; they had questioned his loyalty to democracy; and "such mutual asperities on the wedding eve can hardly be conducive to a happy marriage." The socialists had successfully insisted on creating a tripartite government under de Gaulle rather than accept a commu-nist/socialist government without him. This avoided forcing the socialists to choose between the communists or the MRP, a choice bound to divide the Socialist Party. The ambassador found all this "too reminiscent of similar crises in the past, and the solution is also familiar: a patchwork government. . . . It symbolizes a unity which does not in fact exist."[85]

But even skeptics might have been stunned by how rapidly this settlement unraveled. By most accounts the new cabinet functioned smoothly enough, and Thorez even won grudging respect from the general. The problem for de Gaulle came in the Constituent Assembly—with its authority to challenge his govern-ment over the budget—and ultimately from its constitutional committee, where de Gaulle had no role and which was moving toward a plan he opposed.

De Gaulle's thoughts about Churchill's defeat in the British general election of 1945 some months earlier (as reprised in his memoirs) help explain why the marriage between the general and the Assembly would quickly collapse. Barely concealing the element of projection, here is how de Gaulle responded to "this sudden disgrace inflicted by the British nation upon the great man who had led it to salvation and glorious victory." "Once the war was over," de Gaulle wrote, "public opinion and policy alike cast off the psychology of union, energy and sacrifice and turned once more to interest, prejudice and antagonism. Winston Churchill lost neither his glory nor his popularity thereby, but only the general adherence he had won as a guide and symbol of the nation in peril. His nature . . . his countenance, had become inadequate to the era of *mediocrity.*"[86]

Manifestly, the general felt that "antagonisms" and "mediocrity" would soon envelop him as well. He would make a last try after his investiture by the Constituent Assembly, but was ready to walk away and save himself for a time when the French people would summon him back on his own terms.

De Gaulle faced an Assembly elected by universal suffrage, yet he clung to his aura as a leader above politics who uniquely embodied the national interest. De Gaulle's disdain did not target democracy per se or the electorate but focused on politicians as a class and their parties. As the clear-eyed MRP founder Teitgen put it: "Did not De Gaulle . . . come to confound in the same phobia and the same contempt all the political parties (guilty or innocent) represented in that Assembly, and as a consequence did he not condemn the representative system itself?"[87]

The breakup began with a sharp critique of the government's proposed military budget by socialist deputy André Philip, who moved that it be slashed by 20 percent. To de Gaulle this would be tantamount to a vote of no confidence. A flurry of public recrimination, however, was matched by back channel efforts to cool things down. The critics settled for an interim and token diminution of the budget in lieu of any final action, while de Gaulle stepped back from his threat to resign.[88] The general then went off on a short vacation trip but continued to simmer. When he returned on Sunday de Gaulle convened an emergency cabinet meeting at the Defense Ministry, brusquely informed his ministers that he was resigning, turned on his heels and left the room. He soon made two moves that slightly eased the consternation and anxiety aroused by this grand drama. First, he let himself be talked out of addressing the French people on the radio, leaving others to speculate on his decision, perhaps thereby making his motives more enigmatic and less damaging. Then he indirectly conveyed to a few MRP leaders that his resignation was a personal matter and that he did not expect or encourage the *parti de fidelité* to follow him out the door, presumably because the communists might take advantage of the vacuum.[89]

Whether the MRP would have moved to the sidelines had he bade them do so must remain uncertain; many rank-and-file MRP deputies wished to follow the general, but party leaders talked them around and avoided a schism.[90] The socialist parliamentary caucus similarly chose to stick with tripartism sans de Gaulle, as the deputies voted 60 to 38 to maintain a coalition rather than swing behind an exclusively socialist/communist government.[91] After some strenuous jockeying the PCF withdrew Thorez's bid to replace de Gaulle, and the Assembly named its current president, socialist veteran Félix Gouin, as France's provisional head of state. After the Assembly "invested" Gouin and approved his three-party cabinet, eyes shifted to the Assembly's constitutional committee that had already been at work for several weeks.

That drafting body consisted of 42 deputies appointed on a proportionality formula (12 each for the PCF and MRP, 11 for the SFIO, and 7 others). Still in the middle, the socialists could produce a slim majority on the committee in sole alliance with either of their ostensible partners, a prospect they hoped to avoid. The committee had unanimously chosen socialist Philip as its chair, but he now departed to join Gouin's cabinet, his place as spokesman for the party taken by the rising but untested *résistant* from Arras, Guy Mollet. The MRP's spokesman (and the committee's rapporteur) remained François de Menthon, a law professor and former minister in the GPRF.

While the CNR Common Program was a cement for any tripartite coalition, it did not address the thicket of constitutional issues under debate in the Assembly's constitutional committee. The socialists bobbed and weaved between the MRP and the communists, trying mightily to engineer a compromise consensus. On some matters they broke with the communist gospel for a fully "sovereign" National Assembly and, for example, backed the use of referenda for amending the constitution. But in the end the socialists supported the communists on three of the most basic choices the committee had to make: the final draft called for a unicameral legislature, a weak (ceremonial) president, and the designation of a prime minister by the Assembly rather than the president—a concentration of parliamentary power strongly opposed by the MRP and by de Gaulle. Intensive last-hour attempts at a compromise brokered by Assembly president Auriol came close to success but finally collapsed. The Assembly then approved the draft by a vote of 309 to 249 and set it before the voters.[92]

No constitutional referendum or plebiscite in French history had ever gone down to defeat, and the socialists expected the same outcome. They assumed that the electorate would be desperate to have done with a provisional state of affairs that had lasted almost two years. But with the MRP, the Gaullists, and the Right opposing the draft constitution, the referendum on May 5, 1946, rejected it, as 10.5 million (53 percent) voted no while only 9.4 million (47 percent) voted yes, with about 20 percent of eligible citizens not voting.

After voters rejected the Constituent Assembly's draft, they soon returned to the polls to elect a second Assembly that would try again. But the momentum of the referendum did not translate into a major realignment of party strength (table 5.1). In metropolitan France the PCF held steady in the June election with about 26 percent of the votes and 146 seats; the share of the MRP increased slightly to 28 percent and 160 seats (making it the largest party in the new Assembly); and the SFIO lost ground with only 21 percent of the votes and 115 seats, 20 fewer than it had won in October. A new conservative party called the Parti Républicain de Liberté (PRL) stridently attacked the MRP from the right, and along with other conservative groups won about 13 percent of the votes and 62 seats, while the secularist Radicals—newly allied the with the free-floating UDSR—took 11 percent of the vote but only 39 seats.[93]

The political profile of deputies elected in the overseas constituencies was roughly similar to those in the first Assembly, with one striking exception. The Arab electoral colleges in Algeria this time sent a radical delegation under the banner "Friends of the Manifesto." Led by Ferhat Abbas, its 11 deputies advocated full civic equality for Arabs and autonomy for Algeria, which clashed with prevailing notions in the metropole about Algeria's status as an integral part of France. Abbas demanded that his group be seated between the socialists

Table 5.1. French National Elections in 1945–46 (Metropolitan Seats)

	October 1945		June 1946		November 1946	
	Percentage of votes	Number of seats	Percentage of votes	Number of seats	Percentage of votes	Number of seats
PCF/MURF	26.1	148	26.2	146	28.8	165
Socialists	24.5	133[a]	21.1	115	18.1	91
MRP	25.6	143	28.1	160	26.3	158
Radicals	9.3	31	11.5	39[a]	11.4	54
The Right[b]	14.4	69	12.8	62	15.4	76

Sources: V.-A. Montassier, *Les Années d'après-guerre, 1944–1949* (Paris, 1980), 116–17, 121, 124; J.-P. Rioux, *The Fourth Republic, 1944–1958* (Cambridge, 1987 transl.), 59, 102, 110. For complicated reasons election figures vary slightly from one account to another.
[a] The UDSR allied with the SFIO in October 1945 (adding 10 seats) and amalgamated with the Radicals in June 1946.
[b] Mainly the PRL in June and November 1946.

and the communists.[94] Overall the distribution of seats after the election of June 1946 left the second Constituent Assembly's political coloration roughly similar to that of the first, but the context had changed. The pressure was much greater on the parties to get the job done at last, even as they governed France during the continuing interim.

A Second Try

The new Assembly first had to name the interim prime minister and de facto head of state. Maurice Thorez, the PCF general secretary, was unacceptable to the MRP, and Felix Gouin would not resume the post since the Socialist Party, dismayed by the gap between their electoral ambitions and the results, decided to keep a lower profile for the moment. That left Georges Bidault, the leading figure in the MRP, as a third possibility, provided the PCF doused the vitriol it had showered on his party during the campaign. In due course an exchange of personal letters between Bidault and PCF leaders Thorez and Jacques Duclos registered a new accord. When the latter affirmed their fidelity to the CNR Common Program, Bidault replied that he was especially pleased with their decision to join his cabinet "since you invoked the spirit of the Charter of the Resistance, which is my guide to accomplishing the mission."[95] Invested with near unanimity by the new Constituent Assembly (with the communists abstaining), Bidault formed an almost exclusively tripartite cabinet, with Gouin and Thorez as his vice presidents and the MRP's Robert Schuman as finance minister. Bidault's presidency would last for the six months it took the Assembly to draft and enact a new constitution.

The new constitutional committee again had 42 members, including 12 from the MRP, 11 from the PCF, and 9 from the SFIO. Socialist Philip chaired the committee and Paul Coste-Floret of the MRP was its rapporteur. The new faces included socialist Paul Ramadier, known for his skill in brokering compromises, and Ferhat Abbas. With no formal role in the committee's deliberations, Bidault and the Assembly's president, veteran socialist Auriol, worked from the sidelines to promote an accord. Charles de Gaulle, on the other hand, intervened three times to press his own vision for the new constitution.

Having withdrawn from the public arena since his resignation in January, de Gaulle suddenly burst on the scene with a speech at Bayeux on June 16, the anniversary of the town's liberation. De Gaulle made the case for a strong president of the republic who would in turn appoint a prime minister less dependent on the whims of the Assembly; a two-house parliament; and a strong French Union (also headed by the president), which would firmly anchor France to its overseas colonies. There was nothing anti-republican in the general's speech, but its haughty tone offended the communists and even sympathetic socialists like Blum. Having stirred the pot, the general then resumed his silence. But his ardent supporters built on the Bayeux speech by launching a Gaullist Union without de Gaulle's participation. If they hoped to discomfit the MRP and tip it into the anti-compromise camp, they came close but failed.[96]

To be sure, the MRP also insisted on an upper house of parliament to be elected by a different process than the direct voting for the National Assembly, albeit with more limited powers than the Assembly. The president of the republic, to be chosen jointly by the two houses of the parliament, would designate the prime minister, but with the approval of the Assembly. These departures from the first draft were accepted in principle by the PCF and the SFIO as well, but differences remained over important specifics. When the constitutional committee finally reported out a draft proposal on August 2, its vote was 22 (mainly socialists and MRP) to 0, with 20 pointed abstentions. The PCF geared up to amend certain elements of this draft in the Assembly and perhaps to campaign for a no vote in the ensuing referendum if it did not have its way.[97]

On August 27 de Gaulle called a press conference where he attacked the proposed draft, root and branch. He objected that it did not provide adequate powers to either the upper house or the president; that the design of the French Union was far too vague and weak; and that the executive as a whole lacked sufficient standing and independence. Ironically, however, de Gaulle's bombshell might have saved the constitutional draft in two unintended ways. First, despite the fierce internal disagreement that his intervention set off in the MRP, the party ultimately distanced itself from the general's rejectionist stance and renewed its commitment to compromise with its two partners on the Left. Second, the PCF had framed its reservations about the new draft in fear that it might still pave the way for de Gaulle's return to power. (Virtually the day after de Gaulle resigned in January 1946 the party's Political Bureau deemed him a reactionary and decided that "we must act to make his return to power impossible.")[98] But the general's all-out opposition to the draft at his press conference made it plausible for the PCF to reconsider. With de Gaulle himself leading opposition to the draft, compromise among the tripartist parties could produce a constitution that adequately concentrated republican power in a National Assembly and that finally ended France's provisional state of affairs.

After the scene shifted to the Assembly itself, Auriol engaged in tireless diplomacy to persuade and wheedle the parliamentary groups to enact the draft.[99] Yet sticking points persisted. The nature of the French Union remained the most contentious, murkiest, and least resolvable issue; the character and electoral basis of the upper house ran a close second as a potential stumbling block. It took all the persuasion MRP leaders could muster to secure agreement that would leave provisions for the French Union exceptionally vague in the constitution, with specifics to be determined later by the Assembly and its parliamentary successors.

On the upper house (the Council of the Republic), Ramadier helped broker the final accord. He accepted the idea of an upper house constituted on different lines from the Assembly, "with deeper [local] roots in the country," but insisted that the National Assembly "must have the last word." In other terms, the Council of the Republic should be "a Chamber of Reflection but not of resistance to the Assembly"; it must not be a reconstituted Senate, whose coequal powers had periodically paralyzed governance in the Third Republic. The Council of the Republic would share in the election of the president, but it would have only a suspensive veto on most legislation and none on the budget. Finally, Ramadier urged that the constitution should not specify the mode of election for the upper house, which would be settled in a separate electoral law. After Bidault's intervention, a razor-thin majority of the MRP parliamentary caucus accepted the Ramadier compromise; the Assembly later adopted a protocol for the election of the first Council of the Republic, mainly by departmental electoral colleges most of whose *electors* were to be chosen by universal suffrage in each canton.[100] With such evasions and compromises, the Assembly approved the constitutional draft with palpable relief on September 29 by a vote of 440 to 106, with only the Radicals and the Right voting no.

During the final days of deliberation, MRP leaders tried but failed to persuade de Gaulle to support their efforts at compromise. On the contrary, on the day of the Assembly's final vote de Gaulle made a speech at Epinal to denounce the draft on offer unreservedly. The Gaullist Union, along with the Radicals and the Right, mobilized against the draft for the referendum while the tripartite parties supported it. On October 13, 9,297,000 (53 percent) of those voting approved the draft, while 8,165,000 (47 percent) voted no. But almost eight million eligible voters—disillusioned, weary, confused, cynical?—did not turn out at all. Thus only 36 percent of eligible voters actually approved the constitution, and the Gaullists could argue that the Fourth Republic did not rest on a veritable popular mandate. The party system, they claimed, had discredited itself by foisting this deeply flawed constitution on the nation. Both must be altered, although just how this could be done lawfully short of a massive shift in public opinion remained a mystery.[101] In any case, the provisional would finally yield to the constitutional, to the Fourth Republic.

To recapitulate: coming out of the occupation, de Gaulle's presence naturally loomed above all others, but whether as a unifying or divisive force remained to be seen. His most obvious challenger was the PCF, especially with the sway of communists in the burgeoning CGT. The FN and the MLN Resistance movements seemed well positioned to wield influence, and the Socialist Party, which imploded in 1940, regained momentum by dramatically purging the deputies who had voted for Pétain. All these contenders were at once allies and rivals. Before V-E Day they managed to avoid any serious ruptures and pointed France toward a renewed democratic future.

The regrouping of political forces began in earnest between late 1944 and mid-1945, and sorted out their strengths and weaknesses. The local liberation committees faded from the scene after V-E Day, and the large Resistance movements succumbed to strategic indecision and wavering confidence about their future roles in a normalized republic. Instead of fusing or finding effective postwar orientations, they suffered terminal erosion (in the case of the FN) or fatal political schism (in the case of the MLN). The grandiose but futile Estates General of the French Renaissance in July 1945 marked the last bold flourish of the liberation committees and Resistance movements.

The three badly compromised and fragmented prewar parties of the center and Right failed to remobilize effectively, although they had some success in small town and rural municipal and cantonal elections. But in the national elections of October 1945 and June 1946 for successive Constituent Assemblies, the three progressive parties—the Communists, Socialists, and social-Catholic MRP—decisively carried the day.

The CNR Common Program constituted a cement for tripartite governance, first under de Gaulle's provisional unity cabinet then in the governments formed after he left the stage. Disagreements, tactical maneuvering, and threats to abandon the effort altogether abounded among the three parties, but tripartism endured even after the Constituent Assembly failed to produce a constitution acceptable to all three. After the voters rejected the draft supported by the communists and socialists in the obligatory referendum, the second Constituent Assembly to its credit negotiated the requisite constitutional compromises. As we shall see in chapter 8, tripartism continued, facing the challenges of postwar reconstruction and of implementing the "peaceful revolution" advocated in the Common Program of the Resistance.

6

Postwar Prospects in the U.S.

ROOSEVELT HAD LEFT THE NEW DEAL IN suspended animation after 1940. The president would be re-elected in 1944 essentially as a war leader, after weathering the controversy over whether Henry Wallace should be replaced as his running mate. Although FDR manifestly suffered from ill health, few expected that he would not live to see V-E Day or the end of World War II, let alone that Harry Truman would occupy the White House until 1953. The core questions that run through the remaining two chapters on the US are: how did the Truman administrations serve or fail the progressive agenda, and how fared the CIO—the leading progressive interest group in the US?

This chapter begins with the launching of progressive visions for the postwar in the US, analogues of the CNR Common Program and Labour's *Let Us Face the Future.* We then consider FDR's re-election campaign; Truman's approach to reconversion after V-J Day; the conflicts between big business and big labor during the postwar moment; losing battles by the White House and congressional liberals for extending price controls and enacting a bill to maintain full employment in the future; the impact of the G.I. Bill of Rights; the Republican sweep of Congress in the election of 1946 and its direct result: passage of the anti-union Taft-Hartley labor law.

Two Progressive Visions

As November 1943 came and went, Chester Bowles was worried. The advertising executive and New Deal enthusiast had joined the war effort in 1941 as director of the Connecticut district of the Office of Price Administration

(OPA)—the wartime machine of government employees and volunteers for the 5,400 local boards that supervised rationing and controlled prices. In July 1943 Roosevelt persuaded Bowles to head the beleaguered OPA in Washington, where he quickly mastered most of the agency's political and administrative quicksands. But it was not the relentless challenges of the OPA that now troubled Bowles; it was the next presidential election.

"We were worried that FDR would not run in '44," he recalled, although the odds were that the president would ultimately do so. More to the point, Bowles and his circle in the administration worried over the prospective re-election campaign and the fate of the New Deal. While grand strategy and war-related issues absorbed Roosevelt, these liberal Democrats had started to look beyond the horizon to military victory and the postwar. They knew that the New Deal had only cushioned the Great Depression's devastating effects without really changing "an inoperative, poor-working economy," which had left eight million unemployed after the recession of 1938. Reinvigoration of the New Deal was vital lest America return after the war to that "old stagnant, half-baked economy."

Bowles had good access to the president and sent him a memo before FDR's departure for the Teheran conference with Churchill and Stalin. He urged Roosevelt to visit the troops during that trip and to return home with a speech along the following lines:

> The troops wonder what they're coming back to. They remember their fathers struggling with unemployment. . . . If we can produce this way for the war, why can't we produce this way for peace? This is the message the troops asked me to bring back to you: that they're not coming back to the old days; they're coming back to a different and new America that is dynamic. Therefore, I propose a Second Bill of Rights in the field of economics: the right to a home of your own, the right of a farmer to a piece of land, the right of the businessman to be free from monopoly competition, the right to a doctor when you're sick, the right to a peaceful old age with adequate social security, a right to a decent education...

FDR passed the memo back to his aide Sam Rosenman (Bowles's intermediary in the White House) with the notation: "What the hell do I do about this?" What indeed?[1]

Proposals for reanimating the New Deal had previously come to the White House from the National Resources Planning Board (NRPB), a small agency established by the administration in 1939, led by liberals of various back-grounds, and best described as a group "planning for planning." NRPB reports issued by 1943 included two headed *After the War*. In their way they anticipated the future reports by Beveridge in Britain on social insurance and on full employment, albeit without the public fanfare that Beveridge generated. One report advocated systematic, quasi-Keynesian postwar policies to achieve full employment, while the other linked that goal to "freedom from want" and called for major expansions of social security and the provision of relief.[2] Congressional conservatives rounded on this excrescence of the New Deal, and after a brief legislative battle defunded the NRPB in mid-1943. They could not undo the reports already issued by the board, but they could prevent further attempts to "repeal the law of supply and demand," as the *Wall Street Journal* sneered.[3]

When he returned from the Teheran conference Roosevelt did not deliver the stunning speech that Bowles had proposed. But he later incorporated the input from Bowles and the NRPB into his annual message to Congress in January 1944, where he called for "an economic bill of rights" along those lines.[4] Given this opening, Bowles now urged that each month between January and July the president send over to Congress a legislative proposal elaborating on one of these new "rights." Nothing was likely to get done on Capitol Hill, he knew, but by July Roosevelt would have fashioned a domestic re-election platform for the postwar era. Roosevelt, however, failed to take up the suggestion and sent no such bills over to Congress. And after he accepted renomination for a fourth term in July, a postwar agenda had scarcely any place in his limited campaigning.[5]

The president's inaction reflected his immersion in military and diplomatic issues and perhaps his poor health, but also his political instincts and polling data from Public Opinion Research in Princeton. Some early polls suggested that voters would probably view November 1944 as a wartime election in which they valued continuity of leadership and *not* as a postwar-agenda election, which the president could well lose. Two questions posed in March 1944 asked voters' their expected preferences in November between FDR and the Republican front-runner Thomas Dewey "if the war is still going on?"—FDR 51 percent, Dewey 32 percent, Undecided 17 percent. Alternatively, "if the war is over?"—FDR 30 percent, Dewey 51 percent, Undecided 19 percent. Polling in July pointed in the same direction. Asked "What would you say are the strongest arguments for voting *for* Roosevelt?" 62 percent answered his "superior ability to handle present and future situations," 39 percent specified "knows the war, has war experience," while only 19 percent cited FDR's "past record of handling internal affairs."[6]

The shrinking community of New Deal liberals in Washington were not the only ones pushing for a progressive postwar agenda in 1944. Prodded by its president Philip Murray and vice president Sidney Hillman, the CIO sought to raise the federation's political profile by creating a Political Action Committee. Headed by Hillman, the CIO-PAC hoped to turn CIO union members into CIO voters—a problem dramatized in the mid-term elections of 1942 when an extremely low voter turnout of only 28 million (compared to about 50 million in 1940) produced the most conservative Congress since 1932. Republican gains of 47 House seats reflected the defeat of an estimated 42 "pro-labor" congressmen.

The CIO-PAC faced two organizational problems. First, the CIO's structure, from union locals to city and state CIO councils, did not coincide with the congressional districts in which people voted. But the PAC managed to compile lists of CIO members in those districts, ran voter registration drives at factories, and opened fourteen regional offices to coordinate such efforts. The other problem was posed by the Smith-Connally Act's prohibition of political contributions from union coffers. The PAC found two ways around that ban: it used funds directly allocated by CIO unions for "educational" efforts rather than direct contributions to candidates, and it organized "dollar drives" among union members, whose donations could be channeled to candidates' campaign committees.[7]

The PAC registered new voters; produced pamphlets, flyers, newspaper articles, and radio broadcasts; canvassed neighborhoods; and worked to get out the vote on election day.[8] Until now the national radio networks and most local stations readily gave airtime to the National Association of Manufacturers and to syndicated commentators hostile to trade unions. The CIO-PAC lobbied the Federal Communications Commission to administer its vague regulations more fairly to provide airtime for labor's point of view, and it pressured the station owners trade group, whose industry code had typically served to mute labor's voice.[9] The CIO-PAC's smartly edited *Radio Handbook*—a comprehensive list of issues, tactics, and talking points for broadcasts—probably had more impact than its companion *Speaker's Manual*.[10]

As the CIO-PAC produced a flurry of electoral activism it also crystalized a progressive program for postwar America. Its principal manifesto, *The People's Program for 1944*—like the CNR Common Program in France and the Labour

Party's *Let Us Face the Future*—raised a progressive standard for renewal in the postwar moment. The manifesto, drafted for a CIO conference in June, was then distributed to 12,000 union locals. It opened with lavish praise for Roosevelt but focused on the unfulfilled agenda of the New Deal as the CIO imagined it. The wellspring of *The People's Program* came from FDR's proposed "Economic Bill of Rights," now gathering dust in the White House after his January message to Congress, until the CIO-PAC resurrected it as the center-piece for its campaign.

The manifesto demanded jobs for all with adequate wages; "decent housing to the people at a cost within their means"; provision for all of adequate medical care; equality of educational opportunity; and improved protection from the economic perils of old age, sickness, accident, or unemployment. To achieve such security and well-being, like the Common Program of the French Resistance and the British Labour Party platform, CIO-PAC insisted on "Planning for Plenty": "We reject as false that there is a conflict between the planned utiliza-tion of our national resources and genuine free enterprise." The CIO called for a national planning board and for tripartite industrial councils—a favorite idea of Phil Murray and the UAW's Walter Reuther to advance industrial democracy, but an idea rejected by the administration, as we saw, both before and after Pearl Harbor. Unlike the CNR and the Labour Party, the CIO-PAC did not advocate nationalization, but it did call for the government to act as an employer of last resort should private industry fail to maintain full employment. An additional proposal reflected the program's specific trade union provenance: full employ-ment and the resultant mass purchasing power would be shored up by a guaran-teed annual wage. While the government could not enact this notion, it could encourage its incorporation into collective bargaining agreements.[11]

With the specter of reconversion unemployment imminent, *The People's Program* espoused the temporary extension of wartime price controls, progres-sive taxes, new public works, and the pending Kilgore bill to aid workers displaced from shuttered defense plants. It addressed as well the needs of other constituencies: of farmers for price supports; of small businesses for credit; and of returning servicemen and women for medical care, completion of interrupted education, demobilization bonuses, housing loans, and job placement services. Education figured prominently in the CIO's program, with proposals for federal grants to eliminate inequalities in urban and rural schooling, and between blacks and whites; increased access to higher education; and programs for day care and preschooling. In the section headed "Civil Rights," CIO-PAC supported two contentious anti-discrimination proposals of that time: a permanent federal Fair Employment Practices Commission (FEPC) and an "anti-poll tax bill and elimination of other restrictions on the right to vote."[12]

To Keep or Drop Vice President Wallace?

To hold the Democratic Party to a progressive course in 1944, Hillman, Murray, and the CIO-PAC also supported the renomination of Vice President Henry Wallace at the party's national convention in Chicago, due to begin on July 19. Certain party leaders, on the contrary, hoped to keep the Democrats on a centrist track by muting the party platform and by dropping Wallace as FDR's running mate. An outsider to the party's ranks and a registered Republican before 1932, Wallace never won the trust of big city Democratic bosses or southern barons. True, as FDR's secretary of agriculture he been a dedicated leader, a team player when it counted, and was popular with many kinds of farmers. But as vice president in 1941 he emerged as an outspoken progressive and high-minded internationalist and attracted a new set of antagonists.[13]

It is easy enough to list prominent Democrats who found Wallace's personality baffling, or objected to his pronounced liberalism, or to his sanguine outlook on our Soviet allies. But the principal impetus to replace him arose from a belief that he would harm the ticket among swing voters and might therefore drag the president and his down-ballot allies to defeat in a close election. Absent such suppositions and pressures by key party figures, FDR himself would likely have been comfortable keeping Wallace on the ticket. Roosevelt behaved on this matter in his characteristic style: evasive, manipulative, and pragmatic. He encouraged the prospects of both Wallace and James Byrnes, the former South Carolina senator and current economic stabilization overseer in the White House. But Byrnes held no more appeal to the coterie of party leaders than Wallace: he too might damage the ticket, in this case with his segregationist background and his personal history as a religious convert and divorcee.

The opposition to Wallace gained momentum from the relentless maneuvering of Edwin Pauley, a wealthy California oilman and the conservative finance chairman of the Democratic National Committee (DNC). Pressure to drop Wallace also came from Ed Flynn, the astute boss of the Bronx Democratic machine, and from Robert Hannegan of Missouri, the current head of the DNC.

But Wallace could not be dropped without a replacement acceptable to a consensus of party leaders and to FDR himself.[14]

Abroad for almost two months on missions for the White House, Wallace met with Roosevelt twice upon his return, on July 10 and 11. From those meetings, and from talks with liberal insiders, Wallace had the impression that the president hoped Wallace might stand aside. But Wallace was ready to fight unless FDR told him explicitly that he did not want him on the ticket, something Roosevelt was not prepared to do. The two parted with reassurances by FDR that his next term would be "really progressive."[15] At a White House dinner of the anti-Wallace coterie that evening, however, DNC head Hannegan urged as an alternative Senator Harry Truman, who had few enemies and few negatives. When FDR mused about the possibility of tapping Supreme Court Justice William Douglas, the others reacted "stonily." According to Pauley, FDR finally told Hannegan: "I think you and everyone else want Truman . . . [and] you are the ones I'm counting on to win this election." But when the president saw Wallace again two days later, he still waffled. He told Wallace that while he couldn't put it this way in public, "I hope we will be the same old team"—which FDR then effectively negated by saying that, win or lose at the Chicago Convention, "we'll have a job for you in world economic affairs."[16]

So far Roosevelt had danced around the problem without asking Wallace outright to withdraw or naming a preferred alternative, but he could not evade this decision indefinitely. Hillman told Roosevelt that the CIO was committed to Wallace—unless the president himself indicated a different preference. Roosevelt still kept his options open in a letter he drafted at Hannegan's urging on July 14 to the convention's prospective chair, Senator Jackson: "I have known Wallace for twelve years; I like him and I respect him. . . . I personally would vote for his re-nomination if I were a delegate to the Convention." But, the president continued, "I do not wish to appear in any way as dictating to the Convention. Obviously the Convention must do the deciding. . . . [There should be] two other considerations besides experience and ability: will the nominee strengthen the ticket, and will the nominee meet such opposition in so-called doubtful states as to hurt the ticket."[17]

Despite the intrigues they knew to be swirling around them, neither Wallace nor Byrnes would capitulate. So on July 19 Hannegan prevailed on Roosevelt to put in writing that "I shall be very glad to run with either Harry Truman or Bill Douglas"—to be kept confidential but to be used if necessary at the convention.[18]

Since Douglas had taken himself out of the running, that left Truman. Elected to the Senate in 1934 under the patronage of Kansas City's notorious "Boss Pendergast" and re-elected in 1940, Truman had been a low-keyed but loyal supporter of the New Deal. A veteran of the Great War, he ably chaired a special Senate Investigating Committee in 1941 that exposed mismanagement and profiteering in national defense contracts without creating a general air of scandal or incompetence around the administration.[19]

When the Democratic National Convention convened, party regulars first exerted their moderating influence on the platform committee. Byrnes and Ben Cohen (one of FDR's advisors) had earlier prepared a sketch for the platform. They spotlighted the successes of the New Deal—"[by now] part of the nation's heritage"—and the prodigious achievements of wartime production orchestrated by the president with "the cooperation of free civilian labor and free private enterprise." Looking ahead, the Byrnes-Cohen draft emphasized the veterans benefits pledged in the G.I. Bill, unemployment benefits for those dislocated from wartime industry, and a gradual easing of wartime controls without aggravating the dangers of inflation.

Byrnes had earlier warned Roosevelt that South Carolina and Texas might cause "serious trouble" for the ticket if the Democratic platform for 1944 encouraged Negro voting in the South or questioned school segregation. Under the heading of "Equal Opportunity and Fair Play" the Byrnes-Cohen draft avoided those issues even as it affirmed "religious, civil, and political liberties of all citizens without regard to race, creed or color" and stated that state and federal legislation should protect "freedom from economic discrimination, and freedom from the fear of lynch law." By the time the convention platform committee finished its work, however, the language on civil rights was even more pallid than Byrnes's. Following a salute to FDR's Four Freedoms, the platform merely added the benignly nebulous thought that "racial and religious minorities have the right to live, develop and vote equally and share the rights guaranteed by our Constitution. Congress should exert its full constitutional powers to protect these rights"—an entirely vain expectation. Nor did the platform make any mention of an Economic Bill of Rights for the postwar era.[20]

As for the vice presidency, many convention delegates (including those from the CIO) stood firmly in Wallace's camp. After the vice president made a rousingly liberal seconding speech for FDR's nomination, those delegates mounted a clamorous demonstration, and some observers felt that if the convention had voted that night Wallace might have prevailed. But the power brokers (including "boss" Kelly of host city Chicago) saw to it that the convention adjourned. On the next day they discretely used the "Hannegan letter" to convince Truman that FDR wanted him on the ticket and to lobby wavering delegates. The first ballot tally gave Wallace 429 of the required 589 votes, while Truman polled 319; on the second ballot momentum swung to Truman and the liberals followed in the name of party unity. Wallace himself finally led the Iowa delegation into support of Truman, whom he privately regarded as "a small man of limited background who wants to do the right thing."[21]

The Election of 1944: FDR's Fourth Term

For three months after his renomination Roosevelt enfolded himself in his wartime leadership, barely campaigned, scorned his Republican opponents, and avoided saying anything controversial on matters foreign or domestic. As the election neared, however, the White House asked Bowles to draft a speech about the goal of full employment after the war, and he happily complied with a roadmap to full employment (which he defined as 57 million jobs) that involved redistributive measures to increase purchasing power via tax policy, loans, and subsidies. But once again his proffer seemed to disappear in the Oval Office. Then, without notice, on October 28 the president delivered a version of the Bowles speech in a national radio broadcast from a campaign rally in Chicago.

Roosevelt began with some light jabs at the Republicans, who offered (he claimed) little except personal attacks on him that would "keep the isolationists contributing." He then invoked his patented Four Freedoms refrain, but he used it here as a prologue for resurrecting his proposed Economic Bill of Rights— eight of whose aims he enumerated —as "a new basis of security and prosperity for all." After his usual nod to social harmony (the link between the well-being of workers and farmers and the success of private enterprise), he proclaimed the need after the war for "an adequate program that must provide America with close to 60 million productive jobs." He also pledged to sustain farm income, to end wage controls promptly after the war, and price controls as soon thereafter as possible. After this speech, however, FDR reverted to his preoccupation with grand strategy and showed no inclination to follow it up.[22]

Surrogates of course campaigned for FDR as well. Large ad-buys in the black press by the National Citizens PAC, for example, praised administration intervention against the "vicious race-haters" in the Philadelphia transit strike and lauded FDR's support for the wartime FEPC.[23] The DNC bought national radio time on November 1 for a roundtable of well-known liberals. The panel addressed "the big lie" of Republican red-scare tactics and smears, such as the mendacious linking of Hillman to communist leader Earl Browder. A speech by Hillman, claimed journalist Quentin Reynolds, "sounds far more like a papal encyclical than a Marxist tract." At the end of the broadcast Reynolds quipped that the panelists had tried to dissect the Republican campaign, "But how can you sum up nothing?"[24] In another DNC broadcast to the farm belt Wallace expounded on how the income of dairy and livestock farmers went up and down in tandem with the total payrolls of American workers; now FDR had made that very point in his recent Chicago speech "when he declared for 60 million jobs. . . . [which would] provide the farmers with 60 million well-paid customers."[25]

Just before the election Roosevelt stepped up his own campaign pace. In a broadcast aimed at the Midwest on November 2 "Dr. Win the War" stressed the massiveness of current operations in the Pacific alongside the all-out war being fought in Italy and France and on the verge of moving into Germany. As for the "malignant smears" of his opponents, he would simply ignore them in the hope that "the team-work that we have demonstrated in this war" en route to "a total victory" would carry over into peacetime.[26]

A foray into New England wound up with a rally and pugnacious radio broadcast in Boston's Fenway Park. Roosevelt summoned up memories of the path-breaking Catholic politician Al Smith, the victim of past bigotry that, FDR alleged, was becoming ever-more expansive. Taking a cue from Hollywood's small-unit combat films, the president read out a hypothetical roster of "our fighting men . . . of all races, colors, and creeds: Murphys, Joneses, Cohens, Carusos, Kowalskis, Schultzes, Olsens, Swabodas, and Lowells." He then proceeded with his characteristic mix of jocularity, solemnity, and purposeful vagueness. Domestically, FDR was still running against Hoover (who no longer needed to be named) and standing on the "fortifications" built by the New Deal since 1933. "Can those who fought tooth & nail against [such] progressive legislation during the past twelve years," he asked, "be trusted with its preservation?" For the Republicans promise only, with utmost vagueness, "the biggest house-cleaning in history." Otherwise their campaign is replete with subtle encouragements to "intolerance" and smears—one of their candidates having absurdly declared in Boston that "the Communists are seizing control of the New Deal."

To which the president simply countered: this country and this administration are democratic to the core.[27]

After a strenuous final day of rallies in and around New York City on November 5, Roosevelt closed his campaign the following evening with a serene radio broadcast from Hyde Park. Avoiding all talk of partisan politics, his thoughts went out to American armed forces around the world, to the Gold Star Mothers at home, and to the marvel of the free democratic elections about to occur even as the war raged.[28]

Thus did the campaign run by Roosevelt and the DNC keep it a wartime election, largely avoiding any contentious ideas about the postwar. Roosevelt's sole detour into a progressive discourse about the future came in the Chicago speech—the only time he invoked his proposed Economic Bill of Rights, which he linked on that occasion to the catchy slogan of "60 million postwar jobs." Bowles was prescient on all counts when he glumly expected that FDR "would get re-elected all right, but with no mandate for the postwar period." In due course, he believed, conservatives would effectively insist: "You were elected to win the war and you've won it. Now shut up."[29]

Although FDR won decisively his margin was the smallest yet: 25.6 million votes to Dewey's 22 million (53 percent to 46 percent); he carried 36 states with 432 electoral votes (including New York, California, Pennsylvania, and Michigan, as well as the South) to Dewey's 12 states with 99 electoral votes. The defeat of two isolationist bêtes noires, Senator Nye (N. Dak.) and Representative Fish (of FDR's home district), gave the president special pleasure; Hillman delighted in the defeat of Martin Dies, the chair of HUAC, which had brutally red-baited the CIO-PAC and Hillman personally in its 1944 hearings.[30] But Democrats recouped only about half their net losses of 1942 in the House (their ostensible majority rising to 242 from 190) and maintained but did not increase their majority of 56–38 in the Senate.[31]

The CIO leaders could exult momentarily in the president's re-election and the defeat of a few Republican congressmen in swing districts. Meeting in convention shortly after the election, CIO delegates cheered their lungs out and passed a resolution to put the PAC on a permanent footing. In a note of thanks to Hillman, FDR applauded that move to sustain "the political education and political energy of working people."[32] Clearly CIO-PAC helped put Roosevelt over the top in a few targeted states, but its impact on priority congressional races was not reassuring. After the momentary euphoria passed, two internal postmortems admitted how difficult it had been to create "CIO voters" from the raw material of union membership lists. And after FDR's fourth term, they knew, the CIO would have a much harder time rallying its members at the polls.[33] Historians too consider PAC's performance in 1944 as something of a hollow victory apart from the president's re-election. As Hillman's biographer puts it, "There were signs everywhere that the PAC's victory was less than met the eye."[34]

In any case, by April 1945 Roosevelt was gone. Severe medical problems had been diagnosed before FDR's nomination for another term, but the president had kept the dire prognosis to himself.[35] On April 12 a massive cerebral hemorrhage finally killed him. His new vice president, in his halting way, would in due course take up elements of the liberal postwar agenda—fleetingly crystallized in FDR's Economic Bill of Rights and in the CIO-PAC's *People's Program*—while conservative opponents in both parties would indeed do all they could to stifle such efforts completely.

The Challenges of Reconversion

Wartime economic regulation, to recapitulate, had three major components. The War Production Board (WPB), working with the military procurement agencies, supervised allocation of materials to defense industries, conversion of factories and building new ones, and the terms of defense contracts. The War Labor Board (WLB) had the power to regulate wages and working conditions and to arbitrate serious disputes between management and labor so as to avoid work stoppages. The OPA ran the rationing and price control systems with its network of regional offices and local volunteer boards. Standing above those agencies, the White House in 1943 created a small Office of Economic Stabilization (OES), where James Byrnes became FDR's gatekeeper and conflict adjudicator. With the peace, the NWLB and the WPB would expire, and the OES would be folded into a new Office of War Mobilization and Reconversion (OWMR).

Apart from the G.I. Bill of Rights (see below), Washington had established few concrete policies or mechanisms for demobilization and reconversion after the defeat of the Axis.[36] The administration had assumed that V-E Day would inaugurate a transitional phase in the world war. With fighting only in the Pacific theater, prolonged and brutal as it was likely to be, all-out war production could begin to wind down. In late 1943 a spokesman for the National Association of Manufacturers (NAM) anticipated at least six difficult months of reconversion layoffs as plants converted to peacetime production, but he assumed that "the spread-out ending of the war" between the defeat of Germany and of Japan would permit "partial reconversion" to ease the dislocations. The machine-tool and construction sectors had already reached their peaks in providing for military needs by the end of 1943. In 1944 the huge Brewster military aircraft factory on Long Island closed, and in the spring of 1945 Ford shut down its mammoth bomber plant at Willow Run.[37] Much of the American army in Europe would be transferred to the Pacific after V-E Day, but the military could still contract using the priorities of a pre-established "point system" for an orderly demobilization. Events did not follow those rudimentary scripts.[38] When Truman approved the use of two atomic bombs to bludgeon Japan into surrender, this momentous act brought the entire global war to a sudden end, and few in Washington were prepared for the next steps. Truman shared the glee of troops in the Pacific and those packed into ships from Europe to join them, but like Keynes he might have felt that this was all happening too fast.

Truman organized a broadcast to the nation on August 15, 1945, shortly after V-J Day, to present his reconversion "team." He had just named his close friend Fred Vinson as his secretary of the Treasury, and he had replaced Vinson at the OWMR with another longtime chum, the conservative Missouri banker John Snyder. The president now introduced Snyder as "the man responsible for formulating the high policy of reconversion from peace to war." Alongside Snyder at the microphones stood four holdovers from the wartime agencies: William H. Davis, Byrnes's replacement at the about-to-expire Office of Economic Stabilization; Chester Bowles at the OPA; Joseph Krug at the WPB; and Paul McNutt of the War Manpower Commission.[39]

Snyder's opening remarks would have raised few eyebrows: the administration wanted a stable postwar economy that would avoid either excessive inflation or prolonged unemployment and recession—an economy with job opportunities and a rising standard of living for all. And, he added in a nod toward business, "The war has put a new and higher ceiling on our ideas of production. . . . It has returned to us some of the faith in ourselves."[40]

Snyder then introduced Bowles, who began with some good news: gasoline rationing would be lifted—no more limits, no more coupons. But alas, he added, no new tires would be available to drivers as yet. Rationing of canned fruits and vegetables would end, but not of meat, fats, sugar, or shoes—all as yet too scarce to allow "fair shares" without rationed quotas. Krug for the WPB said that potential hoarding of materials and production bottlenecks still required controls on such scarce materials as tin, crude rubber, textiles, and lumber. But henceforth, he added, no government limits would be placed on production of autos and other durable goods for consumers.

Now Snyder turned to a core issue: "I feel that price stability is vital to orderly reconversion. How do you feel about it Mr. Bowles?" Bowles warmed to the challenge. "We're facing one of the most dangerous periods in our country's economic history," he insisted. Think of the boom-bust fumbling after World War I or of the current inflation in Europe. "We could lose overnight all the ground we've held during these war years." The OPA must continue to guard the prices of food, clothing, rents, building materials, and (in the face of huge pent-up demand) of durable goods as well. Of course, we will lift controls and ceilings as soon as possible. Snyder then asked Davis how wage and price controls fit into his picture. Davis initially responded with the ideal scenario: economic stabilization in the postwar means "steady production with good profits, steady jobs with good wages, and a steady flow of goods at fair prices." He conceded that some shrinkage was bound to occur in pay packets from the highs of war production fueled by overtime, but in their own self-interest workers should now seek only wage increases that can be absorbed by employers without requiring price hikes.[41] This appealing formula briefly became official White House policy, but it was one unlikely to leave any group satisfied. Two days later in a cabinet meeting Secretary of Commerce Wallace indeed argued that wage stabilization in that mode misses the point—which should be "the maintenance of the worker's take-home pay and real wages."[42] Yet to be heard from were the two houses of Congress, the well-honed big business lobbies, the CIO unions in the mass production industries, and the potentially volatile emanations of public opinion.

A first skirmish came while Vinson still headed the OWMR, when Congress spurned his request for benefits for federal and maritime employees reconverted out of a job but ineligible for regular unemployment insurance. Later Congress would bury the broader Kilgore bill for federal unemployment provision for laid-off war workers. In December 1945 Congress renewed the Second War Powers Act of 1942 and the Economic Stabilization Act (the enabling legislation for wartime economic controls), but only for six months and not the minimum of one year requested by the administration.[43]

His back not yet against the wall, Truman addressed the nation just after New Year's Day 1946. His basic goals for the postwar economy remained full employment, with steady jobs at decent wages that maintained workers' purchasing power, and for business, "good profits based on big volume" rather than higher prices. Truman briefly folded into this speech the progressive agenda set out in FDR's Economic Bill of Rights, albeit without referring to it by name: "Reaching that goal means better homes, better food, better health care, better education and security for every citizen." Then the president added a plea for "the same cooperation and teamwork we had during the war years"—at a time when American workers, farmers, businessmen, and consumers wanted an end to the particular wartime constraints that weighed on their own group.[44]

The French and the British faced far more daunting postwar economic challenges than the US, but all three nations feared the specter of an inflationary wage-price spiral deriving from shortages of consumer goods, rising prices, and escalating wage demands by workers seeking to keep pace. Without the need to rebuild a devastated infrastructure or to sustain an export drive, however, the US also had good reason to fear the opposite problem: a deflationary downdraft stemming from the unemployment of laid off war production workers and throngs of returning veterans, with a resultant shortfall in mass purchasing power to sustain the nation's economic capacity. Still, one had to prioritize. Truman essentially left to Congress the matter of government action against potentially prolonged unemployment, while the White House focused on Truman's own two "musts": the extension of price controls and the avoidance of strikes that would disrupt if not cripple production.[45]

Big Labor and Big Business

The administration, however, found itself whipsawed between the aggressive stances of big business and big labor. Business was collectively represented by the NAM and the US Chamber of Commerce, and, in the field, by corporate giants such as GM, Ford, US Steel, Bethlehem Steel, General Electric, Goodyear Tire & Rubber, and International Harvester, which had all recognized unions but were determined to reclaim "the right to manage" and to resist union demands for "excessive" wage increases. Organized labor began the postwar moment with a huge membership base. The AFL dominated the craft unions, the construction trades, and the machinists; the CIO dominated the mass production industries with such relatively new but powerful unions as the UAW, the USWA, and the UE. The unions hoped to lock in their gains from the full-employment and overtime pay packets of the war production economy. Beyond that, however, the CIO unions were committed to progressive politics and an open-ended concept of industrial democracy. The ideals of parity between union shop stewards and company foremen or of tripartite industrial councils were lost causes, but a contested gray zone for negotiation short of such parity lay waiting. Both sides prepared for battle in the postwar moment.

Wilfred Sykes, the president of Inland Steel and chair of the NAM's Postwar Committee, set out the association's perspective in late 1943 in a series of seven syndicated newspaper articles that reached up to 25 million readers. Postwar job prospects would be rosy after some difficult reconversion layoffs ran their course, Sykes believed, but only if business could freely produce, sell, and price the goods desired by consumers and thereby create manufacturing and distribution jobs. If postwar manufacturers regained the freedom they needed, he argued, they will not simply produce the same old unimproved goods but would be developing new materials (metal alloys, plastics, fibers) and new products.

To do so, however, a manufacturer needed large sums of investment capital, and under wartime policy the government "is taking it away from him almost as fast as he takes it in." Confiscatory levels of corporate taxation thus prepared the way for postwar inflation, Sykes argued, since industry would have to raise prices sharply to secure the capital that alone can create jobs and satisfy consumer demand. As quickly as possible after victory, "wage- and job-freezing, materials-priorities, price ceilings and rationing" must end; "there should be a mustering-out day for enterprise as well as for the troops." Focusing on the investment of private risk capital, competition, a free pricing system, and increased productivity, the NAM's fundamental demand amounted to a simple proposition: "After the national emergency it is the duty of government immediately to set enterprise free."[46]

After the war ended, Sykes knew, big business would also have to face down the demands of organized labor. This fight would not center on the recognition of trade unions per se, as it had in the epochal clashes of 1935–41. Rather, it would involve countering union calls for large wage increases. A second front against labor would be in contract negotiations over the rules governing working conditions, assignments of workers, discipline, and grievances. Here a long gestating business slogan emerged alongside its call for liberating free enterprise from wartime regulation: a demand that labor unreservedly recognize business's "right to manage."[47]

For its part, organized labor feared that reconversion layoffs could settle into persistent unemployment once wartime labor shortages evaporated; more generally and urgently, the unions sought to prevent a deterioration in their members' standard of living. In November 1945, Philip Murray marshaled the statistics and arguments for a "substantial" across-the-board pay increase. In wartime, wage scales had barely budged, but the income of industrial workers rose thanks to long work weeks and overtime pay at time-and-a-half. Those conditions had now ended, causing an average decline in take-home pay of 23 percent for employed industrial workers.[48]

During the war, the CIO argued, the productivity of workers had risen by an estimated 23 percent, their wages had increased by only 16 percent because of WLB caps, and the cost of living had risen by 45 percent despite price controls. All the while corporations were amassing huge profits, despite high nominal levels of corporate taxation, thanks to cost-plus contracts, tax write-offs, and federal subsidies for new plants. From this data the CIO calculated that the mass production industries could grant a wage increase of 31 percent and still earn double their profits after taxes compared to the prewar years of 1936–39. In addition to arguments about fairness ("the great disparity between wages and profits"), Murray made a loosely Keynesian macroeconomic case: only a substantial wage increase would "assure the necessary volume of purchasing power to keep the wheels of industry going," thereby bringing good profits for corporations without the need for large price increases.[49]

The looming battle between big labor and big business first erupted in a clash between the UAW and GM. In November 1945 Walter Reuther led the GM division of the United Auto Workers into contract negotiations where he called for a wage hike of 30 percent, coupled with a demand that GM pledge not to raise auto prices since the company could easily fund this pay raise out of accumulated profits. Should the corporation balk, Reuther added a call for GM to open its books to outside scrutiny. GM categorically rejected these demands (especially the insidious notion of "capacity to pay"), and readied itself for a crippling strike. Other massive strikes seemed imminent in the steel and meatpacking industries and likely to come later in electrical manufacturing, coal mining, and the railroads.[50]

* * *

Truman tried to outflank the problem by convening a presidential Labor-Management Conference (LMC) in November—not to settle specific industrial conflicts but to tamp down antagonism and promote cooperation and proce-dural accords between the two sides. Labor's delegates came from the AFL, CIO, UMW, and the railway brotherhoods. Management was represented by the NAM and by the US Chamber of Commerce. (Under its president Eric Johnston in 1942, the Chamber had briefly flirted with a "corporate liberalism" more accommodating to the New Deal and to organized labor. But the NAM had never wavered from its hard line rejectionism and had been preparing since 1943 for the postwar transition with planning committees and public relations campaigns.)[51] Finally, non-voting "public representatives" participated in the LMC as unofficial mediators on the six committees in which the conference did its work.

Intended to promote constructive industrial relations, the agenda of Truman's LMC did not include the wage increase question but only the parameters for collective bargaining. At the opening plenary session, however, Phil Murray moved that the conference help resolve the "all-important wage issue" by endorsing a call for "substantial wage increases . . . to sustain adequate purchasing power." In this démarche Murray drew opposition on all sides—from delegates of the NAM, the Chamber of Commerce, the AFL, and the United Mine Workers—and the motion was sidetracked. At the final plenary wrap-up session on November 30, Murray again urged the conference to endorse a "substantial wage increase" and thereby offer hope to workers and constructive guidance for business in the looming industrial conflicts. When a delegate observed that Murray "was attempting to pull his chestnuts out of the fire for the UAW and the steel workers," the CIO president of course took umbrage and reiterated his rationale: while corporate profits after taxes would remain high, the dangers of a steep drop in national income from inadequate wages and unemployment could best be deterred by injecting substantial wage increases into the economic bloodstream. Murray bluntly called for "a better distribution of wealth," which would still protect "reasonable profits . . . managerial efficiencies, and your investors."[52]

This time William Green of the AFL tried in his fashion to be supportive. After a brief recess to consider his options, Green proposed that the conference endorse "general wage increases to be granted immediately" so as to maintain purchasing power and thereby avoid a recession. But his motion excised the word "substantial," which for Murray remained vital. Ira Mosher, president of the NAM and head of the largest cutlery manufacturer in the US, had more fundamental objections. With limited profits and constraints on raising prices, he argued, how could a corporation offer substantial wage increases? You want to keep up purchasing power, he asked? Then don't call strikes! Even Green's motion, he complained, supported immediate wage increases without reference to worker productivity. So Mosher offered an alternative resolution: that the conference adhere to the agenda and consider neither a national wage policy nor the question of prices. The three motions (NAM, AFL, and CIO) were put to plenary votes, where each commanded only its own set of delegates and failed to be adopted.[53]

Earlier, three of the conference's six committees had deadlocked altogether and issued clashing labor and management reports. In the Committee on Collective Bargaining, management called on labor to avoid "extravagant [initial] demands" and to maintain "good faith" in negotiations. This labor could accept, but not so management's objection to "the use of force" during negotiations—barely coded words for strike and picketing tactics. Labor also opposed the notion that unions should incur draconian penalties if a wildcat strike (by definition a sponta-neous job action) occurred while a contract was in force, even if local union offi-cials had tried to head it off. In the same vein labor opposed the notion of making unions judicially "answerable" for contract violations; Dan Tobin of the AFL teamsters objected that such threats would "crucify" labor unions and could put them out of business. Management's report snidely concluded that labor's view of collective bargaining seemed to entail "eventually reaching a compromise on everything it demanded, no matter how fantastic or prejudicial."[54]

Labor delegates in the Committee on Management's Rights accepted the premise of "the inherent right and responsibilities of management to direct the operation of an enterprise." But labor balked at listing specific management prerogatives in advance, as the latter demanded. In management's eyes, labor assumed that collective bargaining would lead to joint responsibilities, perhaps even to the abomination of joint management committees. Management wanted its prerogatives recognized over such matters as disciplinary actions, seniority issues, and discharges for cause—decisions subject only to *subsequent* chal-lenge when and if contractual grievance procedures provided for such reviews. But labor would not play that game at the conference; it refused to enumerate such management prerogatives because of "the wide variety of traditions, customs, and practices" in various industries and trades. A final disagreement came over management's wish to halt current drives to unionize foremen, which labor refused to discuss. For labor, in sum, the fine points of management's roles in modern industry would "in the main follow, rather than precede, the development of sound industrial relationships."[55]

In the Committee on Representation and Jurisdictional Questions, labor vehemently opposed management's wish to amend the Wagner Act so as to bar "coercive" tactics during the period preceding an NLRB representation election, which would "impose industrial slavery" on the workers. Labor likewise denounced the proposal that upon expiration of a contract management could "question the majority status of the union" and demand a renewal of its mandate. Management proposed that unions be allowed to negotiate only on a plant- or storewide basis instead of larger bargaining units, which would immeasurably weaken the large unions. Finally management wished to introduce various compulsions and legislative mandates to curb jurisdictional disputes among unions, which labor rejected as outside interference.[56]

The other three committees of the LMC agreed on joint reports, but only by avoiding contentious matters. In plenary session the conference did unanimously adopt a toothless motion on fair employment practices. But first, at Murray's urging, it deleted a clause proposed by management that "individual ability, merit and achievement should remain the measure of individual recognition and reward," because that language "might vitiate seniority clauses in existing agreements." Finally, on a matter essential to Truman, the conference could not agree on the automatic use of independent fact-finding panels when collective bargaining or mediation failed in sectors vital to the national economy. Agreement foundered on who should appoint such panels or whether some standing agency of government should wield this power, but above all on labor's traditional rejection of arbitration unless both sides in a specific dispute agreed to it.[57]

Whatever sugarcoating the delegates gave to the conference as it adjourned, the president knew better. "On all the important questions of how to avoid work stoppages," he admitted, "the conference arrived at no accord." While Truman personally sympathized with CIO calls for substantial wage increases without the need for price hikes, he wanted above all to head off economically damaging strikes. But the conference revealed why the CIO and the White House would temporarily part company. Seconded by his secretary of labor Lewis Schwellenbach (a former New Deal senator from Washington state),

Truman looked to mechanisms such as "cooling off periods" and independent fact-finding panels, which organized labor generally opposed. As a strike wave gained momentum Truman found himself in the equivalent of FDR's position during the Little Steel strikes of 1937–38: wishing a plague on both business and labor for not rising above their entrenched positions in behalf of the public interest.[58]

The Postwar Strike Wave

After the Labor-Management Conference deadlocked, strikes proliferated. A cascade of strikes had started in the summer and fall of 1945 with hundreds of localized walkouts by industrial, white-collar, and sales workers across the country. The press heaped derision on a strike by the American Federation of Musicians in defense of its extravagant featherbedding provisions. A wildcat strike in New York by a dissident local of the longshoreman's union (ILA) over the issue of sling-net load sizes paralyzed the New York waterfront and aroused the fury and gutter-fighting talents of the ILA's corrupt president. Elsewhere tens of thousands of oil refinery, timber, and textile workers walked out. And in the new year aggrieved machinists in Stamford, Connecticut, and trolley drivers in Lancaster, Pennsylvania, sparked trade union militancy that culminated in brief citywide sympathy strikes, with similar insurgencies to follow in Rochester, Pittsburg, and Oakland. Hard, conventional methods by employers to combat strikes in those settings provoked the unconventional responses of near-general strikes.[59]

The mass production industries were the main arenas of conflict, however, starting with the UAW's national strike by 190,000 GM workers who had survived reconversion layoffs, and strikes against the large farm machinery companies. In January 800,000 steelworkers, 125,000 packinghouse workers, and 200,000 electrical workers walked off their jobs. The unions eventually settled these strikes with wage increases that fell far short of their opening demands. Reuther's UAW, for example, had initially called for a $1.45 hourly base pay rate over the current $1.12. Well into the long strike, a fact-finding panel that Truman set up on his own initiative recommended a raise of 19½¢ an hour. GM insisted on 18½¢, while Reuther (like the striking British miners in 1926) dug in for that extra penny, but eventually yielded. Similarly, as a USWA staffer later described it, the 1946 steel settlement was one of the "quickie" contracts of that time, "when everybody got an increase of 18½¢ an hour and ran."[60]

No sooner did the combatants in those CIO strikes settle than the coal miners and the railway brotherhoods shut down their industries, creating in Truman's eyes veritable national emergencies. Truman responded to the paralyzing rail strike with a federal seizure of the railroads, but the rail unions continued the strike anyway. In a furious response, Truman asked Congress for authorization to draft the striking rail workers into the army. Cheering the president, the House rushed through approval of the draft measure by a vote of 306–13. But cooler heads prevailed in the Senate, where opposition led by Senators Taft and Wagner resulted in a vote of 70–13 against authorizing that extreme sanction. Meanwhile aggressive mediation by a White House aide finally brought the rail union leaders to settle on lines that Truman had earlier proposed. Truman's threat to draft striking railroad workers infuriated liberals and labor leaders, however, not least his old friend and supporter A. F. Whitney, head of the Brotherhood of Railway Trainmen. Whitney threatened to use the entire treasury of his union to defeat Truman. But the president won back some goodwill in labor's precincts by vetoing the anti-union Case Bill when it later reached his desk.[61]

The Battle over Price Controls

Britain, France, and the US each faced scarcities of food, manufactured goods, and housing in 1945 as they had during the war—far less acute in the US, but for how long and with what consequences no one could say. Much of the income from the full employment and overtime pay of American war production ended up in savings accounts or war bonds, and pent-up consumer demand was a bracing prospect for producers in 1945. But the administration feared that if it abandoned wartime controls prematurely, consumers would chase still-scarce goods at escalating prices before peacetime production could meet demand at reasonable price levels. Hence for Truman the two "musts": avoiding strikes that would impede production and extending price controls.[62]

Like Mendès France in liberated France, and Morrison and Cripps later in Britain, Chester Bowles (head of the OPA) dreaded the social consequences of an inflationary wage-price spiral. The "hold the line" stabilization policies of FDR had prevented one during the war, thanks in part to homemakers volunteering as "price-panel assistants," the indispensable eyes and ears of the OPA to monitor local stores for violations. (A "kitchen gestapo" to their opponents, the women volunteers were for FDR and OPA leaders "democracy in action"; "a first experience of civic responsibility ... of economic citizenship in a modern state"[63]—like the ARP volunteers and fire-watchers in Britain celebrated in similar terms by Morrison and Stephen Spender.) With the peace, restraint by the unions could help counter the danger of a wage-price spiral, but only if price ceilings protected workers from runaway inflation. Bowles assumed that price controls had to last for about two years after the peace, until such time as supplies of everything from steaks and suits to autos and refrigerators could reach sufficient levels.

Conversely, business interests large and small wished to regain their freedom immediately: to compete freely for materials, to manufacture what they wished, and to charge enough for robust profits. Farmers too chafed at OPA price ceilings on their products. Bowles and the OPA became lightning rods for a storm of business and farm lobbying of Congress to loosen wartime regulation and end it altogether as soon as possible. The OPA fought back with its own public relations machinery, and for a while most consumers seemed to support extension of price controls despite claims that OPA regulation was "socialistic" and itself caused the shortages that plagued them. To make matters worse, with the expiration of the WPB, apparel manufacturers, for example, could now make bedspreads not subject to price ceilings instead of the price-controlled shirts and pajamas most needed by the public.[64]

In December 1945 Congress renewed the governing statutes for economic stabilization for six months, far too short a time horizon in the liberal view. The extension left Snyder with considerable power over the economy, but to Bowles, Snyder failed utterly to wield it effectively. In candid letters to Truman, Bowles complained that Snyder did not grasp the interdependent issues of economic stabilization, had succumbed to an "improvised day-to-day policy often entailing retreat ... [and] gave in whenever a hard case arises." The current conflict over steel was a major case in point. US Steel had demanded a 13 percent price increase of $7 per ton to compensate for any wage rise the corporation might accept. Bowles rejected this demand on the grounds that US Steel's peacetime production and sales could easily sustain good profits and higher wages without an exorbitant price rise that would spiral through the economy. US Steel dug in, however, and took the strike because (in Bowles's judgment, which proved accurate) Snyder had signaled to the corporation that he would soon override Bowles and approve the requested price increase as a basis for a settlement.

In light of all this, Bowles tendered his resignation from the OPA. But Byrnes suggested that Truman reestablish the Office of Economic Stabilization by executive order and appoint Bowles as its head, leaving him in a better position to vie with Snyder in formulating stabilization policies that encompassed prices, wages, farm subsidies, and production. Bowles liked the idea, and he stressed to Truman that "you've said the fight against inflation is the most important problem on the home front." Within a few days Truman appointed Bowles as head of a resurrected OES, and named Bowles's liberal ally Paul Porter to head the OPA.[65]

In his new post Bowles tried to promote a temporary grand bargain with big labor. The unions, he proposed, should moderate their wage demands and negotiate new contracts for 5 to 11 percent wage increases (rather than the 18 percent won by the UAW and the USWA after their strikes), and the two labor federations should tender a one-year no-strike pledge. In exchange the administration would promise to hold down the cost of living by continuing farm subsidies and price controls. Bowles won tacit acceptance of this accord from the heads of the AFL and CIO, provided that Truman staged a major event at the White House where he publicly asked for their agreement to promote "orderly stabilization and industrial peace" and to head off "a disorderly race between prices and wages." The circle would close, Bowles hoped, if the dramatic deal prompted Congress to approve a year-long extension of OPA (due to expire at the end of June) without crippling amendments. But Truman would go along only if his secretary of labor agreed, and Schwellenbach had been suddenly hospitalized, was out of reach, and could or would not oblige. The prospect for a grand bargain dissipated.[66]

The odds had been slim in any case that this theatrical initiative from the White House would deflect the assault in Congress on the OPA. Besides direct lobbying, the NAM spent over $3 million in 1946 on newspaper ads, mailings, and speakers blaming scarcities on OPA controls. The NAM, said its ads, "supports price controls by the American housewife, not by bureaucrats in Washington."[67] In May the House voted by 355 to 42 for a one-year extension of OPA with amendments that, to Porter and Bowles, made effective price control impossible. Consumer groups, some veterans organizations, and locals of some AFL and CIO unions organized large protest rallies to save the OPA, but to no avail.[68] Senator

Wagner could not even secure a majority for a "clean" one-year extension of OPA in his own Banking Committee. The amendments to the extension bill lifted the ceilings on many commodities and industrial products immediately or in short order, and they allowed businesses to factor in all kinds of costs besides higher wages in requesting higher prices. The Senate bill with such crippling amendments sailed to passage by a vote of 53–11, a "death sentence for effective economic stabilization," as Wagner put it.[69]

Having lost those battles, Bowles advised Truman to veto the bill and then resigned. Truman gambled that a veto would bring a chaotic but brief interlude without any price controls, which would induce Congress to pass a more effective version. An executive order kept the OPA in business for the moment, but only to pursue earlier infractions. Congress did pass a new extension a month later, but with only marginal concessions to the administration, which still left an "unworkable" system. Truman reluctantly signed the second bill, since the explosive rise of prices and rents in the intervening month had provided a "frightening foretaste" of complete decontrol. But even if the signed bill slightly moderated the number and size of imminent price increases in the first version, it still left the OPA with utterly inadequate enforcement mechanisms.[70]

Steel price rises had already undermined postwar economic stabilization, but the supply and price of meat—with more direct impact on consumers—wrecked it altogether. Wartime rationing had channeled meat to the armed forces and had distributed short civilian supplies fairly, but it had still upset a consuming public deeply attached to meat as a marker of well-being. When price controls expired in July 1946 after Truman's veto, suppliers rushed beef and pork to market, temporarily filling butchers' shelves but at sharply increased prices. Many consumers reacted by boycotting the blatant profiteering.[71] But as a spokesman for livestock growers warned, "You won't get production if you re-control meat." Porter at OPA duly fixed new price ceilings in September, as the second extension bill empowered him to do. But when the new rules went into effect on September 9, meat again vanished from butchers, as the big meat-packing companies held back supplies and cattlemen kept their steers in feed lots awaiting higher prices before they would send them to slaughter.[72]

This mess crested on the eve of the mid-term congressional elections. Democrats now ran scared as public opinion seemed to shift under the weight of alternating dearth and soaring prices for meat, and of the propaganda campaign alleging that price controls themselves caused the problems. Party pressure

finally forced Truman to capitulate. On October 14 he lifted all controls on livestock and meat and ordered the acceleration of decontrol on most everything
else; on November 9, except for rents, he "put the last remaining remnants of the
inflation control program out of its misery." By that time prices had risen 13
percent since July and they kept rising steeply through 1948. As measured by
the Consumer Price Index (with a base of 100 representing average price levels
in 1935–40), prices rose from 130 in December 1945 to 140 in December 1946
and climbed to 170 by the end of 1948.[73]

The Elusive Ideal of Full Employment

In July–August 1945, a solemn but optimistic anticipation of the postwar
moment unfolded at Cornell University with a lecture series rushed into print as
The United States after War. The speakers represented business, labor, agriculture, diplomacy, and education, with the opening lecture entitled "Social Planning
for Tomorrow" by Alvin Hansen—New Dealer, Harvard professor of political
economy, and advocate for Keynesianism. In Washington Hansen had been the
lead author of two reports for the NRPB in 1943 making the case for postwar
economic planning, counter-cyclical government spending to sustain employment, and expansion of social security to bolster purchasing power and a decent
standard of living.[74] Between the potential postwar perils of runaway inflation or
a deep slump, Hansen thought the latter more likely, and his NRPB reports
emphasized "democratic planning for full employment." His Keynesian assumptions challenged traditional wisdom about avoiding deficits and balancing
budgets: "A nation may make itself poor by reducing public debt" at the wrong
time, he warned. To forestall recessions the state should use anticipatory fiscal
policy, borrowing, and running deficits to spend aggressively; during inflationary
booms it could raise taxes and retire public debt.[75]

At Cornell Hansen honed his argument with a new emphasis on the right to a
job as a human right, as already implied in a British white paper on full employment of 1944. The statutory right to a job would be fully compatible with free
enterprise and with freedom of choice by workers, Hansen insisted. In practice
it would depend on a robust economy that generated sufficient demand:
"Adequate total demand means an adequate total outlay whether by individuals,
business, or government for goods and services. . . . The public sector can act as
a balance wheel to [demand generated by] the private sector," most obviously in

construction projects. Likewise, "a broad and comprehensive system of social security and social welfare, combined with a progressive tax structure, acts steadily and continuously as a powerful stabilizing factor. It puts a floor under depression. It acts as a great irrigation system, distributing purchasing power widely over the whole country."[76]

Twice during his lecture Hansen saluted a full employment bill pending in the Senate (S. 380). Formally introduced in January 1945 by Senator James Murray, a New Dealer from Montana, the bill would establish an individual's "right to useful, remunerative, and regular employment" and would authorize federal planning to head off postwar recessions with compensatory spending to help assure that "every man and woman in the country who is willing to work and capable of working has the right to a job."[77] The Murray bill did not provide a numerical definition of "full employment," or the levels of federal expenditure that might be required, or the actual planning mechanisms. Still, "full employment" now moved from being an appealing slogan to a serious if fluid policy initiative, which incorporated the right of an individual to a job. An alert Senator Taft immediately objected that the vision behind this bill was "completely at variance with my whole idea of the American system."[78]

For tactical reasons Murray shifted jurisdiction over S. 380 to Senator Wagner's Banking Committee, while he enlisted a Texas New Dealer to introduce the bill in the House. There, however, the conservative Rules Committee assigned it to the obscure and decidedly unfriendly Committee on Expenditures in the Executive Department, guaranteeing an eventual brawl over the bill. A staffer of Murray's now formed a "continuation group" of aides to line up support in Congress, promote the bill among the public with position papers, and steer it through the shoals of congressional hearings, amendments, and voting. The continuation group included such veteran New Dealers as Hansen and Leon Keyserling from Wagner's staff, along with representatives from liberal religious, women's, and civil rights groups, and the CIO and AFL.[79]

By the summer of 1945 Murray had secured four moderate Republican co-sponsors, and the Banking Committee held its hearings. Nine members of Truman's cabinet testified in favor of the bill, and only four of the sixty-seven witnesses opposed it. The opposition being organized by GM, the NAM, the Farm Bureau Federation, and other business groups essentially bypassed Wagner's hearings and awaited a more friendly forum in the House committee. By a vote of 13–7 the Banking Committee reported out the bill, while its opponents issued a harsh minority report evoking the nefarious influence of such conservative bugbears as J. M. Keynes and Henry Wallace, not to mention Hitler and Stalin, who in their twisted ways had purportedly provided for full employment.[80]

In the Senate floor debate, Democratic co-sponsor Joseph O'Mahoney (Wyo.) tried to reassure his colleagues by underlining his well-known resistance to most deficit spending, his belief that the bill carried no antagonism to free enterprise, and the fact that Congress would have the ultimate say over federal "investment and expenditure" to promote full employment. Along the same lines, a "compromise amendment," adopted by voice vote, embedded the bill's main provisions in additional reassuring language. The final Senate version carried by a vote of 71–10, but conservatives understood that the outcome might well be reversed when the action shifted to the House.[81]

Business opposition dominated the hearings held by the House committee, which resounded with charges that the bill would promote unbridled federal deficits, sap business and investor confidence, undermine private enterprise, prove unworkable, or lead to socialism. The House committee made short work of the bill, voting it down 17 to 3; the chair then named a small subcommittee headed by a conservative southerner to draft an eviscerated replacement. The House substitute eliminated all traces of the right to a job or of executive branch planning for federal spending to maintain employment should a recession loom. The bill did authorize a new White House economic council to provide an overview of the economy and policy recommendations to Congress.

Truman unequivocally backed the Senate version, but Senator Barkley's best efforts in the conference committee did not avail, and the conference version (duly passed by both houses of Congress) was essentially the House substitute. The elusive but inspiriting ideal of "full employment" disappeared from the text and from the bill's very title, now called simply "The Employment Act of 1946." Gone was a government guarantee for the right to a job, along with the Senate's provision for "such volume of Federal investment and expenditure as may be needed ... to achieve the objective of continuing full employment." Instead, hollow language pledged the use of existing "functions and resources" of the government to encourage "maximum employment, production and purchasing power."[82]

The principal innovation that emerged from this legislative battle was a new institution: a three-man Council of Economic Advisors appointed by the president, which could conduct fact-finding and analysis on the state of the economy and issue an annual economic report to be received by a new joint congressional committee. Truman canvassed members of his cabinet about what to do now, and they agreed that he should sign the Employment Act of 1946 into law as better than nothing. The president did so on February 20, gamely stating that "the result is not all I had hoped for, but I congratulate members of both houses. . . . The Employment Act is not the end of the road but the beginning."[83] Senators Murray and Wagner publicly took the same hopeful position. In Murray's words, it offered a president who acted "properly and firmly" a starting point to press for federal interventions against recession and unemployment. Other liberal postmortems lamented the lethal assault by Congress on any Keynesian policy of counter-cyclical measures and the empty formulas of the final version—which is why so many conservatives such as Taft (who insisted that "the economic machine cannot run on federal money") in the end voted for the bill without qualms.[84]

Thus did the administration and its liberal allies lose two great battles over postwar policy, bested by the business lobbies and congressional conservatives in the two parties even before the mid-term election of 1946 swept Republicans into control of Congress. The administration's push for a "clean" extension of OPA succumbed to vigorous business lobbying on Capitol Hill, which angry public demonstrations against sharply rising prices could not offset. The battle over a "full employment" policy with Keynesian teeth ignited rival lobbying campaigns by liberal groups and business interests, and it ended in another defeat. This left Truman signing under duress two drastically emasculated versions of laws he and his progressive allies had sought.

Congressional maneuvering and inaction rather than floor votes buried a third liberal policy initiative for the postwar. The Wagner-Murray-Dingell omnibus bill, first introduced in 1943, anticipated several proposals in FDR's Economic Bill of Rights and the CIO-PAC's *People's Program for 1944*. The bill initially encompassed veterans benefits; major expansions and greater federalization of social security provisions; and a new program for national health insurance.[85] Federalization of social insurance failed first when Congress sidetracked the Kilgore bill for federal unemployment benefits for laid-off war workers. In September 1945 Senator Wagner introduced a bill for federalizing, expanding, and standardizing unemployment insurance for the general population. His proposal came before the southern-dominated Finance Committee, which rejected all its key provisions.[86] National health insurance, the core of the Wagner- Murray-Dingell bill, found strong support in the Truman White House, but faced severely uphill odds in Congress. The battle for national health insurance, and for public housing as well, continued across the postwar moment, as we shall see in chapter 9. The bill's sketch of provisions for veterans, meanwhile, was superseded by the G.I. Bill of Rights in 1944.

The G.I. Bill of Rights

If the rise of the CIO was arguably the most consequential American social movement of the 1930s, the Servicemen's Readjustment Act of 1944 (known, after a brilliant public relations stroke, as the G.I. Bill of Rights) set off a different kind of change in America's social equilibrium. Earlier wartime legislation anticipated the eventual separation of millions of men and women from the armed forces with mustering-out pay, facilities for medical care, rehabilitation services, and disability pensions for the seriously wounded. Under the Selective Service Act, returning veterans could in principle reclaim their peacetime jobs; if that proved impossible or unsuitable, the G.I. Bill now entitled them to special unemployment benefits of $20 for 52 weeks (the "52–20 Club," as the veterans called it) and preferential advantages in seeking new jobs in the public sectors. But two sections of the G.I. Bill of Rights broke genuinely new ground: low-cost, guaranteed loans for purchasing a home or farm or establishing a business; and grants covering tuition and living expenses for veterans resuming or starting college, post-graduate programs, vocational education, or on-the-job training programs.

Washington's planned timetables and "point systems" for phased demobilization between V-E Day and V-J Day were upended by Japan's sudden surrender in August, as pressures for more rapid demobilization swelled both at home and among servicemen abroad—capped by demonstrations in January on some military bases, "Bring Daddy Home" campaigns by military wives, and loud demands by some congressmen.[87] The anticipated flow of returning veterans became a torrent, notwithstanding delays on military bases in the states where men awaited their paperwork and final discharges.

Most of the jobs veterans might hope to resume had been filled by others, and the claims of veterans were bound to clash with civilian seniority or personnel situations in some sectors of the labor force. As in Britain, a desperate housing shortage confronted the veterans, since housing construction and renovation had ground to a halt during the war. Rental vacancies were virtually nonexistent in many locales, while conversion of a few military bases and the use of prefabricated Quonset huts were insufficient palliatives. Similarly, the flow of veterans into post-secondary education initially hit serious snags. Most glaringly, the for-profit vocational education and job-training sectors saw proliferating courses of questionable utility and even outright fraud.[88]

Under the G.I. Bill, college and university campuses across the country pulsated with veterans who overtaxed their faculties, classrooms, and campus housing, and who found that their government stipends for tuition, living expenses, and books did not keep up with rising costs after 1945. Most of Harvard's matriculated students, for example, had left for military service between 1940 and 1945; the university now urged the survivors to return, and about 2,500 did so during the next few years. The university also reached out to new prospects who might never have considered Harvard for themselves (a glossy brochure was called "What about Harvard?"),[89] and hundreds of such veterans applied and won acceptance. The class size of Harvard College in those postwar years ran to 145 percent of prewar levels, peaking in the Classes of '49 and '50 with the campus awash in veterans. The student veterans were older, and over 650 were married compared to the typical dozen or so prewar. They also seemed more worldly and serious than typical undergraduates in the past, as academic honors at graduation reached all-time highs.[90] For all its particularities, the profile of postwar Harvard was typical of large public and private universities, such as the University of Wisconsin and University of Michigan, or Columbia and Syracuse University.[91]

For some veterans, however, the very architecture of the G.I. Bill of Rights featured a forbidding barrier. About 1,154,000 World War II veterans were black, a ratio of one out of thirteen, two-thirds of whom lived in the South while a quarter came from urban centers in the North. They had already been flayed by the rigid segregation and racism in the armed forces during their service. Their status was underscored in 1944 when Congress rebuffed an initiative from the White House to facilitate absentee balloting in the armed forces for the upcoming election. Roosevelt desired a simple and accessible "federal ballot" for the services, but southern power in Congress left absentee service balloting to the customary ministrations of the separate states, tantamount to depriving southern black soldiers of the vote.[92] A surface reading of the G.I. Bill, it is true, seemed to promise its benefits to all qualified veterans regardless of race. In steering the legislation, however, Congressman John Rankin of Mississippi, one of the most vicious racists and anti-Semites in Washington, assured that implementation and oversight of the G.I. Bill were left to state agencies (as in education) and to state and district offices of the Veterans Administration (VA) and the US Employment Service. These local agencies could direct the benefits disproportionately or exclusively to whites in keeping with Jim Crow state laws and local mores. Black veterans in the South and border states would experience frustrations, affronts, and rejections. When not excluded altogether from the potentially transformative benefits of the G.I. Bill in employment, loans, or educational benefits, they were obliged to attend segregated or third-rate institutions, programs, or job-training placements.[93]

Among black veterans who qualified for admission to colleges, perhaps 55 percent were effectively turned away, and of those able to enroll, 70 percent were shunted into overcrowded and understaffed all-black institutions. Meanwhile, discrimination in the building trades and other occupations curtailed job opportunities for blacks who had acquired new skills in the service. The only bright spot seemed to be the "52–20" veterans unemployment benefit, but in the Deep South, administrators used the technicalities of the law to shunt black veterans into menial jobs; if they balked they would be denied the unemployment payments. Blacks did gain some access to temporary housing under the Veterans Emergency Housing Program which, however, was patently inadequate for whites and blacks alike.[94] To be sure, the most tenacious, motivated, or well-placed black veterans capitalized on the educational benefits of the G.I. Bill, and some launched themselves on rewarding careers in law, public service and the like that they might not have otherwise attained.[95]

In the long term, apart from this blight of racial discrimination, the G.I. Bill of Rights reinforced postwar demographic and social trends, notably the "baby boom" resulting from the cascade of wartime and postwar marriages; traditional gendered attitudes about work; and the wish of most veterans to make up for lost time. The acute but temporary problems that followed demobilization generally subsided within three years. As long as building materials remained scarce, for example, builders had incentives to construct more lucrative commercial properties. But when the materials became widely available, home construction took fire with the G.I. Bill's support of private home builders, realtors, and the bankers who made guaranteed loans to finance home purchases by otherwise under-qualified veterans. Some projects for rental housing moved forward as well under local or nonprofit auspices, mostly small-scale but with a handful accommodating thousands of tenants (primarily veterans), such as the initially all-white Stuyvesant Town in New York City. But the great boom stimulated by the G.I. Bill came in suburban development of tract housing, some of mammoth size, such as the initially all-white Levittown projects on Long Island and Pennsylvania that filled with veterans' families.

Overcrowding at colleges and universities eased as their capacities and staffs expanded to meet the demand. By the early 1950s a large cohort of college-educated veterans had passed through these institutions into middle-class occupations, including many unlikely to have pursued such education before the war.[96] At that point a serious side effect abated as well: the severe disadvantaging of female applicants to colleges and universities in the crush of applying and returning veterans. "While women were 40 percent of all college graduates in 1940, their proportion had dropped to only one in four by 1950." For administrators of higher education had decided that the number of women students would, for the time being, "inescapably have to be reduced," as a dean at Cornell put it.[97] As for veterans of the various women's auxiliary services—capped in 1940 at 2 percent of the armed forces—they were eligible for benefits under the G.I. Bill and enrolled in higher proportions than men. But few in number to begin with, they were generally neglected in the transitional and advisory mechanisms of demobilization.[98]

During the postwar moment untold numbers of individual veterans encountered problems great and small in reentering civilian life. Many combat veterans (a decided minority of the 15 million men who passed through the armed forces) repressed their traumatic wartime experience, at what psychological cost to themselves and their families we do not know; the imagined disorientation or maladjustment of individual veterans at any rate became one motif in the postwar film noir genre.[99] But most veterans simply wished to slip back into civilian life, settle down, and move forward.

Veterans organizations might or might not help with those transitions, but they could certainly bolster the collective identity and interests of veterans and thereby magnify their weight in the commonweal. Five major veterans organizations competed for members in 1945: (in order of size) the American Legion; the Veterans of Foreign Wars (VFW), the oldest; the Disabled American Veterans; American Veterans of World War II (AMVETS); and the American Veterans

Committee (AVC)—the last two new and limited to veterans of World War II.[100] We shall closely examine the progressive AVC in chapter 9.

The Election of 1946 and After

During the war FDR tried not to provoke restive conservative forces in Congress, especially as hostile Republicans gained ground in the mid-term election of 1942. With the end of the war, Truman faced the same political landscape. In advocating for a strong full employment bill and a "clean" extension of the OPA, he suffered lopsided defeats on both measures even with his party's nominal control of Congress. Government in the US was manifestly divided as the wartime veneer of patriotic consensus dissipated. Regarded by many as an accidental president ill-suited to fill FDR's shoes, Truman put on a stoic face as the country geared up for its first postwar election in November 1946. Apart from Truman's shaky leadership, FDR's unprecedented four-term presidency favored the prospects of Republicans insisting that "it's time for a change." Truman avoided any direct involvement in the election, and few Democratic candidates would have wished him to campaign for them.

An election-eve survey of contests across the nation by the *New York Times* tried to distill the tenor of the campaign in each state. While most Democrats defended FDR's legacy, Republicans denounced the New Deal but did not call for rolling it back so much as stopping its further progress and ending the New Deal's purported bureaucratic excesses, inefficiencies, and abridgements of individual liberty. Their prime campaign motif seemed to be the "ineptitude" and "bungling" of Democratic Washington. With the slogan "Had Enough?" Republicans harped on the recent meat crisis, the shortages of other goods, and inflation—for all of which they blamed the OPA. Two other bugbears for Republicans were the CIO and alleged communist influence in Washington, occasional Republican themes in the 1944 election. Their candidates sometimes linked the two by denouncing the influence of a leftwing CIO-PAC.[101]

Without FDR's inspirational presence, however, CIO-PAC (as some insiders had feared right after 1944) foundered in its quest to turn union members into reliable progressive voters. To begin with, CIO-PAC had to absorb a shocking setback in the Detroit mayoralty election of November 1945. In this presumed bastion of the UAW and CIO, black and union voters had helped re-elect Mayor Edward Jeffries to a second term in 1941. But in the wake of the Detroit race riot of 1943, which erupted over housing issues and where 34 people were killed, Jeffries repudiated CIO positions against segregated housing and police brutality. In 1945 UAW leaders backed the progressive alternative of their own vice president Richard Frankensteen, who prevailed against incumbent Jeffries in the Democratic primary. But Jeffries then ran on another ticket, and his campaign cynically employed racial slurs, demagoguery, and red-baiting. Black voters went for Frankensteen overwhelmingly, but white union workers from the AFL and CIO, especially of Slavic and of southern US background, deserted Frankensteen in droves. Jeffries won re-election by 274,000 to 217,000 votes.[102]

Subsequently internal dissension erupted in the CIO over how to recalibrate the PAC for the 1946 election. Sidney Hillman wanted to explore unity with other progressive organizations to increase the PAC's clout, but Phil Murray prevailed in opposing that course; he wished to keep PAC's resources entirely in-house and foreclose any possible drift toward a third-party movement. When Hillman died suddenly in July 1946, his assistant Jack Kroll became PAC's director, but he now had to answer to a new four-man board of union secretary-treasurers. Factional conflicts in the UAW also spilled over to the PAC and paralyzed its operations in Michigan. By and large CIO-PAC support proved as unavailing in the 1946 congressional elections as it had in Detroit's mayoral election. In the Republican landslide that November, pro-labor candidates supported by PAC fared poorly as Republicans made record-setting gains in both houses.[103]

In the Senate a Democratic majority gave way to 51 Republicans and 45 Democrats. An 8 percent national swing in aggregate (albeit low turnout) voting lifted Republicans to control of the House, with a net gain of 54 seats, which gave them 245 seats to the Democrats' 188. Since almost all these gains came outside of the South, this electoral upheaval decimated the already thin ranks of progressive Democrats. The Republicans now held almost 75 percent of congressional seats outside the South. Democratic victories in many tightly contested seats in 1944 were now reversed. As in Britain's 1945 general election, swing voting was especially pronounced in suburbs, but there was also a falloff of the Democratic turnout in union districts and among northern black voters.[104] In California an unknown Republican named Richard Nixon smeared and defeated a prominent liberal congressman. The cohort of conservative Republican freshmen senators included three who would excel as demagogic red-baiters: Senators McCarthy (Wisc.), Jenner (Ind.), and Cain (Wash.).

* * *

The election left Truman in a difficult position. He still embraced the spirit of FDR's Economic Bill of Rights, whose agenda he had vaguely invoked in his first State of the Union address in January 1946. After the election that November, in his second State of the Union and his Economic Report of January 1947, he again called for strengthening and extending New Deal innovations: increases and extensions of coverage in social security benefits and in minimum wage levels; a new federal Department of Welfare; a public housing program along the lines of the stalled Taft-Wagner-Ellender bill; a major program for national health insurance; unspecified steps to end racial job discrimination; and a plea against cuts in the progressive income tax. (Taft saw the Economic Report "as a vehicle to recommend a complete social welfare program" in the wake of the New Deal.) But Truman did little to advance this agenda in the hostile environment of the 80th Congress.[105]

On the contrary, the president pursued a temporary détente with the new Congress while its Republican leadership labored to enact their two top priorities: major tax cuts and revisions of federal labor laws. Truman's conciliatory stance stemmed in part from his foreign policy priorities at this juncture, as the president courted the newly converted isolationist stalwart Senator Arthur Vandenberg of Michigan. The senator's ability to nudge some Republican colleagues toward a bipartisan foreign policy for the containment of communism abroad was yet to be tested. For Truman the first steps would be congressional approval of economic aid to a desperate Western Europe and of funds to support his pledge to aid Greece and Turkey in resisting communist pressure.

Truman also sustained his truce with Congress by appointing national commissions to study two inherently contentious issues. The Temporary Commission on Employee Loyalty quickly reported back in March 1947 and prompted the president to create a Republican-supported federal Loyalty Review Board, whose disregard of due process eventually wreaked havoc in the lives of hundreds of progressive public employees. The President's Committee on Civil Rights took longer to issue its report, which became a benchmark in the glacially spasmodic federal movement toward civil rights for blacks. (The loyalty program and civil rights issues will be pursued in chapter 9.)

After extensive wrangling among Republicans and sniping by some Democrats, each house passed a version of the Republican tax cut bill and resolved their differences in conference. The tax cut bill brought a moment of truth for the president. Truman attacked the bill for its inequity, as it gave proportionately far greater relief to the well-off, and for its effect in raising the federal budget deficit, which Truman had pledged to reduce. After both houses passed the bill by large majorities Truman vetoed it, as most of his advisors recommended. He then managed to persuade a handful of wavering Democrats in the House to support him, and a veto-override vote fell short by only two votes.

Taft-Hartley

After Truman's Labor-Management Conference of November 1945 failed to calm the waters of industrial relations, the president riled organized labor during the strike wave of 1946 by not endorsing demands for higher wages that he knew to be legitimate, and by his flailing, coercive interventions against the railroad and coal strikes. But he regained some ground with his veto of the anti-union Case Bill. Truman himself wanted modifications to the Wagner Act to curb potentially abusive union practices and to create mandatory mechanisms for federal intervention to deter disruptive national strikes. In the wake of anti-union campaigning by Republicans in the 1946 election, Truman probably viewed himself as an honest broker who opposed drastic curbs on unions advocated by the Right, yet he agreed that strikes which compromised the nation's economy should be reined in. For now, however, the initiative passed entirely to the Republican-led 80th Congress.

What eventually emerged as the Taft-Hartley law was a moving target once congressional deliberations began. The House version, steered by Representative Fred Hartley (N.J.), grew more punitive with each round of deliberation in committee and on the floor. Both versions of the bill took up an array of anti-union measures long promoted by the NAM. Liberal Democrats and a handful of Republican moderates had little influence on the final draft reported out of conference. (The few punitive provisions finally dropped included a proposed ban on industry-wide collective bargaining, and the outright abolition of the NLRB.)

Outside the ranks of labor, a few stipulations in the final bill might have appeared as consensus reforms, such as bans on jurisdictional strikes and secondary boycotts and the prohibition of closed shops (where only current union members could be hired). Other provisions drew serious objections and not only from the unions. Taft-Hartley turned upside down the intent of Wagner Act, which generally defined unfair labor practices as abuses by employers. Now the unions would fall into the crosshairs of the NLRB and the federal courts, while Taft-Hartley also provided greater recourse for individual workers against unions in their workplaces.[106]

Among other things, Taft-Hartley:

- Authorized injunctive relief for employers in certain strike situations, which broke the taboo against labor injunctions banned by the Norris-LaGuardia Act of 1932.
- Made unions liable for wildcat strikes in violation of existing contracts (when the very definition of such a strike was that workers walked off the job in defiance of their union's official position).
- Prohibited picketing and secondary boycotts against companies to which a struck employer was transferring work or goods, and forbade jurisdictional strikes.
- Eroded union security clauses in contracts by requiring that provisions for union shops be approved by majority vote of all the unit's workers in a secret ballot.
- Authorized states to adopt "Right to Work Laws" that could ban union shops altogether, leaving workers free to refuse union membership or payment of dues.
- Expanded the exclusion of agricultural labor from coverage by the Wagner Act to include most facets of food processing (with their heavily black work forces), while refusing to include racial discrimination as an unfair labor practice.
- Eliminated the card-check method for union organizing as an alternative to a formal and more time-consuming union representation election.
- Required workers to "opt in" for union dues checkoffs instead having them occur automatically under negotiated contracts.
- Prohibited unions from donating to any federal election campaigns.
- Prohibited federal employees from striking.
- Excluded supervisory personnel from joining the unions of workers
- Required union officials (but not their counterparts in management) to sign non-communist affidavits, without which their union would be ineligible for NLRB representation elections.

The impetus for the Taft-Hartley law, its architecture, and its lopsided approval came from a powerful congressional bloc that historian Ira Katznelson calls "the Republican/Southern Democrat anti-union coalition," which crystalized in the 1940s. The Republican side, driven by ideology, aimed to maximize the market freedom and "right to manage" of established big business (as advocated by the NAM) and of newer, smaller entrepreneurial companies that fiercely opposed the encroachments of unions on their turf. Across the aisle the Southern Democrats, motivated primarily by defense of the racial status quo in their region, sought "to insulate the South's [segregated] employment relationships and [discriminatory, low-wage] labor markets from the effective reach of national unions."[107]

The final votes on Taft-Hartley were 320 to 79 in the House and 57 to 17 in the Senate. Some of those votes came from congressmen and senators who might have objected to various provisions in the omnibus bill but believed that a revision in the balance established by the Wagner Act between the rights of employers and of workers was long overdue. Time and court cases would presumably sort out the details, which could be altered later by amendment.[108]

When the final bill emerged from conference, the White House canvassed the heads of cabinet-level agencies on what to do when the bill reached the president's desk. At least two recommended that Truman sign the bill: the head of the Federal Works Agency and Marriner Eccles, a veteran New Dealer speaking for the Federal Reserve's board of governors, which he chaired. ("The Bill has symbolic significance to organized labor," wrote Eccles, "[which is] a more important factor influencing union opposition to the bill than its actual provisions. We do not think the bill will affect adversely the legitimate functioning of unions. But it will provide increased protection to the public and to the workers themselves against abuses and shortsighted practices.") Several cabinet members claimed to be still deliberating and did not take a firm position. Those recommending a veto included the NLRB, the Council of Economic Advisors, the head of the Bureau of the Budget, and the secretaries of labor, of the interior, and of the army.[109]

Meanwhile Truman's aide Clark Clifford contacted leading economists and prominent Democratic lawyers for their opinions about technical aspects of Taft-Hartley. Among the lawyers, Lloyd K. Garrison provided a meticulous all-out assault on the bill. Clifford also had Gael Sullivan, executive director of the DNC, canvass state Democratic officials (chairs, vice chairs, national committeemen and -women) to take the local pulse on whether or not Truman should veto the imminent tax cut bill and Taft-Hartley. Sullivan's personal summary stated that Taft-Hartley, while not "an NAM- inspired slave labor bill," was still "unsound and unworkable." Of Democratic state officials, 95 favored a veto (86 from outside the South), and 68 urged Truman to sign, with roughly similar proportions on the tax bill. Urban party bosses in Chicago, Jersey City, and Pittsburg recommended vetoing Taft-Hartley and signing the tax cut bill, while Ed Flynn of the Bronx declared that "New York State would be lost to the Democrats" unless Truman vetoed both.[110] Clifford also forwarded a tally of letters, cards, and telegrams to the White House about Taft-Hartley as of June 11: 114,909 letters urged Truman to veto and 3,656 to sign. The 390,000 postcards overwhelmingly urged a veto, while telegrams had a ratio of five to one.[111] Organized labor's lobbying efforts against Taft-Hartley showed little difference between the CIO and the AFL.[112]

Clifford provided the president with arguments that might induce him to veto the bill. Talking points circulating in the White House included: (1) Taft-Hartley will encourage anti-union employers to harry, provoke, and weaken unions; (2) "the Act compels good union men to act as strikebreakers against fellow members" because it prohibits workers in Company B from refusing to do work sent across by strike-bound Company A; (3) under Taft-Hartley a majority of *eligible* employees (not of those actually voting) must vote in favor of representation by a union seeking to become their bargaining agent; and (4) curbing union shops could force workers to work alongside people they distrust, such as spies for the bosses, and non-union workers would be treated under Taft-Hartley with greater solicitude than union members.[113]

On June 20 Truman convened his cabinet and told them that he was about to veto this "lawyer's bill" that would create labor strife instead of allaying it, and that "cannot be administered." He went on the radio that night to explain the damage this "shocking piece of legislation" would do by undermining the right to bargain collectively and by imposing excessively harsh restrictions on trade unions. Truman specifically mentioned the re-legitimization of injunctions; the new forms of union liability that would encourage damage suits by employers; how the law would work against union security agreements that have encouraged stable labor relations; and how the ban on political contributions by unions could even prohibit their newspapers from commenting on candidates. Deprived of fundamental rights, the president concluded, workers would have no means of protecting themselves except by striking or by endless lawsuits.[114]

Truman hoped that the inevitable vote to override his veto would fail in the Senate where 32 votes (one-third) would defeat it, and where Minority Leader Barkley could lead a last-ditch fight to uphold the veto. The White House finally did some head-counting, with a tally indicating 28 senators in support of the veto and several "possibles." Truman agreed to see 13 senators personally, but the White House assessment proved faulty and his personal interventions yielded no return. The final Senate vote to override was a dispiriting 68 to 25.[115] In his next official statement Truman could only say that his administration would faithfully execute the new law.

Implementation included a reorganization of the NLRB mandated by Taft-Hartley, which expanded its board of commissioners from three to five members and bifurcated the NLRB's functions between those commissioners and a new, independent office of NLRB general counsel. The general counsel now had authority over NLRB trial examiners and responsibility for defending NLRB decisions appealed to federal courts. (The rationale for this separation was to create space between the investigation of cases and the board's final decisions, between prosecution and judgment, so to speak.) But Truman then made one of the worst appointments of his entire term. Presumably trying to appease the congressional majority, he named as NLRB general counsel Robert Denham—a Republican proponent of Taft-Hartley and a trial examiner for the NLRB who had shown no sympathy for organized labor. From this post Denham could work against the original mission of the NLRB to promote the orderly growth of trade unions and could sabotage efforts to repeal Taft-Hartley.[116]

In its annual report for fiscal 1948, the NLRB tallied a huge number of disputes filed since enactment of the new law (36,735 versus 14,909 for the comparable period in fiscal '47). As predicted by its opponents, Taft-Hartley entangled the unions in a morass of legal proceedings. In the formal allegations of unfair labor practices, however, three-quarters of the charges (2,553) were still being brought against employers, primarily for discrimination in hiring or firing because of union affiliation; the typical charge against the unions (749) was for coercion of employees. The NLRB also supervised 21,277 workplace elections. Almost 18,000 were union-shop authorization polls newly required by Taft-Hartley, which resoundingly approved those negotiated agreements 98 percent of the time. But in union representation elections supervised by the NLRB, the petitioning unions won only 72.5 percent of the time compared to an average of 81.4 percent during twelve prior years under the Wagner Act.[117] All told, from the vantage point of NLRB jurisdiction, Taft-Hartley in its first year did not produce a seismic upheaval in labor relations, but union power was eroding at the margins. Unions were obliged to defend themselves at law with growing frequency. Organizing in the South became more difficult than ever, as well shall see in chapter 9, and Taft-Hartley strengthened management's impulse to act more aggressively in future negotiations.

Two Setbacks for Labour

1. In solidarity with striking coal miners, the Trades Union Congress called a general strike in 1926, which lasted to no avail for nine days. Employer reprisals and enactment of punitive labor laws followed. Credit: NCJ Mirrorpix/Newscom.

2. After the collapse of Ramsay MacDonald's minority government in 1931 and his expulsion from the Labour Party, a snap election brought overwhelming victory for his "National Government" slate. MacDonald remained PM, but Conservatives such as Stanley Baldwin (to MacDonald's right) and Neville Chamberlain (back, second from left) dominated his cabinet. Credit: © Mirrorpix/Newscom.

3. Fifteen years after the bitter split of 1920 at the Socialist Party congress in Tours, socialist Léon Blum and communist Maurice Thorez (second row, fourth and third from the left) rallied together at the *Mur des Fédérés*—a memorial site for the French Left, where hundreds of Communards were summarily executed in 1871. Credit: Photo 12/Alamy Stock Photo.

4. Léon Jouhaux addressed the CGT Paris federation to mark the end of a major schism in the French labor movement dating from 1921. A reluctant Jouhaux finally agreed in 1936 to a merger with the communist CGT-U in the spirit of the Popular Front alliance. Credit: Sueddeutsche Zeitung Photo/Alamy Stock Photo.

5. Harry Hopkins won FDR's approval for a Civil Works Administration to create temporary jobs for millions of the unemployed during the winter of 1933–34. In 1935 Congress enacted a long-term program for work relief known as the WPA. Credit: Franklin D. Roosevelt Presidential Library and Museum.

6. During the signing ceremony for the Social Security Act of 1935, congressmen jockeyed for prominent places in the official photographs, but the act's prime architect, Secretary of Labor Frances Perkins, always held center stage just behind FDR. Credit: Everett Collection/Newscom.

7. The CIO's founding fathers (from the left): Sidney Hillman of the Amalgamated Clothing Workers; John L. Lewis of the United Mine Workers; Lewis's longtime deputy Phillip Murray, who led the Steelworker's Organizing Committee; and John Brophy, head of CIO organizing. Lewis abandoned the CIO in 1941 and Hillman died in 1946, leaving Murray as the CIO's undisputed leader. Credit: © Underwood Archives/The Image Works.

8. Mounted by locals of the fledgling UAW, the West Detroit and Flint sit-down strikes of 1936 against General Motors brought a breakthrough victory for the CIO's project to "organize the unorganized" in the mass production industries. Credit: Courtesy of the UAW.

9. "All Behind You, Winston." The iconic cartoon by David Low captures the intended spirit, if not the day-to-day reality, of Churchill's coalition government, with Labour's "big three"—Attlee, Bevin, and Morrison—abreast of Churchill in the front rank. Credit: David Low/Solo Syndication.

10. Put in charge of civil defense in October 1940 at the height of the Blitz, Herbert Morrison authorized "deep sheltering" in the London subway system and promoted a low-cost indoor air-raid shelter, which could double as a dining table, that protected against falling debris but not a direct hit. Credit: © Imperial War Museums (Q(HS) 102).

11. (left) Cover of the CNR
Common Program (March 1944).

12. (below) Cover of the CIO-PAC
People's Program for 1944 (June 1944).
Credit: Social Movements Collection,
Hamilton Library, University of Hawaii.

13. (opposite) Cover of *Let Us Face the Future*,
Labour's electoral manifesto for 1945.
Credit: People's History Museum.

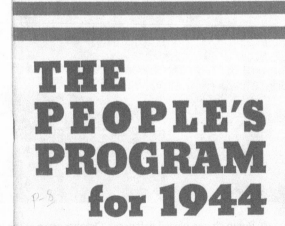

LET US FACE THE FUTURE

A
DECLARATION
OF LABOUR POLICY FOR
THE CONSIDERATION
OF THE
NATION

2d

PUBLISHED
BY
THE LABOUR PARTY

2d

14. In de Gaulle's triumphal procession down the Champs-Elysées after the liberation of Paris, the CNR's social-Catholic president Georges Bidault was on the general's immediate right, but the council as a whole was not invited.
Credit: © Imperial War Museums (HU 66477).

15. Louis Saillant (standing), CGT representative to the CNR, succeeded Bidault as the council's head. A ubiquitous voice for progressive unity in 1944–46, Saillant gradually broke with his mentor Jouhaux to side with the CGT's communists.
Credit: © LAPI/Roger-Viollet/The Image Works.

16. Labour's "big three" savoring the party's unexpected landslide in the election of 1945—with no sign of Bevin's aversion for Morrison or of the latter's long-standing ambition to replace Attlee as party leader. Credit: Getty Images/Popperfoto.

17. On vesting day in 1947 signs went up at mines all across Britain proclaiming the new era of a nationalized coal industry. Credit: Photograph courtesy of the National Coal Mining Museum for England.

18. Nye Bevan touring a new council housing estate built in accord with his vision for low-rise, semi-attached houses rather than high-rise flats, with generous floor space and amenities. Credit: Getty Images/J. A. Hampton.

French Press and Information Service

Constituent Assembly in Session before the election of the Government. Note the empty Government benches.

19. The election of a Constituent Assembly in October 1945 began the formal restoration of republican democracy in France. The Assembly had to designate a provisional head of state, whose cabinet would fill the vacant government front benches, shown here. The Assembly finally chose de Gaulle, but wariness on both sides persisted, and after three months the general abruptly resigned. Credit: Free French Press and Information Service; photo in the author's possession.

20. After Léon Blum's return from Buchenwald in 1945, he and Vincent Auriol (left)—comrades during the Popular Front and the Vichy years—anchored the social-democratic tradition in the revived Socialist Party. As president of the Constituent Assembly, and then as the Fourth Republic's first president, Auriol helped sustain tripartism during France's postwar moment. Credit: Sueddeutsche Zeitung Photo/Alamy Stock Photo.

21. While the NAM campaigned against prolonging price controls and rationing after the war, some veterans and consumers groups organized public demonstrations in support of the OPA. Credit: Wisconsin Historical Society, WHS–10244.

22. The progressive American Veterans Committee advocated for policies to ease the severe housing shortages faced by World War II veterans. Shown here, the Hollywood AVC chapter camped out overnight to dramatize the issue. Credit: Los Angeles Times Photographic Archives (Collection 1429), UCLA Library Special Collections.

23. A symbolic gesture in support of civil rights came when Eleanor Roosevelt persuaded Harry Truman to be the first American president to address the NAACP. The event took place at a large outdoor rally held at the Lincoln Memorial. Credit: National Archives and Records Administration.

24. The administrative boards of France's new social security funds convened in 1947. The inscription reads: "Social security protects the worker and defends him against the social scourges. It gives him the maximum guarantee because it is conceived for him and administered by him." Credit: Copyright Agence France-Presse.

25. Leaders of the Progressive Party before their July 1948 convention: Henry Wallace is flanked by running mate Senator Glen Taylor and party co-chair Paul Robeson. Back row from the left: Rexford Tugwell, head of the platform committee; Congressman Vito Marcantonio; campaign manager and ex-New Dealer "Beanie" Baldwin; Albert Fitzgerald, president of the United Electrical Workers (UE); and Elmer Benson, ex-governor of Minnesota. Fitzgerald, Marcantonio, and Robeson were well known as fellow travelers; Baldwin was likely a concealed communist. Not shown: communists Lee Pressman (secretary of the platform committee) and John Abt (general counsel). Credit: Everett Collection Inc./Alamy Stock Photo.

IUE-CIO NEWS

"IN UNION THERE IS STRENGTH"

CONFUSION

COMMUNIST STYLE

UE is trying to spread confusion among long service GE workers. UE has taken a poll of the workers as to their possibility of winning and found they have lost ground - a lot of ground.

Knowing that all the constructive gains and benefits gotten for GE workers over the years were made under the banner of CIO until 1948. REMEMBER. They are frantic. So they stoop to using the good names of long service workers and try to win votes because of their failure to make any constructive gains since 1948.

But the old timers won't be fooled. The old timers remember UE selling out in 1941 and allowing the company to take away the cost of living bonus - - - without a fight. They remember that UE sold out in 1947 and allowed GE to take away our profit sharing bonus - - - again without a fight. These sellouts have cost GE workers an average of 10 cents per hour.

DEBATE

AMERICAN STYLE

1 - On Sunday, September 2, on a TV show on station WRGB, James B. Carey, president of IUE-CIO challenged Leo Jandreau, Albert Fitzgerald, Julius Emspak or James Matles to a debate on the issues in this campaign. Jandreau and Matles were in the studio at the time.

TO THIS DATE, NOT A SINGLE ONE OF THEM HAS HAD THE GUTS TO ACCEPT THIS CHALLENGE.

2 - On Monday, September 3, Mike Quill, president of the CIO Transport Workers, challenged Matles and Jandreau to debate Quill's charge that Gerhardt Eisler, on orders from the Cominform, ordered Matles to get out of CIO.
TO THIS DATE, NEITHER ONE OF THEM HAS HAD THE COURAGE TO ACCEPT THAT CHALLENGE.

REMEMBER: Not one single UE officer has issued a challenge to debate anyone in IUE-CIO. Not a single UE challenge.

They're cowards.

GE workers, you'll have the chance Friday, Sept. 14th to vote out the cowards, vote out the communists, vote out the un-Americans.

26. When the UE left the CIO in 1949, the federation chartered a competing union (the IUE) led by CIO secretary-treasurer and longtime anti-communist James B. Carey. The rivalry weakened the leverage of electrical workers facing aggressive postwar managements. Credit: Helen Quirini Papers, M. E. Grenander Department of Special Collections and Archives, University at Albany Libraries.

27. Attlee's cabinet mobilized troops to unload vital cargoes such as meat imports (shown here) when longshoremen shut down the docks with wildcat strikes in 1949. Credit: British Pathé.

28. In traditional syndicalist fashion, the breakaway CGT–Force Ouvrière stood "against every form of political sway"—an obvious reference to communist domination of the CGT, which precipitated the schism in December 1947. Credit: Courtesy of Force Ouvrière.

Who Runs America?

the Congress? ★★★ the President?

OR YOU AND THE MAN NEXT DOOR?

RUNNING AMERICA *is the joint job of 150,000,000 people. It's the biggest job in the world today —keeping it running for liberty and for freedom. And the whole world's watching to see whether Americans can do it!*

IN MUCH OF THE WORLD *today, the people have resigned from running their own countries. Others have been quick to step in—first with promises of "security"—and then with whips and guns—to run things their way. The evidence is on every front page in the world, every day.*

FREEDOM COMES UNDER ATTACK. The reality of war has made every American think hard about the things he's willing to work and fight for—and freedom leads the list.

But that freedom has been attacked here recently—just as it has been attacked in other parts of the world. One of the most serious threats to individual freedom has been the threat of Government-dominated Compulsory Health Insurance, falsely presented as a new guarantee of health "security" for everybody.

THE PEOPLE WEIGH THE FACTS. In the American manner, the people studied the case for Socialized Medicine—and the case against it.

They found that Government domination of the people's medical affairs under Compulsory Health Insurance means lower standards of medical care, higher payroll taxes, loss of incentive, damage to research, penalties for the provident, rewards for the improvident.

They found that no country on earth can surpass America's leadership in medical care and progress. They found that able doctors, teachers, nurses and scientists —working in laboratories where Science, not Politics, is master—are blazing dramatic new trails to health for Americans—and for the world.

THE "GRASS ROOTS" SIGNALS CONGRESS. In every community in the Nation, people stood up to be counted on this important issue. Thousands of local women's clubs, civic groups, farm, business, religious, taxpayer, medical, educational and patriotic organ-

izations spoke out—giving the great United States Congress its unmistakable Grass Roots signal from home!

And ever watchful, ever sensitive to an alert people, The Congress saw that signal, and heard the people speak out, loud and plain. That's democracy in action. That's the American way!

Today among the 10,000 great organizations on militant public record against "Compulsory Health Insurance" are:

General Federation of Women's Clubs	American Legion
American Farm Bureau Federation	National Association of Small Business Men
National Grange	United States Chamber of Commerce
Veterans of Foreign Wars	National Association of Retail Grocers
National Conference of Catholic Charities	National Retail Dry Goods Association
American Protestant Hospital Association	American Bar Association

● Doctors of this Nation are grateful that the people refused to be wooed by the fantastic promises of this un-American excursion into State Socialism. ● Doctors of America are dedicated to serve their fellow citizens at home and their comrades in uniform, wherever service to this Nation may take them. ● And the thing they stand ready to fight for—to sacrifice for—to die for—is not the alien way of life of Socialism, but the prideful security of a free and self-reliant people!

THE VOLUNTARY WAY IS THE AMERICAN WAY!

● Throughout the Nation, free men and women, working and planning together, are finding the American answer to every question of medical service, care and cost. Hundreds of Voluntary Health Insurance Plans are in healthy competition—sponsored by doctors, insurance companies, hospitals, fraternal organizations—by industry, agriculture and labor. ● Today in America—70 million people are protected by Voluntary Health Insurance! ● Throughout the Nation, families are insuring themselves against the major costs of illness—at reasonable, budget-basis prices. Voluntary Health Insurance takes the economic shock out of illness. Protect your family now. ● For information, ask your doctor—or your insurance man.

An American's greatest heritage is the right to learn the facts—and to speak his mind. Maintained with honor and used with sincerity—that right will guarantee forever that

You and Your Neighbor Run America!

PHYSICIANS OF THIS COMMUNITY PARTICIPATED IN PAYING FOR THIS SPACE

AMERICAN MEDICAL ASSOCIATION ● NATIONAL EDUCATION CAMPAIGN
ONE NORTH LA SALLE STREET, CHICAGO, ILLINOIS

29. The AMA vehemently opposed any federal program of national health insurance under Social Security. Its media and lobbying campaigns against "socialized medicine" proclaimed that "the voluntary way is the American way." Credit: Courtesy American Medical Association Archives.

PART III

STRUGGLES AND OUTCOMES

7

Building Socialism British Style

LABOUR'S 1945 ELECTORAL PLATFORM, *Let Us Face the Future,* set out ambitious if necessarily vague commitments on housing, social insurance, health care, nationalizations of specified economic sectors, and education (among other domestic issues) and added this telling comment: "There is no good reason why Britain should not afford such programmes, but she will need full employment and the highest possible industrial efficiency in order to do so." Despite the straitened circumstances besetting the nation, once in power Labour did not shrink from its vision and remained confident that the means could be found. We have seen how difficult it proved to maintain the economic underpinning on which Labour's programs depended; several times the country teetered on a veritable financial or economic abyss. Yet buffeted by scarcities of consumer goods and raw materials, negative trade balances, severe deficits in dollar reserves, and the need for yet more austerity, the Attlee government strove mightily to fulfill its pledges.

In 1945 Labour had the advantage of a decisive electoral mandate and party unity. Victorian and interwar Britain had seen fits and starts of reform in such domains as slum clearance and public housing, primary schooling, secondary education, social insurance, and health care. With a wind to its back from wartime enthusiasm over the Beveridge Report of 1943, Labour set out to rationalize and expand that "patchwork" of accretions into comprehensive provisions for a more egalitarian civic order. No longer in the political wilderness or a junior partner in the wartime coalition, Labour had to move past its internal debates of the thirties and early forties and translate policies into acts of Parliament. Would the Labour Party have the political will and the skill to do so effectively?

Addressing the Housing Deficit

In 1945 consensus reigned in Britain that housing must hold a top priority for any government emerging from the general election: 63 percent of respondents to a Gallup Poll in July named housing as the most urgent domestic problem; no other issue scored in double digits.[1] Labour candidates had emphasized housing in their campaigns although the party's manifesto left its prospective policy vague in the extreme. Once in office Attlee's cabinet confronted a dire situation: severe prewar deficits in the quantity and quality of affordable housing, extensive wartime damage to the housing stock, population growth during the war, and the demobilization of veterans needing housing.

British government involvement with housing reached back into the late nineteenth century with a commitment to "slum clearance." In 1890 officials designated blocks of grossly substandard housing for demolition and incentivized local councils to rehouse dispossessed residents more salubriously. A different kind of initiative just after the Great War, in keeping with the hollow rhetoric of that moment, sought to build new "homes fit for heroes." The Housing and Town Planning, or Addison, Act of 1919 authorized three sources of support for publicly built dwellings: modest council subsidies from local rates, regulated rents from tenants, and (in this case) open-ended central government subsidies to meet financial shortfalls. At the same time the government lifted wartime restrictions on private builders, which increased already inflated prices of materials and building methods. Addison's costly program came to an abrupt end after 1923.[2] MacDonald's minority Labour government started a new program for slum clearance in 1930. The substantial infusion of subsidies for demolition and rehousing, however, generally produced five-story blocks of flats in unsightly barracks styles of poor quality. Cumulatively by 1939, successive "slum clearance" programs had demolished only half of the designated sites, and only 300,000 local authority units had been built to replace them. As Orwell showed in *The Road to Wigan Pier* (1937), "squalid," "beastly" slums still dominated working-class housing in the northern mining and industrial regions.

All told, implementation of public housing programs in Britain had been spasmodic, sensitive to shifting political winds and fiscal constraints. The means for meeting acute housing needs kept changing, and government subsidies rose and fell sharply several times during the interwar years. Meanwhile private sector building in the 1930s produced about 2 million new homes, answering to the common preference among the middle classes and better-off workers to be owner-occupiers. This mini-boom in private building relied on nonprofit building societies that, despite the economic slump, took in savings deposits from the steadily employed and recycled them to provide mortgages with the interest tax-deductible.[3]

During World War II, housing experts agreed that even before the first bombs dropped, private builders and public programs had together fallen far short of meeting critical needs for more and better housing, especially in working-class neighborhoods. The war visibly compounded the problem. By V-E Day, bombing and rocket attacks on Britain had damaged around 3.5 million dwellings, including 200,000 totally destroyed, 250,000 standing but uninhabitable, and 250,000 occupied but in need of major repairs.[4] Population had increased during the war by about a million, and around 2.5 million wartime marriages foretold an imminent baby boom putting yet more pressure on the housing stock.

As a stopgap, the coalition government ordered over 120,000 prefabricated units manufactured by war-production methods, which proved helpful but too expensive. Local authorities began to repair severely damaged buildings, a slow process that stretched out into 1949. Meanwhile, the Dudley Report of 1944 from the housing division of the Ministry of Health criticized the design of existing public housing, its cramped space, and its monotony, but the report offered no master plan for the future of housing. A perfunctory white paper of March 1945 spoke only in the haziest terms of the need for 3 to 4 million new homes over the next decade. Then, as it awaited the election in June 1945, the all-Conservative caretaker government put the benchmark for immediate needs after the war at 750,000 new homes.

It would be a lively counterfactual exercise to ask what might have happened in the arena of housing if Attlee had split off the Ministry of Health's housing division, as he had initially contemplated. Or if the prime minister had chosen as minister someone other than Aneurin Bevan, the caustic maverick and backbench critic of the coalition during the war. Would anyone else have fashioned the distinctive approaches to housing and to health care on which Bevan insisted and shepherded to success by the end of his tenure in 1950? In fact

Attlee left the Ministry of Health intact and, in a surprise move, chose Nye Bevan to lead it.

Forgiving Bevan's persistent badgering and occasional outbursts directed at the coalition front bench, Attlee recognized Bevan's sheer intelligence, commanding verbal talent, dedication to Labour, and popularity with the party's constituency branches, which had elected him to the National Executive Committee (NEC) in 1944. A self-schooled Welshman from a coal-mining family, Bevan was one of the few deputies of working-class background whom Attlee could elevate to his own front bench and, at 47, Bevan would be the youngest member of an aging cabinet. Bevan's maverick left-wing past (including his expulsion from the party along with Cripps in early 1939) contrasted on the surface with most other ministers, who had been schooled in the arts of patience and compromise. But Attlee understood that behind "the provocative irresponsibility" Bevan had sometimes displayed, he was thoughtful, serious, and capable of pragmatism.[5] In any case, the alchemy of Attlee's decision was sound. Bevan proved a minister effective in his two domains even if that meant compromising at times with his own maximalist inclinations. In cabinet he was a loyal member of the government but increasingly outspoken in conflicts with others. In effect, with his presence "the big five" of the party in due course became "the big six."

Establishing the National Health Service was Bevan's greatest challenge, but housing unavoidably made immediate claims on his attention. By late 1945 Bevan had drafted Labour's housing program. He directed that scarce building materials, construction labor, available land, and financing all be funneled into public housing for rental to the people most in need. Local councils (over 1,500 in number, ranging from London to rural districts) would erect the public housing, using private subcontractors or "direct labor schemes" as they preferred. The councils had been acquiring land since 1943, had enough in hand by 1946 to construct an estimated 600,000 homes, and already had long waiting lists and the local knowledge to allocate units as they rose. But what type of dwellings would the councils build? And what about private sector building projects?

Bevan was emphatic: the councils would build semi-detached houses for rental rather than apartment blocks. And he insisted that these houses should offer an unprecedented level of comfort despite the higher costs. The Dudley Report of 1944 had recommended that floor space in public housing be expanded from the prevailing 750 to 800 square feet for the typical unit with three small bedrooms to 900 square feet. Bevan fixed that as the new minimum and encouraged houses of 1,000 square feet. He also required a second, upstairs lavatory; wider halls; thicker walls; better insulation; and various small amenities and built-ins for kitchens and other rooms.[6]

To get projects started the local authorities could borrow substantially at low interest (not to exceed 3 percent) from the Public Works Loan Board. Costs for repayment and maintenance would be offset, as in the past, by tenant rents (fixed at modest, sustainable levels that averaged around 10s per week), annual subsidies from local rates, and funding from the Treasury, but in new proportions and higher levels than in the past. In the interwar years the typical annual subsidy per unit from local rates had been £2.15s and from the Treasury £5.10s; now subsidies rose to £5.10s from local rates and £16.10s from the Treasury.[7]

Given the scarcity of building materials (especially of imported timber and of bricks), and the severe attrition of the construction workforce to well under half its prewar size, Bevan prioritized the use of material and labor by placing limits on "speculative building" for purchase. Private projects by builders would require licenses, to be granted in limited numbers so that only one out of every five new houses could be erected for the up-scale market. The Tory opposition bridled at this restriction and urged that the private sector be freed to do what it did best, but Bevan argued that the housing crisis of the postwar moment required planning and coordination: "We have to plan with plannable instruments," he maintained, "and the speculative builder, by his very nature, is not a plannable instrument."[8]

Under the Housing Act of 1946, housing starts multiplied by the summer but not a single unit had yet been completed. Bevan refused to release specific target numbers, despite a clamor for him to do so from the opposition and some Labourites. The apparent lack of progress drew criticism on all sides, most dramatically in the form of squatters. About 40,000 took over abandoned military bases that lacked functioning utilities—actions condoned by local authorities who tried to help make the buildings habitable. Then, in the heart of London, small groups of squatters organized by communists briefly occupied abandoned luxury flats for a few days to make a point.[9] Such worrying episodes stoked debate in Parliament, where Churchill himself led scathing attacks on Bevan from the opposition benches, the two having long detested each other. Within the cabinet some colleagues called for a National Building Corporation with more direct control over the whole process, but Bevan opposed such centralization as a needless layer of bureaucracy. None of this sniping phased him: "I will not be panicked into doing a bad job" remained his standard response. His difficulties on the housing front within the party finally subsided after the annual party conference of 1948, where he beat back a critical motion from the floor.[10]

Around that time Bevan's stubbornness started to pay off. Public housing completions began to mount in 1947 and peaked in 1948 at a record-setting level. By then, however, Bevan faced a different challenge: the financial crisis created by the trade deficit, the dollar shortage, and the convertibility fiasco (discussed in chapter 4), which forced Cripps to order cutbacks in Labour's capital programs for new housing, schools, hospitals, and factories. A rise in defense spending, under pressure from the US, intensified the budgetary strain. But Bevan maneuvered effectively within the cabinet to maintain the forward momentum of his housing program. At the price of some modest trimming he succeeded, and housing retained a steady proportion of roughly 20 percent of Labour's capital budget.[11]

In 1948 Labour spokesmen started boasting of achievement. Issues of the monthly party bulletin featured a page of public housing statistics to demonstrate the steady progress being made from the dead start of 1946. The ministry now had to restrain certain councils rather than goad them into faster action, as the curtailment of hard-wood imports to husband dollar reserves took a toll on the pace of council housing. Still, after the peak of 284,000 houses finished in 1948, completions continued at over 200,000 units annually for the next three years.[12] Labour aggressively brushed off Conservative calls for more private ("speculative") building and mocked Tory claims that long waiting lists for council houses reflected Labour's failure, whereas these lists actually "prove how deplorably under-housed we were in the days of Tory supremacy." In 1949 Labour saw confirmation for its policy in President Truman's public housing victory of 1949.[13]

Bevan did not dismiss the aspiration for home ownership, but at the present time, he observed, "if the ownership of the houses is a denial of somebody else's personality [i.e., need], it is a social affront." Occasionally he went further on the question of class and community. He hoped that someday the councils might build for different income groups in the same housing estate to counteract social segregation, "the unbalanced communities, [where] you have colonies of low-income people living in houses provided by local authorities and you have higher-income groups living in their own colonies." "This segregation of the different income groups is a wholly evil thing from the civilized point of view," he once declared. "It is a monstrous infliction upon the essential psychological and biological one-ness of the community." Alongside his program's concrete results—over 800,000 new public housing units—Bevan left a lofty ideal of community for future inspiration.[14]

The virtues and limits of Bevan's singular contribution to Britain's housing landscape became clear only after the next two decades of housing policy unfolded. Labour's housing policy under Attlee succeeded after a rocky and much-criticized start, but in two ways Bevan's achievement appears retrospectively as a distinctive interlude, even an anomaly. In the first place, the British preference for home ownership rather than rentals would reassert itself and influence government policy once the worst of the housing shortage eased.[15] Bevan implicitly admitted as much in a parliamentary debate in April 1950: "The Tories' demand to 'Let the private builder build,' would not increase the total number of houses. It would merely mean that the better-off would jump the queue. As long as there is a shortage of houses Labour will maintain the ratio of houses to rent and houses for sale, so as to ensure priority for those whose need is greatest."[16] The most urgent shortages left in the war's wake eventually abated, and the two separate "colonies" of housing that Bevan deplored would develop apace.

Second, while public housing continued to expand during the 1950s, its quality evolved regressively and lurched from bad to worse. In 1950 the Conservatives decided to outbid Bevan's record on housing for the coming election. At their party conference the Tories pledged to build 300,000 public housing units in the first full year after they came to power. When they finally won the general election of 1951, Harold MacMillan took charge of housing, where his success put him on track for higher office. MacMillan sped up council building projects, secured a rise in the Treasury's annual public housing subsidy to £36.5s per unit, and oversaw more than 200,000 completions of public housing for three successive years. The Conservatives essentially delivered on their pledged numbers but at the cost of quality: a substantial reduction in average square footage and room sizes, and a scaling back of amenities. In a 1953 white paper MacMillan then announced that private builders would be freed to serve the market for owner-occupiers. Thereafter private housing completions rose steadily, from only 34,000 in 1952, to 113,000 in 1955, to 151,000 in 1959, at which time private completions exceeded local council completions. MacMillan also encouraged upkeep in the private housing stock through improvement grants and eased restrictions on rent increases.[17]

As public housing units kept going up in substantial numbers, however, the proportion of flats to houses was rising, and there lay the crux of the matter. The construction of apartment buildings in public housing grew from less than 25 percent in 1953 to about 50 percent in the 1960s and, as one housing scholar puts it, "The proportion of flats in the built form of very high towers and slabs advanced with astonishing speed from the late '50s." A spurt in high-rise construction peaked in 1964.[18] Thereafter approvals of high-rises declined rapidly—but not before a new landscape took shape in council housing that plagues Britain to this day.

The impetus for high-rise construction had originated in the interwar years with modernist architectural movements of utopian bent seeking new kinds of housing. When translated into actual public policy in the 1950s and 1960s, high-rise, high-density apartment blocks were supposed to compensate for land shortages and high land prices. The largest construction companies lobbied for support of new "industrialized" building methods for high-density construction, which reduced their labor costs and gave them advantages over smaller competitors. For a decade government subsidies rose with the height of the apartment buildings. As housing expert John Short summarizes: "Suggested by architects, promoted by central government and pushed for by the big contractors, the high-rise blocks were touted as the solution to problems of land availability and as a panacea to modernizing the construction industry." For a brief time, he believes, public tower blocks also became symbols of "municipal virility and aggression."

But rethinking eventually set in. High-rises proved costly and the government started cutting subsidies. The partial collapse of a 22-story building in Newham London in May 1967 sealed the retreat. Once imagined as vertical garden cities with blocks of flats in ample open space, and as a check on urban sprawl, high-rise construction initially meshed with the demands of slum clearance. But the actual high-rises that went up on council estates dismayed many tenants, whose common preference for a house with a small garden had been ignored. The buildings came to be regarded as sterile and ugly, ill-designed and shoddy. Tenants in high-rises could not easily keep an eye on their children and had trouble preventing vandalism. "The shiny towers, initially the sign of achievement, became the sign of failure and incompetence," Short concludes.[19] How wise might Bevan's choices have appeared twenty years later to anyone who recalled them? After 1964, Harold Wilson's new Labour government gradually abandoned construction of high-rise council flats, emphasized subsidies for renovating old houses, and encouraged owner-occupation with low-cost mortgages and tax exemptions. By 1970 over 50 percent of British households were owner-occupiers, and council housing estates had become more spatially and socially segregated than ever.[20]

Education: Taproot of Inequality?

There is a grimly ironic and often remarked fact in the history of British education. From seeds planted in a government report of 1926, the Education Act of 1936 had finally raised the school leaving age to fifteen as of September 1, 1939. On that very day, however, German troops invaded Poland, the evacuation of British school children began, and raising the school leaving age was postponed indefinitely.[21] Requiring children to remain in school until age fifteen was intended as an entering wedge for efforts to provide secondary schooling distinct from the often mediocre elementary schools in which most British children lingered until the age of fourteen. Now, with the outbreak of war, everything was frozen in place.

In 1941 R. A. Butler, long interested in education, accepted Churchill's invitation to leave his high profile post with the Foreign Ministry in order to head the Board of Education (the precursor to the Ministry of Education, as renamed in 1944). An upper-class, reform-minded Conservative, Butler understood that rationalizing Britain's educational system would be crucial to any broader social transformations in the war's aftermath. Churchill, who had little interest in educational reform, instructed Butler to lead a holding action that kept schools running as best as possible during wartime evacuations, bombings, and geographic displacements. The prime minister reiterated on several occasions that Butler should avoid initiatives that might disrupt the harmony of the coalition government or arouse the historic vested interests embedded in British education. Butler noted those limiting admonitions and quietly ignored them as he set to work in collaboration with his Labour deputy Chuter Ede, who had a background in education and shared the desire to craft a major education act acceptable to the coalition.

Butler succeeded by choosing his priorities. Above all, he negotiated tactfully but persistently with the three religious interest groups (the Anglicans, the

Dissenters, and the Roman Catholics) that had historically founded the nation's elementary schools and still ran about half of them. His creative diplomacy eventually broke the sectarian roadblocks to reforming Britain's archaic and uneven provision of elementary schooling. Using as leverage the financial straits and deteriorated physical condition of many schools, Butler devised a formula that won over the Anglicans and Dissenters. Each voluntary (i.e., religiously sponsored) school could opt to become a "controlled school"—with all its expenses absorbed by local school boards and rate payers in exchange for oversight, the hiring of most teachers, and a shift to a nondenominational form of Christian religious instruction. If that was unacceptable, a school could instead become an "aided school," which retained some independence in management and curriculum, and responsibility for roughly half of potentially costly capital expenditures, but with operational costs such as teacher salaries assumed by the local boards. Butler hoped to bring Catholic schools under the same umbrella of greater control in exchange for public financing, but he found no willing partners in negotiations with Catholic bishops and notables.[22]

With this major if incomplete rationalization of elementary schooling settled, Butler avoided overreach on other issues that might doom his whole project. His white paper and subsequent parliamentary act affirmed a commitment to raise the school leaving age to fifteen by 1947, and to sixteen when that became "practicable." As a corollary he promised access to secondary education for all, but he effectively left implementation of this fundamental issue to future governments. Given the growing debate over the forms and objectives of secondary schooling, especially among Labourites, Butler would only endorse local experimentation. Meanwhile he renounced any attempt to take in hand the operation of Britain's historic "public schools"—the 150 to 200 selective and expensive private institutions, depending on how one counted, crowned by the well-endowed likes of Eton, Winchester, and Harrow. While their exclusiveness seemed increasingly problematic to many, Butler knew that these bastions of social privilege had droves of loyal alumni ready to defend them in Whitehall and Westminster.[23] Nor, finally, did Butler have much to say about financing, expanding, or democratizing higher education. The resultant Butler Education Act of 1944 was thus a landmark of sorts and a success story in its own terms, but it was also an evasion of other major issues.

Churchill (with Attlee's agreement) consistently tried to postpone action on anything not central to winning the war, which might in turn strain his coalition's political stability. Faced with the Beveridge Report in 1943 and Butler's education white paper in the same year, Churchill considered the former more disruptive and financially onerous to implement. The PM side-tracked the Beveridge Report for the duration, at the cost of the bitter three-day debate in the Commons described in chapter 1. But he allowed the proposed Education Act to move forward in Parliament, since Butler had mollified the religious interests, left the "public schools" alone, and did not propose any contentious blueprint for secondary education. Parliament then adopted the act with substantial bipartisan support, despite rumblings from a vocal minority of Labourites.[24]

Labour's enthusiasm for the Beveridge Report in 1943 worked to the party's advantage as a campaign issue in the general election of 1945, but the Education Act of 1944 largely removed the subject of education from the campaign. In Labour's election manifesto the article on education said only: "An important step forward has been taken by the passing of the recent Education Act. Labour will put that Act not merely into legal force but into practical effect, including the raising of the school leaving age to 16 at the earliest possible moment; [and will back] 'further' or adult education, and free secondary education for all." After the election, education did not rank high on the cabinet's agenda, given the ambivalence in Labour's ranks about how to organize universal secondary education, even as the alternatives took on increasingly sharp definition.

Attlee chose as minister of education Ellen Wilkinson, the left-wing MP who had organized the dramatic Jarrow march against hunger and unemployment in 1936, but who allied with Herbert Morrison and served as his energetic deputy for civil defense during the war. As Minister Wilkinson's top priority was to implement the Emergency Training Scheme (ETS), a crash program put in place in 1944 to train new teachers with expedited twelve-month courses in over fifty special colleges, instead of the normal two-year program in estab-lished institutions. A great success, the ETS by the end of 1950 had turned out about 34,000 new teachers, two-thirds of them male and mostly former members of the armed forces.[25] Under Wilkinson the Education Ministry worked on expanding the provision of free school meals, promoting smaller class sizes, and overseeing the addition of roughly 5,000, mainly prefabricated classrooms to replace facilities damaged by bombing and to meet the expanded demand for schooling that would crest in 1948; a sister program delivered desks and furnishings for the new quarters. As this propulsive activity mounted, however,

Dalton urged that raising the school leaving age to fifteen be deferred from the announced target date of April 1947 to September to ease the financial burden even at the price of terminating schooling for most current fourteen-year-olds. But Wilkinson, as her last major act before her sudden death that February, insisted (under the threat of resignation) that the change take effect in April as promised.[26]

The prospects for secondary education depended in the main on the 150 or so Local Education Authorities (LEAs), with scant direction from the Butler Act or from the Labour government, apart from a requirement to file a development plan with the ministry by the end of 1946. Most LEAs followed the nonbinding recommendations of the Norwood Report of 1943, which Butler had commissioned to explore how universal secondary education might be implemented. With some qualifications, the report supported a three-track system of secondary education to serve the varying aptitudes and vocational needs of British youth as they moved on from primary schooling. The Norwood Commission believed that students could be divided into three "rough groupings" of aptitude and ability, to be sorted around the age of eleven by the standardized examination known as the 11-plus. Different types of secondary schools could then accommodate those disparities rather than cramming all pupils into one common institution and curriculum, which would be too taxing for most and insufficiently challenging for others. The three presumptive tracks comprised the traditionally rigorous, Latin-teaching, Grammar schools (for those likely to enter the learned professions or higher administrative and business positions); Technical schools (for students likely to become skilled craftsmen or mechanics); and "Secondary Moderns"—the catchment institutions for working-class students whose likely future lay in agriculture or unskilled labor, and for whom the curricula of the Grammar or Technical schools would be excessively demanding and pointless. (Of course, Norwood added, "ease of transfer" among the three types of schools should be assured when appropriate for individual students.) Butler's white paper distilled the Norwood perspective down to this bare formula: "After 11, secondary education, of diversified types but of equal standing, will be provided for all children."[27]

The Grammar schools—historically independent, with generally sterling reputations, rigorous curricula, and well-qualified teachers—had long crowned the pyramid of public secondary education in Britain. Founded mainly by endowments from the prospering middle classes in nineteenth-century British towns, they catered primarily to those local constituencies, in contrast to the Etons and Winchesters that drew on a national pool of well-heeled families. By 1945 most Grammar schools had two paths for admissions: roughly half the pupils received scholarships from their LEAs based on the results of the 11-plus examination. The remaining places went to the children of middle-class families that did not make the cut but could afford the fees. Ambitious working-class families had a special regard for the Grammars as a meritocratic portal to social mobility for their bright, hard-studying sons and daughters—children like Mikardo, Wilkinson herself, and other Labourites who had risen from humble origins by way of admission to their local Grammar school.[28]

The "public schools" (i.e., elite private schools), meanwhile, charged high fees and admitted students as they chose, despite some palliative suggestions in a report on "public schools" also commissioned by Butler in 1943. The Fleming Report proposed that a percentage of places in each "public school" be allotted to scholarship boys chosen by their LEAs, based on negotiated accords with individual schools. Most of the "public schools" signaled a receptivity to this scheme in principle, but it turned out that the great majority of the LEAs were reluctant to pay costly subventions for handfuls of individual pupils, even if a school were to accept them and parents agreed to send their anointed sons to those snobbishly forbidding institutions.[29]

The potential alternatives to the three types of tiered and separate public secondary schools were known as "multilaterals" or "comprehensives." Back in 1938 a Board of Education commission had considered endorsing multilateral schools, where all the students would have "the provision of good general education for two or three years . . . [followed by] the organization of four or five 'streams,' so that the pupils at the age of thirteen or fourteen years may follow courses that are suited to their individual needs and capacity." But the commission "reluctantly decided that we could not advocate as a general policy the substitution of such multilateral schools for separate schools of the existing types." Neither the Norwood Commission of 1943 nor the Butler Act endorsed "multilateral" schooling either, but they did recommend experimentation by the LEAs. While the 1944 Education Act thus struck a major blow against the "patchwork" character of elementary schooling across the country, its promise of universal secondary schooling largely left in place the presumption that different types of children should be educated in different types of schools.[30]

The tiered, three-track system could be viewed in the darkest terms. As summarized by Melissa Benn (a later advocate for comprehensives): "Written into this progress [by the Butler Act] was an a-priori separation of the country's children into winners and losers by the age of eleven—a division that predictably shaped itself along class lines. . . . The twin threads of class anxiety and class ambition were woven right through [secondary] school organization" after the war.[31] Generous LEA appropriations for the Grammar schools supported better teachers, curricula, and facilities; prepared their students for standardized exit examinations; and thereby secured for the minority of Grammar students who sought it an exclusive path to the universities to be shared with graduates of the elite "public schools." In the competition for places in the Grammar schools, working-class families had numerous individual success stories but lost out overall to the sons and daughters of professionals and businessmen. Conversely, the majority of students, who either shunned the 11-plus exam or failed to pass it, were likely to end up in Secondary Moderns with thinner curricula and resources and, as Wilkinson feared, where students might well suffer boredom, lack of incentive for self-discipline, or low self-esteem.[32]

Comprehensive secondary schools, where all students shared "a common school life," had been advocated since 1930 by the small but energetic National Association of Labour Teachers (NALT) and by elements in the London County Council, and they were vaguely endorsed as Labour Party policy in the late 1930s. The PLP, however, supported the Butler Act and shied away from embracing comprehensives as the route to universal secondary education. Neither Wilkinson nor her successor could unknot the division of opinion in the party or their own ambivalence over the appeal of freestanding Grammar schools. Both ministers left the matter on the back burner, which meant that advocates for a more principled egalitarian approach like the NALT were generally, though not entirely, stymied.[33]

At the annual party conference in Scarborough in May 1948, for example, two of four motions from the floor about education concerned secondary schooling. One vaguely tried to nudge the party toward comprehensives: "That all secondary schools should be free to develop Grammar and Technical courses without any limitation as to the percentage of pupils in any area taking such courses." A second motion (likely emanating from the NALT) was more confrontational: "That this Conference affirms the principle of the common Secondary School for all, up to the age of 16; the abolition of all fee paying; and the taking into the state system of all private, including so-called Public Secondary Schools." The conference neither adopted the motions nor voted them down but "remitted" them to the national executive "on the understanding that the principles behind them were accepted."[34]

Of necessity, experimentation remained the only way forward. As one education expert put it: there was no likelihood that comprehensives could be widely instituted in the face of prevailing and deep-seated traditions and interests. "My opinion is that our wisest course now is to watch carefully the experiments being made with each type of school, . . . to be guided by the results, and especially by the public reactions to the various types."[35] Since the LEAs retained the major say in financial and policy decisions about secondary education, the field for experimentation lay open.

At the end of 1946 the Fabian Society commissioned a review of the LEA development plans, required by the Butler Act, filed to date. Other than supporting "an adventurous will to experiment" and the "crying need" for more educational research, the review made no recommendations. But it noted that the Education Ministry "seems to consider large multilateral schools with some dubiety, as they have to be built so that they can be subdivided into separate schools if they do not prove a success." In any case, "at the moment parents tend to think that the 'cleverest' children are selected for the Grammar Schools . . . and the least 'clever' for the Modern Schools."[36]

Under the fifty-three development plans filed (one-third of the total LEAs) "the general picture shows the overwhelming preponderance of the Modern school, and acceptance of the policy of segregating secondary school children into Grammar, Modern, and Technical schools," the author concluded. About 12 percent of students would likely be attending Grammars, 41 percent Secondary Moderns, 6 percent Technicals, 10 percent Technical-Moderns, and 27 percent multilaterals or comprehensives. "[But some] LEAs have shown willingness to experiment, and have not accepted the policy of segregation without misgiving"; more than half the LEA's envisioned some move toward bi- or multilateral schools, and London and Middlesex "intend to set up multilaterals, which will swell the proportion of children who are not rigidly segregated." Few LEAs, however, would sanction the disappearance of existing Grammar schools in the name of "administrative unity or in pursuit of a theory of educational equality."[37]

A few plans offered broad arguments for multilateral or comprehensive schools, most notably the London County Council: "We tend to love exclusive aristocracies. . . . [But] we need to create a much wider aristocracy—of those who excel in the art of social living. . . . Education is not a matter merely of intellectual achievement. It is a matter of all-around growth and development. . . . Life in school should promote a feeling of social unity among adolescents of all kinds and degrees of ability." Certain LEAs favored multilaterals because of the flaws in segregating children by the 11-plus examination; or because they "believe that segregation will lead to a caste system in society and to an over-valuation of academic ability"; or because "the greater variety of courses in the same school would enable a curriculum to be chosen for each child which would more exactly fit his abilities and aptitudes than the set course in a Grammar, Technical, or Modern school."[38] The London County Council's Peckham Girls' Secondary exemplified the hopes for multilaterals. "No one specializes in the first two years"; later, informational vocational lectures would be offered to thirteen-year-olds and their parents, and in the third year students "branch off, but they do not become isolated." "Each of the three houses is a cross section of the school. . . . They do not obscure the children's sense of belonging to a year and [to the] school"; all recreational, sports, and outside enrichment activities would be pursued in those larger frameworks.[39]

In the decades after 1951 critiques of intelligence testing and the 11-plus exam fed the broader argument over secondary schooling, especially among aspiring middle-class families whose children failed to make the 11-plus cut and who might be forced to pay high school fees to avoid the reviled Secondary Moderns. When the 1964 election returned Labour to power, Minister of Education Anthony Crosland—a moderate in intraparty politics but a passionate egalitarian—brought to his post an animus against the "public schools," albeit with the paralyzing caveat that parents had a right to pay for the education they wished for their children. Crosland instead targeted the Grammar schools in the public sector. The ministry requested the LEAs to revisit tracking and to consider reorganizing secondary education. Ninety out of 163 took up those matters, and some began to incorporate Grammars into comprehensive schemes that would eventually reduce the number of Grammars from a high of over 1,000 to under 200. "Preservationists" successfully resisted mixed-ability schooling in other LEAs, but by 1974 about 60 percent of secondary students attended comprehensives. Conflict over selection, and over the forms, purposes, and financing of secondary education, would wax and wane through cycles of changing opinions down to the present day.[40]

In 1945 the pipeline for higher education remained extremely narrow at both ends (number of secondary school students qualified for university admission and number of places available). When Labour lost the election of 1951 the situation had not much changed. Limited capacity in the universities reinforced the fact that secondary schooling prepared so few students to seek or qualify for a university education. As Labour prepared for the election in 1950 the party boasted that "in 1939, 13,255 pupils sat for the Higher School Certificate examination [for university admission], and 9,901 passed. In 1948, 29,731 sat, and 20,582 passed."[41] But the prewar baseline was so constricted that this doubling only underlined the problem of limited access to universities.

Before the war all British universities combined enrolled a total of about 50,000 students: roughly one-quarter at the University of London, one-quarter at Oxford and Cambridge, one-quarter in Scotland's four universities, and one-quarter at the red bricks, which like Grammar schools, had local roots and support. Self-governing corporations, universities relied mainly on their endowments and tuition fees for income along with any support that might come from local authorities. In 1911 a national University Grants Committee (UGC) funded by the Treasury began to subsidize universities, in part proportionately to the demonstrated need of each. By the 1930s the subsidy typically provided about a third of a university's income but never more than half. The UGC had no oversight powers but paid site visits every five years to each university. The UGC's reports registered warning signs about duplicated or dubious research by faculty, but they did not lobby for an expansion of scientific teaching or university capacity.[42]

After the war the Treasury replaced some of the elderly members of the UGC with more dynamic academics and added planning for future development to the UGC's brief. Starting in 1946 Treasury support increased, and by 1950 the UGC provided on average about 60 percent of the universities' income.[43] But no impetus for university expansion came from Attlee's government, given the mountain of more immediate claims on public resources. Nor did Labour seriously decry the constricted state of higher education as a major obstacle to long-term social mobility.

The postwar influx of veterans made little dent on the status quo. The coalition government had enacted a Further Education and Training scheme (FET) to provide full tuition and maintenance grants for demobilized members of the armed forces whose post-secondary education at universities or specialized colleges had been disrupted by the war. Of 83,000 FETs awarded between 1945 and 1950, 43,000 went to university students. Compared to the almost 2 million American veterans who attended colleges and universities under the G.I. Bill (roughly 1 in 8 returning servicemen and women), Britain's program touched only 1 in 100 veterans.[44]

For the clarion call that Labour might have raised about a future reform and expansion of higher education we have instead the pamphlet prepared for the education committee of the Fabian Society. The author, who wrote as "Quintus," was identified as a twenty-eight-year-old Oxford man with a distinguished prewar academic record and army service in the ranks and as an officer between 1940 and 1945. With extensive statistics, his inquest offered a bleak overview of university education in 1947 and put forth a simple agenda for expanding higher educational opportunity.

In the near future university capacity must at least double, Quintus argued. Scholarship support—the crucial underpinning of recruitment by merit—was currently the typical British patchwork of well-meaning but inadequate provisions. (Forty percent of students had financial help of some sort before the war, and the proportion briefly rose to perhaps 70 percent as the FET veterans passed through but would then decline.) Quintus argued that comprehensive scholarship aid must support every admitted student who needed it, with an eventual goal of eliminating tuition altogether. Admission must be entirely by merit as opposed to current practices where (as with Grammar schools) "we have not one system of selection of undergraduates, but an uneasy combination of two: the first depending on ability, and the *second on ability to pay.*" And selection by merit need not depend exclusively on standard examinations but could be supplemented by "the use of the interview and possibly other tests," because well-off families gave their offspring advantages in preparation for those examinations.[45]

In anticipation of the general election in 1950 Labour boasted that "the road to university has already been greatly widened," with 80,000 students now enrolled in Britain's universities compared to 50,000 before the war.[46] But the bar had been so high to begin with, and the increase (driven in part by the FET that would shortly end) so modest, that this was not much of an achievement. Plans and support for opening new universities or adding new programs, and for accommodating and aiding substantially more students, did not begin in earnest until 1953 under a dynamic new chairman of the UGC. Only in 1961 did the number of university students finally more than double from prewar levels to 113,000, with plans for up to 60,000 more places by the end of the decade, at which time seven new universities were slated to open.[47]

Forging a National Health Service

The Beveridge Report of 1943 proposed concrete measures to mitigate penurious old age, unemployment, and disability, but Beveridge also identified three other areas for government action outside the purview of his plan for social insurance: a full-employment policy (which Beveridge himself sketched in a subsequent report on his own initiative) to minimize rather than merely palliate unemployment; children's allowances, which (as we saw) the coalition government enacted in 1944; and a National Health Service (NHS) that would provide comprehensive and universal health care for the British people.

The patchwork quality of unemployment insurance schemes or old-age pensions that Beveridge sought to rationalize applied to health care as well. Lloyd George's program in 1913 for "national health insurance" (NHI) became a major feature in that landscape. Opposition from the British Medical Association (BMA) failed to derail the proposal and once Parliament adopted NHI, a threatened boycott by doctors did not materialize. Medical specialists were not involved in the NHI, but the great majority of general practitioners enrolled as "panel doctors," who received standardized capitations (yearly flat fees) paid by the government for each eligible worker who signed up for care. The NHI program, however, did not cover the spouses and children of eligible workers, did not apply to hospitalizations, and had income limits that kept out most of the self-employed and middle classes. While the number of enrolled workers expanded to about 15 million over the next two decades, those exclusions remained in place.[48]

The availability, staffing, management, and finances of hospitals was another patchwork element in British health care. Numerous hospitals had been built in the long nineteenth century, sustained by the growth of local philanthropy and the activity of local public authorities or councils. As a result, two uncoordinated types of hospitals had developed. By 1939 they comprised 1,334 private or voluntary hospitals (among them a score of high prestige teaching hospitals) and 1,771 public or municipal hospitals (including many small facilities for treatment of TB or "fevers").[49] The Ministry of Health, established in 1919, had no significant jurisdiction over either type.

By the eve of World War II, if one looked at this from a national perspective, hospitals constituted a crazy quilt of uneven geographical provision, while access and quality of care for ailing individuals varied starkly according to class and wealth. Access for working people and the poor usually involved a demeaning confinement to charity beds, a relic of times past. As one scholar concludes, the voluntary hospitals acquired over time "a dual character: a service for the rich grew alongside the older charitable services."[50] In any case, most hospitals of both types had fallen into financial straits, notwithstanding a spate of hospital modernization in greater London during the 1930s under the socialist County Council.[51] Income from the endowments that had once sustained the private hospitals provided on average under half their necessary funding by 1939. With war on the horizon, the government scrambled to assemble an Emergency Hospital Service to provide a semblance of subsidy and coordination for the distribution of personnel, equipment and supplies if waves of military or civilian casualties inundated the hospitals as they shortly would.

Two successive coalition ministers of health began to plan for health care after the war. In February 1944 the Conservative Henry Willink circulated a draft white paper, "A National Health Service," potentially comparable to Butler's white paper on education, with the draft of a Parliamentary act intended to follow. But the plan drew criticism from some Labourites for its limitations and headlong resistance in a different spirit from the British Medical Association. Labour's cabinet ministers seemed willing to support the white paper, but only as "a first installment" or "an irreducible minimum" for what they desired. Led by the small but vocal Socialist Medical Association (SMA) and the Fabian Society's Medical Services Research Group, some Labourites insisted on the need for group-practice health centers employing state-salaried physicians who, they hoped, would become the entering wedge for a publicly salaried medical service in the future—the BMA's worst fear. Willink's plan would have permitted part-time private practice for doctors with capitation rosters, but the SMA wished to end the combination of private and public practice. Labourites wanted to end the sale of medical practices (which Willink did not propose), and to regulate where new doctors could practice in order to aid underserved regions. Finally, some Labourties advocated a takeover of the voluntary hospitals as a step toward a unified hospital system.[52]

When Willink published his white paper, resistance from the BMA began in earnest. The association sought to secure the future of private practice and of the voluntary hospitals, and to maximize the freedom and influence of physicians in all corners of any new medical landscape. Acutely hostile to supervision by the untutored laymen of local councils, the BMA pressed for administrative and advisory supremacy by medical professionals. Willink had devised a complex formula for leaving the voluntary hospitals their independence while assuming most of their costs, but the BMA wanted a firmer guarantee. The BMA also sought certainty that the sale of medical practices would not be banned, as well as severe limits on any public power to direct physicians to underserved areas. Willink held extensive negotiations with the BMA, and in due course he modified his proposal to accommodate some of their concerns. As John Pater, an authority on the NHS, concludes of Willink's compromises: "The price [he] paid included not only the abandonment of important elements, such as controls on the distribution of doctors, and the rapid development of [group-practice] health centers, . . . but also the creation of a planning and administrative system of almost unworkable complexity."[53]

The minister's concessions to the BMA, however, only stiffened Labour's reservations about his approach. As the coalition wound down after VE-Day, the Conservatives decided against introducing a Parliamentary act that might galvanize Labour's critique and unleash a debate that could aid Labour in the coming election. But even without that debate—and without being tied to a specific blueprint of its own—Labour now had a promising issue for its election campaign. After Labour's victory, when the time for hard decisions came, instead of Willink in the crosshairs it would be a leading bête noire of the Tories, Nye Bevan.

Since Willink's white paper had foundered, Bevan inherited only a vague consensus for "a comprehensive and universal" health care system free to all citizens and no roadmap for how to get there. The vested interests obstructing any path forward had not changed: the general practitioners skittish about losing their freedom to new types of authority; specialists and consultants who had their own concerns and their private patients; the "voluntary" and the municipal hospitals, with their respective traditions and local constituencies; and, on the left, socialist physicians whose ideal remained a full-time salaried medical service and new group-practice health centers.

Bevan started with the hospitals, the key sites in his eyes for improving medical care, where all citizens, regardless of who they were and where they lived, should have free access to beds and specialists. As things stood, the voluntary hospitals had tottering finances and no public control, and they usually ministered to charity cases and full-pay patients with little in between. Many municipal hospitals were too small, and the elected local councils often ran them in parochial fashion. Bevan abandoned the contorted solutions that Willink had considered and simply proposed to nationalize all hospitals (except the prestigious teaching hospitals), and to create a unified system that transformed their governance and financing. Instead of establishing an independent public corporation to oversee the nation's hospitals, on the model being used for the nationalization of coal and electricity, the Ministry of Health would supervise the new structure directly. But at the next level Bevan adapted the template for coal and utilities by creating fifteen or so regional hospital boards. Dissociated from the elected local councils, the regional boards would have planning responsibilities and supervisory power over new local hospital management committees. Each management committee would in turn oversee the hospitals in a district organized around a "natural hospital area" for their population, such districts numbering 370 by the time the NHS launched.[54]

In the cabinet Bevan faced opposition led by Herbert Morrison, Attlee's deputy prime minister. Morrison's career had long been anchored by his leadership of Labour in the London County Council, and by a vision of democratic socialism expressed in good part through the action of elected local councils. But with a nudge from Attlee, the cabinet came around to Bevan's plan for nationalization and governance by appointed regional boards rather than elected councils.[55]

As for the general practitioners, Labour at its annual conference in 1934 had ostensibly embraced the SMA's call for a full-time salaried medical service in preference to capitations (annual prepaid fees per enrolled patient). But that loosely held party stance did not drive legislative policy after 1945. Instead Bevan proposed only to supplement capitations with small salaries, in order to undergird free choice for patients. (Capitations, as one historian puts it, "encouraged the doctor to provide good service in order to attract and keep the patient who could move if dissatisfied.")[56] Formally the GPs (as well as dentists and pharmacists) would be under contract to local "executive councils," at least half of whose members would be medical professionals. Bevan insisted that dental, hearing, and eye care should be incorporated into the NHS from the outset. Meanwhile, new doctors would be barred from practicing in overserved areas, and the sale of medical practices would be abolished with compensation to current practitioners. On a separate track (a separation much criticized in the future) local authorities would still be responsible for public health services such as ambulances, immunization drives, midwifery, pre- and postnatal care, and home nursing. The NHS would encourage those local authorities to establish new group-practice health centers as well, but given current constraints on construction projects and finances, Bevan made no promises whatsoever about such facilities.

Reluctantly, Bevan agreed that specialists working in NHS hospitals could also have special "pay beds" for fee-paying private patients, which he assumed would win over most specialists and deter a proliferation of private clinics for wealthy patients. Bevan also insisted on funding the NHS from general tax revenue rather than the contributions being levied on citizens and employers for national social insurance. Finally, Bevan asserted that he would consult with spokesmen for the profession but would not "negotiate" with the BMA before he presented a draft of his act to Parliament.

If the BMA could not negotiate, it could certainly lobby on issues of freedom, recompense, and control over physicians in the future health service, and it could attack Bevan's "tyrannical" treatment of the profession. Along with the *British Medical Journal,* Conservative MPs, and Tory newspapers, the BMA amplified the fear that whatever its initial form, Bevan's NHS would evolve into a full-time salaried medical service, where doctors became a branch of the civil service.[57] Concretely the BMA defended the right to buy and sell medical practices, opposed controls over the distribution of physicians, objected to adding any salaries to customary capitations, questioned the treatment of the voluntary hospitals, deplored the inordinate power of the minister under the draft, and balked at the balance between professionals and laymen on supervisory boards. But with Labour's solid parliamentary majority supporting the minister every step of the way, the bill withstood all opposition assaults on the plan and on its much-vilified architect. The act became law on November 6, 1946, with the royal assent, and the "appointed day" for the NHS to launch was to be January 1, 1948, later postponed by the cabinet to July 5.

After the act passed, the BMA polled its members with an obliquely phrased question: "Do you desire the Negotiating Committee to enter into discussions with the Minister on the regulations authorized by the NHS Act?" A negative,

hard-line, vote implicitly committed a doctor to boycotting the service, the ultimate pressure on the government to modify the act's terms. The vote did not
quite register the overwhelming repudiation of the NHS that the BMA's adamant
leaders expected. While 54 percent did vote no, 46 percent endorsed the milder
option of further discussion, but the GPs voted no by nearly two to one. The
battle between the Bevan and the BMA now seemed to simplify: either the
government would amend the act favorably or a mass of GPs seemed likely
shun the NHS when it began in 1948.

Bevan refused to panic, confident that in the end the great majority of doctors
would join. All along he had cultivated support from the three small but prestigious Royal Colleges of physicians, of surgeons, and of obstetricians to
counter the all-out hostility of the BMA, and he now enlisted them to promote
a more temperate exchange of views within the profession. To this end Bevan
made a few adjustments at the margins of his plan, while a commission he
appointed in June 1947 set the actual terms of remuneration for various types
of doctors on the generous side. But into the next year the BMA still insisted
that the act was "so grossly at variance with the essential principles of our
profession that it should be rejected absolutely by all practitioners." To prepare
the ground the BMA held another plebiscite and stated that if more than 13,000
GPs voted against the act, the profession should boycott the NHS en masse.
Bevan countered by arranging a debate in Parliament where he attacked
the BMA's "squalid political conspiracy" and "organized sabotage." While he
offered some conciliatory gestures over two technical sticking points (the status
of medical partnerships and rights of appeal by doctors against sanctions by
their local executive council), he stood fast on abolishing the sale of medical
practices and on adding a small state salary to compensation by capitation for
GPs. His confrontational tone evidently stiffened the backs of the doctors,
however, and in February 1948 the plebiscite showed only 4,084 specialists and
GPs voting for accepting service and 25,340 against![58]

As an impasse loomed, Bevan's supporters at the Royal Colleges of medicine suggested that he should explicitly promise that a full-time salaried service
would never enter through the back door of regulation, and that the modest
salaries supplementing capitations would last three years and become optional
thereafter, so that they served mainly to help new doctors get established. Bevan
effectively made those gestures, and the BMA therefore conducted another poll
in May. This time the outcome was closer. Around 13,000 doctors voted for

accepting service and around 14,000 against, but the negative votes included only 8,500 to 9,500 GPs—far below the 13,000 noes set by the BMA as the threshold for an all-out boycott.[59] The hard line chairman of the BMA now announced its capitulation in a letter to *The Times,* and he pledged that "the profession will do its utmost to make the new service a resounding success."

Bevan's final volley before the launch came during a parliamentary Q and A in June: any rumor that treatments or drugs under the NHS would be inferior to those for private patients was categorically false, he insisted. There would be no more "'panel doctoring' for the less well-off nor anything charitable or demeaning" in their treatment. Warming to a theme in his personal socialist vision Bevan added: "There is nothing of the social group or class in this; and I know you will be with me in seeing that there does not unintentionally grow up any kind of differentiation between those who use the new arrangements and those who . . . do not."[60]

The NHS passed from word to deed with astonishing success. After the launch in July 1948, 95 to 97 percent of the population enrolled in the first few months. About 20,000 GPs (90 percent) joined the NHS as did comparable or higher proportions of specialists, dentists, pharmacists, and opticians. As Bevan's admiring colleague and biographer Michael Foot plausibly maintains, "Few victories in politics have ever been so conclusive. . . . The service won national approval, immediate and lasting."[61] The finances of the NHS, on the other hand, were bound to raise problems, since prior to the launch "it was quite impossible to tell the extent to which this new scheme would be used by the general public." Within a year the initial cost estimates proved much too low given the popularity of the service. While "the cost per prescription is approximately as estimated," a ministry spokesman reported, the volume of prescriptions far exceeded expectations. And "who could have foreseen that a quarter of the population would have rushed to the dentist's chair, a seat not generally chosen for dalliance?" Or that 2 million pairs of spectacles would be prescribed in the first six months. By the end of 1949, 6.8 million dental visits had been logged and 4.5 million pairs of eyeglasses prescribed, both easing the "inarticulate misery and pain" of long neglect. Meanwhile the regional hospital boards and their management committees outspent original cost estimates as they began renovating, hiring, and making salary adjustments. Altogether the costs of the NHS required a supplemental appropriation of £98 million early in 1950 over the original £366 million for the first full year of operation, although administrative costs amounted to only 2.3 percent of the total.[62]

Anxiety over Britain's fiscal straits nonetheless led Morrison and Cripps to urge that NHS costs be reined in, lest they spiral out of control. In October 1949 the cabinet pressured Bevan to accept the principle of a one shilling co-payment on each prescription to raise additional revenue for the service, but also because a small co-payment might "have substantial effect in eliminating unnecessary resort to prescriptions." Bevan deplored this breach in the promise of free medical care, accepted the cabinet's decision instead of resigning, but retained authority over whether or when to implement the charge—something he did not actually intend to do. Cripps also wanted to set a ceiling of £329 million on the NHS for 1951–52 and to require small co-payments on dentures and eyeglasses. Here Bevan drew the line and talked his colleague around.[63]

Likewise troubled by the cost of the NHS, the Conservative minister of health in 1952 appointed a committee chaired by a noted economist to review how the NHS was working. Finally published in January 1956, the report dismissed charges of financial laxity in the NHS and showed on the contrary that its costs had fallen as a percentage of gross national product. Inflation and expanded services, not inefficiency, had led to rising costs. Moreover, the report surprisingly concluded, "It would be altogether premature at the present time to propose any fundamental change in the structure of the NHS." Similarly an independent inquiry by a blue-ribbon medical panel reported in 1962 that the NHS was sound, admirably comprehensive, and had not infringed on the independence of doctors, although it criticized the compartmentalization of general practice, hospitals, and local authority provisions for public health.[64]

Voices from the left also complained about that threefold division, and about the failure to establish group-practice health centers. Bevan's NHS plan had included group health centers, but claims on materials and funding to erect factories, housing, and schools relegated health centers to the lowest priority. A lack of enthusiasm among physicians for health centers reinforced a tepid commitment to such facilities by Bevan and his officials in the ministry. In 1948 Bevan formally released local authorities from the responsibility to plan for health centers, and under his other hat as minister in charge of housing he did not set aside sites for health centers on new public housing estates. Health centers effectively fell by the wayside in Labour's implementation of the NHS.[65]

A leader of the Socialist Medical Association insisted at the 1947 party conference that health centers represented "the symbol to the people of this country of what a Socialist Medical Health Service really means." Deep in Labour Party records one can find traces of the hopes invested in that model for delivery of health care. The proposed Birmingham Health Center, for example, illustrated how a new health center might actually look. Estimated to cost £30,000 and to serve 20,000 people, the center would accommodate five GPs, each with a suite of offices, a joint facility for minor surgical procedures, a dispensary, two dental offices, and quarters where one doctor could be on call at night. But "the present building situation" stymied even the London County Council, which had to shelve plans for building brand-new health centers in each of its nine health districts and settled instead for opening only one "new, specially designed" center in 1952. Worse yet, according to a history of the SMA, the costs of this London facility "would be used as one excuse for not continuing with a health centre programme."[66]

Restructuring proposals kept coming from both sides of the House: to find new formulas for administrative bodies; to shift costs away from Treasury spending and to increase payments into the NHS from National Insurance contributions; to modify the compensation of doctors, dentists, and hospitals (perhaps levying an "hotel charge" on patients who could pay); to expand co-payments. By 1981, with a budget of £8,500 million, roughly 88 percent of NHS funds still came from the Treasury, 10 percent from National Insurance payments to the NHS, and 2 percent from co-pays.[67] Thatcher's governments created incentives to contract out for various NHS services and to privatize some altogether, and Blair's New Labour continued this trend. All told, since 1948 the NHS has been reorganized repeatedly, whittled away at, yet reaffirmed by successive governments under both parties—who often claimed to be saving the NHS from itself: from the prodigality supposedly built into its conception of universal, free health care.[68]

Public Ownership Revisited

With the exception of iron and steel, by 1947 Labour had moved on all nationalizations pledged in its 1945 manifesto. In most cases, after a brief learning curve, the transitions went fairly smoothly. Only the nationalization of inland transport hit a major snag on how to treat independent, short-haul truck drivers who numbered in the hundreds of thousands. After prolonged disagreement, the cabinet decided to leave them out of the new public sector, and state control fell short of the integrated rail and road transport system originally imagined.[69] At the least, public ownership eliminated the private profit motive and stock dividends, and it facilitated planning and coordination. The legislative acts generally stopped short of drastic structural reorganization, however, and ruled out worker parity on managing boards. When Labour's annual conference revisited the subject of industrial democracy in 1948, a motion from the Amalgamated Engineering Union (AEU) urged that administrators in nationalized sectors "be chosen from persons of proven ability and from among organized workers by hand or brain; and that the principle of workers' participation in management, through their trade unions, should be firmly established." Spokesmen for the NEC opposed the notion of workers sitting by right on managing boards. As Jim Griffiths put it: "While it is agreed that the fullest possible use should be made of men of ability drawn from the ranks of the workers, it would be quite wrong to appoint men on any test other than capacity for the job." He recognized that most managers "had been brought up in a capitalist environment," a situation that must gradually change, but "political tests" for such posts were inappropriate. Amicable debate gave way briefly when another motion from the floor called for iron and steel to be nationalized "on the basis of complete workers' control and without compensation"—to which Sam Watson, secretary of the Durham Miner's Federation, scornfully replied that this "smelled of syndicalism with a faint tinge of Guild Socialism."[70]

Whether to proceed with the nationalization of iron and steel and, if so, how to carry it out and on what timetable proved divisive questions. Steel would be the first and only manufacturing industry to be nationalized, as opposed to infrastructure, power, or transport. Coal, railroads, and utilities all needed modernization, new capital, better management, and coordination. The quasi-cartelized steel industry had limited its capacity during the long slump to protect profitability for some owners, but it had performed reasonably well during and after the war, given the huge new demands for its output. If steel, unlike coal, was not "failing the nation"—one ostensible test for nationalization—steel remained one of the "commanding heights" that had to be taken in hand under Labour's program for a planned, high-efficiency mixed economy. But might something short of public ownership give the government sufficient leverage over steel? And would nationalization be worth the struggle with the well-organized steel barons and their free-enterprise Tory supporters?

In Attlee's cabinet, Morrison, on economic and political grounds, advocated a minimalist approach to steel and a postponement of legislation for as long as possible. Initially the cabinet swept aside Morrison's concerns and instructed Minister of Supply John Wilmot to draft a plan. Wilmot ran into adamant resistance from the British Iron and Steel Federation, the industry's trade association, but submitted a proposal to the cabinet to move on public ownership in the parliamentary session of 1947–48 "by a simple acquisition of shares, while retaining the names and forms of the existing companies." The general secretary of the steel workers union, who opposed nationalization of his industry, urged Morrison to reopen the question, and a wavering Attlee allowed Morrison to present an alternative to Wilmot's plan. Morrison's "hybrid" plan stopped short of veritable nationalization and proposed instead a new Iron and Steel Control Board to coordinate the industry, with government power to take ownership of companies held in reserve.[71]

Bevan for one was furious. His district in Wales included one of the leading British steelworks, whose owners had shuttered it during the slump and caused untold misery for many of Bevan's constituents. Reopened by the time the war began, the Ebbw Vale steelworks had performed well, but Bevan was adamant that the interests of private owners should never again wreak such human havoc or hold back an expansion of capacity. Probably no one in cabinet felt as strongly as Bevan on the need for full-scale nationalization of iron and steel.[72] Under such pushback, the divided cabinet finally rejected Morrison's "hybrid" plan but agreed to defer action on steel to the parliamentary session of 1948–49.

A new minister of supply submitted a plan for public ownership of iron and steel that left intact existing enterprises and marketing operations. The government would buy out the shares of 92 companies, but under a new British Steel Corporation no major restructuring of the industry was planned, and no significant form of worker participation in management would be introduced. Opposition in the House of Lords delayed the bill but could not derail it, and the government agreed that vesting day would come in July 1950, after the next general election. As one critic observed, however, the steel bill "removes the profit motive and puts nothing in its place." Few Labour MPs joined Mikardo in urging that nationalization of steel logically be followed by similar measures in the engineering (fabrication) and machine tool industries.[73]

At the party conference of 1948 speakers talked of "pressing on until we emerge from the capitalist wilderness," and the party anticipated that "steel—the citadel of economic power—[would] soon be in the hands of the People." Including iron and steel, about 20 percent of the national economy would soon be under public ownership. Was yet more nationalization needed to achieve Labour's visions for a planned, mixed economy and for greater social equality? Labour's commitment to the "common ownership of the means of produc-tion"—the totemic Clause 4 of the party's 1918 charter document—endured as a slogan. But uncertainty grew over what additional public ownership might accomplish that planning, regulation, and coordination of the private sector could not. To the extent that public ownership would facilitate economic effi-ciency (a "technocratic" doctrine long associated with the Fabian Society), perhaps it had now gone as far as it should. But if nationalization also had the social purpose of curbing the economic and political power of the wealthy few under democratic socialism, then mere efficiency need not suffice as the test, and further nationalizations might well be desirable. In addition, as Morrison later noted, the nationalization acts had done almost nothing so far to address the interests of consumers.[74]

A Fabian Society pamphlet, *More Socialism or Less?,* posed the core ques-tion, as summarized by a reviewer in the party bulletin: "In 1950–55 should we press on with further socialization of industry and services? Or should we mark time and have a breathing space in which to consolidate the progress so far? In the end the authors come down on both sides of the fence."[75] Indeed in most shades of party opinion, from Morrison to Bevan, from the TUC to Keep Left, ambivalence prevailed on the further expansion of public ownership. As the research department at Labour headquarters prepared material for the party's manifesto in the coming election in 1950, it concluded that the obvious targets for public ownership in heavy industry already functioned with reasonable effi-ciency. Nationalization therefore seemed unsuitable for strongholds of British capitalism such as Unilever, airplane manufacturing, auto manufacturing, and chemical industry giants.[76]

Still, the final draft of the manifesto for 1950 called for nationalizing cement and sugar refining because they constituted near monopolies presumably detri-mental to the public interest. Water supply, a scarce basic necessity, "should become a wholly public responsibility." The importing and wholesaling of meat had been supervised by the Ministry of Food during and after the war; now "the present system of distribution should become a permanent public service." Finally the manifesto targeted the large industrial or accident insurance companies that sold individual supplements to new state social insurance provisions: "the Proprietary Companies should be taken out of the realm of private profit and [be] mutually owned by the policyholders themselves instead of by private shareholders."[77]

With its tepid framing and omission of the most weighty manufacturing sectors, the manifesto could easily appear as a shopping list of possibilities without much conviction or coherence. The dissidents of Keep Left, for example, were skeptical. "Our social democracy is now based not merely on public ownership . . . but also on the destruction of arbitrary power, whether exercised by the manager, the bureaucrat or the State. . . . There are more ways of nationalization than whole industry legislation, and more ways of killing the capitalist cat than choking it with compensation! . . . [The state could also] buy up one or more plants, or build new ones to operate in competition with the existing firms in any industry." In sum, other, experimental ways lay open in which to exercise state power within a mixed economy.[78]

In the coming electoral campaign, however, the threat to take cement and sugar into public ownership created backlashes that Labour could ill afford. The inclusion of sugar refining on the list seems in retrospect especially misconceived. True, Tate and Lyle controlled 85 percent of the industry's capacity, but the public had little sense that the giant firm was "failing the nation" in the distribution, quality, or pricing of its popular sweeteners. Tate and Lyle launched a shrewd advertising campaign against nationalization of sugar, featuring the charmingly belligerent icon of "Mr. Cube." Then too Morrison had warned that putting the industrial insurance companies on the list, however persuasive the rationale, would unleash thousands of insurance agents who had day-to-day contacts with voters. Pledging the "mutualization" of the big companies rather than outright nationalization appeased neither the firms like Prudential nor their employees, who (in Morgan's words) "became in effect unpaid Tory propagandists, without producing any obvious changes or benefits with which the voters could identify."[79] Without a coherent strategy going forward in a key area of socialist economic doctrine, Labour entered the electoral campaign of 1950 with these two self-inflicted wounds.

Labour and Communism, at Home and Abroad

Communism, however, was one issue that would not bedevil Labour as it approached the general election. In France and the US the influence of domestic communism, real or imagined, had a great impact on the political postures and fortunes of progressive forces. In Britain the Labour Party's long-established scorn for home-grown communists helped make the case for democratic socialism. Yet Labour insisted that "communist conspiracy is a real danger." How Labour confronted communism at home and abroad aligns Labour with kindred anti-communist progressives in France and the US but also sets it apart.

In the late 1930s the Labour Party (as we saw) would not join the popular front bandwagon. It rejected a bid for affiliation by the Communist Party of Great Britain (CPGB), forbade its members to join front organizations or share platforms with communists, and in early 1939 expelled Cripps and Bevan (the latter readmitted after a brief interval) for noncompliance. Another communist bid for affiliation in 1942, after the awkward period of the Hitler-Stalin pact had ended, also met rejection. With an estimated 45,000 members, the CPGB had significant influence in some trade unions and intellectual circles, but it failed to broaden its base during the war. In 1945 some activists, responding to a murky change in the party line, campaigned for Labour candidates, while the CPGB ran 21 candidates of its own; the latter won around 100,000 votes and just 2 seats, and lost their deposits in 12 districts.[80] So early in 1946 the communists made another bid for affiliation with Labour.

Sustained later by the annual conference, the national executive (NEC) summarily rejected this request. Labour had historically "shown its goodwill towards the workers' regime in Russia" (with early support for recognizing the Soviet Union), but it claimed that the CPGB was actually "an obstacle to friendship with Russia." Whatever Stalin's reasons for the Nazi-Soviet pact had been, for instance, the adherence of the CPGB to the Moscow party line during that desperate period for Britain made CPGB behavior seem manifestly unpatriotic. Labour's rejection statement of 1946 insisted that the Labour Party was the only effective political weapon of Britain's workers; that the CPGB opposed democracy as "a bourgeois fraud"; did not think for itself; and influenced neither opinion nor policy. "Their unquestioning obedience to a party line imposed from above have made their periodical somersaults the laughing-stock of the world, isolated in their little cells, speaking and thinking an alien jargon."

Unable to discredit democratic socialism, the CPGB now sought affiliation only "to try to break up the Labour Movement from within."[81]

"As an affiliated organization," the NEC declared, "the Communists would be able to introduce their bitter sectarian quarrels into every local Labour party branch ... [with] deliberately engineered quarrels over issues of minor importance. They would attempt to drive out in disgust all sections of the Labour Party which disagreed with their private 'party line'... by demagogy and all the methods of caucus control.... Secret meetings of the Communist Party 'fractions' would precede every meeting of a local Labour Party. Parodying democracy by rigid pressure tactics, they would seek to install their nominees in all important offices." The NEC's sense of how British communists would operate "as a fifth column working from within" anticipated in detail the recriminations that roiled the progressives of the American Veterans Committee in the US (see chapter 9).

When the Labour Party came to power in 1945 it hoped (like the tripartite governments in France) to steer between American capitalism and Soviet communism in international relations as well as domestic policy. But Foreign Minister Ernest Bevin (who early on experienced Soviet bullying directly) swung the government increasingly toward its US ally and financial benefactor. In 1947 the Keep Left backbenchers created a stir with a pamphlet criticizing the government's drift away from the party's "third force" stance of 1945. International Secretary Denis Healey countered with a pamphlet defending Bevin's diplomacy. In the simplest terms, Bevin aligned Britain with the US to resist Soviet pressures in Europe and the Middle East, as Britain withdrew from active influence in Greece, Palestine, and Iran. At this uncertain moment Bevin urged Washington to resist isolationist sentiment in the US and commit itself more robustly to countering Soviet diplomatic pressures. Healey noted the "sustained and violent offensive against Britain by her Russian ally ... which aimed at isolating Britain morally as a decadent reactionary power"—the current emphasis in Soviet diplomacy. In this light, "the aim of an Anglo-American understanding is to prevent war by proving to Russia that an aggressive anti-British policy is doomed to frustration."[82] The Keep Left group of course shared the goal of maintaining peace and promoting postwar accord, but it hoped to do so by returning to the mediating, third force posture envisaged by Labour in 1945. At the Margate party conference in May 1947 Healey's pamphlet drew serious criticism, but Bevin's forceful speech helped quash a motion critical of his diplomacy.[83]

The government had also introduced a bill in Parliament to extend conscription for five years. At the party conference anti-militarists opposed this measure, but their motion garnered only 571,000 mandates versus 2,332,000 against. Dissenting Labour MPs in the House then persuaded Attlee to reduce the proposed term of national military service from eighteen months to one year, but by the end of 1948 Parliament restored the eighteen-month term of service.[84] During 1948 events on the ground made Bevin's policy shift all but inexorable: the communist coup in Prague; the Berlin blockade; the rejection by the Eastern bloc of participation in the Marshall Plan for European recovery; and attacks by Western communist parties against the Marshall Plan.[85]

In this evolving environment, Labour backbenchers who continued to defend the Soviet Union and insist on Western culpability for the deepening Cold War fell afoul of the Labour leadership. While the Keep Left group took a far more qualified stand, welcomed the Marshall Plan, and stayed within the bounds of party rules, "hard leftists" ignored party policy, including bans on supporting "fusion movements" of socialists and communists in Italy, Germany, and Poland. Hard left initiatives included the "Nenni Telegram" signed by three dozen Labour MPs to cheer on the "fusionist" socialist leader Pietro Nenni on the eve of the Italian elections of 1948, even though the NEC had endorsed the socialist faction led by Nenni's anti-communist rival. In the wake of the Nenni telegram the Labour Party expelled a prime mover in that affair (Platts-Mills) and later moved against four fellow traveling MPs who continued to fraternize with "fusion" movements on the continent, above all the left-wing polemicist Konni Zilliacus. Elected an MP in 1945, Zilliacus had experience in foreign relations as an official with the League of Nations before the war. An inexhaustible and habitual apologist for the Soviet Union, Zilliacus it is true did not slavishly follow the Moscow line, and he had come to support Tito against Stalin's anathema. But that nuance scarcely mattered to the Labour leadership.[86]

While some Labourites accused the four MPs of being "crypto-communists," Transport House ostensibly came down on them for repeated violations of party discipline. The NEC finally expelled the four in 1949, in the case of Zilliacus only after a heated debate at the party conference. Party leaders enlisted Healey to summarize their case against the maverick as "a shrill-voiced apologist for tyranny," even though he showed occasional "glimmers of schizophrenic realism which distinguish him from complete Kremlin paranoiacs." Healey objected especially to Zilliacus's "malignant contempt for democratic socialists" and scoffed at his "demand for our sympathy for Communism because the French and Italian trade unions are mainly communist."[87] The expulsions ensured that the four MPs were denied Labour endorsement in the next election, and all lost their independent re-election bids.

For its part the Keep Left backbenchers, such as Ian Mikardo, Michael Foot, Barbara Castle, and Richard Crossman, were extremely critical of the Soviet Union and international communism but maintained their belief in a British third force as mediator for the long term. In a critique of Labour Party policy, published in January 1950 on the eve of the election, Keep Left glumly noted socialism's recent setbacks in much of Western Europe and blamed the communists in good part for that situation: "The policy of sabotage pursed by the Communist Parties and their fellow-travellers, has pushed the Continental Socialists into accepting subordinate positions in Right-wing coalitions, and so lost them the support of the working class. Only in Western Germany does a strong Socialist Party, based on the Trades Unions, lead the opposition to a free-enterprise government." Therefore "the most important task of British Labour in Europe is to rally and revitalise the working-class movement in its double battle against reaction and Russian Communism."[88] Keep Left may have been thorns in the side of Labour's leadership but no one could accuse them of being fellow travelers.

Labour's rhetorical assaults on the CPGB and its expulsion of outspoken fellow traveling MPs occurred in the glare of publicity, but another act in this drama initially played out behind the scenes. Reacting in part to revelations of espionage for the Soviets by a British atomic scientist, Attlee continued Churchill's policy of quietly condoning efforts to curb communist influence in sensitive areas, but without resort to public inquisitions or punitive legislation against the CPGB. In May 1947 Attlee formed a Special Cabinet Committee on Subversive Activities to liaise with MI–5 and other security agencies, but late that year Morrison rejected a call from some Tories for a Select House Committee on Un-British Activities. By 1948 some communists had been quietly dismissed from their jobs in the civil service, teaching, and the BBC; others found their career paths blocked.[89]

The internal security issue went public in March 1948 when Attlee announced that civil servants known to be members of the CPGB would not be allowed to engage in work "vital to state security"; if suitable work could not be found they would be fired. Attlee's announcement aroused a tempest in the Civil Service Clerical Association (CSCA) over how the union should respond on behalf of affected members. During the war several important trade unions had cultivated "popular front" unity with communist organizers and union officials. The National Union of Miners famously had a modus vivendi in its leadership ranks between communists and Labour Party stalwarts, as did the Amalgamated Engineering Union, and the CSCA itself.[90]

Civil liberties arguments for freedom of political opinion initially prevailed in the CSCA in opposition to any political purge, and thus in criticism of Attlee's initiative. But the balance soon tilted against the union's communist element as Labour loyalists pivoted to vote communists out of the leadership. This type of conflict erupted in the TUC itself when its General Council recommended barring communists from union offices. Some unions followed that course, including the National Union of Teachers, while others such as the National Union of Miners did not. Even the TGWU—Bevin's old union now led by the bluff Labour right-winger Arthur Deakin—was roiled by this conflict, as some locals balked at turning against their communist activists.[91] But all told, as a monograph on the Labour left argues, "Non-communist left-wing trade unionists were caught in a whipsaw between a crusading Right and a communist Left now not merely profoundly unpopular, but more than ever difficult to defend. As a result the alliance between communist and Labour Left trade unionists shattered irretrievably, and left-wing strength in the trade union movement was broken."[92] Militancy still prevailed in some shop floors and union locals, but (with exceptions like the coal miners union) the popular front amalgam effectively dissipated.

After the defection to Moscow of the "Cambridge spies" Burgess and Maclean in May 1951, top civil servants in Whitehall and leaders of both major parties agreed to put in place more rigorous security screening for sensitive government positions. Under these procedures, which still ruled out any public witch-hunting, 25 civil servants were dismissed for security reasons, another 25 resigned while being investigated, 88 were transferred to non-sensitive work, and others with communist ties found some employment doors closed. But none of these people were publicly named or pilloried.[93]

The Election of 1950

Thirty-five consecutive victories in parliamentary by-elections since the 1945 election sustained Labour's morale, but the party suffered substantial losses in recent rounds of local council elections. With the next general election due no later than mid-1950, Attlee decided against calling an early election in the fall of 1949 (to rekindle the party's energy) or deferring the election as late as possible (to prepare more fully for the campaign). Instead, bowing to Cripps's refusal to introduce his next budget until Labour had received a new mandate, the PM settled on dissolving the current Parliament in early February and holding the election toward the end of the month, although it was historically rare to call a general election in the depth of winter.[94]

Earlier the government had resolved a related matter. The last major redistribution of parliamentary seats dated from 1918. Given the population movements and demographic growth over three decades, the PM decided to proceed with reapportionment by a nonpartisan Boundary Commission, even if it was likely to affect Labour adversely. The Representation of the People Act of July 1948 brought a small reduction in the total number of seats from 640 to 625 (by, among other provisions, abolishing the 12 university seats that had allowed a plural or double vote by university graduates) and introduced new procedures for postal (absentee) voting. Reapportionment increased the number of seats in the Conservatives' traditional South England heartland from 86 to 101, while reducing the seats in London from 62 to 43; this redistribution was bound to yield a net gain of a least 30 seats for the Tories over their 1945 total.[95]

The general election campaign of February 1950 featured party broadcasts on BBC radio and extensive press coverage. The BBC allotted twenty- or ten-minute broadcast segments to Labour and to the Conservatives (five each), to the Liberals (three), and to the Communist Party (one), with the choice spots after the nine o'clock news going to the two major parties. Yet radio did not dominate this campaign, as the BBC gave little coverage to the election in its news broadcasts and arranged for no on-air debates. National and local newspapers lavished attention on the campaign, slinging mud and offering bona fide news in varying proportions. Official party pronouncements, especially the electoral manifestos, provided grist for individual candidates, but what they did with it in their own printed electoral addresses and speeches was up to them. Party leaders tried to help with campaign circuits of the constituencies, most memorably Attlee, whose wife drove him hither and yon across the country in their diminutive automobile. Campaign finance loomed as a sensitive if murky issue, with Labourites uneasy about funds being secretly channeled by business interests into Tory campaigns. All told, however, close students of this election surmise that relatively few votes were changed by the radio addresses, partisan press coverage, or campaign rallies during the three weeks of electioneering. More likely, any swings in voter sentiment probably had occurred before the campaign began, spurred by such episodes as Conservative thrusts during the debate on steel nationalization, the impact of "Mr. Cube" on public sentiment, or a notorious remark by Bevan back in the summer 1948.[96]

On that July day, while Attlee issued soothing remarks on the launch of the NHS, Bevan addressed a mass party rally in Manchester, where he evoked his youthful memories of deprivation and of the demeaning means test for public relief. "That is why no amount of cajolery can eradicate from my heart a deep burning hatred for the Tory Party that inflicted those experiences on me," he declared. "So far as I am concerned they are lower than vermin. They condemned millions of first-class people to semi-starvation." The speech was widely reported for its "bitter hatred" sentiment, but initially only one news-paper (*The Times* of London) picked up the phrase about Tory vermin. Yet that sufficed to set off an avalanche of denunciation over the following weeks. Tories founded a "Vermin Club," and Churchill dubbed Bevan "The Minister of Disease—for is not morbid hatred a form of mental disease?" Plausibly or not, Bevan claimed to have meant only that Labourites wished to stamp out the Tory politicians behind such odious policies and held no animus against half the electorate, as Churchill implied. But the "vermin" phrase, invoked ad nauseam by the Tories, lay heavily over the election.[97]

The campaign was long on hyperbole and short on concrete proposals for the future. Foreign relations provided no significant issues, apart from Churchill's insinuation that he personally could conduct the most productive dialogue with Stalin. The Tories promised to rescind the nationalization of iron and steel and would of course scrap Labour's 1950 "shopping list" for future public ownership. But the Tories did not call into question the public ownership enacted by Labour since 1945 in coal, railroads, civil aviation, electricity, and gas, or Labour's "welfare state" provisions for unemployment insurance, old age pensions, public housing, and the NHS. Much like the US election of 1944, the campaign featured vague but sharp attacks from each side on the political reliability of their opponents. Labour still rallied under the slogan of "fair shares"; ran against the prewar Tory record of mass unemployment and the dole; and evoked the inefficiencies of unbridled capitalism. To those familiar tropes Labourites might add the link between big business interests and

Conservative politicians. As a pamphlet from the Keep Left group put this last point: "The road haulers, the steelmakers, the insurance tycoons, the cement barons, and Mr. Cube have shown us . . . that we are in the midst of a power struggle; and if the other fellow has financial knuckledusters, you can't fight a power-struggle with twelve-ounce padded gloves."[98]

The Tories sneered at socialism; they denounced inept management by the Labour government, unnecessarily prolonged austerities, excessive interference with business activity and individual freedom, and Labour's divisive class rhetoric, "Tory vermin" being exhibit number one. To rebrand the Tory Party and show that it was no longer "the party of mass unemployment," an industrial policy committee chaired by Rab Butler had drafted an *Industrial Charter*, which found its way into Tory policy statements by late 1947. The Conservatives Party would maintain "full employment," albeit with less state intervention and planning, and lower taxation than under Labour. The Conservatives talked of "humanizing free enterprise, not nationalizing it," and they expressed the desire for cooperation with the trade unions and for providing workers with better job security.[99]

Polling day brought a record-breaking turnout of 29 million citizens (84 percent of eligible voters). The outcome doubtless disappointed both sides. The Conservatives and allied groups rebounded by 2.5 million votes from their falloff of 1945, winning 12.5 million votes (43.5 percent), which gave them 299 seats. Labour exceeded its 1945 total by 1.3 million votes, with 13.3 million votes (46.1 percent) but still lost a substantial number of seats: down from 393 in 1945 to 315 in 1950 (table 7.1). The Liberals suffered a particular humiliation: they had run 478 candidates, of whom 319 lost their £150 deposits (forfeit if a candidate did not win at least one-eighth of the votes cast in the constituency), sums covered only in part by an insurance policy from Lloyds. (Labour lost none of its deposits, the Tories 5, and the Communists 97 out of 100.)[100] Including the Liberals (who gained almost 400,000 more votes but won only 9 seats), the sole independent, and the lone communist victor, Labour emerged from the election with a working majority of just 6, which verged on a hung parliament that might fast require a new election. Conservatives called their recovery "a moral victory." In its official postmortem Labour claimed that few of its own voters in 1945 had defected to the Right. Rather, in addition to the effect of reapportioned seats, the outcome reflected new Conservative voters brought out by the lavish use of paid canvassers working in teams, whereas Labour's 279 paid full-time agents were supplemented only by volunteers.

Many victors from both parties won by five-figure pluralities, but Labour amassed the most lopsided victories, as it won 42 seats by over 20,000 votes compared to 8 seats by the Tories and their allies in Northern Ireland. In a sense, then, Labour paid a cost in "wasted" votes with its heavily concentrated support in the mining and industrial regions of Wales, Scotland, and northern England, and in London. Few other trends are discernable in the election's outcome, apart from the larger number of university-educated MPs on both sides of the House. Only 21 women won seats (including 14 from Labour) out of 126 female candidates, down from 24 winners in 1945. Victorious Labourites sponsored by trade unions numbered 111 in 1950 compared to 120 in 1945.[101]

Table 7.1. British General Elections of 1950 and 1951

Election of 1950

Total eligible electorate	34,270,000		
Total votes cast	28,773,000 (84 percent)		
	Number of votes	Percentage of votes	MPs
Conservatives	12,502,000	43.5	299
Labour	13,266,000	46.1	315
Liberals	2,621,000	9.1	9

Election of 1951

Total eligible electorate	34,646,000		
Total votes cast	28,596,000 (82.5 percent)		
	Number of votes	Percentage of votes	MPs
Conservatives	13,718,000	48	321
Labour	13,949,000	48.8	295
Liberals	731,000	2.5	6

Sources: H. G. Nicholas, The British General Election of 1950 (London, 1951), ch.12 and appendix; D. Butler, The British General Election of 1951 (London, 1952), ch.10.

New Rivals: Bevan and Gaitskell

In the opening weeks of the new Parliament with Labour's hairline majority, the Tories employed harassing tactics to demoralize and perhaps bring down the new government. Prolonging sessions of the House or suddenly calling for divisions (votes) late at night meant that Labour had to keep its ranks on call at all times; a taxi careening to a halt in front of Parliament to unload Labour MPs or an ambulance delivering a sick one might alone save the day on such unscheduled votes over minor matters.[102] Eventually the Tories eased up on such tactics, and Attlee's second government lasted over a year and a half. On the touchstone issue of nationalizing steel the PM would not capitulate to Tory demands for a retreat, but otherwise "consolidation" prevailed more than even Morrison might have wished.

One development during Attlee's second government overshadowed routine business and sparring with the opposition: the jolt of the Korean War and the conflicts within Labour it eventually unleashed. Britain's imperial interests and pressures from the US had already led Attlee's first government to far higher expenditures on the military than anticipated. In a pamphlet on the eve of the 1950 election, Keep Left—the group of dissident but loyal backbenchers—complained that "instead of reducing our defence bill, we have begun a rearmament programme which, if continued will involve us in an annual expenditure of at least £1,000 million, and possibly far more"—a deplorable situation in light of more pressing national and global needs.[103]

The Korean War intensified this predicament. Without hesitation the government joined the armed response of the US and UN to the invasion of South Korea in June 1950, which brought 15,000 British troops to Korea by 1951. Keep Left too supported British participation. As Richard Crossman put it, "This is a welcome, if disturbing decision," but the only way to keep faith with the ideal of the UN. Attlee himself shared that same mixed feeling: "It is infuriating," he told the House of Commons, "that after our tremendous efforts since the war . . . we should now have to divert so much of our resources to the armed services." While Keep Left MPs supported a forceful response to communist aggression in Korea, they insisted that "in the long run Communism could not be defeated by military means alone" but by policies to combat poverty and misery around the world.[104] But Korea was first and last a military challenge, and not only in East Asia. Western leaders initially feared that the

Soviet Union had encouraged North Korea's invasion, possibly as a diversion from an impending confrontation in Europe, where Soviet forces had overwhelming numerical superiority. The new rounds of defense spending in the West set off by Korea went in good part to building up NATO forces.

The costs of accelerated rearmament eventually appeared in the next Labour budget, by then the domain of Hugh Gaitskell. Attlee had named economist Gaitskell as a deputy to Cripps after the 1950 election, and in October Gaitskell succeeded the ailing Cripps as Chancellor of the Exchequer. Responding to pressures from the Ministry of Defense and from Washington, Gaitskell proposed greatly increased defense expenditures, along with several tax increases and other measures to help offset the costs. In the process he reopened another budget question, having long worried about the rising costs of the NHS. Gaitskell wanted to limit NHS expenditures, resist large supplementary appropriations, and introduce co-payments for certain NHS services. In the Health Services part of his draft budget he therefore proposed to lower the projected cap on NHS spending and to revive a proviso for co-payments by NHS patients for dentures and eyeglasses, which had been floated but dropped by Cripps in 1949.

In the privacy of the cabinet Bevan (minister of labor since January 1951) attacked the proposed rise in spending on the armed forces and defense production, objected to the lower appropriations for health services proposed by the chancellor, and categorically opposed charges for dentures and eyeglasses under the NHS. By now a mutual wariness between Bevan and Gaitskell had evolved into a deep personal and ideological animus. Gaitskell was not open to substantive compromise on defense appropriations or NHS co-payments. When Bevan made co-payments for dentures and eyeglasses a resignation issue in early April 1951, Gaitskell in effect did the same. At that critical moment Attlee was incapacitated in hospital with an ulcer, Morrison had just been named foreign minister to replace the dying Bevin, and Dalton flitted between both sides. There was no one in the room to mediate effectively or to lay down the law of party unity to the two adversaries. After vacillation by some ministers and several failed attempts to find face-saving compromises, the cabinet endorsed Gaitskell's budget.[105]

Instead of resigning immediately as threatened, Bevan let his critique seep into the open and expand, in part through articles by his friends at the *Tribune*. First, he argued, the exorbitant new appropriations for military production would prove impossible or reckless to implement on that scale, given such constraints in British industry as shortages of machine tools, skilled labor, and raw materials (which the US frantically stockpiled). Second, Bevan insisted that the principle of free medical care under NHS not be breached for such opportunistic pretexts, one small slice at a time. Finally, Bevan taxed Gaitskell with veering off the socialist road instead of redoubling Labour's commitment to its ideals. To Bevan, Britain's achievements since 1945 made it a beacon to the world on how democratic socialism could be built; its principles should be vaunted and amplified, not compromised or muted.[106]

On the first point Bevan was eventually proven right. When the Conservatives came to power in the election of October 1951 they acknowledged that the scale of Labour's military production appropriations in 1950–51 had exceeded Britain's industrial capacity, and they reduced the defense estimates in their own budget. The implication followed that the inexperienced Gaitskell had been unnerved by pressures from his service chiefs and from Washington, had set unreasonable military goals in his first (and only) budget as chancellor, and had in turn caused needless intra-party strife in seeking ways to pay for them. Another (more speculative) implication might be that Labour's defense buildup skewed and thereby undermined Britain's economic performance, which had improved in fits and starts with successful export drives, state-led modernization in certain sectors, and a devaluation of the pound sterling in 1949.[107]

Bevan was also on firm ground when he claimed that colleagues such as Morrison and Gaitskell who groused so much about soaring NHS costs were overlooking the bigger picture. To be sure, NHS expenses in the first two years had far exceeded estimates before the launch, given the huge pent-up demand for medical and dental attention and the heavy costs of reorganizing and improving the hospital service. But the growth in costs was leveling off in 1951 and over the next decade did not present an unsustainable financial burden, given the purpose of the NHS. In April 1951, however, Bevan's arguments on military production budgets and NHS co-payments were hard to prove and failed to win over the cabinet or the PLP.

When Bevan's frustration in cabinet became common knowledge, many in the party, including most of his admirers on the Left, tried to dissuade Bevan from resigning. For almost two weeks he hesitated, but exasperated at failing to extract concessions, he finally sent Attlee his resignation. Had Gaitskell lost the battle in a last-minute reversal by the cabinet, he pledged to go quietly. But

Bevan went clamorously before the House to justify his resignation. In a speech that seems to have been a misconceived and poorly executed performance by the usually superb orator, Bevan let loose a torrent of bitterness against Gaitskell and a myopic egotism. His comments at a PLP caucus the next day were more of the same and made him no new friends, whereas Gaitskell won warm support in the caucus after his own remarks.

Only Harold Wilson (head of the Board of Trade) and one junior minister followed Bevan out the door of Attlee's government. To most of the PLP this rift would not clear the air for socialist principles but would simply weaken the party as it faced another election likely to come soon.[108] In that election, called by Attlee for October 1951, Labour by some measures did well: it polled more votes than the Conservatives (indeed more than any party in British history), and it won a higher proportion of the national vote (48.8 percent) than it had scored in the 1945 landslide, thanks in part to the evaporating Liberal vote (see table 7.1). But the Tories still won the election with a majority of 17 seats.[109]

The Keep Left dissenters had long looked to Nye Bevan as an inspiration but at a distance, as Bevan had been bound by cabinet unity and confidentiality. Now Bevan was free to join them in open dissent, and their coterie quickly became known as "the Bevanites." The Bevanites came into their own after Labour lost the general election of October 1951 and the party went into opposition. Attlee remained as leader of the PLP and of Labour's "shadow cabinet," but the Bevanites gained ground at the party conferences of 1951 and 1952 in the annual election of the 7 constituency branch members of the National Executive's 22-member committee. By the end of conference in 1952 Dalton, Morrison, and Shinwell were gone from the NEC; Bevan (consistently at the top of the poll) and the popular Jim Griffiths were now joined by five Bevanites.[110] Meanwhile the centrist wing of the party, undergirded by the largest bloc-voting trade unions, increasingly defined itself against the Bevanites. Instead of fading out, the conflict of April 1951 took fire.

Bevan hoped to emerge as party leader once Attlee stepped down, and his admirers shared that goal. Mikardo reasonably dubbed Nye "a reluctant Bevanite," however, and denied that the Bevanites had an operational political machine. The Bevanites put their energy into debating issues and policies, and they often disagreed among themselves. Their impact on the party came especially from their numerous public forums (called "brains trusts") held before overflow crowds, their pamphlets, and their articles in the *Tribune*. Their tangible existence as an enlarged version of Keep Left ended in late 1952, however, when the PLP (as it had on past occasions) ordered all unofficial groups within the party to disband on pain of expulsion. Formally, at least, the Bevanites complied, but the contest for dominance in the party continued. Led by the heads of the largest unions, the centrists in the party had settled on Gaitskell as their choice for post-Attlee leader.[111]

In his memoirs Mikardo used the term "haters" to describe the animus of Gaitskell and his trade union stalwarts against the Bevanites. In Mikardo's view, they sought to resolve their rift not by debating the issues but by force majeure. This reached a crescendo in 1955 with a misbegotten attempt by the Gaitskellites to expel Bevan from the party, which Attlee squelched only at the last moment.[112] Attlee then led the party into the 1955 general election, which Labour lost by a greater margin in votes and seats than in 1951. Attlee retired from the leadership and was succeeded by Gaitskell.

Over the next few years the bitter rivalry between Bevan and Gaitskell wound down and surprisingly repaired itself around the issue of nuclear weapons policy. Bevan had vigorously opposed nuclear testing and seemed ready to embrace nuclear disarmament, but he finally shrunk back. At the Brighton party conference of 1957 Bevan startled such allies as Castle, Foot, and Mikardo by rejecting the case for unilateral nuclear disarmament that was starting to gain ground in Britain. He thereby moved closer to US policy, which hinged in good part on nuclear deterrence, and thus to its advocate Gaitskell. In effect Bevan became the foreign minister-in-waiting when Labour next prevailed. Despite strong support in constituency branches, the Bevanite coterie had been fraying since 1955 and the Brighton conference sealed its demise. Grassroots activism on the Left instead found an outlet in the Campaign for Nuclear Disarmament, publicly launched in early 1958 outside the confines of the party. When a general election came in 1959, Bevan and Gaitskell stood together on platforms and posters. But notwithstanding the Suez fiasco that shook the Conservative Party, Labour still lost the election decisively.[113] Bevan's death in 1960 abruptly ended this long-running drama. But memories of Bevan's fighting spirit, socialist ideals, stirring oratory, and remarkable achievements during Attlee's first government grew stronger over the years as an inspirational legacy for Labour.[114]

Three losing national campaigns in a row would be sobering to any major political party and Labour began a period of self-examination and renewed conflict. As an essential symbolic gesture, Gaitskell sought to jettison or revise Clause 4 of the party's 1918 charter, which called for "common owner-ship of the means of production." But by 1960 leadership of several big unions had changed and taken a leftish turn. At conference the effort to scrap Clause 4 failed, while a motion effectively endorsing the Campaign for Nuclear Disarmament carried. Gaitskell vowed to fight aggressively against those two positions, which he saw as barriers to broad electoral support, and he gained some ground at the 1961 conference. Meanwhile Gaitskell beat back Harold Wilson's effort in the depleted PLP to replace him as party leader. But Gaitskell died suddenly in 1963 at the age of fifty-six, devastating his supporters.[115] The talented but excessively nimble Wilson again vied for the party leadership in the PLP, and on the second ballot defeated Jim Callaghan. Wilson went on to lead Labour to victory in the 1964 general election, and he found places in his cabinet for ex-Bevanites, such as Castle and Crossman, alongside centrists, such as Crosland and Healey.[116] The Labour Party was back, a new generation ascendant, albeit one that had experienced World War II as young adults.

In the alternations of political power in the 1940s, '50s, and '60s some histo-rians see a postwar consensus across the mainstreams of Britain's two major parties; coming out of the war, Labour enacted that consensus and at least in attenuated form the Conservatives sustained it for the next two decades. Others challenge this thesis as a "myth of consensus."[117] If the notion of a new consensus is not quite a myth, neither is it the best framework for assessing the import of British-style socialism in the postwar moment. True, the Tories did not attempt to roll back the "settlement" they inherited from the Attlee govern-ments after their narrow victory in the general election of 1951. Labour's legacy included a fully formed welfare state with the NHS at its core; an ambitious public housing program; strong trade union bargaining power; quasi-Keynesian fiscal tactics to sustain purchasing power; a degree of central planning for a mixed economy; and a constant reiteration of egalitarian values. A few of Labour's far-reaching programs no doubt had roots of a sort in the thought and experience of the coalition years of World War II, notably in the contribution of reformist Liberals Beveridge and Keynes. But the forms and transformational heft of Labour's postwar settlement derived in the main from the party's prewar social democratic agenda, its surprisingly decisive victory in 1945, and its hard-fought exercise of power, not least over the NHS, which the medical lobby and the Tories bitterly opposed. After 1951 the Conservatives came to terms with Labour's bedrock achievements but worked steadily to modify them incrementally in favor of free enterprise. Finally, the Thatcher era after 1979 brought an all-out assault on the Attlee settlement—about which a comment in Healey's memoirs is worth pondering: "Thatcherism became possible only when the wartime generation was passing from the stage."[118]

8

Tripartism and Its Aftermath

IT TOOK TWO AND A HALF YEARS for France to exit the provisional state of affairs that began with the liberation of Paris in August 1944. Political forces—old political parties, Resistance movements, new parties—began to regroup with varying degrees of success. But the restoration of democracy started in earnest only with the election in October 1945 of a Constituent Assembly, after the return from Germany of POWs and surviving deportees. When voters rejected the Constituent Assembly's draft constitution in the requisite referendum, another six months elapsed before a second Constituent Assembly reached sufficient compromises to produce a new draft, which won voter approval by a thin margin. During the long provisional interval the CNR Common Program helped undergird de Gaulle's unity government and subsequent tripartite coalitions after the general abruptly exited the scene. Disagreements, sharp elbows, and threats to abandon coalitions abounded within and among the PCF, MRP, and SFIO, and the CGT labor movement harbored such tensions as well. But until the fall of 1947, when a great strike wave brought the experiment to an explosive end, tripartism remained the political framework for France's postwar moment. Successive governments addressed the intractable challenges of postwar recovery—the "battle of production," scarcities of food, and threats of runaway inflation—while they sought to implement the "peaceful revolution" imagined by CNR in such matters as economic controls, social security, housing, and educational opportunity.

Launching the Fourth Republic

After the approval of the second constitutional draft in the referendum of October 1946, elections for a National Assembly with a five-year term followed in November. The results only mildly scrambled the political balance. Communists won the most votes and seats, edging out the MRP, a strong and close second. An erosion in the Socialist vote continued, giving the party only 91 seats, while parties on the right won 76, and the Radicals, 54 (see table 5.1). Formal inauguration of the Fourth Republic, however, had to wait until the election of the new upper house in a complex and time-consuming process; this Council of the Republic would then meet jointly with the National Assembly to choose the president of the republic.

Once the upper house was chosen, the balloting for president of the republic proceeded in January 1947. The MRP put up its veteran legislator Champtier de Ribes and the Right backed its own candidate. In the end the parliamentarians chose socialist Vincent Auriol by a narrow majority. While the post of president lacked the type of powers and independence that de Gaulle had demanded, Auriol made it as proactive as possible. Seeking a government anchored by the three major parties and headed by a socialist prime minister, he sounded out Blum and Gouin, who declined the burden, and then turned to Paul Ramadier, who initially made the same response. But he was Auriol's man and the president refused to take no for an answer. Both Auriol and Ramadier were part of the small generational cohort of prominent socialist veterans (along with Blum, Gouin, Philip, and Jules Moch), which offered an element of continuity from the Third to the Fourth Republic. Auriol shared the view of a later biographer that Ramadier was a man of independent judgment, a reliably hard worker, and a politician thoroughly dedicated to republicanism, although at one point Auriol had to warn him against acting like "an old Third-Republic type" (*un vieux de la IIIème*).[1]

At Ramadier's behest Thorez of the PCF and Teitgen of the MRP, the two vice presidents he named to his cabinet, concerted behind the scenes to smooth cooperation among their potentially antagonistic colleagues—an earnest extra step to make tripartism work.[2] But an array of divisive issues had long since crystalized that would strain that equilibrium, starting with the long-festering problem of shortages, prices, and wages.

Food Supplies, Prices, and Wages

The years of systematic looting by the Nazis of food, fuel, and manufactured goods had left the French people exhausted from the chronic shortages and caloric deficits of rationing under the occupation. But any hopes that material life would quickly improve after the Liberation proved illusory. The GPRF and its tripartite successors struggled to master the converging problems of shortages of vital necessities, disruptions of industrial production, war damage, currency inflation, and budgetary shortfalls. The reconstruction of basic road and rail transport held top priority since so much else depended on that. Next came the "battle for production" in coal mines, utilities, and manufacturing where workers labored hard and long, while their restored trade unions for the moment restrained their urgent demands for higher wages. Over agriculture, most vital to the population's immediate well-being, the state had less sway. It could try to incentivize increased production and could attempt to control the prices of farm products, although that second objective might well clash with the first.

The minister of supply (*Ravitaillement*) had the most thankless post in the government, a prime target of public fury over persistent scarcities and high prices. Between September 1944 and its disappearance as a cabinet-level ministry in January 1947, six men headed the Ministry of Supply. Disorganized and overwhelmed from the outset, the ministry lost 6,000 district officials after the Constituent Assembly drastically reduced its budget in December 1945 under fiscal duress. Food supplies leached into the black market at alarming rates; use of forged or stolen ration books increased; some wholesalers and importers used fraudulent practices and political connections to protect their trafficking.[3]

Overall the ministry's policies incoherently teetered between free market deregulation (generally urged by farmers, *commerçants,* and manufacturers) and strict government control (advocated by industrial and white-collar workers, pensioners, and state employees). The Ministry of Supply initially focused on contracting for imports from the Western Hemisphere, but for various reasons, including inadequate shipping capacity, imports fell short of the anticipated mark. When socialist Christian Pineau took over (May 1945–January 1946) he sought to encourage market mechanisms to curb the corrosive black market. Pineau hoped to stimulate livestock supplies by lifting price caps at the wholesale level while retaining them at the retail level. His successor abandoned that policy and re-regulated wholesale prices—at which point livestock merchants froze their operations (much as happened in the US some months later).[4]

In the fall of 1945 Pineau tried a new policy at the other end of the food chain: he would end the demoralization of bread rationing, while retaining retail price controls on bread! This proved a "catastrophic" decision, since bakers could not meet the unleashed demand for their loaves, with the added problem that farmers sometimes rushed to buy up bread for use as a feed grain. The ministry restored ration cards in January 1946, with an allocation of only 300 grams per day for adults instead of the previous 350 grams.[5] None of this did much to raise agricultural productivity given the structural weaknesses of that sector; for as a report to Bidault later observed, in the US the average farmer fed fifteen people, but in France only five.[6]

Wine too was a problem. When Yves Farge (a prominent *résistant* and independent leftist) became minister of supply in June 1946 he pledged to destroy the black market and to purge compromised bureaus within his ministry. One offender was the beverage division, where accusations surfaced that licenses to import Algerian wine were going to cronies of prominent politicians. The ministry's inspector general found "organized fraud" in that area, and the *scandal des vins* became front-page news when Farge denounced Felix Gouin himself as a protector of compromised officials. It took Gouin almost three years finally to clear his name.[7]

When the three partners reknit the tripartite coalition in June 1946, the two left-wing parties demanded that Bidault convene a national economic conference to address the wage-price problem—an effort that calls to mind Truman's Labor-Management Conference the previous fall. Truman hoped to bring big labor and big business into closer rapport (with "public" delegates as facilitators) for the coming rounds of collective bargaining in the mass production industries. Truman did not include the actual wage rates at issue in the conference agenda, while for Bidault the specifics of agricultural and industrial prices and of wage levels constituted the core problem. Yet the two conferences had similar underlying concerns. For the long term: reconciling conflicting views on how to increase production while raising living standards. For the short term: how to avoid strikes by exasperated workers that could throttle production instead of increasing it. Truman and Bidault both feared that the respective demands by CIO and CGT unions for substantial wage increases would, if rebuffed, unleash such strikes, but if fully conceded set off a destructive wage-price inflationary spiral.

At the National Economic Conference on Prices and Wages (July 4–20, 1946) Bidault reasonably posed as an honest broker seeking to "enhance purchasing power and establish a lasting equilibrium between prices and wages." His opening speech insisted that wage increases should not exceed 15 percent, as against the 25 percent publicly demanded by the CGT to compensate for high prices. Wage hikes above 15 percent, Bidault argued, would force up prices for all consumers, thereby undermining the actual value of the workers' raises. Apart from that line in the sand, Bidault endorsed union demands for maintaining existing wage differentials and for providing extra help to the neediest tiers of workers. He promised to seek a sounder equilibrium between agricultural and industrial prices and, more broadly, in keeping with the CNR Common Program, he advocated an economy "oriented toward the distribution of goods more than toward the accumulation of profits. . . . [and] a constant concern with the collective interest."[8]

Spokesmen for the trade unions, big business, farmers, shopkeepers, and consumers each advanced their well-established positions in detail. Big business emphasized the need to hold down wages and to maintain the profits that alone could finance investment to modernize their enterprises. The *patronat* (employers federation) deplored the unions' "obsession with wage rises" (*une psychose à la hausse*), just when prices (they claimed) were starting to stabilize. In their own bailiwick of industrial production, the *patronat* advocated longer hours and continuation of the temporary six-day week: "The only effective way to increase purchasing power by 25 percent," they provocatively claimed, "is not by raising hourly wages, but by increasing the working day by 25 percent, so as to raise production by a similar amount."[9]

Labor, in contrast, protested that many workers lacked even "the vital minimum," which imperiled their very health. Union delegates called for draconian enforcement of price controls and requiring manufacturers to produce "articles of social utility." They also deplored the excessive numbers of small shops that weighed on economic efficiency. So too did the Mouvement Populaire des Familles, whose position paper complained that "hundreds of thousands of men and women have vanished as producers by virtue of [*du fait du*] the growing number of shopkeepers." Just as Mendès France argued in early 1945, France's proliferation of shopkeepers created inefficiencies in distribution that raised the costs for agricultural and industrial products.[10]

Pressured by restive workers, the CGT ostensibly stuck to its call for a 25 percent catch-up wage increase. But a government surveillance report, claiming knowledge of discussions in the CGT leadership, predicted that "in the last resort" the CGT would hold out for as little as 18 percent; "the *ex-unitaires* [i.e., the communists in the CGT leadership] are currently exhibiting a large spirit of conciliation." Informants also cited a comment by PCF leader Jacques Duclos that "*L'excitation Cégetiste*" was provoked by socialist militants to embarrass communist leaders for their restraint.[11] In the event Léon Jouhaux, the venerable non-communist stalwart of the CGT, did indeed argue at the conference for the 25 percent demand, while Benoît Frachon, the communist co-leader of the CGT, proved more accommodating. "We are not saying: 25 percent or bust," Frachon declared, "nor do we wish to be told: it is 15 percent or nothing, but rather to leave room for a possible compromise." With several side issues related to wage rates also under discussion, including a substantial raise in the minimum wage for the most disadvantaged workers, the conference ultimately fused and fudged its recommendations to approximate a total package of 18 percent.[12]

The most intractable economic problems remained agricultural prices and low agricultural productivity. While agreeing that farmers had to receive higher prices as an incentive to productivity, Bidault resisted retail price guidelines higher than he deemed bearable for staples like flour, meat and milk. But over the next three months Bidault watched helplessly as staple prices soared through his benchmark levels on the wings of continued scarcities. In September he was informed that "official prices in August 1946 have undergone the steepest rise we have seen in years. In comparison to July they have risen by 24 percent," pushed up inexorably by the prices that farmers commanded for grain and livestock. The price of milk was a particularly sensitive barometer. The conference's agriculture committee had recommended a retail price guideline of 10F per liter of milk, but Bidault insisted on holding it to 9F. Absent effective enforcement at either wholesale or retail levels, however, the actual price to consumers hit 11F by October. Only increased agricultural productivity—more manpower, modern equipment, revamped distribution—would mitigate the problem in the long term.[13]

When Bidault's interim presidency ended in December, he left behind an alarming situation in the food supply chain. "What was yesterday simple individual fraud is tending today to become a collective revolt," warned the minister of supply. "Here the wine growers menace the Government; . . . there the leader of a peasant association imagines starving out the capital; somewhere else the bakers go out on strike." In the hope of incentivizing farmers to bring their output to the open market, some municipal and departmental authorities "do not hesitate to decree on their own authority the abolition of all regulation." Worse yet, "the public is astonished that it never sees punished those it knows to be responsible"; at best only the small fish were prosecuted for black market offenses while the big manipulators escaped. What next, asked the minister: Refusals to pay taxes?[14] While comparable to the pressures by various economic interests massed for and against the OPA in the US, one difference was the readier resort to violence in France: assaults on government bureaus and the burning of paperwork, armed attacks on food convoys, theft of ration books.

One of the few pieces of good news Bidault's office received was a comparative assessment of strikes in various countries, which concluded that "in all these countries except France strikes have reached a level never known before." In the US the strike wave of 1946 had resulted in 81 million lost man-days, and in Britain 793,000 man-days had been lost. But with a similar population France had lost only 244,000.[15] Communist restraint in the CGT had so far tamped down worker unrest over the long-running cost-of-living problem, but the restraint could not last indefinitely. The vise was tightening, even as the post-Liberation governments deliberated on other domestic issues such as social security, education, and housing.

Expanding Social Security

In part two of the CNR Common Program on measures to be implemented after the Liberation, pride of place among "indispensable reforms" went to economic renovation, followed by social issues. Sandwiched between a clause on reestablishing independent trade unionism and one on bolstering security of employment, the manifesto called for "a complete plan of social security, designed to assure all citizens the means of existence in all cases where they are unable to procure it by working, and with the management to be carried out by the beneficiaries [*interéssés*] and by the state." By no means a mere afterthought for the Resistance, an overhaul of social security was not a top priority either. Apart from the novel idea of participatory administrative control over social security, the CNR was decidedly vague about the whole subject.[16]

Two major initiatives of the interwar period had begun to replace or modify the previous patchworks of social welfare provision. A law of 1928, as amended and implemented in 1930, established the simulacrum of a national system of social insurance for workers, including medical insurance, modest old-age pensions, and workmen's compensation (disability benefits), but not unemployment insurance. Miners, railwaymen, and utility workers already had special provision for such benefits in their own sectors, and this law extended that net to workers in other commercial and industrial enterprises above a certain threshold of employees. Under the law's core proviso, workers earning below either of two wage thresholds (one for large cities) were required to enroll along with their employers, with each paying in contributions. Initially the new system covered about 13 million workers, but after wage thresholds for compulsory participation were raised, the system by 1940 encompassed close to 20 million workers in commerce and industry.[17]

Unlike in Britain, spouses and dependents were covered by the medical insurance, which extended to hospital and maternity care as well. The law of 1928 also advanced the evolution of hospitals from charitable institutions to public services and a shift in control over those hospitals from local notables to medical professionals and state functionaries. The law gave the insured the right to choose their own doctors, and it ostensibly covered 80 percent of their medical costs. In practice, however, the doctors drove hard bargains with the approximately 1,000 local funds (*caisses*) that administered the benefits, most controlled by mutual societies trying to husband their resources. The system therefore could leave beneficiaries with substantial out-of-pocket costs. Yet with all its limitations, the 1928 law was a big step in the transition from charity or public assistance for the needy to social insurance or social security.

On an entirely different track, in a spirit that combined paternalism and social control, large firms in the 1920s created funds to provide family allowances for the children of their workers. Family allowance benefits provided aid for workers with additional mouths to feed but with no prospect of bringing home higher income. When these employers set aside a portion of their wage costs for this purpose, they in effect redistributed income to workers with children from those without. But only about 20,000 employers in commerce and industry out of 1.5 million participated in the 1920s. Provision of family allowances extended primarily to 1.5 million railwaymen, coal miners, and utility workers; 1.5 million other workers; and 1 million civil servants.

From these parochial beginnings, the family allowance system moved to center stage because of the panic over France's falling birthrate and demographic future after the Great War. By the late 1920s, over half the Chamber of Deputies had joined its pro-natalist caucus, where encouraging families to have more children became a patriotic imperative. In March 1932 the pro-natalists passed a law that transformed the terms for this social provision by requiring all employers in industry or commerce to contribute to a family allowance *caisse,* and by raising the payouts to workers with children. These funds remained entirely separate from the new social insurance system; for their proponents, having children must be regarded as a normal event and not "an insurable risk." Businessmen or mutual societies continued to administer the family allowance *caisses* but now under greater supervision by the Ministry of Labor.

In 1938 the Daladier government pegged the family allowances to average departmental wage levels, and set the benefits at 5, 10, and 15 percent of those figures for the first, second, and third child, respectively, plus a 10 percent supplement for unwaged mothers (*mères en foyer*). Some pro-natalists thus sought to limit the participation of married women in the labor force by calibrating the allocation of benefits to favor stay-at-home mothers. Yet as historian Susan Pedersen shows, this 1938 provision was exceptional; in most respects the family allowance system remained gender neutral in regard to who brought wages into the household.[18]

Under prodding from the pro-natalist lobby, Daladier's government also established a High Commission on Population, which drafted a "Family Code" promulgated shortly before the war broke out. Among other goals, such as curbing abortion and providing loans to young rural couples, the code envisioned expanding the family allowance system to other groups. The basic premise that family income should increase with family size remained in force from the waning years of the Third Republic through Pétain's regime and into the Liberation.

Vichy embraced pro-natalism enthusiastically, adopted the Family Code with small changes, retained the family allowance *caisses,* and ostensibly sought to discourage married women from joining the work force. Yet with an eye to the wives of the 1.5 million POWs languishing in Germany, Vichy went in the other direction by replacing the unwaged mother's supplementary family allowance with a larger benefit for all eligible families living on a single wage. Vichy also tinkered with but did not overhaul the social insurance system, and it set new standards for how hospitals should function and who should control them, which carried over into the Liberation years.[19]

The man who emerged from Free France with responsibility for overhauling social security after the Liberation was Pierre Laroque, appointed by de Gaulle's minister of labor as director general of social security. A high-level technocrat with a background in administrative law, Laroque had served the Council of State and held positions in the Labor Ministry in the 1930s, where his civic values centered on "solidarism"—a quasi-corporatist but democratic doctrine to promote social harmony among otherwise antagonistic interests. Of mixed Catholic-Jewish ancestry, Laroque remained in the position he held at the time of the capitulation but was dismissed in October 1940 after Vichy's first round of anti-Jewish laws, and he soon found his way into the Resistance. Traces of Laroque's "solidarist" ideological predilection can be found in his work for the GPRF and successor governments on social security, but overall he approached his task as a new start in the spirit of the CNR charter.[20]

Laroque's plan, promulgated in an ordinance of October 4, 1945, by the GPRF just before the election of a Constituent Assembly, had four objectives: to universalize French social insurance in stages; to promote social solidarity by the redistributive features of a common risk pool that encompassed the needy and the better-off; to rationalize the social security system by creating a single public fund (*caisse unique*) in each department, which would absorb the family allowance funds as well; and to democratize the management of these *caisses* with representatives of the insured constituting the majority on the administrative boards. To Laroque's surprise each of these objectives proved contentious and none was adopted without modification.

Little argument arose over one feature of Larouque's blueprint: since the French state could not afford to support social security with general tax revenues at this juncture, it would rely almost entirely on contributions to the *caisses* from employers and (as applicable) from the potential beneficiaries. But as historian Peter Baldwin argues in his comparative history of modern welfare states, whereas the Beveridge Plan minimized the redistributive penalty on the better-off with its combination of flat rate contributions and treasury subsidies, the French approach—intended to be more "solidaristic" and hence redistributive than Britain's—produced a sharp backlash from groups heretofore outside the social security system. Managerial white-collar workers (known in France as *cadres*), the self-employed, and members of the professions evinced little enthusiasm for the minimal social security benefits they might gain, whilst their contributions would sustain the benefits of others. The previously uncovered groups might have welcomed incorporation into social security only if its structure mirrored "the hierarchy of remuneration" (in Baldwin's phrase) that they believed their due. Moreover, groups such as coal miners and railwaymen valued their existing "contributory entitlements" and were loath to be folded into a general system.[21]

Pushback to modify Laroque's original plan came from several directions. At the outset pro-natalists and MRP advocates for the family prevailed on de Gaulle to direct that the family allowance *caisses* should remain separate from the social security system, although the employers who paid in the contributions would no longer be in exclusive control these funds.[22]

Laroque first intended to bring the *cadres* into the social security system alongside blue-collar workers since their employers could readily be tapped for contributions. But the *cadres* organized an energetic lobbying group, which succeeded in neutering the redistributive subtext of Laroque's plan. Their amendment established a minimal income ceiling for their employer and employee contributions, above which individuals, if they chose, could contribute to an entirely separate supplementary scheme that entailed no redistribution to other groups. The same kind of drama recurred in 1946 when the government sought to bring millions of self-employed, mainly artisans and shopkeepers, into the social security system. A flurry of opposition developed from the self-employed who wanted their own *caisses,* where risk and benefits would be allocated among their peers.

These successive frays led the government to appoint a commission of experts to reconsider the new structure of social security. The resulting Surleau Report concluded that the problem could only be resolved "within the framework of each of the occupational groups [*professions*] concerned" and recommended that social security should not be one unified, universal system after all. Instead it should comprise separate systems (for workers, independent artisans and the self-employed, the liberal professions, and the agricultural sector) with a fifth system sometime in the future to cover citizens who fell outside those categories. Each scheme would calibrate its benefits according to its particular interests and actuarial considerations. A law of January 1948 codified this huge deviation from Laroque's plan. Authorizing four separate tracks for social security safety nets, it effectively undermined Laroque's embedded ideal of redistributive solidarity.[23]

At the same time, however, the expanded oversight role of the state over social security yielded significant reforms in such matters as the arrangements governing health insurance benefits. Government officials now had the power to oversee negotiations with doctors over the terms of medical insurance. In effect they reversed the way the 1928 law usually operated, where the fee schedules negotiated between individual *caisses* and doctors "became treated as minimum charges after which the patient's responsibility for payment could escalate without limit." Instead, the new schedules set maximum fees, 80 percent of which would be reimbursed, with patients' out-of-pocket costs limited and transparent.[24]

Another dispute over Laroque's plans arose on how to implement the consensus view that administration of the new social security *caisses* should devolve upon the insured themselves. To expedite matters, Laroque proposed to enlist the dominant trade union federation in each department to fill the two-thirds of the seats on each administrative board of a departmental *caisse* allocated to the workers. (In Paris, Lyon, and other urban agglomerations, the departmental *caisse* would subdivide the work with local *caisses*.) This approach to "democratization" would have handed the CGT a virtual monopoly in all but a handful of departments. The Catholic trade union federation (CFTC), seconded by certain MRP deputies, attacked the proposal in the name of greater pluralism. The CGT fought back with charges that the CFTC wished to deliver social security to manipulation by the bosses and religious interests.[25] In the end the government decided to hold competitive elections where slates of workers at the grass roots could vie for those positions.

Participatory administration via election became a consciousness-raising exercise about citizenship and social security. The question remained whether the elections should take place on site in factories or at public polling places. One MRP deputy warned that "if the elections are held in the coercive atmosphere of the factories, there will be no guarantee for the secrecy of the vote."[26] But the convenience and appeal of voting in plants and ateliers prevailed. Only when on-site voting was not possible were public voting bureaus made available.

The first elections for the administrative boards of the departmental social security and family allowance *caisses* of the workers were held in April 1947. For the 124 boards up for election, 7,750,000 workers were eligible to vote of whom 5,790,000 cast their ballots—a robust turnout of almost 75 percent. The CGT's slates won majorities on most boards, but the CFTC with support from many non-communists won a significant presence as well. Under the proportional representation system in use, the CGT won 1,384 seats; the CFTC, 613; and other slates (including mutual societies), 214.[27]

At the next election in June 1950, with balloting held only in public polling places, 69.5 percent of eligible workers voted. By now the CGT had more rivals in the working class. The CGT won 970 seats; the CFTC, 537; the new socialist-linked CGT-FO, 398; and the mutualists and others, 288. The non-CGT vote had grown from 41 percent in 1947 to 56 percent in 1950.[28] In both cases the elections obliged political antagonists to cooperate in a great work of public service, with the elected boards meant to keep the administration of social security sensitive to the needs of the beneficiaries. The complexities of the entire system were legion, with so many separate tracks and so many elements of state oversight intersecting.[29] But French citizens became increasingly attached over the next decades to the diversion of a significant percentage of GDP and personal income into social security contributions to underwrite their benefits.

The Stillbirth of Educational Reform

Before 1789 the French state had no role in the provision of primary education, which depended on the will and capacity of parents or communities to pay for teachers, and on local priests to provide a modicum of supervision. After 1789 primary schooling moved to center stage in revolutionary thinking as a requisite for advancing democracy and equality. By 1793 the revolutionaries proclaimed the right to primary education, and the National Convention decreed that the state treasury would fund schoolteachers, thereby ending their dependence on the volition and resources of parents or local communities. The experiment failed because of hyperinflation in 1795–96 among other reasons; thereafter while *instruction publique* remained a nominal component of the

French civic order, the state retreated from any effective financial support for schoolteachers, and Napoleon allowed primary schooling to revert to its prior status as a product of local demand and a sphere of influence for the church.[30]

Concerned instead with the training of elites, Napoleon founded a new kind of secondary school called *lycées* parallel to existing confessional and municipal *collèges*. In all these secondary schools the tradition of Latin-based humanistic education held a prominent place, under supervision of a new Napoleonic educational bureaucracy known as "the University." Napoleon also created a new institution of advanced education: an École Polytechnique to produce engineers and army officers. Later the Polytechnique became a model for other specialized elite institutions with admission by competitive examination (*concours*).[31]

The long nineteenth century saw periodic attempts to advance the frontier of state responsibility in education with initiatives for teacher training and for state subsidies of public and, at times, private (i.e., Catholic) primary schools. But the evolution of social demand is what ultimately made primary schooling universal across France. The appeal of basic education spread because of its growing utility, as literacy became requisite for such career paths as army NCOs, certain skilled trades, or office work in modern enterprises like railroads and department stores. In that context the Third Republic made primary schooling obligatory and a universal public service in the 1880s, while removing the church from any role.[32] Public primary school teachers—the *instituteurs* and *institutrices* trained at state normal schools—became the field agents, so to speak, of the republic's secular values. Alongside the three Rs they taught about French history and heroes to promote patriotism and civic virtue.

By the twentieth century the principal problem in French education was the divide separating primary from secondary education. Primary schooling was obligatory and universal; its teachers had acquired a modest professional identity that carried esteem in republican circles. Secondary *collèges* and *lycées* had high fees (especially for boarders) and, apart from a small tier of scholarship students, enrolled the children of professionals, functionaries, middle managers, and businessmen. Known as *professeurs,* the teachers held the baccalaureate degree and often the prestigious *aggrégation,* awarded after rigorous examinations following study at a university. By the interwar decades the *instituteurs* of the primary schools and the *professeurs* of the secondary schools had organized into separate trade unions, ever alert to defend their particular interests.

From the point of view of students and their families, a chasm existed between the relatively costly and exclusive secondary schools and the primary schools free to all citizens. By the interwar decades the standard school leaving age was thirteen, but as in Britain that left a limbo of sorts for two years of education beyond elementary schooling properly speaking, yet with no smooth path for advancement to secondary schools for those of modest means who sought it or any incentive for those who did not.

How, then, might the two structures of popular and elite provision be bridged or integrated? Should all children be assured of a useful secondary education, or at least all who desired it? Could secondary education be expanded and reconfigured to absorb much larger numbers of students with more varied aptitudes and occupational futures? Such questions naturally arose in the two waves of progressive politics in France during the Popular Front and the postwar moment. If in the end these efforts had little structural impact on French education, it was not for want of trying. Egalitarian reformers in both periods reached for the stars with comprehensive plans under the banner of "a single school system" or *école unique*.

Before the Popular Front came to power, the Chamber of Deputies in 1928 had voted by a hairline majority of 292 to 286 to endorse the principle of secondary public education free from tuition and had appropriated funds to cover tuition fees for the sixth form (first year) starting in 1930. By 1933 this provision had been extended in principle to tuition for all years, albeit without affecting fees for room and board.[33] At its optimistic inception in the summer of 1936 the Popular Front parliament almost immediately passed a law raising the school leaving age from thirteen to fourteen. Under the Radical minister of education Jean Zay, a lawyer by background and the youngest member of Blum's cabinet, momentum toward the *école unique* gathered force but then stalled.

Zay sought to create a system of continuous tiers rather than two separate orders of education, popular and elite. He wanted elementary schooling to be more clearly defined as ending around age eleven, and to eliminate the later years of instruction that prolonged it in many primary schools. In effect, he proposed a new tier of public education, a kind of middle schooling for all students, but one in which they would not be irrevocably tracked. "Does not social justice demand that, whatever the point of departure, each [student] may go in his chosen direction as far and as high as his abilities permit?"Zay asked.[34]

He therefore proposed that the sixth form (or first year) of secondary education should serve as a "vestibule class" or "orientation year" in which students could sort out their interests while faculty assessed and advised them. As a corollary Zay proposed a core syllabus for all students during that year, which would leave the way open to a choice of a classical, modern, or technical concentration in subsequent years. Students who simply did not wish to proceed further after the age of fourteen could seek a new school leaving certificate.

For their own contrasting professional reasons the trade unions of the *instituteurs* and of the secondary school teachers were both cool to Zay's plan; the latter lobbied vigorously in defense of "the traditions and methods that give all its value to our secondary education." The far-reaching reform plan that Zay submitted to parliament in March 1937 remained tied up in the Chamber of Deputies' education committee, whose unsympathetic chair held the *aggrégation* in classics and defended the rigor and humanistic virtues of traditional secondary education. The best Zay could do was to encourage experimental programs with his objectives.[35]

Educational reform figured prominently as a component of Vichy's new moral order, but if the regime knew what it despised, it vacillated about what exactly to promote. Vichy viewed the *instituteurs* with distrust as freethinkers, socialists, and, in the late 1930s, anti-national pacifists; quickly purged the public schools of Jews and Freemasons; banned the two teachers unions; and closed down the normal schools—"those evil seminaries of democracy"—that trained the *instituteurs* for their invasion of the body politic. Instead, Vichy intended that future teachers would be trained in the same traditionalist baccalaureate programs that led to most middle-class careers. Initially Vichy authorized local authorities to subsidize private Catholic schools, and sanctioned religious instruction on public school premises during the school day. Political shifts within the regime led to revocation of those extreme forms of support for church influence but only to replace them with more qualified versions. Vichy also deflected pressures against the primacy of Latin in secondary school curricula and restored tuition charges for the final two years.[36]

The clause on education in the CNR's agenda of "indispensable reforms" stated only one broad goal: "The effective opportunity for all French children to benefit from the most fully developed education and access to culture, whatever their parents' situation, so that the highest functions will be truly open to all those who have the talents [*capacités*] required to exercise them—thereby promoting a veritable elite, not of birth but of merit."[37]

Under the GPRF and during the political skirmishing of 1945–46, the issue of the Catholic schools loomed as a potential obstacle to tripartite cooperation. Vichy's embrace of subsidies to those schools and breaches of *laicité* (secularism) in the public schools had for the moment tainted the recourse to such overt measures. During the early months of the GPRF André Philip—a Protestant and prominent socialist with an impeccable Resistance record—headed a commission looking into the question of public and private schooling. Less rigid about *laicité* than most socialists, Philip hoped to end "the idiotic rupture" between progressive believers and secularists. But he proved unable to broker an agreement for even modest gestures toward Catholic interests in private schooling.[38] Yet neither the Socialists nor the MRP were ready to turn this into a make-or-break issue.

Leery of the vaguely threatening notion of the *école unique,* the social-Catholics wanted a more tolerant and supportive public policy toward church-sponsored schools, and a constitutional guarantee for freedom of education, or *enseignement libre,* as they called private schooling. The Left would not embed this guarantee in the new constitution nor breach the *laicité* of public schools, but neither did it insist on a public monopoly of education. In effect Socialists and social-Catholics agreed to let sleeping dogs lie, so the contentious question of support for confessional schools jostled but did not shatter their cooperation.[39] The issue, for example, was a proximate cause for the fall of MRP Robert Schuman's cabinet in July 1948. His minister of public health, Madame Poinso-Chapuis of the MRP (the first woman with full cabinet status), collaborated with the religious Schuman on a decree to outflank *laicité* by channeling funds to nongovernmental "family associations." In the name of child welfare (the minister's province), those associations might then provide subsidies for parents who could not afford the fees for the confessional schools of their preference. After parliamentary wrangling the Assembly quashed the decree amid a great deal of hostility by the Socialists toward Madame Minister. But only in 1951 did the endemic tension over confessional schooling erupt full force.[40]

Meanwhile in 1945 the GPRF established a blue-ribbon commission to study the reform of public education, composed of a score of distinguished intellectuals, education professionals, and government officials. Chaired successively by two leftist members of the prestigious Collège de France, the physicist Paul Langevin and the psychologist Henri Wallon, the group was known as the Langevin-Wallon Commission. Its deep explorations and methodical deliberations took over two years, and by the time it published its final report in April 1947 the moment for reform had passed. Parliamentary politicians proved skittish about the report's many technical issues and were besides preoccupied by economic and labor issues. For his part the socialist minister of education Edmond Naegelen had been no help at all, his indifferent behavior aptly described by historian Antoine Prost as "stupefying." The report was saluted as a noble effort and then left on the shelf unimplemented.[41]

Yet Langevin-Wallon warrants consideration for two reasons. First, because it distilled the democratic sentiment and reformist zeal of France's postwar moment and constituted a major effort to flesh out a path toward the CNR's broad objective. Second, because in so doing the report implicitly displayed the tension between two objectives in educational reform that did not easily mesh: full-bore equality of opportunity on one side and a modern society's technological, vocational, and professional needs, which required provision for varied aptitudes and educational options, on the other.[42]

The Langevin-Wallon plan (hereafter L-W) advocated a thorough reconstruction of French education to achieve the potential for social justice in a democracy. In the spirit of the CNR program, it declared that "recruitment [for secondary schooling] today is far too often determined by the social class and financial resources of families. . . . The passage from one level of education to another [therefore] presents great difficulties." An appendix to the report calculated that only 5.5 percent of current students in secondary schools were the children of workers and 5.7 percent of farmers, whereas 29.4 percent had parents in the liberal professions or management cadres.[43]

Taking up where Zay left off, L-W proposed over time to replace the traditional bifurcated schooling with three *cycles* "corresponding to the levels of development, and to which all the children should successively have access." When fully realized, this would yield an integrated system for children between the ages of six and eighteen. The first cycle of primary schooling would cover ages three to eleven—with the three-to-six preschool years a matter of parental discretion, but with state provision of *écoles maternelles* for those who desired them. The second cycle would cover all children aged eleven to fifteen. The curriculum would initially be common to convey "general knowledge," and subsequently more specialized, but "the specialized teaching will include a choice of activities that permits the children to test their tastes and aptitudes. . . . Options properly speaking should come up only in the last years of the second [i.e., middle school] cycle. . . . [And] the passage from one option to another must always remain possible."

Thus L-W did not advocate an equivalent of Britain's make-or-break 11-plus exam for the tracking or streaming of students, but a longer, individualized period of observation, encouragement, and assessment by teachers during the second cycle. To underscore its resistance to premature or arbitrary streaming, the report added this comment on "options": "Since the commission considers that the sixth form is the first step in a period of two years devoted to the obser- vation of the students . . . prior to any kind of scholarly determination, it proposes that no differentiation should separate students during the sixth form. It further recommends that the Latin option as well as the vocational option coincide [only] with entry into the fourth form.[44]

In the third cycle (ages fifteen to eighteen—fourth to first forms) each child would be directed—though not irrevocably—to one of three sections or tracks. The "theoretical section," preparatory for higher education, would offer curricula for classical or modern literary studies, scientific study of various kinds, or tech- nical courses of study. A second section or track would consist of "professional studies" for "the children potentially able to serve as middle managers in commerce and industry." Finally there would be a vocational track for *études pratiques,* such as manual work/study apprenticeships or agricultural studies in rural areas. Parting from the relative rigidity and exclusiveness of traditional secondary schooling in France, the third cycle would thus offer a wider variety of learning options and would permit reevaluation of individual students when appropriate. To make another comparison, the secondary schooling envisaged in L-W was closer in spirit to Britain's multilaterals or comprehensives than to the linked alternatives of prestigious freestanding Grammars and generally inferior Secondary Moderns.

Under L-W schooling would become compulsory until age eighteen, and public education would be free at all levels to promote access to secondary and post-secondary education regardless of a student's social origins. For the same reason free tuition for higher education had to be supplemented by need-based scholarships for expenses. Similarly the apprenticeship track of the third cycle required provision of income replacement (*présalaire*) for working-class or farm children who might normally be earning for their households during those years.[45] The report's main concession to circumstances was to project a five-year period for its gradual implementation, keyed to the dramatic call for gradually raising the school leaving age from fourteen to eighteen. By then the commission hoped that the requisite financial resources, physical infrastructure, and trained teaching personnel would be available, as they certainly were not in 1947.

Little of L-W made its way into law, although as in Zay's day the Education Ministry's bureau of secondary education encouraged experimental classes in a progressive educational spirit. But most teachers disliked the new pedagogy, and the classes petered out after their patron left the bureau. Only at the inception of de Gaulle's Fifth Republic in 1959 would comprehensive educational reform begin in earnest, following a long gestation in sharp debates by the wary teachers unions on other proposals during the 1950s. Among other things, the 1959 law (Berthoin-Debré) finally raised the school leaving age to sixteen and introduced a compulsory two-year "cycle of observation" at the start of secondary schooling.[46] Still, without major changes in the law between 1945 and 1958, enrollment in public secondary schools almost doubled, from around 740,000 to 1,350,000, although "the [customary] social hierarchy was faithfully reproduced."[47] Along with population growth, increasing parental demand brought an incremental expansion of secondary education albeit without major structural or pedagogical change.

Reconstruction and Housing

Unlike Britain, France deferred major housing initiatives in the postwar moment because two urgent problems caused by war damage took priority. First, destruction from the German invasion of 1940, Allied bombing in 1943–44, and the battles across France after D-Day had wrecked the nation's rail, road, and maritime infrastructures. War damage left 22,000 kilometers of inoperable rail lines; destroyed most locomotives and rolling stock; demolished 7,500 road bridges and 4,000 spans over rivers; and laid waste to ports and merchant shipping.[48] For the next three years socialist Jules Moch labored doggedly as minister of transport to revive French transportation networks and to prepare the airline industry for the future. The second priority—the domain of the Ministry of Reconstruction and Urban Planning (MRU)—was to compensate and *temporarily* rehouse the almost two million civilians whose dwellings, farms, or commercial buildings had been badly damaged or totally destroyed from the same military causes.

Apart from gathering information about housing and launching the odd demonstration project of modernist design and prefab methods, most of the MRU's manpower and resources initially went to aid the victims of war damage, the *sinistrés* (disaster sufferers). The flow of battles and targeting by Allied bombing concentrated the damage geographically: over 1,800 communes (out of 38,000) were declared collectively *sinistrés,* including 190 of 334 urban communes above populations of 10,000.[49] At least 269,000 housing units had been totally destroyed along with 130,000 farms and 55,000 commercial/industrial structures, and at least a million other dwellings were seriously damaged.[50] The MRU had to verify every damage claim and process all compensation payments; undertake repairs where possible at state expense; and provide temporary (essentially wooden) housing for the *sinistrés* in direst need. From 1945 to 1947 budgets for the MRU provided ample appropriations for the *sinistrés,* and for little else; thereafter that spending wound down, and other issues could absorb the ministry's attention.[51]

In the tripartite governments that followed de Gaulle's resignation two communists led the MRU between January 1946 and May 1947. François Billoux and his successor continued the ministry's emphasis on clearing debris from the communes *sinistrés,* disarming unexploded bombs, repairing damaged buildings, and providing temporary housing. By the end of 1946 over 400,000 families had been rehoused and 300,000 more had the damaged dwellings they inhabited shored up. The communist ministers developed plans for new public housing initiatives but could not make headway before their tenures ended.[52] Though Billoux did not emphasize this in his retrospective account, the PCF also sought to maintain rent control against pressures to weaken or wind it down.

Stringent rent control had been operative since the emergency of the Great War in 1914. The downside, acknowledged by all sides, was that rent control froze in place a vast array of substandard housing: crowded, unhygienic, and uncomfortable, with an estimated 48 percent lacking running water and 80 percent without indoor toilets. On the upside, this largely inflexible rent control system kept housing affordable for working-class tenants, who clung to their extremely low rents as a vital form of social protection. But rent control also left owners and landlords without incentive or (in many cases) the means to upgrade their properties no matter how deplorable their condition, let alone to enhance the value of their property.[53]

The National Assembly debated rent regulation on and off but could not achieve consensus for two years. The PCF in effect linked support for loosening rent control with the granting of substantial wage increases for workers. The Socialists stopped short of that linkage but advocated other safeguards to protect tenants' tenure and to shield the neediest from excessive rent increases. The MRP hoped to assure small landlords sufficient income for repairs and for a modest return, and to provide a right of recovery should landlords require their property for personal use. The Radicals and conservatives wanted to encourage market mechanisms as much as possible yet without creating a firestorm of aggrieved low-income tenants. After the political balance shifted rightward (see below) the National Assembly in June 1948 finally passed a revision of rent regulation by a vote of 261 yes (mainly the MRP, UDSR, most of the Right) to 192 no (mainly the PCF), with the 90-odd Socialists abstaining.[54]

The key section of the law provided that every housing unit was to be evaluated on an individual basis under a complex technical formula having to do with its size, characteristics, and rent per square meter—a formula known as *surface corigeé*. Officials at the MRU would then calculate a modestly increased rent, and rents could be slightly raised again for each unit at six-month intervals under another complicated formula. Passage of the law was possible in part because the politicians distanced themselves from the actual levels of rent increases for each dwelling by leaving them to faceless officials at the ministry and by assuring that rents would rise only gradually. The Assembly also cushioned the impact with a companion law offering a "housing allocation" to the most demonstrably needy tenants, although the Finance Ministry habitually tried to minimize the funding level for this new subsidy.[55]

During 1945–47, when the *sinistrés* remained the top priority, the MRU erected about 800,000 temporary (wooden) units for them. Before 1949, however, perhaps only 50,000 new units of permanent housing went up under the auspices of the MRU, while private enterprise constructed three-quarters of all new housing, in contrast to the British approach. With the plight of the *sinistrés* on its way to being resolved, the MRU turned to spurring new construction. A law of September 1947 revived a modest interwar public housing program known as HLMs (Habitations à Loyer Modéré or Dwellings at Moderate Rents). Single-purpose local authorities could borrow capital from a state agency to put up new housing at extremely low interest (1 to 2 percent), with the loans repayable over a long period of between forty to sixty years. While the ministry set minimum standards for construction and operation of the housing developments, local authorities had considerable autonomy in erecting them and selecting tenants. Over time some HLM authorities, capitalizing on the law's porous language, used their autonomy to extend tenancies to *cadres* and other middle-class families as well as workers, and in some cases they found ways to sell the apartments to the tenants instead of renting them.[56] All told in the period 1945–53 (leaving aside the temporary housing for *sinistrés*), the MRU recorded almost 500,000 new housing completions from all sources.[57]

After this spate of legislative action on housing, the most interesting personality to head the MRU took over its direction in late 1948. Eugène Petit (known by 1944 as Claudius-Petit, having incorporated his nom de guerre in the Resistance), was originally a cabinetmaker by trade, but through independent study he went on to become a teacher of design in Lyon. Affiliated with social-Catholic groups and with trade unions, and a supporter of the Popular Front, Petit joined the resistance movement Franc-Tireur after the occupation and became its first delegate to the CNR. Obliged to leave France in October 1943, Claudius-Petit joined de Gaulle's Consultative Assembly in Algiers and later in Paris; influenced by Le Corbusier, whom he had met in the 1930s, he won attention for his advanced views on urban planning. In the postwar, he argued, the republic should not simply reconstruct war-damaged areas as they had existed before but should use the most modern design, architectural, and engineering methods in multidisciplinary urban and regional planning to rebuild the nation in a new fashion. Passed over as a possible choice to head the MRU, Claudius-Petit set off with Le Corbusier on a study mission to the US, underwritten by the Foreign Ministry. The pair toured the Tennessee Valley Authority (the New Deal's great triumph in regional development and rural electrification), interviewed its director, and came away much impressed with TVA's "leçon magistrale d'aménagement du territoire."[58]

In September 1948 Claudius-Petit (affiliated politically with the UDSR) was named head of the MRU, and he held that office under eight successive "Third Force" governments until January 1953. To advance his vision for a new approach to regional and urban planning, Claudius-Petit raised the status of the ministry's planning arm; established a new financial agency within the ministry

(the Caisse d'Aménagement du Territoire); and issued a green book (the equivalent of a British white paper) called *Plan national d'aménagement du territoire*. As is evident, his core concept was "*aménagement*," roughly translatable
as planning for development—something essentially beyond reach of the MRU
in its early years. Unable to interest Jean Monnet in co-sponsoring his scheme
for regional planning that combined industrial development and residential
construction, he formed a blue-ribbon ministerial commission instead.

Claudius-Petit long advocated the need to decentralize development away
from the Parisian conurbation and to support local development with state loans
and subsidies. As a start he sought to strengthen the law of eminent domain
for both empty and built spaces in such potential zones, and to enlarge state
supervisory and financial power over local authorities. But the National
Assembly under the "Third Force" political equilibrium was more susceptible
than ever to the sway of local interest lobbying. While Bidault's cabinet of 1950
endorsed Claudius-Petit's policy of planning for decentralized regional development, the Assembly restrained the MRU's powers as well as its appropriations. His regional planning policy had support among urban planners and
architects but lacked sufficient administrative power or funding. The MRU did
relocate farther away from Paris several new factories originally slated for
construction close to the capital, and it funded three demonstration projects for
development zones. But on the whole Claudius-Petit's vision for regional planning of industrial development and residential construction could not take off
and, as he lamented in 1953, was "mis dangeureusement en sommeil."
Sidetracked, he could have added, much like the Langevin-Wallon Report on
educational reform several years earlier.

Tripartism and Its Discontents: The MRP

The plausibility of tripartism in the postwar moment derived in good measure
from the remarkable success of the MRP in party-building and electoral
politics. The founding cohort of social-Catholic *résistants* fostered a progressive orientation anchored in the CNR Common Program, melded with traditional Christian values. The tripartite governments of 1945–47 hoped to make
workers feel integral members of the polity and not a class apart. The MRP
therefore had to respect and work with the PCF as bona fide representatives of
the working class. Some MRP activists perhaps shared with fellow-traveling

intellectuals a sentimentalized solidarity with the proletariat. But unlike such figures as Sartre, who granted "unconditional absolution" to communist actions at home or abroad no matter how questionable or offensive,[59] Socialists and social-Catholics deplored the authoritarianism of Moscow and of the PCF, even as they cooperated with the communists and abided their periodic distemper in cabinet, government agencies, and economic boards.

By 1947 the commitment to tripartist cooperation had frayed on all sides but still endured. In January, for example, the MRP's executive committee after five hours of debate voted six to four with two abstentions to endorse joining the tripartite cabinet that socialist Paul Ramadier sought to form. While the committee "dreaded the activities and exaggeration of the Communists," it decided that the MRP should continue to support *tripartisme*.[60] At the MRP's third National Congress in March 1947 the issue erupted again in a plenary debate over the merits versus the pitfalls of cooperation with the PCF.

The MRP's official report on general policy called for continued cooperation "with all parties that emanate from the people." In the debate that followed, Madame Denesch defended cooperation with the PCF because the MRP must not cut itself off from the working class—and "for the militant worker, there is no distinction between his party [the PCF] and the working class." True, officials who interacted with PCF militants often endured a war of nerves, but the communists also supported reasonable and constructive positions. To break decisively with the PCF in the current climate would be to lapse into isolation, she concluded (to *vifs applaudissements*). In the same spirit, Léo Hamon supported cooperation with the PCF, which "enjoys (wrongly, but even so) immense confidence among the French popular masses, which we cannot help but take into account." "To fulfill our mission as an arbiter rather than one of the opposing forces," he argued, we cannot turn stridently anti-communist.

Speakers on the other side insisted that it was time to say "no to denials and cowardice." They worried about alienating middle-class voters, and about falling into the pattern of the Socialist Party, which "crumbles and unravels from one consultation to another because it sticks too closely to the PCF and gives the impression of being in tow." Former minister of the army Edmond Michelet offered an amendment to change just one word in the official policy resolution: instead of pledging to cooperate with all parties *d'émanation populaire*, he would substitute *d'émanation démocratique*. The delegates understood that he intended this to exclude collaboration with the PCF. They knew that a tempest had previously raged in the Constituent Assembly in 1946 around an MRP proposal for a *statut des partis* that would have required internal democracy in all lawful political parties. The Communists made rejection of that notion nonnegotiable, and the MRP reluctantly abandoned it; Michelet now revived the idea as a rationale for breaking ties with the PCF. In the end, however, the delegates voted down his amendment, which would have put the onus for scuttling *tripartisme* on the MRP.[61]

The new president of the Fourth Republic, for one, welcomed this news since it made the task of holding a coalition government together much easier. As Auriol noted in his journal: "The MRP has affirmed in a recent declaration that it was essential to safeguard the union of the three large parties associated with the government. The participation of the Communists in the government is one of the conditions for the recovery of France."[62] The MRP kept faith with tripartism up to that point despite the discomfort of its leaders and the outright hostility of many in the party's rank and file.

For the MRP Gaullism offered one possible exit from tripartism, but most party activists would not take it. During the grinding battles over the second constitutional draft, the MRP balked at de Gaulle's critique and backed the final compromises. There followed two successive attempts to launch a Gaullist movement in opposition. The short-lived Gaullist Union of 1946, which the general inspired but did not actively lead, campaigned against the second constitutional draft and against the "betrayal" by the MRP in backing it. Speakers at a mass meeting in the Vel d'Hiver shortly before the referendum rounded on the MRP as "The party of recantations, of contradictions, in a word of lies," and attacked party leader Bidault as "a flag-bearer without a flag."[63] When the draft won approval at the polls in October by a narrow margin the Gaullist Union wound down. But in April 1947 de Gaulle himself launched the more potent Rassemblement du Peuple Français (RPF). Undaunted by the fact that the new constitution was now a fait accompli, the RPF insisted that the entire edifice must be scrapped—not by a seizure of power, to be sure, but by forging a new political consensus that could sweep aside all obstacles to a renovation.[64]

The new movement attracted remarkably few prominent figures in the MRP. Initially the RPF formed a Gaullist interparty group in the existing parliament. Edmond Michelet jumped at the chance, seeing "the immense opportunities offered, especially for the youthful MRP by this *Rassemblement* that de Gaulle is proposing."[65] But like the Socialists, the MRP refused permission for its deputies to adopt a "double affiliation," and each deputy had to choose. Even Maurice Schumann refused to bolt, and only Michelet and *L'Aube*'s editor Louis Terrenoire among the top echelon deserted to join the seventy or so deputies in the "Gaullist Intergroup." To justify his choice, Michelet dug out underground writings from 1943 by Teitgen about France's need to free itself from the traditional parties. "In France the political parties are clans when they are not factions," Teitgen had written. "To base the nation's political life on them . . . is to entrust associations dedicated to robbery with guarding the treasure."[66] In the leadership of the MRP that sentiment had now dissipated in the light of experience. To the *résistants* who led the MRP, the uncompromising Gaullist assault on the institutions and spirit of the new Fourth Republic was an adventurism based on a personal mystique that may have saved the country's honor in 1940 but had become irrelevant if not dangerous.[67]

Tripartism and Its Discontents: The Socialists

Socialists certainly did not speak with one voice about their political options either, and historically the SFIO was no stranger to crippling factionalism facilitated by its own internal democracy. After the Liberation the shattered party immediately reestablished itself at an "extraordinary Congress," where it named Daniel Mayer, a disciple of Blum's and the socialist delegate to the CNR, as general secretary and purged the socialist parliamentarians who had voted yes for Pétain. As men and women of a new generation began to join the party in modest numbers, however, the resurrected party relied on familiar structures and on the depleted cadres of party veterans. As one historian has shown, the party's revival was "endogenous rather than exogenous," "a failed opening," "an unfinished renewal," which, among other things, inadequately advanced women.[68] Albert Camus anticipated some of this when he wrote in *Combat* soon after the Liberation that while most Frenchmen were now socialists in spirit, "We were dissuaded from joining the PS by a few of their people and by most of their methods." The intrepid *résistant* Léo Hamon similarly recalled his own choice: "I was turned away from the Socialist Party, like many other *résistants,* by its rigidities, its rejection of the innovations that seemed necessary to us, which excluded the welcoming intellectual attitude that Léon Blum himself would have wished to see prevailing. I joined the MRP."[69]

Nonetheless, if the option of tripartism in the postwar moment rested on the hybrid, center-left leanings of the MRP, the Socialist Party always seemed to be the coalition's fulcrum. In theory socialists had two alternative political choices. They could forge an alliance of the two avowedly Marxist parties. Or they could break with the authoritarian PCF and tilt toward the center in partnership with the MRP and others in search of a French version of the British Labour Party. But the SFIO accepted tripartism as the best way to advance its progressive agenda and to preclude a hardened polarization that would leave the French communists, their quarter of the electorate, and the mighty CGT outside the pale. Accordingly the Socialists refused to participate in any coalition government that excluded either the PCF or the MRP. Superficially, this stance maximized the SFIO's political leverage, but some party activists disliked that straitjacket, as they saw it.

After his return from Nazi captivity, party patriarch Léon Blum had reformulated in books and newspaper columns his humanistic and reformist credo for socialism, which still honored the long-term aspiration of transforming and ultimately replacing capitalism. His devotees in the party were receptive to tripartism. To the more militant left-wingers, however, Blum was a revisionist diluting veritable socialist principles. In their own journals and some departmental federations, they advocated a less equivocal socialist doctrine on the primacy of class struggle, expressed distrust of the MRP (whose clerical-religious ties they exaggerated), and tended to favor a course aligned with the PCF. As Socialist strength, relative to the party's high expectations, ebbed in the election of June 1946 for the second Constituent Assembly, many activists faulted the electoral tactics and propaganda from central headquarters under Daniel Mayer.

These crosscurrents erupted at the thirty-eighth National Congress of the SFIO, August 29– September 1, 1946.[70] By that time Guy Mollet had emerged as the leading critic of the party's status quo. A teacher in Arras before the war and an activist in the SFIO's large Pas-de-Calais federation, Mollet (b. 1905) survived his perilous Resistance activity with the OCM and rose quickly in the post-Liberation party. With a power base as mayor of Arras, Mollet was elected as a deputy to the two Constituent Assemblies, and he led the socialist group on the constitutional drafting committee of the first Assembly. Mollet's insurgency against the status quo at the party congress had three goals. First, to reject the *Rapport Moral*—the annual report on his stewardship and policy—to be presented by

Secretary General Mayer. Second, to win adoption of a policy motion that would affirm more orthodox socialist doctrine. ("The class struggle is not out of date. . . . The whole of our effort must be oriented towards the working class," as one delegate put it.) And finally, to elect a new executive committee that would in turn choose a new secretary general, presumably Guy Mollet.

The dissidents succeeded in rejecting Mayer's *Rapport Moral* by a vote of 2,975 mandates (66 percent) versus only 1,365 in its favor. Mayer then immediately resigned but maintained a conciliatory stance toward the dissidents. At that point the implications of this vote as a dramatic victory for the Left began to dissipate. Two competing policy motions vied for adoption: an essentially anti-tripartist Mollet motion, and an alternative by André Philip with a less doctrinaire statement on class conflict and socialism's goals. Instead of endorsing the Mollet motion, however, the delegates sent the competing motions to a resolutions committee, which took the edge off each and fused them into an old-style synthesis motion. Underneath the ideological currents and the clash of personalities swirling at the Congress, political scientist B. D. Graham writes, "The whole revolt had an unmistakably cathartic character, as if the members were rebelling not so much against their leaders as against their situation and the intolerable frustrations of tripartism." Mollet was "the secretary general of all the discontents," as one delegate later put it.[71] In sum, after the vote to reject the *Rapport Moral,* no consensus emerged on how to proceed.

On its last day the Congress named a new 31-member executive committee, as the delegates voted on a list of 95 declared candidates without resort to any slates. They chose people from various corners of the party, including 18 new faces and only 13 carryovers out of the 23 who stood for re-election. The new executive committee tilted leftward yet it remained fairly well-balanced between dissidents (including the two most outspoken activists) and moderates (including Mayer and several current ministers). The committee's subsequent vote in a secret ballot for a new secretary general was extremely close between the two candidates: Mollet and the veteran Blumiste and current minister Augustin Laurent. The 16 to 14 win for Mollet apparently hinged on the vote of Salomon Grumbach, one of Blum's old allies; Grumbach personally favored Laurent but commented that "it would not be wise to refuse the fullest support to the comrades who had a majority at the Congress."[72]

During the next year Mollet consolidated control over the party apparatus, but he never managed to establish its primacy over the socialist parliamentary deputation on major policy decisions, although he kept trying. Moreover his own mounting ambivalence over communism and revolutionary militancy disrupted Mollet's relations with some of his leftist allies going forward.

Tripartism and Its Discontents: The PCF

The PCF certainly had problems with tripartism after the Liberation, but not with becoming "a party of government." Emerging from the occupation, French communists had huge political capital from their aggressive political and para-military roles in the Resistance, after the problematic interlude of the Nazi-Soviet pact, and from the supreme contribution of their Soviet patron in defeating the Nazis. The party enjoyed a great surge in membership, as did the CGT where communists quickly gained majority support in most trade unions and depart-mental federations. French communists wanted respect, deserved respect after the Liberation, and got it—starting with de Gaulle's GPRF. The specifics for communist participation in coalition governments invariably caused conflicts but compromises allowed that involvement to proceed.

The PCF had two ministers in de Gaulle's provisional unity government (Charles Tillon as air minister and François Billoux as public health minister). After de Gaulle was named acting president by the Constituent Assembly in October 1945, a face-saving compromise allowed him to refuse the key Ministries of Defense, Interior, or Foreign Affairs to a communist. Instead, de Gaulle appointed PCF general secretary Maurice Thorez as one of his four high-ranking ministers of state and specifically tasked him with overseeing a major reform of the civil service. Tillon became minister of armaments, Billoux was named MEN, and communists headed the Ministries of Industrial Production and of Labor. In the cabinet of socialist Gouin, Thorez was one of two vice presidents (along with an MRP leader), and the communists again held major cabinet posts in the economic and social sphere.

The communist ministers of Labor and of Industrial Production had substantial leverage in implementing innovations promised by the CNR: *comités d'entreprise* in factories for worker consultation with management over plant facilities, working conditions, and productivity issues; the nationalization of several sectors, including electricity where, unusually, labor had significant representation on the managing board; promulgation of a coal miner's charter; and initial implementa-tion of new social security laws.[73] Under Ramadier's Fourth Republic cabinet

Billoux was actually named as minister of defense, albeit with the three uniformed services transferred out from under him. Even so, Billoux had charge of planning a major overhaul in the recruitment and organization of the armed forces. Add together the initiatives of communist ministers in these various projects, some largely completed and some unrealized—civil service reform, social security, nationalizations, labor relations, army recruitment—and one sees that participation in cabinets served the purpose of penetrating and reshaping several key French institutions.[74]

Maurice Thorez stood at the center of the party apparatus, of its public image, and of its governmental contingent; he all but embodied the PCF presence in the postwar moment. Of impeccably proletarian status from a coal-mining family (although Thorez had not actually worked in the pits himself), he was, like Ernest Bevin, an ambitious autodidact who could operate effectively in the halls of power.[75] From 1945 until mid-1947 Thorez enjoyed relative freedom from constraint by either Moscow or rival party comrades, although temperamental and ideological differences over the PCF's commitment to proletarian militancy repeatedly surfaced in its central committee.

Thorez had no problem with the party's traditional authoritarianism, its "democratic centralism" and stern discipline. These led the SFIO to reject the PCF's periodic overtures for fusion, even as the socialists remained open to "unity of action." But the PCF was clearly in a popular front mode, its emphasis on national recovery and the expansion of democracy. While the party's base remained as always the working class, the PCF courted intellectuals, elements of the middle class, and especially farmers via its agrarian weekly La Terre (circulation over 300,000) and its local peasant associations. The party was cautious about fiscal or regulatory policies that might alienate the agricultural constituency and in some regions it reaped impressive rural support at the polls.[76]

As a minister of state or vice president in all the tripartite governments between October 1945 and May 1947 Thorez won grudging admiration for his work in the cabinet from most ministerial colleagues, starting with de Gaulle himself. Thorez made a signal contribution to their common cause with his unflinching support—in tandem with party comrade Benoît Frachon of the CGT—for "the battle of production," which required sustained sacrifice by workers. No account of the period omits how Thorez traveled to the northern coal fields in July 1945 where he exhorted the miners to redouble their efforts in behalf of the French people and denounced slackers, absenteeism, and wildcat strikes. This dramatic harangue no doubt raised hackles among over-worked miners, but it served well the party's political propaganda, which insisted on the primacy of the working class in the recovery and future pros-pects of France.[77]

Having renounced any notion of seizing power by force after the Liberation (although that idea could not be definitively banished), the postwar PCF insisted that its route to power lay through democracy—through the ballot box and the powers of a National Assembly whose sovereignty remained supreme.[78] During the successive election campaigns of the postwar moment the communists played rough and dirty. They of course heaped scorn on the collaborationists and reactionaries of the Right, but also on their vacillating Socialist rivals, and espe-cially on the progressive centrists of the MRP. They distrusted and vilified that party as riddled with reactionary ex-Pétainists, clerical influence, and a desire to undo the *laïcité* of French public schooling. But once the dust settled after each round of elections, the communists ultimately reached accommodation with the MRP, even if they hoped eventually to get free of the tripartist formula.[79]

From Tripartism to the "Third Force"

One would need an ingenious Venn diagram to plot the array of domestic and foreign issues intersecting in 1947 that finally shattered France's political equi-librium: the ever-worsening cost-of-living troubles; mushrooming strikes for higher wages by rank-and-file workers; the mounting pressures on the PCF and the CGT to abandon the "battle for production" and back those strikes; an erup-tion of conflict in parliament over Indochina; the mutual hardening of anti-Soviet resolve in Washington and anti-American hostility in the Kremlin; the US proffer of Marshall Plan aid and Moscow's rejection of that assistance as an imperialist trap; the resurrection of the Comintern (now called the Kominform), with a new militant line for Western communist parties. On top of all that, de Gaulle launched his new movement in April 1947, targeting the communists, the Fourth Republic constitution, and the political parties. Little wonder that between May and November 1947 tripartism collapsed and the political balance shifted rightward.

The Indochina problem almost sundered Ramadier's government in March but in the end it did not. Rebellion by nationalists and communists against de Gaulle's initiatives to reclaim French control of Vietnam left a mess for the

Fourth Republic. Ramadier and most of his cabinet wished to negotiate a settlement but only after regaining the upper hand militarily, while the PCF demanded an end to military action and immediate negotiations; the PCF central committee advised its parliamentary deputies to vote against military credits to bolster French forces there. When the matter came before the National Assembly on March 22, however, the PCF deputies abstained and its minister-deputies voted aye for the sake of cabinet unity.[80]

Ramadier above all wished to defend a commitment to block wage increases until a thorough review of prices and wages long scheduled for July. Rank-and-file workers in various sectors insisted that this left them with a desperately declining standard of living, and strikes broke out among postal workers, journalists, and typographers, among others. In April workers occupied two Renault plants in a wildcat strike for a 10F hourly wage increase above the current 25.5F. The strike spread to metalworkers in the Paris region, as the Renault workers voted by a three to two margin to continue the strike. For the moment L'Humanité denounced the wildcat strike, but that was about to change.[81]

Signaling a shift, Thorez told the cabinet that wage increases demanded by the strikers should not be blocked and need not touch off an inflationary wage-price spiral because corporate profits could offset them. Socialist André Philip and MRP Finance Minister Robert Schuman countered that productivity bonuses and continued price controls should suffice for workers until the July review. Backed by the majority of his cabinet, Ramadier would not budge on wage increases and decided to seek a vote of confidence in the National Assembly. On May 4 the Assembly duly voted confidence by 360 to 186, with the communists, including their ministers, voting no and the right-wing PRL abstaining.

Ramadier received conflicting advice on how to respond when he consulted his party's executive commission and the Assembly's socialist caucus. At Mollet's urging the commission voted 12 to 9 that socialists should not participate in any government that excluded the communists; since his cabinet's unity had been shattered Ramadier should therefore resign. The socialist deputies, however, voted by 69 to 9 that Ramadier should not resign lest he create an unpredictable political crisis. The final decision, most agreed, should await a National Council of the party due to convene three days later.[82]

His determination stiffened by Auriol and Blum, however, the PM decided to oust the communist ministers from his cabinet immediately, which was his constitutional prerogative. He informed the PCF ministers that they had effectively vacated their positions by voting against the confidence motion and were no longer part of his cabinet. For Ramadier the ejection was strictly a question of sustaining cabinet solidarity as a prerequisite for viable parliamentary democracy. This outcome startled the communists and some socialists as well, not least Mollet. At the SFIO National Council on May 7, Ramadier declared that "if the Council orders it, I shall hand my resignation tomorrow to Auriol. But in doing so I should feel I was signing the abdication of the Republic." Mollet countered that remaining in a "bourgeois" government without the communists would risk a severe break with the working class. In the end the Council voted against Mollet's view that Ramadier should resign, 2,529 mandates versus 2,125.[83]

Despite the dramatic headlines in the French and Anglo-Saxon press, the ejection of the communist ministers did not seem definitive on either side. The divided socialists again reversed themselves at their party congress in Lyon that August. This time following Mollet's lead, the delegates voted (2,423 to 2,276) that continued participation of socialists in a government without the communists was problematic and would risk "definitively compromising the chances of [real] democracy in our country." Mollet believed that coalition with parties of the center would force socialists into concessions detrimental to the working class, which would bring "a growing discredit" on their heads from which the communists alone would benefit.[84] Ramadier was shaken by the Congress's resolution and wished to resign, not from principle but from weariness, but Auriol refused to accept his proffer. So the skirmishing continued, but in the name of party unity Mollet wisely did not press his slim majoritarian edge to a definitive confrontation.

For its part, the PCF had gambled in May on provoking a ministerial crisis, which boomeranged when Ramadier ejected their ministers. But like de Gaulle when he resigned in January 1946, the PCF assumed that it would return to power soon enough and on better terms. The PCF's basic line of serving the French people as a governing party had not yet changed, either in its public pronouncements or its correspondence with Moscow. "The objective of our policy is to return to the government and utilize the pressure of the masses," wrote *Humanité's* editor Marcel Cachin. But the PCF faced an undertow from the spiraling discontent of the workers and from the escalating hostility between the two superpowers, each looking for backing in Western Europe. By autumn the Cold War split had crystalized in France for all to see over the Marshall Plan and its rejection by the Kremlin as a form of American blackmail. The PCF now revised its narrative; in late August it began to depict its ouster from the government as a result of American pressure and plotting. While historical research since that time has shown this to be unlikely, it remained a plausible notion for the party to exploit.[85]

Making the political situation even more fraught, the Gaullist movement had a stunning success in the municipal elections of October 1947. Candidates under the RPF's banner won 35 percent of the votes, took control of seventeen of France's largest cities, and gained mayoral seats in forty-one departmental capitals.[86] But the MRP's stance formed a dike against the Gaullist tide and reinforced the MRP's cooperation with the socialists. When Ramadier finally resigned in November, the socialists ceded primacy to the MRP in a new government led by Robert Schuman, which extended from the center-left to the center-right. While tripartism had ruptured in May, the definitive break in French political and social life—the end of the postwar moment—came only that fall.

To replace tripartism the socialists, the MRP, the centrists, and the moderate Right came together in a new kind of alignment—just the situation that tripartism had sought to avoid. The new configuration left the communists outside the pale and forming an adversarial society with strong electoral support from workers and other voters.[87] The "Third Force" governments would defend the integrity of the Fourth Republic against the two rejectionist (if mutually hostile) forces of communism and Gaullism. But the "Third Force" coalitions would *not* be a *travailliste* formation of the center-left —the analogue to the British Labour Party that some socialists, progressive MRPs and even some Radicals had wistfully imagined. Of centrist coloration to begin with, the "Third Force" cabinets edged further rightward with almost each new iteration.[88] The seismic shifts in international relations and the explosion of worker discontent that fall became the specific contexts for "Third Force" governance between late 1947 and the next legislative election in 1951.

The Strike Waves of 1947 and 1948

The formation of the Kominform at the end of September and the imposition on its Western parties of a hard line on class struggle and anti-Americanism marked a turning point. It took Thorez some agile maneuvering to sustain his leadership, culminating with a tongue-lashing and self-criticism session in Moscow that November, but retain it he did. In tandem with the party, the CGT too adopted a more militant line, and it abandoned completely its restraint in "the battle of production." After the settlement of the Renault strike, a series of other localized, sometimes wildcat strikes had followed in June. Those strikes ran their course without any major consequences, but after a calculated hiatus during the paid vacations of summer, a new wave of strikes began in September and accelerated dramatically in the autumn. Neither methodically orchestrated nor entirely spontaneous, their main cause remained the desperate need for higher wages, but their import was increasingly political. Frachon, head of the CGT, told Moscow on September 9 that "we have found a very original form of strike movements and we have carried it out on a grand scale," but he added that the CGT was avoiding the risky course of promoting a general strike.

Tension escalated dramatically on November 10 when a 40 percent increase in tram fares decreed by the new Gaullist city authorities in Marseilles provoked a mass protest that turned into a riot. After four demonstrators were arrested, crowds stormed the courthouse to free them and then city hall to eject the mayor. The ensuing melees with the forces of order led to casualties on both sides and a sense of imminent anarchy in the city. Elsewhere militant strikes and workplace occupations proliferated—in the coal fields, auto factories, the metal trades, the building trades, the railroads, post offices, and electrical plants. On November 26 the CGT created a National Strike Committee to coordinate its forces, and announced that over two million workers were on strike. Regional demonstrations and riots also multiplied, for example in Valence where three demonstrators were killed on December 4. The previous night the Lille-Paris express was intentionally derailed, killing sixteen and injuring many more. (The CGT adamantly denied responsibility and subsequent investigations proved inconclusive as to who had caused this tragedy and why.)[89]

The newly seated government of Robert Schuman fought back on two fronts. Spurred on by socialist Minister of the Interior Jules Moch, the cabinet drafted legislation to protect the freedom to work alongside the freedom to strike. Moch believed that "the right to strike is the right to stop work without drawing penal or administrative sanctions. It should not be confused with the right to occupy the workplaces, and still less with preventing workers who do not wish to strike from working." (Parliament passed a law to that effect in due course.) Second, Moch set to work organizing the police and paramilitary forces at his disposal to the best advantage, but also issued orders to avoid excessive force or the use of firearms unless under direct assault. Though his ministry received alarming reports from around the country, Moch was less panicked than some colleagues and more skeptical about the "insurrectionary" intentions or capabilities of the communists. Still, he emerged as the face of repression who proclaimed that "between me and the saboteurs it is a battle without mercy." With informants in the ranks of the PCF and CGT, Moch used his authority most theatrically to thwart a planned occupation of a major power station in Paris that would have plunged the capital into darkness and immobility. But it was harder to end the occupation of the coal mines and the violent clashes between strikers and miners attempting to work. Finally the National Strike Committee, aware that many rank-and-file workers now wanted to end their strikes, issued a back-to-work order on December 9, followed promptly most everywhere except in some of the embattled coal fields.[90]

Staying on through various "Third Force" cabinet shuffles, Moch upgraded and reorganized the forces of order, starting with the paramilitary riot police or CRS (Compagnies Républicaines de Sécurité), established after the Liberation by the GPRF under Interior Ministry control. First Moch disbanded several CRS units for their failure to maintain order in Marseilles, amidst allegations that communists in their ranks had fraternized with the rioters.[91] Later he reorganized the CRS to make them a more effective force and improved the channels of communication with departmental authorities. The Interior Ministry was thus better prepared when a new wave of militant strikes began in October 1948, above all in the coal fields. Moch mobilized the gendarmerie, the CRS, and some military units to face down the coercive tactics of the highly organized strikers. (In the front ranks of clashes with picketers, CRS units were taunted by workers with shouts of "CRS/SS.") By now Moch himself was the outsized ogre of communist propaganda as America's lackey and a vicious strikebreaker. Denouncing Moch and his mentor Blum in November 1948, one PCF deputy plumbed the depths of contempt when he exclaimed in the National Assembly, "The working class hates you, the entire people hates you."[92]

The strike waves of late 1947 and 1948 raised the question then and since: were these strikes "insurrectional"—intended to bring the economy to a standstill by force? to bring down the government? perhaps even a prelude to an armed seizure of power by communists in the midst of the chaos? During the strike waves the anti-communist media endlessly advanced that notion, and the Prague coup of February 1948 no doubt heightened such fears. But even after the recent opening of relevant communist archives in Paris and Moscow, no confirmation of such intent has come to light. The strikes of late 1947 and late 1948 had manifestly political purposes, and many of them featured exceptionally coercive and violent tactics against persons and property. The strikes generated extreme rhetoric and propaganda on both sides. But as Mencherini and other historians have concluded, they were not actually "insurrectional." The recollection of a young railroad worker, who later rose to head the CGT, seems accurate: the strike wave "was simply a matter of action to press for worker demands, with a political significance [as well]: the refusal to abandon French economic sovereignty vis-à-vis the Americans and the Marshall Plan."[93]

Another Schism in the House of Labor

The arc of the postwar moment in France and the paroxysm that ended it are mirrored in the history of the CGT itself, and in a third schism in France's house of labor—following the schism of 1921; the reunification of 1935–36 in the spirit of the Popular Front; the new rupture of the CGT in 1939 after the Nazi-Soviet pact; and a second reunification under Resistance auspices. After the fall of France, Vichy had banned the CGT and the Catholic CFTC, and it decreed a corporatist Charter of Labor that eliminated all genuinely independent trade unionism along with the right to strike. The split of 1939 at first impeded joint action by trade unionists resisting such policies or the Nazi occupation itself. But courageous underground work by individuals on both sides of the CGT divide forged a basis for unity known as the Perreux Accords of April 1943. With the liberation of Paris, individuals from both groups immediately reclaimed the federation's former headquarters and set out to rebuild the CGT of old on the basis of the Perreux Accords.

Léon Jouhaux, still interned in Germany, remained the titular head of the CGT, while Benoît Frachon, the PCF's labor point man during the occupation, acted in his stead as leader. When Jouhaux returned to France in May 1945 the socialist press piously declared that "the CGT has recovered its guide." Louis Saillant, a negotiator of the Perreux Accords, the CGT delegate to the CNR and now its president, seemed a placeholder for his mentor Jouhaux. Saillant was one of five non-communists or *ex-confédérés* on the CGT's reconstituted executive bureau alongside three communists or *ex-unitaires*—which replicated the proportions before the 1939 schism. But as the CGT's membership rapidly swelled to or beyond its high watermark of four million in 1937, and as most of its constituent unions and departmental federations came under communist control, the balance of power inexorably shifted to the *ex-unitaires*. Younger workers were evidently impressed by communist organizational élan and unresponsive to the old syndicalist traditions of independence from political parties, which the communists argued would promote an unhealthy isolation of the working class.[94]

By September 1945 the CGT bureau had expanded to include eight *ex-confédérés* and five *ex-unitaires* or communists, but that was deceptive. Of the former, Saillant was increasingly drawn into the communist orbit despite his formerly close ties to Jouhaux; one was probably a communist "submarine"; one was about to exit trade union work for socialist politics and another member soon passed away, neither of them replaced. By April 1946, when the CGT held its first postwar National Congress, at least 80 percent of the voting units and their delegates were under communist sway. Jouhaux and Frachon were officially co-secretary generals, but Frachon effectively headed the federation, since Jouhaux focused on international missions, and the bureau had tilted into the *ex-unitaire* camp.

Initially the communists had used their growing power prudently but now they began to flex their muscles. For example, the CGT Congress changed the formulas for representation at National Councils and Congresses in a way that favored the seven largest unions and downgraded the influence of smaller non-communist unions, which the *ex-confédérés* like Jouhaux considered a naked power grab.[95]

At the beginning of 1946 the embattled minority (as they were now forced to see themselves) began to organize under the name Force Ouvrière (FO) to advocate for internal democracy and free debate in the CGT. In 1946–47 FO organized caucuses in some workplaces, trade unions, and CGT departmental federations. But their implantation in such venues was generally weak and gained little traction.[96] Amidst growing demoralization FO convened a national conference of about 200 FO delegates on November 9, 1947, to debate what to do next. The consensus—espoused in particular by Jouhaux—was to maintain their presence in the CGT and continue the uphill fight for internal democracy and resistance to any outside influence such as Moscow.

But the National Council of the CGT on November 13 dashed those hopes. By a vote of 857 to 127 the Council, echoing the Moscow line, approved an unqualified condemnation of the Marshall Plan, as against the FO view that the Marshall Plan could benefit France provided there were safeguards for national independence. (Saillant voted with the majority, in effect parting with Jouhaux; thereafter he echoed Moscow's anti-American "peace" line as secretary general of the World Federation of Trade Unions.)[97] A final conflict arose during the strike wave. Dismayed at the violence of the strikers' tactics, the FO group urged the CGT to negotiate with Schuman on measures his government proposed to settle the strikes. Frachon and the National Strike Committee (composed exclusively of *ex-unitaires*) considered this a stab in the back by FO.[98]

On December 18–19, 1947, FO convened a second conference, larger and better organized than the first. Most of the 300 FO delegates came with instructions from their groups, and after an impressively free and open debate the balloting began. Delegates from 15 of the 18 FO caucuses in CGT trade unions and from 37 of 54 CGT departmental federations voted by a decisive majority to create a new labor federation. To the very end Jouhaux wished to avoid that step, to somehow maintain the ideal of syndicalist unity yet to restore the CGT's democratic character. But he finally capitulated and joined his four remaining comrades on the CGT bureau in resigning and clearing out their desks. In *L'Humanité* Cachin railed that FO was simply doing America's bidding in collaboration with Léon Blum.[99]

The aftermath of the break proved discouraging, for as an American official observed a year later, the split had been "unplanned, improvised, and confused." The FO had to establish itself with essentially empty pockets. Its limited funds consisted initially of a subsidy funneled to it by Labor Minister Daniel Mayer and small non-repayable loans from the AFL; later some modest subsidies were probably channeled from the CIA through AFL and CIO contacts. But relations between FO and its US supporters "have been vastly overestimated in France" and were never coordinated, smooth, or decisive.[100] Meanwhile, two unions that FO hoped would bolster its ranks decided not to come over: the venerable typographers union voted by a three to two margin to remain in the CGT, and the schoolteachers voted decisively to be an autonomous union rather than join FO. At the founding congress of the new federation that followed in April 1948 the delegates adopted the organizational template of the 1936 CGT and at

Jouhaux's urging voted for the name CGT-FO. The discourse of the Congress was all about independent, democratic syndicalism. As one enthusiast put it: "In Frachon's CGT one suffocated. In the CGT-FO one can breathe and can work for the future of the working class." But the prediction of the new secretary general that CGT-FO would attract 1.5 million adherents proved wildly optimistic, as it enrolled only 500,000 to 600,000 members as of 1948, although membership in the CGT also started dropping sharply at that time.[101] Yet Force Ouvrière persisted through the ups and downs of succeeding decades and provided unionized workers with an alternative to the CGT should they seek one.

9

The United States: Divided Government, Divided Nation

WHAT WAS LEFT STANDING OF THE NEW DEAL, and of wartime mobilization policies, as full-bore partisan politics erupted in Washington after V-J Day? The early, improvisational responses to the Great Depression by FDR, such as the National Industrial Recovery Act and the Agricultural Adjustment Act (AAA), had long since been nullified by the Supreme Court. The WPA, Harry Hopkins's bountiful program of temporary jobs for the unemployed and support for the arts, had run its stormy course, lingering only in the built environment and collective memory. Popular New Deal programs, such as the Civilian Conservation Corps, had wound down as well. Other New Deal innovations, in contrast, had firmly taken root. From the initial spate of the Hundred Days in 1933 financial and banking reforms, rural electrification and the TVA, agricultural subsidies for farmers salvaged from the AAA all survived. From the "second New Deal" after the mid-term election of 1934 the Social Security Act endured, with its umbrella of federal old-age pensions, unemployment insurance in all the states, and federal funding to the states for aid to their neediest citizens. So too did the twin pillars of New Deal labor law endure: the Wagner Act that facilitated union organizing under supervision of the NLRB, and the Fair Labor Standards Act, with its minimum wage and provisions for overtime pay.

The years of war production left an imprint too. The bargain between big labor, big business, and the state brokered by the administration ("maintenance of membership" for the unions in exchange for their no-strike pledge) reflected FDR's instinctive quest to braid equity and social concord with free enterprise.

The OPA's rationing and price control system embodied a "fair shares" approach to managing scarcities on the home front. Most manufacturing, business, and farm interests demanded that OPA regulation end as soon as possible after the peace, while millions of consumers wished OPA to continue until shortages and price inflation came to a demonstrable end. On the cusp of transition from the war production economy, liberals deemed a "full employment" policy for peacetime (heralded by Roosevelt in one lone speech just before the 1944 election) to be the most urgent extension of the New Deal. They hoped to sustain full employment and combat recessions through federal planning for counter-cyclical "expenditure and investment," coupled with an affirmation of every citizen's right to a job. But as we saw, little came of that hard-fought effort or of the attempt to prolong the OPA for two years after V-J Day. Meanwhile, to the contrary, anti-union sentiment grew in Congress and climaxed in the Taft-Hartley law, enacted by the Republican-controlled 80th Congress elected in November 1946.

This chapter takes up the challenges faced by progressives in veterans organizations, the labor movement, national politics, and the 1948 presidential election. It then considers the fate of Truman's "Fair Deal" program during his second term, the balance of federal action and inaction in such areas as civil rights, housing, social security, education, and national health insurance.

The impact of domestic communism and anti-communism commands a prominent place here. The anti-communist affidavit required of union officials by the Taft-Hartley law of 1947 was an omen, an early warning sign of the tidal wave of anti-communism starting to wash over American political culture. No matter how the CIO acted, dealing with communist influence in its unions would divide the federation. But the problem of communism in American public life went far beyond the confines of organized labor. It erupted most visibly in the Hollywood film studios and the broadcasting industry with their blacklists and in the proceedings of Truman's loyalty review boards for federal employees. Conflict within the American Veterans Committee (AVC) makes for an especially illuminating case study. A diminutive rival to the huge American Legion, the AVC (which peaked at a membership of 100,000) contributed as intended to the nation's progressive activism in the postwar moment. But the AVC soon endured a prolonged tempest over how to deal with communists in its ranks, a problem which would divide and bedevil progressives in general.

Progressives in the Postwar Moment: The Case of the AVC

The national influence and deep social roots of the American Legion initially attracted some progressive World War II veterans into its ranks.[1] But the domination of the Legion by the World War I generation, its grating hyperbole about "Americanism," segregated posts in the South, and reputation for sophomoric antics at its annual conventions repelled many progressives. For Charles Bolté, a founder of the AVC, the Legion in 1945 enshrined "the traditional though unwritten alliance between the middle class and the upper class. . . . It won its points by wrapping itself in the flag, praising God and country. . . . The Legion believed that the prejudices of its time and class were essential truth."[2]

For the next two years AVC member Bill Mauldin hammered home a critique of the Legion in livelier tones. The youthful Mauldin had emerged from the war as a celebrated observer of the American military experience. His cartoons about army life, from boot camp to heavy combat, featured two long-suffering and cynical G.I.s named Willie and Joe. First published in *Stars and Stripes,* the cartoons were syndicated back home and collected by Mauldin's agent in a volume called *Up Front;* rushed into print, the book vaulted onto the best-seller list in 1945 and was optioned for a movie. After his discharge Mauldin drew cartoons about Willie and Joe as veterans. Collected in a volume called *Back Home* in 1947, the book featured a running commentary on the Legion for its strident approach to "Americanism," disdain for civil liberties, racial discrimination, authoritarian governance, and lack of support for public housing, among other failings.[3]

The AVC, on the other hand, had none of that baggage. The programmatic statements of Bolté, Gilbert Harrison, and other founders about their new organization emphasized that "we could not sign over to an older organization our rights and obligations to solve the problems which had not been solved the last time. . . . We need a new organization because we have new problems." The AVC would be "a wholly democratic organization" and its members— "citizens first, veterans second"—an activist, "citizens lobby," in its local branches and nationally, for "a world we want to live in . . . [providing] peace, jobs, and freedom." The AVC would campaign for economic security, racial justice, and world peace for all citizens, alongside "adequate financial, medical, vocational and educational assistance for every veteran."[4]

Like the Legion, the AVC perforce claimed to be nonpartisan and had politically ambitious veterans from both major parties—Willkie Republicans, such as

Harold Stassen, Oren Root, and Jacob Javits, alongside aspiring liberal Democrats, such as FDR Jr.; G. Mennen Williams, future governor of Michigan; Paul Douglas, future senator from Illinois; and Richard Bolling, future congressman from Missouri. The ranks of the AVC included African Americans en route to prominent careers (Franklin Williams and Robert L. Carter, for example), and Hollywood actors (Melvyn Douglas, Burgess Meredith, William Holden, and, briefly, a pre-conversion Ronald Reagan). To be sure, the rival American Legion had on its rolls not dozens of political aspirants but hundreds of governors, congressmen, and senators up to President Truman. Still, the AVC had enough energetic and well-connected activists to make itself heard in Washington.

Many AVC members were not college graduates or heading to college, notably Mauldin himself, and the AVC had numerous community chapters; Brooklyn, New York, had fourteen neighborhood branches by February 1946, which supplied a flow of copy for the borough's newspaper, the *Brooklyn Eagle*. But big public and private universities such as the University of Wisconsin, the University of Michigan, Harvard, Columbia, and Syracuse were the most fertile terrains for the AVC.

Kingman Brewster (later Yale University's president), for example, convened an organizational meeting for the AVC at Harvard in January 1946, and the chapter elected officers that July. The university gave the AVC quarters where it could counsel veterans on their benefits under the G.I. Bill. By November the HU-AVC had a membership of about 600, which peaked at over 800 the following year. The chapter convened a day-long conference on "Problems of Student Veterans" with Boston University's AVC, where inadequate student living allowances under the G.I. Bill headed the list of complaints, followed closely by the shortages and high cost of student housing.[5] The AVC's "Operation Subsistence" national petition campaign garnered roughly a million signatures calling for an increase in student living allowances, which finally passed (after prolonged obstruction by Congressman Rankin) in February 1948.[6]

At Columbia University about 200 student veterans formed an AVC chapter in February 1946 "to express their opinions without supervision of veterans of past wars"; to drown out voices of bigotry and special interests; and to work toward a peaceful and economically secure future. The AVC chapter became the fastest growing student organization in Columbia's history. CU-AVC lobbied for New York City rent control to be extended to college dorms and for the university to cease "profiteering" on dorm and room rents. It supported

striking campus employees, campaigned to raise G.I. Bill subsistence allowances for students, and ran a successful co-op bookstore on campus to hold
down the cost of books. The chapter invited AVC officers like Bolté and FDR
Jr. to speak on the campus, as well as outsiders, such as a British Embassy official who talked about planning in the UK.[7]

As "citizens first, veterans second" AVC chapters addressed non-campus
issues with comparable energy. Pushing back against the NAM's agenda,
AVC chapters rallied behind an extension of the OPA: a reenactment of
the Boston Tea Party preceded an HU-AVC demonstration to "Save OPA." The
AVC supported most front-burner liberal causes, including such civil rights
issues of the day as a permanent FEPC, anti-lynching legislation, and local
voting rights movements, and it promoted interracial chapters in its own organization. It supported the Taft-Wagner-Ellender public housing bill (see below)
and spearheaded the National Veterans Housing Conference in Washington in
February 1948, which the American Legion boycotted.[8] But Truman's loyalty
program (also discussed below) provoked the AVC. The national executive
board (the National Planning Committee) condemned the initiative. So too
did CU-AVC, which "views with disfavor Truman's plans for identifying and
removing subversive elements from government service . . . as a kind of dragnet
that poses a greater threat to our democratic form of government than do the
persons it may be used against," for whom existing criminal laws sufficed
if applicable.[9]

Committed to the irreproachable cause of world peace, to continued cooperation among the Big Three wartime allies, and to a strong United Nations, the
AVC was ill-prepared for the fissures opening up between the Soviet Union and
the United States. Evasion became impossible when Truman proposed to aid
Greece and Turkey in resisting communist pressures to subvert their governments, authoritarian as those regimes might be. The AVC's national executive
board proposed a middle ground: extend economic but not military aid to Greece,
on condition that Greece demonstrates movement toward democracy, and no aid
for Turkey. When AVC branches debated the question, HU-AVC and CU-AVC
both endorsed that middle position. At a CU-AVC forum on future military
service, however, 110 members opposed a peacetime draft while 62 favored it
with qualifications, and almost everyone (167) opposed as excessively milita-
ristic Truman's call for Universal Military Training, which the American Legion
supported.[10]

The AVC's interracial chapters and campaigns against racial discrimination were commonplace in the North but more problematic in the South. The AVC had branches in at least twenty southern locations, but it seems that only Chapel Hill, Nashville, and Atlanta had inter-racial chapters. Atlanta was a center of progressive stirrings in the postwar South and of resistance to the racial demagoguery and reaction also on the rise in Georgia.[11] "Black veterans were founding members of the Atlanta AVC and prominent in the chapter's leadership," according to historian Jennifer Brooks; some had been recruited from the all-black Georgia Veterans League. For some veterans of both races the AVC provided a first experience where whites and blacks were on the same footing. Atlanta's main AVC chapter, with between 125 and 250 members, had plenty of local causes to work on including opposition to the resurgent Ku Klux Klan and to local white supremacists. The AVC and its progressive allies in Atlanta launched voter registration and get-out-the-vote drives, indirectly supporting a liberal governor (soon to be drubbed by a rabid segregationist), and Congresswoman Helen Mankin, who won her Democratic primary but lost the election. Avoiding issues like school segregation, the Atlanta AVC campaigned unsuccessfully to desegregate one softer target, the Atlanta public library.[12]

In 1945 the Communist Party (CPUSA) had urged its veterans to join the American Legion and dismissed the AVC as an elitist group lacking ties to the American masses. In a review of Bolté's 1945 book (delayed by *The Nation* so it could run a rejoinder by an advocate for the AVC alongside) party member Walter Bernstein scoffed that "there is little need today for an organization of intellectuals to act as a steering committee for veterans. . . . A veteran on the picket line has more in common with another striker who was in the last war than he has with a veteran from this war who is inside the plant."[13] The paper published this iteration of the communist line just as that policy was about to change: When it became clear by early 1946 that infiltrating the Legion led nowhere for the CPUSA, the party called on its cadres to join the AVC instead. As the AVC later put it: "In January 1946, after Browder was deposed [as chair of the CPUSA], the line changed. AVC was now a fine progressive organization with a democratic membership. The only trouble with it was that it had a 'reactionary' leadership."[14]

Chapters on and off campuses soon felt the impact of this course change by the CPUSA, and AVC's national leadership began to squirm. At its first national convention in June 1946 founders Bolté and Harrison were elected chair and vice chair—Bolté almost unanimously but Harrison only after a hard fight and close vote against a challenger from the Left.[15] In November the AVC national executive board by a vote of 15 to 4 with 5 abstentions denounced communist infiltration of their organization and the attempt "to exploit the hardships of the veteran in order to further the Party's selfish political ends." The board's pronouncement implied that party members were unwelcome in the AVC's ranks but did not go any further. The worry over communist infiltration (already trumpeted by reactionary journalists) was offset by the belief that all World War II veterans had served their country honorably and that an individual's political views should be no one's business. Whatever the nefarious purposes of communists might be in the AVC, liberal anti-communists at this point did not wish to oust members based on their political beliefs let alone unleash a witch hunt.[16]

The factionalism in certain chapters caused by the new communist presence, however, agitated the organization and demoralized many members who "could not stomach the infighting." In due course the problem roiled campus chapters like those at Columbia and the University of Michigan, but the most vivid account of the havoc wrought by communists on the AVC comes from a community-based chapter in Queens, New York. Julian Franklin had joined other "local boys" only two weeks after his discharge, while he prepared to complete his degree at Queens College, and was elected chapter treasurer. The AVC initially opened an exhilarating passage from mere discussion to real political action, with campaigns for renewal of the OPA, public housing, and an anti-lynching law. But soon new members began showing up who opposed "legalistic delays," such as proper quorums, who sneered at "social democrats," and who denounced the likes of FDR Jr. and Bolté.

Communists had arrived, and they fended off resistance by appeals against (legalistic) "obstructionism," "reactionary positions," and "red-baiting." Franklin, who was briefly cowed by the Spanish Civil War experience and union organizing of the communists' main spokesman, found himself in a quandary. Progressive veterans were caught between the unsettling experience of communist bulldozing in their chapters and the readiness of reactionary opinion to smear the AVC and its goals. "Thinking members, disgusted and beaten down, fell away," but Franklin was told in so many words by communist militants that "they didn't care how small AVC became as long as it remained ideologically correct. . . . Then when the depression comes we will attract a vast following."

Franklin and like-minded veterans finally walked away and established a new AVC chapter in the neighborhood, only to be subjected to cynical attacks by the old chapter. "All too many progressives are so weary of red-baiting that they no longer care to distinguish between Communist and non-Communist progressivism," he concluded when he went public with his sobering experience. "That kind of indifference is the natural result of being caught between Communist domination on one side and indiscriminate persecution of Communists on the other." But one must recognize the Communists' tactics, he concluded, and their "inflexible dogmatism that cannot adjust to the realities of American political life."[17]

The influence of the hard left—the communists, fellow travelers, and First Amendment absolutists—grew especially strong in the AVC's New York Area Council, an umbrella group for 95 regional chapters. Moderates in New York City turned for help to the fierce anti-communist David Dubinsky, head of the ILGWU (AFL). Dubinsky delegated Gus Tyler, a union official and World War II veteran, to take the ILGWU's expertise on battling communists into the AVC. Even Tyler could not get the better of the hard leftists in the NY Area Council, which remained a burr under the AVC's saddle until a showdown in 1948, but Tyler helped liberals organize an "Independent Progressive Caucus" for the long haul and countered communist tactics with stratagems and dirty tricks of his own.[18]

In June 1948 the executive board conducted a poll of AVC members on the communist issue. A majority responded that it was undemocratic to eject the Communists but, on the other hand, the members feared that if the Communists remained they might take over the AVC. The board in any case moved toward barring Communists and as a test case challenged the AVC membership of John Gates, editor of the *Daily Worker* and previously a party point man on veterans affairs. A three-man committee (Michael Straight, publisher of the *New Republic,* FDR Jr., and Robert Nathan) questioned Gates at length and reported to the November 1948 AVC convention in Cleveland that Gates was certainly a Communist but that "in his view his loyalty to his party did not conflict with his pledge of support for our principles."[19]

At the Cleveland convention the liberals of the Independent Progressive Caucus waged an all-out battle with the hard left of the "Progressive Caucus." (The liberals referred to the latter not as "left-wingers" but as "East-Wingers," meaning they took their guidance from the Soviet East.) Despite agonizing over individuals' sacred right to their political opinions, the convention expelled Gates from the AVC. A slate of anti-communists headed by Harrison won the balloting for officers, and the convention then declared membership in the CPUSA to be incompatible with membership in the AVC. The convention also urged the abolition of HUAC and the repeal of Taft-Hartley; opposed the outlawing of the Communist Party; and defended the Marshall Plan.[20]

When the Harvard chapter debated the board's initial anti-communist statement of 1946, a membership meeting approved it by a vote of 74–58. "Subservience to the principles of a conspiratorial and undemocratic organizations is utterly incompatible with membership in AVC," as one veteran put it. Even so, the language of the chapter's approval resolution underscored the AVC's conundrum: "We wish to emphatically dissociate ourselves from the red-baiting tactics of the henchmen of reaction; but we cannot let their bad example dissuade us from our determination to make known our stand."[21] When the AVC national convention in November 1948 voted to expel or bar Communist Party members, some chapters rebelled but HU-AVC supported the move. Yet backing the evolving anti-communist position in the AVC did not plunge the Harvard chapter into a spiral of red-baiting. In March 1948 HU-AVC joined other progressive organizations to lobby against the Barnes Bill, which would have set off a witch hunt in Massachusetts public schools, and against establishing a "Little Dies [HUAC] Committee" in the state legislature. In 1949 HU-AVC lobbied against a new clause in the federal loyalty oath for students in the naval ROTC, which required them "to name persons connected with groups listed as subversive by the Attorney General." This was "a stool pigeon clause . . . [and] a menace to American freedom," which the navy soon revoked.[22]

Factionalism between "the left left-wingers and the right left-wingers" severely disrupted the Columbia University branch. Parallel to alignments in the national AVC, in 1947 a liberal Independent Progressive Group at Columbia stood against a Progressive Caucus, which included the communist contingent and liberals for whom red-baiting was the cardinal sin. With 328 members voting, the Independent Progressives swept the four main chapter offices. But the factional fighting wore away at the patience of many member; when CU-AVC held its next round of elections in May 1948 only 205 cast votes.[23]

After the Cleveland convention in November, a chapter meeting of CU-AVC debated whether to accept the dictate that "Communist Party members are ineligible for membership in AVC" or to disaffiliate from the national AVC over the purge. For the moment a third-way "Build AVC Caucus," headed by the chapter chairman, tried to hold the chapter together under a non-communist leadership embracing all members without regard to political beliefs. But the liberals of the Independent Progressive Caucus prevailed with their view that Communist Party members were driving others away by their extreme positions and delaying tactics.[24] By the time of its next elections in February 1949, the CU-AVC had lost 200 more members, leaving only about 100 dues-payers. The Build AVC Caucus dissolved, "washed up by history" said its spokesman. The Progressive Caucus argued to the end that "the road to fascism is paved with red-baiting," but the liberal caucus prevailed by a vote of 55 to 43. The shrunken chapter slowly faded away; a last trace of CU-AVC was a lively pair of forums it sponsored in spring 1951 on "Conformity and Diversity in American Life."[25]

As in the Harvard and Columbia chapters, the demoralizing struggles over the communist presence helped drive down the national membership of the AVC from its high of about 100,000 to around 20,000 in 1950 and 10,000 by 1953. Various chapters on and off campus petered out, which was bound to happen eventually on campus chapters. But progressive veterans could continue as individual members of the AVC. The organization maintained a lobbying office in Washington and remained a source of activism in some communities. Nor did the AVC lack prominent leadership: Michael Straight (now running the *New Republic*), was elected chairman in 1949–51,[26] and Bill Mauldin in 1953–54. "When travelling around speechifying for Stevenson last Fall," Mauldin recalled, "I noted with some pride that the backbone of most Volunteers for Stevenson outfits consisted in large part of weather-beaten AVC survivors, all toughened idealists."[27] Through the early 1950s the organization remained a visible part of the progressive coalition, especially in the push for racial justice, as it lobbied in Washington and submitted amicus briefs to federal courts on civil rights cases.

Nor did the AVC give up in the South. After Straight was elected national chair, with a black law professor as his running mate, he began a national tour for the AVC in the airplane he owned. In Tallahassee, he found that the all-white Florida State University adjoined the all-black Florida A&M University, and that black students were discouraged from crossing the road from one campus to the other. At an organizing meeting at A&M 150 black veterans turned up. Bill Pawling, a white southerner and AVC's regional organizer, told them that

AVC had no chapter in Tallahassee but that a few white veterans at Florida State had joined AVC as individuals. He invited the black veterans to do the same, "and we could go on from there." The black veterans refused; they wanted an interracial chapter in Tallahassee and appointed an organizing committee.

At Florida State a professor and liberal old-timer warned that "if you go ahead and set up an interracial chapter the authorities in both institutions will be forced to expel every student and faculty member who joins it. You will ruin us." Straight and Pawling hunted down the twenty-odd white AVC members, and four agreed to meet with the black A&M organizing committee. Straight then left town and flew on to Texas (where vigilantes tried to break up two of his meetings); a letter from Pawling soon caught up with him. "Our Tallahassee chapter had been formed," Straight recalled. "It held its first meeting in the second story of a building in the town. Policemen with pistols drawn had broken into the meeting room. They had arrested our members and taken them to jail. There, they were told that they would be expelled from the two colleges unless they disbanded their chapter. They were standing fast." An update came a few days later. "Our chapter chairman had suffered a nervous breakdown. . . . The chapter members refused to disband, under the threat of expulsion from the two colleges, but they had suspended their activities."[28]

Bill Mauldin had flirted with popular front causes after his discharge in 1945, but the cartoonist was not comfortable either with communists or with red-baiting, and he personally embodied the AVC's dilemma all along.[29] During his chairmanship Mauldin helped consolidate a narrative of the AVC's struggle with the communist problem as one of AVC's legacies to postwar liberalism. The AVC's progressive idealism as a democratic "citizen's lobby" of World War II veterans remained at the core, but communist infiltration of the organization had forced itself into the mix early and brutally. Held back at first by an aversion to red-baiting and a respect for the liberty of individual political opinion, the majority finally purged the communists for the dissension and obstructionism they relentlessly caused.

The AVC emerged from this trauma severely diminished but still standing. Commenting on an internal document under discussion in 1953 at the height of McCarthyism, an AVC attorney hoped that "the memo will contain a short disclaimer of any intention to intimate that the only way to prove that one is not a communist is to prove that one is against everything the communists ever stood for or said they stood for. That would be playing straight into the hands of McCarthy and his kind"—an awkward way of stating how the AVC had tried to operate all along. Elmer Davis—the dean of liberal radio commentators and FDR's chief of the Office of War Information during the war—put it more tersely: "Just after the war the AVC had some communists in it, as probably all the organizations had; but the AVC threw its communists out, learning in the process what is a communist and what to do about him. But thereafter the AVC became [i.e., remained] liberal, not reactionary; so the big veteran's organizations feel little fellowship with it."[30] The problem of communist influence of course played out on multiple terrains outside the AVC: in Hollywood and the broadcasting industry; among federal and state government employees; and most consequentially in the CIO.

The CIO and Its Communists

When the war ended the CIO's forty or so unions included about a dozen left-led or "communist-influenced" unions, most small or medium-sized and outside the mass production industries. The left-led United Electrical Workers (UE), on the other hand, did battle with industrial giants such as General Electric and Westinghouse and was the federation's third largest union. In 1945 three of the UE's top officials (Julius Emspak, James Matles, and Ruth Young) were known communists, while Albert Fitzgerald (elected president in 1941) was a steadfast fellow traveler. Similarly, the mercurial Reid Robinson, elected president of the Mine, Mill and Smelter Workers in 1936, was not a party member but an independent leftist apparently more royalist than the king. The Fur and Leather Workers Union and the West Coast Longshoremen and Warehousemen's Union had long-serving communist presidents (Ben Gold and Harry Bridges), both fixtures on the CIO executive board. Most of the communist-influenced unions were relatively democratic in their internal affairs and stood in the progressive vanguard on race relations in the workplace and union hall.[31]

Between 1939 and 1941 the Nazi-Soviet pact discombobulated communists and fellow travelers in the labor movement as the new party line urged them to resist American production in aid of the "imperialist war."[32] In France the Nazi-Soviet pact destroyed the PCF's viability and drove it underground amidst charges of defeatism and treason, while the CGT ousted the federation's communist leaders. In the CIO, however, President John L. Lewis also opposed FDR's tilt toward support for Britain. Lewis not only tolerated the communists and fellow travelers in the CIO but drew on them for political support. When Lewis stepped down after FDR's re-election in 1940, a potentially dicey situation changed with the Nazi attack on the Soviet Union in June 1941. From then on most CIO communists vaulted to the forefront of patriotic commitment for maximal war production, and anti-communist sentiment in the CIO abated if only temporarily.

The steelworkers' top-down organizing and centralized governance eventually marginalized the communists. After the early organizing years, at the founding convention of the United Steel Workers of America (USWA) in 1942, the union's draft constitution stipulated that membership would not be restricted by "race, creed, color or nationality." An amendment from the floor proposed to add "political affiliation" to the mix, but Phil Murray finally cut off a long and heated debate to bury the amendment.[33] In contrast, the United Auto Workers (UAW) bottom-up organizing and local activism bred factionalism around colliding individual ambitions, where communist leverage increased. By the postwar era two rival alliances had taken shape. One bloc coalesced behind Walter Reuther's drive to head the UAW and included ex-socialists like himself, anti-communist Catholic activists, business unionists uninterested in ideology, and a Rank-and-File Caucus that had opposed the wartime communist line on concessions over such issues as incentive pay bonuses. The rival "left-wing" coalition—supported among others by communists and fellow travelers—was headed by two non-communist UAW officials with their own followings, President R. J. Thomas and Secretary-Treasurer George Addes, who united to block Reuther's headlong ambition. With a combination of anti-Stalinist conviction and opportunistic union politics, Reuther now made communist influence in the UAW his wedge issue.[34]

At the UAW national convention in March 1946, the dynamic Reuther defeated the more stolid Thomas in the balloting for president by a razor thin 4,444 to 4,320 votes, but his rivals still controlled the UAW executive board. At the next UAW national convention in November 1947 Reuther's well-honed coalition re-elected him as president by a two-thirds vote, and his allies made a clean sweep of other offices. Although pockets of opposition remained, Thomas and Addes quietly departed. Reuther began to rein in the UAW's hyper-democratic localism, and moved toward a more bureaucratic model of trade union leadership.[35] Murray (who personally preferred Thomas) was leery of Reuther's excessive ambition, but he applauded the end of communist influence in the UAW;

Reuther in turn hoped to eliminate communist power in the national CIO, but without any concession to reactionary forces in America.[36]

Murray had long accommodated the CIO's left-led unions for their effective organizing and honest administration, although he was dubious about the smaller unions that had failed to enlarge their base. Deeply patriotic and Catholic, Murray sympathized with anti-communist Catholic activists in the CIO, but he publicly kept his distance from their Association of Catholic Trade Unionists (ACTU), arguably an organized "outside influence" on the CIO comparable to its communist cells.[37]

Murray repeatedly mediated between communists and anti-communists to maintain labor unity.[38] Some of Murray's top-level appointments, beyond his union brothers from the old days of the UMW, reflected his balancing act. When Roosevelt convoked leaders of industry and labor right after Pearl Harbor for the talks that produced an accord for wartime labor peace, Murray named as the CIO's four representatives two from left-led unions (Emspak and Curran) and two non-communists (Rieve and Thomas).[39] When the UE voted out the young and mercurial anti-communist James Carey as president in September 1941 Murray kept him on at CIO headquarters as national secretary-treasurer of the CIO, while Murray's right-hand man (and eventual successor) in his steel-workers union was the anti-communist David McDonald. But at national head-quarters Murray also employed fellow traveler Len De Caux as director of publicity (with oversight of the *CIO News*) and Lee Pressman as general counsel. A man with well-known communist ties as a young New Dealer in Washington, Pressman served effectively under Lewis and then under Murray as chief legal counsel for the CIO and for the USWA.[40]

As 1946 dawned, splitting the CIO over the issue of communist influence seemed to Murray unthinkable, while in global affairs he believed it incumbent that Big Three unity be maintained in the postwar era. In concert with the British TUC and the French CGT, the CIO helped launch a new World Federation of Trade Unions (WFTU). Excluded from the prewar international labor federation, the Soviet Union's state-run trade union organization had a commanding presence in the WFTU—which is why the AFL boycotted the new organization from the start. Typical of his tightrope walk, Murray sent Pressman and Carey as key members of the CIO's delegation to the WFTU's founding conferences.[41]

At the CIO's national convention in November 1946 Murray backed a motion on political policy designed to contain a growing rift between communist-influenced unions and their antagonists. The resolution required that the delegates "resent and reject efforts of the Communist Party or other political parties . . . to interfere in the affairs of the CIO," but without stipulating any additional threats or sanctions. Similarly, Murray directed McDonald and Pressman to "argue out" what should be done about a proposal to purge communists from the steelworkers' executive board. The resulting compromise stated that the union would not tolerate efforts by outsiders "to infiltrate, dictate or meddle in our affairs," but with language added by Pressman that "we engage in no purges, no witch hunts."[42]

A year later much had changed. The Taft-Hartley law made a sympathetic administration in Washington crucial for both the AFL and the CIO—meaning that a Democratic victory in 1948 must not be imperiled by the third-party movement starting to crystalize around Henry Wallace (see below). Then too Truman had put forward the Marshall Plan (in a manner promising participation by the two labor federations), and this European recovery program won the enthusiastic support of mainstream progressives and trade unionists but bitter opposition from the Soviet Union and its acolytes abroad. A new party line from Moscow demanded that allied parties go all out in opposing the Marshall Plan, and that the CPUSA should encourage formation of an anti-imperialist third party led by Wallace. Communist union officials were supposed to defend that line within the CIO, even if it risked alienating non-communist colleagues and rank and filers of their own unions.[43]

As the Cold War began in earnest and anti-communism gathered momentum, Murray came to believe that the well-known communist presence in the CIO was an albatross whose pro-Soviet tropisms (ordinarily of relatively minor importance) could now drag the CIO to the margins of American life and even threaten its survival. Over the next year Murray rounded on CIO communists and fellow travelers in the leadership who were attacking the Marshall Plan and supporting Wallace's candidacy, thereby jeopardizing the Democrats' long re-election odds. But Murray's turnabout was not yet complete. At the CIO's national convention of October 1947, for example, he invited Secretary of State Marshall to speak—a clear provocation to the left-led unions—but the subsequent resolution (crafted by Pressman for Murray) endorsed US economic aid to Europe without mentioning the Marshall Plan by name.[44]

In January 1948, after Reuther gained control of the UAW, Murray moved to rein in communist and fellow travelers on the CIO executive board by imposing a uniform political line, pro-Marshall Plan and anti-Wallace third party. The board's approval by a vote of 33 to 11 thereby curtailed the political space that the CIO traditionally gave to each national union.[45] Soon after, Murray parted ways with Pressman, his much-valued counsel whose communist ties had not previously disrupted their relationship, after Pressman decided to go all-in with Wallace's third party. (After the 1948 election Pressman described that decision as an enormous "miscalculation." Or as McDonald claims to have told Pressman as he departed: "You have a chance to accomplish some really constructive results within the CIO and the steelworkers. To throw that away for Henry Wallace and the nut fringe around him is to be a damned fool.")[46] Meanwhile John Brophy imposed tighter control by national headquarters over the state and city Industrial Union Councils that oversaw the CIO's political work, since hard leftists had been using some councils as staging grounds for their own agendas. By 1949 such pressures from the top drove the UE to refuse payment of its national dues and effectively to leave the CIO.

Earlier two other communist-influenced unions had moved in the other direction. The National Maritime Union (NMU) was forged on the docks of East Coast ports after years of violent battles with shipowners and rival AFL unions. Small numbers of communist seamen helped shift the balance of support among their comrades to the fledgling NMU, led by the pugnacious Joe Curran who, like President Fitzgerald of the UE, was not a CPUSA member but a thoroughly dependable ally of the party. As Curran brought his union into the CIO, the CPUSA propaganda machine elevated him into a proletarian hero, and the party maneuvered to fill most of the union's staff positions with communists. When the party's leadership became riven by factionalism in the mid-1940s, however, it became harder for Curran to work with communist cadres, especially after the return of William Z. Foster to head the CPUSA in 1945. Few seamen understood these obscure conflicts, but Curran finally found the communists far more trouble than they were worth. Up and down the East Coast at raucous meetings of NMU locals, Curran renounced his union's ties with the party, and in 1948 he expelled their cadres.[47]

Mike Quill, the insistently Irish president of the Transport Workers Union (TWU), headquartered in New York City, for a time gave fealty to the interests of his members and to his CPUSA comrades. Quill had political as well as trade union ambitions; he was as an elected member of the New York's City Council and the president of the CIO Council of New York. By 1948, however, his various constituencies were not meshing. The mayor of New York City insisted on doubling the long-standing 5-cent transit fare as a budgetary necessity and the only way to fund substantial raises for transit workers. Rank-and-file TWU members overwhelmingly favored that hike to fund their raises, but the CPUSA demanded that the fare be held steady. The Wallace third-party issue also intruded—another sign to Quill that CPUSA leaders had become "arrogant" in their directives for militant action. "W. Z. Foster and his wrecking crew," Quill believed, were propelling the communists into isolation and irrelevance with impossible demands. At a mass meeting of his New York City local in April 1948 Quill renounced his communist ties, and in a theatrical gesture shredded a *Daily Worker.* In due course Quill and the TWU fell into line with mainstream CIO positions.[48]

At the CIO's Cleveland convention in October 1949, with the departure of the UE irrevocable, the delegates adopted three resolutions framed by Reuther: barring communists from the CIO executive board; giving the board power to expel affiliated unions with a two-thirds vote; and raising the dues of affiliates to compensate for losses from expelled unions. Murray soon ordered a series of "trials" of the CIO's nine remaining communist-influenced unions. Without due process, much of the testimony simply aligned stances of those unions with the words of the *Daily Worker.* The verdicts of expulsion from the CIO after the hearings were foregone conclusions; McDonald sat on five of the panels and later described them as "kangaroo courts."[49] By mid-1950 ten unions with around a million members were out of the CIO. Liberal Senator Hubert Humphrey then had the nine reports of the CIO panels officially published by his Senate Subcommittee on Labor Relations.[50]

The once formidable UE soldiered on at about half its peak membership, and eventually its much-hounded communist officials broke their ties with the CPUSA to gain some breathing room. But the upheaval had set loose a new CIO rival (known as the IUE), where James Carey finally prevailed. The schism of 1949 in turn encouraged General Electric and Westinghouse to play the two unions against one another (with Washington assuring a leg up to the IUE on security issues in military contracts). Managements toughened their stance in collective bargaining with both electrical workers unions.[51]

In general, corporate management grew more adamant about its "right to manage," and most CIO unions pushed back less than they once had. At Truman's Labor-Management Conference in November 1945, Labor had refused to stipulate and "build fences" around management's prerogatives: "The responsibilities of one party today may well become the joint responsibility of both parties tomorrow," labor delegates insisted. A year later the NAM was back on the attack, reiterating that "exclusive management functions" must be recognized lest collective bargaining become a vehicle for workers to appropriate management functions "rather than a means for negotiating desirable employment conditions." Joint production committees would give unions an unacceptable veto power, while overly rigid seniority rules would erode effective management.[52] With employers so insistent about their "right to manage," the UAW and other unions gradually retreated from pressing for more democratic industrial relations. Instead, the unions concentrated on negotiating expanded benefits packages, higher wages, and cost-of-living increases.[53]

One could take this argument further. Weakened by Taft-Hartley, by the schism with its left-led unions, and by an erosion of shop-floor militancy, the CIO unions drifted into greater accommodation to American corporate capitalism. This set the stage for the CIO's (re-)merger with the larger and less progressive AFL in 1956. Further down the road, the labor movement in the AFL-CIO era would lack the will or the strategy to counter the geographic mobility of corporate capital—the leading factor in hollowing out the base of working-class communities and with them the power of their unions. Meanwhile, another problem for American progressives in general and CIO unions in particular lay in the clash of their official opposition to racial discrimination with the harsh realities on the ground.

The CIO and Race

From its inception the CIO sought to promote racial inclusion and opportunity for blacks without alienating its far larger white membership. In the organizing drives of the 1930s, success for the industrial union model depended on signing up black and white workers across various job categories. The experience of the United Mine Workers had proven that if unions shunned black workers, bosses could use them as pawns and strikebreakers. But once management recognized a CIO union and began collective bargaining, difficulties might arise. Employers with multiracial work forces wished to avoid disruption and to leave intact existing patterns of workplace segregation, where black workers usually held janitorial, warehouse, low skilled, or dirty kinds of factory-floor jobs, with lower pay scales. Most of the new unions did not initially challenge such practices.[54]

Far more than the AFL and most major American institution, however, the CIO officially promoted employment opportunity for blacks, nondiscrimination, and civil rights. In the aircraft industry, for example, the UAW had a more welcoming attitude toward black workers than its rivals in the AFL machinists and boilermakers unions, which maintained segregated, subordinate locals (called auxiliaries) for their black workers, if they accepted them at all.[55] But the CIO could do only so much to turn its members into racially liberal citizens. Hurdles were highest in the South, but difficulty abounded in other regions, especially where white workers had migrated from southern states or were of South- or East-European immigrant backgrounds, whose community mores clashed with CIO hopes to bridge the racial divide.

During the war white workers in some war production plants in Pennsylvania and the Midwest walked off the job in anger when new black hires appeared on their shop floors. In a vicious "hate strike" in 1944, white Philadelphia transit workers violently protested the hiring of a handful of blacks as motormen. Several hate strikes occurred in Detroit's war production factories, although the traumatic Detroit race riot of 1943 involved housing and other neighborhood issues, as did its coda in the race-baiting mayoral election of 1945 discussed above. But all of these incidents demonstrated how problematic the CIO's progressive public stance on race could be.[56] For all the "logic of solidarity" in the CIO's organizing saga, "whiteness" remained an individual advantage not likely to be ceded in plants South or North.[57]

The constitutions of CIO unions usually called for nondiscrimination in employment, but seniority trumped other considerations when it came to job retention or advancement. In their initial contracts unions and management generally agreed on provisions for "departmental" seniority rather than plant-wide seniority that might facilitate occupational mobility for qualified workers regardless of race. The priorities of war production, however, complicated such arrangements: the rapid expansion of the industrial workforce between 1939 and 1944, the concomitant hiring of many women and blacks, and the temporary scrambling of job classifications because of labor shortages for semi-skilled work. When the uncertainties of reconversion began to loom late in 1944, traditional seniority claims became the frontline defense for white workers and the great obstacle for black and female war workers hoping to survive future changes in labor markets.[58]

Phil Murray tried to finesse this serious conundrum. In the pages of Chicago's major black newspaper he insisted that abrogating existing seniority rights in order to preserve the wartime jobs of blacks and women would be badly short-sighted. Murray argued that seniority embodies "a qualified property interest in [one's] job." It constituted in effect a kind of "common law in industry," which enables a worker to tell the boss "you shall not pass me by in promotions indis-criminately because of my race, color, or creed." On the flip side Murray implic-itly addressed "last hired, first fired" practices as well as black discontent over departmental instead of plant-wide seniority. "If seniority principles are not equitably and justly applied," he wrote, "the remedy is to make it work, not to destroy the vehicle." He bluntly warned that were seniority abrogated or eased to preserve the wartime jobs of blacks and women, many white workers would become "not only anti-Negro and anti-woman but anti-union." Murray then approvingly described a conference of women UAW members in Detroit in December 1944, which rejected the relaxation of existing seniority agreements. Instead the women urged the UAW to eliminate discriminatory contract clauses on promotions and upgrades in the future and to maintain seniority lists without reference to gender. In conclusion, the CIO president explained that collective bargaining was in any case not the province of the federation but an autono-mous, "sovereign" right of each union, most of which were adhering for now to existing seniority agreements.[59]

While largely unable to alter discriminatory practices at ground level in the North or South, the national CIO could engage in what has come be known as "rights talk." The vehicle for this progressive mission in race relations was the CIO's National Committee to Abolish Discrimination (the CAD), first created in 1942. Chaired in 1945 by CIO Secretary-Treasurer Carey and directed by black trade unionist George L. Weaver, the CAD in turn oversaw about one hundred state and local CIO anti-discrimination committees.[60] In 1945 the CAD published a comprehensive agenda for the postwar era. The CIO would pursue economic equality (nondiscrimination in employment) in collective bargaining contracts, backstopped by a permanent FEPC. It would lobby legislatively for political equality (nondiscrimination in the right to vote and to seek office). And public social equality (i.e., nondiscrimination in public services and public facilities, including education and "access to all residential areas") would also be pursued legislatively. The CAD drew the line, however, at "private social activities," which would remain entirely outside the realm of CIO suasion, let alone government intervention.[61] The CAD was no more (but no less) than a moral standard-bearer, an educational instrument and lobbying office. It had the ear of the CIO's national executive, which honored the CAD agenda in high profile speeches and convention resolutions. But implementation—action to end discrimination in job placement and advancement, to assure black representation in union councils, or to desegregate plant facilities and union halls where such segregation existed—could come only through action by the CIO's constituent unions and their locals on the ground.

Progress for black workers depended above all on their own determination and resourcefulness in standing up to racism in their workplaces and union halls. But at times it helped to have sympathetic ears at national union or CIO headquarters. The story of George Holloway of Memphis, Tennessee, exemplified both points. Holloway had gone to college for two years, but the jobs he found exposed him to relentless discrimination. In 1946 he was hired as a warehouseman at a new International Harvester (I-H) farm equipment factory in Memphis. After prolonged stalling I-H agreed to an NLRB representation election in April 1948, which the UAW won handily. Because of his education Holloway became recording secretary of the local's negotiating committee and its sole black member.[62]

After the union and I-H negotiated a contract Holloway sat on the local's grievance committee, where the I-H supervisor across the table habitually spoke of "niggers." (After a year management agreed to desist, complementing Holloway for abiding the abuse—presumably as Jackie Robinson had done when he broke the color line in major league baseball.) A UAW field representative later pressed I-H to transfer Holloway to a machinist job for which he was eminently qualified. Thanks to the UAW's national negotiating strategy, I-H eliminated the one-third pay gap between the Memphis plant and its northern factories, and the company granted its workers a pension plan, group health insurance, and more paid holidays.

But all along Holloway's white union brothers in Memphis gave him a hard time. In 1951 his local built a union hall across from the plant but insisted on separate toilets for blacks and whites. Not for the first time, Holloway called Reuther, whose emissary came down to Memphis to desegregate the restrooms, only to have the black/white signs go back up after he left town. National UAW officials returned to Memphis and threatened the local with receivership if it did not relent. The local refused and the receivership lasted for two years, the length of the current contract. Meanwhile the national UAW lobbied I-H to desegregate its in-plant facilities. So the story ends well, but only because Holloway and his staunchest black comrades absorbed and countered a decade of harassment, occasional threats of violence, and repeated frustration. In a comparable story line, the USWA lifted the wages and benefits of all its members North and South, and in the 1950s it worked to end racial discrimination at the huge US Steel works in Birmingham, Alabama.[63]

Set against the massive indifference or outright hostility to notions of racial justice in white American society in the 1940s and 1950s, what then should one emphasize? The restraint and frequent evasions of CIO unions to make good on workplace equity? Or the national CIO's advocacy for racial justice in the public sphere and in the workplace (given voice by its CAD), and the halting steps taken over time in that direction by most of its national unions? A single example certainly cannot stand in for an answer. But George Holloway's story of ground-level racism by management and white fellow workers, black worker grit and resilience, and occasional assistance from UAW headquarters, suggests a positive balance for the CIO's record on race in the postwar moment—a time when Detroit elected a racist demagogue mayor, southern black veterans faced implacable discrimination when claiming lawful G.I. benefits, the remarkable Stuyvesant Town housing development in New York City excluded blacks, and southerners blocked every civil rights bill in Congress.

If the CIO hoped to grow, however, the South beckoned during the postwar moment, notwithstanding the region's charged racial climate. In May 1946, in a fit of optimism, the CIO executive board created a Southern Organizing Committee (SOC) that launched "Operation Dixie," a centralized, multi-union organizing drive headquartered in Atlanta and coordinated by state directors across the South. Murray named Van Bittner, a comrade from UMW days, to direct the SOC, but his deputy, a vice president of the Textile Workers Union of America (TWUA), effectively ran Operation Dixie. The leaders stipulated from the outset that the organizing drive would not be accompanied by political activity. The SOC vetted and hired over 200 organizers, preferably southerners and veterans.

Textile manufacturing had increasingly relocated in the South since the 1930s, and Operation Dixie concentrated on textile mills especially in North Carolina, home to three of the largest textile companies in the nation. Unions involved with tobacco, wood and furniture products, shipbuilding, and oil and atomic energy also hoped to expand their memberships through Operation Dixie. At the outset the CIO provided a million dollars from proportional contributions by member unions to kick start Operation Dixie, and it assumed that as workers signed up their dues would replenish SOC's coffers.[64]

But Operation Dixie soon bogged down into a dispiriting run of failures. Organizers could only operate outside plant gates, and at the textile mills and other plants they had great difficulty recruiting the local activists on whom a successful unionization drive always depended. In that first summer, SOC state directors reported progress at some small companies, but they made no inroads whatsoever at the major textile and wood products factories. And at three mid-sized textile mills where the NLRB held a representation election, the TWUA was routed in all three, in one mill by 105 votes for the TWUA versus 496 votes for "No Union." Workers who had grown up in severe poverty and insecurity repeatedly told organizers: "We don't need you. You're going to cost us our jobs—the best jobs we have ever had."[65] Some workers may have wanted a union, but they were usually reluctant to step forward. Organizers used a metric known as the "throw down rate"—the proportion of leaflets distributed to workers at plant gates that were immediately tossed aside. At the huge Cannon Mills, a bastion of paternalistic social control and SOC's prime target, the throw down rate was reportedly low (implying potentially favorable sentiment about the union), but no further signs of commitment ever materialized.[66]

Southern plant managers knew how to use aggressive tactics with their workers— sanctions, transfers, firings, even threats to close a factory altogether— alternating with paternalistic sweet talk and small preemptive pay raises. Local community establishments and law enforcement seconded the owners' resistance to Operation Dixie and insured that harassment against SOC organizers went unpunished. (As one reported, "I'm beginning to think our problem is to get out of here alive!") Race-baiting, anti-Semitism, and red-baiting were staples in such community hostility: a typical smear claimed that only communists advocated the race-mixing that these outsiders promoted. Even in locations and in sectors with largely white workforces, including the textile mills, racial tension seethed below the surface and greatly complicated SOC's efforts. Red-baiting and race-baiting may have started with employers and community leaders but easily aroused white workers insecure over their industrial jobs and livelihoods. The SOC organizers could not neutralize such a toxic brew.[67]

In all, the failure of Operation Dixie by the end of its first year added to the CIO's woes from the Taft-Hartley law; from the escalating conflict over its communist-influenced unions; and from the rising aggressiveness of managements. Yet the 1948 election ended up providing a reprieve of sorts, perhaps even a reversal, for the seeming downward slope of the CIO in 1947–48.

Who Speaks for the Liberals?

In the first year of Harry Truman's presidency a Congress controlled by his party thoroughly stymied its own liberals as well as a new president hoping to reinvigorate the New Deal. After the mid-term election of 1946 Republicans controlled both houses of Congress for the first time since 1930, and Truman focused on international relations where he could initiate policy. Prodded by his State Department and defense chiefs, Truman advocated an unprecedented peacetime interventionism in Europe with a policy of "containment" against the Soviet Union. First proposing to help Greece and Turkey resist communist pressures, the president generalized this impulse into the "Truman Doctrine": the US would support nations seeking to resist subversion "by armed minorities or by outside pressures." Meanwhile the administration hardened its negotiating stance on the international control of atomic energy, essentially dooming that prospect. With the Marshall Plan for substantial economic aid to help European recovery, Truman pivoted in 1947 to a less bellicose posture. Yet that too accelerated the drift into Cold War when the Soviet Union and its satellites spurned the proffered aid as an American power play and a capitalist snare.[68]

Truman's tough line on resisting Soviet influence dismayed some liberals. Their hope for peace in the postwar world, after all, had been predicated on continuing cooperation among the Big Three, which seemed to be receding into wishful thinking. The potential militarization of "containment" alarmed liberals who feared a drift toward war and who voiced impatience as well with Truman's inability to deliver on domestic issues. Outspoken in deploring Truman's leadership were former vice president Henry Wallace (dismissed from Truman's cabinet as secretary of commerce in September 1946 after he began speaking out accusingly about world peace) and Rexford Tugwell (a top early New Dealer who had returned to academia after serving as the appointed governor of Puerto Rico during the war).[69]

Truman had alienated organized labor by his harsh responses to the railroad and coal strikes in 1946, but his veto of Taft-Hartley in 1947 salved that wound. The Senate override of his veto jolted the AFL and the CIO. Both federations mobilized to win repeal of Taft-Hartley by aggressively backing the Democrats in the next election cycle. Still, while labor leaders saluted Truman's veto, many shared the common view in the press and opinion polls that Truman was out of his depth in the White House, and they hoped to find an alternative to head the Democratic ticket in 1948. Despite those negative vibrations, Truman found in himself a reservoir of confidence, feistiness, and political savvy. Although most Americans had apparently given up on him, Truman expected to win them over and be renominated.

Ex-New Dealers and progressive activists who hoped to be free of Truman organized two rival pressure groups that quickly hardened a latent schism in their own ranks. The Progressive Citizens of America (PCA) crystalized around Wallace's attack on Truman's bellicose foreign policy initiatives and tepid domestic leadership. The PCA's founding core had migrated from the National Citizens PAC—the organization launched by Sidney Hillman in 1944 for middle-class progressives and intellectuals outside the orbit of trade unionism's CIO-PAC. From the start NC-PAC had a popular front aura that aroused some red-baiting.[70] Phil Murray initially welcomed PCA's formation but quickly backed away, uncomfortable with its ultra-leftist tone and zealous about guarding organized labor's independence. Murray opposed any third-party solution to the liberal quandary, and the PCA seemed to be edging in that direction. On the other hand, Albert Fitzgerald, the fellow-traveling president of the CIO's UE, remained one of PCA's staunchest activists.

The PCA's popular front stance entailed repugnance toward "red-baiting"; willingness to welcome communists in pursuit of common purposes; and muting criticism of the Soviet Union. Henry Wallace stated often and honestly that he personally had nothing to do with communism. But when questioned repeatedly by the press about communist influence in the PCA's third party (formally launched in February 1948), he claimed not to know who was or was not a communist, or what made their presence so objectionable, as long as they supported his own cause. While not an apologist for the Soviet Union per se, Wallace directed all his attacks on bellicosity and warmongering toward Washington and Wall Street, regardless of events in the Soviet orbit abroad. Thus he had little to say about the Prague coup of February 1948, and later that year he blamed the Berlin blockade on the US and proposed that America withdraw from West Berlin to defuse the crisis.

For its part the CPUSA initially hesitated over its strategy for the 1948 election: should the party run its own, ideologically pure, candidate for president as it had in the past? Or support the Democrats as it had for FDR's re-election bid in 1944? Or nurture the transition of the PCA into a third party headed by Wallace? For a time some PCA activists in states like California and Illinois tried to keep options open for Wallace as either a potential Democratic presidential nominee or as the standard-bearer of a third party. The uncertainty of the CPUSA finally dissipated under pressure from Moscow. Just after the CIO executive board voted to endorse the Marshall Plan and reject a third party, the CPUSA's central committee decided to back a Wallace-led, anti-imperialist third party. When the new party formally launched in February, America's communists and fellow travelers were all-in, and assumed that Wallace himself would remain indifferent or oblivious to their influence.[71]

A rival liberal organization evolved from the Union for Democratic Action (UDA), a small activist group that supported FDR's interventionist drift in 1941 and in 1945 worked hard for passage of the Full Employment Act. The UDA had set itself apart by refusing membership to communists or participation in events sponsored by the CPUSA. Shortly after the formation of the PCA, the UDA convened an expansion conference. Under a new name— Americans for Democratic Action (ADA)—it promoted a liberal alternative to the PCA's popular front stance. While the PCA had Wallace and Tugwell among its marquee names, the ADA included Eleanor Roosevelt and her son Franklin Jr., Walter White of the NAACP, liberal radio commentator Elmer Davis, and ex-New Dealers such as Wilson Wyatt and Leon Henderson, joined later by Chester Bowles. Phil Murray kept his distance, but Walter Reuther, Emil Rieve, and James Carey brought a CIO presence into the ADA, as did David Dubinsky for the AFL. Reinhold Niebuhr and Arthur Schlesinger Jr. provided some intellectual sheen, while ex-socialist James Loeb (a founder of the UDA) and Joseph Rauh (a labor lawyer and former aide to Wyatt) became the ADA's main spokesmen in the political fray.

Over the next decade the ADA would embody liberal anti-communism and its quandaries. For the moment it denounced communist influence in Wallace's PCA and aggressively opposed the prospect of a third party. Although most members disdained Truman and hoped to be rid of him (mirroring Eleanor Roosevelt's

privately held view), the ADA considered the Democratic Party as the only practical vessel for advancing a progressive agenda with New Deal roots. True,
Wallace's movement advocated a forceful version of that domestic agenda, but in
the ADA's view the Progressive Party (so named by its convention in July 1948)
threatened to siphon off votes from the Democratic ticket and thus help Republican
reactionaries to victory. With its small membership (which peaked at about
18,000) and weak finances, the ADA was unsure about how to proceed. Some
hoped to leverage liberal influence as activists within the Democratic Party
machinery, while others wanted to push the party in a liberal direction by the
force of ideas. Either way, although most ADA members nursed a strong aversion
to Truman, they had no obvious alternative to lead the Democratic party.[72]

Wallace and the Progressive Party

When the PCA formally launched its unnamed third party in February 1948,
communist influence in the Wallace movement became evident during the
special election for a vacant congressional seat in the Bronx, New York. Leo
Isacson, a one-term state assemblyman, militant progressive, and lawyer for
tenants and workers, vied for the seat against the Bronx Democratic machine's
lackluster candidate and two others. Isacson ran under the banner of New York's
American Labor Party, which had just become the state affiliate of Wallace's
new party. Isacson had a good rapport with the district's working-class whites,
blacks, and Jews (who constituted a third of the district's population). Wallace
spoke in the district for him, but Isacson's secret weapon was his 3,000 or so
campaign foot soldiers, filled with cadres of the CPUSA drawn from across the
metropolitan region. In a low-turnout special election they helped carry the day
by canvassing, electioneering with sound trucks, leafleting, and getting out the
vote. Despite pleas for the Democratic candidate by Mrs. Roosevelt and New
York City's mayor, Isacson won with 56 percent of the votes. His victory elec-
trified progressives fed up with the Democratic Party and propelled maverick
US Senator Glen Taylor (Idaho) into Wallace's party, whose vice presidential
candidate he later became. Naturally Isacson's victory panicked other progressives who feared that Wallace's third party could undermine the Democratic
Party in the general election.[73]

Communist influence in the Progressive Party also came into view during
its long platform-drafting process. Rexford Tugwell chaired the 74-person

platform committee, with Lee Pressman as its secretary. (Urged on by the CPUSA's general secretary, Pressman also decided to run as the Progressive Party candidate for a congressional seat in Brooklyn against the pro-labor, pro-Truman Democratic incumbent, in a district where Pressman had lived as a youngster.)[74] The platform committee held public hearings in Philadelphia, open to any and all testimony. Then to forge a final version from various inputs PCA headquarters appointed a small drafting subcommittee. Through most of the process Pressman hovered over successive deliberations and kept the draft on track to reflect key positions of the CPUSA and its patron, the Soviet Union. The platform amplified Wallace's mantra about the nefarious alliance among Wall Street, monopoly capitalism, Washington's militarists, and bipartisan congressional reactionaries. Like Wallace, the platform put the onus entirely on the US for the Cold War and for any future warfare with the Soviet Union. When Tugwell and others suggested making the party's stance on international relations slightly more balanced and thus palatable to the American electorate, communists like Pressman and John Abt (the Progressive Party's general counsel) intervened to block such adjustments.

Still, the platform process, and the tenor of the party convention in July, were not simply matters of communist manipulation. Non-communists in the Progressive Party, after all, constituted the bulk of the platform committee and of the convention itself. With large majorities they accepted the platform, if occasionally in ignorance of what went on behind the scenes. So while it is true that Pressman and his comrades almost never let "divisive" (i.e., anti-Soviet) language slip through into the platform, they were not simply imposing their positions on a cowed membership. As a priority, the communists protected the Soviet Union's image and interests, but Progressive Party activists went along to avoid splitting their movement. As Tugwell observed, they valued "solidarity and the danger of contention" at the party's coming convention.

The 3,000 enthusiastic delegates and alternates to the Progressive Party convention formed an impressive amalgam from all regions, ages, classes, and skin colors. The climax came at a mass outdoor rally that drew 30,000 people, where Paul Robeson sang and Wallace and his running mate Senator Taylor gave their acceptance speeches. On the next and last day, however, a long plenary session on the platform saw a flare-up over the "Vermont motion." One of that state's delegates proposed from the floor the following addition to the platform's section on US-Soviet relations: "Although we are critical of the present foreign policy of the United States, it is not our intention to give blanket endorsement of the foreign policy of any nation [i.e., the Soviet Union]." "The platform as it now stands," the delegate explained, "lays us open to the charge of condemning American foreign policy practically *in toto,* while saying nothing critical of the foreign policy of any other nation." And, he prudently added, "It is not the intention of this resolution to Red-bait or introduce any red herrings." But the motion certainly implied criticism of the Soviet Union, which Pressman and his comrades had so far avoided. From the floor ex-congressman Hugh De Lacy (probably a concealed communist) immediately denounced the proposed addendum as "some kind of phony declaration that doesn't mean anything." Another delegate countered that the Progressive Party did not support "blind friendship" with the Soviet Union: "We are not communists and we don't endorse everything that Russia does." After a half hour, Albert Fitzgerald in the chair cut off the desultory debate and called for a voice vote. Ayes supporting the Vermont motion were heard in the hall, but the nays prevailed.[75]

Communists and fellow travelers thus assured that the platform was uncompromising on US-Soviet relations, but the non-communist majority sustained that position. Like their hero Wallace, they believed that bipartisan reactionaries in Washington and Wall Street had set off the Cold War. As historian Thomas Devine puts it, for the majority of idealistic delegates, "Criticism of the Soviet Union was beside the point and would undermine the fight for peace. . . . The United States still remained responsible for ending the Cold War. Calling attention to Soviet misbehavior was simply a way of shirking that responsibility," even in the mild form of the Vermont motion.

All in all, the communists might have succeeded too well. For they refused to recognize how counterproductive their rigidity on Soviet-American relations might seem when amplified by the press and viewed by the American electorate. On the left, *The Nation* and the *Progressive Magazine* refused to endorse anyone, while the *New Republic* and the leftist *New York Star* endorsed Truman. Several members of the Progressive Party board, including ex-New Dealer Aubrey Williams and left-wing farm activist James Patton, now resigned from the party.[76] Tugwell had worked behind the scenes for less rigidity, and he finally took the matter to Wallace himself, only to be brushed off. But Tugwell's commitment to party unity trumped all, as he accepted a platform plank categorically denouncing the Marshall Plan (a plan he favored if only to a degree) and one advocating independence for Puerto Rico (which contradicted his experience as governor of the territory and his support for the alternative of statehood). As the convention ended, the party dropped Tugwell from its executive committee, and without regret he became an ordinary member. Tugwell then kept a low profile but once or twice conveyed his misgivings. "I am an uneasy member of the Progressive Party worried about control by the wrong people," he said in August. Yet Tugwell would not repudiate or walk away from the party before the election.[77]

Critics on the anti-communist left denounced the politics of Wallace's "dream world," as well as his sometimes abrasive personality and his deficit in political sagacity. The independent radical Dwight MacDonald slammed at Wallace for months in his small but influential journal *Politics,* and in 1948 he collected this material in a volume called *Henry Wallace: The Man and the Myth.* The critique hammered at the role in the PCA of communists or *Stalinoids,* as MacDonald called them. Because "it has taken the liberals a long time to learn the facts of life about Stalinism," he argued, the acceptance of its evils makes Wallace not merely "a good man gone wrong" but a politically dangerous one. MacDonald skewered Wallace's "jumbled" use of language; "Wallace is fuzzy-minded to a degree unusual even in a politician," the critic contended. "He is constantly contradicting himself without ever admitting it." Eleanor Roosevelt, a founder of the ADA who had supported Wallace for the vice presidency in 1940 and 1944, now deplored Wallace's candidacy. "He had never been a good politician, he never has been able to gauge public opinion, and he never has picked his advisers wisely," she claimed. "As the leader of a third party he will merely destroy the very things he wishes to achieve. . . . No one in this country wants a third party as much as the Communists do. . . . We live in a much more complicated world than Mr. Wallace seems to understand."[78]

Truman on the Move

Back at the White House staffers worried over negative views of Truman in the press and opinion polls as a vacillating, inarticulate, and crony-ridden figure. A memo from a small group of aides headed by Clark Clifford (special counsel to the president) sketched a demanding road map for victory. At bottom the "Clifford Memo" called on Truman to pivot firmly toward the liberal side of his ambivalent (not to say Janus-faced) political persona. His veto of Taft-Hartley had begun a reconciliation with organized labor. Now Clifford urged him to win back the nation's middle-class liberals and others by reviving FDR's "second bill of rights" agenda and such policies as national health insurance. Clifford also advised Truman to embrace the civil rights program recently proposed by his own President's Committee on Civil Rights (see below). Going far beyond anything FDR ever fought for, the proposals included a bill to outlaw the poll tax, a federal anti-lynching bill, creation of a permanent FEPC, desegregation of interstate transportation, and an end to discrimination in the armed forces. Wallace's PCA and the ADA of course supported such measures; for these rival progressive groups such civil rights were simply long overdue in a democratic America. For the White House strong advocacy would be tactical as well: a way to win votes from liberals and northern blacks and to preempt any sudden, if unlikely, Republican push for civil rights during the second session of the 80th Congress.[79]

The Clifford Memo assumed that the centrist and internationalist Thomas Dewey (FDR's opponent in 1944 and the governor of New York) would be the Republican nominee rather than a conservative isolationist like Senator Robert Taft. Truman's initiatives for "containment" would serve him well in his re-election campaign, since Dewey was unlikely to challenge them. The South, Clifford opined, could "safely be ignored" in Truman's electoral strategy because Dixie had nowhere else to go. Southern Democrats would not bolt the party even under the shadow of a new civil rights program which, he might have added, they could thwart with their traditional obstructive tactics in Congress. The western states, farmers, and independent voters, on the other hand, had to be actively courted, along with union members, liberals, and the elements of FDR's fragile urban coalitions: Negroes, Jews, Italians, and other Catholic communities. With Wallace likely to launch a third party, the memo insisted that he must be identified with the PCA's communists and marginalized from the American mainstream. But Clifford also advised Truman to recognize the hostility to Wall Street among voters and to dwell on issues like high prices and housing shortages, which could be blamed on congressional inaction under the Republicans.

Truman initially followed Clifford's advice by sending a strong special message on civil rights to Congress in February. Meanwhile his aides liaised with the ADA, which agreed to work on publicity to discredit Wallace, while the White House and the DNC concentrated on the Republicans.[80] In the spring Truman took a cross-country rail trip proposed by Clifford, with a nonpartisan event in California as the destination. The president began to hone a combative style at appearances in small towns from the rear platform of his train in the western states. But Clifford had erred about "ignoring" a southern backlash against White House support for civil rights. Southern governors loudly threatened opposition. Truman recoiled and for the moment backed away from his own program, while Clifford admitted he had been wrong. Dixie along with Wallace's third party now loomed as potential spoilers.

There things stood as the Democratic Party convention in July approached. Liberals had tried and failed to find an alternative to head the ticket. Their favorite prospect (absurd in retrospect) was General Dwight D. Eisenhower, who discouraged such thoughts but did not definitively say no until early July. New Deal veteran and Supreme Court justice William O. Douglas likewise ruled himself out. Going into the convention with no plausible opponent, apart from a token effort by southern segregationists to nominate one of their own, Truman became the inevitable nominee. Liberals now shifted their energy into securing a strong civil rights plank in the party platform. Truman and his firmest supporters wanted to avoid a divisive imbroglio over civil rights, and backed a plank of pious generalities similar to the 1944 platform. But organized labor, the ADA, and big city politicians who needed black votes combined to back an alternative civil rights plank that would include an anti-lynching bill, action to secure black voting rights, a permanent FEPC, and an end to discrimination in the armed forces. Southern delegates would have none of this, and they would not even support the evasive 1944 formula. Instead they proposed an alternative that spoke exclusively about the rights of each state to regulate racial matters and the unconstitutionality of federal interference. The innocuous Truman-backed plank won the platform committee's final approval, but the convention chair agreed that backers of the South's states' rights resolution and of the liberal alternative could each present their minority reports to the convention.

The spotlight now fell on Hubert Humphrey, the youthful and energetic mayor of Minneapolis since 1945 and the main spokesman on the platform committee for the ADA's hundred-odd convention delegates. Humphrey had two credentials for his spot on the ADA executive board. First, during a thorny merger of Minnesota's independent Farmer-Labor Party and the state's weak Democratic Party, Humphrey led a successful fight to bar communists from the merged party.[81] Second, as mayor Humphrey made civil rights a central issue, created a local FEPC, and sponsored a city human relations council to publicize the cause. Just before the convention, Humphrey had won the Democratic-FL Party primary for a Senate seat in Minnesota. Passionately committed to civil rights, Humphrey hoped to curb southern influence in Congress and to undercut the appeal of Wallace to black voters.[82]

But Humphrey faced a dilemma. For he also wanted backing from the national Democratic Party for his Senate campaign, and he feared retaliation from Truman loyalists if he embarrassed the president by leading a floor fight against the platform plank that Truman favored. The night before the showdown Humphrey verged on withdrawing from his starring role, and only some late-night phone calls back home brought him around. At the podium next day Humphrey then outdid himself with a rousing ten-minute speech. To good effect he invoked the international context for civil rights: "For us to play our part effectively [on the world stage] we must be in a morally sound position. . . . Our demands for democratic practices in other lands will be no more effective than the guarantee of those practices in our own country." His address concluded on a stirring note: "To those who say that we are rushing this issue of civil rights I say to them, we are 172 years late. To those who say that this civil rights program is an infringement of states rights, the time has arrived in America for the Democratic Party to get out of the shadow of states rights and walk forthrightly into the sunshine of human rights. . . . I ask my party to march down the high road of progressive democracy."[83]

When they finally voted, the delegates easily defeated the southern states' rights minority plank, 309 to 925. Then the convention voted 651 to 582 to adopt the liberal minority plank, which thereby replaced the tepid clauses of the platform committee. Humphrey had helped turn the tide from the expected close but honorable loss to a startling liberal victory. Watching on TV back in Missouri, Truman famously railed against "crackpot" liberals. But in due course he embraced the platform, even while fearing that this raw sectional conflict presaged the party's defeat. True, only delegates from Alabama and Mississippi stalked out of the convention hall at that point, but the small-scale bolt later mushroomed into a third party led by Governor Strom Thurmond (S.C.), who linked segregation to states' rights.

Back in Philadelphia, after a long grind of nominations, speechmaking, and hoopla, Truman delivered his acceptance speech at the inauspicious hour of 2:00 a.m. Yet he roused the delegates with his fighting spirit, optimism, mockery of the Republicans, and attacks on the pitiful record of their 80th Congress.[84]

With melodramatic effect he now pledged to call that "do-nothing," "rich man's" Congress back into a special summer session to illustrate his point, a tactic advisors had earlier suggested.[85] The 80th Congress had done little more than pass Taft-Hartley and a tax cut favoring the wealthy, with no action on such pressing issues as high prices, farm policy, or housing. Calling out the "do-nothing Congress" proved a potent tactic.

White House aides in concert with the DNC's research staff proved surprisingly effective in scheduling the president's campaign logistics and providing him with talking points, speeches, and feedback. With the hard core segregationists lost to Thurmond's States' Rights Party, and the most defiant leftists lost to Wallace's Progressive Party, Truman's campaign focused on organized labor, farmers, and the big city coalitions. Starting off with a speech to the traditional Labor Day rally in Detroit's Cadillac Square, Truman remained on the hustings continuously until the election.

On his private train Truman traversed much of the country. He concentrated on the midwestern states of farms and heavy industry; Texas and Oklahoma in the Southwest; Kentucky and West Virginia; California; and New York, Pennsylvania, New Jersey, and Massachusetts. Truman made over 170 brief, off-the-cuff speeches in small towns from the rear platform of his train, but never on Sunday! These plain-talking "whistle stops" effectively supplemented the standard rallies and motorcades culminating in speeches at hotel banquet halls, civic auditoriums, and state fairs. Truman's staff coordinated his travels with the local and national press, and often invited reporters onto the train along with local and regional politicians.[86] Truman's foray into New York City at the end of October shrewdly included an unprecedented speech in Harlem and culminated with a rally at Madison Square Garden. Meanwhile surrogates campaigned energetically: running mate Senator Barkley (Ky.) traveled an estimated 150,000 miles by airplane with many stops in the South; Agriculture Secretary Brannan made 80 speeches in farm states emphasizing the administration's commitment to agricultural price supports; Labor Secretary Tobin gave 150 speeches attacking Taft-Hartley.[87]

Truman often accused Dewey of refusing to say where he stood on such issues as high prices, housing, aid to education, and social security expansion. The president recognized that Dewey was running a low-keyed, "safe" campaign. With a comfortable lead in the polls, Dewey kept to the high road; he dodged controversial issues as much as possible, tried to avoid any spontaneous gaffes, and would not descend to Truman's pugnacious style. When Dewey's poll numbers began to slip in October, some staffers urged him to be far more aggressive, but Dewey's self-confidence and desire not to rock the boat prevailed over that sound advice.[88]

The president not only fought like an underdog but paradoxically seemed to be running *against* incumbency— the "do-nothing" 80th Congress and the complacent Dewey all but inhabiting the White House in his own mind. Truman's blunt and clipped verbal manner, his very inelegance (compared to Dewey, not to mention FDR) seemed to appeal to average Americans. He repeatedly depicted Dewey as a bland, evasive elitist in thrall to the NAM (which concerted to kill price controls) and to the wealthy who would have benefited from the "rich man's tax bill" that Truman vetoed. In his final radio address Truman exhorted voters to ask themselves "whether you want a government for all or for the privileged few." And, he added, "I believe that the Constitution, which rightly protects property, is still more deeply pledged to protect human rights."[89]

Truman's Loyalty Boards

One might think that as he ran for re-election Truman would face sustained attacks about alleged communist influence in Washington. Republicans had leveled the charge in 1944 against FDR (who brushed it off with disdain) and against certain Democratic candidates in 1946. By 1948 the agitation over how to deal with domestic communists and fellow travelers in their ranks had enveloped the CIO leadership, the Hollywood studios, and the AVC, among others. After revelations about Soviet atomic espionage, accusations in congressional hearings by former communist couriers included sensational charges of spying against former State Department official Alger Hiss and senior Treasury advisor Harry Dexter White. For the moment, members of the administration vouched for the two influential men.

But could Truman plausibly be accused of being "soft" on communism? His foreign policy initiatives to "contain" international communism served as one layer of insulation. On the domestic front (under conservative congressional pressure) the president had authorized a far-reaching program to certify the "loyalty" of every federal employee, which effectively blunted communists-in-government smears against him in 1948. Truman launched his federal loyalty-security program by executive order in March 1947. Under nominal supervision of the Civil Service Commission, which appointed a Loyalty Review Board, the program sought to identify employees with "membership in, affiliation with or sympathetic association with . . . subversive [groups]." The targets of course included communists who might be spies, but scrutiny fell mainly on fellow travelers—people supportive of communist activity without formal membership in the party, if only to avoid its stringent discipline—and on progressives who had supported popular front organizations in the past.[90]

The program scrutinized over two million federal employees and job applicants during 1947–48; by 1953 the cumulative number under review reached 4,757,000. As step one, each employee had to fill out a loyalty questionnaire from the FBI, which conducted the vetting. The main reference point in FBI scrutiny, in addition to its own files and HUAC's, was the new *Attorney General's List of Totalitarian, Fascist, Communist, and Subversive Organizations*. This list included the CPUSA and its direct offshoots; various communist-supported groups (such as the National Negro Congress, later absorbed into the Civil Rights Congress, which defended persecuted blacks and communists); and popular front groups from the recent anti-fascist past (such as the League of American Writers, defunct after 1943, and the Joint Anti-Fascist Refugee Committee).[91] When the FBI's initial review revealed membership in or contributions to such groups, or other alarm bells, the FBI ordered a full field investigation. The bureau then passed about 26,000 dossiers to departmental loyalty boards set up under Truman's executive order. The boards in turn sent lengthy interrogatories to about three-fourths of the individuals and held formal hearings for over 4,000. (Along the way over 6,000 individuals under investigation resigned, many no doubt to avoid the vetting process or damage to their reputations.) Altogether the loyalty boards adjudicated 17,060 cases in 1947–48: they rated 16,503 individuals as "eligible on loyalty" and dismissed or barred 557.[92]

Given the hyperbole and the vast number of man-hours spent by the FBI to vet the employees and to compile dossiers on the "subversive" organizations, what are we to make of these loyalty reviews? Ultimately the individual case files as much as the statistics put into perspective this demoralizing episode with its erosion of civil liberties. Even in summary form the case files show the prolonged harassment (often lasting years) and the havoc wrought among federal employees of progressive bent. The process no doubt flushed out a few clandestine communists. But as historian Landon Storrs shows, prominent targets included anti-fascist popular fronters, racial justice activists, progressive female activists (whom conservatives held in special contempt), and some ex-New Dealers, especially in labor and consumer agencies, reaching up even into Truman's White House.[93]

In his one major campaign speech devoted to the loyalty review boards, Truman began with the common assumption that no member of the CPUSA should be employed by the federal government. At the time of his speech, Truman explained, among the two million federal employees answering questionnaires, the FBI found that the loyalty of 99.7 percent "was not questionable." Only 0.3 percent required further scrutiny by departmental loyalty review boards which, Truman maintained, operated under legal safeguards against unfounded charges. The boards determined that the overwhelming majority of those individuals too were loyal Americans; the exceptions were fired, and in a handful of cases the FBI initiated criminal prosecutions.[94]

Truman's presentation of his loyalty program was accurate as far as it went: the federal government would not knowingly employ communists; the overwhelming majority of employees were loyal; the review boards had forced out only a small number of federal employees or job applicants. But Truman also elided and evaded. He did not mention the vast expenditure of manpower in the FBI's hunt; the extremely dubious nature of the attorney general's list of subversive organizations; the several thousand employees who resigned under this inquisitorial pressure before any final determination; the fact that cleared individuals were often subjected to subsequent reinvestigations. His speech entirely ignored the anxiety and personal ordeals of patriotic progressive employees. Finally, he misled the public by claiming that the boards' procedures had "legal safeguards," when in fact adverse information often remained anonymous with no opportunity to confront or cross-examine accusers.

In reply to Eleanor Roosevelt, who (along with the AVC and other liberals) objected to the loyalty review on civil liberties grounds, Truman had insisted that the program would not to become a "witch hunt"— unlike the congressional committees conducting their own Red hunts without boundaries or due process, whose public posturing the president scorned. The loyalty boards, he claimed, operated outside the glare of publicity and confirmed the loyalty and patriotism of "the overwhelming number of civil servants." True, he agreed with Mrs. Roosevelt, "It is contrary to American tradition to enquire into the political or philosophical views of anyone ... which is why all of us feel a certain repugnance to this program." But it was necessary in order to root out the "small infiltration of seriously disloyal people." Individuals had an absolute constitutional right to their opinions, he concluded, "[but] no one has a constitutional right to work for the government."[95]

In the end Truman's loyalty program helped insulate him from a mounting anti-communist hysteria. Then too Henry Wallace deflected Truman's potential communism problem by repeatedly denouncing Truman's "containment" policies as warmongering, and by Wallace's obtuseness about communist influence in his own third party. The swirling currents of anti-communism landed mainly on Wallace's shoulders, making Truman and his administration seem in contrast as reliable patriots. (None of that would shield the administration when, after 1950, Senators McCarthy and Jenner brought a breathtaking demagoguery and recklessness to their own Red hunts.)

Election Day 1948

Buoyed by Isacson's victory in the Bronx special election of February and by early opinion polls, the Progressive Party gained ballot access in all but three states (Illinois, Nebraska, Oklahoma), despite the hurdles. After the convention in July, however, the party faced a downward slide and a growing gap between activists and the broader electorate. Postmortems in the press on communist influence cast the Progressive Party in a relentlessly negative light. In the fall Wallace made a campaign swing through several southern states where he would speak only to non-segregated audiences and stoically bore the racist vilification and egg throwing. This rekindled admiration for the man in liberal circles up North but not much for his candidacy. Because the Progressive Party "persists in wrapping themselves in the glory of FDR," nervous ex-New Dealers like Ickes still feared that Wallace might drain off enough liberal voters to jeopardize Truman's chances, even though "Truman is running on the most liberal platform ever adopted by a major party in America."[96]

Some liberal Democrats—such as Congresswoman Helen G. Douglas in California, newcomers Hubert Humphrey and Paul Douglas running for Senate seats in Minnesota and Illinois, and Chester Bowles running for governor in Connecticut—faced the threat of Progressive Party spoilers when they refused to change positions on such issues as the Marshall Plan. In New York Wallace's ALP affiliate ran fourteen candidates, including Isacson and Pressman, in normally Democratic congressional districts, along with Vito Marcantonio, the

ALP's longtime incumbent. Marcantonio ended up as the only Progressive Party congressional candidate in the entire country to win.[97]

Although Dewey led in the final polls of October, Truman won the election with roughly 24 million votes (49.5 percent) to Dewey's 22 million (45.1 percent). Between them the two third parties garnered only 4.8 percent of the vote. Thurmond's States' Rights Party won roughly 1,700,000 votes cast almost exclusively in the South and carried only four Deep South states. The States' Rights (Dixiecrat) candidate had tried but failed to secure the Democratic Party ballot lines in most of the South, and the key electoral states of the region remained in the Democratic fold. Wallace won only 1,160,000 votes, with his highest totals in New York (510,000) and California (190,000). True, he cost Truman the electoral votes of New York, and perhaps of Michigan and Maryland as well, where Wallace's votes exceeded the margin by which Dewey carried those states. But none of this undercut Truman's clear plurality in the national popular vote or his victory in the electoral college.[98]

The alchemy of Truman's victory is probably best explained by the issues he raised and his aggressive campaigning, which played off the bland and evasive campaign of his rival. Dewey might have seemed an ideal candidate with his experience, cautious temperament, and calm under fire.[99] But Truman's well-organized campaign, combative spirit, and blunt talk with a wisp of demagoguery prevailed among most of his targeted constituencies. Using agricultural price supports as a wedge issue Truman attracted farmers who in the past decade had leaned Republican. The CIO-PAC and the AFL's political operation worked hard for the Democrats, and he did well among unionized workers. The big city coalitions forged by FDR in 1936 seemed to hold, and Truman had great success among black urban voters; in NYC he won in Harlem by a margin of 75,000 votes.[100]

Statistically the aggregate vote for congressional Democrats exceeded Truman's by over 5 percent. In 1936 FDR's "coattails" had produced huge Democratic majorities in the House and Senate, and his presence helped the party retain control of Congress for the next eight years. But in 1948 any coattails effect worked the other way, as some Democratic candidates may have helped wavering voters get past their reservations about Truman in a few close states. The election reversed the outcome of the 1946 congressional contest, and the Democrats swept back into control of Congress. In the Senate they gained 9 seats (all outside the South), for a total of 54 to 42. The majority of

Democratic senators, however, were still from the South and border states, and regained the powerful committee chairmanships vested in them by seniority. In the House, Democrats gained 75 seats, giving them a majority of 262 to 172, but outside the southern and border states Republicans still held a 169 to 159 edge. Conservatives from both parties, in other words, could still combine in various configurations to block or water down legislation to reinvigorate the New Deal or to defeat civil rights bills in the name of states' rights.[101]

Civil Rights in the Postwar Moment

As a New Deal senator from the border state of Missouri, Truman won in 1934 and 1940 with the help of black votes in the state's two big cities. But in an address in July 1940 to a group of colored Democrats he cautioned "that I am not appealing for social equality of the Negro. The Negro himself knows better than that . . . Negroes want justice, not social relations. . . . We owe the Negro legal equality . . . and opportunities to better himself." Apart from lauding the New Deal, Truman could say only that FDR in contrast to his predecessors "has appointed more Negroes to responsible governmental positions" and that federal housing programs would benefit blacks.[102] A year later the senator could have added FDR's Fair Employment Practices Commission (FEPC). For with war on the horizon in 1941, labor and civil rights activist A. Philip Randolph—head of the Brotherhood of Sleeping Car Porters (AFL)—organized a campaign against discrimination in employment and in the armed forces and threatened to lead an embarrassing 50,000-person "march on Washington" if the administration failed to act. FDR went just far enough for Randolph to stand down; the president side-stepped completely segregation in the armed forces but issued an executive order creating a temporary FEPC for the war production industries to handle complaints about discrimination against blacks, albeit with cumbersome enforcement powers. Congress later harassed the FEPC, starved it of necessary additional funding, and shut it down in June 1946.[103]

As president, Truman could scarcely do less on civil rights than his illustrious predecessor. For FDR had not advanced civil rights causes (despite relentless nudging from Eleanor Roosevelt), lest he risk retaliation from the southern contingent on his New Deal and wartime priorities. Truman held the same racial attitudes as most regional colleagues yet contemplated support for an anti-poll tax bill, an anti-lynching bill, and a permanent FEPC. His presidency saw seven years of broken field running on civil rights: at moments he forcefully urged congressional action but usually deferred to southern opposition and failed to follow through. On three occasions, however, he issued notable executive orders that broke new ground. Truman's record of action and evasions reflected his personal comfort with the social separation of the races, along with his distress over America's deficit in equal justice and opportunity for blacks and his need to court liberal and black northern votes.[104] As but one example of his ambivalence: Eleanor Roosevelt persuaded Truman in 1947 to address a mass rally of the NAACP at the Lincoln Memorial in her company. The event made him the first US president ever to speak before the preeminent civil rights organization. Yet he wrote privately on the eve of the gathering that Mrs. Roosevelt "has spent her public life stirring up trouble between blacks and whites—and I'm in the middle."[105]

Three vicious assaults on southern black veterans in 1946 aroused Truman's fury. When an NAACP delegation recounted the details of those killings and maimings to the president, Director Walter White observed that Truman's face "became pale with horror." The president concluded that "it is going to take something more than the handling of each individual case after it happens." In March 1947 Truman created a President's Committee on Civil Rights to assess US race relations and to propose an agenda of actions. Presidential aide David Niles and his assistant Philleo Nash recruited the committee's fifteen members, with input from Walter White. They consisted in the main of white moderates "broadly representative of American life . . . and not especially interested persons like myself," in White's words. Chairman Charles E. Wilson, president of General Electric, epitomized such appointees. Only two blacks were included (one a woman), along with another woman, one official each from the CIO and the AFL, three clergymen, and FDR Jr. (who carried the perspective of the AVC). Truman urged Niles to "push [the committee] with everything you have."[106]

The Committee on Civil Rights completed its work in October 1947 and tendered its report, *To Secure These Rights,* under FDR's World War II refrain "freedom from fear," which Truman had earlier invoked. The report combined moral exhortation with a surprisingly forceful program for federal action. The administration and civil rights groups promoted the report extensively in the black and mainstream media; as in the publicity campaign for the Beveridge Report in Britain, *To Secure These Rights* soon appeared in an abridged eight-page pamphlet for wide distribution.[107] On February 2, 1948, Truman sent an impassioned special message to Congress with a ten-point agenda on civil rights, and he intended to follow with an omnibus civil rights bill that his aides were drafting.[108] The momentum abruptly stopped, though, when the southern governors' backlash led Truman to desist from pressing Congress for legislation at that juncture. But *To Secure These Rights* had a life of its own as a benchmark for civil rights organizations, local human relations councils, the CIO's Committee against Discrimination, the black press, the National Council of Negro Women, and some of the black churches.

Meanwhile, however, as in the CIO and the AVC, a rift between liberals and the popular front/communist left hardened among civil rights advocates—a split embodied by Paul Robeson and A. Philip Randolph. The NAACP had long resisted the presence of communists and fellow travelers and therefore shunned even Paul Robeson.[109] A star black college athlete, mesmerizing singer, renowned stage and screen actor, and left-wing activist, Robeson had led an "American Crusade against Lynching" in September 1946, which drew on progressive Hollywood star power for support and publicity. Although the NAACP would not work with him, Robeson had access to the White House at that time and met with the president over the lynching issue. But when the locus of Robeson's activism shifted to the communist-influenced Civil Rights Congress, the White House twice rebuffed delegations led by Robeson.[110]

A. Philip Randolph, a militant crusader for black rights in his own way, ended up on the other side of the divide from Robeson. To open an economic front in the civil rights movement, Randolph had been a founder of the National Negro Congress (NNC) in 1936. Without objection, communists helped with funding and strategy. But at the NNC's 1940 convention the communists became obtrusively domineering and imposed the CPUSA anti-Roosevelt line in the wake of the Nazi-Soviet pact. Dismayed at that brusque turn, Randolph memorably stated that "Negroes cannot afford to add to the handicap of being *black* the handicap of being *Red*"; he "would not be a member of the NNC, or any other organization which was a Communist Front."[111] Defunct by 1948, the NNC was absorbed by the Civil Rights Congress, and the rift continued. In January 1950 Roy Wilkins of the NAACP convened a national Emergency Civil Rights Mobilization in Washington representing fifty-odd church, labor, and civil rights organizations. The 1,000 delegates were to spread out and lobby Congress for passage of an FEPC bill, currently stalled in the House Rules Committee. The NAACP made sure to inform the White House that the Emergency Mobilization "emphatically rejected the support and cooperation of the extreme left-wingers . . . and [in particular] the party-line Civil Rights Congress."[112]

Despite its name, Wilkins intended the Emergency Mobilization to establish a permanent umbrella group for advocates of civil rights. The January conference did not find the right organizational formula for that purpose, but a second try, steered by Wilkins and Randolph in late 1950, created a permanent coalition of civil rights constituencies, which called itself the Leadership Conference on Civil Rights (LCCR). With headquarters in Washington, the LCCR sought to harness the energies of established institutions in black communities, such as churches and women's clubs; interracial advocacy groups; and allies in organized labor, white churches, liberal Jewish groups, and the ADA (whose operative Joseph Rauh became the LCCR's counsel). Over the next two decades the LCCR coordinated the lobbying of Congress and publicity for the cause, but it failed completely in the 1950s on its key issues: abolishing the poll tax (which in any case was fading in importance), federal prosecution of lynching, desegregating interstate public transportation, and establishing a permanent FEPC.

After FDR's temporary FEPC for the war production industries closed down, creating a permanent FEPC with "cease and desist" powers became a priority for civil rights advocates. But an FEPC also loomed as the epitome of threats to "the southern way of life": to states' rights, traditional social controls over labor, resistance to unions, and even to racial segregation itself.[113] Advocates came nearest in 1950 when the House approved a bill for a "voluntary" FEPC rather than the "compulsory" version with strong enforcement powers championed by liberals but opposed by Republicans taking their cue from Senator Taft.[114] Even that weak House bill, however, threatened the total resistance of the South to civil rights. The FEPC bill dealt with discrimination and equal opportunity in the workplace, and proponents insisted that the bill was not a Trojan horse for social integration. But that fear lingered. A Louisiana banker and Democratic loyalist, for example, sought reassurance that FEPC legislation "does not apply toward social equality, as the States Rights leaders would have us believe, but is a question of employment only." A White House aide replied that during House debate on the FEPC bill even Harlem Congressman Adam Powell insisted that "this deals only with employment discrimination. Nowhere does it mention or sanction interference with segregation or any social customs, or in fact discrimination in any place but on the job."[115] Even so, after the House approved the weak FEPC bill, a southern filibuster killed it in the Senate.

The Senate remained the graveyard for all civil rights legislation, since unlimited debate could be halted there only by a "cloture" vote requiring two-thirds of
senators present and voting. Cloture on civil rights always fell short. In the
1940s the House, for example, passed bills to abolish the poll tax three times,
but in each case cloture votes in the Senate failed and the bills died. Liberals
advocated the democratic option of cutting off unlimited debate by majority
vote, but in 1950 conservative Republican senators joined their Democratic
counterparts to raise the bar even higher by requiring 64 votes (two-thirds of the
entire Senate) for cloture—a move denounced by liberal Republican Wayne
Morse as "an unholy alliance with Southern Democrats."[116] On occasion
Republicans backed mild civil rights bills. The RNC, for example, made a
cloture vote in the Senate on the (weak) FEPC law a party issue, either in good
faith or to embarrass the Democrats. The NAACP then entreated the White
House and the DNC to twist the arms of uncommitted Democrats. But successive cloture votes on the FEPC bill in May and July fell short by 52–32 and
55–33, respectively.[117]

Desegregating the Armed Forces

The Selective Service Act of 1940 had authorized the drafting of black men
into the army, with a 10 percent limit on the total of black conscripts and volunteers, lest the armed forces be inundated with black recruits. From induction
onward, almost everything proceeded on segregated tracks, including incorporation of black troops into all-black units, assignment of white officers to
command them, and deployment of black units for support and logistical tasks
rather than for frontline combat side-by-side with white troops.[118] Tensions
created by segregation ignited emotional, even violent confrontations on some
military bases.

In its way Washington was sensitive to the issue. As part of Frank Capra's
Why We Fight documentary film series, commissioned by the army in 1942 to
motivate its draftees, the famed director planned to include a film on "the Negro
Soldier," intended for black units but which might end up being shown to white
troops as well. As one film historian explains, the army was in a bind: "It wanted
to make a movie that would convince skeptical African American men and their
families that this was their war too, but only if it could avoid the subject of
racism altogether and find a narrative of inclusion that would somehow manage

not to unsettle any white GIs."[119] *The Negro Soldier,* co-written by black activist Carlton Moss, celebrated the role of blacks in America's history and military experience, from Crispus Attucks to the Great War and into the present. Through the induction process, training, and deployment, the men (and women auxiliaries) may have been segregated, but the film portrayed them without the demeaning stereotypes of blacks almost universal in Hollywood movies.[120]

Capra's production team was told to play down possible combat roles for black troops in World War II, but the film showed black recruits training at length and strenuously for action should circumstances require it. In early 1945, right after the Battle of the Bulge, platoon-sized units of black soldiers volunteered to be rushed into frontline combat alongside depleted white units. The black soldiers fought well, but this interlude created no movement in the War Department to end the inefficiencies and degradations of military segregation.[121]

In October 1947 A. Philip Randolph formed the Committee against Jim Crow in Military Service and Training, as the administration prepared to renew conscription (which had lapsed for over a year) or alternatively to replace it with Truman's pet proposal for UMT (Universal Military Training). Inspired by the spirit of Gandhi and the tradition of boycotts in black communities, Randolph advocated civil disobedience against military segregation. He warned the White House that draft-age blacks might in numbers refuse to serve in a segregated military, and that people like himself would risk punishment by encouraging them to refuse.[122]

On March 31 Randolph testified to that effect before the Senate Armed Services Committee with a fierce attack on the toxically anti-democratic character of segregation. "Negro youth have a moral obligation not to lend themselves as world-wide carriers of an evil and hellish doctrine," he declared. "I pledge myself to openly counsel, aid and abet youth, both white and Negro, to quarantine any Jim Crow conscription system, whether it bears the label of UMT or Selective Service. . . . I shall call upon all Negro veterans to join this civil disobedience movement and to recruit their younger brothers in an organized refusal to register or to be drafted. . . . In resisting the insult of Jim Crowism to the soul of black America, we are helping to save the soul of America." Randolph ended his testimony with a cry of exasperation: "Finally let me say that Negroes are just sick and tired of being pushed around and we just don't propose to take it, and we do not care what happens."[123]

Southerners in Congress counterattacked with the common and demeaning justifications of military segregation: that Negroes were inherently cowardly and lacked the courage for combat; that aptitude testing shows they lack the intelligence for leadership or for proficiency in technical military roles; that desegregation would disrupt unit cohesion and morale. Southerners threatened to bottle up the renewal of conscription unless it incorporated segregation. Once again Truman was in the middle.

The president soon made up his mind, and issued Executive Order 9981 on July 26, 1948, making it his administration's stated policy to assure "equality of treatment and opportunity for all persons in the armed services without regard to race, color, religion, or national origin." Randolph objected to the ambiguity of a statement that talked of prohibiting discrimination but not of desegregation. When he received reassurance from Truman's emissary Senator McGrath that desegregation was indeed the goal, he called off civil disobedience.[124]

Executive Order 9981 initiated an effort to cajole the Pentagon into cooperation. Truman assigned that task to a small Committee on Equality of Treatment and Opportunity in the Armed Services. His committee was not to study the problem but rather to pressure the three branches of the armed forces to design and institute policies for integrated training and deployment—and for equality of opportunity for promotions. On Niles's suggestion Truman named as the committee's chair Charles Fahy—a former solicitor general, who had defended the internment of Japanese-Americans during the war as a military necessity and was "a reconstructed southern liberal on race." Fahy faced mulish resentments to this new layer of oversight on the civilian and military chiefs in the Pentagon. For two years, turf battles persisted between Fahy, the secretary of defense, and successive secretaries of the army. The navy (where blacks had served on the same ships as whites but in inflexibly subordinate roles, such as mess stewards) seemed relatively cooperative, as did the newly autonomous air force. But Secretary of the Army Kenneth Royall, a southern segregationist, proved an inflexible defender of the status quo, and Truman eventually forced him to resign. Fahy then worked doggedly to overcome the Army's continuing institutional resistance.[125]

By the time the committee submitted its final report (*Freedom to Serve*) in May 1950, the dam had broken in principle. The report formally gave the lie to justifications for segregation based on aptitude testing, assumptions about the unsuitability of blacks for combat or command, and disruptions of effectiveness that desegregation would purportedly bring to the military.[126] Relatively little had actually changed in the navy, and virtually nothing in the army, but Fahy had overcome the army's resistance to the very idea of integration, and implementation was now a matter of time.[127] True, that time would seem long in coming. Michael Straight, AVC national chair, for example, wrote several times to Secretary of the Army Pace and to David Niles in 1951 about persistent discriminatory practices. Pace replied that the proportion of blacks in the army had broken through the old 10 percent cap to 14 percent, but he acknowledged that "the Army continues to employ all-negro units and that the race of negro personnel is [still] shown on assignment orders." The Army would not dismantle black units all at once, he wrote, but would be moving in that direction. A general noted that the Far East command was being actively integrated while bases in the US "present problems of greater magnitude. . . . But we think that time has run out on this matter."[128] Full desegregation in training, in deployment to bases at home and abroad, and in assignments would take about another two years.

Impetus to speed up integration indeed came from the Pacific theater. The Korean War began suddenly in June 1950, and before the front eventually stabilized, the US-UN forces had survived near annihilation twice over. In their utterly ill-prepared first months of the war, US forces were driven back to a shrinking perimeter around the port of Pusan. Then, after a counteroffensive swept through North Korea to the border with China, a massive Chinese army crossed the Yalu River and drove US forces back to South Korea. Initially the black units rushed over from occupied Japan were slated for their usual support roles in the rear. But the bloody fighting and repeated withdrawals forced commanders to put black replacements into the front lines. Later deployed north, black units engaged in brutal combat in freezing weather during the ensuing retreat. Since most of his black troops performed well in combat, Eighth Army commander Matthew Ridgway became the leading uniformed advocate for military integration, and within a year a majority of the Eighth Army's infantry companies were effectively integrated.[129]

Within this larger story, the fate of the historic black 24th Infantry Regiment is a sobering case study. Deployed in 1950 for occupation duty in Japan, the regiment was shipped to Korea at the nadir of US fortunes in the Pusan perimeter. Units from the regiment were quickly slotted into frontline combat, and for the next year they fought up and down the Korean peninsula. Along the way some companies won their engagements, displayed notable bravery, and suffered high casualty rates. At other points positions collapsed into routs, and indiscipline sullied the regiment's image to the point where it was slated to be disbanded. Decades later, however, a revised official history of the 24th Regiment explained the unit's mixed record by exposing the racial biases of various white officers up to the regimental command, the tactical ineptitude and poor leadership of those officers, and the comparable performance of other regiments under similar conditions.[130]

Alongside EO 9981 on integrating the armed services, Truman issued a companion executive order in July 1948 to ban discrimination in hiring and promotion in the federal workforce. Unable to secure from Congress an FEPC covering the private sector, Truman could at least promote equal employment opportunity in the military and civilian establishments under his direct authority. Discrimination was pervasive in the federal workforce, and Negro employees also faced segregation of facilities in the South and in Washington, DC. When Chester Bowles left the OPA to head the Office of Economic Stabilization in February 1946, for example, he relocated to the Federal Reserve Building where he found that he could not lunch with three Negroes on his staff who were barred from the building's cafeteria—a practice he soon ended.[131]

Ending discrimination in the federal workforce did not arouse the overt resistance that met Truman's initiative to desegregate the army, but the slow pace and bureaucratic obstacles in the field were comparable. The executive order called for fair employment boards in the regional districts of various federal agencies. When a memo forwarded to the White House from an employee in the Denver office of the Budget Bureau complained about "widespread disregard of the executive order barring discrimination in his region," David Niles commented that the boards "might be encouraged to move in the direction of more *affirmative action* toward the development of fair employment practices." One knotty problem: local "fair employment officers" in federal agencies served only part time—presumably devoting little time to the matter. Niles proposed that the Civil Service Commission send out its own officials to oversee the process in the larger agencies. The chair of the national Civil Service Commission's Fair Employment Board agreed in principle, yet cautioned against "interposing the CSC between these employment officers and their departmental chiefs." Despite such bureaucratic intertia, CSC headquarters affirmed that slow progress was being made, especially with the help of "welfare organizations of minority groups" that developed cases for redress.[132]

Truman's Stewardship of the New Deal Legacy

Two bookends bracket the fate of Truman's Fair Deal program during his second term. The Housing Act of 1949 became his signature victory, while the defeat of national health insurance, alongside the failure of all civil rights legislation in Congress, stood as his foremost setback.

The New Deal's Public Works Administration had built a modest 25,000 units of public housing, but FDR's priorities for recovery and relief lay elsewhere. For Senator Robert F. Wagner of New York, that consummate urban liberal, however, the mass of substandard tenements in the cities was an affront that had to be remedied. In 1935 Wagner failed to win passage of a new program for slum clearance and public housing, to be financed by large capital grants, but after the election of 1936 he tried again. This time he proposed financing through federal loans and small annual subsidies for local housing authorities. Opposition in both houses halved the commitment of Wagner's bill and inserted limits on building costs (and therefore on quality), but the bill finally passed in 1937, and established the US Housing Authority in Washington to oversee federal public housing programs.[133]

Facing an acute postwar housing shortage after the wartime halt in home construction (including most public housing), Truman and congressional liberals backed a substantial new program for federal housing aid, with slum clearance and public housing as its centerpiece. A one-off co-sponsorship by Republican Senator Taft and conservative Democrat Ellender (La.) gave unusual impetus to the effort, and the Taft-Wagner-Ellender bill passed the Senate. But intense opposition to public housing by the home builders' and realtors' lobbies blocked the bill in the House. Under the same influences Congress scuttled wartime controls over building materials and dispatched to any early grave the Veterans Emergency Housing Program directed by New Dealer Wilson Wyatt.[134]

When the Democratic-controlled 81st Congress convened in January 1949, the shortage of affordable housing remained acute, despite the start of mass produced tract housing in such suburbs as the Levittowns built primarily for veterans. Truman first wrangled a fifteen-month extension of rent control from

Congress to protect tenants from extortionate rent increases in a market with scarcely any vacancies. With the support of urban liberals, the administration then proposed a target of one million new units of public housing over seven years, to be financed by $1 billion in federal loans and $500 million in capital grants to local housing authorities.

Negotiations began in the Senate over the target number for public housing units. To Truman's proposed one million, Taft countered with 600,000 over eight years. In an unusual spirit of compromise the Senate Banking Committee (with 10 votes from each side of the aisle) settled on 800,000 units over six years. As a last resort to derail the bill, two conservative Republican senators moved an amendment cynically designed to peel away Southern Democratic support by forbidding racial discrimination in public housing. Facing a cruel tactical dilemma, most northern liberals opposed the amendment, lest the whole bill fail. They joined Southern Democrats to defeat the amendment 49–31, after which the Senate passed the housing bill 57–13.[135]

Unwilling to follow Taft on this issue, conservative Republicans in the House fought public housing on principle. They shared the extreme views of the real estate and home-building associations in behalf of unfettered private enterprise and opposed any federal program for housing poor people. When a rare parliamentary maneuver pried the bill loose from the obstructive House Rules Committee, the realtors and home builders redoubled their lobbying against this "socialistic scheme." An amendment to strip the public housing title from the larger bill failed by the narrowest margin, 204 to 209 votes. Only then did the bill finally pass, 227 to 186, in what Taft called "an historic occasion." With a stark divide in the House between congressmen from urban districts and those from rural ones, the 45 congressmen from the South's more urbanized districts backed the public housing provision and apparently tipped the outcome.[136]

The Housing Act of 1949 included titles that expanded federal mortgage insurance for private housing and others to support slum clearance and construction of public housing. The Housing Act thus avoided choosing between reliance on private enterprise or substantial planning and funding for housing from Washington. (In contrast, as we saw, Bevan made that choice in Britain's postwar moment by requiring licenses for private builders that restricted homes for the private market to one out of every five units going up.) Instead the US Housing Act of 1949 converged around one goal that both sides could embrace: economic stimulus from construction of all sorts.[137]

Title I of the Housing Act on urban renewal or slum clearance turned out to be its most significant provision. On sites procured by local housing authorities under eminent domain, and paid for with taxpayer money, Title I vaguely called for "predominantly" residential construction. But it simultaneously directed that localities should offer "maximum opportunity for the redevelopment of project areas by private enterprise," and it set no limit on the profits of such ventures. The Housing Act thus opened a door to private builders and investors on land cleared under urban renewal procedures, in addition to public housing for the working poor. Under the vague language of the act, in concert or collusion with local housing authorities and politicians, developers could erect office buildings, market-rate housing, or even convention centers and the like in urban renewal areas. In the end far more poor people lost their homes to the bulldozers under urban renewal than were later accommodated in public housing projects.[138]

In legislative annals Democrats touted the Housing Act of 1949 as a major win for the Fair Deal agenda because of Title II on public housing. But in the long run the act miscarried in that respect as well. Year-to-year appropriations for public housing began to fall short of the targets almost immediately with the budgetary strains of the Korean War. By 1964 only 356,000 units had been built.[139] Worse yet, most of the public housing built under federal auspices was of dubious design and poor quality. Stringent income limits for eligibility ensured that public housing projects would become enclaves of the very poor and of racial minorities, including "problem families," which most local authorities lacked the capacity to screen out.

Wagner's Housing Act of 1937 had restrained the construction of high-rise buildings for public housing. But in the 1950s the "towers in the park model" became the norm. Most public housing projects went up on slum clearance sites isolated from surrounding communities on open expanses of land. Their sponsors used new cost-saving design techniques for column-and-slab construction that produced grim, high-rise buildings. Many such projects were cut off from customary street life, and residents had trouble supervising their children outside or deterring vandalism. In the years ahead most local housing authorities lacked the funds to maintain the buildings properly, especially their roofs and elevators, although the huge New York City Housing Authority did a far better job than most others on tenant selection, policing, and building maintenance through the 1960s.[140]

Public housing in Britain, as we've seen, eventually ended up in similar disrepute. The two countries started with an identical problem in 1945—a prewar mass of substandard or slum housing—and relied on local authorities for the construction and management of public housing, as did France in due course. But Nye Bevan insisted that most new public housing estates in Britain comprise low-rise, semi-attached houses with small gardens. His ministry also set relatively generous standards for the size of apartments and their amenities. But when British housing policy and funding formulas shifted in the late 1950s to 1960s, the high-rise, slab model came to dominate new public housing estates and soon obliterated Bevan's version of public housing. In the US the misfortunes of high-rise public housing materialized more quickly thanks to the limitations of the Housing Act of 1949 and the flawed approach of most local planners and politicians who implemented the act.

The few other legislative victories that Truman won for his Fair Deal agenda also came in 1949, the first year of his second term. A rosy summary of the first session of the 81st Congress by House Majority Leader John McCormack hailed both the Housing Act and the liberalization of Social Security (passed in the lower house, with likely approval to come in the Senate).[141] Expanded eligibility for federal old-age pensions encompassed new occupational categories that added an estimated 11 million people to the 35 million currently enrolled. They included 4.7 million non-farm self-employed; state and local government employees choosing to opt in; such occupations as salesmen and taxi drivers; and 700,000 full-time farm-workers. Pension payouts would increase by about 70 percent, which raised the average old-age pension from $26 a month to $45, with small incremental increases in Social Security taxes to underwrite pensions going forward.

McCormack also cited long overdue congressional action to raise the federal minimum wage from 40 cents an hour to 75 cents, directly benefiting an estimated 1.5 million workers, and to fine-tune the overtime provisions of the Fair Labor Standards Act. Enacted over vocal anti-labor sentiment, this House bill made some exceptions to the original exclusions of domestics and farm laborers—the majority of the black labor force—from minimum wage and overtime laws. Later Senate action, however, scaled back those changes and still left most such workers outside the modest protective umbrella of the New Deal.[142]

Senate Majority Leader Scott Lucas struck comparable upbeat notes, but had to acknowledge defeat in two areas. First, not only did the Senate fail to repeal

Taft-Hartley, but it failed by one vote to rescind even the law's revival of injunctions, which the Democrats' allies in organized labor especially detested. In that 44–46 vote, the opposing majority came in the main from 32 Republicans, but enough Democrats defected to derail the repeal.[143] Second, the Senate blocked every civil rights initiative after Lucas led a losing fight to amend the rules on cloture motions. As noted above, that skirmish ended up *increasing* the hurdle to cloture by requiring 64 votes (two-thirds of the entire Senate) to cut off debate. Anti-poll tax and FEPC legislation that passed in the House died in the Senate. Liberals now chaired a few committees or subcommittees in each house and held hearings on other civil rights proposals, such as a permanent Commission on Civil Rights or the prohibition of segregation on interstate transportation, but those causes too stalled out in those committees or on the floor. Likewise, Congress rejected a government reorganization plan urged by Truman that would have created a new Department of Welfare. Nor would it agree to immigration reform, statehood for Alaska and Hawaii, or home rule for the District of Columbia. By the last year of Truman's term, the only "civil rights" measure passed by Congress that Truman could sign into law was a bill setting September 17 as annual Citizenship Day.[144]

Federal Aid to Education?

In 1945 George Zook gave an endowed lecture at Harvard on the role of the federal government in education. An educational sociologist, college president, briefly FDR's commissioner of education, and now head of the American Council on Education, Zook reviewed the traditional control over education by the states under the Tenth Amendment's "reserved powers" clause. He then enumerated federal initiatives that had nonetheless arisen over the years such as the Morrill Act land grants for colleges; the office of the US Commissioner on Education, which gathered statistics and made recommendations about best practices; educational programs under the Agriculture Department, such as "extension" courses for farmers; and the federal construction of school buildings under the New Deal's WPA. Without suggesting that the federal government in any way supersede control by the states over education, Zook advocated substantial federal funding for the states to offset inequality in educational provision caused by large variations in the demand for schooling (school-aged children per 1,000 population) or per capita income in the states to pay for it.

Zook gave special attention to inequities in provision of education for Negros and whites in the South, which targeted funding from Washington could help overcome.[145]

Federal aid to promote educational opportunity formed one heading in FDR's "second bill of rights" and in the CIO-PAC's *People's Program for 1944,* which specified the educational tiers that required federal support, from preschooling to college. Truman now took up the cause of federal aid to education, although his concern about budget deficits restrained his zeal. When Congress considered the question, however, conservatives opposed most forms of federal aid to education. In the end Congress passed only a bill for construction aid to about 600 school districts impacted by high densities of federal employees, defense workers, or military families dwelling on property exempt from local taxes. The Senate also approved grants-in-aid to the neediest school districts for maintenance and operations, but the House rejected any such role for the federal government as its Education Committee killed the Senate bill by a vote of 13 to 12.[146]

Higher education, however, seemed a different matter. The G.I. Bill's tuition and subsistence grants to veterans for post-secondary schooling put a spotlight on the strengths and deficiencies of the nation's provisions for higher education. Truman appointed a commission in July 1946 to study how to expand and support higher education in America, with an eye to "the functions of higher education in our democracy."[147] The president chose none other than George Zook to head this Presidential Commission on Higher Education, and its twenty-eight members included Nobel Prize–winning physicist Arthur Compton, college presidents Milton Eisenhower and Sarah Blanding, and liberal Methodist bishop G. Bromley Oxnam. Their staff harvested exhaustive data, and the commission generated a host of recommendations. Completed in December 1947, its report warmed to the subject under such rosy headings as Education for All, Education for Free Men, Education Adjusted to Needs, and the Social Role of Higher Education in a Democracy. The report then addressed two clusters of issues. One concerned expanding and equalizing individual opportunity for higher education and ending discrimination against prospective students based on race, creed, national origin, sex (treated only in passing), social class, or ability to pay. The commission then turned to institutional needs: the organizing, staffing, and financing of higher education, public and private, for both teaching and research.[148]

In visionary fashion, the commission championed two-year community colleges, general education in undergraduate curricula, and external support of university research. The report called for equalizing educational opportunity for all citizens regardless of income or race, and in particular for eliminating Jewish quotas at selective colleges. The report acknowledged that the dual college systems for whites and blacks in the South could not be easily conjured away; for now, the resources of the black colleges had to be enhanced and equalized. Still, the report urged colleges and universities "to act as pioneering agents of leadership against discrimination" and (by implication) to contemplate the eventual integration of colleges in the South.[149] Four of the commission members registered a brief dissent on that matter. While recognizing the idealism of their colleagues, they insisted that "the facts of history" could not be ignored: separation of the races in the South was so deep-seated that challenging segregation even in such a highly oblique fashion would be counter-productive. "We believe," wrote the four dissenters, "that pronouncements such as those of the Commission on the question of segregation jeopardize the efforts [to ameliorate the black colleges], impede progress, and threaten tragedy to the people of the South, white and Negro."[150]

Truman presumably did not expect a report so sweeping and impossible to implement. On one level *Higher Education for American Democracy* echoed the landmark reports of Truman's two presidential committees on civil rights (*To Secure These Rights* and *Freedom to Serve*). All three sought to end discrimination and promote equality of opportunity—except that desegregating higher education in the South was not part of the liberal agenda. Even the major civil rights organizations pursued that objective on the separate and more discreet track of legal challenges in the courts. Moreover, the report on higher education was too airily idealistic yet too dense to be of practical political use. Still, its data, analysis, and advocacy would be mined in the future by reformers at individual colleges, foundations, state education authorities, and federal agencies.[151]

In the event the commission's report was buried much like the far-reaching 1947 Langevin-Wallon report on transforming French education. The sprawling Zook report also aligned with arguments in the Fabian Society's concise pamphlet of 1947 on expanding university education in Britain, opening its doors to new kinds of students, and underwriting their costs—none of which were implemented in Britain's postwar moment either.[152]

The Struggle for National Health Insurance

Upon retiring as secretary of labor after Roosevelt's death, Frances Perkins exchanged letters with Justice Frankfurter. "I had, as you know, a program in mind," she wrote. "The program is almost accomplished. Everything except health insurance, dear Felix, that I had on my original list."[153] Dropped from the Social Security Act under pressure from the American Medical Association (AMA), national health insurance remained for liberals a missing limb in the New Deal welfare state. The Wagner-Murray-Dingell omnibus bill of 1943 included a call for national health insurance, but conservatives repeatedly blocked it. Small lobbying groups of heterodox physicians, medical researchers, liberal officials, and philanthropists like Mary Lasker had long backed national health care insurance. Grouped under Senator Wagner's aegis in 1944 as the Committee on the Nation's Health (CNH), they advocated that cause as well as federal support for medical research and medical education. Truman's November 1945 address to Congress added his strong support for all those goals.[154]

In early 1946, James Murray, chairman of the Senate Committee on Public Welfare, geared up to push again for prepaid national health insurance "to relieve American families of the burden of medical costs and to assure the nation-wide availability of adequate medical care." For current data on potential costs, modalities, and problems, Murray enlisted Isidore Falk, head of research and statistics in the Social Security Administration. Falk documented the economic insecurity caused by the potentially high costs of medical care and surveyed current practices in a score of countries, most of which mandated some form of government-sponsored health insurance. Like Truman and Murray, Falk called for the broadest coverage of earners and their dependents (some 80 to 90 percent of the population), along with arrangements for the neediest citizens who could not pay contributions into any new federal insurance system.[155]

Falk believed that Washington should set the system's general policies, but the actual administration should devolve to regional advisory councils made up in the main of medical professionals, which would determine how to pay health care providers. They could choose to compensate physicians by a capitation system, fees-for-services (at uniform levels for all GPs), or even a straight salary. National insurance would also cover lab services, medicines, hospitalization, dental care, and home nursing. Having tried to estimate the costs, Falk then outlined options for financing the scheme by contributory payments, by general government revenues, or a combination of both. The knottiest question concerned what amount of annual personal income might be subject to a new contributory tax for federal health insurance: should it be $3,000, now the income limit for Social Security deductions? Or $5,000, so as to incorporate more middle-class earnings? Or no limit at all, obliging wealthy citizens to support the system to the fullest extent?[156]

In the end Senator Murray could not persuade his committee to report any bill to the Senate floor, and his prospects further receded when the Republicans took control of the 80th Congress. Truman, however, did not concede defeat. In 1947 he appointed Oscar Ewing as head of the Federal Security Agency, which oversaw the Social Security Administration. One of Clark Clifford's informal band of liberal advisors, Ewing advocated federal health care insurance and held a dim view of the AMA, "which didn't want the government to have a thing to do with medicine, and opposed every bill that was introduced."[157] At Truman's request Ewing prepared a comprehensive report on the state of the nation's health, "on the possibilities for raising the health levels of the American people," and on "the most practicable methods of achieving such goals."[158]

Two developments complicated Ewing's task. The National Health Assembly that convened in May 1948 at the president's request brought 800 "professional and community leaders" to Washington to scrutinize the nation's health care. The conference underlined the shortage of medical personnel and facilities but would not endorse compulsory health insurance under Social Security. Instead it recommended an expansion of private insurance plans along with special federal aid to states for their neediest citizens.[159] Second, the current Republican chair of the Senate Committee on Public Welfare had commissioned the Brookings Institute think tank to examine the health insurance issue, and Brookings too endorsed the voluntary approach.

Senator Murray then requested Michael Davis, director of the CNH lobbying group, to assess the Brookings Institute report. Unsurprisingly, Davis concluded that the report contained a parade of dubious claims about the difficulties of creating a compulsory national insurance scheme. Davis focused on the "voluntary/compulsory" strategy recommended by Brookings: a law compelling individuals to join voluntary (i.e., private) insurance plans, similar to state requirements of drivers to purchase auto accident insurance. Davis argued that the convoluted Brookings plan would be cumbersome to administer and exorbitant in oversight costs as it placed this responsibility in private hands rather than public authority. It would also leave hanging how to deal with bad risks (i.e., very sick people) and with the needy, whom private insurance plans would not cover; the inevitable means tests for citizens left out of the private plans, moreover, "are neither politically valid nor decently humane."[160]

Ewing gamely acknowledged the opinions of the National Health Assembly and of Brookings, but like Davis he found reasons enough to argue that relying on private insurance would be a mistake. "The facts make it clear that, at a maximum, only about half the families in the US can afford even a moderately comprehensive health insurance plan, on a voluntary basis. The net result, then, would be to leave without adequate protection the very groups—those with incomes below $3,000—whose plight the Nation needs most to remedy in order to raise the country's level of health."[161] In a press conference and radio speech Truman endorsed Ewing's temperate, well-packaged, and decisive report and made national health insurance under Social Security a signature issue on the hustings.

After the Democratic victory in 1948 the AMA went into panic mode and launched an all-out drive to defeat the push by Truman, Ewing, and Senator Murray for a compulsory national health insurance plan as a leg of Social Security. The AMA vowed to expend its entire treasury in opposition, and it assessed each member $25 to enlarge its war chest. To rally public and congressional opinion, the AMA hired Whitaker and Baxter to carry their flag. Initially a West Coast public relations and advertising firm, the company had evolved as political consultants and the country's leading specialists in negative campaigning. Unlike the AMA's behind-the-scenes lobbying in 1935, the AMA's campaign in 1949–50 was clamorously public. It saturated newspapers, magazines, and radio with advertisements; enlisted sympathetic businessmen to place their own ads; and sponsored speaker's bureaus, billboards, and the like. Physicians across the country lobbied local businesses and civic leaders to contact their congressmen, and their patients found stacks of AMA pamphlets in waiting rooms with similar requests.[162]

The simple core message fashioned by Whitaker and Baxter endlessly insisted that Truman's plan was "socialized medicine," while "the Voluntary way is the American way." Their publicity raised alarms about the financial burdens and the services that might or might not be delivered by "socialized medicine," speciously implying, for example, that patients would no longer be able to choose their own doctors. The AMA's publicity and lobbying campaign exceeded those of the realtors and home builders against public housing, or of the NAM against the OPA and the full employment bill in 1946. Along with business groups, the National Federation of Women's Clubs, and the American Legion, even the National Medical Association with its 4,000 black physicians embraced the AMA's campaign. The mismatched and underfunded CNH did what it could to counter the AMA's arguments and smears, but to no avail. The battle continued into 1950 as liberals looked to the congressional election to improve their position, while the AMA kept up the pressure to prevent that outcome. In October 1950 alone the AMA spent over $1 million and recruited business allies to spend another $2 million to flood the press and air waves with ads denouncing "socialized medicine." Liberals lost ground in the election, and the AMA could claim victory.[163]

Any chance of compromise had evaporated by 1949–50. Senator Murray and Michael Davis had briefly considered the idea of a two-tiered system, with compulsory health insurance for those earning under $5,000 that left wealthier citizens free to purchase private insurance if they wished. Perhaps that half loaf might appease the AMA and allow other bills for federal support of medical education, medical research, and hospitals to go forward. The AFL president, William Green, for one, indicated that as the price for national health insurance he could accept the exemption of the highest earners "whom doctors want to retain as luxury-income, strictly private practice patients."[164]

Truman too had briefly contemplated compromise when he asked Ewing to convene the National Health Assembly. But the Southern Democrats at that point were furious with the president over the civil rights issue and seemed ready to balk at any federal initiatives on health care. Meanwhile conservatives in both parties opposed the administration's executive reorganization plan, which would have created a cabinet-level Department of Welfare almost certain to be headed by their bête noire Oscar Ewing. As Ewing recalled in an oral history, "They did not want me given a higher platform from which to argue for national health insurance." Both the Senate and House rejected the reorganization plan decisively and with it, implicitly, Ewing's health insurance plan.[165]

In keeping with his deference to congressional prerogatives, Truman did not intervene once it became clear that opinion in the 81st Congress doomed the idea of national health insurance. The proposal finally died not by a negative vote but by the stubborn inaction of Murray's own Senate Subcommittee on Health Legislation, which would not agree on any bill for health insurance under Social Security. By default that left the field clear for the private insurance companies and "voluntary" plans. The Senate went on to endorse federal funding for local public health authorities, for medical education, for medical research, and for hospital building. But the House would not support this agenda except for hospital construction, seemingly everyone's favorite form of federal expenditure for health care.[166]

Funding for hospital construction had been the modest substitute in 1935 for national health insurance under Social Security. In 1946 Congress reanimated that program with the bipartisan Hill-Burton Hospital Survey and Construction Act. The act provided federal grants and loans to the states (especially states with low per capita income) for improving and expanding community hospital facilities. Lister Hill was a New Deal, segregationist senator from Alabama, the son of a surgeon, and an astute congressional negotiator. His bill stipulated that states should fund up to but no more than 4.5 hospital beds per 1,000 population; that the hospitals could not exclude blacks unless "separate but equal facilities" were available; that states were expected to provide matching funds; and that they were to encourage their hospitals to offer free treatment for people who could not pay. But mechanisms for enforcing those requirements were at best nominal.

In 1949 the one health care bill that both houses of Congress sent to the president provided fine-tuning and additional funding for Hill-Burton. This construction (or public works) program initiated no structural changes in America's health delivery system and left doctors fully in charge of their hospitals—which is why the AMA did not oppose the bill; under Hill-Burton public aid for health care did not entail much public control. Later, however, critics would complain that Hill-Burton created a surplus of uncoordinated, ill-distributed hospital beds, and that it indirectly encouraged costly, hospital-based treatments.[167]

One last round in the battle over public health insurance lay ahead before Truman left office. Ewing and Arthur Altmeyer (head of the Social Security Administration) concluded by 1951 that the best they might achieve was a program to support health care for retired social security pensioners and their survivors, who faced the most costly medical problems. Even this scaled-back goal, however, aroused the AMA, which insisted that a better plan already existed for that population: "The American medical system, which has made this the healthiest great nation in the world." Truman convened yet another presidential commission, which proved more supportive of the AMA than of progressives. Senator Murray nonetheless introduced a bill for federal hospital insurance for the elderly, but it too went nowhere.[168]

The CNH continued its modest lobbying, incurred some blatant red-baiting, gradually wound down, and closed its doors in March 1956. As director Davis summarized: "We all believe that the Committee accomplished a good deal in national legislation relating to hospitals, research, public health and the care of persons on public assistance. Our advocacy of national health insurance helped in reducing opposition to these secondary measures. The main accomplishment, however, has been to put the idea of health insurance firmly on the administrative and political map." The CNH had also worked "to coordinate AFL and CIO policies on health matters"—a task no longer necessary with the impending merger of the two federations. Looking ahead, the question remained "What do we get for our [private] health insurance money?" Davis personally favored "comprehensive medical services and group practices," like the Health Insurance Plan in New York.[169]

As its letterhead in 1956 indicates, the CNH had been a mix of progressives and moderate allies standing up to the AMA's onslaught against "socialized medicine" and against persistent conservative opposition to expanding Social Security. As the CNH closed down, that letterhead radiates a nostalgic quality. The organization had five honorary vice presidents: George Meany, head of the AFL; Walter Reuther, head of the CIO; "Red" Methodist bishop G. B. Oxnam; Gerard Swope, president of GE in the 1930s and an exemplar of corporate liberalism; and the godmother of progressives, Eleanor Roosevelt. The board of directors included nine, presumably liberal, physicians; several veterans of organized labor; and a smattering of former New Dealers whom we have encountered, such as Sam Rosenman, Morris Cooke, farm leader J. G. Patton, and Mary D. Keyserling. Senator Wagner had died a decade earlier, but his son and namesake, now the liberal mayor of New York City, had taken his place.

Over time progressives would regroup and the AMA would become less monolithically hostile to federal support for health care. Private insurance companies retained control over health insurance, but in 1965 the enactment of

Medicare provided federal hospital and medical insurance under Social Security for men and women over sixty-five years of age—an entitlement now as indispensable and popular as Social Security retirement pensions but still a far cry from the quest of Ewing, Senator Murray, and Truman for universal national health insurance.

Conclusion: Three Scenarios, One Story?

AS THE THREE WESTERN ALLIES CROSSED the threshold of victory after profoundly different wartime experiences, their postwar moments were bound to vary as well. What, then, do the parallel accounts and comparative perspectives of this book offer? The answer begins at the point when victory first came into view. Independently from one another, progressives in the three countries held comparable values and agendas for postwar change, which they encapsulated in three manifestos: the *Common Program* of the clandestine National Council of the Resistance (CNR) in early 1944; the Labour Party manifesto for the 1945 British general election, *Let Us Face the Future;* and *The People's Program for 1944* of the CIO-PAC for the US election of November 1944. When aligned (as they have never been), these three programs—so close in time, so similar in content, so resonant with comparable aspirations—constitute a new portal into the postwar moment. This book presents the preoccupations and language of each program in its national context; recounts the ensuing struggles of progressives in Britain, France, and the US against the inertia and the conservative forces of their own societies; and examines in detail some of their achievements and failures. Domestic postwar struggles in each country form three distinct scenarios, but they constitute a single story as well, foreshadowed by the common themes in the three manifestos.

In his classic plea for comparison, the great historian Marc Bloch acknowledged that weighing commonalities and differences was "not an easily traveled road." Nor, he insisted, should comparisons be lightly undertaken:

They are valuable only when they are based upon factual studies which are detailed, critical, and well-documented. . . . [But they] will save the scholar from attributing excessive importance to local pseudo-causes and, at the same time will develop his sensitivity for specific differences. . . . More or less unconsciously every national tradition of historians has elaborated its own vocabulary . . . in which issues are problematized. Different [national] schools of historiography almost never ask the same questions.[1]

For Bloch, in sum, comparison is an antidote to parochialism and, at the extreme, to questionable civic or historiographical assumptions about national exceptionalism. But equally important, comparison helps illuminate national particularities. I have cast this book in three parallel narratives that convey the distinctiveness of each national experience in the postwar moment. But I have done so throughout in a comparative spirit, with a mind to the commonalities implicit in the three manifestos of 1944–45. In this final chapter assessing changes accomplished, fumbled, or stymied in the three nations, comparison is the priority.

Before considering the postwar moment, however, two preliminary themes in the book invite a final look. First, on what became the most urgent predicament facing the democracies after 1935: could progressives find a path for standing up to Hitler without setting off the catastrophic war that most of them dreaded? Second, could they maintain a sufficient degree of wartime unity?

Equivocal Responses to Aggressive Fascism

In the three historic democracies, the major progressive forces during the 1930s—the Labour Party, the French Socialist Party, and the Roosevelt administration—faced a common challenge as they looked beyond their own borders. After the Great War progressives nursed a visceral antiwar sentiment if not outright pacifism, but in the 1930s aggressive fascism clouded that certainty. Almost as soon as the Popular Front took power in France, for example, the Spanish Civil War revealed a fault line in Léon Blum's cabinet. Blum and his partners all sympathized with the Spanish republicans, but the cabinet split over actively aiding them. Key ministers from the Socialist and from the Radical parties believed that aid would set off an arms race likely to provoke a war with the fascist powers supporting Franco in the Spanish cockpit. To hold the Popular Front together, and despite his personal "agony," Blum agreed to nonintervention and a notional international arms embargo on both sides of the Spanish conflict. In Britain the Labour Party, a minority opposition, did not have to make a comparable decision of state. But in deference to its socialist comrades in France, Labour supported the ruling Conservatives and backed the arms embargo. In the US, FDR welcomed the policy of nonintervention and the arms embargo.

Could war be avoided as Hitler's aggressiveness mounted? The Munich crisis and its aftermath revealed the chasm in the French socialist camp between the minority of Blumist anti-appeasers ("war mongers" to their opponents) and the growing strength of the Faureist pacifist wing (ostriches to their rivals). After the Popular Front collapsed Daladier helped negotiate appeasement at Munich and then asked for a vote of confidence back home. As a minority in their parliamentary deputation, the Blumists bowed to traditional party discipline and reluctantly voted confidence on Munich. But when Daladier changed course and led France into vigorous rearmament, the Socialists seemed left behind, immobilized by the hardening schism between anti-militarists and anti-appeasers. The final denouement of that divide arguably came after the fall of France, when a large majority of socialist parliamentarians voted yes on plenary powers for Pétain in July 1940, as did a far larger majority of Radicals. Earlier, after the Nazi-Soviet pact, the French Communist Party, the third element of the Popular Front, had gone its own way, pivoted from its bellicose anti-fascism, and turned its back on the coming "imperialist war." This posture provoked government repression and drove the party underground. Thus by May 1940 the official French stand against Hitler came not from the Left but from nationalist conservatives like the new PM Paul Reynaud and his sub-cabinet appointee, General Charles de Gaulle.

In Britain, Labourites initially split much like the French socialists over how to respond to aggressive fascism. But in contrast, the balance in the Labour Party gradually swung against the pacifists and anti-militarists, the functional equivalent of the Faureists in the SFIO. Prodded by Bevin and Dalton, the party conference of 1935 forced the resignation of doctrinaire pacifist leader Lansbury. Labour MPs later denounced and voted against the Munich pact, reversed their traditional anti-military budget votes, and backed rearmament, although they drew the line at peacetime conscription. In May 1940 Labour MPs joined Tory dissidents to help bring down the reviled Chamberlain. They then joined Churchill's coalition government and helped the new PM stave off the last gasp of appeasement sentiment in his war cabinet: the possibility of a negotiated peace with Hitler under the duress of Dunkirk and the capitulation of France.

Well into his second term Roosevelt conducted foreign policy in a relative comfort zone. Although he chafed at the straitjacket of the Neutrality Acts, the president avoided confrontation with the isolationists of both parties. Behind the scenes FDR reinforced appeasement by urging Chamberlain and Hitler to negotiate an accord at Munich. But in 1940 the president began his incremental tilt toward support of Britain; asked for revision of the Neutrality Acts; and called for serious rearmament, including peacetime conscription, adopted in 1940 by a bipartisan vote in Congress. This tilt gained momentum after the fall of France, but it also drew fierce opposition from a range of isolationists. After FDR's re-election, as the latter feared, his policy crystalized into all-out support of Britain short of war, which brought lend-lease assistance and then naval escorts for merchant convoys across the Atlantic, a prelude to war with Hitler.

Domestic Unity in Wartime

Pursuit of the war against the Axis required a substantial degree of internal unity in Britain, the US, and *France Combattante*—a unity that the Nazis had long since imposed on Germany. In wartime Britain an electoral truce came first, then a coalition government in which Attlee agreed to play by Churchill's rule: "Everything for the war, whether controversial or not, and nothing controversial that is not *bona fide* needed for the war." Labour ministers led an overhaul of civil defense, mobilized workers male and female for war production with relatively little resort to compulsion, improved aspects of their treatment on the job, and infused wartime austerity with a "fair-shares" spirit. A serious political fray broke out over Labour's push to nationalize the coal mines and to impose coal rationing under wartime conditions, both of which Churchill finally rejected. And in 1943, when rank-and-file Labour MPs rebelled against their own coalition ministers to demand immediate implementation of the Beveridge Report on social insurance, they came close to fracturing their party, the coalition government, or both, but the crisis passed without such dire effects. Coalition continued to V-E Day.

In France, the small and disparate local seeds of the internal Resistance initially developed from the ground up without any semblance of coordination. A first step in unifying the internal Resistance came with the fusion of three movements in the unoccupied zone (Combat, Libération-Sud, and Franc-Tireur). In parallel fashion, militants from the communist and the non-communist factions of the CGT labor federation, which had split apart in 1939, clandestinely negotiated the Perreux Accords to reunify the CGT for the post-Liberation future. Meanwhile de Gaulle's emissary Jean Moulin worked tirelessly to create a National Council of the Resistance (CNR), an umbrella group for the internal Resistance, including the communists, which would in turn recognize de Gaulle as leader of the Resistance, internal and external. The CNR cemented a structure for coordinating the "secret army" (FFI) to support Allied forces (including Free French divisions) when they invaded France to expel the Germans. Equally important, the CNR forged a progressive Common Program for the post-Liberation era, ratified unanimously by the CNR council after debate and redrafting.

In the US, FDR avoided confrontations with Congress over most domestic issues after 1938, and when war loomed he too implicitly followed the Churchill-Attlee guideline. One potential threat to national unity arose from demands by black activists to end racial discrimination in the armed forces and in the war production industries. FDR felt it safe to disregard the first demand but established a temporary FEPC to defuse the second. As wartime economic agencies evolved, most were headed by industry executives (often "dollar-a-year-men") with no connection to the New Deal, apart from such exceptions as Chester Bowles at the OPA. At the prompting of Bowles and others, however, the president in January 1944 proposed to Congress an Economic Bill of Rights to assure "freedom from want" in America, a notion earlier heralded in FDR's war-aims ideal of the Four Freedoms. Roosevelt then put aside this vision for the postwar as he turned back to war-related matters, but the new CIO-PAC fleshed out the president's sketch for a second bill of rights in its *People's Program*, which anchored the CIO's campaign for FDR's re-election. In contrast, the president himself treated the election of 1944 as a vote on his war leadership rather than a potentially contentious battle over a postwar agenda. Implicitly Churchill would approach his bid for re-election eight months later in much the same spirit. Neither of these commanding figures, of course, would lead their nations into the postwar moment.

Into the Postwar Moment: The Economic Sphere

Progressives entered the postwar moment intent on using government to promote economic efficiency, to expand provisions for social welfare, and to advance equality alongside the individual liberties rescued from the Axis assault. The challenges of reconversion and reconstruction, however, immediately diverted progressive energies into defensive battles. The specter of an inflationary price-wage spiral loomed over all three nations: pent-up consumer demand that could not yet be satisfied, especially shortages of foods, formed one side of the problem; demands from workers for substantial wage increases and the potential for crippling strikes to secure such raises formed the other side. To combat the threat, Attlee's cabinet, Truman's administration, and France's tripartite governments—all generally well disposed to organized labor— sought to hold the line against worker demands they deemed excessive while trying to deter profiteering and the black market. As de Gaulle's first minister of the national economy in 1944–45, Pierre Mendès-France campaigned with moral zeal, on the air waves and in the halls of power, to manage food and fuel shortages, rationing, and currency problems in ways that shielded the most vulnerable citizens against the depredations of inflation and the black market. In the US a great battle for public opinion and for votes in Congress raged in 1946 over extending wartime rationing and price controls by the OPA. In Britain the Labour government not only maintained price controls but extended rationing to include even bread. Meanwhile Stafford Cripps imposed export drives that sent British manufactured goods like cars abroad in exchange for hard currency to purchase desperately scarce food, raw materials, and machinery. Inflation buffeted the three societies, but in the end their governments avoided, if barely, the severest type of wage-price inflationary spiral.

Struggles in the political, electoral, and legislative arenas of the three democracies refracted clashing economic interests—manifest in Truman's ill-fated Labor-Management Conference (November 1945) and George Bidault's National Economic Conference (July 1946). In 1945–46 big business was better organized and big labor more assertive in the US than in Britain or France, but less so in the years ahead. The steel and sugar cartels in Britain, not to mention the British Medical Association, for example, would fight the prospects of nationalization in their sectors aggressively. In France agricultural interests undermined price controls by collusion with black-market channels or by simply withholding their products from consumers to await better prices (a strategy followed by US cattlemen and meatpackers in 1946). The *patronat* (the French equivalent of the NAM) proved resilient in defending their interests as cabinets came and went.

The war production economies of Britain and the US required planning and economic mobilization on a vast scale, presumed by most corporate interests to be temporary expedients that would end with the peace. For British and American progressives, however, state intervention and "democratic planning" to promote economic efficiency remained as vital in peacetime as during the war, and France's postwar governments embraced that notion as well.

Nationalization of a few sectors, pledged in the CNR and Labour Party manifestos, proceeded apace in Britain and France. Attlee's government nationalized the Bank of England, civil aviation, coal mines, electricity, and natural gas by creating independent public corporations that sat atop regional supervisory boards. The buyout of shareholders removed the private profit motive, but the government expected those sectors to be self-sustaining and beyond political influence going forward. Labour thus rejected a statist/corporatist model or one that brought worker representation to upper management. Nationalizations could promote economies of scale and smoother labor relations (as under the Miner's Charter) but were not intended to transform the social relations of work or of consumption. And when the time neared to deal with iron and steel, the very purpose of Labour's pledge to take that industry into public ownership came under question within its own ranks, parallel to pushback from the well-organized steelmakers. After much backing-and-filling Attlee proceeded anyway. But no further nationalizations took place after his re-election in 1950, despite the vague targeting in that year's party manifesto of sugar, cement, and industrial insurance.

In France the social-Catholic MRP, in concert with its socialist and communist partners, rejected the writ of unrestrained free market economics. The tripartist governments nationalized Renault, coal, electricity, gas, and a few large banks and insurance companies, usually in some version of the independent public corporation model. While specific measures for nationalization varied in each sector, all went beyond the most modest option of simply replacing existing private boards of directors, but none went as far as control by a full-blown state bureaucracy (*étatisation*).[2] In the US, while a faction of the miner's union had advocated nationalization of the coal mines in the 1920s, public ownership was no longer a policy option by the 1940s. The lone exception was rural electrification and regional planning under the New Deal's Tennessee Valley Authority, which some progressives hoped to extend to other underdeveloped regions.

For all the dramas of nationalization in Britain and France, the broader grail of planning to promote economic modernization and increased productivity is what anchored progressive agendas in all three democracies. In Britain, for example, the Labour government supported a score of consultative Working Parties in various industries outside the nationalized sectors, reminiscent of the NRA's abortive aim to establish "voluntary" industry codes in 1933. But Labour's efforts at national planning for investment, productivity, and "manpower budgets" retained an ad hoc quality and did not settle into a durably effective institutional structure.[3] In contrast, the Monnet Commission in France, with a more limited and technocratic mandate, established significant state input on investment and modernization of heavy industry, including cement, coal, and steel. The Plan (Monnet) Commission then helped channel the disbursement of Marshall Plan aid in France, and it later facilitated Western Europe's six-nation coal and steel community (the Schuman plan), a forerunner to the European Economic Community. Arguably economic planning in France proved more successful after 1946 than did Labour's vaunted commitment to planning since the mid-thirties.[4]

With the experience of the Great Depression etched in the collective memory, progressives aggressively took up the notion of fostering full employment. If we consider aims and efforts rather than outcomes, the US was no exception in this matter. Congressional liberals, led by Senators James Murray and Robert Wagner, with Truman's backing, fought mightily to pass a full employment bill in 1946. Their bill would have affirmed the right of every able-bodied citizen to a job; mandated federal officials to study economic trends in order to anticipate recessions; and authorized planning for Keynesian-style interventions (via public works and fiscal policy) to preempt the potential effects of recessions on employment. Conservatives, supported by NAM lobbying, ultimately sank the full employment bill as well as Truman's push for a "clean" two-year extension of wartime OPA price controls. But the utterly hollow Employment Act of 1946 that Congress passed instead did include one small piece of the original proposal: a new Council of Economic Advisors attached to the White House, enjoined to issue an annual economic report. Optimistic progressives such as

Murray and Wagner claimed to see the council as a potential instrument for initiatives to sustain full employment in the future, which finally happened if only in the mid-1970s.[5]

In the United States, returning veterans loomed larger in society than their counterparts in Britain, let alone the 1.5 million dispirited French prisoners of war returning from Germany after five years of captivity and idleness. (For those soldiers liberated at last, the French government provided little more than repatriation, reception centers, modest maintenance stipends, and a new ministry in Paris.)[6] In 1944 Congress enacted the G.I. Bill of Rights, the most consequential postwar policy in the US, under conservative auspices but with progressive support: the racist committee chairman John Rankin of Mississippi steered the bill through the House, with major input in the drafting from lobbyists for the American Legion. Apart from other provisions, the G.I. Bill subsidized veterans resuming interrupted higher education, as did Britain albeit on a proportionately much smaller scale. But uniquely, the G.I. Bill also supported veterans seeking to *begin* post-secondary education, including college, graduate school, or vocational training. The expansive impact of the G.I. Bill on educational opportunity, social mobility, and home ownership (via government subsidized, low-interest bank mortgages) is justly seen as a landmark in modern American history, but typically racial discrimination was built into the architecture of the law. In the South, employees of the relevant federal and state agencies administered the G.I. Bill's education, job placement, housing, and other provisions as rigid segregationists, and they could skew or altogether nullify its benefits for black veterans in the region.

Three Versions of Postwar Politics

Commonalities in progressive goals among the three allies perforce found expression in very different political contexts. Success at the polls was necessary if not always sufficient to move decisively in either a progressive or conservative direction. In mature democracies, after all, swings of opinion were likely sooner or later to bring stalemate or reversals that made a steady course of long duration problematic.[7] In that sense the endpoint of the postwar moment lay roughly between 1948 (for France) and 1951 (for Britain and the US).

Labour's decisive victory in 1945, and the party's solid alliance with the TUC, gave Attlee's first government (1945–50) a high degree of stability as it faced the problems of reconstruction and recovery. True, the ensuing dilemmas often mired the cabinet in argument and indecision, yet only once did Attlee's leading colleagues seriously consider trying to replace him, and the PM deftly quashed that intrigue. In general, once the cabinet finally reached a consensus— such as reneging on convertibility of the pound sterling, embracing a "wages policy," devaluing the pound, going ahead with steel nationalization, cutting capital spending under financial duress, or backing Bevan's contentious approaches to public housing and to national health care—party discipline sustained those decisions. With its razor-thin majority, Attlee's second Labour government (1950–51) was far less productive. On the contrary, cabinet policy debates spawned deep conflict in the party between centrists supporting Hugh Gaitskell and leftists clustered around Nye Bevan. Neither would come to power as the Conservatives prevailed across the next decade in three successive elections.

Liberated France offered up searing dramas that its American and British allies did not experience: the street battles of the Parisian uprising; the engagements by FFI units with retreating Germans across the country; the violent settling of local scores; and the painful memories of Vichy repression and Resistance martyrdoms. After the war only France had to reestablish a new republican framework and reinstitute an electoral democracy, both of which required great expenditures of political energy.

Under de Gaulle's leadership and then without him, successive governments in 1945–47 rested on an unprecedented political configuration generated by the Resistance: tripartite coalitions of communists, socialists, and the new social-Catholic MRP. Even with fading electoral clout across those years, the socialists remained the fulcrum of tripartist governance, but the latter depended even more on the MRP's progressive leadership and on the communists' decision to act as a "party of government." As he had long promised, de Gaulle— acknowledged all around as head of the provisional government after August 1944—reestablished democracy in France with a referendum authorizing a Constituent Assembly and providing for its election in October 1945. Then, to his frustration, the parties took over, and the general brusquely removed himself from the scene three months later. The Constituent Assembly initially failed to agree on a constitutional draft acceptable to the tripartist partners; backed only by the socialists and communists, the draft was voted down in the ensuing referendum. With the election of a second Constituent Assembly, similar in political complexion to the first, however, tripartism reknit itself and reached it apogee as the three parties compromised sufficiently to produce a new constitutional draft. De Gaulle adamantly opposed that draft as well, but this time the voters approved it, even if narrowly and with a large abstention rate. By the start of 1947 France finally passed from the provisional to the constitutional.

Was de Gaulle right to disdain the Fourth Republic from its inception? Hindsight can be invoked to support his case. The failed French efforts to reconquer Vietnam (initiated by de Gaulle himself in 1945) produced a nearly fatal political impasse in 1953–54, which Mendès France managed to resolve by agreement with Hanoi. Then successive rebellions in Algeria by Arabs and by European extremists created a paralyzing crisis for Paris in 1958, which the Fourth Republic parliament exited by recalling de Gaulle to power and extinguishing itself.[8] But such later crises, which did feed off the structural weaknesses and sour political dynamics of the 1950s, have weighed too heavily in assessing tripartism's achievements in the postwar moment, not least its democratic constitutional compromise on the second try.

The Resistance had temporarily united a spectrum of French citizens ranging from communists to Catholics. With the regrouping of political forces and the consolidation of republican parties after the Liberation, the institutional force of the Resistance faded, as the major movements imploded or wound down. Part two of the CNR's Common Program provided a cement for tripartist governance, but the program's impetus for renewal dissipated after tripartism collapsed in late 1947, although Gaullists and other groups continued in their own ways to honor the Resistance in symbol and memory.[9]

It is tempting to believe that America moved in an opposite political direction from France and Britain in the postwar moment, given the fading of the New Deal after 1938, the legislative defeats of progressive initiatives in Congress in 1945–46, and the Republican sweep of Congress in the election of November 1946. On its face that mid-term election ratified a U-turn away from the domestic legacy of the New Deal, whatever FDR's achievements and ineffable evasions are reckoned to have been.[10] Yet the Republican 80th Congress produced only two major acts, both vetoed by Truman. Congress narrowly upheld his veto of a large tax cut favoring the wealthy but overrode his scathing veto of the Taft-Hartley Act, which reined in union rights even as Britain and France enhanced them. The battles were on, but as yet far from decisive.

When black activists and their liberal allies demanded a federal anti-lynching law and a permanent FEPC, Truman largely avoided confronting adamant southern opponents of such civil rights legislation. But the president executed astute flanking maneuvers with executive orders. First he appointed a presidential committee in 1946 to review the state of race relations. The committee's well-publicized report fused a surprisingly strong civil rights agenda with a compelling moral rationale. Then in 1948 Truman pledged to end discrimination in the armed forces and appointed a small committee to oversee and accelerate the Pentagon's implementation of that policy. The work of those two committees, along with an executive order against racial discrimination in the federal workforce, became foundational building blocks for future, if glacial, progress on the most besetting problem of equity in the US.

The progressive side of Truman's complex political persona dominated his re-election bid in 1948. His well-run campaign, feisty spirit, and derision of the "do-nothing" 80th Congress appealed to a wide range of voters, and the election not only gave Truman a second term but returned Democratic majorities in Congress. States' rights segregationists failed to derail the Democratic Party in most of the South, while Henry Wallace's third-party challenge on the left collapsed amid a backlash against communist influence in his campaign.

In all, then, the 1946 congressional election did not prove to be the decisive U-turn from the New Deal that it may have seemed at the time. Two responses from the British Labour Party to Truman's dramatic victory in 1948 underscore that point and deserve attention for their comparative perspective. Party headquarters at Transport House approvingly reprinted excerpts from Truman's address to Congress on January 5, 1949, after his re-election:

> We believe that our economic system should rest on a democratic foundation and that wealth should be created for the benefit of all [said the president]. . . . Our minimum wages are far too low. Small business is losing ground to growing monopoly. Our farmers still face an uncertain future. . . . Five million families are still living in slums and fire-traps. . . . Proper medical care is so expensive that it is out of reach of the great majority of our citizens. Our schools in many localities are utterly inadequate. Our democratic ideals are often thwarted by prejudice and intolerance.

The editors of Labour's monthly bulletin then commented: "We are not suggesting that Mr. Truman is a Socialist. It is precisely because he is not that his adumbration of these policies is significant. They show that the failure of capitalism to serve the common man . . . is not, after all, something we invented at Transport House to exasperate Mr. Churchill." The party's Keep Left dissidents had an emphatically positive view: "Fortunately the re-election of President Truman has shown that the American people are more progressive than most of their newspapers and Congressmen. The Fair Deal, backed by a politically conscious labour movement, is based on . . . moral principles which inspire our socialism. . . . Over a wide field the Truman Administration and the Labour Government have the same interests and ideals—and the same enemies."[11]

The grinding battles of 1945–46 resumed during Truman's second term, since new Democratic majorities in Congress did not mean liberal majorities— far from it. Under the banner of his "Fair Deal"—Truman's campaign to enhance surviving New Deal programs and enact some missing pieces—the president confronted relentless opposition from shifting cross-party alliances of conservatives. Between 1949 and 1952 he lost the big battle for national health insurance, killed thanks to the AMA's mendacious crusade against "socialized medicine." Nor did progressives manage to repeal key provisions of Taft-Hartley or to enact civil rights bills such as a federal anti-lynching law and a permanent FEPC. Other liberal causes did carry, including a delayed victory for a major public housing initiative in 1949; an enlargement of groups covered by Social Security; and long overdue increases in old-age pensions and in the federal minimum wage. The years between 1949 and 1952 also saw the gradual implementation of Truman's executive orders desegregating the armed forces and the federal workforce. Across the postwar moment in America, in other words, neither progressive advance nor conservative rollback held a definitive upper hand, although the latter's southern segregationist variant remained implacable.

Unions and Governments

In relations between political progressives and organized labor, mutual support was strongest in Britain yet not entirely without problems. The rapport between Democratic administrations and US trade unions proved bumpier than in Britain but in the end a source of strength for both sides. In France the relationship of government to trade unions hit bottom during Vichy, became mutually supportive after the Liberation, but came to a sharp parting of the ways in late 1947.

Despite limits on their freedom of action, trade unions enjoyed security and growth under the war production regimes of Britain and the US. As Churchill's minister of labor, Ernest Bevin preserved the rudiments of collective bargaining in wartime. Workers earned good overtime pay in the factories, and many saw improvements in workplace facilities. When Labour came to power, the Attlee government revoked the punitive features of the Tory Trade Unions Act of 1927 and restored automatic dues checkoffs for the party from union members. The "contentious alliance" of the party's industrial and political wings held firm, with union-sponsored MPs still a solid if proportionately smaller phalanx in Labour's parliamentary presence. The largest unions controlled the TUC's General Council, and union delegations to Labour Party conferences usually exercised a moderating bloc vote. The high point for cooperation between the party's two components came when the TUC accepted Cripps's proposal in 1948 for a "wages policy" that imposed government guidelines for negotiated wage increases to hold back inflation. Such prior restraint violated the TUC's bedrock principle of unimpeded collective bargaining, but by a narrow margin the TUC agreed to support *their* government with this concession.

The TUC of course had its fissures. Arthur Deakin, Bevin's successor as head of the huge TGWU, anchored the right wing of the Labour Party and conducted a running battle with radical shop stewards who used "smash and grab" tactics (as he put it) against management and national union officials. Within his own union Deakin faced militant dockers who ignored official hierarchies and launched crippling wildcat strikes. In the clash of the 1950s over the party's future between the leftish Bevanites and the centrist Gaitskellites, the trade union vote at conference supported Gaitskell, whom the PLP chose as party leader after Attlee stepped down in 1955. But in the 1960s the union block vote turned leftish, ceased pulling the party toward the center, and stymied Gaitskell's attempt to revoke the party's historic Clause 4 commitment to public ownership of the means of production.

Just after Pearl Harbor FDR brokered his bargain between government, big business, and big labor: the AFL and the CIO agreed to a no-strike pledge for the duration in exchange for maintenance of membership, which translated into expanding union rolls from new hires. In the war production economy corporate profits accumulated from cost-plus contracts and federal subsidies for new plants, while the unions contended with the War Labor Board's Little Steel Formula that limited wage increases. But as in Britain most workers earned good overtime pay that kept factories running around the clock. Dissidents in the CIO, especially in the UAW, saw the administration's labor policies as one sided; resisted incentive bonuses in lieu of wage increases; denounced the no-strike pledge as a form of unilateral disarmament; and rumbled about creating an independent labor party. But Phil Murray helped hold the UAW and the CIO to the no-strike pledge and to links with the Democratic Party.

After V-J Day, American workers feared that their standard of living would decline with reconversion layoffs, disappearing overtime pay, and vulnerability to rising prices. Murray and Walter Reuther made the case for substantial wage raises that corporations could fund from their accrued profits without raising prices unduly—a notion of "ability to pay" that management categorically rejected. Waves of strikes in many sectors and regions erupted across the country; strike rates and work days lost in the US proportionately far exceeded those of Britain and France in 1946. But as strikes against General Motors and US Steel idled hundreds of thousands of workers, they provoked little violence on either side of the picket lines, although strikes against General Electric brought some sharp clashes. The autoworkers, steelworkers, and electrical workers eventually settled their strikes for less than demanded, usually for an 18.5-cent hourly wage increase. But subsequent national strikes by the mine workers and the railway brotherhoods provoked bitter attacks by Truman on those unions for imperiling the nation's economy. Attlee's cabinet would later break a comparably disruptive dockers' strike by calling up troops to unload maritime cargo. But the Senate prudently blocked Truman's move to take over the railroads and draft striking workers into the army. Truman's ill-conceived response naturally infuriated organized labor, which turned on the president for a time.

Overall, however, despite frustration in the unions at the lack of unqualified support from either FDR or Truman, organized labor found allies in the White House when congressional conservatives enacted punitive labor laws. The two Democratic presidents vetoed the Smith-Connally War Labor Disputes Act of June 1943; the Case Labor Relations Bill of 1946; and the Taft-Hartley Act of 1947, although Congress overrode the first and third of those vetoes. The AFL and the CIO had backed FDR for his fourth term; notwithstanding Truman's hostile acts in 1946, his perceived political weaknesses, and his dim prospects, both federations eventually rallied to Truman in 1948 and helped him to victory. Institutionally the relationship between progressive Democrats and the trade unions had no counterpart to the Labour Party's "contentious alliance," yet functionally in the elections of the 1940s the relationship worked much the same way.

For French workers, in contrast, the war brought a stunning assault as Vichy dissolved the CGT and the small Catholic CFTC along with all republican political parties. Vichy's Charter of Labor essentially banned independent trade unionism and the right to strike, and the STO conscripted hundreds of thousands of Frenchmen for work in Germany. In 1943 the Resistance countered with a reverse image to Vichy's project: the CNR's clandestine sixteen-member council included delegates for the CGT and the CFTC[12] alongside those of eight Resistance movements and six republican "political families." CGT delegate Louis Saillant, named to the CNR's five-man bureau, succeeded Georges Bidault as CNR president after the liberation of Paris. In 1945–46 French trade unions experienced a spectacular growth in numbers, and communists soon controlled over two-thirds of the unions. In the name of national recovery, CGT unions carried a patriotic "battle for production" into coal mines, factories, and transport and joined most public sector unions in moderating wage demands. On their side the tripartist governments adhered to the CNR Common Program: they reinforced trade union rights; revamped and extended provisions for social security and national health insurance (albeit with separate *caisses* for workers, professionals, and the self-employed rather than the one universal system advocated by some); introduced elections by workers for places on their departmental social security boards; and facilitated input by workers on shop-floor issues in new *comités d'entreprise.*

Communist support for wage restraint lasted for about two years but then unraveled from the bottom up. Steadily losing ground to rising prices, dissident workers (postal employees and Renault workers, to begin with) bypassed their union leaders to mount wildcat strikes, much like the stevedores in Britain. By late 1947 the CGT changed course completely: a CGT National Strike Committee backed a wave of often violent strikes—economic at bottom but with explosive political overtones.

Communism, Organized Labor, and Political Culture

How, then, did communism affect the labor movements and, more broadly, the domestic political cultures of the three democracies? In the wake of the Bolshevik Revolution, newly minted French communists joined other radicals to oppose the CGT's reformist leadership under Léon Jouhaux. As a traditional syndicalist, Jouhaux bridled at outside interference in the CGT's affairs, and his wing of the federation pushed the radicals out in 1921, parallel to the schism in the Socialist Party at Tours that gave birth to the PCF. When the Left regrouped to form the Popular Front in 1935, Jouhaux at first resisted a return of the communist *unitaires* to the CGT. But by 1936 he agreed to head a reunited federation and led the CGT with good faith until the Nazi-Soviet pact of 1939 caused yet another rupture. (Clandestine negotiations during the occupation known as the Perreux Accords laid the groundwork for repairing that second split.)

When the CGT and the PCF changed course in fall 1947 and effectively went into opposition, a minority of non-communist comrades who had been caucusing under the banner of Force Ouvrière (FO), with Jouhaux their elder statesman, became casualties of the new militancy. The CGT's majoritarian communist leaders brushed aside FO's calls for moderation, as the CGT council condemned the Marshall Plan unreservedly and supported a violent strike wave despite the reasoned protests of the FO minority on both counts. Finally, with considerable reluctance, the FO dissidents departed from the CGT in the last days of 1947. This third twentieth-century schism in the French house of labor between communists and their adversaries produced a small but long-lived rival federation that called itself CGT-Force Ouvrière.

Across the Atlantic, the founders of the CIO had also been wary of interference in the CIO's affairs—starting with moves by the AFL to discourage their organizing drives in the mass production industries. Lewis, Hillman, Murray, and most of the original CIO movers finally bolted from the AFL in 1937 to get on with their mission and by 1938 formed a rival federation. Some of the best CIO organizers were communists, and communists and fellow travelers won the leadership of several CIO unions. A clash between Catholic CIO activists and communists waxed and waned between 1939 and 1947—a conflict that Phil Murray long and effectively mediated for the sake of CIO unity. But when the new party line from Moscow in late 1947 required CPUSA opposition to the Marshall Plan along with all-out support for Wallace's third-party movement, Murray and the CIO executive board turned decisively against the federation's communist-influenced leaders. By a vote of 31 to 11 in January 1948 the board demanded that all member unions desist from opposing the European Recovery Plan and from supporting Wallace's third party, lest it wreck Democratic electoral prospects. (The defection from the communist orbit of Joe Curran's seamen's union and Mike Quill's transport workers union exemplified the problem posed for the CIO's communists and fellow travelers by the hard line of the CPUSA under William Z. Foster.) By 1950 a major schism had sundered the CIO. The largest left-led union, the United Electrical Workers (UE), withdrew from the CIO in 1949, and the CIO executive board subsequently expelled nine smaller communist-influenced unions. Once a great asset in "organizing the unorganized," CIO communists and fellow travelers had become an albatross, which Murray and his allies would no longer abide.

As a thought experiment, one might consider the schismatic CGT-FO in France as a reverse image of the communist-influenced CIO unions in the US. Dominant in the CGT by 1946, communists increasingly dismissed the federation's democratic and syndicalist traditions, and bullied or ignored the dissenting minorities clustered in the Force-Ouvrière caucuses. Conversely, the CIO executive board demanded that member unions follow the board's majoritarian political line of early 1948. The FO adherents finally felt themselves pushed out of the CGT, just as the UE felt pushed out of the CIO. The aggressive Moscow line of fall 1947 would seem to be the common factor in the CGT and CIO schisms, which weakened the hand of organized labor in both countries.

Conflicts between communists and anti-communists in organized labor spilled over into the World Federation of Trade Unions (WFTU), the new international labor association founded in 1945. Excluded from the international organization of the interwar years, the Soviet Union was a major presence in the WFTU from the start, and for that reason the resolutely anti-communist AFL boycotted the organization. But the TUC, the CIO, and the CGT (led at that point by Jouhaux) were founding partners of the WFTU. By 1949, however, as the WFTU became a hot site for Cold War skirmishing, the CIO and the TUC bolted and helped found a rival international federation. In the rump, communist-dominated WFTU, General Secretary Louis Saillant loomed large. Once Jouhaux's disciple, and the CNR's face of progressive unity in France in 1944–46, Saillant had broken with his mentor by 1947, and as a fervent fellow traveler trumpeted the Soviet's anti-imperialist peace line in the WFTU throughout the 1950s.[13]

Domestic communism held a relatively minor place in the TUC and in British political culture. The Labour Party consistently rejected overtures for affiliation from the CPGB in the 1930s and 1940s, and scorned its subservience to

Moscow. During the Attlee years Labour expelled four hard-left or fellow-traveling MPs for their indiscipline, but the Keep Left dissidents (and later the Bevanites) had little sympathy for fellow travelers let alone the CPGB. Several trade unions did maintain a popular front atmosphere through the 1940s with a safe harbor for their valued communist comrades. But except for the sprawling miner's union, communists were evicted from most union leadership positions by the early 1950s.

After the Nazi invasion of the Soviet Union in June 1941, French communists brought an infusion of militant energy and organizing skill into the Resistance. Their momentum and influence kept growing after the Liberation, and communism became more central in the social and political landscape of France than it ever had before. For almost three years the PCF operated as a "party of government" in the postwar moment and sustained tripartism. Then the PCF ministers broke government unity in a confidence vote and socialist PM Ramadier ousted them from his cabinet in May 1947. By the fall, under Moscow's new line, the PCF went into all-out opposition. Their erstwhile partners in tripartism from the MRP and SFIO had hoped to preclude the isolation of French communists, to deter the hardening of an adversarial communist subculture. In this the socialists and social-Catholics had now utterly failed; politically unmoored, they ended up as participants in blandly centrist and unstable anti-communist, anti-Gaullist "Third Force" governments.

In the US, domestic communism (proportionately even smaller in members than the CPGB) had a vastly disproportionate impact on American political culture. Under growing assaults by HUAC, the American Legion, and Truman's loyalty review boards—with the attorney general's new list of "subversive" front organizations in hand—communists, fellow travelers, and progressive activists from many walks of life faced harassment and exclusion. Red-baiting became especially blatant in Hollywood and in the broadcasting industries with their proliferating blacklists.

American communists, however, were not simply the victims of persecution in the postwar moment. As happened during the popular front days of the mid-thirties and early forties as well, communists could disrupt progressive anti-fascist and civil rights organizations for their own purposes. Hence, for example, A. Philip Randolph's decision to break with the National Negro Congress, which he had helped found, over communist bullying in 1940, or the NAACP's long conflict with Paul Robeson. Above all, CPUSA willfulness finally split and weakened the CIO. Most dismayingly from the perspective of this book, communist tactics deeply roiled and severely weakened the progressive American Veterans Committee, as its reactionary foes could not. Yet the anti-communist backlash of the late 1940s was merely act 1. After 1950, anti-communism became an all-consuming political maelstrom with the rise of McCarthyite demagoguery and witchhunting, untethered to the reality of a shriveled communist presence in American public life.

Reflections on the Long Game

Are the progressive quests of the postwar moment still relevant in the twenty-first century? During a spirited London march against austerity and racism in July 2016, members of Momentum—a British social movement on the left flank of the Labour Party—carried placards proclaiming the rally's main themes: "FOR HEALTH, HOMES, JOBS, EDUCATION."[14] Here is a powerful piece of evidence for the persistence of issues on the progressive agendas of the 1940s. The challenges of assuring good health care for all, affordable housing, decent-paying jobs, and educational opportunity unsurprisingly resurface time and again in Britain, France, and the US in new iterations and changing contexts.

The Momentum marchers might have been unaware of how their themes echoed the call of the Beveridge Report in 1943 to face down the "five giants" or obstacles to a "comprehensive policy of social progress." In Beveridge's distinctive terminology, the obstacles to social well-being were Want (POVERTY), Disease (HEALTH), Squalor (HOMES), Idleness (JOBS), and Ignorance (EDUCATION). Beveridge's report on social insurance addressed only the problem of Want, with a comprehensive blueprint for income security: unemployment insurance, old- age and disability pensions. Across the Atlantic FDR had long believed that he provided Americans with a comparable safety net against poverty in the Social Security Act of 1935. Later, the president included freedom from want among the Four Freedoms he heralded as a moral basis for the Allied cause in World War II. After 1945 Britain's Labour government and the tripartite governments in France overtook the US by enacting new, comprehensive social security systems that incorporated child allowances and national health care.[15]

Meanwhile, the UN's Commission on Human Rights worked to universalize the norms of liberty, including freedom from want. Chaired by Eleanor Roosevelt, the commission debated several drafts and finally agreed on the text for a Universal Declaration of Human Rights, adopted in late 1948 by a General Assembly vote where the Soviet bloc abstained along with South Africa and Saudi Arabia. The Declaration's normative but nonbinding prescriptions for societies around the world incorporated basic social and economic rights (articles 22–26) along with the personal and political liberties that the Nazis had obliterated, although not the right to self-determination for colonial peoples.[16]

Momentum's slogan in 2016, which evoked four of the obstacles still blocking the path to social progress, did not specify the vexing complications of the present century piled atop traditional conservative pressures to cut back state regulatory action, to lower taxes, and to curb government spending: unprecedentedly huge income inequality;[17] unimpeded flows of capital, management strategies, and technology in businesses around the globe; resultant new kinds of structural unemployment; and the strains of immigration and of multiculturalism. But in raising four of the key issues that progressives had confronted in the 1940s, Momentum's demands implicitly addressed some of those newer complications as well.

Britain's comprehensive NHS, created after Nye Bevan's epic battle with the BMA, stood as Labour's foremost achievement in the postwar moment. Funded by general revenues, the NHS covered the entire population of citizens who chose to sign up (approximately 96 percent), nationalized both public and voluntary hospitals, and incorporated the vast majority of general practitioners and specialists into the system. Yet even before its launch in 1948 the NHS came with problems. Bevan conspicuously failed to establish the group-practice health clinics envisioned by socialist physicians as the system's capstone. Then the Attlee government qualified its pledge of comprehensively free health care with contentious proposals to charge small fees for prescriptions or for eyeglasses and dentures. Those passing episodes made virtually no dent on the development and popularity of the NHS, which successor Conservative governments in 1951–64 sustained. In the long term, however, changing political tides and anti-statist ideologies engulfed the NHS. Both Thatcher and Blair's New Labour whittled away at the growth of NHS budgets, pursued cost-shifting initiatives, and outsourced certain functions. Most visibly, underfunding of the NHS caused severe overcrowding of facilities and unendurably long waiting periods for certain treatments and surgeries. Paradoxically, perhaps, health care still led the list of issues in Momentum's rally decades later.

In France that would not be the case. The health care component of postwar social security reform combined private medical practice and government health insurance for everyone in a different way. Unlike the original NHS, funded from general revenues, postwar French health care was linked from the outset to the various social security funds (*caisses*) into which employers and employees, the self-employed, and professionals paid their contributions. These state-regulated, public insurance funds negotiated fee schedules with medical providers (often unionized) for the entire range of treatments, and they paid the bills directly to practitioners or by reimbursing patient outlays. With repeated fine-tuning over the years, this system remains notable not only for its universality, but for its transparent and low pricing, prompt reimbursements, and absence of heavy administrative costs. By most accounts, French citizens and medical practitioners alike embrace their system, which according to the World Health Organization ranks at or near the top in medical outcomes.[18] Unlike in Britain and the US, French health care is not presently in a state of crisis.

In twenty-first-century America the belief remains strong in some quarters (as proclaimed by the AMA since the 1930s) that US medicine is the best in the world. But private, profit-making insurance companies rule over US health care. Most citizens get health insurance from plans offered by employers, paid for in varying proportions by contributions from employers and employees, often with high deductibles and co-payment requirements. Patients and practitioners alike detest the administrative interference by insurance companies between patients and providers and resent the mountains of costly overhead and paperwork. For a disgracefully large swath of citizens—the uninsured and the inadequately or precariously insured—the troubles are far worse: stark limitations on access to decent health care with consequent high and unchecked rates of illness and morbidity.

The roots of this depressing exceptionalism lie in the setbacks to progressive proposals in the 1930s and 1940s, starting with the exclusion of national health insurance from the original Social Security Act of 1935 under lobbying pressure from the AMA. In 1944–45 Congress would not pass the Wagner-Murray-Dingell omnibus reform bill, with its centerpiece of national health insurance. When such advocates as Truman, Senator Murray, and Oscar Ewing revived the push for national health insurance in 1948–50, the AMA's fierce publicity campaign against "socialized medicine" buried their efforts. At the end of that prolonged losing struggle, however, liberals prioritized two limited goals for the future: federal co-funding of health care provision in the states as an entitle-ment for the neediest citizens (Medicaid), and single-payer federal health and hospital insurance under Social Security for citizens over sixty-five years of age (Medicare)—both enacted in the next progressive political wave of 1965–66. Thereafter the insurance companies successfully lobbied against any compre-hensive public insurance option let alone a national single-payer plan for health care in the mode of Medicare—all of which leaves a deep and tangled crisis in access to affordable health care today.[19]

Interwar governments in the three countries spasmodically enacted "slum clear-ance" to replace substandard housing for the working classes with low-cost public housing. Segments of all three societies, however, nursed a strong desire for home ownership. In postwar Britain Nye Bevan understood that preference but largely ignored it, as he prioritized new rental housing for the working classes. Bevan limited building licenses and access for private builders to scarce mate-rials, while overseeing construction by local authorities of low-rise semi-attached houses with small gardens. With relatively generous standards of floor space and amenities these homes met at least part of the desperate postwar need for afford-able rental housing. Bevan's restraints on private builders fell away in the 1950s under succeeding Conservative governments, even as the Tories continued to fund new public housing but shifted to a preference for high-rise tower blocks.

In the US progressives faced intense ideological opposition to public housing from associations of realtors and home builders, but the Truman administration finally won passage of a major public housing program in 1949, along with new infusions of mortgage insurance for homebuyers and a green light for bull-dozers to initiate "urban renewal" for public and private development. France delayed postwar public housing only because of more urgent priorities for reconstructing transport and aiding the war-damaged *sinistrés,* but in 1948 France too funded local authorities to construct public housing. In all three countries much of the public housing that went up in the 1950s–60s comprised high-rise buildings sterile in design and shoddy in execution; physically isolated from traditional neighborhood life; segregated by race, income or both; ineffec-tively managed (with notable exceptions); and poorly maintained for want of adequate resources going forward.[20]

Meanwhile urban and regional planners in all three countries nurtured new visions of town planning to combat urban sprawl, and to meet demands for decent housing through suburban development. With the G.I. Bill and other types of FHA mortgage insurance, the US government did the most to open new (racially segregated) paths to suburban home ownership. On the public housing front, the federal government eventually gave up on building new housing projects, and it even authorized local authorities to demolish some of the most notorious projects in cities like Chicago and St. Louis. Instead the Department of Housing tendered rent vouchers to aid needy working-class families in securing affordable housing. But this sound policy proved easy to defund when the political climate grew more aggressively conservative. Meanwhile, traditions of state and local initiative in the US persisted. New York State's exemplary Mitchell-Lama program of the 1960s–70s, for example, incentivized private developers on urban renewal sites with low-interest loans and tax abatements to construct limited-profit, means tested, rent-regulated housing for middle- and working-class households.

If we jump to the present day, the dearth of affordable housing seems worse than ever, especially in the great metropolitan areas where glaring income inequality permeates the built environment—not simply through the renovation of existing housing by new high-income residents (gentrification) but in the proliferation of luxury housing sky-high in price and design. London, Paris, New York—where millions of workers made their livings and resided for generations—are fast losing their diversity as the less wealthy are priced out of their customary neighborhoods. Assuring affordable housing is, in new contexts, as much of a challenge as in 1945.

Reconstruction needs in Britain and France, and pent-up consumer demand in all three countries, precluded mass unemployment in the postwar moment. But the specter of the Great Depression lingered vividly in the collective memory, alongside the opposite fear of runaway inflation. Commitment to "full employment" (usually defined as unemployment of no more than 5 percent) figured prominently in progressive thought in all three countries. In America, the Wagner-Murray full employment bill of 1945–46 would have proclaimed the right to a job and authorized planning for counter-cyclical government spending on public works to combat future recessions and unemployment. After major brawls, both houses of Congress defeated the bill, but in the realms of content and advocacy the bill matches anything put forward in Britain or France.

The 1950s and 1960s are remembered in Britain, France, and the US as relatively prosperous decades notable for economic growth and good (usually unionized) jobs in manufacturing, mining, construction, public services, and white-collar work. During the last quarter of the twentieth century, however, the structure of employment began to change drastically. Managements exported jobs to cheaper labor markets around the globe starting in such sectors as textiles, clothing, and footwear, moving on to consumer electronics, steel, and automobiles, and more recently to such sectors as call centers for customer service, software coding, and basic accounting. Unimpeded flows of capital across national borders sought the highest profits for investors and rewarded new styles of corporate management insensible to social contracts with their workers or communities. The resulting structural unemployment is most visible in the "rust belts" of heavy industry in the American Midwest, northern England, and Northeastern France, where some union halls have become sites of mourning for the good "middle-class" manufacturing jobs of the past (as Americans like to call them).

The fallout from these economic changes has taken an especially dismal if paradoxical turn in France. In the 1950s–70s, protective employment terms and social benefits, largely legacies of the postwar moment, became entrenched and generous for middle- and working-class people on the job. But the protected classes (including public employees, *cadres,* industrial workers, and transport workers) enjoyed their prerogatives at the expense of later cohorts vainly seeking good permanent jobs, including women, immigrants, and the younger generations. Structural unemployment in France has hovered for years at a seemingly immoveable 10 percent, while youth and young-adult unemployment remains frozen at about twice that level, with even higher rates among those of immigrant background.[21] Some in the French Socialist Party long advocated a 35-hour workweek to create more jobs by spreading the work around. Finally enacted in 2000, the 35-hour week has no doubt enhanced leisure time for the steadily employed (and with it the French sense of their unique *savoir vivre*), but little evidence suggests that the law has helped create permanent new jobs.[22]

The refractory new jobs question, different than the cascading joblessness of the Great Depression or the painful unemployment of earlier business cycles, hangs over the future in Britain, France, and the US. Angry demands to bring back decent jobs or to create new ones of similar caliber amount at the moment to little more than a cri de coeur. Construction of public works and infrastructure repair are much discussed as means to mitigate employment problems. But how are they to be paid for, when such projects cannot be easily squared with conservative demands for reducing public debt, cutting taxes, and reining in government spending?

Conservatives and "neo-liberals" call for deregulating business and finance as much as possible so as to unleash the potential of private enterprise large and small to create jobs. Progressives counter by advocating substantially higher minimum wages, but they must fight off the unproven claim that high minimum wages or guaranteed employee benefits are "job killers." Another much-touted form of palliation is to retrain the casualties of job losses in new skills for new types of jobs. But experience suggests that vocational retraining sometimes (often?) becomes a state-funded boondoggle for the providers of such services, with scant long-term advantage to many hapless trainees.[23] For future generations, hope for decent jobs might depend on better literacy and digital skills from more effective secondary education, or on making post-secondary education affordable to all who seek it: two immense challenges, which bring us to Momentum's final rubric.

In Britain and France the school leaving age, finally raised to fourteen before the war, still doomed the mass of children to enter adulthood without veritable secondary education. The postwar governments, while ready to raise that threshold further, could not agree on a model to promote educational opportunity for children of varied abilities and interests alongside existing paths to higher education or remunerative careers. Defenders of the *lycées* and *collèges* in France and of the comparable Grammar schools in Britain—where curricula usually featured the teaching of Latin—stymied visions for more inclusive types of secondary schools.[24] In France during the Popular Front, Education Minister Jean Zay proposed in vain a new system for continuous tiers of primary, middle, and secondary schooling to promote social mobility and educational opportunity. With painstaking attention to detail, the postwar Langevin-Wallon Commission revivified Zay's model, but its report of 1947 got shunted aside as well, a counterpart, one might say, to the Wagner-Murray full employment bill as an unfulfilled progressive benchmark. Progress in French educational reform began only after 1959 under de Gaulle's Fifth Republic.

In Britain members of the Labour Party split between partisans of multilateral or comprehensive high schools and supporters of the Grammar schools (which some Labourites had attended, usually on scholarships, and fondly recalled). Comprehensives gained ground in Britain only because control over educational policy devolved onto the 150-odd Local Education Authorities, which could experiment with local options. But LEAs that retained their Grammar schools instead of folding them into new comprehensives had to establish manifestly inferior Secondary Moderns to accommodate most other students. The challenge of structuring secondary education in Britain lasted long into the twentieth century with ongoing battles over comprehensives versus Grammars, and over the rigid streaming of the 11+ exam.

In the US the states and counties shared control over secondary education. The normative school leaving age had reached sixteen by the 1940s, and the nineteenth-century democratic ideal of the "common school" had migrated to high schools as well. In the South and border states, needless to say, any such evolution came with rigid racial segregation at all levels, unmodified until the 1960s.[25]

Higher education commanded the most attention in the US postwar moment, while only rattling on the progressive fringes in Britain and France. The flood of American veterans starting college with benefits from the G.I. Bill enlarged paths for social and economic mobility. Truman's Commission on Higher Education advocated a permanent expansion of higher education, reforms in its quality, enhancement of its variety, and promotion of equality in educational opportunity regardless of race, creed, ethnicity, gender, or ability to pay. But like the Langevin-Wallon Report in France, the report of Truman's commission went nowhere. In Britain higher education scarcely appeared on the Attlee government's radar. The Fabian Society, however, tried to nudge the Labour government with a forceful, fact-filled brief for expanding university education in Britain, opening its doors to new kinds of students, and underwriting their costs. Only in later decades, however, did Britain and France open new university campuses and expand older ones, perhaps under the influence of American higher education.

In the US of the late 1950s and 1960s federal aid for research, and strong support in most states for their own public universities, drove the expansion of higher education. No other state quite duplicated California's master plan, with its three tiers of local two-year community colleges, four-year state colleges, and research universities, which grew in number from the original two at Berkeley and UCLA to eight. But many states adopted that model to one degree or another and created a great boom for higher education in the 1960s for potential students and faculty alike.

If we jump to the twenty-first century we find an extremely troubled landscape in higher education on at least two fronts. First there is the crisis in affordability for students. In Britain and the US, reduced funding of higher education at the national and local levels, despite escalating costs in the 1980s to 1990s, has spurred a great surge in tuition rates at public institutions as well as private ones, and a consequent cost-shifting to student borrowing that lumbers countless students with unsustainable debts. (One symptom of the cost squeeze in all three nations is the way their universities chase after full-paying foreign students.) A potential crisis of viability also afflicts higher education in the three nations: what should be the veritable purposes of higher education in a world of mutating occupational structures? What pedagogical innovations can meet the needs of today's students? (One symptom of this preoccupation: the rise of private, for-profit institutions focused entirely, and often fraudulently, on vocational objectives, whose customers too are eligible for large student loans.) To put it differently, how can new vocational imperatives be fused with the best intellectual traditions of teaching and scholarship, if they can be at all?[26]

In the three historic democracies there have been many way stations and influences in the trajectories of progressive forces. During the early twentieth century the Labour Party emerged as the chief rival of Britain's Conservatives; the Popular Front rekindled the egalitarian tradition of the French Revolution without its violence; and in the US, FDR harvested diffuse progressive impulses for reform into the sustained experimentation of the New Deal. I have argued here for assigning a prominent place in progressive lineages to the postwar moment, not simply for Britain (where the case is obvious after the election of 1945) but for France and the US as well. I have documented and assessed the achievements of those years as well as the failed efforts, some of which at least left markers for future struggles.

Progressive social movements and politicians have resisted dogmas about the supremacy of individual interests and the unalloyed virtues of free markets. They have responded as advocates for the commonweal's general interests, and for society's vulnerable and disfavored citizens. Perhaps the core aspirational value in the progressive camps can be called "social solidarity." True, that ideal is inherently unstable and problematic. The notion of interconnectedness is always subject to disruption from contradictory pressures—social, economic, cultural, ethnic, or religious. We have seen how competing claims stymied progressives during the postwar moment—as in clashes between blacks and whites in some CIO unions; in arguments over comprehensives versus

Grammars in Britain and over the role of traditional *lycées* in France; in desires for home ownership versus desperate working-class needs for affordable rentals; in conflicts over the potential inflationary impact of higher wages reasonably demanded by workers. The list can go on. But overall, political leaders like Clement Attlee, Vincent Auriol, and Harry Truman—not to mention men like Nye Bevan, Pierre Mendès France, or Phil Murray[27]—usually articulated their beliefs in a spirit of social solidarity and tried to act on them during the postwar moment despite the obstacles and the odds.

ACKNOWLEDGMENTS

IN THE EARLIEST STAGES OF THIS PROJECT, encouragement from colleagues was singularly important. For I was leaving behind decades of research, writing, and professional camaraderie in the fields of eighteenth-century history, the French Revolution, and the Napoleonic era. I first tested the waters in 2004 with an undergraduate seminar at Columbia called "From War to Peace: Britain and France in the 1940s," although I intended my research to cover the three historic democracies ultimately victorious against the Nazis. The responses of colleagues with whom I first discussed this project, among others Alan Brinkley, Susan Pedersen, Kim Munholland, and Robert Dallek, proved reassuring.

With the advice of two veteran bookmen, Donald Lamm and John Wright, I eventually drafted a prospectus with two purposes: to crystalize my thinking into a detailed and feasible outline, and then to obtain a publisher's commitment. Chris Rogers, at that time executive editor at Yale University Press, signed up the book and offered sound advice for its progress. While the book took far longer to complete than either of us anticipated, I produced a complete first draft in 2016. Chris having by then retired, my new editor, Adina Berk, insisted that I cut the manuscript substantially and make its arguments more explicit. For this apt response I am grateful to Adina, and the book is more reader-friendly for her counsel. In the round of revision that followed I had the inestimably effective aid of my wife, Nancy Woloch, who had recently published a prize-winning book of her own, who made countless suggestions for cutting and improving my manuscript.

At various points along the way my Columbia colleagues Ira Katznelson and Vicki de Grazia offered strong encouragement, as did the late American labor historian Judith Stein. Geoffrey Field read a first draft of my British chapters and provided extraordinarily useful suggestions. Two college classmates became surrogates for the general readers I hope to reach. Joe Krieger (a physicist) read several chapters and urged me on with his sustained interest. Ira Jolles (a lawyer) heard me out over lunch on many occasions and thus helped me clarify my arguments. My son David Woloch (a public policy official in New York City) did the same, while my son Alex Woloch (an English professor in California) read various chapters at long distance and gave me valuable reactions.

I presented an overview of "Three Progressive Visions" in several venues: a lecture at the annual meeting of Britain's Society for French History in 2012, whose hosts at York University I thank; the Intellectual and Cultural History Seminar at CUNY organized by Jerrold Seigel and Richard Wollin; and the Workshop on 20th Century Society and Politics at Columbia, convened by Ira Katznelson and Adam Tooze. I submitted a draft of my last French chapter to the NYC Area Workshop on French History (organized by Jeff Horn), where the comments by such twentieth-century experts as Herrick Chapman, David Schalk, and Irwin Wall were supportive as well as insightful.

Two librarians at Columbia, Jean LaPonce and Bob Scott, offered vital assistance as did administrators at Sciences Po in Paris, which in the early 2000s controlled access to the papers of the MRP in the Archives Nationales. I also thank the editors of *French History* in Britain, who published my paper on the MRP between 1944 and 1948, which I then drew on for the book. At the far end of this odyssey I worked to maximize the value of the illustrations for the book, with the skillful assistance of Suzie Tibor, who tracked down variant images, and secured the requisite permissions and high-res images. For spot-on copyediting I thank Eliza Childs, and for managing production issues, Margaret Otzel.

Finally, to bring things full circle, I offer a dedication of sorts to the five veterans of my extended family who fought in World War II, all as it happens in the European theater. I was too young to register their departures but old enough to appreciate their returns in 1945, for all had survived. My uncle Milton Kramer (whom I knew best) served in the Army Air Force ground crew for the entirety of the war, from North Africa to Sicily and through the Italian campaign. He returned to civilian life with relish, was active in a veterans organization for several years, and over the decades attended his unit's reunions. My uncle Raymond Woloch and second cousin Bernie Kaplan were both in the Army signal corps; Raymond ended up in General Bradley's command unit. Those three were the lucky ones. Somewhat younger, my cousin-in-law Dan Levine and my second cousin Eli Kramer were assigned to the infantry pools that funneled replacements into depleted units after the D-Day invasion. In keeping with the odds stacked against such green infantrymen, both were grievously wounded during the Allied pursuit of the Nazis across France and Germany. Dan finally emerged from the military hospitals severely hobbled by permanent injuries. Eli was advancing atop a tank when both his arms were mangled by a direct hit. Like sailor Harold Russell in *The Best Years of Our Lives,* Eli ended up as one of the rare bilateral hand amputees in the American armed forces. A high-spirited youth when he entered the army, his personality remained unbroken, and it was Eli who comforted his shaken kin back home rather than the other way around.

New York City
November 2017

NOTES

Abbreviations Used in Notes

A.N.	Archives Nationales (Paris)
B.F.O.	British Foreign Office series (online): "Conditions and Politics in Occupied Western Europe 1940–45": France
CU Oral History	Columbia University Oral History Collections
DHFDR	*Documentary History of the Franklin D. Roosevelt Presidency,* (ed.) George McJimsey (Bethesda MD: University Publications of America, 2001–), 43 vols.
DHTP	*Documentary History of the Truman Presidency,* (ed.) Dennis Merrill (Bethesda MD: University Publications of America, 1995–), 35 vols.
FACT	new title for *Labour Party Bulletin,* Vols. VII–VIII (1949–50)
Free France	Free French Press and Information Service, NYC, 1942–45
LC	Library of Congress, Manuscript Division
LPB	*Labour Party Bulletin,* Vols. V–VI (1946–48)
Wieviorka, *Oral Histories*	Olivier Wieviorka (ed.), *Nous Entrerons dans la Carrière: De la Résistance à l'Exercice du Pouvoir* (Paris, 1994)

Prologue

1. A.N. 72 AJ 64, doss. MRP: "Projet d'introduction à une Action Révolutionnaire des Jeunes Français," typescript by Gilbert Dru of the MRL [mid-1944].
2. H. Noguères, *Histoire de la Résistance en France* (Paris, 1981), V: 185, 330–31. Also J.-M. Domenach, *Gilbert Dru, celui que croyait au ciel* (Paris, 1947).
3. A.N. 72 AJ 64: "Paris Est Libre" (MRL handbill).
4. C. Bolté, *The New Veteran* (NY, 1945), chs. 1–4, 6–7; Gilbert Harrison Papers, LC: Box 2.
5. D. Healey, *The Time of My Life* (London, 1989), chs. 2–3; also K. Morgan, *Labour People, Leaders and Lieutenants, Hardie to Kinnock* (Oxford, 1987), 313–16.

Chapter 1. Labour's Long Apprenticeship

1. See T. Wright and M. Carter, *The People's Party: The History of the Labour Party* (London, 1997), chs. 1–2, and D. Tanner, P. Thane, and N. Tiratsoo (eds.), *Labour's First Century* (Cambridge, 2000).

2. M. Worley (ed.), *Labour's Grass Roots: Essays on the Activities of Local Labour Parties and Members, 1918–45* (Burlington VT, 2005), chs. 1, 2, 7, 10, 12; Worley, *Labour inside the Gate: A History of the British Labour Party between the Wars* (NY, 2005), ch. 1; on the ILP's disaffiliation, 142–44.

3. A. J. P. Taylor, *English History, 1914–1945* (Oxford, 1965), 125–29.

4. J. Lovell and B. C. Roberts, *A Short History of the T.U.C.* (London, 1968), chs. 4–6; L. Minkin, *The Contentious Alliance: Trade Unions and the Labour Party* (Edinburgh, 1991), part 1.

5. P. Renshaw, "The Depression Years, 1918–31," in B. Pimlott and C. Cook (eds.), *Trade Unions in British Politics: The First 250 Years* (London, 1991).

6. Alan Bullock, *Ernest Bevin: A Biography,* abr. edn., ed. B. Brivati (2002), chs. 5–7; Lovell and Roberts, *Short History of the T.U.C.,* chs. 5–6; Renshaw, "Depression Years."

7. Tanner, Thane, and Tiratsoo, *Labour's First Century,* 395.

8. Besides Bullock's indispensable biography, see J. T. Murphy, *Labour's Big Three* (London, 1948), chs. 3, 12.

9. Bullock, *Ernest Bevin,* 138–39 on Transport House.

10. See D. Marquand, *Ramsay MacDonald* (London, 1977); K. Morgan, *Labour People: Leaders and Lieutenants, Hardie to Kinnock* (Oxford, 1987), 39–53.

11. Wright and Carter, *People's Party,* 54–60; Morgan, *Labour People,* "The Planners," 107–18.

12. P. Seyd, *The Rise and Fall of the Labour Left* (London, 1987), table 3.2: Total Individual Party Membership (1928–1985). The threshold for affiliation for a party branch was 250 members.

13. M. Worley (ed.), *Labour's Grass Roots,* 4–27, 118, 253–4; S.Fielding, P. Thompson, and N. Tiratsoo, *England Arise! The Labour Party and Popular Politics in 1940s Britain* (Manchester, 1995), 8–11.

14. Marquand, *MacDonald,* 668–70, 779–81.

15. Worley, *Labour inside the Gate,* ch. 3.

16. L. Beers, *Your Britain: Media and the Making of the Labour Party* (Cambridge MA, 2010), 142–43, 148–49, 158–59, 189–94.

17. E. Hughes, *Sydney Silverman: Rebel in Parliament* (London, 1969), 8–14.

18. B. Pimlott (ed.), *The Political Diary of Hugh Dalton, 1918–40, 1945–60* (London, 1986), 196.

19. M. Ceadel, *Semi-detached Idealists: The British Peace Movement and International Relations* (NY, 2000), 318–19.

20. P. Clarke, *The Cripps Version: The Life of Sir Stafford Cripps* (London, 2002), 62, 64; *Dalton Political Diary,* 181 (19 Jan 1934).

21. Quoted in H. Winkler, *British Labour Seeks a Foreign Policy, 1900–1940* (New Brunswick NJ, 2005), 176 n35.

22. See B. Pimlott, *Labour and the Left in the 1930s* (Cambridge, 1977), part 4.

23. Winkler, *British Labour,* 121–22.

24. *Dalton Political Diary,* 200; B. Pimlott, *Hugh Dalton* (London, 1985), 235.

25. K. Harris, *Attlee* (London, 1982), 152–55; Winkler, *British Labour,* 135–38; Hughes, *Sydney Silverman,* 64. On Lansbury, M. Ceadel, *Pacifism in Britain, 1914–1945* (Oxford, 1980), 278.

26. Pimlott, *Labour and the Left,* 143–53; J. Campbell, *Nye Bevan and the Mirage of British Socialism* (London, 1987), ch. 6; Clarke, *Cripps Version,* 73–81. Bevan soon sought and was granted readmission.

27. Hughes, *Sydney Silverman,* 64–75.

28. Left-wing publisher Victor Gollancz published the book by Michael Foot et al. in July 1940 and reprinted it in 1945 for the general election. (See J. Lewis, *The Left Book Club* [London, 1970], 125.) By then, Conservatives countered with Tory MP Quintin Hogg, *The Left Was Never Right* (London, 1945), esp. chs. 7–9, which attacked Labour contortions over foreign policy, rearmament and conscription in the 1930s.

29. Fielding, Thompson, and Tiratsoo, *"England Arise!,"* ch. 3; S. Brooke, *Labour's War: The Labour Party and the Second World War* (Oxford, 1992), ch. 2.

30. A. Calder, *The People's War: Britain, 1939–1945* (London, 1969), ch. 2; R. Mackay, *Half the Battle: Civilian Morale in Britain during the Second World War* (Manchester, 2002), 46–50; G. Field, *Blood, Sweat, and Toil: Remaking the British Working Class, 1939–1945* (Oxford, 2011), 10–24, 33–36.

31. G. Stewart, *Burying Caesar: Churchill, Chamberlain and the Battle for the Tory Party* (London, 1999), 404–20; Taylor, *English History, 1914–1945,* 472–75; Harris, *Attlee,* 172–78.

32. See A. Roberts, "The Tories versus Churchill during the 'Finest Hour,'" in his *Eminent Churchillians* (London, 1994).

33. Labour Party Conference, 1940, 123–25.

34. Stewart, *Burying Caesar,* 421–36, esp. 432; J. Lukacs, *Five Days in London, May 1940* (New Haven CT, 1999), chs. 2–4.

35. N. Harman, *Dunkirk: The Patriotic Myth* (NY, 1980), 9–13.

36. J. B. Priestley, *Postscripts* (London, 1940), 3–4; Harman, *Dunkirk,* 164–65.

37. See V. Brome, *J. B. Priestley* (London, 1988), 241–76; J. Cook, *Priestley* (London, 1997), chs. 20–21; A. Calder, *The Myth of the Blitz* (London, 1991), 196–204.

38. Priestley, *Postscripts,* 33, 35, 46.

39. Ibid., 36–7, 80, 90. Cf. A. Aldgate and J. Richards, *Britain Can Take It: The British Cinema in the Second World War* (Oxford, 1986), 225–28, and P. Stansky and W. Abrahams, *London's Burning: Life, Death and Art in the Second World War* (Stanford CA, 1994), 122, on the comparable "robust Socialist patriotism" of filmmaker Humphrey Jennings and writer George Orwell.

40. Priestley, *Postscripts,* 96–100.

41. Cook, *Priestley,* 188–89; Brome, *Priestley,* 250–52; A. Briggs, *The War of Words,* Vol. III of *The History of Broadcasting in the United Kingdom* (Oxford, 1995 edn.), 192–94, 292–94, 540–41.

42. See J. M. Lee, *The Churchill Coalition, 1940–1945* (London, 1980), chs. 1–2, 4.

43. I. McLaine, *Ministry of Morale: Home Front Morale and the Ministry of Information in World War II* (London, 1979), chs. 2–5; M. Yass, *This Is Your War: Home Front Propaganda in the Second World War* (London, 1983).

44. See P. Stansky, *The First Day of the Blitz, September 7, 1940* (New Haven CT, 2007).

45. Quoted in Stansky and Abrahams, *London's Burning,* 50.

46. B. Donoughue and G. W. Jones, *Herbert Morrison: Portrait of a Politician* (London, 1973), ch. 20.

47. P. Ziegler, *London at War, 1935–1945* (NY, 1995), chs. 6–10; Tom Harrisson, *Living through the Blitz* (NY, 1976), ch. 5; Calder, *People's War,* ch. 4; R. Mackay, *The Test of War: Inside Britain, 1939–1945* (London, 1999), 123–36; Field, *Blood, Sweat, and Toil,* 57–70, on sheltering in the tubes.

48. Broadcast of Nov 3, 1940, in Morrison, *Prospects and Policies* (NY, 1944), 152–57.

49. Donoughue and Jones, *Herbert Morrison,* ch. 21.

50. B. D. Vernon, *Ellen Wilkinson, 1891–1947* (London, 1982), 186–88; M. Perry, *"Red Ellen" Wilkinson: Her Ideas, Movement and World* (Manchester, 2014), 355–61.

51. See Harrisson, *Living through the Blitz,* chs. 6–7.

52. Stansky and Abrahams, *London's Burning,* part 2; Aldgate and Richards, *Britain Can Take It,* 225–28; Calder, *Myth of the Blitz,* ch. 11. The film was completed in 1942.

53. Morrison, New Year's Eve broadcast 1941, in *Prospects and Policies;* Mackay, *Test of War,* 129–31; Donoughue and Jones, *Herbert Morrison,* 293–96, 307; Vernon, *Ellen Wilkinson,* 189–90.

54. S. Spender, *Citizens in War and After* (with 48 color photographs by John Hinde) (London, 1945), 15 and passim.

55. Morrison, *Prospects and Policies,* 170.

56. Bullock, *Bevin,* chs. 11–12, 14; Field, *Blood, Sweat, and Toil,* ch. 3, esp. 119–23.

57. D. Barnes and E. Reid, "A New Relationship: Trade Unions in the Second World War," in Pimlott and Cook, *Trade Unions in British Politics,* 137–55; H. Pelling, *A History of British Trade Unionism,* 3rd edn. (London, 1976), 303–4.

58. Bullock, *Bevin,* 258–9; 290–91, 317–18.

59. Barnes and Reid, "New Relationship," 146–47; Mackay, *Test of War,* 205–6.

60. Field, *Blood, Sweat, and Toil,* 129–31, 139–55; Bullock, *Bevin,* 276–77; Calder, *People's War,* 116, 235–36.

61. Bullock, *Bevin,* 295; R. Taylor, *The Trade Union Question in British Politics: Government and Unions since 1945* (Oxford, 1993), ch. 1.

62. H. L. Smith (ed.), *Britain in the Second World War: A Social History* (Manchester, 1996), ch. 4; Field, *Blood, Sweat, and Toil,* 101–4; Barnes and Reid, "New Relationship," 147–49; Campbell, *Nye Bevan,* 132–34.

63. H. Nicholson, *The War Years, 1939–1945:* Vol. II of *Diaries and Letters,* ed. N. Nicholson (NY, 1967), 231–32; E. Shinwell, *I've Lived through It All* (London, 1973), 175.

64. Taylor, *English History,* 649–50; Clarke, *Cripps Version,* 342–70; Pimlott, *Dalton,* 348–49.

65. Bullock, *Bevin,* 303–5.

66. P. Addison, *The Road to 1945: British Politics and the Second World War* (London, 1975; 2nd edn., 1994), 253–54.

67. K. Jefferys (ed.), *Labour and the Wartime Coalition: From the Diary of James Chuter Ede, 1941–1945* (London, 1987) (hereafter *Ede Diary*), 28, 105; H. Morrison, *An Autobiography* (London, 1960), 230; on the Tories, Addison, *Road to 1945,* 229–35.

68. S. Brooke, *Labour's War,* 59–72; *Ede Diary,* 75; Shinwell, *I've Lived Through It All,* 174; Fielding, Thompson, and Tiratsoo, *"England Arise!,"* ch. 3.

69. *Ede Diary,* 135–36, 29, 33, 35, 61, 135; Brooke, *Labour's War,* 72–79.
70. Nicholson, *War Years,* 192 (Dec 4, 1941).
71. B. Pimlott (ed.), *The Second World War Diary of Hugh Dalton, 1940–45* (London, 1986) (hereafter *Dalton Wartime Diary*), 423, 432 (May 6 and 12, 1942); Pimlott, *Dalton,* 354; *Ede Diary,* 71–73.
72. *Dalton Wartime Diary,* 433–37, 444–45, 450–51.
73. Pimlott, *Dalton,* 354–56.
74. Lee, *Churchill Coalition,* 109; Pimlott, *Dalton,* 358; Brooke, *Labour's War,* 80–88.
75. *Ede Diary,* 107, 113, 118–19; Calder, *People's War,* 353–54.
76. See the indispensable José Harris, *William Beveridge: A Biography* (Oxford, 1977; 2nd edn., 1997), chs. 16–17; N. Timmins, *The Five Giants: a Biography of the Welfare State* (London, 1995), part 1; Addison, *Road to 1945,* ch. 8; Calder, *People's War,* 525–32; Mackay, *Half the Battle,* 231–40; McLaine, *Ministry of Morale,* 181–85.
77. *Social Insurance and Allied Services: Report by Sir William Beveridge* (American edition reproduced photographically from the English edition) (NY, 1942), 6–7, 11.
78. Ibid., 153–72. In 1944 Beveridge produced an unofficial report to promote full employment, which he had addressed earlier in a comparison of social security in Britain and America: "Social Security: Some Trans-Atlantic Comparisons," *Journal of the Royal Statistical Society,* CVI (1943), 312–16.
79. See Churchill's mulish "Promises about Post-War Conditions," Jan 12, 1943, in K. Jeffreys (ed.), *War and Reform: British Politics During the Second World War* (Manchester, 1994), 97–8.
80. *Dalton Wartime Diary,* 553. Cf. Addison, *Road to 1945,* 233.
81. *Ede Diary,* 119n.
82. *Dalton Wartime Diary,* 553–54, 558; *Ede Diary,* 120; Nicholson, *War Years,* 281–82.
83. *Ede Diary,* 121–22, 124; *Dalton Wartime Diary,* 555.
84. *Dalton Wartime Diary,* 554–55, 560–61; *Ede Diary,* 122–24, 126.
85. Morrison, *Autobiography,* 230.
86. On education, see Brooke, *Labour's War,* 187–201, and the discussion below in chapter 7.
87. S. Pedersen, *Family, Dependence, and the Origins of the Welfare State: Britain and France, 1914–1945* (Cambridge, 1993), 208–19, 326–36.
88. Ibid., 336–56. (The average weekly wage for men was 121 shillings in 1945, p. 345.)
89. Paul Addison's influential *The Road to 1945* made the case for a new mood of consensus during the war, spanning reform elements of the Conservative Party and the mainstream of Labour. But in light of subsequent political battles, others have plausibly treated this notion of a new consensus as something of a myth. See H. Jones and M. Kandiah (eds.), *The Myth of Consensus: New Views on British History, 1945–64* (NY, 1996).
90. Brooke, *Labour's War,* chs. 4–5.

Chapter 2. The Travails of the French Left

1. See J. Merriman, "Contested Freedoms in the French Revolutions, 1830–1871," in I. Woloch (ed.), *Revolution and the Meanings of Freedom in the Nineteenth Century* (Stanford CA, 1996), 173–211; W. H. Sewell, Jr., *Work and Revolution in France: The Language of Labor from the Old Regime to 1848* (Cambridge, 1980), chs. 9–12.

2. M. Dreyfus, *Histoire de la C.G.T.: Cent ans de syndicalisme en France* (Brussels, 1995), 37–75; R. Magraw, *Workers and the Bourgeois Republic* (Cambridge MA, 1992).

3. B. George, D. Tinant, and M.-A. Renauld, *Léon Jouhaux dans le mouvement syndical français* (Paris, 1979).

4. D. Ligou, *Historie du Socialisme en France, 1871–1961* (Paris, 1962), part 2; G. Lefranc, *Le Mouvement Socialiste sous la troisième république*, Vol. I (Paris, 1963–77).

5. C.-E. Labrousse, "Preface: Le Socialisme et la Révolution française," in J. Jaurès, *Histoire Socialiste de la Révolution français*, Vol. I (Paris, 1969 edn.), 9–34.

6. See R. Kedward, *France and the French: A Modern History* (NY, 2006), 59–61.

7. Dreyfus, *CGT,* 77–112; Magraw, *Workers,* ch. 4.

8. S. Courtois and M. Lazar, *Histoire du Parti communiste français* (Paris, 1995), 50–67.

9. Ligou, *Socialisme,* 321.

10. Reprinted in A. Kriegel (ed.), *Le Congrès de Tours, 1920: Naissance du Parti communiste français* (Paris, 1964), 249–53.

11. R. Wohl, *French Communism in the Making, 1914–1924* (Stanford CA, 1966), 180–3, 188.

12. The text in Kriegel, *Congrès de Tours,* 140–41.

13. Full text in Kriegel, 101–36; excerpts in J. Lacouture, *Léon Blum* (trans. G. Holoch, NY, 1982), 131–44.

14. Dreyfus, *CGT,* 113–26; Wohl, *French Communism,* 236–44; Magraw, *Workers,* 191–94.

15. Dreyfus, *CGT,* 121–26; Wohl, *French Communism,* 279–84. Organized labor further fragmented with the formation in 1919 of the CFTC, a small Catholic trade union federation.

16. P. J. Larmour, *The French Radical Party in the 1930's* (Stanford CA, 1964), chs. 1–2, 4; S. Hoffmann, "Paradoxes of the French Political Community," *In Search of France* (NY, 1963), 3–34.

17. A. Cole and P. Campbell, *French Electoral Systems and Elections since 1789* (Brookfield VT, 1989), ch. 4. By the eve of the 1936 election, the SFIO deputation was down to 97, primarily because of the defection/expulsion of the "neo-socialists," discussed below.

18. E. Weber, *The Hollow Years: France in the 1930s* (NY, 1994), esp. chs. 1, 5, 9.

19. Blum, "La Déviation Néo-Socialiste," *L'Oeuvre de Léon Blum* (Paris, 1954–), Vol. 1928–34: 543–81; Weber, *Hollow Years,* 116–17; J. Colton, *Léon Blum: Humanist in Politics* (NY, 1966), 85–87; J. Moch, *Une si longue vie* (Paris, 1976), 98; Georges et al., *Léon Jouhaux,* 32–43.

20. *New York Times* and *The Times* (London), Feb 7, 1934; Weber, *Hollow Years,* 127–41.

21. See B. Jenkins, "The Six Février 1934 and the 'Survival' of the French Republic," *French History,* XX (Sep 2006), 333–51.

22. A. Prost, "Les Manifestations du 12 février 1934 en province," in J. Bouvier (ed.), *La France en mouvement, 1934–1938* (Paris, 1986), 12–30.

23. Courtois and Lazar, *Histoire du PCF,* 118–20; Georges et al., *Léon Jouhaux,* 123n.

24. Dreyfus, *CGT,* 150–62; Georges et al., *Léon Jouhaux,* 111–57.

25. See M. Cachin, M. Thorez, and A. Marty, *The People's Front in France* (NY, 1935), a pamphlet rushed into translation.

26. "Le Pacte d'Unité d'Action" (Jul 1934); "Plate-forme d'action commune du PS et du PC" (Sep 1935); and "Le Programme du Rassemblement Populaire" (Jan 1936), reprinted in Blum, *L'Oeuvre,* Vol. 1934–37: 222–29.

27. See J. Touchard and L. Bodin, "L'État d'opinion au début de l'année 1936," and R. Rémond and J. Bourdin, "Les Forces adverses," in P. Renouvin and R. Rémond (eds.), *Léon Blum, chef de gouvernement, 1936–1937* (Paris, 1967/1981), 49–68, 137–59.

28. Blum, *L'Oeuvre,* 234–44.

29. On first/second round electoral dynamics, see A. Bleton-Ruget, "Comportements et espaces électoraux: L'exemple du département de la Saône-et-Loire, 1906–1956," in Bleton-Rouget and S. Wolikow (eds.), *Voter et élire à l'époque contemporaine* (Dijon, 1999), 168–70.

30. See Blum's retrospective essay "Exercice et conquête du pouvoir" (Nov 1947), in *L'Oeuvre,* Vol. 1945–47: 427–37; and Colton, *Blum,* 71–73.

31. J. Jackson, *The Popular Front in France: Defending Democracy, 1934–38* (Cambridge, 1988), 85–104; Bouvier (ed.), *La France en mouvement,* 62–112; G. Lefranc, *Histoire du Front Populaire, 1934–1938* (Paris, 1965), 139–80.

32. See N. Greene, *Crisis and Decline: The French Socialist Party in the Popular Front Era* (Ithaca NY, 1969), chs. 2–3; Larmour, *Radical Party,* part 2; and especially S. Berstein, "Le Parti radical-socialiste, arbitre du jeu politique français," in R. Rémond and J. Bourdin (eds.), *La France et les Français en 1938 et 1939* (Paris, 1978), 275–306.

33. K. Mouré, "'Une Eventualité Absolument Exclue': French Reluctance to Devalue, 1933–1936," *French Historical Studies,* XV (Spring 1988), 495–505.

34. I. Wall, "The Resignation of the First Popular Front Government of Léon Blum, June 1937," *French Historical Studies,* VI (Fall 1970), 544–45.

35. J. Moch, *Rencontres avec Léon Blum* (Paris, 1970), 234–38.

36. Ibid., 238–41; G. Lefranc, *Histoire du Front Populaire,* 255–82; Lacouture, *Blum,* 378–90; and especially J. Laniel, *Jours de Gloire et Jours Cruels, 1908–1958* (Paris, 1971), 96–97, who mentions G. Mandel and L. Jacquinot as receptive to Blum's idea.

37. Jackson, *Popular Front,* 162–63, 175–77.

38. Ibid., 212. Cf. Berstein, "Le Parti radical-socialiste."

39. M. Bilis, *Socialistes et Pacifistes: L'intenable dilemme des socialistes français, 1933–1939* (Paris, 1979), 173–96.

40. Cited in Lacouture, *Blum,* 310.

41. Lacouture, *Blum,* 305–35, 349–58; Colton, *Blum,* ch. 8.

42. Jackson, *Popular Front,* 205–7.

43. See R. Gombin, "Socialisme et pacifisme," in *La France en 1938–1939,* 245–60; Bilis, *Socialistes et Pacifistes,* 79–98 on Faure.

44. Jackson, *Popular Front,* 195–98, 201, drawing on the work of R. J. Young.

45. Greene, *Crisis and Decline,* 216–24; Billis, *Socialistes et Pacifistes,* 246–47, 256–57.

46. Blum, *L'Oeuvre,* Vol. 1937–40: 220–21.

47. There is no record of the voting in the caucus, but Greene plausibly identifies 86 socialist deputies who supported Faure (including Gouin and Spinasse) and 29 who supported Blum's anti-appeasement position (including Auriol, Moch, and Philip): *Crisis and Decline,* 244–45n.

48. Moch, *Rencontres avec Blum,* 250–52.

49. Dormoy, Nov 3, 1938, cited by Greene, *Crisis and Decline,* 232.

50. Ibid., 240–51; B. D. Graham, *Choice and Democratic Order: The French Socialist Party, 1937–1950* (Cambridge, 1994), 224–42.

51. B. Singer, "From Patriots to Pacifists: The French Primary School Teachers, 1880–1940," *Journal of Contemporary History,* XII (Jul 1977), 424–27.

52. Greene, *Crisis and Decline,* 259–72; Graham, *Choice and Democratic Order,* 235–42; Ligou, *Socialisme,* 242–55. The small band of Bataille Socialiste militants balked at the synthesis motion.

53. See R. Rémond and J. Bourdin (eds.), *Eduard Daladier, chef de gouvernement* (Paris, 1977).

54. Courtois and Lazar, *Histoire du PCF,* 167–72.

55. *Strange Defeat,* Marc Bloch's influential eyewitness account (published posthumously in 1948), described the demoralizing atmosphere at the front in 1939–40, and the sclerotic qualities of the French military establishment, but also the will to fight and the expectation of victory among many Frenchmen. Recent studies include E. R. May, *Strange Victory: Hitler's Conquest of France* (NY, 2001), 3–12, 449–84; J. Jackson, *The Fall of France: the Nazi Invasion of 1940* (Oxford, 2003), ch. 5; and J. Blatt (ed.), *The French Defeat of 1940: Reassessments* (Providence RI, 1998).

56. Jackson, *Fall of France,* 226–27.

57. Moch, *Rencontres avec Blum,* 262n, 265–70.

58. Jackson, *Fall of France,* ch. 3, esp. 138–42; J.-P. Azéma, *From Munich to the Liberation, 1938–1944* (Cambridge, 1979/1984 transl.) ch. 2.

59. See R. Paxton, *Vichy France: Old Guard and New Order, 1940–1944* (NY, 1972), ch. 1.

60. See Colton, *Blum,* ch. 13.

61. Moch, *Rencontres avec Blum,* 271–73; Blum *L'Oeuvre,* Vol. 1940–45: Mémoires (Fragments), written in captivity after his arrest in September and devoted to the events of 1940.

62. N. Castagnez, *Socialistes en République: Les parlementaires SFIO de la IVe République* (Rennes, 2004), 27–32; Moch, *Rencontres avec Blum,* 275–76 and n. For a list of the eighty: D. Mayer, *Les Socialistes dans la Résistance* (Paris, 1968), 174–75.

63. G. LeBéguec and E. Duhamel (eds.), *La Reconstruction du Parti Radical, 1944–1948* (Paris, 1993), 17–21.

64. Socialists voting no who became prominent in post-Liberation politics included Auriol, Blum, Gouin, Moch, Moutet, Philip, Ramadier, and Tanguy Prigent; Marx Dormoy was assassinated in late 1940. Prominent Radical resistors included Bastid, Mendès France, and Zay from the *Massilia* contingent. (Zay and the conservative Mandel, both Jews, were murdered in 1944.) The behavior of parliamentarians before and after the armistice, and their postwar fates, is analyzed comprehensively by O. Wieviorka, *Orphans of the Republic: The Nation's Legislators in Vichy France* (Cambridge MA, 2009 transl.).

65. P. H. Teitgen, *Faites entrer le témoin suivant, 1940–1958: De la Résistance à la Ve République* (Rennes, 1988) (hereafter Teitgen, *Memoirs*), 16–25; A. Philip, "Resistance," in *France and Britain,* no. 11 (Aug 1942).

66. See M. Viorst, *Hostile Allies: FDR and Charles de Gaulle* (NY, 1965). Also Henri de Kerillis, the maverick anti-Munich conservative, *I Accuse de Gaulle* (NY, 1946 transl.).

67. See F. Kersaudy, *Churchill and de Gaulle* (London, 1981), and J. Lacouture, *De Gaulle: The Rebel, 1890–1944* (NY, 1990 transl.), part 3.

68. The indispensable history of Free France is J.-L. Crémieux-Brilhac, *La France Libre: De l'appel du 18 Juin à la Libération* (Paris, 1996). This historian-witness, an escaped

prisoner of war, made his way to England and served as secretary of Free France's propaganda committee.

69. Crémieux-Brilhac, *La France Libre,* 195–98.

70. Ibid., 198–210; Lacouture, *De Gaulle: The Rebel,* 308–19; J. Jackson, *France: The Dark Years, 1940–1944* (Oxford, 2001), ch. 16.

71. Following Philippe Burrin's pioneering work, R. Gildea, *Marianne in Chains: Daily Life in the Heart of France during the German Occupation* (NY, 2003) and R. Vinen, *Unfree French* (New Haven CT, 2006) emphasize this theme in their exemplary studies.

72. C. Michelet, *Mon Père Edmond Michelet* (Paris, 1981), 63–86.

73. *Conseils à l'occupé* reprinted in Mayer, *Socialistes dans la Résistance,* 177–80; M. Sadoun, *Les Socialistes sous l'occuption: Résistance et collaboration* (Paris, 1982), 126–29.

74. See H. R. Kedward, *Resistance in Vichy France: A Study of Ideas and Motivation in the Southern Zone, 1940–1942* (Oxford, 1978), ch. 6; H. Frenay, *The Night Will End* (NY, 1973/ 1976 transl); and the memoirs of Teitgen, C. Michelet, and Claude Bourdet. Emmanuel d'Astier, the founder of Libération (Sud), had been a right-wing activist in his younger days, but he had swung sharply leftward by 1940. In the occupied zone conservative nationalists dominated the major Resistance groups, apart from Libération (Nord).

75. Courtois and Lazar, *Histoire du PCF,* 179–85; J. Fauvet, *Histoire du Parti communiste français,* 2nd edn. (Paris, 1977), 281–334; J. Sweets, *The Politics of Resistance in France, 1940–1944: A History of the Mouvements Unis de la Résistance* (Dekalb IL, 1976), ch. 4; Gildea, *Marianne in Chains,* ch. 10.

76. Colton, *Blum,* chs. 14–15; Lacouture, *Blum,* part 3; Blum, *L'Oeuvre,* Vol. 1940–43.

77. Sadoun, *Socialistes sous l'occupation,* ch. 2; Paxton, *Vichy France,* 276–79.

78. Mayer, *Socialistes dans la Résistance,* 22, 66–68, and Document XI, 195.

79. "French Socialist Policy," *France and Britain,* no. 11 (Aug 1942), published in London by French exiles of the Groupe Jean Jaurès.

80. MUR letter to the CAS, Apr 15, 1944, cited in Sweets, *Politics of Resistance,* 169–70.

81. Compare *France and Britain,* no. 1 (Fall 1940), and no. 7 (Dec 1941); A. Philip, "Resistance," ibid., Nov 1942; "Rapport de Félix Gouin à Léon Blum" (Oct 1942), in Mayer, *Socialistes dans la Résistance,* 201–10.

82. Mayer, *Socialistes dans la Résistance,* 74–110; Sadoun, *Socialistes sous l'occupation,* 184–88.

83. D. Cordier, *Jean Moulin: La République des Catacombes* (Paris, 1999), 81–157, and A. Clinton, *Jean Moulin, 1899–1943: The French Resistance and the Republic* (Basingstoke, 2002), chs. 8–9. Cordier was an aide to Moulin in London and had access to important documents.

84. See Sweets, *Politics of Resistance,* ch. 2; Clinton, *Moulin,* ch. 9.

85. R. Dallek, *Franklin D. Roosevelt and American Foreign Policy, 1932–1945* (NY, 1979), 362–66, 376–79. See also W. L. Langer, *Our Vichy Gamble* (NY, 1947/1966), chs. 7–10, and Viorst, *Hostile Allies,* chs. 5–8.

86. De Gaulle declared his democratic intentions in March 1942 to Christian Pineau, a trade-unionist leader of Libération (Nord), who would shortly return to France. See Lacouture, *De Gaulle: The Rebel,* 381–83.

87. C. Bourdet, *L'Aventure incertaine: De la Résistance à la Restauration* (Paris, 1975), 205.

88. Ibid., 215–18; H. Noguères, *Histoire de la Résistance en France de 1940 à 1945*, Vol. III (Paris, 1967), 171–77; R. Hostache, *Le Général de Gaulle, Jean Moulin et la Création du C.N.R.* (Paris, 1989), chs. 4 and 7; Sweets, *Politics of Resistance*, ch. 5.

89. Mayer, *Socialistes dans la Résistance*, 62–73; "Socialism Underground: The Need for Political Parties," *France and Britain*, Mar 1943.

90. See J. Debû-Bridel, *De Gaulle et le Conseil National de la Résistance* (Paris, 1978), 20–22; Bourdet, *L'Aventure incertaine*, 212–15; Cordier, *Moulin*, 214–66, 301–6, 365–87; "Temoignage de Pierre Meunier," in *Jean Moulin et le Conseil National de la Résistance* (Colloque de l'Institut d'Histoire du Temps Présent, 1983), 66–68; Clinton, *Moulin*, 163–67. On Brossolette, see G. Piketty, *Pierre Brossolette: Un héros de la Résistance* (Paris, 1998).

91. Cordier, *Moulin*, 378–87; Crémieux-Brilhac, *France Libre*, 532–34; Hostache, *De Gaulle et le CNR*, ch. 7; Courtois and Lazar, *Histoire du PCF*, 188–96.

92. These two suggestive modifiers come from Moulin (see appendix 2 in *Jean Moulin et le CNR* [Colloque], 184); Cordier, *Moulin*, 387–401; Crémieux-Brilhac, *France Libre*, 534–44; Hostache, *De Gaulle et le CNR*, 183–200.

93. Debû-Bridel, *De Gaulle et le CNR*, 27–39, and Courtois and Lazar, *Histoire du PCF*, 191.

94. J.-C. Demory, *Georges Bidault, 1899–1983* (Paris, 1995), chs. 5–8.

95. See D. DeBellescize, *Les Neuf sages de la Résistance: Le Conseil Général d'Etudes dans la clandestinité* (1979); the overview by A. Shennan, *Rethinking France: Plans for Renewal, 1940–1946* (Oxford, 1989), part 1; and the *cahiers* of the OCM republished after the Liberation by Blocq-Mascart in *Chroniques de la Résistance* (1945).

96. The invaluable monograph of Claire Andrieu, *Le Programme Commun de la Résistance: Des idées dans la guerre* (Paris, 1984) reproduces six successive proposals along with the final version.

97. Ibid., 83–96.

98. Ibid., "Texte définitive," 172–75.

99. Ibid., 41–42. In fact only Joseph Laniel persisted in opposition past this first canvass. Conservative Louis Marin's odd choice for a surrogate on the CNR was Jacques Debû-Bridel, who by 1943 had swung sharply leftward and would edit the Front National's newspaper after the Liberation. (See Debû-Bridel, *De Gaulle et le CNR*, 23–25, 75–98.)

100. J.-J. Becker, "Le PCF," and S. Berstein, "La SFIO," in C. Andrieu, L. LeVan, and A. Prost (eds.), *Les Nationalisations de la Libération: De l'utopie au compromis* (Paris, 1987).

101. The OCM's position paper on the planned economy took a more reserved line, which the CNR's final phrasing could nonetheless accommodate. "Le secteur dirigé (plutôt que nationalisé)" would include "les enterprises auxquelles l'Etat imposera ses directeurs en plus de ses directives." The organization of such enterprises could take various forms, ranging from a state monopoly "fonctionnarisé" to "des formes plus souples," the latter being preferable in the OCM's eyes. *Chroniques de la Résistance*, 309–26, esp. p. 318.

102. Andrieu, *Programme Commun*, ch. 2.

103. On the COMAC, see Hostache, *De Gaulle et le CNR*, ch. 11.

104. For the Vichy administration and its collapse in the Loire region, see Gildea, *Marianne in Chains*, chs. 7, 12–14.

105. Lacouture, *De Gaulle: The Rebel*, 518–27; Crémieux-Brilhac, *France Libre*, chs. 35–36. For de Gaulle's speech, J.-L. Crémieux-Brilhac (ed.), *Ici Londres: Les voix de la liberté, 1940–1944*, 5 vols. (Paris, 1975–76), V: 47–48.

106. See Crémieux-Brilhac (ed.), *Ici Londres*, V: 32–35 and 41–44 ("messages d'alerte" of Jun 1 and "messages d'exécution" of Jun 5).

107. G. Bolloré [Bollinger], *Commando de la France Libre: Normandie 6 Juin 1944* (1983).

108. Crémieux-Brilhac, *France Libre*, ch. 39.

109. See Y. Farge, *Rebelles, soldats et citoyens: Carnet d'un Commissaire de la République* (Paris, 1946), on the departments around Lyon, and F.-L. Closon, *Commissaire de la République du Général De Gaulle: Lille, Septembre 1944–Mars 1946* (Paris, 1980). For overviews, see Azéma, *From Munich to the Liberation*, ch., 6, and Jackson, *Dark Years*, chs. 22–23.

110. J.-P. Rioux, *The Fourth Republic, 1944–1958* (Cambridge, 1987 transl.), 43–48.

Chapter 3. The Roosevelt Era

1. R. Zieger, *The CIO, 1935–1955* (Chapel Hill NC, 1995), 9–12.

2. G. Gerstle, *American Crucible: Race and Nation in the Twentieth Century* (Princeton NJ, 2001), chs. 2–3.

3. See Burton K. Wheeler, *Yankee from the West* (NY, 1962), 296.

4. D. Kennedy, *Freedom from Fear: the American People in Depression and War, 1929–1945* (Oxford, 1999), chs. 2–3.

5. J. E. Smith, *FDR* (NY, 2007), 250–51.

6. See F. Friedel, *F.D.R. and the South* (Baton Rouge LA, 1965).

7. Smith, *FDR*, 275–77; Kennedy, *Freedom from Fear*, 96–98.

8. Smith, *FDR*, 292–95.

9. Ickes, for example, sought Frankfurter's advice for appointments to his Interior Department's legal staff (J. N. Clarke, *Roosevelt's Warrior: Harold L. Ickes and the New Deal* [Baltimore, 1996], 40).

10. A. M. Schlesinger, Jr., *The Age of Roosevelt*, Vol. II: *The Coming of the New Deal* (Boston, 1958), prologue, esp. 20–21. Fine books on the Hundred Days by J. Alter, A. J. Badger, and A. Cohen appeared in 2007–8.

11. Wheeler, *Yankee from the West*, 314.

12. K. Davis, *FDR: The New Deal Years, 1933–1937* (NY, 1986), chs. 6–7; Schlesinger, *Coming of the New Deal*, chs. 4, 22.

13. F. Perkins, *The Roosevelt I Knew* (NY, 1946), 192–99.

14. Schlesinger, *Coming of the New Deal*, 110.

15. J. J. Huthmacher, *Senator Robert Wagner and the Rise of Urban Liberalism* (NY, 1968), ch. 9, esp. pp. 143–51.

16. Schlesinger, *Coming of the New Deal*, chs. 6–10; Davis, FDR: The *New Deal Years*, ch. 7; Perkins, *Roosevelt I Knew*, 200–201.

17. H. Ickes, "Public Welfare: Projects of Reconstruction," in *The Federal Government Today: A Survey of Recent Innovations and Renovations* (NY, 1938), 25–27; Perkins, *Roosevelt I Knew,* 269–76.

18. The FDIC insured bank accounts; FERA, the new federal relief agency, will be discussed below; the National Youth Administration (NYA) provided assistance for youths; the Civilian Conservation Corps (CCC) established "boot camps" where youths worked on forestry and conservation projects.

19. A. M. Schlesinger, Jr., *Age of Roosevelt,* Vol. III: *The Politics of Upheaval* (Boston, 1960), part 1; Kennedy, *Freedom from Fear,* ch. 8; Davis, FDR: The *New Deal Years,* ch. 10.

20. "Cradle to grave" is often ascribed to the Beveridge Report, but the text did not use that phrase. When FDR read of the Beveridge Plan in 1943 he asked: "Why does he get credit for this cradle to grave insurance? It is my idea. . . . It is the Roosevelt Plan." See Perkins, *Roosevelt I Knew,* 278–84.

21. Ibid., 286–91.

22. A. J. Altmeyer, "Social Security: Insurance against Economic Hazards," in *Federal Government Today* (1938), 32–33.

23. The CES (permanently) deferred consideration of its "tentative proposals" to set standards for health insurance plans and to offer subsidies to states that sponsored them, until the CES staff and "the technical experts of the AMA" could undertake a "cooperative study." (*Report to the President of the Committee on Economic Security* [Washington DC, 1935], 41–43.) Congress later filled in some of the blank space with subsidies to states for building hospitals. See P. Starr, *The Social Transformation of American Medicine* (NY, 1982), 266–79.

24. G. T. McJimsey (ed.), *Documentary History of the Franklin D. Roosevelt Presidency* (Bethesda MD, 2001–) (hereafter DHFDR), Vol. V: Social Security: signing statement by FDR.

25. See A. Altmeyer, "Social Security," 31–36.

26. DHFDR, V: Vincent Miles speech; Chamber of Commerce pamphlet for employers, Sep 1935.

27. Beveridge reflected on the New Deal's Social Security Act in Beveridge, "Social Security: Some Trans-Atlantic Comparisons," *Journal of the Royal Statistical Society,* CVI (1943), 305–21.

28. For sharp criticisms, see M. Leff, "Taxing the 'Forgotten Man': the Politics of Social Security Finance in the New Deal," *Journal of American History,* LXX (Sep 1983), 359–81.

29. Lump sums went to workers who retired at age 65 before annuity payouts were to begin in 1942.

30. Speeches by John Winant and Vincent Miles in DHFDR, V.

31. Altmeyer, "Social Security," 34–35.

32. Charles Wyzanski of the Labor Department, one of the act's principal architects, rationalized these exclusions on the grounds of administrative difficulties.

33. I. Katznelson, *When Affirmative Action Was White: An Untold History of Racial Inequality in Twentieth-Century America* (NY, 2005), 42–50. Also H. Sitkoff, *A New Deal for Blacks: The Emergence of Civil Rights as a National Issue* (NY, 1978), 52, 74.

34. H. Hopkins, *Spending to Save* (NY, 1936), 108–17.

35. DHFDR, XXX [CWA]: planning memos, Docs. 6–7, and Doc. 16: "Proceedings of General Meeting," Nov 15, 1933.

36. Ibid.: Mayflower Conference Minutes: Doc. 16.

37. Hopkins, *Spending to Save,* 113–14, 120–21.

38. DHFDR, XXX: Doc. 22: Conference on Emergency Needs of Women, Nov 20, 1933; S. Ware, *Beyond Suffrage: Women in the New Deal* (Cambridge MA, 1981), ch. 5.

39. DHFDR, XXX: Doc. 122: Relief Census of Oct 1933. On the relief rolls in 79 cities in 1934, 20 percent of recipients were blacks and 25 percent women (Hopkins, *Spending to Save,* 160–61).

40. DHFDR, XXX: Doc. 16: Mayflower Conference; Doc. 39: CWA staff meeting, Dec 6, 1933.

41. Ibid.: Docs. 75 and 90: Douglas to FDR, Jan 24, 1934; NY Governor Lehman to FDR, Jan 17, 1934; FDR to Lehman, Feb 10, 1934.

42. R. Sherwood, *Roosevelt and Hopkins: An Intimate History* (NY, 1950), 65–66; Kennedy, *Freedom from Fear,* ch. 9. A FERA report of Jun 26, 1934, showed about 4.5 million families on state relief rolls; 47 percent of the relief dossiers opened in April were ex-CWA workers. (DHFDR, XXX: Doc. 122.)

43. G. McJimsey, *Harry Hopkins: Ally of the Poor and Defender of Democracy* (Cambridge MA, 1987), ch. 5; Clarke, *Harold L. Ickes,* 138–45; Sherwood, *Roosevelt and Hopkins,* 68–71.

44. Hopkins, *Spending to Save,* 168–75.

45. Ibid., 115.

46. See S. Quinn, *Furious Improvisation: How the WPA and a Cast of Thousands Made High Art out of Desperate Times* (NY 2008), chs. 5, 14–17.

47. Perkins, *Roosevelt I Knew,* 188–89.

48. Fireside Chat, Jul 24, 1933.

49. DHFDR, VIII: Doc. 333.

50. J. Auerbach, *Law and Liberty: The La Follette Committee and the New Deal* (Indianapolis, 1966), ch. 5, esp. p. 101.

51. Huthmacher, *Wagner,* 189–98.

52. Katznelson, *When Affirmative Action Was White,* 55–61.

53. D. Brody, "The Emergence of Mass Production Unionism" [1964], in Brody, *Workers in Industrial America: Essays on the Twentieth Century Struggle* (NY, 1993), 106–11.

54. C. Phelan, "William Green and the Ideal of Christian Cooperation," in M. Dubofsky and W. Van Tine (eds.), *Labor Leaders in America* (Urbana IL, 1987).

55. D. Brody, "Mass Production Unionism"; J. Brophy, *A Miner's Life* (Madison WI, 1964), 244–52; W. Galenson, *The CIO Challenge to the AFL: A History of the American Labor Movement, 1935–1941* (Cambridge MA, 1960), ch. 1.

56. Dubofsky and Van Tine, "John L. Lewis and the Triumph of Mass-Production Unionism," in *Labor Leaders in America;* Brophy, *Miner's Life,* ch. 13; S. Fraser, *Labor Will Rule: Sidney Hillman and the Rise of American Labor* (NY, 1991), chs. 8–11.

57. Zieger, *CIO,* ch. 2.

58. Ibid., ch. 3; Brody, "Mass Production Unionism."

59. A languishing AFL craft union (the Amalgamated Iron and Steel Workers) was down to a few thousand members by 1936, when it "authorized" SWOC to organize the industry.

60. R. Filippelli, "The History Is Missing, Almost: Philip Murray, the Steelworkers, and the Historians," in P. Clark et al. (eds.), *Forging a Union of Steel: Philip Murray, SWOC, and the United Steelworkers* (Ithaca NY, 1987), 1–12.

61. D. J. McDonald, *Union Man* (NY, 1969), 91–101, 104. McDonald was a UMW aide to Murray, who appointed him secretary-treasurer of SWOC.

62. Ibid., 102–4; D. Brody, "The Origins of Modern Steel Unionism: The SWOC Era," and M. Dubofsky, "Labor's Odd Couple: Philip Murray and John L. Lewis," in Clark et al. (eds.), *Forging a Union of Steel*, 13–44.

63. Auerbach, *La Follette*, 138, 121–28, 135–37; McDonald, *Union Man*, 104–19.

64. McDonald, *Union Man*, 121–22, 143–44.

65. Brody, "Origins of Modern Steel Unionism"; McDonald, *Union Man*, 145–47; Galenson, *CIO Challenge*, ch. 2.

66. See C. Johnson, *Maurice Sugar: Law, Labor, and the Left in Detroit, 1912–1950* (Detroit, 1988), chs. 5–6.

67. On Pressman, M. Kempton, *Part of Our Time: Some Ruins and Monuments of the Thirties* (NY, 1955/1998), 59–60. State legislatures began passing anti-sit-down laws in 1937, and in 1939 the Supreme Court's *Fansteel* decision overturned an NLRB finding and declared that the sit-down "was an illegal seizure of the buildings" (Galenson, *CIO Challenge*, 143–48).

68. N. Lichtenstein, *Walter Reuther: The Most Dangerous Man in Detroit* (Urbana IL, 1995), chs. 4–5; Zieger, *CIO*, 46–54; Johnson, *Maurice Sugar*, chs. 6–7; Brophy, *Miner's Life*, 269–72.

69. Lichtenstein, *Reuther*, chs. 6–7; Johnson, *Maurice Sugar*, ch. 8; Zieger, *CIO*, 97–100; Fraser, *Hillman*, 417–20.

70. W. Leuchtenburg, "The Election of 1936," in his *The FDR Years: On Roosevelt and His Legacy* (NY, 1995).

71. See N. Woloch, *A Class by Herself: Protective Laws for Women Workers, 1890s–1990s* (Princeton, 2015), chs. 2–5. The major exception was *Muller v. Oregon* (1908), which the court upheld.

72. W. E. Leuchtenburg, *The Supreme Court Reborn: The Constitutional Revolution in the Age of Roosevelt* (NY, 1995), ch. 4; K. S. Davis, *FDR: Into the Storm, 1937–1940* (NY, 1993), chs. 1–3.

73. Wheeler, *Yankee from the West*, ch. 15; Clarke, *Roosevelt's Warrior*, ch. 12; radio addresses by Senator Green (R.I.) and Senator Guffey (Pa.) in DHFDR, I ["Packing" the Supreme Court]: 476–80, 687–94; Huthmacher, *Wagner*, 221–24.

74. Explanations of Roberts's switch reflect contrasting scholarly perspectives on US constitutional history, labeled for convenience "internalist" (doctrinal shifts in court thinking) and "externalist" (the impact of political contexts on court decisions). See "AHR Forum: The Debate Over the Constitutional Revolution of 1937," in *American Historical Review*, CX (Oct 2005), 1046–1115, with a fine centerpiece article by L. Kalman and comments by A. Brinkley, W. Leuchtenburg, and G. E. White.

75. Leuchtenburg, *Supreme Court Reborn*, ch. 5.

76. See J. T. Patterson, *Congressional Conservatism and the New Deal: The Growth of the Conservative Coalition in Congress, 1933–1939* (Lexington KY, 1967), chs. 1–6. In 1938 conservatives killed FDR's proposal for reorganizing and expanding the executive branch.

77. DHFDR, XXVI [Response to Recession 1937–38]: Doc. 50: Keynes to FDR (Feb 1, 1938); Doc. 56: US Conference of Mayors (Apr 8, 1938) recommending a WPA appropriation of $3 billion to combat resurgent unemployment.

78. Ibid.: Docs. 57, 59, 79, 81: Drafts of FDR's radio address, Apr 12, 14, and Jun 24, 1938.

79. Davis, *FDR: Into the Storm*, 255–65, 277–95, 351–64; Leuchtenburg, *Franklin D. Roosevelt*, 271–74; Patterson, *Congressional Conservatism*, 250–91; and R. Polenberg, "The Decline of the New Deal, 1937–1940," in J. Braeman, R. Bremner, and D. Brody (eds.), *The New Deal: The National Level* (Columbus OH, 1975), 246–66.

80. See R. Dallek, *Franklin D. Roosevelt and American Foreign Policy, 1932–1945* (NY, 1979), part 2: "The Internationalist as Isolationist, 1935–1938"; J. Doenecke and M. Stoler (eds.), *Debating Franklin D. Roosevelt's Foreign Policies, 1933–1945* (Lanham MD, 2005), 5–43, 113–45.

81. Davis, *FDR: Into the Storm*, 15–16.

82. Text in Doenecke and Stoler, 100–03.

83. DHFDR, XXIV [The Czech Crisis, 1938]: Docs. 97–98, 125, 192, 197–98, 201.

84. Dallek, *FDR and Foreign Policy*, 181–82; Davis, *FDR: Into the Storm*, 402–11.

85. See M. Jonas, *Isolationism in America, 1935–1941* (Ithaca NY, 1966).

86. DHFDR, IV [Neutrality, 1939], Doc. 141: "Three Fallacies" (draft of undelivered radio address).

87. See S. Casey, *Cautious Crusade: Franklin D. Roosevelt, American Public Opinion, and the War against Nazi Germany* (Oxford, 2001), ch. 1.

88. McJimsey, *Harry Hopkins*, 119–31.

89. DHFDR, XIII [Election of 1940]: Doc. 24: Ickes to FDR, Jul 16, 1940.

90. On Wallace's capitulation to traditionalists in the Agriculture Department in 1935 and the ouster of the AAA's left-wing general counsel Jerome Frank and his aides, see *The Diary of Rexford G. Tugwell*, (ed.) M. V. Namorato (NY, 1992), 198–217; Kempton, *Part of Our Time*, 55–58; Davis, *FDR: The New Deal Years*, 475–81.

91. DHFDR, XIII: Doc. 28: report on the convention by Paul Wickard.

92. FDR worried that Hitler would demand that France turn its fleet over to Germany, but the Führer did not push the French into that "nightmare" scenario. See W. Langer, *Our Vichy Gamble*, ch. 1; Davis, *FDR: Into the Storm*, 556–61; Lacouture, *De Gaulle: The Rebel*, 199.

93. N. Moss, *Nineteen Weeks: America, Britain, and the Fateful Summer of 1940* (NY, 2003), 267–74, 296–302; Dallek, *FDR and Foreign Policy*, 243–50.

94. DHFDR, XIII: Doc. 32: DNC pamphlet; Doc. 40: DNC radio broadcast by Ickes.

95. For the campaign, see Davis, FDR: *Into the Storm*, ch. 16; Kennedy, *Freedom from Fear*, 451–64; Smith, *FDR*, ch. 21.

96. See M. A. Stoler, *Allies in War: Britain and America against the Axis Powers, 1940–1945* (NY, 2005); chs. 1–3; Dallek, chs. 10–11; J. Meacham, *Franklin and Winston: An Intimate Portrait of an Epic Friendship* (NY, 2003), part 1; K. S. Davis, *FDR: The War President, 1940–1943* (NY, 2000), parts 1 and 2.

97. In his fireside chat of Dec 9, 1941, FDR denounced Nazism at several turns and anticipated America's war with them, but (as yet) spoke only of "complete victory" against Japan.

98. J. M. Blum, *V Was for Victory: Politics and American Culture during World War II* (NY, 1976), 231–34; Davis, *FDR: The War President,* 597–600, 647–53.

99. D. N. Nelson, *Arsenal of Democracy: The Story of American War Production* (NY, 1946); B. Catton, *The War Lords of Washington* (NY, 1948); R. Polenberg, *War and Society: The United States, 1941–1945* (Philadelphia, 1972), chs. 1 and 6; Blum, *V Was for Victory,* ch. 4; Davis, *FDR: The War President,* 435–59.

100. Zieger, *CIO,* 102–10, 133–40; Dubofsky and Van Tine, "John L. Lewis."

101. *Wharton Assembly Addresses 1937* (Philadelphia, 1937), 71–77.

102. M. L. Cooke and P. Murray, *Organized Labor and Production: Next Steps in Industrial Democracy* (NY, 1940), 5–6, 48, 54, 59–60, 63, 241, 244–48, 256–57, 260–65. For Cooke's background, see Fraser, *Hillman,* 131–36, 172–74, 268–70. Even if the two SWOC staff economists thanked in the preface provided Murray with his material, the book ends with an extended "author's dialogue" in Murray's distinctive voice.

103. W. Reuther, *500 Planes a Day: A Program for the Utilization of the Automobile Industry for the Mass Production of Defense Planes* (Washington DC, 1941), with an introduction by Murray; also in H. Christman (ed.), *Walter P. Reuther: Selected Papers* (NY, 1961), 1–12. See esp. Lichtenstein, *Reuther,* ch. 8.

104. "Complete Transcript of Joint Press Conference by C. E. Wilson . . . and Walter P. Reuther . . . March 31, 1942," pp. 4–8 and passim, mimeographed typescript (CU Library #230 W69).

105. Fraser, *Hillman,* ch. 16.

106. Zieger, *CIO,* ch. 6; N. Lichtenstein, *Labor's War at Home: The CIO in World War II* (Cambridge, 1982), ch. 4.

107. K. Starr, *Embattled Dreams: California in War and Peace, 1940–45* (NY, 2002), 5–6, 123–28; Lichtenstein, *Labor's War,* 53–66; Zieger, *CIO,* 127–33.

108. A. Brinkley, *The End of Reform: New Deal Liberalism in Recession and War* (NY, 1995), ch. 8; Fraser, *Hillman,* 480–94; Polenberg, *War and Society,* 20–21, 34–36, 118–21; Davis, *FDR: The War President,* 622–27; Blum, *V Was for Victory,* ch. 4.

109. See Gallenson, *The CIO Challenge to the AFL,* chs. 16, 19.

110. Lichtenstein, *Labor's War,* 96–98, 102–6.

111. Ibid., 136–38, 145–50.

112. DHFDR, XV [Coal Strikes, Labor, and the Smith-Connally Act]: Doc. 90: memo to Ickes, May 7, 1943.

113. Ibid.: Docs. 157 and 161.

114. Ibid.: Doc. 153: Green and Murray to FDR Jun 16, 1943. Also Docs. 160 and 207: Green to FDR, Jun 14 and 26; and Docs. 146 and 212: Murray to FDR, Jun 15 and 26.

115. Polenberg, *War and Society,* 168–70.

116. A. Clive, *State of War: Michigan in World War II* (Ann Arbor MI, 1980), 76–89; Lichtenstein, *Labor's War,* 146–56, 194–97.

117. McDonald, *Union Man,* 165–68. See also Brinkley, *End of Reform,* ch. 9.

Chapter 4. Labour's Moment

1. See P. Stansky, *The First Day of the Blitz* (New Haven CT, 2007); P. Addison and J. Crange (eds.), *Listening to Britain: Home Intelligence Reports on Britain's Finest Hour, May–September 1940* (London, 2010); and G. G. Field, *Blood, Sweat, and Toil: Remaking the British Working Class, 1939–1945* (Oxford, 2011), ch. 2.

2. LPB, Jul 1946, 7. An extremely useful source, the *Labour Party Bulletin* was a monthly publication available to party members, which provided views from the leadership in Parliament and Transport House to explain what the government was doing. Downplaying although not ignoring internal debates, it published feature articles, parliamentary speeches, reports, party proceedings, book notes, and government statistics. It prepared activists for the difficulties ahead but kept Labour's distinctive values and aspirations in view. Starting in 1947, a separate section of the *Bulletin* (Part II) chronicled the undertakings of Labourites in local government.

3. S. Orwell and I. Angus (eds.), *Collected Essays, Journalism and Letters of George Orwell*, Vol. III: *As I Please, 1943–45* (NY, 1968), 200–201, 207–8, 251–52.

4. M-O's archives therefore constitute a goldmine of qualitative source material about daily life before, during, and after the war. See the introduction to A. Calder and D. Sheridan (eds.), *Speak for Yourself: A Mass-Observation Anthology, 1937–1949* (London, 1984), and J. Hinton, *The Mass Observers: A History, 1937–49* (Oxford, 2013).

5. A. Allport, *Demobbed: Coming Home after the Second World War* (New Haven, 2009), 1–49.

6. *The Journey Home: A Report Prepared by Mass-Observation for the Advertising Service Guild* (the fifth of the "CHANGE" Wartime Surveys) (London, 1944), 114–23.

7. Ibid., 14–21, 52, 106–11.

8. T. Harrisson, "Who'll Win" [1944], in Calder and Sheridan, *Speak for Yourself*, 210–18.

9. Cf. Orwell, "London Letter to *Partisan Review*" [December 1944], in *As I Please*, 293–99.

10. In "Who'll Win?" Harrisson noted that the Gallup Poll pointed in the same direction.

11. J. Campbell, *Nye Bevan and the Mirage of British Socialism* (London, 1987), ch. 10.

12. L. Minkin, *The Contentious Alliance: Trade Unions and the Labour Party* (Edinburgh, 1991), 58–61.

13. *Dalton Wartime Diary*, 858–66; *Ede Diary*, 215–19.

14. R. J. Wybrow, *Britain Speaks Out, 1937–87: A Social History as Seen through the Gallup Data* (London, 1989), 10–11.

15. R. McKibbin, *Parties and People: England, 1914–1951* (Oxford, 2010), 114–19.

16. A. Calder, *The People's War: Britain, 1939–45* (London, 1969), 546–54.

17. Fielding et al., *England Arise!*, ch. 3, "Party Politics in Wartime."

18. *Let Us Face the Future: A Declaration of Labour Policy for the Consideration of the Nation* (1945). See also F. W. S. Craig (ed.), *Conservative and Labour Party Conference Decisions, 1945–1981* (West Sussex, 1982).

19. Celticus [A. Bevan], *Why Not Trust the Tories?* (Gollancz, 1944), 78.

20. Helpful perspectives include K. Morgan, *Labour in Power, 1945–51* (Oxford, 1984), ch. 1; *England Arise!*, ch. 4; D. Marquand, *Britain since 1918: The Strange Career of British Democracy* (London, 2008), 60–116; McKibbin, *Parties and People*, ch. 5.

21. *Gallup Poll: Great Britain, 1945,* 109–11. A poll in late June showed 47 percent for Labour, 41 percent for Conservatives, and 10 percent for Liberals.

22. J. Lawrence, *Electing Our Masters: The Hustings in British Politics from Hogarth to Blair* (Oxford, 2009), 130–37; *Gallup Poll, 1945,* 113; B. Pimlott (ed.), *The Political Diary of Hugh Dalton, 1918–40, 1945–60,* 356–60; K. Harris, *Attlee* (London, 1984), 256–7; R. B. McCallum and A. Readman, *The British General Election of 1945* (Oxford, 1947/1964), chs. 7–9.

23. D. and G. Butler, *British Political Facts, 1900–1985* (NY, 1986), 226; McCallum and Readman, *General Election of 1945,* ch. 15 for the statistics; S. Fielding, "What Did the People Want? The Meaning of the 1945 General Election," *Historical Journal,* XXXV (1992), 623–39.

24. G. McDermott, *Leader Lost: A biography of Hugh Gaitskell* (London, 1971), 23.

25. See L. Martineau, *Politics and Power: Barbara Castle, a Biography* (London, 2000), chs. 1–4.

26. McAllum and Readman, *General Election of 1945,* 274.

27. Ian Mikardo, *Backbencher* (London, 1988), 72.

28. *Management by Consent: A Report by a Committee Appointed Jointly by ASSET and the Fabian Society* (Fabian Research Society, pamphlet no. 125: Gollancz, May 1948).

29. Mikardo, *Backbencher,* 77–79.

30. Lawrence, *Electing Our Masters,* 149.

31. On the early bursts of dissidence, see Morgan, *Labour in Power,* 61–63.

32. P. Williams, *Hugh Gaitskell: A Political Biography* (London, 1979), 16–26; McDermott, *Leader Lost,* 8.

33. See K. O. Morgan, *Labour People: Leaders and Lieutenants, Hardie to Kinnock* (Oxford, 1987), "The Planners," 107–19.

34. B. Brivati, *Hugh Gaitskell* (London, 1996), 36–40; Williams, *Gaitskell,* 75–78.

35. Brivati, *Gaitskell,* 55, 60–61, 67: 17,899 votes vs. 7,497 Tory and 3,933 Liberal.

36. After Attlee stepped down in 1955, Gaitskell and Wilson would be chosen as successive party leaders. Two other 1945 freshmen would lead the party after them: leftist Michael Foot and centrist Jim Callaghan. See portraits of the four in K. Morgan, *Labour People.*

37. H. Morrison, *An Autobiography* (London, 1960), ch. 18.

38. Harris, *Attlee,* 262–66. Morrison, *Autobiography,* 245–47, gives an implausibly benign version of this brief tempest.

39. Bullock, *Bevin,* 384–85.

40. P. Williams (ed.), *The Diary of Hugh Gaitskell, 1945–1956* (London, 1983), 11–16. The lone trade unionist at the dinner was George Brown.

41. *Gallup Poll, 1945,* 112, 121–22.

42. See the maddeningly vague essays by H. Morrison, "The State and Industry," and B. Wooton, "Freedom under Planning," in *Can Planning Be Democratic? A Collection of Essays Prepared for the Fabian Society* (Bombay, 1945).

43. P. Hennessy, *Never Again: Britain, 1945–1951* (NY, 1993), ch. 5; A. Cairncross, *The British Economy since 1945: Economic Policy and Performance* (Oxford, 1995), ch. 2; J. Foreman-Peck and R. Millward, *Public and Private Ownership of British Industry, 1820–1990* (Oxford, 1994), ch. 8.

44. On the Working Parties, see LPB, Jun 1947, 74–79; N. Tiratsoo and J. Tomlinson, *Industrial Efficiency and State Intervention: Labour, 1939–51* (London, 1993), ch. 4; and M. Dupree, "The Cotton Industry: A Middle Way between Nationalisation and Self-Government?" in H. Mercer, N. Rollings, and J. D. Tomlinson (eds.), *Labour Governments and Private Industry: The Experience of 1945–51* (Edinburgh, 1992), 137–61.

45. For the unveilings, see LPB, Dec 1946, 2–3; Mar–Apr 1947, esp. 34–36; May 1947, 57; Mar 1948, 45–47. For a painstaking and persuasive overview: J. Tomlinson, *Democratic Socialism and Economic Policy: The Attlee Years, 1945–1951* (Cambridge, 1997), chs. 4 and 6.

46. R. Skidelsky, *John Maynard Keynes: Fighting for Freedom, 1937–1946* (NY, 2001), 375–79.

47. Ibid., ch. 12, "Averting a Financial Dunkirk"; Hennessy, *Never Again,* 94–99.

48. *Gaitskell Diary,* 28–29. Shinwell's lame memoirs do little to counteract this judgment.

49. R. Brady, *Crisis in Britain: Plans and Achievements of the Labour Government* (Berkeley, 1950), ch. 3; D. Greasley, "The Coal Industry: Images and Realities on the Road to Nationalisation," in R. Millward and J. Singleton (eds.), *The Political Economy of Nationalisation in Britain, 1920–1950* (Cambridge, 1995).

50. D. Kynaston, *Austerity Britain, 1945–51* (London, 2007), ch. 8; Harris, *Attlee,* 334–37.

51. LPB, Feb 1947, 36; P. Addison, *Now the War Is Over: A Social History of Britain, 1945–51* (London, 1985), 179–85.

52. *Gaitskell Diary,* 57, 75, 79–80, 84–89, 109; Brady, *Crisis in Britain,* 128–31.

53. LPB, Nov 1946, 3.

54. LPB, Feb 1947; Addison, *Now the War Is Over,* ch. 7 and illustration no. 82.

55. See, D. Hughes, "The Spivs," in M. Sissons and P. French (eds.), *Age of Austerity* (London, 1963); I. Zweiniger-Bargielowska, *Austerity in Britain: Rationing, Controls, and Consumption, 1939–55* (Oxford, 2000), part 4; and M. Roodhouse, *Black Market Britain, 1939–1945* (Oxford Scholarship Online, 2013).

56. LPB, Aug and Nov 1946. See Zweiniger-Bargielowska, *Austerity in Britain,* parts 1 and 4, and on snoek, the memorable essay by Susan Cooper, "Snoek Piquante," in Sissons and French (eds.), *Age of Austerity.*

57. LPB, Sep 1947, 114–19.

58. LPB, Dec 1946, 2.

59. Morgan, *Labor in Power,* 342–47; B. Pimlott, *Hugh Dalton* (London, 1985), 433–34, 484–85, 487–91; Hennessy, *Never Again,* 97–98, 299–305.

60. The key study is P. Clarke, *The Cripps Version: The Life of Sir Stafford Cripps, 1889–1952* (London, 2002), ch. "Cripp's Moment." After Cripps became Chancellor, the Ministry of Economic Affairs was quietly folded.

61. LPB, Nov 1947, 154–57; Dec, 169.

62. LPB, Aug 1947, 99–102.

63. LPB, Oct 1947, 130–33, 144; Nov 1947, 154–57; Dec 1947, 162–69.

64. Recall the expression of relief by Pimlico's citizens to be free of the "Cripps feeling" in the film comedy *Passport to Pimlico* (Ealing Studios, 1949), when their London neighborhood was suddenly revealed to be a dependency of Burgundy. In the film a government spokesman vainly deplores that rationed goods and products meant for export were being freely hawked in the suddenly sovereign enclave.

65. LPB, May 1948, 67–69.

66. Apr 1950 quoted by Clarke, *Cripps*, 483–84; also 488–89 and 493–502 ("From Marx to Keynes").

67. LPB, "The Flattening Curve," Dec 1948, 178–82; Tiratsoo and Tomlinson, *Industrial Efficiency and State Intervention*, ch. 7. See also Addison, *Now the War Is Over*, 193–95; Hennessy, *Never Again*, 377–78; and P. Burnham, *The Political Economy of Postwar Reconstruction* (London, 1990), 97–100.

68. *Gaitskell Diary*, 106, 112, 114.

69. LPB, Nov 1948, 167.

70. For Labour's investment in this vision of socialism, and its shortfalls, see Fielding et al., *England Arise!*, chs. 4–5.

71. Minkin, *Contentious Alliance*, 60–67.

72. R. Taylor, *The Trade Union Question in British Politics: Government and Unions since 1945* (London, 1993), 48–55; and K. Coates, "The Vagaries of Participation, 1945–1960," in B. Pimlott and C. Cook (eds.), *Trade Unions in British Politics: The First 250 Years* (London, 1991), 159–64.

73. See, e.g., *Gaitskell Diary*, 53–54, 58.

74. To this end Harold Wilson warned that in considering applications for increased prices, his officials at the Board of Trade would "take a very austere line on profits." LPB, Mar 1948, 37.

75. Hennessy, *Never Again*, 367–76; Morgan, *Labour in Power*, 379–88.

76. See R. Taylor, "Trade Union Freedom and the Labour Party: Arthur Deakin, Frank Cousins and the Transport and General Workers Union, 1945–64," in B. Brivati and R. Heffernan (eds.), *The Labour Party: A Centenary History* (NY, 2000). Also Taylor, *Trade Union Question*, 51–58; R. Hyman, "Praetorians and Proletarians: Unions and Industrial Relations," in *Labour's High Noon: The Government and the Economy, 1945–51* (London, 1993), 172–88.

77. Kynaston, *Austerity Britain*, 478–85; Morgan, *Labour in Power*, 374–77; Hyman, "Praetorians and Proletarians," 179–89; J. Phillips, *The Great Alliance: Economic Recovery and the Problems of Power, 1945–1951* (London, 1996), chs. 2–3.

78. Minkin, *Contentious Alliance*, and E. Shaw, "Lewis Minkin and the Party-Unions Link," in J. Callaghan, S. Fielding, and S. Ludlam (eds.), *Interpreting the Labour Party: Approaches to Labour Politics and History* (Manchester, 2003), 166–81.

79. On struggles within the TGWU: Phillips, *Great Alliance*, ch. 5.

80. LPB, Mar–Apr 1947, 37.

Chapter 5. Starting Over, with de Gaulle or without Him

1. *Free France*, VI: Aug 1, 1944: 96–103; Nov 14: 362–64. This compendious magazine—well informed and surprisingly balanced—was published (monthly or bimonthly) in NYC between April 1942 and December 1945 by the Free French Press and Information Service.

2. D. Merrill (ed.), *Documentary History of the Truman Presidency*, 35 vols. (Bethesda MD, 1995–) (hereafter DHTP), Vol. II: 166: Doc. 13: Joseph Davies to HST, Jul 3, 1945.

3. Charles de Gaulle, *The Complete War Memoirs of Charles de Gaulle* (original edn., 3 vols., 1955–59; one vol. transl., NY, 1967), 895–98.

4. See J. Debû-Bridel, *De Gaulle et le CNR* (1978), chs. 12–13.

5. *Free France,* VI: 230.

6. De Gaulle, *War Memoirs,* 688–89; "French Press Comments on Lille Speech," *Free France,* Nov 1, 1944, 318–19; J. Gaer, *The First Round: The Story of the CIO Political Action Committee* (NY, 1944), 302: citing the *New York Daily Mirror.*

7. "No more names!" complained socialist CNR member Daniel Mayer. "France needs a platform!" cited in *Free France,* VI: 278.

8. De Gaulle, *War Memoirs,* 505–7.

9. Polling summarized in J.-P. Rioux, *The Fourth Republic, 1944–1958* (Cambridge, 1987 transl.), 40–41.

10. *Free France,* VI: Dec 1, 1944, 426.

11. F.-L. Closon, *Commissaire de la République du Général de Gaulle: Lille, Septembre 1944–Mars 1946* (Paris, 1980), 73–76, on the acquittal by a jury of the notorious collaborationist editor Tardieu in the Nord department because of "extenuating circumstances."

12. *Free France,* VI: Aug 15, 1944, 50: address of Jul 25, 1944.

13. See H. Lottman, *The Purge: The Purification of French Collaborators after World War II* (NY, 1986), 223–28.

14. *Free France,* VI: Oct 1944, 349–51.

15. O. Wieviorka, *Orphans of the Republic: The Nation's Legislators in Vichy France* (Cambridge MA, 2009 transl.), ch. 5 and epilogue, esp. pp. 320 and 340; N. Castagnez, *Socialistes en République: Les parlementaires SFIO de la IVe République* (Rennes, 2004), part 1.

16. Y. Farge, *Rebelles, soldats et citoyens: Carnet d'un Commissaire de la République* (Paris, 1946), 228–31.

17. "Problems of the Purge," *Free France,* VI: Dec 1, 1944, 425–27; "Problem of the Purge" (editorial), VII: Jan 1, 1945, 1–4; Pascal Copeau in the Consultative Assembly, quoted in ibid., VII: Jun 1, 1945, 558–59.

18. See the overviews by Rioux, pp. 33–42, and A. Kaspi, *La Libération de la France: Juin 1944–Janvier 1946* (1995), ch. 7.

19. J. Lacouture, *Pierre Mendès France* (NY, 1984 transl.), chs. 4–6; E. Roussel, *Pierre Mendès France* (Paris, 2007), chs. 5–8.

20. *Free France,* VII: May 1945, 449.

21. Quoted in Roussel, *Mendès France,* 161.

22. See Lacouture, *Mendès France,* ch. 7: "Minister of Rigor," and Roussel, *Mendès France,* ch. 9: "Un cheval qu'on n'attelle pas."

23. P. Mendès France, *Oeuvres Complètes,* II: *Une Politique de l'Économie, 1943–1954* (Paris, 1984): "Lettre de démission au Général De Gaulle, 18 Janvier 1945," 115–25.

24. "French Ministers' Differences," *Times* (London), Jan 22, 1945; "French Minister Threatens to Quit," *New York Times,* Jan 21. But see Roussel, *Mendès France,* 174.

25. Mendès France, *Oeuvres Complètes,* II: "Les causeries radiophoniques," 73–113.

26. Ibid., 77, 79–80, 90, 98, 112.

27. See his exchange of letters with socialist Adrien Tixier (Feb 12 and 14, 1945); his "Note au Gouvernement sur le marché noir et l'inflation" (Mar 26); his parting draft letter to de Gaulle and his letter to Pleven (Mar 29 and Apr 4), in Mendès France, *Oeuvres Complètes,* II: 125–29, 138–46, 148–52.

28. Apart from the two principal biographies, see F. Bloch-Lainé and J. Bouvier, *La France Restaurée, 1944–1954: Dialogue sur les choix d'une modernisation* (Paris, 1986), chs. 1–2.

29. British Foreign Office Series (online): "Conditions and Politics in Occupied Western Europe, 1940–45: France" (hereafter B.F.O.): 371/49077–0004: Adrian Holman to Bevin, Sep 6, 1945.

30. *Free France*, VI: Nov 1, 1944, and VII: Jan 1, 1945.

31. Wieviorka, *Orphans of the Republic*, 214–17.

32. J.-J. Becker, *Le Parti Communiste veut-il prendre le pouvoir?* (Paris, 1981), 146–59.

33. See M. Dreyfus, *Histoire de la C.G.T.* (Brussels, 1995), 213–26; A. Narritsens, "Léon Jouhaux et l'unité de la CGT, 1940–1947," in *Léon Jouhaux: D'Aubervilliers au prix nobel* (Paris, 2010), 107–20.

34. Bourdet, *L'Aventure incertaine*, 390–91. Bourdet later described his preference as "a freemasonry" of Resistance veterans. See his oral history in Wieviorka, *Oral Histories*, 364–65.

35. *Free France*, Dec 15, 1944, 501–2.

36. Wieviorka, *Orphans of the Republic*, 94, 316–27. In contrast, an overwhelming majority of parliamentarians in the centrist Radical Party, 171 in all, had voted full powers for Pétain. But when the Radical Party held its own congress in December, it purged only 38 of the most compromised men.

37. *Free France*, Dec 15, 1944, 499–500.

38. S. Berstein et al. (eds.), *Le Parti Socialiste entre Résistance et République* (Paris, 2000), part 3: esp. J. Vigreux, "Le comité d'entente socialiste-communiste."

39. *Free France*, VII: Dec 15, 1944, and VIII: Oct 1, 1945, 198; J.-J. Becker, "L'anticommunisme de la SFIO," in Berstein, *Parti Socialiste.*

40. A.N. 72 AJ 64, doss. MLN; *Free France*, VII: Mar 15, 1945, 312–13; Bourdet, *L'Aventure incertaine*, 402–7.

41. *Free France*, and the oral history: *Pierre Villon: Résistant de la première heure*, (ed.) C. Willard (Paris, 1983), 135–36.

42. See Lacouture, *De Gaulle: The Ruler*, 16–17; *Pierre Villon*, 116–18.

43. B.F.O. 371/49146–0004: Report on the FN Congress, Feb 12, 1945; *Free France*, VII: Jan 15, 1945, 98–101.

44. *Pierre Villon*, 132–36.

45. *Free France*, VII: Mar 15, 1945, 314–15.

46. *Pierre Villon*, 133–37. A different view of the situation is offered by Pierre Hervé, a dedicated *résistant* and a prominent young communist but a free-thinking one, who advocated an FN-MLN merger in the name of Resistance unity. Still, Hervé believed that the FN's communist leadership did not actually desire a merger with the MLN: "Comment aurait-il voulu confier ses finances à un movement uni?" Wieviorka, *Oral Histories*, 205–6.

47. See R. Vinen, *Bourgeois Politics in France, 1945–1951* (Cambridge, 1995), 183–99, and E. Duhamel, "L'UDSR à la Libération ou la rénovation en politique," in C. Franck (ed.), *La France de 1945: Résistances, retours, renaissances* (Caen, 1996), 49–57.

48. *Free France*, VII: Mar 1, 1945, 250; Closon, *Lille*, 160–61.

49. Andrew Shennan cites a notable report on educational reform in *Rethinking France: Plans for Renewal, 1940–46* (Oxford, 1989), 182.

50. *Free France,* VII: Mar 1, 1945, 250–51; VIII: Aug 14, 1945, 99–100.

51. R. Bichet, *La Démocratie Chrétienne en France: Le Mouvement Républicain Populaire* (Besançon, 1980), 9–30. Bichet was a founding father of the MRP.

52. A.N. 72 AJ 64, doss. MRP: "Paris Est Libre" (handbill); typescript of Gilbert Dru's "Projet" outlining a set of values and a course of action for social-Catholics after the Liberation, which he did not live to see. Cf. J.-M. Domenach, *Gilbert Dru, celui qui croyait au ciel* (1947).

53. De Menthon to Bidault, Apr 2, 1944, cited in P.-H. Teitgen, *Faites entrer le témoin suivant, 1940–1958: De la Résistance à la Vème République* (Rennes, 1988), 328 (hereafter Teitgen, *Memoirs).*

54. Cited in B. Béthouart, *Le M.R.P. dans le Nord-Pas-de-Calais, 1944–1967* (Dunkerque, 1984), 97. See also P. Letamendia, *Le Mouvement Républicain Populaire: Histoire d'un grand parti français* (Paris, 1995), 273–98; Bichet, *La Démocratie Chrétienne,* 45–54.

55. A.N. 457 AP 143, doss. MRP Comm. Exécutif: Notes sur l'Orientation du MRP, Jul 30, 1946. Cf. the party's founding manifesto reprinted in Teitgen, *Memoirs,* 333–35.

56. Teitgen in Wieviorka, *Oral Histories,* 85.

57. A.N. 350 AP 14 [MRP Papers]: 2nd National Congress bulletin; A.N. 350 AP 9, doss. "Propagande." There is dispute over party membership. J.-D. Durand, *L'Europe de la Démocratie Chrétienne* (Paris, 1995), 274, and Letamendia believe that the party had only about 125,000 members at its apex in 1946—but this might refer to actual dues payers rather than nominal members. According to Closon (*Lille,* 163), in its Nord department bastion, the party had 147 local branches with 24,000 members in 1945.

58. I. Woloch, "Left, Right and Centre: The MRP and the Post-War Moment," *French History* (2007), 85–106.

59. See, e.g., J. Quellien, "La Résistance dans le Calvados en 1945: L'exemple d'un échec politique," in C. Franck (ed.), *La France de 1945: Résistances, retours, renaissances* (Caen, 1996), 59–71.

60. V.-A. Montassier, *Les Années d'après-guerre, 1944–1949* (Paris, 1980), 111–12; G. Vincent, *Les Français, 1945–1975: Chronologie et structures d'un société* (1977), 25; *Free France,* VIII: Jul 1 1945, 34, for Interior Ministry numbers; *Le Monde,* Jun 4, 1945, cited in *Free France* VIII: Jul 1, 1945. For the fragmentation of the Right, see J.-P. Thomas, "Réseaux et enjeux des droites en 1944–1945," in G. Richard and J. Sainclivier (eds.), *La Recomposition des droites en France à la Libération, 1944–1948* (Rennes, 2004), 137–50.

61. *Free France,* VII: May 15, 1945, 499, and Jun 1, 1945, 546.

62. "The Cantonal Elections" (editorial), *Free France,* VIII: Oct 15, 1945, 205–6, 208. On the "moderate" (i.e., conservative) parties, see C. Bougéard, "Les Droites dans les élections cantonales de 1945 et 1949," in *La Recomposition des droites,* 257–62. Cf. M. Boivin, "Les Élections de 1945 dans la Manche: Continuité ou changement?" in *La France de 1945,* 249–60.

63. Radio addresses of Sep 4 and 22, summarized in *Free France,* VIII: Oct 1, 1945, 201–2, and B.F.O. 371/49007–0016: Holman to F.O., Sep 25.

64. B.F.O. 371/49077–0004: Holman to Bevin, Sep 10, 1945, p. 5, and the invaluable account by Gordon Wright, a young American diplomat on the scene, *The Reshaping of French Democracy* (Boston, 1948), 78–84.

65. Facsimile of the ballot form reprinted in *Free France,* VIII: Nov–Dec 1945, 240.

66. A temporary federation of seven groups including remnants of the prewar Alliance Démocratique and Fédération Républicaine.

67. B.F.O. 371/49078: Oct 22, 1945, includes a diagram mapping the positions of the various parties and alliances. Radio broadcasts of Oct 4 by spokesmen for the three major parties summarized in B.F.O. 371/49007–0029.

68. A. Cole and P. Campbell, *French Electoral Systems and Elections since 1789* (Aldershot, 1989), 72–78, 179–80; *Free France,* VIII: Sep 1, 1945, 137–38.

69. B.F.O. 371/49076–0042 and 371/49007–0008 and 0013: telegrams from Duff Cooper to F.O., Sep 5, 1945 and from Holman, Sep 11 and 15; B.F.O. 371/49007–0021: Holman to Bevin, Sep 29.

70. These figures are a composite of sorts since, of the eight sources I consulted for this basic information (Rioux, Kaspi, Cole and Campbell, Vincent, Montassier, Graham, Wright, and *Free France*), no two give exactly the same numbers, agreeing only on the total of 522 seats for Metropolitan France.

71. *Free France,* VIII: Nov–Dec 1945, 242, and the local scholarship in *La Recomposition des droites,* especially by J.-P. Thomas, J. Vavasseur-Desperriers, and F. Audigier.

72. B.F.O. 371/49078–0011: Cooper to Bevin, Oct 30.

73. Bichet, *La Démocratie Chrétienne,* 76–79. On the women see, A.N. 350 AP 13: Dec 13, 1945, and for context H. Footitt, "The First Women *Députés:* Les 33 Glorieuses?" in H. R. Kedward and N. Wood (eds.), *The Liberation of France: Image and Event* (Oxford, 1995), 129–41.

74. Bichet, *La Démocratie Chrétienne,* 74–76. "A Machine to Harvest Pétainists"—false, but at least clever; "Lies, Reaction, and Perfidy"—utterly gratuitous. See also British consular reports from Marseilles, Rouen, and Lyon: B.F.O. 371–49078–0003, Oct 1945; and P. Boyer, "Les droites vues par le PCF: Le discours sur le MRP, le PRL et le RPF, 1946–1947," in *La Recomposition des droites,* 73–78.

75. B.F.O. 371/49078–0006 and 0011: Cooper to Bevin (Confidential), Oct 24 and 30, 1945; B.F.O. 371/49007–0033: Cooper to F.O. Oct 13, on the opening of the MRP's campaign.

76. Closon, "Les Partis Politiques, July–August 1945," in *Lille,* 163–66.

77. Letamendia, Vinen, Rioux, and Wieviorka, among others, plausibly emphasize the longer trajectory, while J.-D. Durand and B. Béthouart (with due qualification) stress its first progressive incarnation. For the party's decline, see L. Ducerf, "Le MRP face au RPF, un traumatisme mal surmonté," in *La Recomposition des droites,* 229–39.

78. B.F.O. 371/49078–0006: Cooper to Bevin, telegram and formal report, Oct 24, 1945, italics added.

79. Ibid.: Cooper to Bevin, Oct 30. For the maneuvering of the "pragmatists" in the PCF, see I. Wall, *French Communism in the Era of Stalin: The Quest for Unity and Integration, 1945–1962* (Westport CT, 1983), ch. 2.

80. B. D. Graham, *The French Socialists and Tripartisme, 1944–1947* (Toronto, 1965), ch. 2.

81. See Teitgen and Schumann in Wieviorka, *Oral Histories.*

82. A.N. 350 AP 77: R. Lecourt, "Monolithisme," in Bulletins d'information du groupe parlementaire, Jul 7 and 31, 1946.
83. See B.F.O. 371/49078–0012 and 0017: Cooper to F.O., Nov 2 and 9, 1945; Bichet, *La Démocratie Chrétienne*, 84–86.
84. Lacouture, *De Gaulle: The Ruler*, ch. 9; Graham, *French Socialists and Tripartisme*, ch. 3.
85. B.F.O. 371/49078–0038: Cooper to Bevin, Nov 22, 1945; B.F.O. 371/49079–0026: Dec 19.
86. De Gaulle, *War Memoirs*, 899–900, italics added.
87. Teitgen, *Memoirs*, 302–3.
88. Kaspi, *La Libération de la France*, ch. 14; Graham, *French Socialists and Tripartisme*, ch. 3.
89. See Lacouture, *De Gaulle: The Ruler*, 105–24; G. Elgey, *La République des Illusions, 1945–1951* (2nd edn., 1993), 79–176.
90. Teitgen, *Memoirs*, appendix 3: Commission Exécutive du MRP, 20 Janvier 1946, pp. 567–75.
91. Wright, *Reshaping French Democracy*, 132–33.
92. Ibid., ch. 5; Graham, *French Socialists and Tripartisme*, ch. 4.
93. Vincent, *Les Français, 1945–1975*, 30; Montassier, *Années d'après-guerre*, 120–21; J.-P. Rioux, *The Fourth Republic, 1944–1958* (Cambridge, 1987 transl.), 101–2. Again the numbers vary slightly from one account to another.
94. Wright, *Reshaping French Democracy*, 191, 202, 204–5.
95. A.N. 457 AP [Bidault Papers], 141: Thorez and Duclos to Bidault, and response, Jun 1946.
96. Lacouture, *De Gaulle: The Ruler*, 129–33.
97. Graham, *French Socialists and Tripartisme*, 190–95.
98. S. Courtois and M. Lazar, *Histoire du Parti communiste français* (Paris, 1995), 225.
99. A.N. 457 AP 143, doss. SFIO: Auriol to Mon Cher Président et Ami [Bidault], Sep 2, 1946.
100. A. Fonvieille-Vojtovic, *Paul Ramadier, 1888–1961: Élu local et homme d'état* (Paris, 1993), 318–21; Graham, *French Socialists and Tripartisme*, 220–24; Wright, *Reshaping French Democracy*, 205–16.
101. Montassier, *Années d'après-guerre*, 49–54, 121–23; Wright, *Reshaping French Democracy*, 217–30.

Chapter 6. Postwar Prospects in the United States

1. Chester Bowles, CU Oral History, 165–66. Bowles's published memoir *Promises to Keep: My Years in Public Life, 1941–1969* (NY, 1971) jibes with his earlier oral history, but the latter is often blunter and more illuminating.
2. Alvin Hansen, *After the War: Full Employment—Postwar Planning* (Washington DC: NRPB, rev. edn., Feb 1943), and *U.S. NRPB: After the War: Freedom from Want—Toward Security* (Washington DC, 1942), a 62-page report that summarized the full version of 640 pages. On the NRPB, see A. Brinkley, *The End of Reform: New Deal*

Liberalism in Recession and War (NY, 1996), 245–60, and I. Katznelson, *Fear Itself: the New Deal and the Origins of Our Time* (NY, 2013), 372–80.

3. Quoted in J. M. Blum, *V Was for Victory: Politics and American Culture during World War II* (NY, 1976), 239.

4. On the later trajectory of this clarion call, stressing its origins in the NRPB but eliding Bowles's pivotal role, see C. R. Sunstein, *The Second Bill of Rights: FDR's Unfinished Revolution and Why We Need It More Than Ever* (NY, 2004), ch. 4. Cf. Bowles, *Promises to Keep,* 118–19.

5. Bowles, CU Oral History, 167–68.

6. S. Casey, *Cautious Crusade: Franklin D. Roosevelt, American Public Opinion, and the War against Nazi Germany* (NY, 2001), 150, 166–68. Cf. J. M. Blum's more confusing account of polling advice and FDR's tactical predilections: *V Was for Victory,* 255–62.

7. J. C. Foster, *The Union Politic: The CIO Political Action Committee* (Columbia MO, 1975), esp. 22–27; and S. Fraser, *Labor Will Rule: Sidney Hillman and the Rise of American Labor* (NY, 1991), ch. 17.

8. See the compendium of CIO-PAC pamphlets along with running commentary by its publications director in 1944: Joseph Gaer, *The First Round: The Story of the CIO Political Action Committee* (NY, 1944).

9. E. Fones-Wolf, *Waves of Opposition: Labor and the Struggle for Democratic Radio* (Urbana IL, 2006), 112–18.

10. Gaer, *First Round:* "The Radio Handbook" (311–57) and "The Speakers Manual" (358–402).

11. "The People's Program," in Gaer, 185–212.

12. See also "The Negro in 1944," in Gaer, 449–78.

13. Blum, *V Was for Victory,* 262–92.

14. DHFDR, XXXIV [Election of 1944]: Doc. 216, Pauley's MS recollections, 1950 (740–56).

15. J. M. Blum (ed.), *The Price of Vision: The Diary of Henry Wallace, 1942–1946* (Boston, 1973), 360–67.

16. Pauley's MS recollections; Blum (ed.), *Wallace Dairy,* 367.

17. DHFDR, XXXIV: Doc. 31: Jul 14, 1944, 168–71. The cover page on the first draft bore the note: "to sink in files—top secret." Also Docs. 36 and 37: memos of phone conversations by White House secretary; and Doc. 214: Hannegan's widow to S. Rosenman in 1950, confirming her husband's appeal to FDR to tone down his favorable remarks about Wallace in the Jackson letter.

18. Ibid.: Doc. 41: FDR to Hannegan, Jul 19, 1944; Doc. 215: recollections of M. Connelly to S. Rosenman, Jan 1950.

19. D. Kennedy, *Freedom from Fear: the American People in Depression and War, 1929–1945* (NY, 1999), 790–92.

20. DHFDR, XXXIV: Docs. 24, 34, and 53: Byrnes to FDR, Jun 1 and Jul 6, 1944; and Democratic National Platform.

21. Ibid.: Doc. 216: Pauley's MS recollections; Blum (ed.), *Wallace Diary,* "Recollections of the Chicago 1944 Convention," 367–71; J. E. Smith, *FDR* (NY, 2007), 619.

22. DHFDR, XXXIV: Doc. 148: radio address in Chicago, Oct 28, 1944 (553–57); Bowles, CU Oral History, 170, 173.

23. DHFDR, XXXIV: Doc. 58, Aug 1944. Hillman was the chair of both CIO-PAC and NC-PAC, a parallel organization for liberals outside the unions. On these racial issues see chapter 9.

24. Ibid.: Doc. 107: Oscar Cox to Harry Hopkins: memo of suggested talking points, Oct 16, 1944; Doc. 156: transcript of DNC broadcast round table, Nov 1, 1944.

25. Ibid.: Doc. 176: transcript of Nov 4 broadcast.

26. Ibid.: Doc. 162: broadcast from the White House, Nov 2.

27. Ibid.: Doc. 168: Fenway Park address, Nov 4.

28. Ibid.: Doc. 173: broadcast of Nov 6.

29. Bowles, CU Oral History, 169–70.

30. *Report of the Special Committee on Un-American Activities House of Representatives . . . Report on the C.I.O. Political Action Committee* (Washington DC, Mar 1944), esp. 1–9, 59–65, 73–79.

31. Kennedy, *Freedom from Fear,* 793.

32. DHFDR, XXXIV: Doc. 200: FDR to Hillman, Nov 15, 1944.

33. Foster, *Union Politic,* 40–44.

34. Ibid.; Fraser, *Hillman,* 536–37, who notes that of 28 states where the PAC was involved in congressional campaigns, it may have affected outcomes in only 11.

35. J. Lelyveld, *His Final Battle: The Last Months of Franklin Roosevelt* (NY, 2016), prologue and chs. 7–10.

36. See B. Catton, *The Warlords of Washington: The Inside Story of Big Business versus the People in World War II* (NY, 1948), chs. 16–19; R. Polenberg, *War and Society: The United States, 1941–45* (Philadelphia, 1972), ch. 8; Brinkley, *End of Reform,* 235–40.

37. W. Sykes, *The Postwar Prospect: A Series of Seven Newspaper Articles* (NAM, 1943), "The Prospect for Postwar Jobs," 3–6; N. Lichtenstein, *Walter Reuther: The Most Dangerous Man in Detroit* (Urbana IL, 1995), 222.

38. D. Ross, *Preparing for Ulysses: Politics and Veterans during World War II* (NY, 1969), chs. 2 and 6.

39. DHTP, IV: [Demobilization & Reconversion]: Doc. 19, radio address Aug 15, 1945.

40. DHTP, IV: broadcast of Aug 15, 1945, 203–4.

41. Ibid., 205–11, 219–24.

42. Ibid.: Doc. 21: cabinet meeting, Aug 17, 1945.

43. Ibid.: Doc. 79: administrative history of the Economic Stabilization Program (1945–52), 814–16.

44. Ibid.: Doc. 38: HST radio broadcast, Jan 3, 1946.

45. Ibid.: Doc. 45: HST statement of Apr 3, 1946.

46. Sykes, *Postwar Prospect,* 7–31.

47. H. J. Harris, *The Right to Manage: Industrial Relations Policies of American Business in the 1940s* (Madison WI, 1982), chs. 2–3 are indispensable.

48. P. Murray, *The CIO Case for Substantial Pay Increases* (Washington DC, Nov 1945), 14.

49. Ibid., 3, 5, 16–19.

50. For overviews R. H. Zieger, *The CIO, 1935–1955* (Chapel Hill NC, 1995), 212–27, and Lichtenstein, *Walter Reuther,* ch. 11.

51. *Postwar Conditions and Trends,* (ed.) N. Sargent, secretary of the NAM (NY, 1943–1944), 4–9, 36–38. Also R. M. Collins, *The Business Response to Keynes, 1929–1964* (NY, 1981), 88–93, 110, 118–22; Harris, *Right to Manage,* 110–11.

52. *President's National Labor-Management Conference Official Transcripts* [mimeo-graphed] (Washington DC, 1945): plenary session, Nov 30, 1945, 114–24.

53. Ibid., 123–38.

54. *Industrial Peace: A Progress Report on Behalf of the 36 Business Men Who Represented American Management at the President's LMC, November 5–30 1945* (NAM: Washington DC), 14, and Final Reports of the Committee on Collective Bargaining, 59–65. This 104-page publication frames the LMC entirely from the NAM's perspective, but it presents side by side all the final committee reports from labor and management. Tobin's remarks in *LMC Official Transcripts,* 143.

55. *NAM Industrial Peace,* 23–24, 66–73; Harris, *Right to Manage,* 75, 84 on supervisory unionism.

56. *NAM Industrial Peace,* 74–84.

57. Ibid., 55–58.

58. A. F. McClure, *The Truman Administration and the Problems of Postwar Labor, 1945–1948* (Rutherford NJ, 1969), chs. 3–5.

59. G. Lipsitz, *Rainbow at Midnight: Labor and Culture in the 1940s* (Urbana IL, 1994), part 2.

60. O. Brubaker, quoted in J. Herling, *The Right to Challenge: People and Power in the Steelworkers Union* (NY, 1972), 11; Zieger, *CIO,* ch. 8; Lichtenstein, *Walter Reuther,* ch. 11; J. G. Goulden, *The Best Years, 1945–1950* (NY, 1976), 110–18.

61. D. McCullough, *Truman* (NY, 1992), 493–506; Goulden, *Best Years,* 121–27; Huthmacher, *Wagner,* 328–31; J. Patterson, *Mr. Republican: A Biography of Robert A. Taft* (Boston, 1972), 307–8.

62. DHTP, IV: Doc. 45: statement by HST, Apr 3, 1946.

63. Quotes in M. Jacobs, *Pocketbook Politics: Economic Citizenship in Twentieth-Century America* (Princeton, 2005), 205–7.

64. Bowles, *Promises to Keep,* 149, 130, 134.

65. DHTP, IV: Docs. 40–41: Bowles to HST, Jan 24, Feb 6 and 8, 1946; Bowles, *Promises to Keep,* 138–41.

66. Bowles, *Promises to Keep,* 152–53; Bowles, CU Oral History, 220–23.

67. E. Fones-Wolf, *Selling Free Enterprise: The Business Assault on Labor and Liberalism, 1945–60* (Urbana IL, 1994), 33–35.

68. On rising prices during and after the war, the OPA, consumer responses, and business pressures, see Jacobs, *Pocketbook Politics,* chs. 5–6, and L. Cohen, *A Consumers' Republic: The Politics of Mass Consumption in Postwar America* (NY, 2003), chs. 2–3.

69. *New York Times,* April 19 and 29, 1946; Huthmacher, *Wagner,* 326–27; Goulden, *Best Years,* 100–104. Patterson, *Mr. Republican,* 308–12. Taft had long been hostile to OPA and to Bowles.

70. DHTP, IV: Docs. 47 and 52: Truman's veto message of June and signing statement of July; Doc. 82: interim executive order.

71. "Buyer's Strike Gains Support as Prices Soar," *Brooklyn Eagle,* Jul 11, 1946, and "32 Boro Groups Back Buyer's Strike," ibid., Jul 17; "Buyers' Strikes Spreading as Prices Continue to Rise," *New York Times,* Jul 12, 1946.

72. J. Boylan, *The New Deal Coalition and the Election of 1946* (NY, 1981), ch. 8. Also Goulden, *Best Years,* 105–7, and DHTP, IV: Doc. 44.

73. DHTP, IV: Doc. 55: HST address, Oct 14, 1946; Bowles, *Promises to Keep*, 152–57.

74. R. Collins, *The Business Response to Keynes*, chs. 4–6; R. Lekachman, *The Age of Keynes* (NY, 1966), chs. 5–7, esp. pp. 126–37 on Hansen.

75. Hansen, *After the War—Full Employment, Postwar Planning* (rev. edn.: Washington DC, [Feb] 1943), 2, 8, 16–17, 21. On the NRPB, see note 2, above.

76. *The United States after War: The Cornell University Summer Session Lectures* (Ithaca NY, 1945), 17–19, 21–25, 33.

77. Not to be confused with "the right to work" in the conservative lexicon, which meant the right to be employed without having to belong to or pay dues to a trade union.

78. S. K. Bailey, *Congress Makes a Law: The Story behind the Employment Act of 1946* (NY, 1950) is the indispensable study, which D. E. Spritzer, *Senator James E. Murray and the Limits of Postwar Liberalism* (NY, 1985), ch. 5, usefully supplements. Taft's comment in Spritzer, 107.

79. See Bailey, *Congress Makes a Law*, ch. 5.

80. Ibid., 117–18.

81. Ibid., 107–28; Spritzer, *Murray*, 109–113.

82. Bailey, *Congress Makes a Law*, ch. 11.

83. DHTP, IV: Bureau of the Budget Analysis (474–6) and HST signing statement (829–30).

84. Huthmacher, *Wagner*, 297–99, 318–19; Spritzer, *Murray*, 115–16; Brinkley, *End of Reform*, 261–64. Taft supported a new office to monitor the economy but insisted that public spending was not the solution to unemployment: radio address, Aug 7, 1945 in C. E. Wunderlin, Jr. (ed.), *The Papers of Robert A. Taft* (Kent OH, 2003), III: 66–69.

85. Spritzer, *Murray*, 125–28; Huthmacher, *Wagner*, 294–95, 319–22.

86. Katznelson, *Fear Itself*, 386–88.

87. See Ross, *Preparing for Ulysses*, ch. 6.

88. K. J. Frydl, *The GI Bill* (Cambridge, 2009), ch. 4: "Scandal and the GI Bill."

89. J. R. Thelin, *A History of American Higher Education*, 2nd edn. (Baltimore, 2011), 263–64.

90. G. Graff, "The Men & the Boys: How Veterans Altered the Campus Fabric," *Harvard Crimson*, Jun 5, 2000, and T. Serkin, "Class of 1949: From Barracks to Books," ibid., Jun 7, 1999.

91. K. W. Olson, *The G.I. Bill, the Veterans, and the Colleges* (Lexington KY, 1974), ch. 5 on the University of Wisconsin; Syracuse University Archives and Records online: "Enrollment Statistics for 1943–4 through 1951–2 Present Dramatic Evidence of the Impact of Returning Veterans."

92. Katznelson, *Fear Itself*, ch. 6.

93. D. H. Onkst, "'First a Negro . . . Incidentally a Veteran': Black World War Two Veterans and the G.I. Bill of Rights in the Deep South, 1944–1948," *Journal of Social History*, XXXI (Spring 1998), 517–43; Katznelson, *When Affirmative Action Was White*, ch. 5; Frydl, *GI Bill*, ch. 5.

94. C. Bolté and L. Harris, *Our Negro Veterans* (NY, [March] 1947). The process of exclusion in GA, MS, and AL is recovered in harrowing detail by Onkst ("'First a Negro'").

95. See S. Mettler, *Soldiers to Citizens: The G.I. Bill and the Making of the Greatest Generation* (Oxford, 2005); G. C. Altschuler and S. M. Blumin, *The GI Bill: A New Deal for Veterans* (Oxford, 2009), ch. 5; R. F. Saxe, *Settling Down: World War II Veterans' Challenge to the Postwar Consensus* (NY, 2007), ch. 5.

96. With due qualification Olson, *G.I. Bill,* ch. 9, and the books by Mettler and by Altschuler and Blumin are upbeat on the opportunities for veterans opened by the G.I. Bill.

97. S. M. Hartmann, *The Home Front and Beyond: American Women in the 1940s* (Boston, 1982), ch. 6, esp. 107; Altschuler and Blumin, *G.I. Bill,* 118–28 on Cornell; Thelin, *Higher Education,* 267.

98. Mettler, *Soldiers to Citizens,* ch. 9; M. Murray, "Made with Men in Mind: The G.I. Bill and Its Reinforcement of Gendered Work after World War II," in T. A. Thomas and T. J. Boisseau (eds.), *Feminist Legal History: Essays on Women and Law* (NY, 2011), 84–99.

99. Saxe, *Settling Down,* ch. 3.

100. C. Hurd, "Readjustment," *New York Times,* Jun 30, 1946, 30. See also "4 Vet Groups Accept Council Bid to Speak," *Harvard Crimson,* Mar 1, 1946.

101. *New York Times,* Nov 3, 1946.

102. A. Meier and E. Rudwick, *Black Detroit and the Rise of the UAW* (Oxford, 1979), chs. 4–5; H. L. Moon, *Balance of Power: the Negro Vote* (NY, 1948), 147–56; B. Nelson, "Autoworkers, Electoral Politics, and the Convergence of Class and Race: Detroit, 1937–1945," in K. Boyle (ed.), *Organized Labor and Ameridan Politics, 1894–1994* (Albany NY, 1998); Foster, *Union Politic,* 59–60.

103. Foster, *Union Politic,* ch. 3.

104. J. Boylan, *New Deal Coalition and the Election of 1946,* chs. 9–10.

105. See S. M. Hartmann, *Truman and the 80th Congress* (Columbia MO, 1971), chs. 1–3.

106. On this point, see R. H. Zieger and G. J. Gall, *American Workers, American Unions: the Twentieth Century* (Baltimore, 2002 edn.), 154–59.

107. Katznelson, *Fear Itself,* 388–402, esp. 396–97.

108. R. A. Lee, *Truman and Taft-Hartley: A Question of Mandate* (Westport CT, 1966/1980), ch. 3.

109. DHTP, IX [Taft-Hartley]: Doc. 55, Jun 18, 1947, and 395–96, 417–18.

110. Ibid.: Docs. 44–45, Jun 14, 1947, and 286, 288, 291.

111. Ibid.: Doc. 35. Comparable but different figures as of Jun 14 are given in Lee, *Truman and Taft-Hartley,* 81.

112. For the AFL's comprehensive critique, see G. S. Roukis, *American Labor and the Conservative Republicans, 1946–1948* (Garland, NY 1973/1988), 127–29; and Dave Beck [vice president of the AFL Teamsters], "What Labor Wants," *American Legion Magazine,* May 1947, 11, 26–31: "Vindictive labor laws in the guise of promoting industrial peace are a far more serious threat to our American system of free enterprise than all the Communists and crackpots combined. . . . The right to strike must not be infringed."

113. DHTP, IX: Doc. 70, 511; Doc. 32, Secretary of the Army Patterson; Doc. 50: L. K. Garrison (370–71).

114. Ibid.: Doc. 59: radio address Jun 20, 1947.

115. Ibid.: Doc. 49, 325–29.

116. See Lee, *Truman and Taft-Hartley,* ch. 8.

117. DHTP, IX: Doc. 72: NLRB annual report to Congress for fiscal year 1948 (Aug 1947 to Jun 30 1948), Feb 7, 1949. Slightly different figures on representation elections are given by M. Goldfield, *The Decline of Organized Labor in the United States* (Chicago, 1987), table 11: NLRB Election Results, 1935–84 (90–91).

Chapter 7. Building Socialism British Style

1. H. Cantrill, *Public Opinion*, 115.

2. A. J. P. Taylor, *English History, 1914–1945* (Oxford, 1965), 147, 206; S. Merrett, *State Housing in Britain* (London, 1979), 31–51; J. R. Short, *Housing in Britain: The Postwar Experience* (London, 1982), 33–38; R. H. Duclaud-Williams, *The Politics of Housing in Britain and France* (London, 1978), 154–55; G. Orwell, *The Road to Wigan Pier* (Penguin edn., 1989), ch. 4.

3. Short, *Housing in Britain*, 39–41.

4. M. Foot, *Aneurin Bevan*, Vol. II: *1945–1960* (Paladin edn.: London, 1975), 63–65.

5. In addition to Vol. II of the indispensable biography by Bevan's comrade Michael Foot, see J. Campbell, *Nye Bevan and the Mirage of British Socialism* (London, 1987), 149–52, and K. Morgan, *Labour People* (Oxford, 1987), 204–19.

6. See *The Labour Party Speakers' Handbook, 1949–50* (London, [Oct] 1949), 371–73, which gives the size of the average postwar unit as 934 sq. ft. at the end of 1949. D. Donnison and C. Ungerson, *Housing Policy* (Penguin edn., 1982), 143, put the average size by the end of 1951 at 1,050 sq. ft.

7. Foot, *Bevan*, II: 73; Short, *Housing in Britain*, 44–47.

8. Foot, *Bevan*, II: 69–71.

9. P. Addison, *Now the War Is Over: A Social History of Britain, 1945–51* (London, 1985), 55–56, 65–69.

10. LPB, Jun 1948, 95–96.

11. See "Castles in the Air," FACT, Dec 1950, 180–81. (In January 1949 the LPB was renamed FACT.)

12. Foot, *Bevan*, II: 94.

13. *Speakers' Handbook, 1949–50*, 354–75; "Homes for the People," FACT, Oct 1949, 152–53; "Waiting for Houses," FACT, Apr 1950, 46, and "Housing," 50.

14. *Speakers Handbook, 1948–49*, 20; Campbell, *Nye Bevan*, 163–64.

15. On the preference to own one's home, see P. Scott, *The Making of the Modern British Home: The Suburban Semi and Family Life between the Wars* (Oxford, 2013), chs. 4–5.

16. FACT, Apr 1950, 50.

17. Short, *Housing in Britain*, 47–54; Merrett, *State Housing*, 246–52; Duclaud-Williams, *Politics of Housing*, 177; Donnison and Ungerson, *Housing Policy*, 148.

18. Merrett, *State Housing*, 126–31, 248–49; also Short, *Housing in Britain*, 107–10.

19. Short, *Housing in Britain*, 109–10; Merrett, *State Housing*, 126–31; S. Muthesius and M. Glendendinning, *Tower Block: Modern Public Housing in England . . .* (New Haven CT, 1993), sect. 3: Breakdown.

20. Pat Thane, "Labour and Welfare," in D. Tanner, P. Thane, and N. Tiratsoo (eds.), *Labour's First Century* (Cambridge, 2000), 108.

21. R. A. Butler, *Art of the Possible: The Memoirs of Lord Butler* (London, 1971), 92.

22. Ibid., chs. 5–6; K. Jeffreys (ed.), *Labour and the Wartime Coalition: From the Diary of James Chuter Ede, 1941–1945* (London, 1987), 139–45, 148–49, 164–65, 174–85.

23. These "public schools" belonged to either of two self-selecting associations, one of private school governing boards and one of headmasters.

24. S. Brooke, *Labour's War,* 184–202; P. Addison, *The Road to 1945: British Politics and the Second World War* (rev. [Pimlico] edn., London, 1994), 171–74, 237–39; N. Timmins, *The Five Giants: a Biography of the Welfare State* (London, 1995), ch. 4.

25. See FACT, Feb 1949, 22; Sep 1950, 134–35.

26. B. D. Vernon, *Ellen Wilkinson, 1891–1947* (London, 1982), ch. 10; M. Perry, *"Red Ellen" Wilkinson: Her Ideas, Movement, and World* (Manchester, 2014), 372–77, 380–82; Addison, *Now the War Is Over,* 151–56; P. Hennessy, *Never Again: Britain, 1945–1951* (NY, 1993), 155–62.

27. Excerpts from Norwood and Butler's white paper in J. Stuart Maclure (ed.), *Educational Documents: England and Wales, 1816–1963* (London, 1965), 198–209.

28. H. C. Dent, *Change in English Education: A Historical Survey* (London, 1952), 70–76; Vernon, *Ellen Wilkinson,* 224–25; Perry, *Red Ellen,* 377–80; Addison, *Now the War Is Over,* 143–44, 163–66.

29. S. J. Curtis, *Education in Britain since 1900* (London, 1952), ch. 6; Addison, *Now the War Is Over,* 166–69; Timmins, *Five Giants,* 85–86, 95–96.

30. Maclure, *Educational Documents,* 196–98; Hennessy, *Never Again,* 157–62.

31. Melissa Benn, *School Wars: The Battle for Britain's Education* (London, 2011), 37–41, 44; D. Bourn, "Equality of Opportunity? The Labour Government and the Schools," in J. Fyrth (ed.), *Labour's Promised Land? Culture and Society in Labour Britain, 1945–51* (London, 1995).

32. Benn, *School Wars,* 42–3, 48; Vernon, *Ellen Wilkinson,* 220–21.

33. R. Baker, *Education and Politics, 1900–1951: A Study of the Labour Party* (Oxford, 1972), 66–73, 86–88, 93–97; Brooke, *Labour's War,* 185–203; D. Rubinstein, "Ellen Wilkinson Reconsidered," *History Workshop* (1979), 162–67.

34. LPB, Jun 1948: II, 94–95.

35. Dent, *Change in English Education,* 11–12, 93–94.

36. Joan Thompson, *Secondary Education for All: A report prepared for the Fabian Society's Education Committee* (London, [April] 1947). These LEA reports covered about 750,000 secondary pupils out of 2.5 million nationally.

37. Ibid., 7–9.

38. Ibid., 10–12, 17.

39. LPB, Oct 1948: II, 152–53.

40. Timmins, *Five Giants,* 237–47, 297–303, 318–20; Benn, *School Wars,* 37, 50–58, 71–72, 89–90, 96–97.

41. *Speakers' Handbook, 1949–50,* 339.

42. J. Carswell, *Government and the Universities in Britain: Programme and Performance, 1960–1980* (Cambridge, 1985), ch. 1. Carswell was a Treasury official dealing with higher education. See also Curtis, *Education in Britain,* ch. 7.

43. FACT, Sep 1950, 135.

44. Ibid.; and A. Allport, *Demobbed: Coming Home after the Second World War* (New Haven CT, 2009), 157–58.

45. Quintus, *Universities and the Future: A Report Prepared for the Education Committee of the Fabian Society* (London, Oct 1947), 18–21, 32–33.

46. *Speakers' Handbook, 1949–50,* 342–43.

47. Carswell, *Government and Universities*, 14–18; Dent, *Change in English Education*, 48; the Robbins Report on Higher Education of 1963 in Maclure, *Educational Documents*, 288–300.

48. J. E. Pater, *The Making of the National Health Service* (London, 1981), ch. 1.

49. Timmins, *Five Giants*, 104.

50. H. Eckstein, *The English Health Service: Its Origins, Structure, and Achievements* (Cambridge MA, 1958), chs. 1–2.

51. M. Weinbren, "Sociable Capital: London's Labour Parties, 1918–45," in M. Worley (ed.), *Labour's Grass Roots* (Aldershot, 2005), 205.

52. S. Brooke, *Labour's War*, 203–13; J. Stewart, *The Battle for Health: A Political History of the Socialist Medical Association, 1930–51* (Aldershot, 1999), ch. 8; Pater, *National Health Service*, ch. 4; Eckstein, *English Health Service*, ch. 6.

53. Pater, *National Health Service*, 87–90, 104; Eckstein, *English Health Service*, 147–50.

54. C. Webster, "Birth of the Dream: Bevan and the Architecture of the NHS," in G. Goodman (ed.), *The State of the Nation: The Political Legacy of Aneurin Bevan* (London, 1997), 107–9, 128–29; Pater, *National Health Service*, 108–9, 120, 148; Hennessy, *Never Again*, 137–40; Timmins, *Five Giants*, 113–18.

55. Foot, *Bevan*, II: 131–33; Webster, "Birth of the Dream," 121–25.

56. Timmins, *Five Giants*, 122.

57. Foot, *Bevan*, II: 139–40; Pater, *National Health Service*, 129–30.

58. See Foot, *Bevan*, II: ch. 4; Pater, *National Health Service*, 137, 150–64; Hennessy, *Never Again*, 141–43.

59. H. Eckstein, *Pressure Group Politics: The Case of the British Medical Association* (Stanford CA, 1960), ch. 4; on the vote: Pater, *National Health Service*, 162–63 and Hennessy, *Never Again*, 143.

60. "Doctors and Patients," LPB, Jul 1948: I, 104–5.

61. Foot, *Bevan*, II: 210–11; *Speakers' Handbook, 1949–50*, 305.

62. FACT, Mar 1949, 36–37; Feb 1950, 24; Apr 1950, 51.

63. Morgan, *Labour in Power*, 161–62, and especially Campbell, *Nye Bevan*, 180–85.

64. Foot, *Bevan*, II: 212–15; Timmins, *Five Giants*, 205–7, 294.

65. Eckstein, *English Health Service*, 248–52.

66. Stewart, *Battle for Health*, 195–97; LPB, "Birmingham's Health Centre," Sep 1948: II, 136–37; LPB, Aug 1948: II, 120–21.

67. Pater, *Making of the National Health Service*, 184–86.

68. See Timmins, *Five Giants;* P. Kerr, *Postwar British Politics* (London, 2001), 176–77; and P. Thane, "Labour and Welfare," in *Labour's First Century.*

69. See Morgan, *Labour in Power*, 107–8.

70. LPB, Jun 1948: I: "Scarborough Conference," 82–86.

71. B. Donoughue and G. W. Jones, *Herbert Morrison: Portrait of a Politician* (London, 1973), 400.

72. Foot, *Bevan*, II: 216–26; Campbell, *Nye Bevan*, 199–201.

73. Morgan, *Labour in Power*, 110–21.

74. N. Ellison, *Egalitarian Thought and Labour Politics: Retreating Visions* (London, 1994), ch. 2, and M. Francis, *Ideas and Policies under Labour, 1945–1951: Building a*

New Britain (Manchester, 1997), ch. 4. On consumers, see Morrison's comment at the Margate conference in FACT, Nov 1950, 166.

75. FACT, Jan 1949, 14.

76. Francis, *Ideas and Policies,* 72–73.

77. "Let Us Win Through Together," in I. Dale (ed.), *Labour Party General Election Manifestos, 1900–1997* (London, 2000), 66–67, 68, 70. For the rationales on Industrial Assurance, see FACT, Jan 1950, 8–9, and Feb 1950, 37–41.

78. *Keeping Left: Labour's First Five Years and the Problems Ahead, by a Group of Members of Parliament* (London, Jan 1950), 4–6, 28–30. See also Morrison's friendly foreword to I. Mikardo, *The Choice for Britain: The Labour Case* (London, 1950).

79. Morgan, *Labour in Power,* 121–27; H. G. Nicholas, *The British General Election of 1950* (London, 1951), 71–74.

80. G. Field, *Blood, Sweat, and Toil: Remaking the British Working Class, 1939–1945* (Oxford, 2011), 357–58, 366–68.

81. *The Labour Party and Communist Affiliation: A Statement by the NEC of the Labour Party* [2 pp.] (Transport House, Mar 1946). See also Harold Laski's long-winded pamphlet on the historical differences between authoritarian and democratic socialism. *The Secret Battalion: An Examination of the Communist Attitude to the Labour Party* (Transport House, Apr 1946).

82. [D. Healey,] *Cards on the Table: An Interpretation of Labour's Foreign Policy* (Transport House, May 1947); D. Healey, *The Time of My Life* (London, 1989), 96–105, 114.

83. A. Bullock, *Ernest Bevin: A Biography,* abr. edn., (ed.) B. Brivati (London, 2002), 536–38, 597; E. Pearce, *Denis Healy: A Life in Our Times* (London, 2002), ch. 8; I. Mikardo, *Backbencher* (London 1988), 66–67 on Keep Left.

84. LPB, Mar–Apr 1947: I, 42–43; Jun 1947: I, 68; Aug 1947: I, 108; R. Vinen, *National Service: Conscription in Britain, 1945–63* (London, 2014), 40–49.

85. See J. Callaghan, "Towards Isolation: The Communist Party and the Labour Government," in Fyrth (ed.), *Labour's Promised Land?,* 95–98.

86. J. Schneer, *Labour's Conscience: The Labour Left, 1945–51* (Boston, 1988), ch. 5; also Donoughue and Jones, *Herbert Morrison,* 433–34.

87. D. Healey, "The Zilliacus Mystery," FACT, Dec 1949, 182–83.

88. *Keeping Left,* esp. 26–27.

89. S. Parsons, "British 'McCarthyism' and the Intellectuals," in Fyrth (ed.), *Labour's Promised Land?,* 226–35.

90. N. Fishman, *The British Communist Party and the Trade Unions, 1933–1945* (Aldershot, 1995), ch. 12.

91. J. Phillips, *The Great Alliance: Economic Recovery and the Problem of Power, 1945–1951* (London, 1996), ch. 4 on the TGWU.

92. Schneer, *Labour's Conscience,* 134–40; Parsons, "British McCarthyism," 232–33.

93. P. Hennessy and G. Brownfield, "Britain's Cold War Security Purge: the Origins of Positive Vetting," *Historical Journal,* XXV (1982), 965–73.

94. See K. Harris, *Attlee* (London, 1982), 436–41; P. Williams (ed.), *The Diary of Hugh Gaitskell, 1945–1956* (London, 1983), 138–50 (hereafter *Gaitskell Diary*).

95. FACT, Apr 1950, 55–56; Nicholas, *General Election of 1950*, ch. 1. In 1945 Labour averaged 30,500 votes per seat won while the Conservatives averaged 46,800; in 1950 each party would average around 42,500 votes per seat won.

96. Nicholas, *General Election of 1950*, chs. 6–7; D. Butler, *British General Elections since 1945* (Oxford, 1995 edn.), 2.

97. See Foot, *Bevan*, II: ch. 6.

98. Nicholas, *General Election of 1950*, chs. 8–9; *Keeping Left*, 29.

99. See J. Ramsden, *The Age of Churchill and Eden, 1940–57* (London, 1995), 144–58, 163–68; A. Taylor, "Speaking to Democracy: The Conservative Party and Mass Opinion from the 1920s to the 1950s," and P. Dorey, "Industrial Relations as 'Human Relations': Conservatism and Trade Unionism, 1945–64," in S. Ball and I. Halliday (eds.), *Mass Conservatism: The Conservatives and the Public since the 1880s* (London, 2002), esp. 79–88 and 143–46.

100. FACT, Apr 1950, 55–62; Nicholas, *General Election of 1950*, ch. 12 and appendix (by D. Butler).

101. FACT, Apr 1950, 55–62; Nicholas, *General Election of 1950*, chs. 3, 12, and appendix.

102. See D. E. Butler, *The British General Election of 1951* (London, 1952), 12–14; Ramsden, *The Age of Churchill*, 218–26.

103. *Keeping Left*, 18–19.

104. FACT, Sep 1950, 120–22; Vinen, *National Service*, 286–87 on Korea.

105. Under a diary entry dated Apr 30, 1951, Gaitskell summarized the previous two months of maneuvering over the budget in cabinet. P. Williams (ed.), *Gaitskell Diary*, 238–47.

106. See Morgan, *Labour in Power*, ch. 10, and Campbell, *Nye Bevan*, chs. 15–16.

107. Hennessy, *Never Again*, 404–19.

108. Campbell, *Nye Bevan*, 240–45; F. Williams, *A Prime Minister Remembers* (London, 1961), 243–49.

109. Butler, *General Election of 1951*, ch. 10.

110. M. Jenkins, *Bevanism: Labour's High Tide: The Cold War and the Democratic Mass Movement* (Nottingham, 1979), 129: Castle, Wilson, Driberg, Crossman, and Mikardo.

111. Mikardo, *Backbencher*, 108–9 and ch. 9; L. Martineau, *Politics and Power: Barbara Castle, a Life* (London, 2000), ch. 5; Jenkins, *Bevanism*, chs. 5–7, 12; Campbell, *Nye Bevan*, parts 6 and 7.

112. See *Gaitskell Diary*, ch. 7: "Bevan Expelled?"

113. Butler, *British General Elections since 1945*, 14–19.

114. See Goodman (ed.), *Political Legacy of Aneurin Bevan*, esp. B. Castle, "A Passionate Defiance."

115. T. Wright and M. Carter, *The People's Party: The History of the Labour Party* (London, 1997), ch. 5. Cf. the panegyric by G. McDermott, *Leader Lost: A Biography of Hugh Gaitskell* (NY, 1971).

116. See D. Marquand, *Britain since 1918: The Strange Career of British Democracy* (London, 2008), ch. 7; Wright and Carter, *People's Party*, chs. 6–7; Tanner, Thane, and Tiratsoo (eds.), *Labour's First Century*.

117. For this fecund if irresolvable historiographical debate, see P. Hennessy and A. Seldon (eds.), *Ruling Performance: Postwar Administrations from Attlee to Thatcher* (Oxford, 1987), chs. 1–3 (esp. "The Road from 1945" by Paul Addison, the pioneer of the

consensus view); H. Jones and M. Kandiah (eds.), *The Myth of Consensus: New Views on British History, 1945–64* (NY, 1996); J. Lawrence and M. Taylor (eds.), *Party, State and Society: Electoral Behaviour in Britain since 1820* (Aldershot, 1997), chs. 6–7; and R. McKibbin, *Parties and People: England, 1914–1951* (Oxford, 2010), 164–76.

118. Healy, *Time of My Life*, 73.

Chapter 8. Tripartism and Its Aftermath

1. A. Fonvieille-Vojtovic, *Paul Ramadier, 1888–1961: élu local et homme d'État* (Paris, 1993), 322–23, 327–28.

2. P.-H. Teitgen, *Memoirs*, 357–58; Fonvieille-Vojtovic, *Ramadier*, 330.

3. A.N. 457 AP [Bidault Papers], 142, doss. Ravitaillement: "Exposé sur le Ravitaillement," May 1, 1946. F. Grenard, *Les Scandales du Ravitaillement* (Paris, 2012) is the leading authority. For local case studies, M. Koreman, *The Expectation of Justice: France, 1944–1946* (Durham NC, 1999), ch. 4.

4. V.-A. Montassier, *Les Années d'après-guerre, 1944–1949* (Paris, 1980), 213–14; Pineau oral history in Wieviorka, *Oral Histories*, 271.

5. Grenard, *Scandales du Ravitaillement*, 195–98, 205–9.

6. A.N. 457 AP 141, doss. Prix: "Note pour le Président," Sep 12, 1946.

7. Grenard, *Scandales du Ravitaillement*, 220–28.

8. A.N. 457 AP 141, doss. Conférence Nationale Économique: "Objet de la Conférence" and opening address by Bidault.

9. Ibid., doss. Appels de groupements: Conseil National du Patronat Français to G.B., Jun 19, 1946.

10. Ibid., Resolutions by CGT and CFTC; Mouvement Populaire des Familles to Bidault, Jun 25.

11. Ibid., Ministre de l'Intérieure, Sûreté Nationale: Direction des Renseignements Généraux, 5ème Section, Jul 3, 1946.

12. [Pharos] *Les Archives Internationales*, no. 77 (Sep 1946), and "Rapport Général" by P. Lamour, both in A.N. 457 AP 141.

13. A.N. 457 AP 141, doss. "Politique d'Économie Générale."

14. A.N. 457 AP 142, doss. Ravitaillement: Minister to Bidault, Dec 9, 1946.

15. A.N. 457 AP 141, "Notes pour Mon. le Président," Sep 16, 1946.

16. C. Andrieu, *Le Programme Commun de la Résistance: Des idées dans la guerre* (Paris, 1984), 158, 166, 174; A. Shennan, *Rethinking France: Plans for Renewal, 1940–1946* (Oxford, 1989), ch. 9; B. Valat, *Histoire de la Sécurité Sociale, 1945–1967: L'État, l'institution, et la santé* (Paris, 2001), 30–41.

17. T. B. Smith, *Creating the Welfare State in France, 1880–1940* (Montreal, 2003), ch. 5; P. V. Dutton, *Origins of the French Welfare State: The Struggle for Social Reform in France, 1914–1947* (Cambridge, 2002), ch. 4.

18. S. Pedersen, *Family, Dependence, and the Origins of the Welfare State: Britain and France, 1914–1945* (Cambridge, 1993), 357–59, 371.

19. Ibid., 386–88, 408; Smith, *Creating the Welfare State*, 155–56; P. Nord, *France's New Deal from the Thirties to the Postwar Era* (Princeton, 2010), 176–84, 210–11 on the persistent eugenicist and racialist strains of pro-natalist thought.

20. See E. Jabbari, *Pierre Laroque and the Welfare State in Postwar France* (Oxford, 2012), esp. 7–9.

21. P. Baldwin, *The Politics of Social Solidarity: Class Bases of the European Welfare State, 1875–1975* (Cambridge, 1990), 158–86.

22. See Nord, *France's New Deal,* 169–70, 187–88.

23. See H. Galant, *Histoire Politique de la Sécurité Sociale française, 1945–1952* (Paris, 1955), 114; Baldwin, *Politics of Social Solidarity,* 171, 174–86; Dutton, *Origins of the French Welfare State,* 217–19; Jabbari, *Laroque,* 150–55; Nord, *France's New Deal,* 167–72.

24. Valat, *Histoire de la Sécurité Sociale,* 84–92; Dutton, *Origins of the French Welfare State,* 216–17.

25. Gallant, *Sécurité Sociale,* 123–24.

26. A.N. 457 AP 141, doss. Sécurité Sociale: H. Meck to Bidault, Jul 19, 1946.

27. Galant, *Sécurité Sociale,* 116–28; Dutton, *Origins of the French Welfare State,* 215–16. The election results for the boards of the family allowance *caisses* were proportionately comparable.

28. Galant, *Sécurité Sociale,* 148–50, 182–83.

29. See Valat, *Histoire de la Sécurité Sociale,* ch. 6: "Le Partage du Pouvoir entre l'État et les Caisses."

30. I. Woloch, *The New Regime: Transformations of the French Civic Order, 1789–1820s* (NY, 1994), chs. 6–7.

31. In the postwar moment a new National School of Administration (ENA) took its place among the elite *grandes écoles.* See Nord, *France's New Deal,* 189–213.

32. E. Weber, *Peasants into Frenchmen: The Modernization of Rural France, 1870–1914* (Stanford CA, 1976), ch. 18.

33. J. E. Talbott, *The Politics of Educational Reform in France, 1918–1940* (Princeton, 1969), 166–69; A. Prost, *L'Enseignement en France, 1800–1967* (Paris, 1968), 415–17.

34. Quoted in Talbott, 215.

35. A. Prost, *Du Changement dans l'école: Les réformes de l'éducation de 1936 à nos jours* (Paris, 2013), 29–43. Also Talbott, *Politics of Educational Reform,* 225–38; Prost, *L'Enseignement en France,* 417–19.

36. R. Paxton, *Vichy France: Old Guard and New Order* (NY, 1972), 153–60; J. Jackson, *France: The Dark Years, 1940–1944* (Oxford, 2001), 154–57.

37. Andrieu, *Le Programme Commun,* 174. For other plans, see Shennan, *Rethinking France,* 172–80.

38. L. Hamon, "Tribute," in L. Philip, *André Philip* (Paris, 1988), 260–61; Prost, *Du Changement dans l'école,* 70.

39. See Talbott, *Politics of Educational Reform,* 188–204, for prewar debates between Catholic traditionalists and more conciliatory social Catholics; Shennan, *Rethinking France,* 180–82; J. Girault, "La SFIO et le monde enseignant," in S. Berstein et al. (eds.), *Le Parti Socialiste entre Résistance et République* (Paris, 2000), 294, 298–301.

40. J. Moch, *Une si longue vie* (Paris, 1976), 302–4. On the set-to in 1951, see R. Quilliot, *La S.F.I.O. et l'exercice du pouvoir, 1944–58* (Paris, 1972), 392–410.

41. Prost, *Du Changement dans l'école,* 58–63; Girault, "La SFIO et le monde enseignant," 296–97.

42. A. D. Robert, "La Quatrième République et les questions de l'égalité et de la justice dans l'enseignement du second degré: Le changement sans la réforme," *Revue française de pédagogie*, no. 159 (Apr 2007), 9; J.-M. Donegani and M. Sadoun, "La Réforme de l'Enseignement Secondaire en France depuis 1945: Analyse d'une non-décision," *Revue française de science politique*, XXVI (1976), 1127–30.

43. All citations are from the 34-page summary (exposé) of the L-W Report, available online at http://escales.enfa.fr/wp-content/uploads/sites/7/2009/03/Plan-Langevin-Wallon.pdf.

44. Ibid., 31.

45. Ibid., 4–5.

46. Prost, *Du Changement dans l'école*, 52–63; Robert, "Le changement sans la réforme," 9–15.

47. Rioux, *Fourth Republic*, 411–21; G. Vincent, *Les Français, 1945–1975* (Paris, 1977), 285, 292; Robert, "Le changement sans la réforme," 15–16; Talbott, *Politics of Educational Reform*, 230; Prost, *L'Enseignement en France*, 460–61.

48. D. Voldman, *Reconstruction des villes françaises de 1940 à 1954: Histoire d'une politique* (Paris, 1997), 25.

49. Ibid., 32.

50. J.-P. Flamand, *Loger le Peuple: Essai sur l'histoire du movement sociale* (Paris, 1989), 195. Voldman (p. 25) gives a higher estimate of damaged dwellings.

51. Voldman, *Reconstruction des villes françaises*, 307–17. On the impressive Noisy-le Sec demonstration project, see N. C. Rudolph, *At Home in Postwar France: Modern Housing and the Right to Comfort* (NY, 2015), 25–32, and Voldman, 225.

52. F. Billoux, *Quand nous étions ministres* (Paris, 1972), 107–14.

53. Flamand, *Loger le Peuple*, 196; Rudolph, *At Home in Postwar France*, 17–21.

54. R. H. Duclaud-Williams, *The Politics of Housing in Britain and France* (London, 1978), 33–51.

55. Ibid.; Voldman, *Reconstruction des villes françaises*, 338–39.

56. Duclaud-Williams, *Politics of Housing*, 130–34.

57. Ibid., 124–27 and table VIII.1, p. 149; Voldman, *Reconstruction des villes françaises*, 328.

58. For these paragraphs I draw on Benoit Pouvreau's seminal article, "La Politique d'aménagement du territoire d'Eugène Claudius-Petit," *Vingtième Siècle*, no. 79 (2003), 43–52.

59. See T. Judt, *Past Imperfect: French Intellectuals, 1944–1956* (Berkeley CA, 1992) 209–13.

60. V. Auriol, *Journal du Septennat* I (Paris, 1970), 35.

61. A.N. 350 AP 15 [MRP Papers], IIIème Congrès National, Rapport de Politique Général, and plenary session of Mar 16, 1947.

62. Auriol, *Journal* I, Mar 20, 1947, 159n.

63. A.N. 457 AP 143, doss. "Union Gaulliste."

64. See B. Lachaise, "La Création du Rassemblement du Peuple Français," in S. Berstein and P. Milza (eds.), *L'Année 1947* (Paris, 2000), 327–37.

65. E. Michelet, *Le Gaullisme: Passionnante aventure* (Paris, 1962), 113.

66. See A.N. 457 AP 143, doss. "Union Gaulliste"; E. Michelet, *Le Gaullisme,* 102. For the MRP's hostility toward this 'traitor,' see C. Michelet, *Mon père, Edmond Michelet* (1981), 160–4.

67. Michelet offered a plausible psychological insight about his former comrades in the MRP: "Dans cette satisfaction d'entrer dans les rangs 'républicains' d'où ils avaient été chassés depuis toujours, ils adopteraient tous les défauts d'un régime dont ils n'oseraient pas demander la réforme profonde de crainte de ne pas passer pour suffisamment républicains." *Le Gaullisme,* 91.

68. N. Castagnez, *Socialistes en République: Les parlementaires SFIO de la IVe République* (Paris, 2004), 51–73, 109–11.

69. Camus in *Combat,* Sep 8, Oct 1, and Nov 10, 1944; Hamon, "Temoignage," in Philip, *André Philip,* 263. (Hamon, the Resistance nom de guerre of L. Goldenberg, was not a Catholic.) Claude Bourdet similarly comments on the rigidity of the PS after the Liberation, although Bourdet was "very hostile" to the MRP as well: Bourdet's oral history in Wieviorka's, *Oral Histories,* 364–66.

70. See B. D. Graham, *French Socialism and Tripartism,* ch. 5, esp. pp. 198, 207, 210, and Graham "The Succession Crisis of 1946" in a more detailed study: *Choice and Democratic Order: The French Socialist Party, 1937–1950* (Cambridge, 1994) ch. 6.

71. Quoted in D. Lefebvre, *Guy Mollet, Le Mal Aimé* (Paris, 1992), 112.

72. Graham, *Choice and Democratic Order,* 355–65.

73. See F. Billoux, *Quand nous étions ministres,* ch. 2, and I. Wall, *French Communism in the Era of Stalin: The Quest for Unity and Integration, 1945–1962* (Westport CT, 1983), ch. 2. On the nationalizations, see C. Andrieu, L. Le Van, and A. Prost (eds.), *Les Nationalisations de la Libération: De l'utopie au compromis* (Paris, 1987), part 4, and esp. 330–38 on the EDF.

74. Buton, "L'Éviction des ministres communistes," in Berstein and Milza (eds.), *L'Année 1947,* 344–47.

75. For an evocative portrait of Thorez by a militant insider who later broke with the party, see A. Kriegel, *The French Communists: Portrait of a People* (Chicago, 1972 transl.), 214–23.

76. S. Courtois and M. Lazar, *Histoire du Parti communiste français* (Paris, 1995), 240–2, 230–1.

77. Ibid., 219; Wall, *French Communism,* 35.

78. See J.-J. Becker, *Le Parti Communiste veut-il prendre le pouvoir?* (Paris, 1981), ch. 3.

79. Courtois and Lazar, *Histoire du PCF,* 221–22.

80. Fonvieille-Vojtovic, *Ramadier,* 333; Buton, "L'Eviction."

81. G. Lefranc, *Le Mouvement Syndical de la Libération aux évenements de Mai–Juin 1968* (Paris, 1969), 47–50. The Renault strike was settled on May 9.

82. Auriol, *Journal* I, 204–18; Fonvieille-Vojtovic, *Ramadier,* 333–36; Graham, *French Socialists and Tripartism,* 261–63.

83. Lefebvre, *Mollet,* 113–15; F. Lafon, *Guy Mollet: Itinéraire d'un socialiste controversé, 1905–1975* (Paris, 2006), 336–47; "French Socialists Endorse Ramadier by Narrow Vote," *New York Times,* May 7, 1947.

84. Lefebvre, *Mollet,* 116–18; Lafon, *Mollet,* ch. 9, in detail.

85. Courtois and Lazar, *Histoire du PCF*, 251–53; Buton, "L'Eviction," 348–55; Wall, *French Communism*, ch. 3.

86. Lachaise, "La Création du RPF," 333.

87. Cf. R. Mencherini, *Guerre Froide, Grèves Rouges: Parti communiste, stalinisme et luttes sociales en France. Les grèves "insurrectionnelles" de 1947–1948* (Paris, 1998), 245–60.

88. Thus when Radical André Marie replaced Schuman as PM in July 1948, he named prewar conservative Paul Reynaud as minister of finances, and Joseph Laniel as a sub-cabinet secretary of state. Marie's government fell about a month later because the Socialists and some of the MRP would not support Reynaud's fiscal and economic proposals. The ensuing cabinet crisis was resolved two weeks later when the old-line Radical Henri Queuille became PM. His cabinet included the first right-wing PRL deputy to be named as a minister and the rising rightist Antoine Pinay in a sub-cabinet post.

89. The most comprehensive analysis is R. Mencherini, *Guerre Froide, Grèves Rouges*. For a tally of violent confrontations, see also E. Kocher-Marboeuf, "Le Maintien de l'Ordre Public lors des Grèves de 1947," in *L'Année 1947*, 383–87.

90. Moch, *Une si longue vie*, ch. 15; E. Méchoulan, "Le Pouvoir Face aux Grèves 'insurrectionnelles' de Novembre et de Décembre," in *L'Année 1947*, 390–408; and G. Ross, *Workers and Communists in France: From Popular Front to Eurocommunism* (Berkeley, 1982), 49–61.

91. In a preface to Mencherini's volume, the noted historian Maurice Agulhon recalls the book he co-wrote in 1971 exonerating the CRS units from Marseilles from the charges that led to their cashiering.

92. Cited in Annie Kriegel's autobiography *Ce Que J'ai Cru Comprendre* (Paris, 1991), 438.

93. Georges Séguy oral history in Wieviorka, *Oral Histories*, 237.

94. D. Lefebvre et al., *19 Décembre 1947: Force Ouvrière* (Paris, 1997) (hereafter *FO*), 63–64; M. Dreyfus, *Histoire de la C.G.T.: Cent ans de syndicalisme en France* (Paris, 1995), 214–16. Dreyfus dismisses the commonly used figure of 5 million CGT members in 1946 as far overstated.

95. Lefranc, *Mouvement Syndical*, 26; Lefebvre, *FO*, 92–99; Dreyfus, *CGT*, 223–24.

96. Lefebvre, *FO*, 119–20; Dreyfus, *CGT*, 221–26.

97. A. Bergounioux, *Force Ouvrière* (Paris, 1975), ch. 7; Lefebvre, *FO*, 131–41; Lefranc, *Mouvement Syndical*, 51–55. The unpublished paper "Louis Saillant" by J.-M. Pernot is the sole monograph on this elusive figure; www.ihs.cgt.fr/IMG/doc/presentation_de_la_conference.doc.

98. Lefebvre, *FO*, 147–52, 194; Dreyfus, *CGT*, 230–32.

99. Lefebvre, *FO*, 166–70; Bergounioux, *Force Ouvrière*, 87–89. On Jouhaux's resistance to a schism, see the contributions of M. Dreyfus, A. Narritsens, and D. Lefebvre to *Léon Jouhaux: d'Aubervilliers au prix nobel* (Paris, 2010), 97–129.

100. See the analysis based on American archives by I. Wall, *The United States and the Making of Postwar France, 1945–1954* (Cambridge, 1991), 97–113.

101. Lefebvre, *FO*, 174, 185, 193–97; Bergounioux, *Force Ouvrière*, 90–92; Dreyfus, *CGT*, 238–39.

Chapter 9. The United States

1. See "Student Forum," *Columbia Spectator,* Mar 29, 1946: letter from Ernest Kinnoy.
2. C. Bolté, *The New Veteran* (NY, 1945), ch. 5.
3. B. Mauldin, *Back Home* (NY, 1947), chs. 5–6; T. DePastino, *Bill Mauldin: A Life Up Front* (NY, 2008), ch. 6. Cf. J. Gray, *The Inside Story of the Legion* (NY, 1948), chs. 5–7, 9–10.
4. "Where Do We Go from Here: A New Organization of Veterans Gives Its Answer," AVC pamphlet, 1945; Gilbert Harrison Papers, LC: Box 2: letters from 1941; Bolté, *New Veteran,* chs. 6–7, 9–11; R. F. Saxe, *Settling Down: World War II Veterans' Challenge to the Postwar Consensus* (NY, 2007), ch. 4.
5. *Harvard Crimson,* Jan 11, Jul 12, Nov 6, 7, and 12, 1946; Mar 25, 1949; D. Halberstam, "College AVC Chapter Spent Stormy Half-Decade as Crusader, Reformer," ibid., Mar 14, 1952.
6. Ibid., Apr 25, Jul 12, 1946; Feb 28, 1948; Mar 25, 19 49; Olson, *G.I. Bill,* 64–65.
7. *Columbia Spectator,* Feb 15, 20, 26, Oct 4, 8, 11, 15, 1946; Mar 13, 1947.
8. *Harvard Crimson,* Apr 25 and Jul 12, 1946; Feb 28, 1948; *New York Times,* Jul 12, 1946. Cf. R. O. Davies, *Housing Reform during the Truman Administration* (Columbia MO, 1966), ch. 4; "From Foxhole to Rathole," *Brooklyn Eagle,* Apr 26 and May 19, 1946
9. *Columbia Spectator,* Mar 25, 1947; Mar 24, Apr 28, Oct 3, 1948.
10. *Harvard Crimson,* Mar 9 and 10, 1947; *Columbia Spectator,* Mar 25, 1947; Apr 28, 1948.
11. J. Egerton, *Speak Now against the Day: The Generation before the Civil Rights Movement* (Chapel Hill NC, 1995), 328, 339–41, 375, 557–60; J. Brooks, *Defining the Peace: World War II Veterans, Race, and the Remaking of Southern Political Tradition* (Chapel Hill NC, 2004), 73–74, and 193 note 35; K. Frydl, *GI Bill* (Cambridge, 2009), 255–57.
12. Brooks, *Defining the Peace,* 45–46, 49, 55–56, 62–63, 193–94 notes 35 and 39.
13. "The New Veteran," *The Nation* CLXII (Jan 19, 1946), 65–67, including: W. Bernstein, "Attacking Mr. Bolté," and M. Miller, "Rebutting Mr. Bernstein." See also Gray, *Inside Story of the Legion,* chs. 1, 11; W. Bernstein, *Inside Out: A Memoir of the Blacklist* (NY, 1996), 140–43.
14. Mauldin Papers, LC: Box 2: L. Lauterstein to A. Rice, AVC Executive Director, Dec 18, 1953.
15. *New York Times,* Jun 16 and 17, 1946; M. Straight, "The Greatest Guys in the World," *New Republic,* Jul 1, 1946, 926–27; and D. James, "The Battle of A.V.C.," *The Nation* CLXIV (Jun 14, 1947), 706–8.
16. R. Minott, *Peerless Patriots: Organized Veterans and the Spirit of Americanism* (Washington DC, 1962), 105–6; R. L. Tyler, "The American Veterans Committee: Out of a Hot War and into the Cold," *American Quarterly,* XVIII (Autumn 1966), 422–27.
17. J. Franklin, "Why I Broke with the Communists," *Harper's Magazine,* CXCIV (May 1947), 412–18. This article is cited in passing by Minott and by Saxe, but it has never been mined for its revelatory details and insights. (I have known Julian Franklin as an esteemed colleague and friend for over forty years.)

18. On Gus Tyler, see M. Straight, *After Long Silence* (NY, 1983), 236–37; Saxe, *Settling Down,* 149–50. Cf. James, "Battle of A.V.C.," 706–8.

19. On the poll, Minott, *Peerless Patriots,* 105–6. On the labyrinthine struggle over the NY Area Council, R. Tyler, "Out of a Hot War," 425–33; *Brooklyn Eagle,* Oct 10, 1948; *Columbia Spectator,* Nov 16, 1948. On the Gates case, Straight, *After Long Silence,* 238–39.

20. *AVC Bulletin* III (Dec 1948) in Gilvert Harrison Papers, LC: Box 5.

21. *Harvard Crimson,* Nov 7, Dec 5, 1946.

22. Ibid., Mar 4, 1948; Nov 30, Dec 6, 1949.

23. *Columbia Spectator,* Oct 15 and 18, Nov 15, 1946; Apr 16 and 22, May 13, 1947; May 11, 1948.

24. Ibid., Mar 24, Apr 28, Oct 3, Dec 4, 1948; May 5 and 12, 1949.

25. Ibid., Nov 16, Dec 14, 1948; Feb 17 and 23, 1949; Oct 19, 1949.

26. Michael Straight, whose family published the liberal *New Republic* magazine, joined the British CP while a student at Cambridge in the 1930s and was recruited by Anthony Blunt to spy for the Soviet Union. Straight returned to the US and held jobs in Washington before his induction into the air force. By 1942 he broke with communism and put his experience with the KGB behind him but did not acknowledge it publicly for years to come. (See J. E. Haynes and H. Klehr, *Venona: Decoding Soviet Espionage in America* [New Haven CT, 1999], 152–57, and A. Weinstein and V. Vassiliev, *The Haunted Wood: Soviet Espionage in America in the Stalin Era* [NY, 1999], ch. 4.) Allied with the liberals of the AVC, such as Bolté and Harrison, Straight's secret past likely festered in his psyche and perhaps caused some erratic behavior. But the contention by R. Perry, *Last of the Coldwar Spies: The Life of Michael Straight* (NY, 2005), that Straight remained an agent of the KGB in the postwar years (as against Weinstein's account from the Venona files) is unpersuasive.

27. Mauldin Papers, LC: Box 2: Mauldin to A. Rice, 28 Nov 1953.

28. Straight, *After Long Silence,* 245–46.

29. DePastino, *Mauldin,* 218–19, 227–37, 263–68.

30. Mauldin Papers, LC: Box 2: Lauterstein letter; Elmer Davis in *AVC Bulletin* IX (Feb 1954), 4.

31. The positive case is made by S. Rosswurm (ed.), *The CIO's Left-Led Unions* (New Brunswick NJ, 1992), introduction, and J. Stepan-Norris and M. Zeitlin, *Left Out: Reds and America's Industrial Unions* (Cambridge, 2003). On the UE, see R. W. Schatz, *The Electrical Workers: A History of Labor at General Electric and Westinghouse, 1923–60* (Urbana IL, 1983), part 4; and the dueling oral histories of Emspak and James Carey in CU Oral History.

32. See B. Cochran, *Labor and Communism: The Conflict that Shaped American Unions* (Princeton, 1977), ch. 7: "Political Strikes in the Defense Period."

33. D. J. McDonald, *Union Man* (NY, 1969), 156.

34. K. Boyle, *The UAW and the Heyday of American Liberalism, 1945–1968* (Ithaca NY, 1995), esp. 28–34; H. A. Levenstein, *Communism, Anticommunism and the CIO* (Westport CT, 1980), ch. 10; R. Keeran, *The Communist Party and the Auto Workers Unions* (Bloomington IN, 1980), chs. 9–10; Cochran, *Labor and Communism,* ch. 10; N. Lichtenstein, *The Most Dangerous Man in Detroit: Walter Reuther* (Urbana IL, 1995), ch. 11.

35. Cochran, *Labor and Communism*, 272–79. Cf. Stepan-Norris and Zeitlin, *Left Out*, ch. 4.

36. Reuther, "How to Beat the Communists" (*Colliers*, Feb 28, 1948) in *Walter E. Reuther: Selected Papers* (NY, 1961), 22–35.

37. D. P. Seaton, *Catholics and Radicals: The Association of Catholic Trade Unionists and the American Labor Movement* (Lewisburg PA, 1981), ch. 7; S. Rosswurm, "The Catholic Church and the Left-Led Unions," in Rosswurm (ed.), *CIO's Left-Led Unions;* Cochran, *Labor and Communism*, 289–93; G. Gerstle, *Working-Class Americanism: The Politics of Labor in a Textile City, 1914–1960* (Cambridge, 1989), ch. 9. In 1941 the UE's convention censured the interference of the ACTU and did not reelect ACTU's candidate James Carey as UE president.

38. There is no biography of Murray, but see P. F. Clark et al. (eds.), *Forging a Union of Steel: Philip Murray, SWOC, and the United Steelworkers* (Ithaca NY, 1987).

39. See Emspak, CU Oral History, 282–90.

40. Pressman believed that if Murray had replaced Carey ("who didn't represent anything") as CIO secretary-treasurer in 1941, it would be claimed that the Reds were running the CIO. Pressman, CU Oral History, 405–07.

41. See Carey, CU Oral History, 268–99, 335–50.

42. Levenstein, *Communism, Anticommunism and the CIO*, ch. 11; R. H. Zieger, *The CIO, 1935–1955* (Chapel Hill NC, 1995), 253–61; McDonald, *Union Man*, 184–85. McDonald's memoir is opinionated and blatantly self-justifying yet contains nuggets of useful detail about Murray, the USWA, and the CIO.

43. Cf. J. Gates, *The Story of an American Communist* (NY, 1958), 114–16. After he broke with the party in 1956, the former editor of the *Daily Worker* observed that the party "made it easier for the expulsion policy [of the CIO] to be carried through [later]" by its insistence that CIO communist leaders oppose the Marshall Plan and support Wallace's candidacy.

44. M. Kempton, *Part of Our Time: Some Ruins and Monuments of the Thirties* (NY, 1955/2004), 74–76.

45. DHTP, XIV [Running from Behind]: Doc. 11: FBI to the White House, Feb 7, 1948, 112–15, with detail on the eleven executive board members who favored "Stalin's candidate" Wallace, but noting that "the CIO trend was definitely anti-communist."

46. G. J. Gall, *Pursuing Justice: Lee Pressman, the New Deal, and the CIO* (Albany NY, 1999), chs. 7–8; McDonald, *Union Man*, 195–96.

47. On Curran see Kempton, *Part of Our Time*, ch. 3, and Levenstein, *Communism, Anticommunism and the CIO*, 253–64.

48. J. B. Freeman, *In Transit: The Transport Workers Union in New York City, 1933–1966* (Oxford, 1989), 296–302. In January Quill still took the communist line in the key vote by CIO executive board.

49. McDonald, *Union Man*, 211.

50. 82nd Congress (Document no. 89), *Report of the Senate Subcommittee on Labor . . . on Communist Domination of Certain Unions* (Washington DC, Oct 1951).

51. Schatz, *Electrical Workers*, chs. 8–9; Zeiger, *CIO*, 277–93; Levenstein, *Communism, Anticommunism and the CIO*, chs. 14–17; Cochran, *Labor and Communism*, chs. 10–12. In exasperation Rosswurm, p. 15, calls the IUE a "bastard union."

52. *Should Labor Be Given a Direct Share in the Management of Industry? A Study for Use in Preparation of Debates among College and University Students* (NAM Industrial Relations Department, Nov 1946) [CU Library D261. N2174].

53. See, e.g., M. Goldfield, *The Decline of Organized Labor in the United States* (Chicago, 1987), chs. 10–11, esp. 226–27; Boyle, *UAW,* ch. 4; Zieger and Gall, *American Workers,* ch. 6; S. Amberg, "The CIO Political Strategy in Historical Perspective: Creating a High-Road Economy in the Postwar Era," in K. Boyle (ed.), *Organized Labor and American Politics, 1894–1994: The Labor-Liberal Alliance* (Albany NY, 1998).

54. In a symposium on race and the CIO (*International Labor and Working-Class History,* no. 44, Fall 1993) Michael Goldfield lauds the positive record of the CIO's left-led unions on race in workplace and union affairs and is unsparing on the racism of UMW and USWA officials (pp. 9–13). Judith Stein counters that Goldfield's view "distorts the actual course of southern unionism by ignoring the [negative influence of the] AFL, magnifying the differences within the CIO, and elevating the significance of the communist-led unions" (pp. 51–63).

55. M. E. Reed, *Seedtime for the Modern Civil Rights Movement: The President's Committee on Fair Employment, 1941–1946* (Baton Rouge LA, 1991), ch. 9.

56. R. C. Weaver, *Negro Labor: A National Problem* (NY, 1946), esp. 215–19 and 229–31 on segregated AFL locals; 127–30 and 231–34 on CIO unions; and 222–24 on "hate strikes." Also A. E. Kersten, *Race, Jobs, and the War: The FEPC in the Midwest, 1941–46* (Urbana IL, 2000), "Wartime Hate Strike Data," 143–44.

57. B. Nelson, *Divided We Stand: American Workers and the Struggle for Black Equality* (Princeton, 2001), xxxi–iv and chs. 5–6.

58. See R. Milkman, *Gender at Work: The Dynamics of Job Segregation by Sex during World War II* (Urbana IL, 1987), ch. 7; D. Montgomery, *Workers' Control in America: Studies in the History of Work, Technology, and Labor Struggles* (Cambridge, 1979/1988), 140–43, 149–51, on the unions' long struggle for seniority rights and the CPUSA's contrary plea in 1945 for a kind of affirmative action for black workers.

59. "CIO Head Opposes Seniority Revision," *Chicago Defender,* January 27, 1945, pp. 1, 4.

60. See Zeiger, *CIO,* 155–61 on CAD's founding and wartime years.

61. *National CIO Committee to Abolish Discrimination: Report of the Director Adopted March 13, 1945* (Washington DC, 1945), esp. 3–4, 7–8, 12.

62. I draw on the remarkable oral history edited by M. K. Honey, *Black Workers Remember: An Oral History of Segregation, Unionism, and the Freedom Struggle* (Berkeley CA, 1999), 154–65, 171–78.

63. J. Stein, *Running Steel, Running America: Race, Economic Policy and the Decline of Liberalism* (Chapel Hill NC, 1998), 15–18, 41–52.

64. Zieger, *CIO,* "Facing South," 227–41, and B. Griffith, *The Crisis of American Labor: Operation Dixie and the Defeat of the CIO* (Philadelphia, 1988), 18–25.

65. Griffith, *Crisis of American Labor,* 32–38. On the relative improvement in the lives of many Southern textile workers in the 1940s, and their unease over Operation Dixie, see T. J. Minchin, *What Do We Need a Union For? The TWUA in the South, 1945–55* (Chapel Hill NC, 1997), chs. 2–3.

66. Griffith, *Crisis of American Labor,* 61.

67. Zieger, *CIO,* 237–41; Griffith, *Crisis of American Labor,* 72–79; Minchin, *What Do We Need,* 37–44.

68. See A. A. Offner, *Another Such Victory: President Truman and the Cold War, 1945–1953* (Stanford CA, 2002), chs. 5–9.

69. R. G. Tugwell, *A Chronicle of Jeopardy, 1945–55* (Chicago, 1955), chs. 2–4; J. M. Blum (ed.), *The Price of Vision: The Diary of Henry A. Wallace, 1942–1946* (Boston, 1973), 661–69; R. J. Walton, *Henry Wallace, Harry Truman, and the Cold War* (NY, 1976), ch. 2.

70. One journalistic denunciation in 1944 claimed that of NC-PAC's founding cohort of 141 personalities, 110 were associated with Communist front organizations. See J. Gaer, *The First Round: The Story of the CIO Political Action Committee* (NY, 1944), 213–21, defending NC-PAC.

71. J. R. Starobin, *American Communism in Crisis, 1943–1957* (Cambridge MA, 1972), chs. 6–7, esp. 139–52 and 162–67; DHTP, XIV [Running from Behind]: Doc. 66: ADA Publicity Dept.: "Henry Wallace: The Last Seven Months of His Presidential Campaign," 633–35.

72. S. M. Gillon, *Politics and Vision: The ADA and American Liberalism, 1947–1985* (NY, 1987), chs. 1–2; A. Hamby, *Beyond the New Deal: Harry Truman and American Liberalism* (NY, 1973), 224–29.

73. The authoritative study is now T. W. Devine, *Henry Wallace's 1948 Presidential Campaign and the Future of Postwar Liberalism* (Chapel Hill NC, 2013), 71–82. See also Z. Karabell, *The Last Campaign: How Harry Truman Won the 1948 Election* (NY, 2000), 68–71.

74. Gall, *Pressman,* 238–43, 247–50.

75. Devine, *Henry Wallace,* 172–77; Walton, *Henry Wallace, Harry Truman,* 237–40; Karabell, *Last Campaign,* 179–80; Starobin, *American Communism,* 192–94, and 298 notes 60 and 61. For a final and obscure flap over the Macedonian issue and communist influence, see Devine, 177–78.

76. DHTP, XIV: Doc. 66, 610–12.

77. Ibid., 604–05; Devine, *Henry Wallace,* 195–99; Walton, *Henry Wallace, Harry Truman,* 317–21.

78. *Politics,* Mar–Apr and May–Jun 1947; *Henry Wallace: The Man and the Myth* (NY, 1948), esp. 168–83; E. Roosevelt, "Plain Talk about Wallace," *Democratic Digest* XXV (Apr 1948), 2ff.

79. DHTP, XIV: Doc. 8: memo from Clifford to HST, Nov 19, 1947, 62–104. See also Karabell, *Last Campaign,* 34–39.

80. DHTP, XIV: Doc. 66. The ADA submitted two reports on Wallace and his campaign to the White House in manuscript before publishing them as attack pamphlets.

81. J. L. Sundquist, *Dynamics of the Party System: Alignment and Realignment of Political Parties in the United States* (Washington DC, 1983), 249–51; Devine, *Henry Wallace,* 69. Former Farmer-Labor governor Elmer Benson, now chairman of the Progressive Party, had opposed Humphrey and recently called him "a fascist at heart."

82. T. N. Thurber, *The Politics of Equality: Hubert H. Humphrey and the African-American Freedom Struggle* (NY, 1999), chs. 1–2.

83. Ibid., 58–64; Gillon, *ADA,* 47–50.

84. D. McCullough, *Truman* (NY, 1992), 632–44; A. Busch, *Truman's Triumphs: The 1948 Election and the Making of Postwar America* (Lawrence KA, 2012), 104–13 and appendix.

85. DHTP, XIV: Doc. 27: memo of Jun 29, 1948, probably by Sam Rosenman.

86. Ibid.: Campaign schedule Sep 1–Nov 5, 637–42; Doc. 72: "Recollections of the 1948 Campaign" by William Bray, 796–99.

87. Busch, *Truman's Triumphs,* 130–35.

88. Ibid., ch. 5; Karabell, *Last Campaign,* chs. 15–16.

89. DHTP, XIV: Doc. 70: "Charles Murphy's Recollections" re speeches in Flint and Louisville, 704, 734–35, and Doc. 67: radio address, Nov 1, 1948, 677–78.

90. Executive Order 9835 in A. Hamby (ed.), *Harry S. Truman and the Fair Deal* (Lexington MA, 1974), 191–97; Landon R. Y. Storrs, *The Second Red Scare and the Unmaking of the New Deal Left* (Princeton, 2013), appendix 3: Chronology.

91. R. J. Goldstein, *American Blacklist: The Attorney General's List of Subversive Organizations* (Lawrence KA, 2008), chs. 1–2; G. Horne, *Communist Front? The Civil Rights Congress, 1946–56* (Rutherford NJ, 1988); and F. Folsom, *Days of Anger, Days of Hope: A Memoir of the League of American Writers, 1937–1942* (University Press of Colorado, 1994). The League's roughly 800 members ranged from Hemingway and Van Wyck Brooks to Dashiell Hammett and several communist screen writers.

92. E. Schrecker, *The Age of McCarthyism: A Brief History with Documents* (Boston, 1994), ch. 7 and Documents 7 and 9; Storrs, *Second Red Scare,* appendix 4: Statistics.

93. Storrs, *Second Red Scare,* appendix 2: Case Files, and ch. 4. Among individuals discussed: ex-New Dealers Mary McLeod Bethune, Wilbur Cohen, Mordecai Ezekiel, Isador Lubin, Paul Porter, and the centerpiece of Storrs's analysis: Leon Keyserling (currently on Truman's Council of Economic Advisors) and his activist wife Mary Dublin Keyserling, both repeatedly investigated and ultimately cleared. Also E. Franklin Frazier, Ralph Bunche, Dorothy Kenyon, Caroline Ware, and Philleo Nash, a White House aide and point man on racial issues in 1947–48.

94. DHTP, XIV: Oklahoma City speech, Sep 28, 1948, 648–53.

95. S. Neal (ed.), *Eleanor and Harry: The Correspondence* . . . Truman Library online, Docs. 34 and 35: Nov 13 and 26, 1947.

96. DHTP, XIV: Doc. 52: Ickes to Sam Rosenman, Oct 14, 1948, and "An Appeal to the Liberals of America," 456–58.

97. Marcantonio and Isacson each garnered 36.9 percent of the vote, Pressman a disappointing 22.2 percent. Only Marcantonio's plurality sufficed to eke out a victory.

98. Devine, *Henry Wallace,* 272–76; DHTP, XIV: Doc. 66: "Retreat to Reality"; Busch, *Truman's Triumphs,* 229–30; Karabell, *Last Campaign,* 293–94.

99. See Busch, *Truman's Triumphs,* ch. 5.

100. DHTP, XII: Doc. 54: W. White to O. Chapman, Dec 15, 1948; Doc. 69: memo from P. Nash.

101. Busch, *Truman's Triumphs,* ch. 6; I. Katznelson, *Fear Itself: The New Deal and the Origins of Our Time* (NY, 2013), 329–30, 384–88, 442–44.

102. D. S. Horton (ed.), *Freedom and Equality: Addresses by Harry S. Truman* (Columbia MO, 1960): Address of Jul 14, 1940 to the National Colored Democratic Association in Chicago, 4–6.

103. Reed, *Seedtime for the Modern Civil Rights Movement,* introduction, chs. 1, 10; R. M. Dalfiume, *Desegregation of the U.S. Armed Forces: Fighting on Two Fronts* (Columbia MO, 1969), 115–23.

104. See R. Shogan, *Harry Truman and the Struggle for Racial Justice* (Lawrence KA, 2013). chs. 3–5.

105. Neal (ed.), *Eleanor and Harry:* Doc. 21, editor's note; J. E. Taylor, *Freedom to Serve: Truman, Civil Rights, and Executive Order 9981* (NY, 2012), 78.

106. DHTP, XI [The Truman Administration's Civil Rights Program (vol. 1)]: Doc. 43: HST to A. G. Clark, Jul 20, 1946; Doc. 45: W. White to D. Niles, Sep 26, 1946; Doc. 48: Clark to Niles; Docs. 55 and 56: drafts of presidential statement; Doc. 139: W. White, "The President Means It," Dec 2, 1948. For an overview, see Shogan, *Harry Truman,* chs. 6–7.

107. DHTP, XI: Docs. 126 and 140; Doc. 70: minutes of PCCR 1st meeting; DHTP, XII [Civil Rights (vol. 2)]: Doc. 14: Niles to HST, Feb 11, 1948.

108. Truman, *Freedom and Equality,* 9–17 (Feb 2, 1948).

109. G. Jonas (a decades-long NAACP official), *Freedom's Sword: The NAACP and the Struggle against Racism in America* (NY, 2005), ch. 5, esp. 149.

110. Taylor, *Freedom to Serve,* 69–70 on 1946; DHTP, XI: Doc. 42: Robeson to Niles, Sep 23, 1946, 118–22; DHTP, XII: Doc. 38, Aug 5, 1948, 124, and Doc. 53, Dec 14, 1948, 201–4.

111. P. F. Pfeffer, *A. Philip Randolph: Pioneer of the Civil Rights Movement* (Baton Rouge LA, 1990), 36–40; W. H. Harris, "A. Philip Randolph, Black Workers, and the Labor Movement," in M. Dubofsky and W. Van Tine (eds.), *Labor Leaders in America* (Urbana IL, 1987), esp. 269–70.

112. DHTP, XII: Doc. 91: Nash to Clifford, Jan 1950, and Spingarn to Clifford: Dec 19, 1949, 422–25. On the NNC and CRC see Goldstein, *American Blacklist,* 99–101, 106–9, 143.

113. Katznelson, *Fear Itself,* 188–93, with copious quotations from segregationist senators.

114. T. N. Thurber, *Republicans on Race: The GOP's Frayed Relationship with African-Americans, 1945–1974* (Lawrence KA, 2013), 6–17.

115. DHTP, XII: Doc. 98: Chandler to Feeney, Feb 2, 1950, and response, Mar 1, 1950, 443–46.

116. Thurber, *Republicans on Race,* ch. 1, esp. 28–29.

117. DHTP, XII: Doc. 61: telegram from Randolph to HST, Jan 28, 1949, and telegram from W. White to HST, Jan 25, 1949; DHTP, XII: Doc. 102: Spingarn to White House, May 15, 1950; Thurber, *Republicans on Race,* ch. 1.

118. Dalfiume, *Desegregation of the U.S. Armed Forces,* chs. 3–5.

119. M. Harris, *Five Came Back: A Story of Hollywood and the Second World War* (NY, 2015), 135–36, 303–8. Also K. Kruse and S. Tuck (eds.), *Fog of War: The Second World War and the Civil Rights Movement* (Oxford, 2012), 110–13.

120. *The Negro Soldier* (War Department Special Service Documentary: Apr 1944), available on DVD.

121. Shogan, *Harry Truman,* 145–46.

122. DHTP, XII: Doc. 21: Randolph to Clifford and response, Feb 27 and Mar 18, 1948; Pfeffer, *Randolph,* ch. 4, esp. 138–39.

123. Taylor, *Freedom to Serve*, 80, 89, 92, and "A. Philip Randolph's testimony on Civil Disobedience, March 31, 1948," 151–54.

124. Pfeffer, *Randolph*, 147–48.

125. Taylor, *Freedom to Serve*, ch. 5, esp. 99–105; Shogan, *Harry Truman*, 149–61.

126. *Freedom to Serve: Equality of Treatment and Opportunity in the Armed Services. A Report by the President's Committee* (Washington DC, 1950), esp. ch. 2.

127. Ibid., chs. 3–5 and appendices.

128. DHTP, XXXI: Doc. 212: Straight to Niles, Jan 24, 1951, and earlier telegrams; Doc. 214: Frank Pace to Niles, Feb 21, 1951; Doc. 218: Gen. McAuliffe to Straight, Sep 11, 1951, 807, 818–19, 826–28.

129. Shogan, *Harry Truman*, 157–59; Taylor 109–10. Harlem Congressman Charles Rangel (*And I Haven't Had a Bad Day Since* (NY, 2007), 60–69) vividly recalls the fight for survival by his black unit in North Korea.

130. See W. T. Bowers et al., *Black Soldier, White Army: The 24th Infantry Regiment in Korea* (Washington DC: Center for Military History, US Army, 1996) (online).

131. Bowles, *Promises to Keep*, 144.

132. DHTP, XII: Doc. 101: Niles to D. Dawson (an administrative assistant to HST), Feb 1950, 457–62; Doc. 103: Chair of Fair Employment Practices Board of the CSC to Dawson, May 26, 1950, 466–69.

133. J. J. Huthmacher, *Senator Robert Wagner and the Rise of Urban Liberalism* (NY, 1968), 206–16, 224–29; M. I. Gelfand, *A Nation of Cities: The Federal Government and Urban America* (NY, 1975), 60–64.

134. R. O. Davies, *Housing Reform during the Truman Administration* (Columbia MO, 1966), chs. 3–6.

135. Ibid., 104–8. Cf. Katznelson, *When Affirmative Action Was White*, 48–50.

136. Davies, *Housing Reform*, 110–14.

137. A. Wolfe, *America's Impasse: the Rise and Fall of the Politics of Growth* (NY, 1981), 82–88.

138. See the critique of urban renewal by M. Anderson, *The Federal Bulldozer* (NY [1964], 1967 edn.), esp. xix, ch. 1, and 65–70, and Gelfand, *Nation of Cities*, 144–56.

139. Davies, *Housing Reform*, 136.

140. For the negative case on high rise design and its effects, see R. Plunz, *A History of Housing in New York City* (NY, 1990/2016), ch. 8: "The Pathology of Public Housing." A more positive assessment of NYCHA, from its origins through the 1960s, is offered by N. D. Bloom, *Public Housing That Worked: New York in the Twentieth Century* (Philadelphia, 2008), esp. introduction and part 2.

141. DHTP, XV [the Fair Deal]: Doc. 23: remarks of Majority Leader McCormack on the 81st Congress, first session, Oct 19, 1949.

142. Ibid., Doc. 23: pp. 171–73; Doc. 37: "The Monumental Achievement of the Democratic 81st Congress," Jul 23, 1950, 239–40.

143. Ibid., Doc. 24: Majority Leader Lucas, Oct 17, 1989, 175–84; Doc. 79: 446–47.

144. Ibid., Doc. 38: Summary of the Status of Legislation, Jun 10, 1950; Doc. 79: Major Legislative Actions of the 82nd Congress, second session; Doc. 84: Final Report on Legislative Recommendations of the President Aug 8 1952, 479–80.

145. G. Zook, *The Role of the Federal Government in Education* (Cambridge MA, 1945), esp. 49–51.

146. DHTP, XV: Doc. 37: McCormack, Sep 1950, 239; Doc. 24: Status Report Senate, Oct 1949, 184; Doc. 49; Status Report House, Jan 1951, 319; Doc. 84: White House Final Report, Aug 1952.

147. "Letter of Appointment of Commission Members," in *Higher Education for American Democracy: A Report of the President's Commission on Higher Education* (NY, 1948).

148. Ibid., parts 1–4. On gender, see L. Eisenmann, *Higher Education for Women in Postwar America, 1945–1965* (Baltimore MD, 2006), 51–54.

149. *Higher Education . . . Report*, part 2, 25–39.

150. Ibid., part 2, 29n. The dissenters included D. S. Freeman, biographer of Robert E. Lee, and Compton. With an eagle eye, Jon Taylor, *Freedom to Serve*, 70–72, cites this brief comment.

151. See J. R. Thelin, *A History of American Higher Education* (Baltimore MD, 2011), 268–72, and P. A. Hutcheson, "Setting the Nation's Agenda for Higher Education: A Review of Selected National Commission Reports, 1947–2006," *History of Education Quarterly,* XLVII (Aug 2007).

152. As discussed in chs. 8 and 7, respectively.

153. Perkins Papers, CU Library, Box 26: June 7, 1945.

154. The foundational monograph is M. M. Poen, *Harry S. Truman versus the Medical Lobby: The Genesis of Medicare* (Columbia MO, 1979). P. Starr, *The Social Transformation of American Medicine* (NY, 1982), 266–89, provides an astute overview.

155. [I. Falk,] *Health Care Insurance: A Social Insurance Program for Personal Health Services* (G.P.O., Jul 1946), introduction by Murray, foreword by Falk (xi–xiv), and 19–20. Also D. Spritzer, *Senator James Murray and the Limits of Post-War Liberalism* (NY, 1985), ch. 6.

156. [Falk,] *Health Care Insurance,* ch. 5, 147–66.

157. O. Ewing, Oral History (1969), Truman Library online, p. 177.

158. O. Ewing, *The Nation's Health: A Report to the President* (Washington DC, Sep 1948), iii–iv.

159. Ibid., 75–76.

160. [M. Davis], *Committee on Labor and Public Welfare of the 80th Congress* (G.P.O., Jun 1948), esp. 15–17.

161. Ewing, *Nation's Health,* 8–11, 37–52, 63–114, quote from p. 85.

162. Poen, *Truman versus the Medical Lobby,* ch. 6 is indispensable.

163. *The Voluntary Way Is the American Way* (Chicago: AMA National Education Campaign, 1950); Poen, *Truman versus the Medical Lobby,* ch. 6. On the AMA more broadly, see D. M. Fox, *Health Policies, Health Politics: The British and American Experience, 1911–1965* (Princeton, 1986), 84–86, 153–58.

164. Poen, *Truman versus the Medical Lobby,* 117–26; Green quoted on p. 119.

165. Ewing, Oral History (1969), 173–89. On the congressional votes, K. Doherty and J. Jenkins, "Examining a Failed Moment: National Health Care, the AMA, and US Congress 1948–50" [Jan 2009] (University of Virginia, online).

166. Poen, *Truman versus the Medical Lobby,* 161, 167, 177–82.

167. See Starr, *Social Transformation of American Medicine,* 347–51; Fox, *Health Policies,* 123–31, 166–68; Wolfe, *American Impasse,* 88–92.

168. Ewing, Oral History; Poen, *Truman versus the Medical Lobby,* 188–201.

169. CNH: Davis to Mary Lasker, Mar 14, 1956, Truman Library online. Henry Kaiser was the CNH's treasurer.

Conclusion

1. Marc Bloch, "Toward a Comparative History of European Societies" [1928], in F. C. Lane and J. C. Riemersma (eds.), *Enterprise and Secular Change: Readings in Economic History* (Homewood IL, 1953), 519–521.

2. C. Andrieu et al. (eds.), *Les Nationalisations de la Libération: De l'utopie au compromis* (Paris, 1987), esp. A. Prost, "Une Pièce en Trois Actes," and C. Andrieu, "Des Nationalisations Disparates."

3. N. Tiratsoo and J. Tomlinson, *Industrial Efficiency and State Intervention: Labour, 1939–51* (London, 1993), chs. 3–8, and J. Tomlinson, *Democratic Socialism and Economic Policy: The Attlee Years, 1945–1951* (Cambridge, 1997), chs. 4–8 and 12–13.

4. F. Bloch-Lainé and J. Bouvier, *La France Restaurée, 1944–1954: Dialogue sur les choix d'une modernisation* (Paris, 1986); S. B. Wells, *Jean Monnet: Unconventional Statesman* (Boulder CO, 2011), chs. 4–5.

5. In 1978 a Congress under Democratic control finally passed the Humphrey-Hawkins Full Employment and Economic Growth Bill, in gestation since 1974. The bill acknowledged the primacy of private enterprise and of Federal Reserve monetary policy in maintaining a healthy economy, but it empowered the executive branch to set numerical goals for tolerable levels of unemployment and inflation. If unemployment exceeded the target, the government, in Keynesian fashion, could "create a reservoir of public employment."

6. [H. Frenay,] *Ministère des Prisonniers, Déportés et Refugiés: Bilan d'un Effort* (Paris, Sep 1945); F. Cochet, "Des Retours 'Decalés': Les Prisonniers de guerre et les requis du travail," and C. Lewin, "La Constitution de la Féderation Nationale des Combattants Prisonniers de Guerre," both in C. Franck (ed.), *La France de 1945: Résistances, retours, renaissances* (Colloque de Caen, 1996), 141–52, 175–92.

7. See D. Runciman, *The Confidence Trap: A History of Democracy in Crisis from World War I to the Present* (Princeton, 2013), chs. 1–3.

8. The best overview remains J.-P. Rioux, *The Fourth Republic, 1944–1958* (Cambridge, 1987 transl.).

9. See the oral histories collected by O. Wieviorka (ed.), *Nous Entrerons dans la Carrière: De la Résistance à l'exercise du pouvoir* (Paris, 1994), and B. Lachaise (ed.), *Résistance et Politique sous la IVème République* (Bordeaux, 2004).

10. See, e.g., A. Brinkley, *The End of Reform: New Deal Liberalism in Recession and War* (NY, 1996), epilogue; D. Ciepley, *Liberalism in the Shadow of Totalitarianism* (Cambridge MA, 2006), esp. ch. 6 and conclusion; I. Katznelson, *Fear Itself: The New Deal and the Origins of Our Time* (NY, 2013), introduction; J. Cowie, *The Great Exception: The New Deal and the Limits of American Politics* (Princeton, 2016), introduction—which all emphasize, among other themes, the erosion of the New Deal under the imperatives of the "warfare state" and the national security state.

11. "Going Our Way?" FACT, Feb 1949, 18; *Keeping Left: Labour's First Five Years and the Problems Ahead: By a Group of Members of Parliament* (London, 1950), 25.

12. Founded in 1919, the CFTC (Confédération Française des Travailleurs Chrétiens) had 400,000 members in 1937 and after the Liberation grew to about 800,000 by 1947. The CFTC was not part of the Popular Front and was not invited to the Matignon labor negotiations in 1936, but the CFTC gained a kind of official recognition from the CNR.

13. See F. Romero, *The United States and the European Trade Union Movement, 1944–1951* (Chapel Hill NC, 1992 transl.), part 2; "The Story of W.F.T.U." in FACT, Apr 1949, 60–64; and L. Saillant [general secretary of the WFTU], *The Activity of the World Federation of Trade Unions and the Tasks Arising for the Trade Unions . . . and in Defence of Peace* (London, 1953) [CU Library 267 W89].

14. "We Are Many: Tom Crewe Goes among the Corbyn Supporters," *London Review of Books,* Aug 11, 2016, 13.

15. See H. J. Kaye, *The Fight for the Four Freedoms: What Made FDR and the Greatest Generation Truly Great* (NY, 2014), and N. Timmins, *The Five Giants: A Biography of the Welfare State* (London, 1995), for the British trajectory between 1942 and 1992.

16. See M. A. Glendon, *A World Made New: Eleanor Roosevelt and the Universal Declaration of Human Rights* (NY, 2001), chs. 7–10 for the conflicts that swirled around this project; J. Winter, *Dreams of Peace and Freedom: Utopian Moments in the Twentieth Century* (New Haven CT, 2006), ch. 4, highlighting the vision of René Cassin; and S. Moyn, *The Last Utopia: Human Rights in History* (Cambridge MA, 2010), ch. 2, who argues for the "irrelevance" of the human rights idea to the postwar moment because of the Declaration's ambiguities and purely normative character. Noting the influence of the "Christian personalism" espoused by theologian Jacques Maritain in debates over the Declaration, Moyn argues persuasively that Christian Democrats in the 1950s espoused new European institutions on human rights as potential counterweights to claims over individuals by democratic welfare states as well as authoritarian states. (This view is amplified in Moyn, *Christian Human Rights* [Philadelphia, 2015] and M. Duranti, *The Conservative Human Rights Revolution: European Identity, Transnational Politics, and the Origins of the European Convention* [Oxford, 2017]. The books are assessed by U. Greenberg, "Against Conservative Internationalism," *Dissent* [Spring 2017], 181–86.)

17. See N. Lichtenstein, "Review Essay," *Journal of American History,* CII (Sep 2015), 500–4, on C. Gordon's interactive website *Growing Apart: A Political History of American Inequality;* T. Noah, *The Great Divergence: America's Growing Inequality Crisis and What We Can Do About It* (NY, 2012).

18. T. R. Reid, *The Healing of America: A Global Quest for Better, Cheaper, and Fairer Health Care* (NY, 2010), ch. 4: "France: the Vital Card."

19. See J. Quadagno, *One Nation Uninsured: Why the U.S. Has No National Health Insurance* (Oxford, 2005), esp. chs. 6–8.

20. Nicholas Bloom argues that the huge NYC Housing Authority was a notable exception in the 1950s–60s to the typically poor management and maintenance of public housing projects by other local authorities in the US: *Public Housing That Worked: New York in the Twentieth Century* (Philadelphia, 2008), part 2.

21. T. B. Smith, *France in Crisis: Welfare, Inequality and Globalization since 1980* (Cambridge, 2004), esp. 185–98.

22. At the depths of the Great Depression New Deal Senator Hugo Black proposed a 30-hour work-week law to spread jobs around in the US. FDR did not back that bill but his NRA urged voluntary agreements in various industries to pare down work weeks to encourage more hires.

23. This was already evident in fraudulent for-profit vocational training schools and on-the-job training programs supported by the G.I. Bill: K. J. Frydl, *The GI Bill* (Cambridge, 2009), ch. 4. See also G. Lafer, *The Job Training Charade* (Ithaca NY, 2002), chs. 3 and 7; and for anecdotal evidence in contemporary France the remarkable film of 2015 *The Measure of a Man* (*La Loi du Marché*).

24. The insularity of national historiography on education is especially striking when it comes to this common issue in Britain and France.

25. When pressure mounted, after years of delay, to implement the Supreme Court ruling of 1954 against "separate but equal" schools for blacks, southern whites deserted their public schools in droves to found all-white private academies for their children. Resistance spread north when residential segregation no longer sufficed for de facto school segregation, as courts ordered integration by busing children between school districts.

26. On the contemporary crises in British higher education, see S. Head, "The Grim Threat to British Universities," *New York Review of Books,* Jan 13, 2011, 58–64, and S. Collini, "Sold Out," *London Review of Books,* Oct 24, 2013, 3, 5–12.

27. For retrospective views by Bevan and Mendès France on a range of issues, see the dialogues conducted by the magazine *L'Express* and published as *Rencontres: Nenni, Bevan, Mendès France* (Paris, 1959), esp. chs. 1, 2, 5.

INDEX